THE
PROFESSIONAL
GARDE MANGER

THE
PROFESSIONAL
GARDE MANGER

A GUIDE TO THE ART OF THE BUFFET

David Paul Larousse

John Wiley & Sons, Inc.
New York • Chichester • Brisbane • Toronto • Singapore

Beneath the candelabra, beneath the five tiers bearing toward the distant ceiling, pyramids of homemade cakes that were never touched, spread the monotonous opulence of buffets at big balls; coralline lobsters boiled alive, waxy chaud-froids of veal, steely-tinted fish immersed in sauce, turkeys gilded by the oven's heat, rosy foie gras under gelatin armor, boned woodcock reclining on amber toast decorated with their own chopped insides, and a dozen other cruel colored delights. At the end of the table two monumental silver tureens held clear soup the color of burnt amber. To prepare this supper the cooks must have sweated away in the vast kitchens from the night before.

—Guiseppe Di Lampedusa, *The Leopard* (1960)

Publisher: Margaret K. Burns
Senior Editor: Claire Thompson
Associate Managing Editor: Donna Conte
Copy Editor: Elizabeth Knighton
Photography: Marshall Gordon
Food Styling: Susan Beach and D. P. Larousse
Illustrations: Carol Nunnelly

This text is printed on acid-free paper.

Library of Congress Cataloging in Publication Data:
Larousse, David Paul, 1949–
     The professional Garde Manger / by David Paul Larousse ; foreword by Peter Van Erp.
          p.   cm.
     Includes bibliographical references.
     ISBN 0-471-10603-8 (cloth : alk. paper)
     1. Quantity cookery. 2. Cookery (Cold dishes) 3. Garnishes (Cookery) 4. Buffets (Cookery) I. Title.
TX820.L37   1996
641.7′9—dc20   95-41073

Printed in the United States of America

10 9 8 7 6 5

CONTENTS

FOREWORD

Between 1972 and 1981, while working as senior instructor at the Culinary Institute of America, I operated the Dutchess Valley Club in Pawling, New York. During each academic year a student was invited to live and work at the club as an apprentice, which included various duties—runner, bartender, waiter, *commis,* and *plongeur.* The club was in some ways an extension of the CIA—a culinary frustration outlet, I have called it, where I endeavored to fine tune the initial training of these apprentices. The Americans proved to me, a native of Holland, that they could be as good as Europeans as long as they were given the right training and instilled with pride built on a foundation of excellent culinary fundamentals. I endeavored to select students I felt were equipped to pass on the torch, so to speak, of the classical methods and dishes I had learned during my early years in the profession. Today, when I look back on my tenure at the club, I am genuinely proud of my small legacy of former apprentices—of the individuality I encouraged in them and of their various accomplishments—and very proud that they have grown into an illustrious group.

David Larousse spent a year with me at the club, and in this book I see vestiges of concepts and recipes that were part of his experience there. Like others, he received a broad training, which stressed not only cooking but larger elements of learning the trade: developing professionalism; the complexity of balanced culinary practice; progressing from good sauces to great sauces. Always inherent in the ambiance there was the importance of classical cuisine, that it is not only a name, but also a code; that a soubise is an approach to cooking, and Oysters Villeroi is a direction—change that dish in any way, and it is no longer Oysters Villeroi.

Of course, one does not learn through a cookbook alone, but a truly good cookbook can augment those things that must be learned by doing. The garde manger has changed radically over the years, and there has long been a need for a comprehensive text to address the subject. Armed with this expansive reference, a serious student of the discipline has on hand a compendium of classical procedures, dishes, and contemporary trends, as well as photographs and illustrations revealing a considerable body of information. With hard work and perseverance, a student can thus move expeditiously toward the development of a solid repertoire in fine garde manger work.

Peter Van Erp
New York City, 1995

PREFACE

It has been more than two decades since I stood in the Advanced Garde Manger class, sculpting apple birds and coating twenty-five pound roasted turkeys with chaud-froid sauce. It was in this class, one of the most popular in the second-year curriculum at the Culinary Institute of America, that I first glimpsed the artistic possibilities in the realm of the cold kitchen.

My repertoire since then has grown and evolved, as have the styles of cold kitchen production. The jellied white-sauce-coated turkeys and hams that we so painstakingly decorated during our training are today more frequently seen in formal competitions than on hotel buffets. Heavy, mirrored platters with row upon row of pâtés and galantines arranged before a backdrop of carrot and green bell pepper palm trees are also gone—fortunately, in this case—and tomato roses have fallen out of fashion with our realization that serving a rolled strip of tomato skin is rather déclassé, no matter how visually stunning. The 1950s-style salads with cottage cheese and canned pineapple on a bed of iceberg lettuce garnished with a maraschino cherry also fortunately failed to gain any lasting popularity, as did many of the overprocessed ingredients we were told at school were the wave of the future. However, some of the exquisite dishes typical of classical garde manger—dishes such as *Pâté de Foie Gras en Brioche, Consommé Madrilène, Oeuf en Gelée* and gorgeously decorated individual timbales filled with a fine mousse or salad—have also fallen on hard times. We have raised our level of sophistication in many ways, and we have worked hard to keep labor costs—and hence profits—in line, but we are losing many fine dishes. What does this mean for classical cuisine? Is it on the verge of extinction, or is it already extinct? Are there any great eateries in this world still offering classical dishes in their cold food and small dish production? Will they continue to do so in the next millennium?

Such a state of affairs is the way of the world. Trends come and go, and change is inevitable. Some of the specific causes of these changes, even some human-caused environmental tragedies, ostensibly could not have been avoided. Consider two of the most expensive and gastronomically prized food ingredients that are traditionally stored within the realm of the garde manger: truffles and caviar. *Tuber melansporum,* what the Italians call *la perle della cucina* and the French call a *black diamond,* is an incredible gastronomic delicacy. It figures significantly in classical cookery, including the garde manger. Yet between the nineteenth and twentieth centuries, 90% of the forests of Europe were cut down, which diminished the truffle harvest, at best always a challenge, and has made truffles today a rarity both difficult to obtain and priced beyond reason (currently $500 to $800 per pound). The fate of caviar is equally unfortunate. Because of an abundance of sturgeon in North American waters in the late nineteenth century, there was a considerable caviar industry in the United States. But Americans had little taste for it; caviar sandwiches were often given away gratis in saloons along with a five-cent glass of beer. Incredibly, almost all American-produced caviar was exported to Europe, competing quite well with the Russian product. When the Swiss hotelier César Ritz popularized Russian caviar at his fine Parisian hotel, interest in the North American variety waned. The Russian revolution of 1917 also caused a temporary cessation of caviar production for a period of seven years. Subsequently, with pollution and the damming of rivers on both continents—destroying the sturgeon spawning grounds in North America and turning areas of the Caspian Sea into large mud flats—both the quantity and quality of caviar has been seriously affected, limiting availability and driving up the price.

The reality of these tragedies—and they are tragedies in every sense of the word—makes it impossible to revive truly classical cookery in our time. Yet that is not necessarily our intent or our desire. "Change is good," a friend once insisted, and she was correct: in all things, it is wise to exist in the moment, to remain flexible so as to be able to move with change. If at the same time we can maintain a cognizant connection with the traditions of the past, then we can keep those traditions alive by honoring the dishes and customs that have withstood the test of time. The issue of the vanishing truffle is a test, a challenge to perform a dance, so to speak, that allows us to maintain that connection, while forever evolving and changing our approach as well as our culinary offerings. This dance will forbid the use of black olives—a shameful substitute for the black pearl of the kitchen—but it will allow us to use an artificial truffle for decoration purposes *only*, and encourage us to change the dishes that need to be changed based on the availability or unavailability of important ingredients. "Use what you have," was the dictum a martial arts teacher taught me, and it is an important one. It can lead us to achieve a balance that gives a taste of *haute cuisine* within the style of our designated *cuisine moderne*, and to bring garde manger into the next millennium.

In contemporary garde manger change is a double-edged sword. It has allowed many a foodservice operation to survive in a time of belt tightening and to keep pace with the growing challenge to provide cost-effective buffet and banquet productions. We have had to sacrifice some classical traditions, but the exquisite artistry that is the earmark of a talented garde manger department is reflected in the eyes of an ever-widening and appreciative audience. Alive and well are the dramatic centerpieces raised above the buffet sanctuary—ice carvings and sculptures fashioned from tallow, salt dough, and weaver's dough; the high-tech oval mirrors displaying exquisite layouts of charcuterie, salads, canapés, fresh fruit, and cheese; the multiple small courses that make casual and satisfying evening fare in cafés, bistros, trattorias, and tapas bars, where the kitchen action is fast and furious and the visual imagery of the work produced is often stunning.

This text fills a need to outline the repertoire of dishes and items that make up the contemporary garde manger kitchen. The origin of the dishes and techniques within are gleaned from the hands-on experience of the author over a period of more than two decades; they include dishes learned from more experienced practitioners, as well as personal innovations. Here also are traditional dishes, part of a body of work referred to as classical cuisine, whose style and ingredients have been passed down to us. Some of these dishes are complex and labor-intensive, but are nevertheless included in order to acquaint the student with the history and tradition of the artful works that emanate from the garde manger.

In addition, elements of contemporary garde manger production are presented, ranging from canapés and finger sandwiches, to fish, game, and poultry items presented on mirrors, boards, and marble slabs; from seasonal fruit layouts with *mukimono* centerpieces, to elegantly simple cheese boards with sweeping geometric lines; from breathtaking ice carvings (the most transient culinary medium of all) to stunning tallow and salt dough *pièce montées*. It is our hope that, armed with this abundant work, aspiring garde manger practitioners will be able to apply themselves in the garde manger kitchens of the world, to build their repertoires, develop their styles, and keep this most exciting area within the culinary craft alive and thriving.

D. P. Larousse
San Francisco, California

ACKNOWLEDGMENTS

I am very pleased to thank a number of manufacturers and distributors of food products, tableware, and equipment for graciously lending or donating their products for photography, specifically (in alphabetical order) Bruce Aidells, Aidells Sausage Co., San Leandro, California (sausages for charcuterie photograph); Ulrich Honigausen, B.I.A. Cordon Bleu, Inc., San Carlos, California (porcelain and ceramicware); Debby Smith, Director of Marketing, Boudin Bakery, San Francisco, California (Fernando Padilla bread sculptures); Ron Morris, Director of Marketing, B.R. Cohn Olive Oil, Glen Ellen, California (Sonoma extra virgin olive oil and champagne vinegar); Dominic Palazzolo, Chef/Owner, Bread Effects Culinart, Cincinnati, Ohio (tallow and bread sculptures); Patrick A. Martin and Bill Baker of The Cambridge House, Santa Barbara and San Francisco, California (smoked salmon); Cynthia T. Puccio, Frette Fabrics (napkins), New York, New York; Tim Ecker and Ernie Gilmer, Gourmet Display, Seattle, Washington (faux marble and acrylic platters); Charles Canny and Dave Browning, Hobart Corporation, Inc., Burlingame, California (electric meat slicer); Gary Holleman, Corporate Chef, Indian Harvest Specialtifoods, Inc., Bemidji, Minnesota; Robert King, Robert King Associates, San Francisco, California (dinnerware and table linens); Joyce Smith, Marcel & Henri Charcuterie Française, San Francisco, California (pâtés and terrines); Jim Stevens, President, Maytag Dairy Farms, Newton, Iowa (Maytag blue cheese); Jim Nueske and Gilbert Thompson, Nueske Hillcrest Farms, Wittenberg, Wisconsin (country ham); Lauren Peck and Betsy Neville, Neville/Peck Communications, Pine Ridge, Illinois (Le Creuset cookware and serviceware); Nick and Daniel Sciabia, Nick Sciabia & Sons, Modesto, California (olives and olive oil); Dan Wallace, Southland/Superior Farms, Vernon, California (lamb saddle and precooked boneless lamb leg); Robert J. McAniff, Vice President of Sales, and Sue McCarthy, National Bridal Director, Towle Silversmiths, East Boston, Massachusetts (silver tray and serviceware); Linda Funk, Director, National Product Communications, Wisconsin Milk Marketing Board, Madison, Wisconsin (Wisconsin cheese).

Special thanks to members of the California Culinary Academy: Hervé Biavant, Executive Chef, for the loan of two enormous silver platters for the pâté photographs; Mark Davis, Chef Instructor, for invaluable information on sculpture and centerpieces, and preparation of charcuterie and weaver's dough; Robert "Butcher Bob" Fanucchi, butchery instructor, for charcuterie; Mary Goglio, Librarian, for assistance with research material.

Many thanks also to Marshall Gordon, photographer extraordinaire and infamous humorist; Susan Beach (food and prop styling); Kaitlin Gould (photo support team); Louis Szathamary, Chef Laureate, Chicago, Illinois; Peter Hausin, Proprietor, Palmilord, Les Herbiers, France (technical data on foie gras production); Lars Kronmark, Chef Instructor, Culinary Institute of America, St. Helena, California division; Bruce Kaplan of the U.S.D.A. Food Safety and Inspection Service; staff members of Rio Hotel and Casino, Las Vegas: Walter Worotylko, Executive Sous-Chef; Steven Buffone and Valentina Columbo, Garde Mangers; Timothy A. Emert, Executive Chef, Luxor Hotel, Las Vegas.

I also wish to acknowledge Peter Van Erp, native of Rotterdam, Holland, currently teaching at Brooklyn City College, Brooklyn, New York. Chef Van Erp was one of my instructors and Executive Chef at the Culinary Institute of America, Hyde Park, New York (1970–1982). I also had the opportunity to work with him from 1975 to 1976 when he headed up the kitchen at the Dutchess Valley Rod & Gun Club, Pawling, New York, a private establishment with a gastronomically knowledgeable clientele. From 1972 through 1981, Van Erp used that kitchen as his own training center for one student each year, hand-picked from among his students at the Institute. It was a very special opportunity, and, in large part, the beginnings of this book lie in my year as his apprentice.

CHAPTER 1

INTRODUCTION

A Brief History of Banquets

Banquets have typically functioned to bring people together for the purpose of celebrating birth, marriage, fortuitous weather, and other positive manifestations of nature. Banquets have also commemorated past events, marked family members' deaths, celebrated military conquests, honored individuals for their accomplishments, given thanks for the good things of life, and joined people together to affirm mutual ideas or concerns in the artistic, literary, political, or religious arena. Through its ceremonial role in human affairs, we can examine the history of banquets and subsequently come to understand the function and importance of the garde manger kitchen.

All ancient cultures had some form of banquet tradition, just as modern cultures do today, with both noteworthy similarities and unequivocal differences in customs and styles depending on the particular era and culture. Ancient cultures were considerably more sophisticated than we tend to believe, yet no less superstitious than we know, even if those superstitions were based on then unknown scientific realities. The ancient Egyptians, for example, were quite careful in their choice of foods, and this selectivity was based on a common-sense understanding that the manner in which nourishment was taken was clearly and directly related to good health and illness. They also exhibited an awareness of the importance of hygiene, by virtue of ushering arriving guests into an area separate from the main banquet room, where they washed feet and hands. As they moved into the main banquet hall, servants would make an offer of flower wreaths, and a drink of some kind, served in a small ornamental cup, a *tahbal*, from which the modern word *timbale* is derived. Musicians, acrobats, dancers, and/or pantomimists often entertained during such an event, and seating was informal. Food was served in baskets, brought from the kitchen and passed among the guests and then placed in strategic locations from which guests could help themselves. The custom of bringing in a coffin containing a mock skeleton was not unusual and was a way of heightening the guests' appreciation of material and terrestrial abundance.

The Assyrians, an aggressive culture, typically celebrated military victories. Although their manners were savage by some standards, their inclinations were gregarious, and their celebrations might last as long as a week. The palace doors were left open to all who desired to join the celebration, and at least one reigning king was known to have sent out food and drink to sentry personnel around the city who were unable to attend. These celebrations were not without their intrigue, according to tales of an incident in the eighth century B.C. Sardanapalus—one of the last descendants of Semiramis, the founder of Babylon—was more a self-indulgent fop than a warrior and preferred remaining in the company of eunuchs and concubines to engaging in military campaigns. He was also a cross-dresser, and his effeminate manner made him very unpopular with other officers. During a banquet he hosted to celebrate a military victory, Sardanapalus was harshly abducted and banished to a palace in a faraway city. Desperate after two years in exile, he set fire to the place, killing himself, his eunuchs, and servants, and destroying all his treasures.

Athenaeus, the ardent chronicler of Greek culture, wrote of the Persian kings' banquet tables, indicating that many different animals were consumed as food—horse, camel, ox, ass, deer, ostrich, goose, and cock—some of which were roasted whole. Athenaeus gives us a glimpse of these banquets, which also lasted for days at a time: "White, green, and hyacinth colored tapestries were attached with cords of fine scarlet linen with silver rings to marble columns. The couches were silver and gold on floors of alabaster and streaked marble. Drinks were poured into gold cups of different shapes and there was an abundance of wine."

The Greeks were superstitious, believing that to interrupt a banquet before all necessary rituals were played out was to risk loss of favor with their gods. Wearing white robes was intended to please the gods, as was the practice of guests' washing hands and feet before entering, and numerous solemn invocations of family, home, and nation were performed before the celebration could begin. Young girls, singing, playing the lute and the harp, and dancing, were part of a Greek banquet and, according to Plutarch, a means of preventing quarrels and disagreements.

The debauchery and excess practiced in ancient Rome is legendary, thanks to some of the surviving literature from that era, as well as our twentieth-century films on the subject. The reality, however, is that such excess was practiced by a small minority of wealthy patricians, whereas the majority of the citizenry of Rome and her colonies felt that paying too much attention to matters of food and drink was a wicked luxury. Still, the stories are fascinating. Helioglabus was known for serving precious stones in dishes of food: favas with amber, lentils with pearls, peas with grains of gold. Nero had ceilings that opened to shower flower petals on his guests; Lucullus sent explorers to sea in search of new and exotic foods; and

Apicius spent enormous sums on his appetite and lavish entertaining. We are fortunate to have *Apicius de re Coquinaria* (The Book of Apicius), still in printed form. Marcus Gavius Apicius (80 B.C. to 40 A.D.) was a personality of some note who took his food seriously and cultivated a scientific attitude toward the subject. He created many original dishes—among them râgouts, several cakes, and numerous sauces—many of which he became famous for; he also endowed a school for the teaching and promotion of cooking and culinary ideas. According to Athenaeus, Apicius was a person "... very rich and luxurious, for whom several kinds of cheesecake are named. [And] he spent myriads of drachmas on his belly." In truth, this work was not written by Apicius himself, but by an unknown author or authors during the latter part of the third century A.D. Nevertheless, it influenced the cooking styles of the European continent well into the seventeenth century. Apicius brought further notoriety to himself when he discovered that he was down to his last 10 million sesterce (about $70,000; though some historians claim it was 40 million sesterces, about $280,000). Concluding that life would no longer be worth living, he ingested poison at a banquet especially arranged for the event.

Another important source of our information on the styles of cooking and eating during Roman reign comes from Gaius Petronius, also known as *Petronius Arbiter* since he was considered an "arbiter" of fashion. Petronius was a Roman courtier and satirist, and the author of *Cena Trimalchionis* (Trimalchio's feast), one of the best known pieces of literature to survive from this era. Trimalchio was a braggart, drunk, and wife-beater, given to staging extravagant banquets in order to show off his transformation from former slave to successful entrepreneur. Trimalchio and, later, Petronius both ended their lives in the Apician mode—at a self-staged final banquet-funeral.

As the culture of Rome declined, her power and influence ebbing with it, scores of tribes fought over territory and treasure for a period of several hundred years. The fortunes of a tribe could be lost on a battlefield in a matter of hours or days, while to the victor came both the spoils of combat and the burden of maintaining a position of strength. After such incidents there was inevitably a banquet to celebrate victory and feed a hungry army. Some groups, such as the Gauls (Gallo-Romans), having been under territorial dominion of the former Roman empire, for the most part modeled their banquets on the Roman style. The Romans had introduced the use of spices and a modicum of previously unknown table manners.

But there were few real gastronomic changes, and by modern standards the Gauls ate poorly. Meat and fish were often boiled together; it was not until much later that the custom of cooking them separately was adopted. Meals were long, but some citizens disdained Roman indolence and seated themselves on wooden benches or stools instead of reclining on couches. As for their banquets:

> The table, ornamented with incrustations, is round, covered with a fine tablecloth. The architricline announces that dinner is served. The guests wash their hands, which they will do again after the first course. They put on special robes and sandals, unfold their napkins if they have brought them, for the host does not provide these. Then they take their places around the table.
>
> To satisfy all the senses, the dining-room is strewed with leaves of laurel, ivy, verdant vinebranches; both the guests and the servants are crowned with flowers. Garlands of roses hang from the handles of canthares. Large baskets, placed on the table as well as on the abacus, or sideboard, are full of bunches of cytisus, saffron, privet, marigolds and rosemary, and their fragrance mingles with that of Arabian aromatics smoldering in the three-legged brazier.
>
> The slaves bring in a great quantity of meat, roast or boiled, which is carved with great skill and dexterity by servants in charge of this job. A salver (repositorium) is placed in the centre of the table and various dishes are put on it one after the other: fresh eggs, quarters of beef, mutton, pork, goat, all seasoned with yolks of egg, black pepper, brine, cumin, salt from the salt mines, or residue from boiled seawater. After having consumed endless number of various dishes, the guests are served hot or cold tarts, honey cakes, soft cheese, grilled escargots, chestnuts, figs, Gaul peaches, and fresh and dried grapes. At the end of the meal hot mulsum is brought in once again and the slaves distribute toothpicks of feathers, wood and silver.
>
> (Emile De la Bédolière, *Histoire des Moeurs et de la Vie Privée des Français*, Lecou, 1847).

When Charles ("the Hammer") Martel (688–741) became mayor of the Frankish Palace at the age of 27, he established a political foothold that would lead to the establishment of the Franks as the early rulers of Europe. His son, Pepin the Short, deposed the last of the Merovingian rulers (Childeric III) and continued working toward consolidating the Frankish kingdom. At his death in 768, his two sons, Carolman and Charlemagne inherited the empire. Carolman died in 771, and Charlemagne carried on his father's work of uniting a kingdom. Charlemagne was an enigma in his time. He stood six feet, four inches, an enormous height in his day, had a high, squeaky voice, and lived to the unheard-of age of 72. He was a formidable military strategist and warrior as well as a visionary. He established schools, promoted the arts, and oversaw the restoration of many literary and artistic works left behind by long-vanished cultures of antiquity. Many of the territorial jurisdictions he established in the eighth century remain in place to this day. Concurrent with his efforts to create a nation of literate and prosperous people, the First Lord of the Table introduced some elements of refinement in matters of dining within his court. In the dining room, stone walls were covered with ivy, the floor was strewn with silver lilies, crimson poppies, and red roses, and the air was scented with perfumes. He was the first to invite women to sit at the table with men, although only on the condition that they did not offend with nauseating odors or noxious perfumes. He also introduced a fruit compote as an accompaniment to meats, and at his court people were instructed to eat with the point of the knife, not with the fingers. They may or may not have washed their hands before dining, depending on which historical account one reads, but it is generally agreed that they practiced drinking wine from a communal goblet, passed hand to hand around the table. Beyond the monarch's table, however, hygienic and culinary rules were nonexistent, and among the general populace quantity was still preferred to quality and piles of meats followed one after the other.

After his death in 814 the protocol established by Charlemagne continued to evolve in some measure, though only at the royal tables, where such luxury could be afforded. For the average citizen, the Middle Ages was a period of uncertainty, misery, and predictions of a dire future lasting more than five hundred years. Famine, a common reality, was so dreadful at times that cannibalism was the only alternative to starvation. Raoul Glaber, a ribald monk of the eleventh century wrote, "Cannibalism is rife particularly in certain sections of the center of France, the most underprivileged areas. On the highroads, the strong seize the weak; they tear them apart, roast them and eat them. Bands of men roam the countryside in groups attacking lonely wayfarers, attacking whole families and strolling minstrels with their children, killing them and selling their flesh in the nearest market."

At the royal courts, however, luxury, pageantry, and abundance were the order of the day. Guests washed hands with perfumed water and were handed a napkin by a young page—something considered a great honor, and the order in which it was performed related to a guest's ranking. As guests entered a dining area, they were announced by either trumpet or bell, also depending on their social ranking. After seating, some form of grace was said. Then the first course was brought in with great pomp, sometimes announced by a flourish of trumpets. The dishes were tasted and/or touched with a talisman before serving to guard against poisoning. A typical menu consisted of a soup, fish, roasted game (peacock, pheasant, or swan) and a roasted meat, and a dessert, which might include fresh and dried fruit, creams, pastry, and hippocras (spiced wine). At the conclusion of the meal, the table was cleared, guests washed hands again, and entertainment began, featuring various jesters, jugglers, minstrels, and poets, during which the guests were offered additional aromatized wines and sweetmeats.

In the late fifteenth and early sixteenth centuries, banquet and dining styles evolved into the fledging haute cuisine that would peak in the nineteenth century. Large imported gold and silver serving pieces, French porcelain, and Italian glassware embellished tables covered with fine linen. It was also at this time that banquets took on enormous magnitude in numbers of people and quantity of food served. In 1549, a banquet given in Paris in honor of Catherine de Médici (1519–1589; queen of France 1533–1589), queen to King Henry II, featured a menu that included, in part, no less than 700 capons, chickens, cranes, egrets, herons, partridges, peacocks, pheasants, pigeons, swans, and turtle doves; this was in addition to various rabbit, pork, and veal dishes and a vast quantity of vegetables, including artichokes, asparagus, broad beans, and peas. A mere 14 years old when she married Henry, Catherine had brought with her a retinue of cooks, bakers, and confectioners and a battery of kitchen equipment and marvelous novelties, which captivated both the aristocracy and the masses. The queen was a glutton, her preferences running to—among other things—cockscombs, kidneys, truffles, artichoke heart fritters, and zabaglione. Her presence sparked a gastronomic renaissance in France, which included a renewed interest in dessert, thanks in part to the Marquis Cescare Frangipani, who presented an almond-flavored genoise (sponge cake) as a pledge of eternal love to the young Catherine before she left Italy for France.

Henri III (1551–1589; king of France 1574–1589), son of Catherine de Médici, further promoted the use of a two-pronged fork, which his mother had introduced, as a way to prevent spotting the delicate ruff that encircled the necks of gentlemen. (His tablecloths were typically pleated in a similar fashion.) Interestingly, the fork did not gain widespread use until the reign of Louis XIV, because the cooks of that time contended that it spoiled the taste of food.

French cookery continued to evolve, reaching a certain pinnacle under the Bourbon kings (1589–1850). During the reign of Louis XIII (1610–1645), however, there was an effort to harmonize and simplify. Relative to the simplification promoted by Auguste Escoffier at the turn of the twentieth century, the result was hardly an uncomplicated cuisine, but in its day it was reflective of a ritualized respect for the abundance of the table. Meals were organized into eight courses, as illustrated by the following menu for a banquet during the reign of Louis XIV (1643–1715):

First course: soups, sliced meats, sausages

Second course: courts-bouillons, fritters, game, ham, ox tongue, farces, hot pâtés, salads, melons

Third course: capons, partridges, pheasants, woodcocks, pigeons, turkeys, hares, rabbits, and lamb, all roasted with oranges and lemons, and garnished with olives

Fourth course: larks, ortolans, thrushes, snipe, and sweetbreads

Fifth course: salmon, trout, pike, and carp, all cooked in pastry, and crayfish and turtle

Sixth course: various vegetable dishes, fruit in syrups, and creams

Seventh course: pastries and fresh fruit

Eighth course: preserves, dried and crystallized fruit, fennel in sugar, sugared almonds.

Louis XV (1715–1774) was himself interested in cooking and on occasion hosted "little suppers," where he and his male compatriots would prepare a dinner themselves with servants present only for serving. Official royal events of the time, however, were incredibly pompous and drawn out with a haughty kind of ritual. Even after all the initial ceremonial pomp only the king and courtiers of a certain rank dined, while others waited their turn. The following excerpt of a description of a banquet in 1722, on the occasion of the anointing of the king, gives the reader a glimpse of such formalities:

> In one of the halls of the archepiscopal palace, five tables were laid. The king's table had four steps leading to it, under a purple velvet canopy with golden fleur-de-lys. The four other tables were occupied by peers, ecclesiastical officials, ambassadors, and chamberlains. On the left of the royal table, a tribune had been erected, from which the Duchess of Lorraine watched the ceremony. During the sumptuous banquet the Duchess could see all these dishes filing past without being able to touch them. She quietly nibbled biscuits, with which she was fortunately provided, and offered them to the princes seated near her, who by this time were also beginning to reach the end of their tether.

The little dinners and suppers that Louis XV enjoyed preparing became even more popular toward the end of the eighteenth century, and the menus of these mini-banquets reflected the modern-tending philosophies of personalities such as Antoine Carême, Jean Avice, and Languipière (the latter two were also mentors to Carême). The grandiose and sumptuous banquets still took place, but the popular spin-off of smaller, more intimate dinners resulted in a legacy of notable affairs that remain a part of the literature of this time. One such dinner was hosted by Antoine-Auguste Parmentier (1737–1817), economist, pharmacist, and agronomist, who is credited with popularizing potatoes as a nutritional foodstuff. The menu was composed of twenty different potato dishes, and among the guests was Benjamin Franklin. During the winter of 1803, when there were no fish to be had in Paris, Charles-Maurice de Talleyrand-Périgord (1754–1838) arranged for his butler to carry in a huge poached turbot for his guests, to stumble on the way to the table, and to drop the fish to the floor. The guests were horrified, of course, only to see a second fish brought in directly. Grimod de la Reynière (1758–1838) was also known for grand dinners, though a bit on the eccentric side. He once sent out invitations to 22 guests in the form of his funeral announcement. These guests at his "mortuary dinner" were required to pass through a series of pretentious formalities; they ultimately arrived at a banquet hall, where they found an empty coffin standing behind each guest's chair.

Among the most celebrated hosts of this period was Alexandre Dumas (*père*, 1802–1870), author of *The Three Musketeers*, *La Grand Dictionaire de la Cuisine* (still in print), and numerous other published works. In 1844, Dumas began hosting a weekly dinner. On Wednesdays, at 11:00 P.M., 15 guests, most of them from the theatrical world, came to his home and dined on a soup, a game pie, a roast, and a salad. These meals continued for two years, during which time *The Three Musketeers* was serialized in *Le Siècle*. That Dumas had considerable interest in culinary matters is clear from some of his literary observations, such as: "The omelette is to haute cuisine, what the sonnet is to poetry."

There was one particular supper during this time that received enormous press and notoriety. Madame Vigée-Lebrun, a painter, had invited 15 friends to hear a reading by the poet LeBrun, and during that reading there was a passage describing a Greek dinner. Someone suggested that this dinner be prepared, and after the reading Madame went about making the arrangements. After giving her cook instructions for the evening's menu, she and her girlfriends created some quick costumes out of the material she used to drape her models. They borrowed some urns and vases from the count de Parois, wove laurel branches into wreathes, and, in all, created an ambiance as close as possible to their visualization of ancient Greece. At 10:00 P.M. the other guests arrived, and they all had a splendid little Greek supper. In the days that followed, rumors of the opulence and expense of this affair spread like wildfire, including estimates of its cost as high as 80,000 francs. In her memoirs, Madame wrote of this supper stating that it was a pleasant and amusing evening with her friends, that nothing spectacular took place, and that it cost her the incredible sum of 15 francs.

During this period, the table was more than a place to ingest fuel for the body; it was a common meeting ground where all manner of business and human interaction was conducted. The princes, dukes, and ministers who occupied important posts under Louis XVI met daily at open tables maintained variously in Paris, Versailles, and Fontainebleau. The king and his family made a habit of dining out on Sundays, in an area where they could be watched by their public. "As dinner-hour came, one met these good people on the stairs. Having seen the Dauphine eat her soup, they were dashing to see the princes eat their boiled beef, and then rushed, out of breath, to watch the Ladies eat their desserts. This spectacle gave happiness to the provincials" (from Madame Campan's *Memoirs*). Whether the "provincials" derived happiness from standing around watching the aristocracy stuff themselves is a matter of opinion, for it was not much later that Louis and his family found themselves imprisoned, soon to be casualties of the Reign of Terror. If ever an insurrection was forced by hunger bordering on starvation, with the starving proletariat gathering on Sunday afternoons to watch their sovereign and his family satiate themselves, the French Revolution was it. Yet even in prison the king and his family were fed quite well: "Dinner consisted of three soups, four entrées, three roasts, four sweets, a plate of fancy cakes, three compotes, three dishes of fruit, three loaves of bread with butter, one bottle of Champagne, one small carafe of Bordeaux, and four cups of coffee."

The early nineteenth century saw the publication of two important books on the culinary craft: In 1808, the first edition of *Manuel des Amphitryons* was published, penned by Grimod de la Reynière; and in 1825 *Le Physioligie du Goût* (The Physiology of Taste, or Meditations on Transcendental Gastronomy), by Jean Anthelme Brillat-Savarin (1755–1826).

11

De la Reynière's work was as eccentric as its author, filled with both wit and gastronomic guidelines, including laws governing banquets. Having lived through the horrors of the Revolution and the Reign of Terror, he wrote the *Manual* as a sort of instruction guide for a new society. Few copies exist, but Brillat-Savarin's work—which enumerates various rules for proper food, dining etiquette, and the art of arranging banquets harmoniously—translated by the late M. F. K. Fisher, is still in print today. Brillat-Savarin was also the mayor of Belley, deputy to the Estates General, and magistrate in the Supreme Court of Appeals. During the Revolution he had fled France to escape the Tribunal, first to Switzerland and later to America, where he played the violin on city streets to survive. *Le Physiologie du Goût* appeared in bookstores in October 1825, and though the first edition did not bear the name of the author, the book was an immediate success.

In 1765,* Boulanger opened the first restaurant in Paris on the rue Bailleul. The sign outside his shop read, "Boulanger sells magical restoratives," which is what he called the offerings on his menu, all of which were soups. The sign also said, *"Venite ad me; vos qui stomacho laboratis et ego restaurabo vos."* (Come to me, all whose stomach cries out, and I will restore you.) When he added a dish of lamb shanks in white sauce, the local *traiteurs* (caterers) filed a suit against him—he was not a member of their organization—to prevent him from serving any dishes more ambitious than soup. Parliament ruled in his favor, and the publicity was such that Parisians rushed to his place to taste the new offering. Louis XV even served the dish at Versailles.

Antoine Beauvillier opened another restaurant in 1782 but was forced to close during the Revolution. The Revolution radically changed the way people dined, including the opulent banquets of the royal houses. It was at this time that restaurants began to flourish, and through the nineteenth century they became essential centers of culture. One of the most famous was Rocher de Cancale, first opened in 1795 and taken over by restaurateur Alexis Baleine in 1804. (An original menu can be seen in the Escoffier Museum in Villeneuve-Loubet, a small village south of Nice, France.) This restaurant was known for its oysters (from the oyster beds off the coast of Cancale), *Sweetbreads à la Financière*, and *Sole Normande*, which was created there by the chef Langlais in 1837. Another

---

* (Since he was believed to be a baker, Boulanger has come to be known by that word, while his true name has been lost.)

celebrated café was Café Anglais, which opened in 1802 in honor of the Peace of Amiens, a treaty between England and France. When Adolphe Dulgléré took over the kitchen, it acquired a great gastronomic reputation: *Potage St. Germain, Sole Dugléré,* and *Pommes Anna* were all created there at this restaurant, and all of these dishes are known and prepared today. Other cafés of note included Cafés à l'Académie, des Aveugles, Bignon, Brébant, Cadran Bleu, du Caveau, des Chartres, de Flore, de Foy, Hardy, de Madrid, Napolitain, d'Orsay, de la Paix, de Paris, Philippe, de la Régence, Riche, Tortonis, des Variétés, Véfour, and La Vente Libre (for women only).

The end of the nineteenth century marked the end of a long era of evolution in the style and substance of banquets. Oscar Tschirsky, the celebrated waiter and maître d'hôtel at the Waldorf-Astoria from 1892 until 1943, once wrote: "The dinner most representative of the lavish nineties, I think, was that given by Randolph Guggenheimer, then president of the Municipal Council, in February 1899. It was served at a cost to the guests of $250 a plate. Nightingales sang in a grove of rose trees, grape arbors surrounded the banquet room, and a rare vintage of brandy, bottled before the French Revolution, was opened. Forty guests were present." The menu was as follows:

Oyster Cocktail

Lemardelais à la Princesse

Green Turtle, Bolivar

Basket of Lobster

Colombine of Chicken, California Style

Roast Mountain Sheep with Chestnut Purée

Jelly • Brussels Sprouts Sauté

New Asparagus with Cream Sauce

Fancy Sherbet

Diamond Back Terrapin

Ruddy Duck

Orange and Grapefruit Salad

Fresh Strawberries and Raspberries

Vanilla Mousse

Bonbons • Fruits

Coffee

Twentieth-century banquet styles were unintentionally inaugurated on September 22, 1900, at the Tuileries Gardens. The Affaires des Congrégations was attended by 22,295 guests. In order to serve this number, the staff assembled included 1,800 maîtres d'hôtels, 3,600 waiters and cooks, 300 dishwashers, and 6 pages. Serviceware for this event included 95,000 glasses, 60,000 forks and spoons, 250,000 plates and dishes, 8,000 tablecloths, and 30,000 napkins. Provisions included 5,000 pounds (2,250 kg) of beef fillet, 5,000 pounds (2,250 kg) of pheasants, over 4,000 pounds (1,800 kg) of salmon, 5,000 pounds (2,250 kg) of duckling, 1,300 quarts (1,235 L) of mayonnaise, 5,000 pounds (2,250 kg) of fowl, 2,000 pounds (900 kg) of grapes, 10,000 peaches, 4,000 figs, 6,000 pears, 4,000 apples, 20,000 plums, 60,000 petits fours, 50,000 bottles of wine, 3,000 quarts (2,850 L) of coffee, 1,000 quarts (950 L) of liqueurs.

One can imagine the excitement and awe that must have accompanied the execution of such an enormous event in the first year of a new millennium. But did the caterers of the Affaires des Congrégations realize the size to which various expressions of the foodservice industry would grow? In one of my earliest cooking positions, I was part of a two-man team in charge of all the cold foods for a buffet that fed 600 guests every Sunday evening during that summer season. Some years later—nearly ninety years after the Affaires des Congrégations at Tuileries Gardens—I was involved in the production of three buffets, three sit-down dinners, and three rodeos over a period of six days, each event serving 8,500 guests. Today there are hotel operations in North America where as many as 30,000 meals are served each day, every day of the year, and three-fourths of those meals are served as a buffet. What these numbers indicate is sufficient activity and interest, creating a multitude of work possibilities for any aspiring garde manger willing to invest the time and effort.

DEFINING THE GARDE MANGER

Ludwig Bemelmans began working as a *commis* at the Ritz Carlton in New York City in 1914. In a tale from a collection of his stories (*La Bonne Table*, David Godine Publishers, 1989), he gives the following description of the garde manger, circa 1916: "I had been sent to the kitchen to get small sandwiches for some tea guests. The man who makes these sandwiches is called the *garde manger*. Instead of ovens, this cook has only large iceboxes, in which he keeps caviar, pâté de foie gras, herrings, pickles, salmon, sturgeon, all the various hams, cold turkeys, partridges, tongues, the cold sauces, mayonnaise. To order the sandwiches, the commis had first to write out a little slip, announce the order aloud, go to the coffeeman at the other end of the kitchen for the bread, and finally bring the bread to the garde manger to be spread with butter, covered and cut into little squares."

Traditionally, the garde manger department was a part of a kitchen that created attractive and tasteful dishes utilizing the parts of meat, game, poultry, and fish that the primary kitchen did not use. The loins, tenderloins, fillets, and center cuts were all used by the main kitchen, and what remained was sent to the garde manger for innovation. This ever-uncertain supply of raw foodstuffs with which to work explains why farces—pâtés, terrines, galantines, mousses, and other ground meat-poultry-fish items—are typically created in the garde manger area. Although in modern times the garde manger department continues to be a place of innovation, utilizing secondary and peripheral foodstuffs for cold food items for placement on buffets, it is also that part of the kitchen where showpieces are produced—fashioned from ice, tallow, salt dough, and unleavened bread dough (dead, or weaver's, dough). Here is where the culinary artist has an opportunity to express him- or herself.

In contemporary kitchens, food production is not always strictly divided between the garde manger and the other areas of the kitchen. A large hotel feeding several thousand guests daily requires a large and separate kitchen—sometimes referred to as the pantry—for the specific production of cold food items. At the other end of the spectrum, a 100-seat restaurant that offers dishes on its menu typical of the garde manger does not have sufficient volume to house a separate garde manger production area. Thus, in a kitchen staffed with four to six persons, everyone shares duties as production requires. Typically, the garde manger department is responsible for producing the following cold food items:

- Hors d'oeuvres: canapés; finger sandwiches; salads; appetizers, small courses, and side dishes
- Numerous varieties of farces (forcemeats), such as pâtés, mousses, and terrines
- Charcuterie: primarily, sausages; smoked meat, game, fish, and poultry; and dry-cured fish (traditionally, smoking and curing were performed by a butcher)
- Buffet centerpieces composed of ice, tallow, salt dough, weaver's dough; still life arrangements of fruits, vegetables, and other props (pasta, beans, nuts, dried fruit, bottled oils

15

and vinegars); cut and sculpted fruits and vegetables (*muki-mono*).

The garde manger area is also a place where some food items are reapplied (not reused) to a secondary product. The practice, a holdover from the traditional function of this production area, is still in place today. It is important for two reasons: It helps in ensuring fiscal profitability of the kitchen operation while maintaining a level of culinary excellence, and it allows exploration of the unlimited creative possibilities. The *peripheral* food items previously designated for a different purpose—often carelessly referred to as leftovers—are used in canapés and pastries, soups and salads, mousses and terrines. And although some ingredients are originally earmarked for a different use, a focus on culinary excellence is still maintained—something that the management team and all the individual members of the brigade are responsible for. Consider this illustration: Imagine a roasted veal loin or top round, prepared for a Friday evening banquet. Roasts remaining from such an event, when chilled, can be utilized in a Saturday afternoon sandwich special or in a platter of *Vitello Tonnato* for a Sunday afternoon buffet. Thin-sliced veal, napped with a sauce of mayonnaise, shredded tuna, mashed anchovies, cornichons, and parsley and garnished with capers and sliced lemon, is a well known and savory traditional dish of Italian origin. Poached or roasted chicken, diced, combined with finely diced celery and scallion, seasoned with tarragon, bound with mayonnaise, and stuffed into scooped-out apples, becomes California Apples; poached salmon fillet, broken into fine flakes, topped with dill-flavored vinaigrette, and garnished with pickled cucumber and lightly blanched fresh green peas, becomes a Salmon Salad, Scandinavian Style; fresh asparagus, peeled and lightly blanched—or broccoli—cooked again to al dente, chilled, dressed with vinaigrette, and sprinkled with sieved hard-cooked eggs, creates Asparagus, or Broccoli, Mimosa; baked potatoes are transformed into German-Style Potato Salad when peeled, sliced, dressed with crisp bacon and vinaigrette, and topped with minced parsley; slightly undercooked penne, combined with carefully cut and blanched vegetables and garbanzo beans, lightly dressed with mayonnaise, balsamic vinegar, topped with minced fine herbs, and garnished with a vegetable julienne, is re-created into Chilled Summer Pasta Primavera; cut salad greens simmered in a velouté, puréed, chilled, and creamed, becomes Chilled Cream of Lettuce Soup. These are only a few examples of how food supplies remaining from a previous function can be transformed.

The preceding illustration also emphasizes the importance of the chef garde manger's possessing a broad international repertoire. Traditional garde manger styles have always been based on western European food styles, typically German (well known for charcuterie), French (farces), Scandinavian (cured and marinated fish), and Swiss (the best of German and French styles). In melting-pot North America, contemporary garde manger styles are influenced by a variety of Asian cultures—Chinese, Japanese, Korean, Thai, and Vietnamese—as well as those "south of the border," principally Mexican. A familiarity with all of these influences is essential to understanding the creative possibilities, and those with the knowledge to incorporate these influences within their repertoires are worth their weight in caviar.

At the same time, in today's actual practice, many dishes traditionally prepared in the garde manger department are being "farmed out"—that is, purchased outside the kitchen operation. This is a fairly recent development, spurred by the need to maintain tight labor cost controls. As food and labor costs rise, it becomes increasingly difficult to retain numerous brigade members (culinary staff) with extensive classical training and broad repertoires. And as market tastes change, today's clientele have become more interested in the modern and "latest" styles of food that give them a satisfactory sense of good value for their money spent. Hence, kitchen operations are forced to maintain a delicate balance between highly qualified key brigade members, and a less experienced staff who are dedicated to the profession and willing to learn. Although this trend may appear as leading to the slow demise of the traditions of classical Western cooking, it is in reality a shift in production styles—and it has given birth to a whole new industry of specialty producers who can supply classical-style foods to any kitchen operation when such dishes are called for. At the major food trade shows held in the United States annually, dozens of manufacturers from around the world show their products to the men and women in the profession. These products are the kinds of items that garde manger departments need on occasion, but not frequently enough to maintain the high-cost staff necessary to prepare them. Such items include pâtés and terrines of every imaginable variety (including vegetable pâtés); excellent sausages, both smoked and fresh, made not just from pork but from poultry and seafood as well; naturally produced country hams and other pork by-products; ready-made centerpieces fashioned out of bread, tallow, and salt dough. For future garde mangers, the growth of this industry opens new career possibilities, but not necessarily in a kitchen in the traditional sense.

There is no question that the garde manger department is one of the most exciting and creativity-driven places in which to practice the culinary craft; it offers an opportunity to work as an artist in a food medium. At the same time, such an environment can also be one of high stress, where one can experience frustration and burn-out resulting from a constant demand for eye-dazzling and palate-luscious foods that sometimes disappear in a mad rush of diners toward the buffet table. There is a constant and never-ending responsibility for the garde manger to produce visually appealing and fiscally viable buffets, highlighted by artistic works of art done in ice, tallow, and dough. This is no place for the uninitiated or the fragile food artists of the world. Working in a creative zone where one is free to unleash one's artistic vision demands not just creativity, but the ability to remain eminently well organized and cool under fire. Anything less can lead to frustration and early burn-out. If you are a student of the culinary craft who savors the prospect of fulfilling your artistic inclinations in a medium of cold food production, your enthusiasm is a valuable commodity. Remember, though, you will at times be pushed to your limits and challenged on many fronts. You who are an impetuous artist must also be:

- A dedicated and hard-working culinary professional
- A cool-headed manager who excels at delegating responsibility
- A source of inspiration for co-workers to do their creative and innovative best

How does an interested person learn these skills? After some type of formal training, he or she joins the garde manger department in a hotel operation and begins gaining actual work experience. In some cases, there is a formal apprenticeship program with a specifically organized system of working through the various stations within that department. In addition to initial interest, this undertaking demands both dedication and an eternal willingness to learn. An ongoing willingness to learn is the earmark of every man or woman who ultimately finds him- or herself in a position of responsibility and honor in a creative kitchen. Understanding the elements of professionalism is essential in the process of learning and working with others in the highly charged environment of the Garde Manger. Professionalism, which is both an attitude and a way of conducting oneself in a work environment, is sometimes more important in the garde manger department than in other departments. Here, creative work is continually in progress and the action is often fast and furious. No matter what your co-worker's attitudes, your professionalism demonstrates to others a level of commitment and a personal focus on excellence. What does it mean to be a professional? Consider the following list.

Elements of Professionalism

- Focus on the job at hand, and perform all tasks and responsibilities to the best of your ability.
- Wear clean and well-pressed proper attire, and maintain good personal hygiene.
- Practice being a good listener. (This promotes teamwork, esprit de corps, and camaraderie.)
- Avoid profanity, crude jokes, and gossip. No matter how tough things are, make an effort to accentuate the positive.
- Remember, the foodservice industry is a *service industry*. Customer-oriented service is the best advertising for any service business.
- Learn to wind down after each work day by cultivating conversation with friends and co-workers, reading, and other constructive activities.
- Establish a steadfast rule: Never consume alcohol during a work shift.
- Physically demanding work does not take the place of healthful exercise. Set aside time weekly to maintain good physical fitness.
- Do all things in moderation. (It takes 21 consecutive days to develop a new habit.)
- Arrive at work punctually and stay until the last customer is served.

Not all kitchens adhere to guidelines like these. In every profession there are pockets of enlightenment and harmony, as well as places where personal biases and ego-driven personalities get in the way of a focus on excellence. All students of the culinary arts are encouraged to find a niche where their creativity can flower, and where co-workers consider the following important but simple guidelines as a valid communal affirmation to be adhered to by all:

Kitchen User's Guide

- If you open it, close it.
- If you get it out, put it away.

- If you turn it on, turn it off.
- If you move it, put it back.
- If you spill it, wipe it up.
- If you get it dirty, clean it up.
- If you unlock it, lock it up.
- If you break it, get it fixed.
- If you care about it, treat it as your own.

Finally, if a question arises about who is responsible for what job, remember the story about Everybody, Somebody, Anybody, and Nobody:

> There was an important job to be done, and Everybody was sure that Somebody would do it. Anybody could have done it, but Nobody did it. Somebody got angry about that, because it was Everybody's job. Everybody thought Anybody could do it, but Nobody realized that Everybody wouldn't do it. It ended up that Everybody blamed Somebody when Nobody did what Anybody could have done.

PLANNING, BANQUET THEMES, AND BUFFET SET-UP

THE IMPORTANCE OF PLANNING

For professionals currently employed in the garde manger or pantry production area within a hotel, restaurant, private club, or catering operation, there are generally established menus and operating systems in place, orchestrated by the executive chef and his or her closest subordinates (sous-chef, chef Garde Manger, banquet chef, chef pâtissier). Nevertheless, the better the members of the production and service staff, both front and back of the house, are acquainted with the details of these functions, the more easily the buffet set-up will be accomplished and the more smoothly banquet events will unfold. Detailed planning, of course, is essential to the successful execution of any such event.

Having hosted, organized, and/or prepared food for scores of events over a period of more than two decades, I have been involved in some very spectacular banquets. Some have been shining examples of detailed planning executed with pinpoint precision; others have been disasters and near-disasters, examples of embarrassing debacles, sometimes the fault of no one person or circumstance.

In 1977 I participated as a food server for a banquet to raise money for a local theater organization in San Francisco. The event was held in a downtown department store, and the theme was a Roman bacchanal. The owner of the department store donated the space, and a very fine caterer was hired to create five unique buffets, each on a separate floor of the building. The foodservice on each of four floors reflected a particular theme: a farmer's market, a fish market, a pig roast, and a confectionery. On the fifth floor a three-piece band played rousing dance sets before a portable dance floor. Each floor also had its own bar, with libations in tune with its theme: light wines and nonalcoholic punch for the markets, robust wines and liquors for the roast, champagne and cognacs for the confectionery, and a full bar on the fifth floor. Service personnel (including me) were dressed in white silk togas that came to the middle of the thigh and leather sandals that tied up to the top of the calf. The planning for this event was a phenomenal task, in addition to the preparation of an enormous menu, importation of a myriad of props and serviceware, and scores of service personnel to be orchestrated. Several magnificent creatures—I recall a young leopard, an ostrich, a panda, and several parrots—were brought in from the San Francisco zoo and paraded around to add to the ambiance of the bacchanalian theme. The caterer was highly organized and composed a working script, with each task, ranging from the most obvious to the most insignificant, written out in detail with specific times and individuals assigned to each task. As a result, this event unfolded with nary a hitch and was a success in all respects. Preplanning was the key to that success.

In 1981, I worked as a service person for the same caterer, this time at a fund-raiser held by a local museum. The keynote speaker at this sit-down banquet for 250 potential donors was Henry Kissinger, so the audience was a fairly sophisticated one; service personnel wore white tuxedos with white gloves. The major problem was in the work area—essentially, there was no such area—and the event was designed to compensate for this lack. The main course consisted of a teriyaki-marinated chicken brochette. The marinating of the chicken, in soy sauce, ginger, and marin (sweetened sake), expedited the cooking operation; upright rolling racks with electric heating units were intended to complete the process. The rest of the menu consisted of foods already prepared, to be served cold. The racks were plugged in at the designated time so that they would become hot enough to complete the cooking of the chicken. Service was initiated and the entrées for the guests at the first table were set in place. These guests immediately informed the hostess of a lukewarm and insufficiently cooked main course. When the hostess came running to the caterer to tell him of the problem, the poor man was so mortified that he nearly expired on the spot. Because no one had thought to check the condition of the food as it went out to the first table, no one was aware that the heating racks had put an overload on the electrical system of the museum, which was not engineered for such use, and the primary panel of circuit breakers had shut down. An experience like this cannot be anticipated, but preplanning and quick thinking can prevent disaster. Fortunately, the caterer had brought along several portable hibachis and a case of canned sterno. The workers quickly set up the hibachis just outside the exit door of the museum, fired up the sternos, and began frantically grilling 500 chicken teriyaki skewers (two per person). Fortunately, the hostess, an amenable personality, kept things cool in the dining room while the catering staff worked like mad people to get the food out hot and fast. Of course, it was planning that saved the day—thinking about every possible eventuality and being prepared for as many worst-case scenarios as possible.

BANQUET THEMES

Because banquets have traditionally been held as celebrations of events, achievements, holidays, and other occasions, a theme is often incorporated as a way of highlighting the reason for the celebration. Working around a theme invites innovation in room props, table decorations, costumes, and even behavior (play-acting). The number of possible themes is infinite, and when creative interplay between the host and the kitchen staff or caterer gets rolling, there is no limit to the kinds of props that can be used to create an exciting ambiance. The dining room manager or maître d'hôtel is usually in charge of this area, although a creative garde manger department may have some specialty items that can be used as props. (Most medium- to large-size cities have a professional company that rents props.) In a well-organized operation, these two areas—front and back of the house—coordinate their creative efforts. The following are some suggested themes, with accompanying ideas for props:

Theme: All-American Buffet or Barbecue

In the Banquet Room: American flags; red, white, and blue crepe paper streamers; red checkered tablecloths; posters reflecting Revolutionary War themes; picnic baskets; Shaker-style and bentwood chairs and furniture; reproductions of turn-of-the-century newspapers and popular sheet music.

22

On the Buffet Table: Miniature paper American flags; red, white, and blue confetti and carnations; ice cream maker; wooden butter churn; antique apple peeler; Colonial American platters; toy antique autos; antique bottles; glass milk bottles filled with colored sand, marble, or glass beads; washboards.

Theme: Asian Festival or Chinese New Year Celebration

In the Banquet Room: Travel posters of Asian destinations; a kimono (hanging); Oriental masks; empty rice sacks; braided garlic; large paper parasols, paper dragons, and paper lanterns; bamboo poles.

On the Buffet Table: Chopsticks; raw rice; gingerroots; star anise; bunches of scallions; hot serrano or Thai chili peppers; bamboo steaming trays; Chinese long-handled wire strainers and other smallwares; bottles of saki, *ng ga pi,* and *mui kwe lu* (Chinese liquors); small ceramic or metal Buddhas; hibachi grills; boxes of loose tea.

Theme: Autumn Wine Harvest or Halloween Masquerade

In the Banquet Room: Dried bundles of straw; pumpkins and carved jack o'lanterns; dried gourds and turban squashes; open produce boxes; weathered wood apple crates filled with apples; dried Indian corn; scarecrow; bales of hay; horror film posters; mock spider webbing; plastic human skeleton.

On the Buffet Table: Wicker baskets filled with apples; dried leaves; miniature pumpkins; witch's hat and broomstick; candles; baseball bats, balls, and gloves; professional baseball team pennant flags; baseball cards; cinnamon sticks, nutmegs, star anise, and gingerroots; gold-foil-wrapped chocolate coins; candy corn; dried fruit; whole cranberries.

Theme: Chicago 1920s Speak-Easy

In the Banquet Room: Felt gaming table covers; moonshine jugs; mannequin clothed in 1920s attire; empty violin cases; plastic machine guns; colored foil streamers; ticker tape.

On the Buffet Table: Cigarette holders; black tablecloth and white napkins; cue sticks and billiard balls; poker chips; playing cards; imitation pearl necklaces; sequins and confetti; cigar boxes; copies of old mystery novels (such as those by Raymond Chandler, Dashiell Hammett, and Rex Stout).

Theme: Fifties Rock and Roll Bash

In the Banquet Room: Posters and old LPs of pop musicians (Chuck Berry, Bo Didley, Jerry Lee Lewis, Elvis Presley, etc.); old acoustic and electric guitars; varsity sweaters; fraternity jackets; pompoms; balloons; tubes of "Brylcreem" (in the bathroom); automobile hubcaps; fifties magazines; posters of James Dean, Marlon Brando, and Buck Rogers.

On the Buffet Table: Fifties 45 RPM records; metal-wheel roller skates; furry dice mini-pillows; jelly beans; Hostess chocolate cupcakes and Twinkies (unwrapped); small bottles of Coke.

Theme: Greek Festival or Mediterranean Wedding Reception

In the Banquet Room: Travel posters of Greece and Adriatic destinations; posters of Greek and Roman ruins; posters of Anthony Quinn and scenes from *Zorba the Greek;* fishnets and cork buoys; olive branches and date palms; urns of various shapes and sizes; rope macramé hangings; sailing tackle, nautical flags.

On the Buffet Table: Jars (labels removed) filled with olives, pepperoncini, and gardinia; bottles of olive oil and Retsina wine; Chianti in straw-wrapped bottles; small cork buoys; olive branches and bay leaves; rubber fish; lobster, mussel, and clam shells; terra-cotta pots filled with lemons and/or bunches of grapes; small pieces of marble; bunches of dried grape leaves; sardine and anchovy cans (unopened); model ships; sailing caps; nylon rope; nautical charts.

There is no limit to the banquet themes that can be developed, depending on budget and client preferences. Consider: a Black Tie New Year's Eve Dinner Party; an Eighteenth-Century Masked Ball; an Erotic/Exotic Ball; a Golden Years of Hollywood (1930s Banquet); a King Arthur and the Knights of the Round Table Party; a Mardi Gras/Carnivale Dinner; a Thousand and One Arabian Nights Party; a 1980s Inside Trader LBO Gala; a Sixteenth-Century Florentine Renaissance Dinner; a Tail-Gate Party (Picnic at the Stadium); a Turn-of-the-Century European Café; a Roman Bacchanal; a Wild West Square Dance; or a Winter Solstice Game Buffet.

Although a specific theme often provides an opportunity to gather props and innovate to create an ambiance, the room and table props do not always have to be perfectly coordinated with the theme of a banquet. In some cases, a banquet may not have a specific theme. Arranging various items, such as the following, in the banquet area can give a sense of abundance and festivity.

For the Room: Arrange balloons; large pieces of colorful cloth, twisted and tied with contrasting cloth, hung above and around the table area; crepe paper streamers; stacks of wooden wine and produce crates; movie posters; ancient maps or globes of the world; numerous wicker baskets in different sizes, shapes, and colors, hung above and behind the buffet; dried sausages or salamis, also hanging near the buffet; braided dried chili peppers and garlic; dried flowers.

For the Table: Display baskets or acrylic (clear plastic) containers filled with lemons and limes and/or seasonal fruits and vegetables; baskets of uncut decorative breads and rolls; unshelled nuts, dried fruit, whole raw cranberries, and dried beans (kidney, black, red, pinto, etc.) sprinkled on the table; uncooked pasta (spaghetti, linguine, fettucine, cappellini, etc.) in tall cylindrical jars, uncooked pasta (fusilli, penne, rigatoni) in squat cylindrical jars; copper smallwares (pots and pans) and earthenware terrines; unopened bottles of wine or specialty beers; small wicker baskets.

SETTING UP THE BUFFET SERVICE AREA

The arrangement of tables and dishes on the buffet table is coordinated by the dining room manager or maître d' and the chef garde manger. In an operation where a buffet is a regular event, a standard format is generally followed, which is flexible enough to adjust according to the number of guests expected. For a small buffet accommodating 50 individuals dining all at once, a single line is adequate. One offering of each dish on the buffet menu is sufficient for the first round of guests, with a second platter brought from the kitchen when that on the buffet is one-half to two-thirds consumed. The separate plateware station at the starting point of the buffet indicates to the guests where they are to begin. Two or three 8- to 12-foot-long banquet tables are arranged end to end in a straight line (various angled configurations may be used when the number of guests exceeds 50). If serving personnel are scheduled to assist in serving—always a gracious touch—space should be allowed along the side of the table opposite to where the guests will line up, where servers can stand to help serve and direct guests along the buffet line. The straight or angled table setup can be varied with a large round table between the rectangular tables, and numerous other variations on shape and layout can be used, depending on the size of the buffet and the size of the space.

The center of the buffet table layout should be reserved for a centerpiece: an ice, tallow, or salt dough carving or a large bouquet of flowers. This display is set on a *riser,* so that it is the highest point in the buffet. A riser is simply a sturdy square or rectangular box—wine crates make excellent risers—preferably six-sided for strength, draped loosely with a tablecloth. All such showpieces and other props should be placed toward the back of the table and generally higher than the table surface so as not to interfere with access to the food. The food items on either side of the centerpiece should be slightly lower, with each consecutive item slightly lower, until the last items at the two far ends of the buffet, can sit directly on the table. Risers can be used innovatively, breaking up the spatial order of the buffet, giving a sense of spontaneity within a logical organization, adding interest and attracting the eye.

For any given course, props are interspersed between the dishes, whether theme related or otherwise (see "For the Table" on page 25). Remember to place these items so that they do not interfere with access to the food.

The use of signage depends on the clientele. For most buffets, small folded cards, or cards inserted into small plastic card holders or specially designed upright metal holders, with the names of the dishes printed or clearly hand-lettered in one consistent language, is a welcoming touch. In other cases, however, such as in small private venues where the clientele is more sophisticated, signage would be inappropriate, as if assuming that such knowledgeable individuals are unable to recognize fine classical cookery.

When the number of guests exceeds 50, table configurations change to accommodate a larger menu. Access to the table may begin at either of the two ends or in the center, with two identical "mirror image" setups, each beginning at both ends of the table and ascending to a high point in the center of the table. The decision on the direction of traffic is generally determined by seating logistics, as well as the shape and size of the room. A buffet can also be freestanding, with identical food offerings in four quadrants: two long sets of tables—two or more tables set end to end—positioned parallel, with space between them for servers. Guests can then begin the buffet at any of the four corners. Of course, there are even larger buffet setups, such as one feeding 8,500 guests over a period of five hours on three separate evenings. In this case, an enormous room was the setting, featuring ten separate freestanding stations, each with a facade and/or awning, and guests moved about the room from station to station. Each of several stations represented a cultural region of the world—California, China, France, Germany, Greece, Italy, and Japan—and other stations exclusively featured beverages, bread, dessert, and shellfish.

Whatever the layout of the tables, they must be properly draped. When tablecloths are used, they should fall to within an inch of the floor in front and should be placed in such a way as to conceal uneven edges and seams, with no gaps where overlaid. An *underliner* should be used beneath each tablecloth; this is a soft, thick cloth that lessens noise in the room. Also available are well-designed draping systems, featuring pleated skirts with prefabricated ruffles, which attach to the upper outside corner of a table. These steps are taken to ensure the appearance of a well-designed, well-appointed, and well-organized food station, telling guests that they are welcome and assuring them that the evening has been well planned for their enjoyment.

MENU DEVELOPMENT

THE STRUCTURE OF MENUS

A buffet offering presents, in banquet form, all the dishes offered on an à la carte menu. In other words, the buffet contains *all* of the dishes on a given menu laid out in an attractive manner, from which dining guests may select for themselves directly. The same number and variety of dishes may be offered on a printed menu in a restaurant, but each is ordered from a service person, who places that order in the kitchen, where it is subsequently prepared *à la carte* ("to the order"). The differences between the two are that a buffet allows visual perception of all the dishes on a menu arranged on a buffet table, from which the dining guests choose, select, and deliver back to their own table; and ordering from an à la carte menu requires a written and verbal description of the dishes, the placing of an order, the preparation of the dish, and delivery from kitchen to the guests by service personnel. It is for these reasons that buffet menus should be very carefully attended to in both design, order, and presentation.

Dining styles in North America are much influenced by the French *haute cuisine,* and by reviewing menus from the past, we are able to gain an understanding of the customs of times past. This is not to say that haute cuisine is superior or eternally admirable—it has its high points and its excesses.

Haute cuisine has changed and evolved over a period of nearly four centuries, and these changes affected the rules governing the formulation of menus. Consider, for example, a banquet in 1656 for Louis XIV (1638–1715), hosted by Madame la Chancelière at her Château de Pontchartrain. The menu included roughly two dozen different dishes served in each of six courses, yielding an incredible total of 168 different dishes. Of course, not everyone ate from each and every dish—the dishes were simply laid out on a table, course by course, from which guests could choose their preferences.

More than a century later, the French Revolution (1789–1799), one of the bloodiest insurrections in Western history, so greatly changed the style of governance that styles of eating and dining were also significantly changed. By the nineteenth century national affairs had settled down, and in 1808, Grimod de la Reynière published his *Manuel des amphitryons*, which included 20 menus, each averaging roughly 24 dishes served in six courses. Although every banquet was unique and featured a menu created for a specific event, all were based on a definite organization of courses, which is outlined in the following synopsis of a classical menu (the apéritif, technically not a course, is included for definition because it is a common prelude to dining).

Apéritif	From the Latin *aperire*, meaning "to open" (the appetite); any beverage, from champagne to clear beef broth, technically qualifies as an apéritif. The beverages prepared from plants and roots that are known to have this "opening" effect (used in such brands as Cynara, Dubonnet, Lillet, Vermouth, and Punt e Mes), are predinner cocktails with a typically bitter and sweet flavor. In truth, however, their consumption is more of a social ritual than a gastronomic prelude. In their manufacture the essences of the plants and roots are dissolved with alcohol, which also neutralizes their beneficial effect.
Hors d'oeuvre froid	Generally consists of charcuterie (cold cuts), marinated fish (Gravlax, herring, sardines), or raw vegetables (bagna cauda, crudités).

Potage (soup)	A typical starter course for dinner, in two parts: a clear soup (bouillon or consommé), followed by a puréed and/or creamed soup.
Hors d'oeuvre chaud (hot)	Literally, "outside of the main piece." Typically served as the first course at a luncheon, or during the cocktail hour at a dinner.
Poisson (fish)	Braised or poached, with appropriate sauce and garnish.
Relevé (remove)	Refers to "removing" the preceding dish. Generally consists of a large roast, such as a rib or baron of beef or braised meat dish, with appropriate garnish.
Entrée chaude (hot) *Entrée froide* (cold)	Although *entrée* has come to mean "main course," its actual meaning is "beginning." These courses traditionally followed the fish course and preceded the roast. There were few restrictions on what such a course consisted of, though it was often a dish prepared in a sauce—everything from fish, shellfish, and caviar to goose liver, eggs, and vegetables; from terrines, quenelles, and pastries to quiche, timbales, and tartlets.
Sorbet (flavored ice)	A soft, fat-free ice, made from fruit juice or purée, wine, spirits, liqueur, or an infusion (such as mint). It is designed to clear the palate for ensuing courses.
Rôt (roast)	Usually poultry or winged game, but fairly open to interpretation, depending on the nature of the meal. This course is sometimes followed by a cold meat course, such as goose liver (foie gras) in aspic. In modern times this term has evolved to *rôti*.
Salade	Generally a plain lettuce salad, with oil and vinegar or lemon.
Entremet (side dish) *Legume* (vegetable)	A course served after the roast, either a vegetable dish or a cold fish, shellfish, goose liver, or poultry

item. (The *entremetier*, literally, the "middle man," on the hot cooking line in a typical kitchen prepares the vegetable dishes for all the hot line stations.)

Fromage (cheese)	An unadorned cheese offering, always served before a sweet dessert.
Entremet de douceur chaud or *douceur froid*	*Entremet* means "side dish," and *douceur froid*, "sweet cold." Hot varieties included crêpes, fritters, poached fruit, sweet omelets, and hot soufflés; cold varieties included bombes, cakes, chilled fruit, ices and ice cream, meringues, mousses, pastries, and puddings.

Of course, fine dining menus in modern times are significantly less expansive than the preceding classical menu and generally consist of the following courses:

Appetizer	A simple hot and/or cold small dish
Soup	Clear or thick
Fish or Shellfish	Hot or cold
Primary Course	Main dish (entrée in modern times)
Salad	Lettuce greens, sometimes with herbs and/or vegetable garnish (cucumber, radish, tomato), with a simple vinaigrette
Cheese	Several unadorned varieties offered at tableside and cut to order
Dessert	Fruit and/or pastry

Note: In many quarters of the Western world there has been a recent trend toward lowering dietary saturated fat. This practice seems to be most prevalent in North America, where a dinner may consist of three courses: a single *appetizer*—a small dish, a soup, or a salad; a *main course*—either fish, shellfish, or a heavier dish; and a *dessert*—any number of typical dessert dishes, or cheese with fruit as the final course. Serving the salad *after* the primary course and the serving of a cheese course are both European customs.

The order of food items on a buffet, essentially the same as the order of the food offered on a menu at any sit-down dinner or in an à la carte restaurant, begins from the starting point on the line: hors d'oeuvres, soups, salads, light dishes (entrées), primary dishes (heavier entrées), cheese, fruit, and dessert. All dishes within any of these categories are arranged in the order of digestibility (light to heavy)—vegetable, fish, fowl, pork, veal, game, lamb, and beef; digestibility also relates to their order in terms of method of preparation—raw (salads), poached (fish and poultry), roasted and fried (poultry and meat), raw and baked (fruit and pastry).

Other traditional guidelines that are important to be aware of, even if one does not follow them to the letter, are as follows:

- Consider the following proportions in developing a buffet menu:

  One or two soups

  One roasted item carved at the table (with accompaniments and/or sauces)

  One braised or sautéed dish

  Two hot starches

  Two hot vegetable dishes

  Two to four specific salads, with appropriate sauces (or basic greens with several garnishes and two sauces—one mayonnaise based, one vinaigrette based)

  One fresh fruit platter

  One cheese platter with vegetable or fruit garnishes

  A bread station with three to six bread varieties

  A dessert station with three to six desserts

- A single food item should not appear twice on the same menu. If broccoli appears in a soup, it should not be served as a vegetable; if a fruit appears in a salad, it should not appear in a dessert (candied fruit in ices and creams is an exception).
- When developing the salad portion of a buffet, divide salads into separate categories, then select the salad ingredients in such a way that they do not conflict with other items on the buffet menu. Suggested salad classifications are as follows: grain, fruit, pasta, potato, seafood, smoked or roasted meat, boiled or roasted vegetables.
- Avoid placing same-colored foods adjacent to one another; for example, poached halibut next to rice pilaf or boiled potatoes; braised celery next to a lettuce salad. Work toward harmonizing color cadence.
- Avoid using similar sauces on the same buffet. If a béarnaise sauce is served with a meat dish, avoid the use of Dutch sauce (hollandaise) for a vegetable dish; if Chicken Hunter Style is served, it would not be appropriate to serve a roast with a Portuguese or Zingara sauce, and so on.
- Plan only one deep-fried item per menu, whether croquette, fritter, or potato, for example.

- Vegetable garnishes accompanying hot dishes should be served separately, so as to maintain their serving appearance (dignity) and their heat.
- At service time, serving utensils must *never* be inserted into food items. They should be placed alongside the dish they are intended to serve, on a napkin or doily with underliner, so that a guest is the first to touch a dish. If subsequent guests leave a utensil in a dish, that is their prerogative.

All of these guidelines aside, menu composition is a very personal and deliberate experience, and more than just listing dishes according to a client's needs and budget. Even Auguste Escoffier believed that menu composition was one of the most challenging tasks for any restaurateur. In some ways it may be considered a juggling performance, balancing numerous criteria, including:

- What the client has in mind
- The styles of a given operation
- The personality of the client's guests
- Market availability of food items
- The season of the year and weather
- The capabilities of the kitchen

MENU COMPOSITION

Menu composition is also a form of communicating—not just the dishes on a menu, but the kitchen's philosophy as well. Lars Kronmark, a colleague and very fine and experienced garde manger, believes there is a tendency among guests at a buffet to overmix food varieties. During his European training and experience, he recounts, it was considered highly inappropriate to dine in this manner and there was a commonly accepted protocol when dining at a buffet. Thus, people adhered to commonsense customs that specified taking small amounts of food on each trip to the buffet table, in the order in which they were organized, and consuming them leisurely. In the realm of menu composition, Lars further believes that those preparing a buffet have a responsibility to inform guests of the guidelines that govern dining from a self-service buffet. Hence, the order in which food is arranged on the buffet table, the props used to designate these divisions, and signage (if used) are all significant communications.

The conception of new dishes and the nomenclature applied to them are also important forms of communication. Classic dishes, that is, dishes that have withstood the test of time, are frequently named after an individual (Roast Rack of Veal, Prince Orloff; Peach Melba), a place or city (Waldorf Salad; Salade Niçoise), a style (Sole Bonne Femme; Omelette à la Ménagère), a locale or country (New England Clam Chowder; Crème Anglaise), or an event (Baked Alaska; Chicken Marengo*). Titles of this kind lend character and nobility to a dish, connecting it to the inspiration from which it was created. A common contemporary style of naming a dish employs nomenclature in the form of a near-detailed description of the method of cooking. In my opinion, this is a groundless and egotistical approach, even though it may be intended to elucidate for the dining guest all the ingredients of the dish. Part of the pleasure of dining is the adventure of uncovering new treasures, of revealing ancient mysteries, of discovering the previously undiscovered. Reading a menu with a descriptions such as "Grilled Free-Range Sonoma Mountain Squab Stuffed with a Pomogranate and Rice Stuffing and served with a Red Pepper Purée Butter Sauce," I yearn for "Breast of Unknown Poultry Wrapped in an Enigma of Chard with Mystery Forest Greens." In this style, selecting a dish so described becomes both a chore and a distraction from the interaction and conversation in progress among the guests at a table. An understated approach to naming menu items is superior and far more elegant than listing the ingredients and methods of preparation, all separated by endless, precise prepositions. Somewhere between the two styles is a happy medium. There is nothing wrong with simply naming a dish *Roast Chicken, Pommes Frites*, or *Grilled Salmon, Garden Style* and allowing the recipient to be pleasantly surprised with the actual presentation and components of the dish.

The ability to compose a menu and the appropriate application of a name to a dish are skills that come from hands-on practice and a broad knowledge of dishes and cooking styles. Studying old menus from recent history is a good exercise for developing these skills. Leonard Beck once wrote, "There should be no need to argue that the kitchen window is a good observatory from which to watch the course of history" (*Two Loaf-Givers*, Library of Congress, 1984). Past menus are anthropological relics of a sort—small windows into kitchens of the past through which we are able to view habits, customs, and styles of dining. The nomenclature used,

---

* Baked Alaska was created to commemorate the Alaska Purchase in 1868; Chicken Marengo was created for Napoleon by his chef Dunand, following the Battle of Marengo on June 14, 1800, in which Napoleon defeated Austria.

variety of dishes, and even the graphic layout can be extremely informative when one is challenged with innovating a contemporary menu. They can also be quite humorous, in revealing culinary inaccuracies or the styles of their day. Presented here are a number of menus offering a glimpse into styles of the past and how these styles have evolved. They span a period from early nineteenth-century Paris to San Francisco, circa 1991. (*Please note:* (1) unless otherwise indicated, some of these menus include hot dishes not necessarily prepared in the garde manger kitchen; (2) capitalization of menu items in some of the older menus may not be accurate by modern standards but are left as they were printed then; (3) English translation is provided by the author for some French menu items.)

PAST MENUS, 1811–1991

A dinner for Napoleon I and family, Paris, France, 1811:

LES POTAGES

Consommé au macaroni • Potage à la purée de marrons
Consommé with Macaroni • Puréed Chestnut Soup

LES RELEVÉS

Pièce de boeuf bouilli garnie aux legumes
Boiled Beef with Vegetables

Brochet à la Chambord
Pike in Chambord

LES ENTRÉES

Côtelettes de mouton à la Soubise
Mutton Chops, Soubise

Perdreaux à la Montglas
Partridge Montglas

Fricassée de poulets à la chevalier
Creamed Chicken Stew, Chevalier

Filets de canard au fumet
Duck Fillets in Natural Broth (au jus)

LES RÔTIS

Chapon au cresson
Capon with Watercress

Gigot d'agneau
Roast Leg of Lamb

LES LEGUMES

Choux-fleur au gratin
Cauliflower au Gratin

Céleri-navet au jus
Celery and Turnip in Broth

LES ENTREMETS AU SUCRE

Crème au café
Coffee Pudding

Gelée d'orange
Orange Jelly

Génoise décorée
Sponge cake

Gaufres à l'allemande
German Wafers

The historic "Three Emperors Dinner" at Café Anglais, Paris, June 7, 1867, in honor of Alexander II (the Russian czar), his son, the future Alexander III, and Wilhelm I (king of Prussia):

LES SOUPES

Impératrice et Fontanges

LES HORS D'OEUVRES

Soufflé à la reine
Chicken Soufflé

LES REMOVES

Filet de sole à la vénitienne

Escalopes de turbot au gratin

Carré de mouton, purée de bretonne
Rack of Mutton with Bretonne Bean Purée

LES ENTRÉES

Poulet à la portugaise
Chicken Portugese Style

Pâté de caille
Quail Pâté

Homard à la parisienne
Lobster, Paris Style

Sorbets de champagne
Champagne Ice

LES RÔTI

Canard à la rouennaise
Duck, Rouen Style

Canapés d'ortolon

LES ENTREMETS

Aubergines à l'espagnole
Eggplant Spanish Style

Asperges en branche
Whole Asparagus

Cassolettes princesse
Princess Casseroles

LES DESSERTS

Bombes glacées
Molded Ice Cream

LES VINS

Retour de l'Inde Madère
Château-Margaux 1847

Château-Lafite 1847
Château-Latour 1848

Chambertin 1846
Champagne Roederer

A supper menu composed by Auguste Escoffier, chef at The Savoy Hotel, October 30, 1895:

Consommé poule-au-pot • Consommé de tortue au Madère

———————————————

Huîtres favorite

———————————————

Cailles pochés à la richelieu

Noisettes d'agneau fines herbes

Brochette d'ortolans

Suprême de volaille Jeannette

Parfait de foie-gras

Salade mignonne

Timbale d'ecrevisses américaine

Asperges nouvelles

Biscuits glacés

Bénédictins rosé

Friandises • Fruits

A luncheon menu aboard the *SS George Washington*, June 14, 1922 (hors d'oeuvres, cold buffet, and salads only):

HORS D'OEUVRES

Chicken Salad with Asparagus Tips • American Lobster Salad

Stuffed Egg with Mayonnaise • Smoked Eel • Rollmops

Table Celery • Pickled Walnuts and Olives • Radishes

COLD BUFFET

Breast of Turkey, Cranberry Sauce • Roast Gosling, Apple Sauce

Saddle of Veal, Potato Salad • Leg of Lamb, Mint Sauce

Prime Rib of Beef, Jardinière

Boiled Ham • Virginia Ham • Smoked Ox Tongue

Assorted Fresh and Smoked Sausage

SALADS

Potato • Cole Slaw • Red Beets

A luncheon served aboard the Empress of Scotland, a train on the Canadian Pacific Railway, 14 September 1922:

LUNCHEON

Anchois à la Russe • Queen Olives

Sardines à l'huile

Scotch Broth • Fillet of Whitefish, Tomato Sauce

Mutton Cutlet, Reforme

Pot Roast of Beef, Paysanne

Purée of Turnips • Boiled and Mashed Potatoes

COLD BUFFET

Hareng en Tomate

Galantine de Dinde • Boar's Head

Mosaïque Roll

Salad

Tapioca Pudding • Compote of Rhubarb and Custard

Cheese: Canadian and Cheddar

Coffee

A New Year's Day menu from Schrafft's restaurant (a well-known "diner"-style restaurant of its day), New York City, January 1, 1933:

SPECIAL DINNER

Fresh Shrimp Cocktail

Cream of Tomato Soup

Melba Toast

Queen Olives

Minute Steak with Broiled Mushroom Caps

Glacé Sweet Potato

New Peas in Cream

Hot Gingerbread

Endive and Orange Salad

Old Fashioned Strawberry Shortcake

Beverage

Assorted Cream and Peppermint Wafers

A luncheon menu from the Fujiya Hotel, Miyanoshita, Hakone, Japan, May 6, 1937:

RELISHES

Hors d'Oeuvre Variés

SOUP

Potage Galicienne

FISH

Sole au Colbert

ENTRÉES

Corned Beef Hash, Poached Egg

Chicken Georgina

Crab Curry and Rice

FROM GRILL TO ORDER

Lamb Chops Bouquetière

VEGETABLES

Haricots Verts au Beurre • Cucumber Romaine

Boiled Potatoes • Pommes Pailles

COLD BUFFET

Cold Ham (Poland) • Suckling Pig • Corned Tongue

SALAD

Salade Tomate Ravigote • Lettuce (Grown in the Hotel Garden)

SWEET

Crème Caramel au Chocolat • Granite d'Ananas

CHEESE

Kraft (Canadian) • Gorgonzola

Assorted Fresh Fruits

Coffee

From a "Farewell Dinner," *RMS Queen Mary,* August 8, 1937:

Honeydew Melon frappe

Salami and Mortadella Sausage • Herrings à la Tomate

Proscuitto Ham • Byron Salmon • Eggs Mayonnaise

Anchovy Croûte

Consommé Rejane • Cream of Mushrooms

Chicken Halibut, Sauce Victoria

Fillets of Sole Chesterfield

Timbales Talleyrand

Sweetbread Croquettes St. Cloud

Roast Quarters of Lamb, Mint Sauce

Green Peas Sauté au Beurre

Cauliflower, Cream Sauce • Egg Plant Lyonnaise

Boiled and Roast Potatoes

Roast Aylesbury Duckling, Apple Sauce

TO ORDER FROM THE GRILL

Sirloin Steak garni

Loin Pork Chop, Apple Ring

Salads—Escarole • Dixie

French and Russian Dressing

Regence Pudding

Pears Hêlene • French Pastry

Chocolate and Vanilla Ice Cream and Wafer

Oranges • Pears • Apples

Coffee

A dinner menu from Locke-Ober's, a restaurant in Boston, October 28, 1939 (appetizers, soups, and salads only):

HORS D'OEUVRES

Half Grapefruit • Hearts of Artichoke on Lettuce

Fresh Shrimps Cocktail • Saucisson d'Arles • Radishes •
Queen Olives

Sea Food Cocktail • Tomato Juice • Tuna Fish, Colbert

Fresh Crab Flakes Cocktail • Bismark Herring •
Canapé of Caviar

Lobster Cocktail • Clam Juice Cocktail • Imported Sardines
on Lettuce

OYSTERS AND CLAMS

Medium Cotuit • Large Cotuit

Little Neck Clams • Cherry Stone

SOUPS

Chicken Soup, Family Style • Cream of Fresh Mushrooms

Onion Soup au Gratin • Bisque of Lobster

Clear Green Turtle Soup au Sherry

SALADS

Endive with Beet • Endive with Egg • Lobster Salad

Deep Sea Food • Lettuce and Tomato • Chiffonade

Watercress • Russian Celery Mayonnaise

Cabbage • Vegetable Salad Waldorf

A luncheon menu of the disciples of Antonin Carême, Paris,
France, 1959:

Foie Gras Parfait

Sole Soufflé Abel Luquet

Saddle of Lamb Antonin Carême

Cointreau Ice

Cold Sliced Nantes Duck with Orange

Selection of Cheeses

Omelette Duc de Praslin

A menu from Topnotch, a restaurant and ski lodge, Stowe, Vermont, February 20, 1975 (appetizers only):

APPETIZERS

Iced Wedge of Seasonal Melon with Imported Prosciutto Ham

Quiche Lorraine Maison

Smoked Salmon Romanoff

Filet of Herring in Sour Cream à la Bohémienne

Tureen of Summer Fruits with Kirsch

Pâté de Foie Gras Strasbourgeoise

Shrimp Cocktail Victoria, Topnotch Sauce

APPETIZER SPECIALS

Alaskan King Crabmeat and Avocado Cocktail

Chopped Chicken Livers

Vermont Cheese Fritters

A menu from a hunt buffet dinner, Dutchess Valley Rod and Gun Club, Pawling, New York, January 3, 1976 (Peter Van Erp, chef de cuisine):

LES FRIVOLITÉES CHAUD ET FROID

Buffet Froide • Cold Buffet

Le Saumon de Gaspé en Bellevue, Sauce Verte
Poached Gaspé Bay Salmon, Herb Mayonnaise and Cucumber Baskets

---

Les Aiguilettes de Gigot de Chevreuil en Gelée, Montmorency
Leg of Roebuck, Poached Apples and Cherry Aspic

Le Pâté St. Hubert en Croûte, Sauce Yorkshire
Game Pâté in Pastry, Yorkshire Sauce and Sage Aspic

Salade des Champignons de Paris, Vinaigrette à l E'stragon
Button Mushrooms in Tarragon Vinaigrette

Buffet Chaud • Hot Buffet

Consommé de Tortue Claire Truffe, au Armagnac
Clear Turtle Soup with Truffles and Armagnac

Les Aiguiettes de Canard Sauvage, Sauce Poivrade
Sliced Wild Duck Breast, Pepper Sauce

Le Civet de Selle de Chevreuil, Grand Veneur
Braised Roebuck Saddle, Chief Ranger Sauce

Les Perdreaux en Chartreuse, à l'Ancienne
Partridge Braised in White Wine with Savoy Cabbage Timbales

Le Faisan Rôti, d'Environs, Gastronome
Local Roast Pheasant with Chestnuts, Truffles, and Chanterelles

---

**Le Turban de Riz Sauvage, Fonds d'Artichauds et Delices
du Bois**
Wild Rice Ring with Artichoke Bottoms and Assorted Wild Mushrooms

Choux Rouge Braisée, Normande
Braised Red Cabbage, Normandy Style

Les Endives de Bruxelles, Étuvées • Marrons Glacée
Braised Belgian Endive • Glazed Chestnuts

Fromage Assortis • Assorted Cheese

Les Petits Four

Demi-tasse • Les Digestifs

Coffee • Assorted Liqueurs

A banquet menu from the World Trade Club of San Francisco, honoring a recipient of an annual achievement award, April 21, 1978:

Scandinavian Delight

Double Beef Consommé Mille Fantilles

Cheese Straws

Selected Roasted Rib Eye of Beef

Creamed Horseradish Sauce

Royale Potatoes

Artichoke Bottom Clamart

Strawberries Romanoff

Macaroons

Cafe Noir

A menu from Buffet de la Gare, a café in Strasbourg, France, May 1978 (cold dishes only):

LES ENTRÉES

Oeuf à la Russe
Russian Style Egg

Assiette de crudités
Plate of Raw Vegetable Salads

Assiette de charcuterie
Plate of Cold Cuts

Pâté en croûte, crudités
Pâté in Pastry, Raw Vegetable Salads

Assiette de jambons assortis
Plate of Assorted Hams

Parfait de foie gras de Strasbourg
Strasbourg Goose Liver Mousse

LES SALADES

Salade de saison

Salade de tomates

LES PLATS DU JOUR

Le demi avocat aux crevettes
Half Avocado with Shrimp

La Coquille de saumon mayonnaise
Salmon in a Seashell with Mayonnaise

L'Artichaut tiède, sauce vinaigrette
Warm Artichoke, Vinaigrette

Le Saumon frais fumé, toasts et beurre
Fresh Smoked Salmon, Toast and Butter

A luncheon menu from The Pacific-Union Club, San Francisco, October 6, 1978 (appetizers and soups only):

Crab Legs, Mustard Mayonnaise

Small Olympia Oysters in Own Juice

Pâté de Foie • Eastern Oysters on Half Shell

Jumbo Prawns Supreme, Cocktail Sauce or Mustard-Mayonnaise

Pickled Herring Filet • Sardine Canapé • Half of Avocado

Shrimp, Fines-Herbes • Tomato Juice • Smoked Salmon

New England Seafood Chowder

Jellied Consommé • Consommé Volaille

A luncheon menu from the Banker's Club, San Francisco, December 7, 1978 (appetizers, soups, and salads only):

APPETIZERS

Proscuitto and Sliced Melon in Season • Pâté Maison in Aspic

Crab Legs and Avocado Piquante • Marinated Herring in Wine Sauce

Morro Bay Shrimp Cocktail • Celery Victor with Crab or Shrimp

Hearts of Lettuce • Smoked Salmon, Melba Toast

Blue Point Oysters on the Half Shell

Castroville Artichoke Bottom Stuffed with Crab or Shrimp

SOUPS

Chilled Strawberry Soup

Cold Vichyssoise

Cold Gazpacho

Consommé Celestine

French Onion Soup, Gratinée

SALADS

SALAD JONAS—
Crisp Garden Greens
with Chicken, Ham,
Shrimp, Egg and Caviar

STUFFED AVOCADO—
with Dungeness Crab or
Bay Shrimp, Garni

CARNELIAN SALAD—
Romaine with Choice of
Crab, Prawns or Sliced
Breast of Turkey

THE WAISTLINER—
Fresh California or Exotic
Fruits and Berries with
Cottage Cheese or Sherbet

A luncheon menu from The Jockey Club, Ritz-Carlton Hotel, Washington, D.C., May 5, 1986 (appetizers, soups, salads, and cold specialties only):

APPETIZERS

Beluga Caviar

Crabmeat Cocktail, Sauce Dijonnaise

Smoked Scottish Salmon

Belon Oysters in Ice, Sauce Mignonette

Chilled Gulf Shrimp

Terrine de Campagne Maison

Prosciutto Ham and Melon

Artichoke Vinaigrette

Baked Clams Casino

Escargots Bourguignonne

SOUPS

Onion Soup Gratiné

Consommé Double au Xèrès

New England Clam Chowder

Crème Sénégalaise

Vichyssoise

SALADS

Jockey Club

Hearts of Palm

Bibb Lettuce

Asparagus Vinaigrette

Wilted Spinach and Mushrooms

COLD SPECIALTIES

Stuffed Avocado with Crabmeat

Steak Tartar

Chicken and Julienne Vegetable Salad

Sunset Salad "Lorenzo"

Seafood Salad, Jockey Club

Assorted Fine Cheeses with Fresh Fruit

Fresh Fruit Salad with Honey Pepper Dressing

A dinner menu from the Grill Room at the Connaught Hotel, London, England, September 3, 1987 (appetizers, soups, and eggs only; Michel Bourdin, Chef de cuisine):

HORS D'OEUVRES

Oysters "Christian Dior" Charentais Melon

Pithivies aux Blanc de Poissons "Bonne Femme"
White Fish Tart, Simple Family Style

Salade Caprice des Années Folles
Whimsical Salad of the Wild Years*

Smoked Trout • Smoked Scotch Salmon

Pâté de Turbot Froid au Homard, Sauce Pudeur

Avocado Cocktail • Kipper Pâté Terrine Connaught

Foie Gras Frais Préparé par le Chef • Asperges Vertes
Fresh Goose Liver Prepared by the Chef • Green Asparagus

Jambon de Parme • Feuilleté aux Asperges Vertes
Parma Ham • Green Asparagus in Puff Pastry

POTAGES ET OEUFS

Consommé Chaud • Consommé en Gelée Cole Porter
Hot Consommé • Chilled Consommé Cole Porter Style

Crême d'Artichaut Froide ou Glacé au Parfum de Périgord
Chilled Cream of Artichoke or Perfumed Ice of Périgord

Consommé de Volaille à la Royale
Chicken Consommé with Egg Custard

Soupe à l'Oignon • Oeuf en Gelée Stendahl
Onion Soup • Egg in Aspic, Stendahl Style

Oeufs Pochés Bénédictine

Poached Eggs Benedict

* Author's translation.

A dinner menu from Campton Place, San Francisco, October 2, 1991 (appetizers and salads only):

APPETIZERS

Young Potato and Vidalia Onion Soup

Tomato Gazpacho with Grilled Lobster and Cilantro Cream

Tuna Tartar with Citrus Vinaigrette, Mustard Greens and Hot Pepper Oil

Open-Face Smoked Chicken Ravioli with Wild Mushrooms and Sage Marscapone

Homemade Mozzarella, Eggplant and Vine Ripe Tomatoes with Crispy Sweet Onions

Parma Prosciutto with Smokey Onion Vinaigrette and Gingered Apricots

Seared Foie Gras with Peppered Peached and a Corn Pancake

SALADS

Salad of Field Greens with Lemon Vinaigrette

Frisee Salad with Sun-Dried Tomato, Anchovy and Eggplant Relish Croutons

Caesar Salad with Parmesan Croutons

Contemporary Menus (designed by Lars Kronmark and the author)

A menu for an All-American Barbecue:

APPETIZERS

Blue Point Oysters on the Half Shell, Mississippi Delta Cocktail Sauce

Buffalo-Style Chicken Wings • Smoked Mackerel, Horseradish Mayonnaise

SOUPS

Corn Chowder • Philadelphia Pepper Pot

MAIN COURSES

Grilled Turkey Steaks, Cajun Butter and Cranberry-Orange Relish

Glazed Smithfield Ham, Pickled String Beans

Baked Bluefish, Buena Vista

VEGETABLES

Sweet Potato and Pecan Pie • Baked-Stuffed Potato

Steamed Broccoli • Buttered Succotash • Creamed Peas and
Pearl Onions

SALADS

Hearts of Romaine, Thousand Island Dressing

Potato Salad with Beer Vinaigrette • Marinated Black-Eyed
Peas

CHEESES

Rouge et Noir Camembert • Maytag Blue Cheese • Oregon
Tillamook

DESSERTS

Apple Brown Betty • Strawberry Shortcake

Pecan Pie • Mincemeat Pie

Coffee

A menu for an Asian Festival or Chinese New Year's Celebration:

Fried Spring Rolls • Pickled Eggplant

Ten Vegetable Soup • Hot and Sour Soup

Cantonese-Style Codfish Cakes • Szechwan Duck

Hoisan Sauce • Ginger and Lemon Soy Sauce

Tea-Smoked Chicken • Broccoli Beef

Barbecued Spare Ribs • Sweet and Pungent Tofu

Steamed Baby Bok Choy • Garlic Spinach

Sticky Rice • Shrimp Fried Rice

Melon Shells with Brandied Fruit • Iced Fresh Pineapple

A menu for an Autumn Wine Harvest or Halloween Masquerade:

Jul Glögg • Hot Rum Toddies

Cream of Chestnut Soup • Pumpkin Bisque

Braised Rabbit with Prunes • Beef Brisket Braised in Cider

Roast Rock Cornish Game Hen, Wild Rice and Grape Stuffing

Stewed Tomatoes with Summer Squash • Buttered Parsnips • Apple Chutney

Roasted Beets, Orange Glaze • Braised Leeks and Wild Mushrooms

Pound Cake with Dried Cherries • Baked Apple Stuffed with Chesnuts

Pear and Dried-Cranberry Pie • Candy Apples

A menu for a Chicago 1920s Speak-Easy Party:

Champagne Cocktails • Deviled Eggs • Russian Caviar with Blinis

Oyster Shooters • Canadian Smoked Salmon

Iced Vichyssoise, Louis Diat • Asparagus Mimosa

Hearts of Kentucky Limestone, Baby Shrimp, and Green Goddess Dressing

Porterhouse Steak, Maître d'Hôtel Butter

Grilled Double Lamb Chops, Mint Jelly

Pork and Shrimp Kebabs, Creole Rice

Carrots Vichy • Creamed Spinach • Scalloped Potatoes

Roasted Fondant Potatoes • Parmesan Duchess Potatoes

Rice Pudding with Golden Raisins • Chocolate Mousse

New York-Style Cheesecake • Bananas Foster • Crêpes Suzette

50

A menu for a Fifties Rock and Roll Bash:

Whipped Peanut Butter with Ritz Crackers

Bologna Finger Sandwiches on Wonder Bread

Mayonnaise and Parmesan Cheese Toasts • Pigs in a Blanket

Jack Cheese Kabobs • Onion Soup Dip with Potato Chips

Hot Velveeta Cheese Triangles • Tuna Melts

Beef and Barley Soup • Alphabet Chicken Soup

Mom's Meat Loaf • Broiled Sliced Spam

Lumpy Mashed Potatoes • Corn Fritters, Maple Syrup

Jell-O Mold with Fruit Cocktail • Kool-Aid Ice

Lollypop Lemonade • Sugar-Glazed Popcorn

A menu for a Greek Festival or Mediterranean Wedding Reception:

Antipasti del Giorno • Bagna Cauda • Asparagus Wrapped
in Coppa

Jellied Consommé, Portugese Style • Minestrone Milanese

Assorted Poached Shellfish with Rémoulade and Cocktail
Sauces

Capri Island Squid Salad • Octopus with Lemon and Basil

Deep-Fried Smelts, Ravigote

Roasted Capon with Lemon and Rosemary

Vitello Tonnato

Braised Lamb Shanks, Greek Style

Braised Spinach with Garlic and Capers • Fried Zucchini

Herbed Orzo • Risi Bisi • Baked Polenta, Naples Style

Toasted Ligurian Foccacia

Roasted Bell Peppers, Buffalo Mozzarella, and Basil

Spinach Salad, Greek Style • Gemelli Pasta Salad, Primavera

———————————

Tiramisu • Baklava • Tangerine Tart

A contemporary California menu:

Salmon Tartar Canapés • Jicama and Chorizo Canapés

Oysters on the Half Shell, Raspberry Mignonette

Black Bean Cakes, Avocado Salsa

———————————

Avocado Soup, Champagne • Chicken Congee

———————————

Cous-Cous, Grilled Eggplant, and Currant Salad

Arugela and Red Bliss Potato Salad, Grainy Mustard
Vinaigrette

Mesclun Greens, Sun-Dried Tomato Vinaigrette

———————————

Dungeness Cracked Crab, Mustard Mayonnaise

Scallop and Red Bell Pepper Brochette, Citrus Beurre Blanc

———————————

Broiled Skirt Steak, Roast Shallots and Garlic

Roasted Baby Chicken, Red Wine Vinegar Butter Sauce

Broiled Center-Cut Pork Chops, Pear Butter

Turkey and Apple Sausage with Warm Red Cabbage Salad

Mesquite-Grilled Prawns, Papaya Salsa

———————————

Mixed Grilled Vegetables, Chipotle Aïoli • Artichokes au
Gratin

Zucchini Pancakes • Grilled Polenta Triangles

———————————

Laura Chenel Chèvre • Dried Sonoma Jack Cheese

———————————

Chocolate Decadence • Blueberry Cobbler

Fresh Seasonal Berries in Pastry Tulip

RECIPES FOR THE CONTEMPORARY MENUS

A menu for an All-American Barbecue:

Appetizers

MISSISSIPPI DELTA COCKTAIL SAUCE

(FOR BLUE POINT OYSTERS ON THE HALF SHELL)

1 cup (240 mL) ketchup
¼ cup (60 mL) celery, finely diced
¼ cup (60 mL) prepared horseradish

1 tablespoon (15 mL) lemon juice
2 teaspoons (10 mL) Worcestershire
Tabasco or hot sauce to taste

BUFFALO-STYLE CHICKEN WINGS

Cut chicken wings into thirds, reserving the wing tips for stock. Wash well in cold water, and pat dry. Deep-fry at 375° F (190° C) until light brown, and drain on absorbent paper. Sprinkle liberally with Tabasco, then sprinkle with a spicy mixture of salt and cayenne pepper, and continue baking in a preheated 375° F (190° C) oven until golden brown.

HORSERADISH MAYONNAISE

(FOR SMOKED MACKEREL)

Mayonnaise blended with grated prepared horseradish (squeezed dry), flavored with a little lemon juice, and finished with chopped parsley.

Soups

CORN CHOWDER

4 slices bacon, ¼-inch (6-mm) dice
2 tablespoons (30 mL) butter
1 small Spanish onion, ¼-inch (6-mm) dice
1 stalk celery, ¼-inch (6-mm) dice
1½ (360 mL) cups whole kernel corn

1½ (360 mL) cups Red Bliss potatoes, cut into ¼-inch (6-mm) dice
3 cups (720 mL) chicken stock
1 cup (240 mL) half-and-half (light cream)
1 tablespoon (15 mL) Worcestershire sauce
salt and pepper to taste

- Sauté the bacon in a large soup pot until golden brown. Pour off the fat and discard.
- Add the butter, onion, and celery, and sauté 5 minutes. Stir in the corn and potatoes.
- Add the chicken stock, and simmer until the potatoes are tender (about 30 minutes).
- Purée half of this mixture in a blender or food processor, then return to the remaining half and bring to a simmer.
- Add the cream and Worcestershire, bring to a boil, and season to taste with salt and pepper.

PHILADELPHIA PEPPER POT

1 pound (450 g) tripe, cut into 1-inch (25-mm) pieces
1 ham hock
1 ham knuckle
2 quarts (1.9 L) white veal (or chicken) stock
1 leek leaf
4 sprigs thyme
1 bunch parsley stems
2 bay leaves
½ cup (120 mL) fat back, finely diced
1 medium onion, medium diced
2 stalks celery
1 tablespoon (15 mL) black peppercorns, crushed
2 cups (480 mL) potatoes, peeled and medium diced
salt to taste

- Place the tripe in a pot, covered with water and a teaspoon of salt. Bring to a boil, simmer for 30 minutes, then drain and rinse in cold water. Return the tripe to the pot and cover with the stock. Tie the leek and herbs together with cotton string and add to the stock, along with the ham, and simmer for 1½ hours. Remove the herbs and discard. Remove the ham pieces, pull off the meat, coarsely chop and set it aside, and discard the bones.
- Render the fat back in a heavy-gauge soup pot. Add the onion and celery, and sauté. Add the pepper, the tripe and stock, and the potatoes, and simmer until the potatoes are tender. Add the ham, and season to taste with salt.

Main Courses

GRILLED TURKEY STEAKS, CAJUN BUTTER AND CRANBERRY-ORANGE RELISH

For turkey steaks, use a boneless, skinless raw turkey breast, with the tenderloin removed (save for another use). The steaks are cut across the width, 1- to 2-inches (25- to 50-mm) thick, depending on how wide they are. The pieces are then pounded to a uniform width, seasoned with salt and pepper, dusted with flour, brushed with oil, and grilled or broiled.

Cajun butter is made by blending ¼ pound (113 g) soft unsalted butter with 2 to 3 tablespoons blended Cajun-style spices, such as white and cayenne pepper, chili powder, filé powder, garlic, and thyme. Wrap in parchment paper in a 1½-inch round cylinder and refrigerate. To serve, cut slices, remove the paper, and place on top of the steaks.

CRANBERRY-ORANGE RELISH

zest of 1 orange
1 tablespoon (15 mL) unsalted butter
6 tablespoons (90 mL) sugar
1 cup (240 mL) dry sherry
1 cup (240 mL) dry white wine
½ cup (120 mL) orange juice
2 cups (480 mL) whole fresh (or frozen) cranberries

- Sauté the zest in the butter for 3 minutes. Add all the remaining ingredients, except the cranberries. Simmer until the mixture is reduced by half. Add the cranberries and simmer until the mixture is thick and smooth and all the cranberries have opened. Cool, cover, and refrigerate until ready to use.

GLAZED SMITHFIELD HAM, PICKLED STRING BEANS

Score the outside of a Smithfield (or other good bone-in ham), and rub on a paste made from 1 part mustard and 1 part light brown sugar, blended together. Bake until well caramelized.

For the String Beans

1 pound (450 g) green (or green mixed with yellow) string beans
1 tablespoon (15 mL) salt
3 cups (720 mL) champagne vinegar
1 cup (240 mL) water
1 teaspoon (5 mL) salt
½ cup (120 mL) sugar
¼ teaspoon (1.25 mL) whole cloves

1 teaspoon (5 mL) mustard seeds
1 teaspoon (5 mL) coriander seeds
1 teaspoon (5 mL) black peppercorns
1 bay leaf
2 sprigs oregano
4 garlic cloves, crushed

- Place the string beans in a colander, sprinkle with salt, and allow to sit for 3 hours.
- Combine the remaining pickling ingredients in a saucepan, bring to a boil, and simmer for 5 minutes. Rinse the salted vegetables in cold water, and drain. Place the brine over the vegetables, cool, cover, and refrigerate. Marinate 24 hours before serving.

BAKED BLUEFISH, BUENA VISTA

Cut a fresh bluefish fillet into individual portions, and sprinkle both sides with salt and pepper. Place in a buttered pan or casserole dish. Top each portion with a slice of red onion, a slice of tomato, and a slice (ring) of green pepper. Splash some white wine over the fish, cover, and bake in a moderate oven for 20 minutes.

Vegetables

SWEET POTATO AND PECAN PIE

3 large eggs
¾ cup (180 mL) brown sugar
¼ cup (60 mL) molasses
½ cup (120 mL) heavy cream
pinch of salt
½ teaspoon (2.5 mL) grated gingerroot

½ teaspoon (2.5 mL) nutmeg
3 cups (720 mL) boiled sweet potatoes, peeled and mashed
½ cup (120 mL) chopped toasted pecans
1 9-inch (230-mm) unbaked pie shell

- Combine all ingredients, except the potatoes and pecans, in a large bowl, and beat until smooth. Add the potatoes and pecans, and blend in. Spread into the pie shell, and bake at a preheated 450° F (232° C) oven for 15 minutes. Reduce heat to 325° F (163° C), and bake another 30 minutes.

BAKED-STUFFED POTATO

Slit open the tops of baked potatoes, lengthwise down the center, and scoop out the pulp. Mash this with some butter, cream, salt, white pepper, and nutmeg. Place this mixture into a pastry bag with a No. 6 star tip, and pipe back into the shells. Bake until the tops are golden brown. (Additional ingredients can be included, such as finely minced green onions, crumbled cooked bacon, chives, minced herbs, and so forth.)

BUTTERED SUCCOTASH

Equal parts lima beans and whole kernel corn, sautéed in butter and seasoned with salt and white pepper.

CREAMED PEAS AND PEARL ONIONS

3 cups (720 mL) green peas
1½ cups (360 mL) pearl
  onions
1 small Spanish onion,
  peeled and coarsely
  chopped
¼ teaspoon (1.25 mL)
  nutmeg
2 whole cloves

1 bay leaf
2 cups (480 mL) hot milk
4 tablespoons (60 mL)
  unsalted butter, clarified
3 tablespoons (45 mL) all-
  purpose flour
salt and white pepper to
  taste

- Blanch the peas in boiling salted water until al dente (if frozen, thaw by immersing in hot water and draining). Drop the pearl onions into boiling water, cook until al dente, then drain and cool. Slice the ends off the onions, remove the outer skin, and set aside.
- Heat the milk in a heavy-gauge, noncorrosive saucepan, along with the Spanish onion, nutmeg, cloves, and bay leaf.

Stir the butter and flour into a smooth paste, and beat into the hot milk. Bring to a simmer and cook 5 minutes, while stirring continuously. Season to taste with salt and pepper, strain, and add the peas and onions. Bring to a boil, adjust seasoning, and serve.

Salads

HEARTS OF ROMAINE, THOUSAND ISLAND DRESSING

2 small heads romaine lettuce
1 cup (240 mL) mayonnaise
1 cup (240 mL) strained chili sauce or ketchup
½ cup (120 mL) green and red bell pepper, cut into 1-inch julienne
2 vine-ripened tomatoes, cored and cut into eight wedges each
1 bunch watercress

- Cut and remove the bottom 1 inch of the heads of romaine. Split each one in half lengthwise, and trim the outside edges and top to create a clean single portion. Rinse in cold water, drain well, and refrigerate until ready to serve.
- Rinse the watercress well in cold water and drain. Trim the stems and refrigerate until ready to serve.
- Combine the mayonnaise, chili sauce or ketchup, and bell pepper, and blend thoroughly. Place the romaine halves on individual plates, drizzle with sauce, and garnish with the tomatoes and a bunch of watercress.

POTATO SALAD WITH BEER VINAIGRETTE

2 pounds (900 g) small Red Bliss potatoes
½ cup (120 mL) red onions, sliced paper thin
2 tablespoons (30 mL) chopped chives
½ cup (120 mL) olive oil
1 shallot, minced
1 tablespoon (15 mL) Dijon-style mustard
3 tablespoons (45 mL) chopped parsley
salt and pepper to taste
¼ cup (60 mL) white wine vinegar
½ cup (120 mL) beer

- Cook the potatoes in lightly salted boiling water until tender but firm. Drain, peel, and slice ¼ inch (6 mm) thick.
- Place the olive oil, shallot, mustard, parsley, salt, and pepper in a blender, and purée. Bring the vinegar and beer to a boil, and add to the purée.
- Toss the potatoes and onions with the vinaigrette, and garnish with the chives.

MARINATED BLACK-EYED PEAS

1 pound (450 g) dried
   black-eyed peas
1 small onion, cut in half
2 sprigs thyme
2 bay leaves
½ cup (120 mL) olive oil

¼ cup (60 mL) white wine
   vinegar
2 bunches scallions, finely
   sliced
½ cup (120 mL) chopped
   parsley
salt and pepper to taste

- Cover the beans abundantly with water, and soak overnight. Drain, rinse, and cull and remove any damaged beans. Place in boiling salted water, along with the onion, thyme, and bay leaves. Simmer until tender but still firm (1 to 1½ hours). Drain, remove and discard aromatics, cool, and set aside.
- Combine the beans and remaining ingredients, blend thoroughly, and adjust seasoning with salt and pepper.

Desserts

APPLE BROWN BETTY

4 Granny Smith apples
2 cups (480 mL) finely
   diced white bread (no
   crusts), lightly toasted
¾ cup (180 mL) sugar
½ teaspoon (2.5 mL) ground
   cinnamon

¼ teaspoon (1.2 mL)
   nutmeg
¼ teaspoon (1.2 mL) cloves
¼ cup (60 mL) melted
   unsalted butter
4 tablespoons (60 mL)
   unsalted butter

- Core and peel the apples, cut into thin slices, and place in a large bowl. Add half the diced bread, the sugar, spices, and melted butter. Toss, then place in a lightly buttered pan or casserole dish. Sprinkle the remaining diced bread onto the mixture, and top with thin slices of the remaining butter. Bake at 375° F (190° C) for 30 to 45 minutes.

STRAWBERRY SHORTCAKE

Cut a biscuit in half lengthwise, place on a plate, and top with sliced strawberries macerated lightly with sugar. Place the other biscuit half on top, and cover with sweetened whipped cream.

PECAN PIE

1 9-inch (230-mm) unbaked pie shell
1 cup (240 mL) pecan halves
2 eggs
½ cup (120 mL) dark corn syrup
1 cup (240 mL) brown sugar
3 tablespoons (45 mL) rum
pinch of salt
3 tablespoons (45 mL) unsalted butter

- Beat the eggs, syrup, sugar, rum, and salt until smooth. Place the nutmeats in the shell, and pour the sugar mixture over them. Arrange thin slices of butter on top, and bake in a preheated oven at 450° F (232° C) for 10 minutes. Reduce the heat to 325° F (163° C) and bake about 30 minutes, or until filling is firm.

MINCEMEAT PIE

½ cup (120 mL) raisins
⅓ cup (80 mL) brandy
3 Granny Smith apples, peeled, cored, and medium diced
1 small orange, rinsed and finely ground
¼ cup (60 mL) lemon juice
1 cup (240 mL) sugar
½ teaspoon (2.5 mL) salt
1 teaspoon (5 mL) cinnamon
½ teaspoon (2.5 mL) mace or nutmeg
¼ teaspoon (1.2 mL) cloves
¼ teaspoon (1.2 mL) ginger
½ cup (120 mL) melted unsalted butter
1 unbaked deep-dish pie shell, with dough for the top

- Heat the brandy, pour it over the raisins, and allow to sit 30 minutes. Add the remaining ingredients and blend thoroughly. Fill the pie shell with this mixture, and seal with the remaining dough. Bake at 450° F (232° C) for 15 minutes. Reduce the heat to 350° F (176° C) and bake about 30 minutes, or until top is golden brown.

A menu for an Asian Festival or Chinese New Year's Celebration:

FRIED SPRING ROLLS

¼ cup (60 mL) peanut oil
6 ounces (170 g) ground lean pork
6 ounces (170 g) raw shrimp, finely diced
½ cup (120 mL) mushrooms, finely diced
2 tablespoons (30 mL) soy sauce
pinch of sugar
1 cup (240 mL) celery, finely diced

4 ounces (113 g) fresh mung bean sprouts, well rinsed
1 teaspoon (5 mL) salt
2 teaspoons (10 mL) cornstarch, dissolved in 2 tablespoons (30 mL) saki or dry sherry
12 egg roll wrappers
1 quart (960 mL) vegetable oil

- Heat half the oil in a hot pan until it begins to smoke. Add the pork and sauté for about two minutes. Add the shrimp, mushrooms, soy sauce, and sugar, and cook until the shrimp turn red. Remove from the fire and set aside.
- Heat the remaining oil until smoking, and sauté the celery for several minutes. Add the bean sprouts and the salt, and cook briefly. Add the pork mixture, bring to a boil, add the cornstarch, and blend thoroughly. Cook about 1 minute, and set aside to cool.
- Place about ¼ cup of filling diagonally on a wrapper. Shape into a cylinder measuring roughly 1 inch by 4 inches (25 mm by 100 mm), and bring one corner of the wrapping around the filling, tucking it in firmly at the bottom. Fold the two outside ends around the sides, and tuck firmly as well. Brush the remaining dough with water, and roll the cylinder up securely. Set aside, covered with plastic wrap until ready to fry.
- Deep-fry at 375° F (190° C) until golden brown, and hold in a 250° F (121° C) oven until ready to serve.

PICKLED EGGPLANT

2 large eggplants
1 cup (240 mL) fresh mint
   leaves, coarsely chopped
10 garlic cloves, pressed

salt and balsamic vinegar as
   needed
½ cup (120 mL) olive oil

- Wash the eggplants, then slice them lengthwise, about ¼ inch (6 mm) thick (discard the outermost slices from each eggplant).
- Place a slice of eggplant on the bottom of a glass casserole dish with slightly angled-out sides, measuring approximately 8 inches by 3 inches (200 mm by 75 mm) at the top, and 4 inches (100 mm) deep. Spread the slice with some of the garlic, and sprinkle lightly with salt, vinegar, and some of the mint. Repeat this procedure, pressing down each subsequent slice gently, until all the eggplant is used.
- Place another casserole dish on top of the eggplant, and weight it down. Allow all this to sit at room temperature for 24 hours, draining the pickle periodically (the salt draws moisture out of the eggplant).
- Drain off any remaining moisture, and transfer the eggplant to a clean casserole dish. Pour the olive oil over the pickle, cover, and refrigerate until ready to serve.

TEN VEGETABLE SOUP

Prepare a garnish of 2 cups (480 mL) of vegetables, half cut into perfectly square and consistent dice measuring ¼ inches (6 mm) on each side, and the other half cut into small spheres with a pea (pois) scoop. Vegetable selection can include carrot, celery, jicama, leek, green peas, scallion, and zucchini. Minimally blanch each vegetable separately, then serve in 3 pints (720 mL) of hot, very clear beef or chicken broth.

HOT AND SOUR SOUP

¼ pound (113 g) ground
   lean pork
4 medium-large shiitake
   mushrooms, cut into fine
   julienne

4 dried hot red chili
   peppers
1 quart (960 mL) chicken
   stock
½ teaspoon (2.5 mL) salt

62

3 tablespoons (45 mL) soy
sauce

½ cup (120 mL) bamboo
shoots, rinsed and cut
into fine julienne

2 tablespoons (30 mL) cornstarch, dissolved in ½ cup
(120 mL) white wine
vinegar

1 egg, lightly beaten

¾ cup (180 mL) tofu, cut
into ¼-inch (6-mm) dice

1 tablespoon (15 mL)
sesame seed oil

2 scallions, finely diced

- Sauté the pork, mushrooms, and hot peppers until fully
  cooked. Drain well. Combine the stock, salt, soy sauce, and
  bamboo shoots, and bring to a boil. Add the cornstarch, and
  simmer until thickened (about 1 minute). Add the egg and stir.
  Add the tofu, and serve topped with sesame oil and scallions.

CANTONESE-STYLE CODFISH CAKES

2 tablespoons (30 mL)
gingerroot, grated

1 cup (240 mL) saki

¼ cup (60 mL) scallions,
finely diced

¼ cup (60 mL) bacon, finely
diced

1 pound (450 g) boneless,
skinless codfish, cut into
1-inch (25-mm) pieces

3 egg whites

3 tablespoons (45 mL) soy
sauce

¼ cup (60 mL) peanut oil

2 garlic cloves, sliced very
thin

¼ cup (60 mL) dry sherry

1 tablespoon (15 mL) corn
starch

1½ cups (360 mL) rich
chicken stock

2 tablespoons (30 mL)
hoisan sauce

- Place the fish in the freezer for 30 minutes. Simmer the ginger, scallions, and bacon in the sake, until about 3 tablespoons of liquid remain. Set aside to cool.
- Place the ginger mixture, fish, egg whites, and soy sauce in
  a food processor and purée, using the pulse switch.
- Shape the fish farce into 1-inch (25-mm) round balls,
  slightly flattened on one side, and refrigerate for 1 hour.
- Sauté the fish balls in the peanut oil until golden brown on
  the flattened side. Remove the fish balls from the pan, then
  add the garlic to the pan and sauté briefly. Add the stock,
  hoisin, and fish balls, and bring to a simmer. Dissolve the
  cornstarch in the sherry, add to the liquid, and simmer for 1
  minute. Serve on a bed of steamed greens.

SZECHWAN DUCK

2 4- to 5-pound (1-kg) ducks, well washed and completely dry
4 tablespoons salt
2 tablespoons (30 mL) Szechwan peppercorns, crushed
2 tablespoons (30 mL) grated gingerroot
3 scallions, finely diced

¼ cup (60 mL) soy sauce
1 tablespoon (15 mL) ground allspice
1 cup (240 mL) vegetable oil
10 tablespoons (150 mL) kosher salt
2 tablespoons (30 mL) whole black Szechwan peppercorns

- Combine the salt, pepper, ginger, scallion, soy sauce, and allspice, and rub both ducks vigorously, inside and out, with this mixture. Refrigerate overnight, uncovered.
- Place the kosher salt and peppercorns in a pan, and roast in a preheated 350° F (176° C) oven until the salt is light brown. Remove and grind with a mortar and pestle, or in an electric spice grinder, and set aside.
- Heat the oil, and brown the ducks on all sides. Transfer to a roasting pan with rack, and roast in a preheated 375° F (190° C) oven for 45 minutes. Allow the ducks to rest for 15 minutes, then cut off the thighs and split the bodies in half lengthwise. Cut the thighs and body halves into 1-inch (25-mm)-wide pieces, serve with the toasted salt and pepper mixture, and garnish with scallion brushes.

HOISAN SAUCE

Hoisan sauce is a thick, spicy, sweet sauce, sold in jars and cans in Asian grocery stores. It can be served directly as is, or thinned with a little wine, sherry, stock, and/or soy sauce.

GINGER AND LEMON SOY SAUCE

Combine 2 parts soy sauce with 1 part white wine vinegar, and season with ginger juice (squeezed from grated ginger) and a little lemon zest.

TEA-SMOKED CHICKEN

1 4½-pound (2-kg) roasting
  chicken
2 tablespoons (30 mL) salt

1 cup (240 mL) loose
  Chinese-style tea leaves
sesame seed oil as needed

- Wash and dry the chicken, then rub inside and out with salt. Cover and refrigerate overnight.

- Place the chicken in a steaming basket over a wok or cast iron skillet, or in a large pot with a rack. Cover and steam the chicken for 45 minutes.

- Remove the chicken and its rack, and sprinkle the tea leaves in the bottom of the wok or skillet. Heat over a medium fire until the leaves begin to smoke, then place the chicken on top of the leaves. Cover and set into a 350° F (176° C) preheated oven for 30 minutes. Remove the thighs, cut the body lengthwise in half, then cut the thighs and body halves into 1-inch-wide pieces.

BROCCOLI BEEF

1 pound (450 g) flank steak
¼ cup (60 mL) rice wine
¼ cup (60 mL) soy sauce
1 teaspoon (5 mL) sugar
2 teaspoons (10 mL)
  cornstarch

1 bunch broccoli, cut into
  small flowerettes
6 thin slices peeled
  gingerroot
¼ cup (60 mL) peanut oil

- Cut the flank steak in half lengthwise (as in butterflying), and then into small rectangular pieces. Combine the wine, soy sauce, sugar, and cornstarch, pour over the steak, and marinate several hours.

- Heat the oil in a wok or pan, and stir-fry the broccoli 1 minute. Remove with a slotted spoon and set aside. Add the ginger, cook briefly, then remove and discard. Drain the meat, pat dry, and stir-fry about 3 minutes, or until the meat is no longer pink. Add the broccoli, blend, and serve.

BARBECUED SPARE RIBS

1 side pork ribs (about 2 pounds/900 g), cut in half lengthwise
½ cup (120 mL) soy sauce
¼ cup (60 mL) white wine vinegar
¼ cup (60 mL) rice wine

3 tablespoons (45 mL) sugar
2 tablespoons (30 mL) hoisan sauce
4 large garlic cloves, pressed

- Combine the marinating ingredients, and marinate the ribs overnight.

- Preheat an oven to 375° F (190° C). Attach a hook to each end of the rib slabs (can be fashioned from plain, uncoated coat hangers), and hang from an oven rack placed at the highest level. Place a roasting pan, filled with 1 inch (25 mm) of water, on the bottom of the oven to catch drippings. Roast for 45 minutes, then turn the oven to 450° F (232° C) and continue roasting another 15 minutes, or until the spareribs are dark brown. Remove from the oven, and separate the ribs by cutting between the bones.

SWEET AND PUNGENT TOFU

peel of 1 orange, coarsely cut
1 garlic clove, crushed
2 tablespoons (30 mL) peanut oil
½ cup (60 mL) red wine vinegar
½ cup (60 mL) rice wine vinegar
1½ cups (180 mL) pineapple juice
½ cup (60 mL) dark brown sugar
½ cup (60 mL) tomato ketchup
2 tablespoons (30 mL) soy sauce

2 level tablespoons (30 mL) cornstarch, dissolved in ½ cup (120 mL) stock or water
2 tablespoons (30 mL) sesame oil
2 to 3 cups (480 to 720 mL) vegetable garnish (equal parts carrots—sliced on the bias with a fluted knife—onions and green peppers, cut into small squares, and pineapple, cut into small triangles)

- Sauté the orange peel and garlic in the oil for several minutes. Remove and discard.

- Add the vinegars, pineapple juice, sugar, ketchup, and soy sauce, and bring to a boil. Add the cornstarch, bring to a boil again, and adjust seasoning by adding additional sugar, vinegar, and/or water. Strain and set aside.

- Heat the sesame oil until smoking, and stir-fry the vegetables (excluding the pineapple) several minutes. Add the sauce and the pineapple, and bring to a boil. Place the tofu in a bowl or platter, and pour the sauce over it.

STEAMED BABY BOK CHOY

Bok choy means "white vegetable," and the leaves of this plant are similar to Swiss chard. They should be trimmed of imperfections and well rinsed before steaming.

GARLIC SPINACH

Remove the stems from thoroughly rinsed fresh spinach. Heat a little oil in a sauté pan, and cook the spinach until well wilted. Add some pressed garlic, cook a few more minutes, and season to taste with salt and pepper.

STICKY RICE

Short-grain rice, also known as glutinous rice, is the same variety used in Japanese cookery. It is very starchy and should be well rinsed in warm water several times before cooking. It is poured into lightly salted boiling water (slightly less than 2 parts water to 1 part rice), brought to a boil, then turned down to a very low heat, and cooked 10 minutes. It is then allowed to sit another 20 minutes. (Because this rice is too starchy, it should not be used for a fried rice dish.)

SHRIMP FRIED RICE

¼ cup (60 mL) peanut oil
2 eggs, lightly beaten
½ cup (60 mL) shrimp meat, cut into medium dice

½ cup (60 mL) green peas, blanched al dente (or thawed, if frozen)

67

3 cups (720 mL) cooked long grain rice	salt to taste
	2 scallions, finely sliced

- Heat 1 tablespoon (15 mL) of the oil in a Teflon pan, and pour in the eggs, allowing them to spread over the pan. When the eggs set, flip over, cook another 10 seconds, then remove to absorbent paper. Trim the edges square, and cut the square into julienne strips roughly ¼ inch × 2 inches (6 mm × 50 mm), and set aside.
- Pour the remaining oil into a wok or sauté pan, and stir-fry the shrimp 1 minute. Add the peas, cook briefly, then add the rice and blend thoroughly. Season to taste with salt and garnish with the scallion.

MELON SHELLS WITH BRANDIED FRUIT

Cut the melons lengthwise into quarters, and scoop out the seeds and loose flesh. Cut out the remaining flesh in one piece, by carefully cutting between the flesh and the outer shell (cut halfway through from one side, then halfway through from the other side). Cut these pieces into cubes, combine with equal portions of loquats, kumquats, and litchis, and macerate for 1 hour by splashing with brandy. Drain and serve in the melon shells.

ICED FRESH PINEAPPLE

Trim the ends of the leaves of a pineapple, and rinse well. Cut lengthwise into quarters, and cut out the pineapple flesh, leaving the fibrous core piece intact. Cut this severed piece widthwise into ¼-inch (6-mm)-wide pieces, and replace in the pineapple shell. Slide the slices outward, alternating sides, and serve on a bed of crushed ice.

A menu for an Autumn Wine Harvest or Halloween Masquerade:

JUL GLÖGG

4 bottles dry red wine	1 fifth (1 L) vodka
1 cup (240 mL) sugar	10 cardamom seeds, shelled

10 whole cloves	1 cup (240 mL) slivered
10 black peppercorns	almonds
1 cinnamon stick	1 cup (240 mL) raisins

- Wrap the cardamom seeds, cloves, and peppercorns in a piece of muslin.
- Place the sugar in a saucepan with 3 cups of wine, and dissolve over medium heat. Add the spice sachet and the remaining ingredients, cover, and heat over a low flame. Serve in a heated chafing dish.

HOT RUM TODDIES

Heated rum and water, sweetened with sugar, and flavored with cinnamon, clove, and/or other spices.

CREAM OF CHESTNUT SOUP

Whole fresh chestnuts, peeled, boiled in chicken stock until tender, puréed, and blended with a light chicken velouté, finished with cream.

PUMPKIN BISQUE

Peeled and seeded pumpkin flesh, boiled in chicken stock until tender, puréed, and blended with a light chicken velouté, seasoned with nutmeg, and finished with cream.

BRAISED RABBIT WITH PRUNES

Cut up a skinned and fully dressed rabbit, dust with seasoned flour, sauté until golden brown, and braise in dry red wine with bouquet garni. Add 1½ cups (360 mL) pitted prunes and 1 cup (240 mL) medium julienned carrots during the last half hour of cooking.

BEEF BRISKET BRAISED IN CIDER

Sear a well trimmed and seasoned (with salt and pepper) beef brisket in vegetable oil. Set the beef aside, dust the pan with flour, stir, add 1 part apple cider, 1 part beef stock, and a little tomato paste, and blend. Return the beef and add a bouquet garni, and simmer for 2 hours or until tender.

ROAST ROCK CORNISH GAME HEN, WILD RICE AND GRAPE STUFFING

Prepare a stuffing with a sautéed mixture of scallions and mushrooms, blended with cooked wild rice, long grain rice, kasha, and seedless grapes. Season with salt and pepper, stuff into oven-ready game hens, and secure with toothpicks. Rub the outside of the hens with butter, and roast.

STEWED TOMATOES WITH SUMMER SQUASH

Flavor vine-ripened or canned sliced tomatoes with a sautéed mixture of onion, summer squash (and/or zucchini), garlic, fresh herbs, celery salt, and white pepper.

BUTTERED PARSNIPS

Remove the tops and peel the skin from parsnips, blanch in boiling salted water, sauté in butter, and season with salt, pepper, and nutmeg.

APPLE CHUTNEY

2 cups (480 mL) white wine
   vinegar
½ cup (120 mL) water
1 cup (240 mL) brown
   sugar
2 large garlic cloves, thin
   sliced
¼ cup (60 mL) ginger,
   peeled and sliced paper
   thin
1 teaspoon (5 mL) (6 g) salt

¼ teaspoon (1.2 mL) white
   pepper
4 dried hot red chile
   peppers
1 medium red onion, cut
   into medium dice
1 large lemon, seeded and
   sliced thin
1 cup (240 mL) raisins
4 Granny Smith apples,
   peeled, cored, and sliced
   thin

- Place all the ingredients, except the apples, in a noncorrosive pan. Bring to a boil, and simmer until thick and syrupy. Add the apples and continue cooking another 5 minutes. Remove from the fire, cool, then cover and refrigerate until ready to serve.

ROASTED BEETS, ORANGE GLAZE

Wash unpeeled beets, and place in a roasting pan with a little water. Place in a 375° F (190° C) oven for 1 hour, or until tender. Cool, then peel and slice. Serve warm, topped with a sauce made with orange juice, sugar, and vinegar, lightly thickened with cornstarch.

BRAISED LEEKS AND WILD MUSHROOMS

Cut well-rinsed leeks into large dice, and sauté in butter without browning. Add mushrooms (chanterelles, morels, shiitakes, and/or other varieties), sauté briefly, and dust lightly with flour. Add a squeeze of lemon juice, moisten with chicken stock, and season with salt and white pepper. Blend well, and simmer about 5 minutes.

POUND CAKE WITH DRIED CHERRIES

Serve sliced pound cake with a side of dried cherries rehydrated in brandy and sugar.

BAKED APPLE STUFFED WITH CHESTNUTS

Core some tart apples, and stuff with a filling made from chestnut paste mashed with a little butter and sugar. Splash with white wine, cover, and bake until tender.

PEAR AND DRIED-CRANBERRY PIE

Prepare as for apple pie: peel and core pears, and hold in lemon bath; drain, cut into slices, toss with brown sugar, cinnamon, and nutmeg, and place in an unbaked pie shell; sprinkle with dried cranberries, dot with pieces of unsalted butter, top with a sheet of dough, brush with water, sprinkle lightly with sugar, and bake in a preheated 375° F (190° C) oven about 30 minutes, or until the top is golden brown.

A menu for a Chicago 1920s Speak-Easy Party:

DEVILED EGGS

Hard-cooked eggs, split in half lengthwise, yolks mashed with mayonnaise, drained pickle relish, salt, and pepper; piped back into the eggs, tops sprinkled with paprika.

RUSSIAN CAVIAR WITH BLINIS

Fine Russian caviar is best served with iced vodka and plain blinis.

Blinis

½ pound (227 g) buckwheat flour
½ pound (227 g) all-purpose flour
1 cup (240 mL) warm milk
¾ ounce (21 g, about 1 teaspoon) granulated yeast
¼ teaspoon (1.23 mL) salt
¼ teaspoon (1.23 mL) sugar
¼ cup (60 mL) sour cream
2 small eggs, beaten
¼ cup (60 mL) heavy cream, warm
clarified butter as needed

- Sift the flours into a large bowl. Dissolve the yeast, salt, and sugar in the milk. Make a well in the flour, add the milk mixture, and blend thoroughly with the flour. Let sit 30 minutes in a warm place.
- Add the sour cream, eggs, and cream, and blend thoroughly into a smooth batter. (Texture should be similar to pancake batter, and can be adjusted as needed with additional warm milk or flour.) Ladle into 3–4-inch (76–100 mm) round pancakes on a nonstick pan or griddle greased with the clarified butter and cook on both sides until golden brown. Serve with caviar and sour cream.

OYSTER SHOOTERS

2-ounce (60-mL) shot glasses filled with cocktail sauce, a little vodka, and an oyster, topped with a little more cocktail sauce.

CANADIAN SMOKED SALMON

Arrange smoked salmon on a serving plate, and garnish with finely diced onion, cornichons, and capers placed in butter lettuce cups, lemon wedges, and toasted baguette slices.

ICED VICHYSSOISE, LOUIS DIAT

4 medium leeks, coarsely chopped and well rinsed
2 tablespoons (30 mL) unsalted butter
3 cups (720 mL) chicken stock
2 cups (480 mL) potatoes, coarsely chopped

salt and white pepper to taste
1 cup (240 mL) heavy cream
¼ cup (60 mL) sour cream
2 tablespoons (30 mL) chives, minced

- Sauté the leeks in the butter until tender. Add the stock and potatoes, and simmer until the potatoes are soft. Purée in a blender or food processor, return to the fire, add the cream, and bring to a boil. Season to taste with salt and white pepper, and set aside to cool.
- When chilled, check for seasoning (a squeeze of lemon juice can sometimes bring up the flavor if it is a little flat). Serve in a supreme dish, or in a well-chilled bowl. Top with a tablespoon of sour cream, and sprinkle with chives.

ASPARAGUS MIMOSA

Peeled, blanched, and chilled asparagus, topped with vinaigrette and garnished with sieved hard-cooked egg yolks and minced hard-cooked egg whites.

HEARTS OF KENTUCKY LIMESTONE, BABY SHRIMP, AND GREEN GODDESS DRESSING

Wash and dry the limestone lettuce hearts, cut in half, and place cut side up. Nap with the sauce, and garnish with baby shrimp.

Green Goddess Dressing

2 cups (480 mL) mayonnaise

¼ cup (60 mL) tarragon (or white wine) vinegar

8 anchovy fillets, drained and minced

2 scallions, finely sliced

⅓ cup (80 mL) minced parsley

¼ cup (60 mL) chives, finely minced

- Combine all ingredients thoroughly.

PORTERHOUSE STEAK, MAÎTRE D'HÔTEL BUTTER

Maître d'hôtel butter is made with softened unsalted butter, blended with salt, white pepper, lemon juice, and chopped parsley. It is rolled into a cylinder in parchment paper, refrigerated, and sliced as needed.

PORK AND SHRIMP KEBABS, CREOLE RICE

Cubed pork loin or shoulder can be marinated before broiling/grilling, or simply seasoned with salt and pepper. Vegetable garnish on the kebabs can include mushrooms, pearl onions, bell peppers, pineapple, zucchini, and/or other vegetables. Creole rice is a spicy rice, garnished with diced onion, bell peppers, and tomatoes.

CARROTS VICHY

Thinly sliced carrots cooked in lightly sugared water, flavored with butter and seasoned with salt, white pepper, and chopped parsley.

CREAMED SPINACH

Stemmed and well-washed spinach, blanched in boiling salted water, drained and squeezed dry, coarsely chopped, and cooked in a little cream sauce, seasoned with salt, white pepper, and nutmeg.

SCALLOPED POTATOES

Slice peeled potatoes ⅛-inch (4-mm) thick, and layer in a buttered casserole dish, seasoning each layer with salt and white pepper. Pour milk over the potatoes, dot with pieces of butter, and bake in a preheated 350° F (176° C) oven about 1 hour, or until all the milk has been absorbed.

ROASTED FONDANT POTATOES

Large Russet or Red Bliss potatoes, tournéd ("turned") into a large olive shape, rubbed with butter, seasoned with salt and pepper, and roasted golden brown.

PARMESAN DUCHESS POTATOES

Mashed potatoes enriched with cream and butter, seasoned with salt, white pepper, and grated Parmesan cheese, piped out into rosettes, 2½- to 3-inches (60- to 75-mm) high, then baked until golden brown.

RICE PUDDING WITH GOLDEN RAISINS

Long grain rice, well rinsed, cooked in milk (2 parts milk to 1 part rice) along with sultanas, seasoned with sugar and nutmeg.

CHOCOLATE MOUSSE

5 ounces (142 g) semi-sweet chocolate	6 tablespoons (90 g) unsalted butter, soft

75

5 egg yolks
¼ cup vanilla sugar (60 mL)
¼ cup (60 mL) dry sherry

1½ cups (360 mL) heavy
   cream, whipped

- Place the chocolate in a double boiler, and melt over low heat. Beat in the butter until smooth, and set aside to cool.

- Beat the yolks, sugar, and sherry in a stainless steel bowl over barely simmering water, until thick and approximately double in volume. Remove from the fire, stir in the chocolate mixture, and allow to cool.

- Gently fold in half the whipped cream, and when completely blended, fold in the second half. Pipe out into champagne saucers or other serving dishes, and refrigerate until firm. Garnish with a whipped cream rosette and sprig of mint.

NEW YORK-STYLE CHEESECAKE

¼ pound (113 g) graham
   cracker crumbs
2 tablespoons (30 mL)
   sugar
½ teaspoon (2.5 mL) ground
   cinnamon
6 tablespoons (90 mL)
   melted butter
1½ pounds (680 g) cream
   cheese, soft

3 eggs
1 cup (240 mL) sugar
½ teaspoon (2.5 mL) vanilla
   extract
3 cups (720 mL) sour cream
3 tablespoons (45 mL)
   sugar
½ teaspoon (2.5 mL) vanilla

- Combine the crumbs, sugar, cinnamon, and butter, and blend until smooth. Press into the bottom of a lightly buttered, round spring-form pan, and refrigerate.

- Beat the cheese, adding one egg at a time. Sprinkle in the sugar, then ½ teaspoon (2.5 mL) of vanilla, and beat until smooth. Place in the pan, taken from the refrigerator, and bake in a preheated 375° F (190° C) oven for 20 minutes.

- Beat the sour cream, sugar, and the second ½ teaspoon (2.5 mL) of vanilla until smooth, and spread over the top of the cheesecake. Turn the oven up to 500° F (260° C) for 5 minutes. Remove and allow to cool, then refrigerate several hours or overnight before serving.

BANANAS FOSTER

Prepared at tableside: bananas sliced, heated with butter and sugar, flamed with rum, and served over vanilla ice cream.

CRÊPES SUZETTE

Prepared at tableside: Brandy, orange juice, orange zest, and sugar are cooked to a syrup, with whole butter beaten in. Basic crepes are coated with the sauce, folded into quarters, and served with the remaining sauce.

A menu for a Fifties Rock and Roll Bash:

MAYONNAISE AND PARMESAN CHEESE TOASTS

Mayonnaise and Parmesan cheese blended together, spread on sliced white bread, baked in a moderate oven until golden brown, and then trimmed and cut into squares.

PIGS IN A BLANKET

Small cocktail franks wrapped in strips of prepackaged biscuit dough, and baked until golden brown.

JACK CHEESE KABOBS

Jack cheese, 1-inch (25-mm) cubes, pierced with bamboo skewers, interspersed with green olives stuffed with pimento.

ONION SOUP DIP WITH POTATO CHIPS

Powdered onion soup mix blended with sour cream, and served with potato chips.

HOT VELVEETA CHEESE TRIANGLES

Sliced American cheese placed on sliced white bread, baked until melted, trimmed of crusts, and sliced in half diagonally.

TUNA MELTS

Spread basic tuna fish salad onto toasted English muffins, top with a thin slice of tomato, cover with a slice of Cheddar or American cheese, and bake until melted.

BEEF AND BARLEY SOUP

A strong, clear beef broth made with beef shanks, garnished with diced shank meat and cooked barley.

ALPHABET CHICKEN SOUP

A strong, clear chicken stock, with the addition of medium-diced vegetables and alphabet noodles.

MOM'S MEAT LOAF

¼ cup (60 mL) vegetable oil
1 cup (240 mL) onions, finely diced
2 tablespoons (30 mL) ground poultry seasoning
½ cup (120 mL) dry bread crumbs
¾ cup (180 mL) milk
¼ cup (60 mL) chopped parsley

2 eggs, beaten
1 teaspoon (5 mL) salt
½ teaspoon (2.5 mL) black pepper
¼ cup (60 mL) Worcestershire sauce
2½ pounds (1,125 g) ground beef

- Sauté the onions in the oil until tender. Add the poultry seasoning, blend, and set aside.
- Combine the crumbs and milk, blend and set aside. Combine all ingredients with the ground beef, and mix thoroughly. Take a tablespoon of the mixture, fry it, and taste for seasoning.

- Roll the meat loaf in lightly oiled parchment paper, and shape into a 4-inch- (100-mm) wide cylinder. Bake in a preheated 350° F (176° C) oven, for 45 minutes. Carefully remove the parchment paper, and continue roasting for 30 minutes or until internal temperature reaches 165° F (74° C).

BROILED SLICED SPAM

Remove the Spam from its can, cut into ¼-inch- (6-mm) thick slices, season with salt and pepper, place on a pan, and broil on both sides until lightly browned.

At the Fly by Night Club in Spenard, Alaska (just outside Anchorage), the purchase of a bottle of Dom Perignon is accompanied by a Spam dinner on the house.

LUMPY MASHED POTATOES

Peel the potatoes and boil in lightly salted water until tender. Drain thoroughly, then mash manually or with an electric mixer, being sure to leave a few bits unmashed. Season with salt, white pepper, butter, and a little hot milk.

CORN FRITTERS, MAPLE SYRUP

1 cup (240 mL) milk
5 tablespoons (75 g)
   unsalted butter
pinch of salt
¾ cup (180 mL) whole
   kernel corn

1 cup (240 mL) flour
4 eggs
1 pint (480 mL) maple
   syrup (or as needed)

- Heat the milk, butter, salt, and corn until the butter is melted. Add the flour, and stir until completely smooth and the mixture balls up and pulls away from the sides of the pan (add additional flour if necessary).
- Add the eggs, one at a time, and beat until blended.
- Scoop out 2 tablespoon size pieces, place on a lightly buttered pan, and bake in a preheated 350° F (176° C) oven for 30 minutes, or until golden brown. (The fritters can also be deep-fried at 375° F/190° C.) Serve with warm maple syrup.

79

JELL-O MOLD WITH FRUIT COCKTAIL

Prepare three Jell-O flavors (strawberry, orange, and lemon), and allow to cool to room temperature. Fill large coffee cups with a half-inch-deep layer of strawberry Jell-O, and refrigerate until fully set. Add another inch of the same, along with some finely cut and drained canned fruit (peaches, pears, mandarin oranges, and/or other fruits), and refrigerate until set. Pour in 1-inch of the orange Jell-O, more fruit, and allow to set. Repeat with the lemon flavor. Allow to set, then dip in hot water for several seconds, invert, and serve with Cool Whip.

KOOL-AID ICE

Prepare a sorbet in an electric ice cream machine, using liquid Kool-Aid.

LOLLYPOP LEMONADE

Add small hard candies to a pitcher of lemonade.

A menu for a Greek Festival or Mediterranean Wedding Reception:

ANTIPASTI DEL GIORNO

Antipasti del Giorno refers to a variety of small dishes in a Mediterranean style, based on availability of ingredients, the weather, and the mood of the cook. Some suggested dishes include: sliced cheese, such as fontina, provolone, Asiago, Pecorino Romano; grilled or roasted vegetables, such as bell peppers, eggplant, fennel, garlic, leeks, onions (*see color plate, Hors d'Oeuvres, Greek Style*), zucchini; marinated vegetables, such as artichoke hearts (*see Figure 1.1; see also color plate, Hors d'Oeuvres, Greek Style*), garbanzo, red kidney beans, leeks, lentils, mushrooms; hummus, sliced tomatoes with anchovies, broccoli with Gorgonzola mayonnaise, veal scallopine with tuna mayonnaise, roasted bell peppers with sliced buffalo mozzarella.

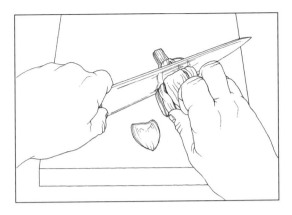

Slice off the bottom of the artichoke.

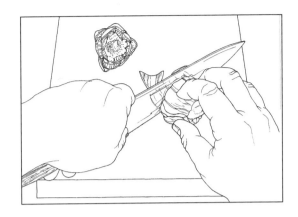

Slice off the top of the artichoke (artichoke should be approximately 1–1½ inches long).

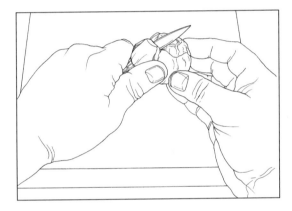

Trim around the bottom edge with a paring knife, removing the tough outer leaves.

Figure 1.1
Paring an Artichoke Down to the Heart

BAGNA CAUDA

Bagna cauda means "hot bath." This is a specialty of the Piedmont region in Italy, typically served during Christmastime and often containing shaved white truffles. The bath consists of 4 parts olive oil, 4 pressed garlic cloves, 1 part mashed anchovies, 1 part capers, 1 part grated cheese, and ground black pepper. It is heated in a chafing dish and served with freshly cut vegetables, typically cardoons (a relative of celery) and artichoke hearts and bottoms, though other vegetables can be substituted (red, orange, yellow, and green bell peppers; Belgian endive leaves and hearts; cucumber sticks; celery spears, among others.)

ASPARAGUS WRAPPED IN COPPA

Coppa is a dry-cured ham shaped like a large salami. It is sliced very thin and wrapped around the bottom halves of peeled, blanched, and chilled asparagus spears.

JELLIED CONSOMMÉ, PORTUGUESE STYLE

A tomato-flavored chicken consommé served chilled.

MINESTRONE MILANESE

A vegetable soup, made with ingredients on hand, typically kidney beans, cabbage, carrots, garlic, leeks, onions, peas, spinach, tomatoes, and turnips, cooked in diced and rendered fatback, simmered in stock, garnished with cooked pasta, and served with grated cheese.

ASSORTED POACHED SHELLFISH WITH RÉMOULADE AND COCKTAIL SAUCES

Poached shrimps and mussels, and shelled crabmeat, lobster, and scallops, served with two or more sauces—one mayonnaise based, another tomato based.

CAPRI ISLAND SQUID SALAD

¼ cup (60 mL) scallions, very finely sliced

¼ cup (60 mL) celery, medium dice

¼ cup (60 mL) carrot, medium dice

¼ cup (60 mL) red bell pepper, medium dice

1½ cups (360 mL) olive oil

½ cup (120 mL) lemon juice

2 tablespoons (30 mL) water

6 garlic cloves, pressed

2 tablespoons (30 mL) basil, minced

salt and white pepper to
   taste
1 pound (450 g) squid

1 bunch curly endive
2 lemons, cut into 8 wedges
   each

- Blanch the diced carrot in boiling salted water for several minutes, until tender but firm.
- Remove the cartilage from the squid body, and the inner part of the tentacles. Slice the body into ¼-inch (6-mm) thick slices, and cut the tentacles into ½-inch (12-mm) pieces. Blanch in boiling salted water, with a little white wine, until fully cooked. Drain, cool, and set aside.
- Beat the olive oil, lemon, water, garlic, basil, salt, and pepper in a bowl.
- Marinate the squid and the scallions, celery, carrots, and red bell pepper in the marinade, and refrigerate overnight.
- Cut the endive into 1-inch (25-mm) pieces, and arrange as a bed on one large, or four individual, serving plates. Place the marinated salad on top, and garnish with lemon wedges.

OCTOPUS WITH LEMON AND BASIL

Purchase octopus ready to cook (skinned, with innards, eyes, and mouth removed), and serve with olive oil mixed with chopped basil, and plenty of lemon wedges.

DEEP-FRIED SMELTS, RAVIGOTE

Dredge fresh (or frozen) smelts in seasoned flour, deep fry until golden brown, and serve with ravigote sauce (olive oil, white wine vinegar, mustard, tarragon, chives, parsley, chervil, onion, and capers).

ROASTED CAPON WITH LEMON AND ROSEMARY

Wash and dry capons, and rub the inside cavities with salt, pepper, sliced lemons, and sprigs of rosemary. Rub the exteriors with butter or oil, season with salt and pepper, and roast until golden brown. Remove the lemons and rosemary from the interiors, and carve or cut up for service.

VITELLO TONNATO

A cold dish of sautéed veal scallopine, napped with a sauce consisting of mayonnaise, flaked tuna fish, lemon juice, capers, cornichons, and chopped parsley, and garnished with parsley and thinly-sliced lemons.

BRAISED LAMB SHANKS, GREEK STYLE

4 lamb shanks
6 garlic cloves, cut in half lengthwise
salt and pepper to taste
¼ cup (60 mL) olive oil
1 cup (240 mL) onions, large dice
1 cup (240 mL) carrots, large dice
1 cup (240 mL) celery, large dice
1 cup (240 mL) leeks, well rinsed, large dice
12 garlic cloves, peeled
¼ cup (60 mL) flour
1 bottle dry red wine
¼ cup (60 mL) tomato paste
2 sprigs rosemary
2 sprigs thyme
2 bay leaves

- Preheat an oven to 400° F (205° C).
- Cut several crosses into the flesh of the shanks, using a paring knife. Insert the garlic cloves. Rub the lamb shanks with olive oil, and season with salt and pepper. Place in a heavy-gauge roasting pan or large cast-iron skillet, and roast 30 to 40 minutes, or until well browned.
- Remove the lamb shanks from the pan and set aside. Place the pan on the stove, and sauté the onions, carrots, celery, leeks, and garlic about 10 minutes, stirring continuously. Add the flour and blend in. Add the wine, tomato paste, and herbs, and bring to a boil. Return the lamb shanks to this mixture, turn the oven down to 350° F (176° C), and cook for 1 to 1½ hours, turning the shanks every 15 minutes. (The meat should be very tender.)

BRAISED SPINACH WITH GARLIC AND CAPERS

Cleaned and stemmed spinach, sautéed with garlic and capers.

FRIED ZUCCHINI

Zucchini cut into 3-inch (75-mm) julienne strips, dusted with seasoned flour, dipped into beaten egg, dredged with bread crumbs seasoned with herbs, and deep fried at 375° F (190° C) until golden brown.

HERBED ORZO

Orzo is the Greek name for a pasta in the shape of rice. In French it is called *langue d'oie* (bird's tongue), and in Italian *puntetti* (points). It is cooked al dente, then sautéed in butter or olive oil, and seasoned with chopped herbs.

RISI BISI

Risotto or long grain rice pilaf, garnished with diced ham and onion, and green peas.

BAKED POLENTA, NAPLES STYLE

Cooked and chilled polenta, cut into ½-inch (12-mm) thick slices, layered as lasagna, with meatless tomato sauce, mozzarella cheese, and pork or chicken cracklings (deep-fried or roasted strips of skin), and baked.

TOASTED LIGURIAN FOCCACIA

Foccacia can be purchased in a bakery, or prepared from the following recipe:

½ ounce (14 g) granulated yeast
2 cups (480 mL) warm water (110° F/43° C)
1 tablespoon (15 mL) sugar

5 cups (1,200 mL) bread flour
1 tablespoon (15 mL) salt
¼ cup (60 mL) olive oil
3 scallions, finely diced

- Dissolve the yeast and the sugar in the warm water, and allow to sit 10 minutes. Add the salt and the flour, and work into a ball (add more flour if needed). Knead well for 10 minutes on a lightly floured board (or beat in an electric mixer with a dough hook) until smooth and elastic. Roll into a ball, place in a lightly oiled bowl, brush with olive oil, and allow to rise in a warm place until doubled in volume. Punch down, and allow to rise again.

- Press the dough into a lightly oiled sheet pan (about 10 × 16 inches/250 × 400 mm), and press down with knuckles, making indentations all over the dough. Brush lightly with oil, sprinkle on the scallions, and bake in a preheated 400° F (205° C) oven 45 to 55 minutes, or until golden brown.

ROASTED BELL PEPPERS, BUFFALO MOZZARELLA, AND BASIL

Rub bell peppers with oil, and bake at 450° F (232° C) until they turn brown and black. Remove to a bowl and cover with plastic (or wrap in a plastic bag), and allow to sit 10 minutes. Remove the skin and seeds from the peppers, rinse, and refrigerate. Serve interspersed with sliced buffalo mozzarella and fresh basil leaves, sprinkled with salt and fresh black pepper, and drizzled with olive oil and balsamic vinegar.

SPINACH SALAD, GREEK STYLE

Cleaned and stemmed spinach, combined with thinly-sliced red onion, kalamata olives, crumbled feta cheese, fat capers, and dressed with a vinaigrette made with olive oil, red wine vinegar, garlic, salt, and black pepper.

GEMELLI PASTA SALAD, PRIMAVERA

Cook gemelli (or other pasta) to al dente, drain, and chill. Combine with finely cut and blanched baby (or grown-up) vegetables—such as artichoke bottoms, carrots, leeks, peas, zucchini, and chopped herbs (basil, oregano, parsley, and so forth)—bound lightly with mayonnaise and a little vinegar, and seasoned to taste with salt and pepper.

86

TIRAMISU

A light sponge cake, layered with pastry cream, soaked with espresso, and dusted with powdered sugar.

BAKLAVA

3 cups (720 mL) water
1 cup (240 mL) sugar
½ cup (120 mL) honey
1 cinnamon stick
1 lemon, quartered and seeded
1 package frozen phyllo dough

1 cup (240 mL) melted butter
2 cups (480 mL) walnuts, chopped and toasted
½ teaspoon (2.5 mL) ground cinnamon
½ teaspoon (2.5 mL) ground cloves

- Simmer the water, sugar, honey, cinnamon stick, and lemon, until a medium thick syrup remains. Set aside.
- Brush 6 sheets of phyllo with butter, and place in a baking pan. Top with the nuts and spices, then top with another 6 sheets of buttered dough.
- Bake in a 350° F (176° C) oven for 20 to 30 minutes, or until golden brown. Remove and set aside. Strain the syrup and pour over the baked dough, cut and serve.

TANGERINE TART

A sweet pastry tart, baked, spread with pastry cream topped with mandarin orange wedges arranged in concentric circles, and glazed with currant or apricot jelly.

A contemporary California menu:

SALMON TARTAR CANAPÉS

Slices of toasted pumpernickel, spread with butter, topped with a layer of finely minced raw salmon seasoned with lemon juice, salt, white pepper, and dill, cut into squares or diamonds, and garnished with a red onion and poached lemon zest.

JICAMA AND CHORIZO CANAPÉS

Slices of jicama, ¼ inch (5 mm) thick, cut into small star shapes, spread with a paste made with goat cheese and salsa verde, each topped with a slice of chorizo, and garnished with a red pepper spear.

OYSTERS ON THE HALF SHELL, RASPBERRY MIGNONETTE

Raspberry Mignonette consists of 4 parts raspberry vinegar, 1 part dry white wine, seasoned with salt, coarsely ground black pepper, minced shallot, and basil leaves.

BLACK BEAN CAKES, AVOCADO SALSA

For the Salsa

1 small cucumber, peeled, seeded, and cut into small dice
1 tomato, peeled, seeded, and cut into small dice
1 small onion, peeled and cut into small dice
1 yellow bell pepper, seeded, and cut into small dice
2 green jalapeño peppers, seeded and cut into small dice

½ cup (120 mL) lime juice
3 tablespoons (45 mL) minced cilantro leaves
1 tablespoon (15 mL) olive oil
1 ripe avocado, peeled, seeded, and cut into medium dice
salt to taste

• Combine all the ingredients, and allow to marinate 3 hours.

For the Bean Cakes

1 pound (450 g) black beans
1 tablespoon (15 mL) salt
2 tablespoons (30 mL) unsalted butter
¾ cup (180 mL) diced onion
2 garlic cloves, pressed
⅔ cup (160 mL) flour

2 egg yolks
1 teaspoon (5 mL) minced thyme leaves
2 tablespoons (30 mL) chopped parsley
salt and pepper to taste
olive oil as needed

- Rinse and cull the beans, and soak in cold water overnight. Drain, place in a pan with 2 quarts (2 L) water and the salt, and cook until tender. Drain, cool, and set aside.
- Sauté the onion in the butter until soft. Add the garlic, cook briefly, then add the flour and blend thoroughly. Place in a food processor along with half the beans, and the eggs, and purée.
- Mash the remaining beans by hand (with a mashing tool or ricer), and combine with the purée. Add herbs, and season with salt and pepper. Shape into individual cakes, measuring roughly 3 × ½ inches (12 × 75 mm), and press together firmly. Refrigerate at least 1 hour before cooking.
- Dust the cakes lightly with flour, and sauté in the oil until crisp on both sides. Place in a warm oven until ready to serve.

AVOCADO SOUP, CHAMPAGNE

2 cups (480 mL) milk
1 cup (240 mL) fresh white
  bread crumbs
4 large ripe Haas avocados,
  peeled and seeded
1 quart (960 mL) dry champagne

juice of 1 lemon
salt to taste
½ teaspoon (2.5 mL)
  nutmeg
1 cup (240 mL) heavy
  cream, whipped
4 sprigs of mint

- Soak the bread in the milk for 1 hour. Place in a blender or food processor with 1 avocado and 1 cup (240 mL) of champagne, and purée. Transfer to another bowl.
- Purée the remaining avocados, interspersing the rest of the champagne and the lemon juice. Blend all, and season with salt and nutmeg. Fold in half the whipped cream, then serve garnished with a dollop of whipped cream and a sprig of mint (*see color plate, Chilled Soups*).

CHICKEN CONGEE

½ cup (120 mL) long grain
  rice
1½ quarts (1.5 L) rich, clear
  chicken stock

1 cup (240 mL) short grain
  (glutinous) rice
1 cup (240 mL) cooked
  chicken breast, shredded
  into fine julienne

10 romaine lettuce leaves, cores removed and cut into large squares

salt to taste

¼ cup (60 mL) sesame oil

- Rinse the long grain rice, and simmer in the chicken stock until tender. Drain the rice from the stock, reserving the stock, and set the rice aside.
- Rinse the short grain rice, and simmer in the stock until soft and mushy. Do not drain. Transfer to a blender and purée. Return to the fire, and add the cooked rice, chicken, and lettuce, and season to taste with the salt. Drizzle a little of the oil on top at service.

Cous-Cous, Grilled Eggplant, and Currant Salad

Grill or broil ½-inch (12-mm) thick slices of eggplant, seasoned with salt and pepper, and brushed with oil. Pour boiling water over currants, allow to sit 10 minutes, then drain off and discard the water. Cut the eggplant into a medium julienne, and combine with cooked cous-cous and currants. Season with mint leaves, salt, and white pepper, and moisten with olive oil and vinegar.

Arugula and Red Bliss Potato Salad, Grainy Mustard Vinaigrette

Combine cooked and peeled Red Bliss potatoes with arugula cut into a broad chiffonade, dress with a vinaigrette made with grainy mustard, and season to taste with salt and pepper.

Mesclun Greens, Sun-Dried Tomato Vinaigrette

Mesclun greens refers to a blend of lettuces, such as arugula, frissee, mache, red and green oak, mizuno, red and green romaine, olorosa, radicchio, baby savoy spinach, tango, and tat soy. Dress the greens with a vinaigrette made with dried tomatoes reconstituted with boiling water, drained, and cut into julienne.

DUNGENESS CRACKED CRAB, MUSTARD MAYONNAISE

A Northern Pacific specialty; the crabs are boiled, drained, and cooled, then served whole with cracking pliers, mustard-flavored mayonnaise, and heated sourdough bread.

SCALLOP AND RED BELL PEPPER BROCHETTE, CITRUS BEURRE BLANC

Sea scallops and red pepper squares, blanched in boiling water, are skewered, broiled or grilled, and served with a sauce made by reducing minced shallot, strained lemon, lime, and orange juice, and beating in unsalted butter.

BROILED SKIRT STEAK, ROAST SHALLOTS AND GARLIC

Skirt steak is a narrow, grainy portion of meat from the breast of cattle, similar to flank steak, though a little more tender. It should be marinated in red wine, herbs, and spices, and grilled or broiled. Shallots and garlic are peeled, tossed in olive oil, salt, and pepper, roasted until soft and caramelized, and deglazed with balsamic vinegar.

ROASTED BABY CHICKEN, RED WINE VINEGAR BUTTER SAUCE

This sauce, served with roasted baby chicken, is a beurre blanc, prepared by reducing minced shallots, red wine vinegar, and red wine, and beating in unsalted butter.

BROILED CENTER-CUT PORK CHOPS, PEAR BUTTER

Pear butter, served with broiled center-cut pork chops, is made the same as apple butter: Peeled and cored pears are steamed with a cinnamon stick and a little white wine, then mashed, and slowly simmered until dark brown and thick.

TURKEY AND APPLE SAUSAGE WITH WARM RED CABBAGE SALAD

A turkey and apple sausage can be prepared using the recipe for Duck and Cranberry Sausage as a guideline (see Charcuterie, page 325) or by purchasing a good quality sausage already prepared, or prepared to your specification by a local butcher or meat purveyor (see the Appendix, "Specialty Suppliers"). Grilled or poached, it goes well with this red cabbage salad.

Red Cabbage Salad

1 small head red cabbage, cored and finely shredded

¼ cup (60 mL) olive oil

½ cup (120 mL) basalmic vinegar

½ cup (120 mL) chicken stock (or water)

2 tablespoons (30 mL) brown sugar

2 tablespoons (30 mL) capers, minced

- Heat the oil, vinegar, stock, and dissolve the brown sugar. Pour over the cabbage, add the capers, and toss.

MESQUITE-GRILLED PRAWNS, PAPAYA SALSA

Prawns (or shrimp) can be seasoned as desired, then grilled or broiled with the shells on and served with this salsa.

Papaya Salsa

1 ripe papaya, peeled, seeded, and medium diced

1 small red bell pepper, medium diced

1 small red onion, finely diced

½ cup (120 mL) minced cilantro leaves

¼ teaspoon (1.2 mL) ground cumin

pinch of salt

the juice of 3 to 4 limes

- Combine all the ingredients, and allow to marinate refrigerated for 24 hours.

92

MIXED GRILLED VEGETABLES, CHIPOTLE AÏOLI

Vegetables to be grilled should be trimmed of ends, seeds, and, in some cases, skin (notably carrots), washed well, brushed with olive oil, seasoned with salt and pepper, then grilled. Once marked on the grill, the cooking can be finished in a hot oven. (They can also be roasted instead of grilled.) Virtually any variety of vegetable can be grilled (or roasted), including carrots, fennel, leeks, onions, bell peppers, sweet potatoes, summer and patty pan squash, zucchini, and so on.

Chipotle peppers are dried and smoked jalapeño peppers, available dried or canned and packed in a tomato-based sauce. Reconstituted from the dried state or drained from a can, they are then pounded into a paste, beaten with oil and egg yolks—as for mayonnaise—and seasoned with salt and vinegar.

ARTICHOKES AU GRATIN

Coat cooked artichoke hearts and bottoms with a little cream sauce, top with a mixture of grated cheese and dry bread crumbs, and bake until lightly browned.

ZUCCHINI PANCAKES

Combine 2 parts shredded zucchini and 1 part mashed potatoes. Shape into individual cakes, dust with flour, and sauté in olive oil or clarified butter. Hold in a moderate oven until ready to serve.

GRILLED POLENTA TRIANGLES

Pour hot, cooked polenta into a pan to a thickness of ½ inch (12 mm). When it has set and is chilled, cut into triangles, dust with flour, sauté in olive oil, and hold in a moderate oven until ready to serve.

CHOCOLATE DECADENCE

1¼ cups (300 mL) water
12 ounces (340 g) granu-
lated sugar
12 ounces (340 g) dark
chocolate
14 ounces (400 g) bitter
chocolate
1 pound, 2 ounces (510 g)
soft butter

12 eggs
6 ounces (170 g) granulated
sugar
3 cups (720 mL) heavy
cream
2 tablespoons (30 mL)
sugar
toasted hazelnuts, crushed
dark chocolate shavings

• Bring the water and 12 ounces (340 g) of sugar to a boil. Add the chocolate (dark and bitter), and stir over medium heat until melted. Remove from the fire, add the butter, and blend thoroughly.

• Beat the eggs and 6 ounces (170 g) of sugar until light yellow and roughly doubled in volume. Fold in the chocolate mixture, blend, then pour into a buttered and lightly floured 9-inch (230-mm) cake pan. Cover the top with a sheet of buttered parchment paper cut to size. Bake in a preheated 350° (176° C) for 40 minutes. Allow to cool before removing from the pan, then refrigerate.

• Whip the cream and the 2 tablespoons (30 mL) of sugar until stiff. Decorate with the whipped cream, toasted hazelnuts, and chocolate shavings.

BLUEBERRY COBBLER

For the Filling

1 tablespoon (15 mL)
cornstarch
pinch of salt
⅛ teaspoon (.6 mL) ground
allspice
⅛ teaspoon (.6 mL) ground
cinnamon
1 tablespoon (15 mL) sugar

2 teaspoons (10 mL) lemon
juice
1½ cups (360 mL) blueber-
ries
⅔ cup (150 mL) grape juice
3 tablespoons (45 mL)
unsalted butter, cut into
½-inch (12-mm) cubes

For the Dough

⅓ cup (75 mL) flour
⅓ teaspoon (1.7 mL) baking
   powder
2 pinches of baking soda
pinch of salt

1 tablespoon (15 mL) but-
   ter, cut into ½-inch pieces
5 teaspoons (25 mL) buttermilk
1 egg, beaten
powdered sugar as needed

For the Filling

- Sift the dry ingredients together. Whisk in the grape juice until smooth. Place in a saucepan with lemon juice and berries, and bring to a boil. Cook for several minutes, then remove from the fire. Beat in the butter until fully emulsified.

For the Dough

- Sift the dry ingredients together. Add the butter, and rub the mixture together until it resembles coarse meal. Add the buttermilk and stir until just incorporated. Do not overmix.
- Preheat an oven to 400° F (205° C).
- Roll out the dough on a floured surface to a thickness of ⅜ inch (10 mm).
- Lightly butter an ovenproof casserole dish. Pour in the fill-ing. Set the dough over the top, trimming the edges. Brush with egg and bake for 15 minutes, or until golden brown. Sprinkle with powdered sugar at service.

FRESH SEASONAL BERRIES IN PASTRY TULIP

Pastry Tulip

⅔ cup (160 mL) sugar
½ cup (120 mL) egg whites
½ cup (120 mL) clarified
   unsalted butter

¾ cup plus 2 tablespoons
   (210 mL) flour, sifted

- Beat the sugar and egg whites together until the sugar is dis-solved. Sprinkle in the flour, and beat until smooth. Add the butter and blend in. Allow to sit for 30 minutes.
- Heat an oven to 450° F (232° C). Brush a pan lightly with butter, and spread about 3 tablespoons of batter into a cir-cle 6 inches (150 mm) in diameter. Place in the oven, and bake 6 to 8 minutes, or until the circle is light brown and the edges are golden brown. Remove from the oven, and re-

move the pastry using a flexible metal spatula. Place immediately over an inverted coffee cup, and gently press down, creating a wavy-edged inverted cup. When it has set (takes about 1 minute), lift off the cup, and set aside in a safe place. Repeat this procedure to create four tulips. Fill berries macerated in a little sugar and brandy, and top with whipped cream.

ELEMENTS OF BUFFET PRESENTATION AND DESIGN

PLATTER COMPONENTS

Food items produced in the garde manger and arranged for buffet service on acrylic mirrors, silver platters, wooden boards, and marble slabs are one of the benchmarks of a great garde manger department. It is, in effect, a large forum in which garde manger practitioners can show off their best work.

A platter presentation can consist of virtually any food item, modified for this large format. Pâtés, galantines, and roulades (farces rolled into cylinders, then baked or poached) are typically served in such a format, but any variety of food item can be presented in this way: antipasti, salads, roasted or smoked meats and poultry, charcuterie, cured or poached fish and shellfish, cheeses, and fresh fruit. (In formal competition, there are very strict guidelines for components. The following are some loose guidelines, but, for precise specifications, please consult any regional chapter of the American Culinary Federation.)

The components of most platters consist of five elements:

1. *Grosse Pièce or Centerpiece:* The *grosse pièce,* literally "large piece," is a partial piece of a primary food item, such as a pâté, galantine, or roulade, from which slices of that item are cut. A grosse pièce may act as *centerpiece,* or a centerpiece may consist of an entire cold roast (e.g., capon, chicken, turkey, veal loin) decorated with chaud-froid or aspic, or both, from which slices of the cold roast cascade down onto and along the platter arrangement. A centerpiece may also consist of one or more wedges or blocks of cheese, with slices of cheese layered from those wedges or blocks; a large cut or carved piece of fruit (usually melon or pineapple), from which flows cleanly cut fruit slices; or a sculptural piece fashioned out of bread, bread dough, salt dough, or carved vegetables (mukimono).

2. *Sliced Grosse Pièce:* Slices of the primary food laid out in harmonious linear and curvilinear lines. When the center-

piece consists of an entire roast or another item, slices of food may not come directly from that item.

3. *Garnishes:* Pieces that complement and accompany the slices of grosse pièce and that must harmonize with that primary food item.

4. *Flow Salad:* A salad that serves as a complementary dish and as an element that can tie the other components together; it must harmonize with the primary food item, as do garnishes.

5. *Cold Sauce:* Cumberland sauce is the traditional sauce accompaniment to roasted game and large joints of meat, as well as meat and game farces; other sauces based on mayonnaise, vinaigrette, or soy sauce are used, as they pertain to a dish. They can be served on the platter in a *socle*, a small food container fashioned out of food, or off the platter in a "gooseneck" sauce server or sauce boat.

Of course, some food presentations will vary slightly from these guidelines. For example, a large salad is a presentation unique in itself; there is no flow salad needed for cheese, and it may or may not be sliced, depending on the style of presentation; fruit does not require a flow salad (although a fruit salad could be worked into a fruit presentation).

DEVELOPING A STYLE

The components and style of any platter is uniquely individual. Choices of primary food, accompaniments, and salad ingredients, as well as the layout itself, are based on personal preference and the creative bent of the individual involved. Everyone develops a style based on his or her own paradigms, artistic vision, and experience—there are no absolutes in the culinary universe, nor is there an absolute criteria for taste. I recall a 19-year-old some years ago who was always coming up with wild and eclectic combinations of foods. That summer he had innovated strawberry mayonnaise to accompany an appetizer dish of smoked salmon. It did not seem to work for me then—nor does it now—but who is to say that strawberries and smoked salmon might not be a fine gastronomic experience for someone who cherishes those two foods? A maturing of style in the culinary trade and foodservice industry, it seems to me, accompanies a move toward the honest and the simple (as in less is more). In the restaurant trade, however, "simple" often equates with boring and mundane, and service with a pinch or two of arrogance may be considered chic. So restaurants and other foodservice operations seeking to make an impression may find an unusual style that can be perceived as the latest innovation. This is the reality of competition in the foodservice business.

In the garde manger, one develops a style of food choices, combinations, and layout that follow an inner vision. It is often not something that can be described clearly; indeed, some of the finest presentations defy explanation. There is an almost magical process that unfolds for each individual practitioner that is difficult to explain. Johann von Goethe, the eighteenth-century poet and dramatist, once wrote: *"We murder when we dissect."* Every detail and nuance of a culinary offering does not require verbalization; there should remain some mystery in the *process* of a creation.

In an attempt to understand the indescribable, I recall a conversation with a colleague, a very fine Danish chef trained in the European tradition, who once confided to me what he thought about "California cuisine." He said: *"They just throw everything up in the air, and however it falls on the plate, that's it. That's California cuisine."* I found this humorous, yet not without some truth. Of course we were both working in California at the time, which meant that we both represented a part of the problem and the solution. But it was clear that he had arrived at an important truth about cooking, something that explains the *je ne sais quoi* (the *I don't know what*) that happens when someone creates victuals that are visually beautiful and perfectly balanced in all aspects. Jean Camous, the late Henri Charpentier's mentor, referred to *"an intelligence of tremendous significance in the philosophy of a chef—the intelligence of the inner man"* (as revealed in Charpentier's 1934 autobiography, *Life à La Henri*). It is not so much a conscious thought process as it is a *feeling* for the proper balance between taste, texture, cadence, color, and flavor; when developed over a period of years, it simply springs from the inner person. If this proper balance is there, then all of the steps—from design, to procurement, to preparation, to execution and delivery—will be in tune with this inner philosophy, and the resulting work will clearly reveal this.

For the student of the garde manger (or the culinary craft), what is required is a dedication to the profession and a willingness to learn. *Practice makes perfect,* and the more platters one prepares, the more one endeavors to study the work of colleagues past and present, the better one becomes at achieving a balance of color, shape, texture, and taste; and from this a philosophy will develop. When I look at snapshots of my own work in the early years (for this reason, it is of the utmost importance to photograph one's work whenever and wherever possible), I see that they clearly lack the level of sophistication and presence that could be found in my later work. Like any skill, the more one practices it, the more one achieves a deeper level of accomplishment.

While there are no hard-and-fast rules or precise guidelines that communicate how visually beautiful edible works are created, there are some general guidelines and important considerations that will lead to the development of successful large-platter presentations:

- Sketch the basic layout of a presentation before setting the items in place. This can be done in a journal or on larger format (such as baker's parchment paper); in either case, the sketch should be saved so that these layouts can be modified and returned to later for reference.
- Consider the placement of all components: grosse pièce, centerpiece, individual slices, garnishes, flow salad, and sauce. (In competition, this exercise is essential, and it is performed repeatedly—first with paper cutouts and later with actual food—in order to allow little room for error when the final platter is presented for judging.)
- Numbers of component items—grosse pièce slices and garnishes—should match.
- Keep it simple: "The best cooking is the simplest cooking" (Paul Bocuse).
- Acrylic mirrors, silver trays, wooden boards, and marble slabs must be clean and smudge-free.
- Sliced items should flow from large to small, in the same order in which they are cut (mixed-size portions of sliced items tend to look like leftovers).
- The ingredients of garnishes and the flow salad should harmonize with the main item.
- All items should be edible. (If toothpicks or bamboo skewers are used to secure a centerpiece, they should be out of sight; in competition, they are strictly forbidden.)
- Allow a border of 2 inches from the edge and sufficient "negative" space. (*Negative space* is a term used in various art disciplines. It refers to an open area of paper or canvas not utilized, that is, empty. This open area serves as a way of bringing the viewer's visual attention into a work rendered in some art medium—watercolor, acrylic, oil paint, pastel, etc. The same technique is utilized on large platters, as well as on smaller individual dishes. Its subtlety directs the eye to the food item being offered.)

- A layer of aspic, known as a "chamise," was in the past placed onto the surface of a mirror or a platter, in order to prevent contamination from the platter to the foods served. Nowadays, a chamise, if used at all, is used only in formal culinary competition; in such a case, it *must* be perfectly sharp, clean, and smudge-free—not an easy task.
- Avoid leafy items that wilt (e.g., basil, lettuce, mint, flat-leaf parsley).

LAYOUT PATTERNS FOR PLATTER PRESENTATIONS

The organization of items on a platter is important for two reasons: (1) The visual attractiveness of the food displayed draws the eye of the dining patron toward it (it looks good to eat) and (2) the items are laid out in an order so that each portion can be taken in an orderly manner, leaving the platter still attractive to subsequent guests.

While every garde manger has his or her own style, there are some basic guidelines that underlie the approach. Some suggestions and illustrations follow:

- Platters come in a variety of materials and shapes:

  Materials: The smaller ones, measuring roughly 6 square feet (1.8 square meters) in area, are made of ceramic, silver, or stainless steel; the larger ones, measuring roughly 10 square feet (3 square meters), are made of reflective acrylic with plastic borders (lightweight acrylic has replaced glass mirrors, which are heavy and fragile).

  Shapes: Generally restricted to square, rectangular, round, and oval; some of the modern acrylic forms come in teardrop and a variety of elliptical shapes.

  Consideration should be given to the material, size, and shape of a platter, relative to the food items: silver is the most elegant, while ceramic is rustic, marble is classic, and stainless steel and acrylic are modern.

- The pattern of a layout on a platter of any size or shape can be either symmetric or asymmetric, depending on one's style and preference. Neat symmetry, with straight and perpendicular lines, and a centerpiece or grosse pièce in a central place, is clean and balanced; asymmetry, with diagonal lines and curves, and a centerpiece or grosse pièce off-center, is harmonious within a context of imbalance (it appears spontaneous but is still well ordered). Both approaches have their place.

100

- Remember to allow sufficient room for negative space. An overloaded platter, while efficient as far as the kitchen is concerned (it requires fewer trips back and forth between kitchen and dining room), is ungracious in style. Allowing open space not only draws the eye into the presentation but also adds a feeling of elegance.
- One should be cognizant of color harmony, shapes and textures, and the flow of the lines of the food when selecting food items for placement on a platter. While these criteria will all be based on the style of the person creating the work, one should seek a comfortable level.
- Be careful with flow salads that are marinated; they can weep, leaving puddles of the marinade on the platter. Such food items should be well drained before placement.

Figures 1.2 through 1.11 show a number of possible arrangements of sliced food items on large serving platters and mirrors. The specific ingredients are incidental to their arrangements; one is free to arrange various dishes in any pattern one chooses, and of course the possible variations are endless. Individual portions, and the larger *grosse pièce* from which those portions are cut, may or may not be coated with chaud-froid or collé, depending on the recipe for the dish. All portions and larger pieces, however, are nearly always coated with aspic.

Note: In food competition, the rule is that the number of garnishes should equal the number of slices. In actual practice, the rule may be overlooked. In all but three of the following illustrations, numbers of components match.

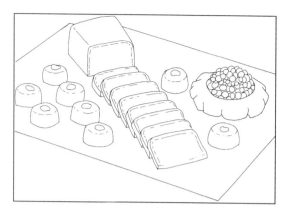

A poultry terrine, partially sliced, with the slices laid out diagonally. Garnish consists of flavored aspic jelly formed in individual savarin molds, filled with sour cream; in the right corner is a turban squash, scooped out, and filled with a mixed vegetable salad, cut with a medium Parisienne scoop ("noisette").

Figure 1.2

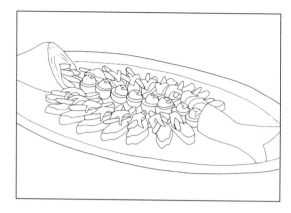

Two boneless and skinless salmon fillets are cut into individual portions, poached, and then arranged in two curvilinear lines, separated by a central row of stuffed hard-cooked eggs. At either end sit the poached head and tail of the same fish.

Figure 1.3

A curvilinear line of sliced fish roulade, garnished with a circle of stuffed squid on croutons and mussels stuffed with shrimp and vegetables; in the right corner is a cabbage scooped out and filled with carved vegetable flowers.

Figure 1.4

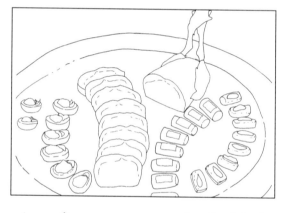

A curvilinear arrangement of a sliced duck galantine, accompanied by three garnishes: stuffed Roma tomatoes, stuffed palm hearts, and glazed sweet potatoes.

Figure 1.5

A beef tenderloin, stuffed with a farce, roasted, sliced, and arranged in the center in two overlapping circles. It is topped with a sliced palm heart salad and garnished with small tartlets filled with vegetable salad and sliced jicama topped with cherry tomato and basil.

Figure 1.6

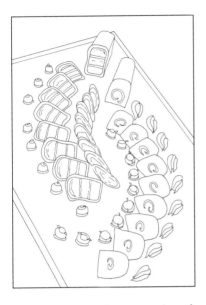

A salmon pâté (en croûte) and a terrine (wrapped in nori), arranged in two curvilinear lines, and accompanied by four different garnishes: two varieties of stuffed cherry tomatoes, sliced stuffed zucchini, and egg wedges topped with poached shrimp.

Figure 1.7

A sliced duck galantine arranged in an "S" layout. Three carved melons filled with fruit and a bunch of grapes highlight one end of the platter; garnishes include orange-wedge shells filled with herb cream and topped with an orange segment, and cucumber socles stuffed with ham mousse.

Figure 1.9

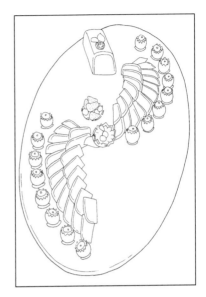

A sliced liver terrine arranged in two double, overlapping curvilinear lines, garnished with stuffed eggs. In the center are two orange halves decorated with fruit.

Figure 1.8

Slices of a fish terrine are laid out in a straight line, with two outside curvilinear lines of individual poached salmon portions garnished with egg yolk paste and a piece of green pepper. Vegetable flow salad sits in two half-circle puff pastry croustades, surrounded by two lines of stuffed cherry tomatoes.

Figure 1.10

The slices of three different fish roulades (two prepared in half-circle molds and one in a straight-sided tart mold) are arranged in three curvilinear rows, with the convex side of each row facing inward. Garnishes consist of half hard-cooked eggs on cucumber slices and butterflied shrimp on croutons.

Figure 1.11

2

COLD SAUCES AND MARINADES

MAYONNAISE

There are numerous tales of the origin of mayonnaise, including that it was created by the duke of Richelieu (or by his chef) in honor of the duke's successful capture of Port Mahon on the island of Minorca on June 28, 1756. The sauce was subsequently dubbed *Mahonnaise*. Antoine Carême claimed that the word was derived from *manier*, the French verb meaning "to stir": "Some people say mayonnaise, others mahonnaise, still others bayonnaise. It makes no difference that vulgar cooks should use these words, but I urge that these three terms never be uttered in our great kitchens and that we should always denominate this sauce with the epithet, magnonaise." Other etymologists trace the origin of mayonnaise to Bayonne, France, with the original name Bayonnaise. *Moyeu*, old French for "middle," referred to the middle of an egg—the yolk. *Bayonne* eventually combined with *moyeu*, they say, evolving into the name we currently use for this cold, egg-yolk-emulsified sauce. And Robert Sokolov, author of *The Saucier's Apprentice*, adds to the confusion with a theory of his own: "It seems to me improbable that no one has yet proposed a fourth solution to the problem. Since most sauces are named after places (Béarnaise, Hollandaise, Piémontaise, Anglaise), it is logical that mayonnaise refers to one also. Unfortunately, there is no town of Mayonne; however, there is a city at the western edge of Normandy, called Mayenne. Who is to say that mayonnaise did not begin as mayennaise?"

BASIC MAYONNAISE

3 egg yolks
½ teaspoon (2.5 mL) dry
   mustard
3 tablespoons (45 mL)
   white wine vinegar or
   lemon juice

1 pint (480 mL) olive oil
salt and white pepper to
   taste

- Beat the yolks, mustard, and 1 teaspoon (5 mL) of vinegar or lemon juice in a stainless steel bowl, using a wire whip.
- Add the oil in a slow, steady stream, whipping continuously. Alternate the oil with the rest of the vinegar/lemon juice as the sauce thickens.
- Season to taste with salt and white pepper.

Note: Basic mayonnaise is typically served with hard-cooked eggs served cold; roasted or braised meat served cold; calf's head (*Tête de Veau*); poached and pan-fried poultry; cold rice dishes; chilled poached fish and shellfish; crudités and salads.

MAYONNAISE DERIVATIVES

AÏOLI

4 to 6 large garlic cloves,
   split in two
2 egg yolks
salt and white pepper

⅓ cup (80 mL) mashed
   potato
the juice of ½ lemon
1 cup (240 mL) olive oil

- Pound the garlic in a mortar until it is a smooth paste. Add the egg yolks, salt, pepper, and potato. Continue pounding, while adding the oil in a slow, steady stream. Intersperse with the lemon juice. When the oil is completely emulsified, adjust the seasoning with salt and pepper.

The word *aïoli* is a combination of *ail* (garlic) and *oli* (Provençale dialect for oil). Léon Daudet (1867–1942), one of the greatest gastronomes of his time, contended that the culinary use of garlic achieved its peak of perfection in aïoli. Frédéric Mistral, who founded the journal *L'Aïoli* in 1891, wrote: "Aïoli epitomizes the heat, the power, and the joy of the Provençale sun."

ALEXANDRA MAYONNAISE

Mayonnaise prepared with hard-cooked sieved egg yolks, seasoned with dry mustard, and garnished with chopped chervil.

AMERICAN MAYONNAISE

Mayonnaise blended with puréed lobster meat.

ANDALUSIAN MAYONNAISE

Mayonnaise blended with tomato purée, garnished with diced bell pepper.

ANTIBE MAYONNAISE

Mayonnaise blended with tomato purée and anchovy paste, garnished with chopped tarragon.

BULGARIAN MAYONNAISE

Mayonnaise blended with thick, cold, puréed tomato sauce, garnished with diced celery root (poached in lemon and white wine).

CALIFORNIAN MAYONNAISE

Heavy cream blended with tomato ketchup, seasoned with Worcestershire Sauce, Tabasco, paprika, and lemon juice.

CAMBRIDGE MAYONNAISE

2 hard-boiled egg yolks, pressed through a sieve
1 anchovy fillet, well mashed
½ teaspoon (2.5 mL) dry mustard
⅛ teaspoon (.6 mL) cayenne pepper
¼ cup (60 mL) white wine vinegar
1 cup (240 mL) olive oil

1 teaspoon (5 mL) tarragon, minced
1 teaspoon (5 mL) dill, minced
1 tablespoon (15 mL) parsley, minced
1 tablespoon (15 mL) capers, drained
salt and white pepper to taste

- Beat the yolks, anchovy, mustard, cayenne, and 1 tablespoon (15 mL) of vinegar in a stainless steel bowl, using a wire whip.
- Add the oil in a slow, steady stream, whipping continuously. Alternate the oil with the remaining vinegar as the sauce thickens.
- Add the herbs and capers, and season to taste with salt and white pepper.

CASANOVA MAYONNAISE

Mayonnaise blended with hard-cooked egg yolks, chopped tarragon, and minced truffles.

CHANTILLY MAYONNAISE

Mayonnaise made with lemon juice, blended with unsweetened whipped cream just before service.

Note: Chantilly mayonnaise is typically served with poached sweetbreads, and with poached or pan-fried poultry.

EPICUREAN MAYONNAISE

Mayonnaise blended with puréed cucumber (seeded and peeled), anchovy paste, and puréed mango chutney.

FRANKFURT GREEN SAUCE

Frankfurt Green Sauce is a dish typical of Hessen, a region near the center of Germany, between Westfallen and Thürigen. A shorter version of this recipe can be prepared by using mayonnaise and yogurt as a base and seasoning it with pickle, onion, mustard, garlic, and lemon. This sauce is typically served with boiled beef and pâtés.

3 hard-cooked egg yolks
1 garlic clove, pressed
1 tablespoon (15 mL) Dijon-style mustard
the juice and zest of one lemon
¼ cup (60 mL) each of the leaves of the following herbs, minced: chervil, chives, dill, flat-leaf parsley, sorrel, watercress, and tarragon
1 cup (240 mL) corn oil
½ cup (120 mL) sour cream
¼ cup (60 mL) sour pickle, finely diced
¼ cup (60 mL) onion, finely diced
salt and pepper to taste

• Combine the yolks, garlic, mustard, lemon zest, a little of the lemon juice, and the herbs. Pour the oil in slowly, while beating continuously. Intersperse the oil with the remaining lemon juice. When all the oil is incorporated, add the sour cream, pickle, and onion and blend thoroughly. Season to taste with salt and white pepper.

110

GENOA MAYONNAISE

Mayonnaise prepared with lemon juice (instead of vinegar), blended with a paste made from pistachios, almonds, basil, sage, and parsley (*see color plate, Salmon Trout in Aspic*).

Note: Genoa Mayonnaise is typically served with braised or baked fish.

GLOUCESTER MAYONNAISE

Mayonnaise seasoned with Worcestershire sauce, garnished with diced or grated fennel root, and finished with sour cream.

GREEN MAYONNAISE

1 cup (240 mL) mayonnaise
1 teaspoon (5 mL) tarragon
  leaves, minced
1 teaspoon (5 mL) parsley,
  minced
1 teaspoon (5 mL) water-
  cress leaves, minced
1 teaspoon (5 mL) basil
  leaves, minced

- Combine all ingredients in a bowl and blend thoroughly (*see color plate, Crudité*).

Note: Green mayonnaise typically accompanies shellfish served cold and hard-cooked eggs served cold.

VINCENT MAYONNAISE

1 part green mayonnaise blended with 1 part tartar sauce.

GRIBICHE SAUCE

2 hard-boiled egg yolks,
  pressed through a sieve
2 hard-boiled egg whites,
  cut into fine julienne
½ teaspoon (2.5 mL) dry
  mustard
3 tablespoons (45 mL)
  white wine vinegar
1 cup (240 mL) olive oil
2 cornichons
1 tablespoon (15 mL) small
  capers, drained

111

1 tablespoon (15 mL) tarragon leaves, minced

1 tablespoon (15 mL) chervil, minced

1 tablespoon (15 mL) parsley, minced

salt and white pepper to taste

- Beat the egg yolks, mustard, and 1 tablespoon of vinegar in a stainless steel bowl, using a wire whip.
- Add the oil in a slow, steady stream, whipping continuously. Alternate the oil with the remaining vinegar as the sauce thickens.
- Add the cornichons, capers, herbs, and egg white. Season to taste with salt and white pepper.

Note: This sauce is typically served with poached fish and shellfish served cold; poached calf's head served cold (*Tête de Veau*).

HAMBURG MAYONNAISE
(MAYONNAISE À LA HAMBOURGEOISE)

Mayonnaise with the addition of lemon zest, a pinch of sugar, and a splash of Madeira.

Note: Hamburg mayonnaise is typically served with grilled or broiled meat or poultry.

HORSERADISH MAYONNAISE

Mayonnaise blended with grated prepared horseradish (squeezed dry), flavored with a little lemon juice, and finished with chopped parsley.

Note: This mayonnaise is typically served with roasted beef or smoked fish.

HORSERADISH SAUCE II

½ cup (120 mL) heavy cream

2 slices fresh white bread, crusts removed and shredded (or grated) into crumbs

⅓ cup (80 mL) sour cream

¼ cup (60 mL) prepared horseradish, squeezed dry

salt and white pepper to taste

- Combine all the ingredients and blend well, seasoning to taste with the salt and white pepper. Cover and refrigerate 1 hour before serving.

Note: This sauce is typically served with roast rib of beef, grilled or broiled meat, or poultry.

LA VARENNE MAYONNAISE

1 small shallot, minced
3 tablespoons (45 mL) olive oil
½ cup (120 mL) mush-rooms, roughly chopped
salt and white pepper to taste

¼ cup (60 mL) white wine
1 cup (240 mL) mayonnaise
1 tablespoon (15 mL) pars-ley, minced
1 tablespoon (15 mL) chervil, minced

- Sauté the shallot in the oil for several minutes. Add the mushrooms, salt, and pepper, and continue sautéing. Add the white wine.
- Using a slotted spoon, transfer the mushrooms to a chopping board, and mince. Return to the sauté pan and simmer, stirring frequently until the mixture is fairly dry. Set aside and allow to cool.
- Thoroughly blend together the mayonnaise, 2 tablespoons (30 mL) of the mushroom mixture, and the herbs. Season to taste with salt and white pepper.

Note: This mayonnaise is typically served with poached fish, served cold.

LEGHORN MAYONNAISE

Mayonnaise made with hard-cooked egg yolks (instead of raw yolks), blended with anchovy paste, seasoned with a little nutmeg, and garnished with chopped parsley.

LOUIE SAUCE

Mayonnaise blended with heavy cream and strained chili sauce (in proportions of 4 or 3 to 1), garnished with minced onion and green pepper, and seasoned with a touch of cayenne pepper and lemon juice.

Note: Louie Sauce is typically served with Shrimp or Crab Louie, a salad dish unique to San Francisco, consisting of a bed of lettuce topped with poached shrimp or Dungeness crab-meat, garnished with tomatoes, olives, and hard-cooked egg wedges. The sauce is served separately.

MANDRELKREN MAYONNAISE

Mayonnaise made with pounded almonds blended with egg yolks, seasoned with a little salt and sugar, then beaten with oil and vinegar (as for basic mayonnaise).

MARSEILLE MAYONNAISE

Mayonnaise blended with a purée of sea urchins.

MEXICAN MAYONNAISE

Mayonnaise blended with anchovy paste, garnished with diced red and green bell peppers.

MUSKETEER MAYONNAISE

1 shallot, minced
½ cup (120 mL) dry white
    wine
1½ tablespoons (22 mL)
    meat glaze

¼ teaspoon (1.2 mL)
    cayenne
2 tablespoons (30 mL)
    chives, minced

- Simmer the shallot and wine until reduced to about 2 tablespoons (30 mL) of liquid. Add the glaze and cayenne, and stir until smooth. Set aside, and allow to come to room temperature.
- Add the reduction and the chives to basic mayonnaise, and blend thoroughly.

Note: This mayonnaise is typically served with cold meats.

ORIENTAL MAYONNAISE

Mayonnaise blended with a Middle Eastern-style tomato fondue.

Tomato Fondue
¼ cup (60 mL) olive oil
1 shallot, finely diced
½ cup (120 mL) onion, finely diced
2 garlic cloves, pressed
½ cup (120 mL) red and green bell peppers, medium dice

pinch of saffron
2 sprigs thyme
1 cup (240 mL) tomato purée
1 cup (240 mL) diced, peeled tomatoes, with their juice
salt and white pepper to taste

- Sweat the shallot and onion in the olive oil for 10 minutes. Add the garlic, peppers, saffron, and thyme, and sauté another 5 minutes. Add both tomato ingredients and simmer about 20 minutes. Remove the thyme stems, season to taste, and allow to cool. Blend with mayonnaise as desired.

RÉMOULADE SAUCE

1 cup (240 mL) mayonnaise
1 tablespoon (15 mL) Dijon-style mustard
1 anchovy fillet, mashed to a paste
1 tablespoon (15 mL) tarragon leaves, minced

1 tablespoon (15 mL) chervil or parsley, minced
2 cornichons, finely diced
1 tablespoon (15 mL) small capers, drained

- Combine all ingredients in a bowl and blend thoroughly.

Note: This sauce is typically served with poached fish and shellfish served cold, fine julienned celery root salad (see "Celery Root Rémoulade" in Chapter 6), crudités and salads, and hard-cooked eggs served cold.

ROQUEFORT MAYONNAISE

Mayonnaise with crumbled or mashed Roquefort cheese added, thinned as needed.

Note: This mayonnaise is typically served with crudités and salads.

ROUGEMONT MAYONNAISE

Mayonnaise seasoned with additional mustard, garnished with chopped tarragon.

ROUILLE

Boiled mashed potatoes, blended with olive oil and fish stock, seasoned with minced chili peppers, seasoned with salt and pepper.

ROUILLE, PROVENÇALE STYLE

1 large red bell pepper
2 red jalapeño peppers
olive oil as needed
2 egg yolks
4 large garlic cloves,
   pressed

⅓ cup (80 mL) mashed
   potato
salt and white pepper to
   taste
1 cup (240 mL) olive oil
the juice of 1 lemon

- Preheat an oven to 400° F (205° C). Rub all the peppers with the olive oil, place on a pan, and roast until they are very dark brown. Remove from the oven, wrap in a plastic bag, and allow to sit 10 minutes. Separate the flesh from the peels and seeds; rinse in cold water and set aside.
- Purée the peppers, yolks, garlic, salt, and pepper in a food processor. Add the potato and, using the pulse switch, add the olive oil in a slow, steady stream, alternating with the lemon juice. Adjust the seasoning with salt and pepper.
- Purée the egg yolks, bell pepper, garlic, salt, and pepper in a food processor. Using the pulse switch, add the potato, then the olive oil in a slow steady stream, alternating with the lemon juice. Adjust the seasoning with salt and pepper.

Note: This sauce is typically served with poached fish and octopus; it is also spread on toasted croutons to accompany bouillabaisse and may include puréed fish livers with traditional bouillabaisse or puréed chicken livers with a chicken bouillabaisse.

RUSSIAN MAYONNAISE

1 cup (240 mL) mayonnaise
1 tablespoon (15 mL) Dijon-
    style mustard
¾ cup (180 mL) ketchup or
    strained chile sauce

2 tablespoons (30 mL)
    white wine vinegar
3 tablespoons (45 mL)
    osetra, sevruga, or
    choupique caviar

- Combine all the ingredients together, except the caviar, and blend thoroughly. At service, ladle some of the sauce over the appropriate salad, and sprinkle the caviar on top of the sauce.

Note: This recipe is the modern version. The classical version is made with lobster tomalley (liver), cooked, and pressed through a sieve.

Russian mayonnaise is typically served with poached fish served cold, crudités, and salads.

SARDAL SAUCE

3 hard-cooked egg yolks
2 tablespoons (30 mL)
    heavy cream
2 tablespoons (30 mL)
    minced truffles
pinch of salt

pinch of white pepper
1 cup (240 mL) olive oil
juice of 1 lemon
2 tablespoons (30 mL)
    Cognac

- Beat the egg yolks, cream, truffles, salt, and pepper with a wire whip. Add the oil slowly, beating continuously, alternating it with the lemon juice. Add the Cognac, and adjust the seasoning.

Note: This sauce is typically served with poached fish served cold or with grilled meat.

SPANISH MAYONNAISE

Mayonnaise seasoned with garlic, additional mustard, and paprika, and garnished with finely diced ham.

BRESSE MAYONNAISE

Spanish mayonnaise flavored with Madeira and orange juice, seasoned with cayenne pepper, and finished with puréed sautéed chicken livers.

SWEDISH MAYONNAISE

Mayonnaise blended with apple sauce that has been cooked with white wine, garnished with grated horseradish.

Note: This mayonnaise is typically served with pork.

TARTAR SAUCE

1 cup (240 mL) mayonnaise
2 tablespoons (30 mL)
   onion, minced
1 hard-cooked egg yolk,
   pressed through a sieve

2 tablespoons (30 mL)
   chives, minced

- Combine all ingredients in a bowl and blend thoroughly.

Note: This sauce is typically served with hard-cooked eggs served cold; poached fish served cold; fried fish and oysters; rice served cold; large tournéed potatoes (*Pomme Pont-Neuf*).

TRIANON MAYONNAISE

Mayonnaise blended with tomato purée and white onion purée (cooked first in a little white stock or white wine, then drained), garnished with diced cornichons and red bell pepper.

TYROLIAN MAYONNAISE

Mayonnaise blended with tomato purée.

VALENTINE MAYONNAISE

Mayonnaise seasoned with additional mustard, blended with grated horseradish and chopped tarragon.

VERDI SAUCE

1 cup (240 mL) spinach
    leaves, well rinsed,
    blanched in boiling
    water, and squeezed dry

¾ cup (180 mL) mayonnaise
¼ cup (60 mL) sour cream
3 tablespoons (45 mL) cor-
    nichons, finely diced

- Mince the spinach into a very fine purée, then blend with the remaining ingredients.

WATERCRESS MAYONNAISE

1 bunch watercress leaves,
    well rinsed, stems
    removed
2 egg yolks

juice of 1 lemon
salt and white pepper to
    taste
1 cup (240 mL) olive oil

- Combine the watercress, yolks, half the lemon juice, salt, and pepper in a food processor.
- Use the pulse, or on/off, switch, and incorporate the oil slowly and carefully, alternating it with the remaining lemon juice. Adjust seasoning with salt and pepper.

Note: This mayonnaise is typically served with poached or soft-boiled eggs or poached fish served cold.

CONTEMPORARY INNOVATIONS

DUTCHESS VALLEY MUSTARD DRESSING

1 cup (240 mL) mayonnaise
1 cup (240 mL) sour cream
¼ cup (60 mL) moutarde de
    Meaux

¼ cup (60 mL) champagne
    vinegar
salt and white pepper to
    taste

- Combine all ingredients and blend thoroughly.

119

GREEN GODDESS DRESSING

1 cup (240 mL) mayonnaise
1 garlic clove, pressed
3 tablespoons (45 mL)
mashed anchovy
3 tablespoons (45 mL)
minced chives
1 tablespoon (15 mL) lemon
juice

3 tablespoons (45 mL) tarragon vinegar
½ cup (120 mL) heavy cream
⅓ cup (80 mL) chopped parsley
salt and pepper to taste

• Combine all ingredients and blend thoroughly.

HERB CREAM

½ cup (120 mL) mayonnaise
¼ cup (60 mL) half-and-half
2 tablespoons (30 mL)
white wine vinegar
1 teaspoon (5 mL) basil
leaves, minced

1 teaspoon (5 mL) parsley,
minced
1 teaspoon (5 mL) tarragon
leaves, minced
salt and white pepper to
taste

• Combine all ingredients and blend thoroughly. Season to taste with the salt and white pepper.

Note: This sauce is designed for service with an appetizer dish consisting of roasted Red Bliss potatoes and roasted bell peppers.

LIME MAYONNAISE

1½ cups (360 mL) mayonnaise
5 tablespoons (75 mL) lime
juice

¾ cup (180 mL) half-and-half
salt and white pepper to
taste

• Combine all ingredients and blend thoroughly. Cover and refrigerate until ready to serve.

Note: This mayonnaise is designed for service with grilled or fried fish.

MUSTARD-PECAN MAYONNAISE

1 cup (240 mL) mayonnaise
5 tablespoons (75 mL)
  grainy mustard

½ cup (120 mL) toasted
  chopped pecans
the juice of 1 lemon

- Combine all ingredients and blend thoroughly. Cover and refrigerate until ready to serve.

Note: This mayonnaise is designed for service with a main dish consisting of fried catfish.

PECAN MAYONNAISE

Three parts mayonnaise, seasoned with 1 part grainy Dijon-style mustard and a little lemon juice, garnished with 2 parts toasted chopped pecans, seasoned with salt and white pepper.

Note: This mayonnaise is designed for service with an appetizer dish consisting of fried okra.

SUN-DRIED TOMATO MAYONNAISE

1 cup (240 mL) mayonnaise
½ cup (120 mL) crème
  fraîche or sour cream
½ cup (120 mL) oil-packed
  sun-dried tomatoes,
  drained and cut into
  small dice

juice of ½ lemon
1 garlic clove, pressed
2 tablespoons (30 mL) basil
  leaves, minced

- Combine all ingredients and blend thoroughly. Cover and refrigerate until ready to serve.

Crème Fraîche

2 cups (480 mL) heavy
  cream
½ cup (120 mL) buttermilk

½ cup (120 mL) sour cream
  or yogurt
¼ teaspoon (5 mL) salt

- Combine all ingredients in a clean noncorrosive saucepan, blend thoroughly, and bring to a temperature of 100° F (38° C).
- Transfer to a clean stainless steel bowl, cover, and set into an oven heated only by the pilot light. Leave for 12 hours.
- Refrigerate for 24 hours. Carefully remove the thickened top part (this is the crème fraîche), and discard any liquid left at the bottom. Cover and refrigerate until ready to use.

THOUSAND ISLAND MAYONNAISE

1 cup (240 mL) mayonnaise
¾ cup (180 mL) strained
   chili sauce or ketchup
¼ cup (60 mL) green and
   red bell peppers, finely
   diced

¼ cup (60 mL) scallion,
   sliced paper thin

• Combine all ingredients and blend thoroughly.

THREE-HERB MAYONNAISE

½ cup (120 mL) mayonnaise
¼ cup (60 mL) half-and-half
2 tablespoons (30 mL)
   white wine vinegar

1 teaspoon (5 mL) each,
   minced basil, parsley, and
   tarragon
salt and white pepper to
   taste

• Combine all ingredients and blend thoroughly. Season to taste with the salt and white pepper.

VINAIGRETTE

The word *vinaigre,* literally "sour wine," is a combination of *vin* (French for "wine," from the Latin *vinum*), and *aigre* (French for "sour," from the Latin *acer,* meaning "sharp").

Vinegar is actually more than just sour wine. It is a fermented product requiring nearly as much care as wine. White or red wine is fermented in oak barrels, using a "mother," a strain of bacteria that consumes the alcohol in the wine, turning it into acetic acid. This fermentation, which requires roughly six months, is followed by a careful filtering of the vinegar, then adjusting the acid content by adding water and/or wine.

Orléans, France, an important wine transport center on the Loire River, is also the French vinegar capital (a vinegar merchant's corporation was established there in 1394). Today, the "Orléans method" is the name applied to this careful fermentation process, whereas the "German method" refers to industrial production of vinegar, a short distillation method requiring one to three days. The differences in flavor and aroma between the two, of course, are significant.

BASIC VINAIGRETTE

1 cup (240 mL) olive oil
⅓ cup (80 mL) red or white
  wine vinegar

⅛ teaspoon (.6 mL) salt
⅛ teaspoon (.6 mL) white
  pepper

- Combine all ingredients in a bowl and blend thoroughly with a wire whip.

EMULSIFIED VINAIGRETTE

3 cups (720 mL) olive oil
1 cup (240 mL) champagne
  vinegar
2 garlic cloves, peeled
1 small shallot, peeled and
  chopped
1 tablespoon (15 mL) Dijon-
  style mustard

½ teaspoon (2.5 mL) salt
¼ teaspoon (1.2 mL) pepper
½ cup (120 mL) parsley
  leaves, well rinsed
½ cup (120 mL) water

- Place all ingredients in a blender and purée. Adjust seasoning with salt and pepper.

Note: This sauce is very much a "taste as you go" creation—more an approach, rather than a strict recipe. One finds a balance between oil and vinegar to suit one's taste (the water is used to cut the acidity of the vinegar). The amounts of garlic and mustard can be increased or decreased as desired, and additional parsley, an emulsifying agent, can also be added to increase viscosity.

RAVIGOTE SAUCE

½ cup (120 mL) olive oil
¼ cup (60 mL) white wine
  vinegar
½ teaspoon (2.5 mL) Dijon-
  style mustard
½ teaspoon (2.5 mL) tar-
  ragon leaves, minced
½ teaspoon (2.5 mL) fresh
  chives, minced

½ cup (120 mL) parsley,
  minced
½ cup (60 mL) chervil,
  minced
2 tablespoons (30 mL)
  onion, very finely diced
1 teaspoon (5 mL) small
  capers, drained

- Blend all ingredients thoroughly in a stainless steel bowl.

Note: This sauce is typically served with hard-cooked eggs served cold; poached fish served cold; grilled meat; or poached or pan-fried poultry.

ROQUEFORT VINAIGRETTE

1 garlic clove, split in half
½ cup (120 mL) olive oil
3 tablespoons (45 mL)
white wine vinegar

⅓ cup (80 mL) mashed
Roquefort cheese
salt and white pepper to
taste

- Rub the garlic clove around the inside of a clean wooden bowl, then discard the garlic.
- Pour in the oil, vinegar, salt, and pepper, and blend thoroughly. Add the cheese and blend again.
- Add the desired quantity of cut, washed, and dried romaine or butter lettuce, toss, and serve.

Note: This sauce can be made with Gorgonzola or other varieties of blue cheese (please change its name accordingly). It can also be made ahead of time, then applied at the time of service.

ASIAN-STYLE VINAIGRETTE

1 cup (240 mL) peanut oil
1 tablespoon (15 mL)
sesame oil
1 tablespoon (15 mL) gingerroot, grated
1 garlic clove, crushed

¼ cup (60 mL) plain rice
vinegar
2 tablespoons (30 mL) soy
sauce
2 tablespoons (30 mL)
water

- Place all ingredients into a blender and purée. Adjust seasoning with additional water, soy sauce, and vinegar.

CORIANDER-LIME VINAIGRETTE

1 cup (240 mL) olive oil
¼ cup (60 mL) champagne
vinegar
¼ cup (60 mL) lime juice
1 jalapeño pepper, seeds
removed, and roughly
chopped

½ cup (120 mL) cilantro
leaves, well rinsed and
dried
½ cup (120 mL) mint leaves,
well rinsed and dried
½ teaspoon kosher salt
½ teaspoon black pepper

- Purée the ingredients in a blender. Cover and refrigerate until ready to use.

CREAM VINAIGRETTE

½ cup (120 mL) heavy
    cream
¼ cup (60 mL) red wine
    vinegar

pinch of salt
pinch of white pepper

- In stainless steel bowl, gently blend the vinegar into the cream and season with salt and pepper. Cover and refrigerate until ready to use.

GINGER VINAIGRETTE

2 cups (480 mL) olive oil
¼ cup (60 mL) white wine
    vinegar
juice of 1 lemon
½ teaspoon (2.5 mL) salt

¼ teaspoon (1.2 mL) white
    pepper
3 tablespoons (45 mL) gin-
    gerroot, grated

- Place all ingredients into a stainless steel bowl, and blend thoroughly. Cover and refrigerate until ready to use.

LEMON-BASIL VINAIGRETTE

1 cup (240 mL) olive oil
¼ cup (60 mL) lemon juice
½ teaspoon (2.5 mL) lemon
    zest
3 tablespoons (45 mL) bal-
    samic vinegar

2 tablespoons (30 mL)
    water
2 shallots, chopped
salt and white pepper to
    taste

- Place all ingredients into a blender and purée. Cover and refrigerate until ready to use.

ORANGE VINAIGRETTE

1 shallot, minced
1 teaspoon (5 mL) Dijon-
    style mustard
the zest of 1 orange
1 cup (240 mL) olive oil

⅓ cup (80 mL) champagne
    vinegar
2 tablespoons (30 mL)
    orange juice
salt and white pepper to
    taste

- Place all ingredients in a blender and purée. Cover and refrigerate until ready to use.

SAFFRON VINAIGRETTE

¼ teaspoon (1.2 mL) saffron
  threads
¼ cup (60 mL) dry white
  wine
1 cup (240 mL) olive oil
¼ cup (60 mL) champagne
  vinegar
1 small shallot, minced

1 garlic clove, pressed
1 teaspoon (5 mL) parsley,
  minced
½ teaspoon (2.5 mL) Dijon-
  style mustard
juice of 1 lemon
salt and black pepper to
  taste

- Simmer the wine and saffron until reduced by half. Set aside to cool.
- Blend all ingredients thoroughly in a stainless steel bowl. Season to taste with the salt and pepper. Cover and refrigerate until ready to serve.

SUN-DRIED TOMATO VINAIGRETTE

¼ cup (60 mL) oil-packed
  sun-dried tomatoes, cut
  into ¼-inch dice
1 cup (240 mL) olive oil
  (some from the tomatoes)
⅓ cup (80 mL) red wine
  vinegar

2 tablespoons (30 mL)
  water
1 small shallot, roughly
  chopped
½ cup (60 mL) parsley
  sprigs, well rinsed
pinch of salt
pinch of black pepper

- Place all ingredients, except the diced tomatoes, in a blender and purée. Add the diced tomatoes and adjust seasoning with water, salt, and pepper.

THREE-ONION VINAIGRETTE

½ cup (120 mL) red onion,
  roughly chopped
2 large shallots, minced
¾ cup (180 mL) champagne
  vinegar
2 cups (480 mL) olive oil

2 tablespoons (30 mL)
  water
salt and black pepper to
  taste
6 scallions, sliced paper
  thin

- Place all ingredients, except the scallions, in a blender and purée. Add the scallions, cover, and refrigerate until ready to serve.

TOASTED CUMIN VINAIGRETTE

1 cup (240 mL) olive oil
½ cup (120 mL) sherry wine
   vinegar
2 tablespoons (30 mL)
   cumin seeds

2 tablespoons (30 mL)
   Dijon-style mustard
½ teaspoon kosher salt

- Toast the cumin seeds on a pan in a 350° F (176° C) oven for about 15 minutes. Grind to a powder with a mortar and pestle, or in an electric spice grinder.
- Place all the ingredients in a blender and purée. Cover and refrigerate until ready to serve.

TOMATO VINAIGRETTE

1 cup (240 mL) olive oil
¼ cup (60 mL) balsamic
   vinegar
2 tablespoons (30 mL)
   tomato paste, dissolved
   in 2 tablespoons (30 mL)
   warm water

1 teaspoon (5 mL) thyme
   leaves, minced
1 teaspoon (5 mL) capers,
   drained
salt and pepper to taste

- Blend all ingredients thoroughly in a stainless steel bowl. Season to taste with the salt and pepper, then cover and refrigerate until ready to serve.

WALNUT VINAIGRETTE

⅓ cup (80 mL) walnut oil
⅔ cup (160 mL) olive oil
¼ cup (60 mL) white wine
   or champagne vinegar
juice of 1 lemon

2 tablespoons (30 mL)
   water
¼ teaspoon salt
¼ teaspoon black pepper

- Place all ingredients in a blender and purée. Cover and refrigerate until ready to serve.

MARINADES AND MISCELLANEOUS COLD SAUCES

A marinade is a liquid, seasoned with various aromatics, in which meat, poultry, game, or vegetables are steeped. Marinades are generally made up of one or more of the following ingredients:

Oil (olive, peanut, walnut; flavored oils such as sesame and chili pepper)

Acid (wine, brandy, vinegar, citrus juice)

Aromatics (mirepoix, leeks, herbs, and spices)

Although its function is primarily to flavor, a marinade can provide some tenderizing by virtue of the acid ingredient (vinegar, citrus juice, and/or wine). When only their flavor is intended, the aromatics should be tied up in cheesecloth (forming a spice sachet) so that they can be removed before the marinated food is cooked. Some marinades are cooked, others are uncooked. In both cases, however, the marinating should be done in noncorrosive vessels, such as stainless steel, glass, or ceramic (avoid plastic and aluminum). The length of time a food is marinated varies: a sauerbraten is marinated refrigerated for up to three days; chicken breast or lamb loin, at room temperature for a few hours.

MARINADE RECIPES

BEER MARINADE

1 pint (480 mL) beer
juice and zest of 4 limes
4 garlic cloves, crushed
½ cup (120 mL) scallions, minced
¼ cup (60 mL) cilantro, minced

6 dried red chili peppers
1 teaspoon (5 mL) ground cumin
pinch of salt
pinch of black pepper

• Combine all ingredients and blend thoroughly.

Note: This marinade is suitable for marinating chicken, pork, or beef.

GIN-LIME MARINADE

½ cup (120 mL) olive oil
1 cup (240 mL) gin
the juice of 12 limes
¼ cup (60 mL) water
4 garlic cloves, pressed

2 sprigs rosemary
½ teaspoon (2.5 mL) ground
  cumin
salt and white pepper to
  taste

• Combine all ingredients and blend thoroughly.

LEMON MARINADE

the juice and zest of 3
  lemons
3 tablespoons (45 mL) olive
  oil
2 garlic cloves, crushed

1 sprig fresh thyme or rosemary
salt and black pepper to
  taste

• Combine all ingredients and blend thoroughly.

Note: This marinade is suitable for marinating chicken, veal, or fish.

OIL, LEMON, AND HERB MARINADE

1 cup (240 mL) olive oil
1 cup (240 mL) peanut oil
3 lemons, sliced paper thin
6 garlic cloves, crushed

2 tablespoons (30 mL)
  cracked black pepper
1 cup (240 mL) basil, parsley, cilantro, and marjoram, roughly chopped

• Combine all ingredients and blend thoroughly.

Note: This marinade, innovated by Jasper White, was designed to marinate one chicken, cut into 8 to 10 pieces, then grilled.

RED WINE MARINADE I

1 quart (1 L) red wine
1 large onion, sliced very
  thin
3 garlic cloves, crushed
¼ cup (60 mL) parsley,
  roughly chopped

1 bay leaf
¼ cup (60 mL) olive oil
salt and black pepper to
  taste

- Combine all ingredients and blend thoroughly until the salt is dissolved.

Note: This marinade is suitable for marinating beef or lamb.

RED WINE MARINADE II

1 quart (1 L) red wine
1 cup (240 mL) red wine
  vinegar
¼ cup (60 mL) water
1 large onion, sliced very
  thin
1 medium carrot, peeled,
  sliced very thin
1 rib celery, sliced very thin

4 garlic cloves, crushed
2 bay leaves
1 bunch parsley stems,
  trimmed and tied
  together
1 tablespoon (15 mL) black
  peppercorns
12 juniper berries
¼ cup (60 mL) salt

- Combine all ingredients and bring to a boil. Remove from the fire and allow to cool to room temperature before using.

Note: This marinade is suitable for marinating large cuts of beef or game (venison, boar, or mutton).

SOY SAUCE MARINADE

1 cup (240 mL) soy sauce
1 cup (240 mL) mirin
  (sweet Japanese wine)
3 tablespoons (45 mL)
  sesame oil
2 garlic cloves, pressed

2 tablespoons (30 mL) gingerroot, grated
1 bunch scallions, trimmed
  and cut on the bias very
  thin

- Combine all ingredients and allow to marinate 1 hour for steaks, 30 minutes for fillets.

Note: This marinade is suitable for marinating high-fat fish, such as bluefish, mackerel, salmon, shad, swordfish, and tuna.

SZECHWAN GRILLING MARINADE

¾ cup (180 mL) soy sauce
¼ cup (60 mL) water
¾ cup (180 mL) dry white
  wine
3 garlic cloves, crushed

1 tablespoon (15 g) gingerroot, grated
1 teaspoon (5 mL) Szech-
  wan peppercorns,
  crushed

1 star anise
2 tablespoons (30 mL)
  medium dry sherry
1 teaspoon (5 mL) sesame oil

2 tablespoons (30 mL) dark
  brown sugar

- Combine and simmer all ingredients in a saucepan for 10 minutes. Set aside and allow to cool.

TOMATO MARINADE

1 pint (480 mL) tomato
  juice
1 medium onion, sliced
  very thin

2 tablespoons (30 mL) basil
  leaves, minced
1 bay leaf
salt and black pepper

- Combine all ingredients and blend thoroughly.

Note: This marinade is suitable for marinating veal or pork.

YOGURT MARINADE

2 cups (480 mL) yogurt
¼ cup (60 mL) cilantro,
  minced

zest of 2 lemons
2 garlic cloves, pressed
salt and black pepper

- Combine all ingredients and blend thoroughly.

Note: This marinade is suitable for marinating chicken or fish.

MIGNONETTE RECIPES

APPLE CIDER MIGNONETTE

1 small shallot, minced
3 tablespoons (45 mL)
  Granny Smith apple,
  finely diced

1 tablespoon (15 mL) black
  pepper, coarsely ground
½ cup (120 mL) cider (or
  champagne) vinegar

- Blend all ingredients thoroughly in a stainless steel bowl. Cover and refrigerate at least 1 hour before serving.

Note: This sauce is typically served with oysters or other shellfish on the half shell.

RASPBERRY MIGNONETTE

1 cup (240 mL) raspberry
    vinegar
¼ cup (60 mL) dry white
    wine
1 teaspoon (5 mL) black
    pepper, coarsely ground

1 teaspoon (5 mL) salt
1 shallot, minced
1 tablespoon (15 mL) fresh
    basil leaves, fine chiffon-
    ade

- Blend all ingredients thoroughly in a stainless steel bowl. Cover and refrigerate at least 1 hour before serving.

MINT SAUCE

¾ cup (180 mL) champagne
    vinegar
¼ cup (60 mL) water
2 tablespoons (30 mL)
    sugar

pinch of salt
2 cups (480 mL) fresh mint
    leaves, rinsed and cut
    into fine chiffonade

- Bring the vinegar, water, sugar, and salt to a boil. Stir until the sugar and salt are dissolved. Place half of the mint leaves in a glass or stainless steel bowl, and pour the hot liquid over them. Allow to marinate overnight.
- Strain the liquid, discarding the mint. Add the remaining mint and serve.

Note: This sauce is a typical English accompaniment for roast lamb leg.

TOMATO-BASED SAUCES

COCKTAIL SAUCE I

1 shallot, minced
½ cup (120 mL) dry white
    wine
1 cup (240 mL) ketchup or
    strained chili sauce
1 tablespoon (15 mL)
    Worcestershire sauce
2 to 3 tablespoons (30 to 45
    mL) prepared

horseradish, squeezed
    dry
2 tablespoons (30 mL)
    lemon juice
¼ teaspoon (1.2 mL) celery
    salt
¼ teaspoon (1.2 mL)
    Tabasco sauce

• Simmer the shallot and wine until nearly dry. Blend together with the remaining ingredients. Refrigerate until ready to serve.

COCKTAIL SAUCE II

½ cup (120 mL) onion, coarsely chopped
2 garlic cloves
6 tablespoons (90 mL) apple juice concentrate
1 cup (240 mL) ketchup
¼ cup (60 mL) tomato paste
½ cup (120 mL) champagne vinegar
juice of 2 lemons

2 tablespoons (30 mL) white Worcestershire sauce
2 tablespoons (30 mL) prepared horseradish, squeezed dry
salt and cayenne pepper to taste
water as needed

• Purée all of the ingredients in a food processor or blender (use water to thin the sauce if necessary). Refrigerate until ready to serve.

BARBECUE SAUCES

Although cooking over charcoal is one of the most ancient of cooking methods, the barbecue method is of American origin, associated with the conquest of the western regions of North America. This cooking style was subsequently exported to Europe. The origin of the word may be the Haitian *barbacoa*, meaning "grill," or the French *de la barbe à la queue* ("from the beard to the tail"), referring to the method of roasting an entire animal on a large spit.

Barbecue sauce and barbecuing are two separate entities. The former generally refers to a tomato-based marinade, whereas the latter is a method of grilling over charcoal and/or aromatic woods (alder, grape, hickory, mesquite, and herb stems, among others) and employing any number of marinades. The three sauces that follow are well suited to beef, pork, or poultry. Marinate the ribs or other parts overnight, then grill, using the sauce to baste.

BARBECUE SAUCE I

1 cup (240 mL) tomato
  ketchup
¼ cup (60 mL) dark brown
  sugar
3 tablespoons (45 mL)
  orange marmalade
2 scallions, sliced paper
  thin
1 garlic clove, pressed

1 tablespoon (15 mL) gin-
  gerroot, grated
1 tablespoon (15 mL) soy
  sauce
¼ cup (60 mL) water
2 tablespoons (30 mL) red
  chili paste
juice and zest of one lemon
¼ cup (60 mL) parsley,
  minced

- Combine all ingredients in a stainless steel bowl. Add chicken, beef, or pork ribs and marinate, covered and refrigerated, for 2 days.

BARBECUE SAUCE II

¼ cup (60 mL) duck or
  chicken fat
1 medium Spanish onion,
  peeled and minced
1 bunch scallions, green
  tops removed, and
  minced
½ cup (60 mL) green bell
  pepper, minced
5 garlic cloves, pressed
2 cups (240 mL) ketchup

¼ cup (60 mL) Worcester-
  shire sauce
¼ cup (60 mL) cider vinegar
½ cup (120 mL) beer
2 tablespoons (30 mL)
  Dijon-style mustard
3 tablespoons (45 mL) dark
  brown sugar
1 teaspoon (5 mL) red chili
  paste
1 teaspoon (5 mL) ground
  cumin

- Sauté the onion, scallions, pepper, and garlic in the fat for five minutes. Combine with the remaining ingredients in a stainless steel bowl and blend thoroughly.

BARBECUE SAUCE III

1 medium onion, finely diced
¼ cup (60 mL) olive oil
½ cup (120 mL) dry white
  wine
zest and juice of 1 lemon

1 cup (240 mL) ketchup
¼ cup (60 mL) dark brown
  sugar
2 tablespoons (30 mL)
  orange marmalade

3 garlic cloves, pressed
1 tablespoon grated ginger
2 tablespoons (30 mL)
  Worcestershire sauce

1 teaspoon (5 mL) dried red
  chili pepper flakes
1 tablespoon red chili pepper paste

- Sauté the onion in the olive oil over medium heat, covered, for 5 minutes. Add the white wine and simmer until reduced by three-fourths. Set aside to cool.
- Combine all the remaining ingredients, along with the onion and wine, and blend thoroughly. Cover and refrigerate until ready to use.

MISCELLANEOUS SAUCES

CREOSAT RELISH

¼ cup (60 mL) olive oil
¼ cup (60 mL) Worcester-
  shire sauce
2 tablespoons (30 mL)
  Dijon-style mustard
2 tablespoons (30 mL)
  white wine vinegar
1 teaspoon (5 mL) thyme
  leaves, minced
2 bay leaves
¼ cup (60 mL) cucumber,
  peeled, seeded, and cut
  into ¼-inch (6-mm) dice

¼ cup (60 mL) green bell
  pepper, cut into ¼-inch
  (6-mm) dice
¼ cup (60 mL) red onion,
  cut into ¼-inch (6-mm)
  dice
¼ cup (60 mL) tomato, cut
  into ¼-inch (6-mm) dice
2 tablespoons (30 mL) cornichon, cut into ¼-inch
  (6-mm) dice
2 tablespoons (30 mL)
  capers, drained

- Combine the oil, Worcestershire, mustard, vinegar, thyme, and bay leaves and blend thoroughly. Add the remaining ingredients and marinate 3 days.

Note: This sauce is typically served with grilled meats. (Its liquid part is sometimes referred to as "English Sauce.")

CUMBERLAND SAUCE

1 cup (240 mL) currant jelly
½ cup (120 mL) port wine
1 shallot, minced
1 tablespoon orange zest

1 tablespoon lemon zest
1 teaspoon (5 mL) grated
  gingerroot
pinch of cayenne

- Blanch the zest in boiling salted water. Simmer the remaining ingredients for 10 minutes. Add the zest, allow to cool, and refrigerate until ready to serve.

Note: This sauce is typically served with game, game pâtés and terrines, or ham, all served cold.

DRIED FRUIT COMPOTE

1 cup (240 mL) sugar
2 cups (480 mL) dry champagne
1 cup (240 mL) red wine vinegar
1 stick cinnamon
¼ teaspoon (1.2 mL) ground cinnamon
4 cloves
½ lemon, sliced very thin

zest of half an orange
½ pound (227 g) pitted prunes, cut in half
½ pound (227 g) dried apricots, cut in half
½ pound (227 g) sultana (golden) raisins
½ pound (227 g) dried figs, cut in half

- Simmer all the syrup ingredients, except the dried fruit, for 5 minutes. Add the dried fruit, and continue to simmer for 5 minutes. Remove from the fire and allow to cool.

Note: This sauce is typically served as a side dish with grilled, broiled, or sautéed sausages.

RHUBARB COMPOTE

2 tablespoons (30 mL) unsalted butter
1 shallot, minced
2 cups (240 mL) rhubarb stalks, cut into medium dice
½ cup (120 mL) sultana (golden) raisins

¼ cup (60 mL) sugar
¼ cup (60 mL) dry white wine
zest and juice of 1 lemon
1 teaspoon (5 mL) gingerroot, grated

- Sauté the shallot and rhubarb in the butter for several minutes. Add the remaining ingredients, and simmer for 30 minutes. Remove from the fire, cover, and refrigerate until ready to serve.

Note: Rhubarb Compote typically accompanies duck sausage (page 336).

CHAPTER 3

COLD SOUPS

One day, in seventeenth-century France, as an unnamed peasant girl was about to carry a bowl of hot broth to a prisoner, she felt remiss in bringing such meager fare to the man. Searching for additional sustenance, she found a handful of dried bread and dropped it into the broth. The dried bread soaked up the warm liquid, effectively thickening it, and thus was soup invented.

Today there are a vast number of soups, well over one thousand, divided broadly into two groups—*clear* and *thick*. Clear soups are subdivided into *broths* and *consommés;* thick soups into *puréed, creamed,* and *velvet* soups. Velvet soups constitute a slight deviation from velouté sauces (*velouté* is French for "velvet"), and because they are so similar to creamed soups, the category has been omitted.

Inasmuch as the garde manger department is technically charged with the production of cold soups, some of the superior varieties are included here. Soup is an important food and is often served as a first or second course (before, after, or in lieu of an appetizer) or as the main course for a light supper. The preparation of cold soup is particularly challenging, because it is served chilled and an underseasoned chilled savory liquid can be flavorless on the palate and a disastrous beginning to a meal. On the other hand, a properly prepared and served chilled soup can be an inspiring gastronomic experience. I am reminded of the first time I experienced Consommé Madrilène. It took me a while to appreciate the ruby-tinted, port- and tomato-flavored, shimmering, translucent beef jelly I served up in an iced supreme serving dish for clientele at the private club where I served as a young commis. But once my eye and palate came to understand that jellied food does not necessarily mean sweet and fruity (as in Jell-O), it is a very fine gastronomic experience.

CLEAR SOUPS

The foundation of cold, clear soups is consommé. Whether made from fish, fowl, game, beef, or lamb, it must be crystal clear and completely fat free. The following recipe for chicken consommé can be modified to suit recipe needs.

CHICKEN CONSOMMÉ

1½ gallons (5.7 L) rich chicken stock, cold

3 pounds (1,350 g) chicken bones, backs, and necks

2 pounds (900 g) coarsely ground chicken meat

6 egg whites, briefly beaten with 1 cup (240 mL) dry white wine

1 celery stalk, trimmed, rinsed, and finely chopped

1 Spanish onion, finely chopped

1 small leek, white part only, finely chopped and well rinsed

1 small bunch parsley stems, trimmed, rinsed, and finely chopped

1 bay leaf

1 sprig thyme

- Combine all the ingredients in a heavy-gauge stockpot and blend thoroughly. Place over a medium fire, and gently stir once every few minutes, until the mixture gets warm (about 110° F/43° C).

- When the broth just barely begins to simmer, turn the fire down low enough to maintain the barest simmer. Allow to simmer for two hours.

- Using a perforated skimmer, very gently cut and lift out a portion of the "raft" that has formed on top. Using a ladle, remove the clear broth beneath the raft, and strain it through at least four layers of muslin (cheesecloth).

- Allow the consommé to sit; then gently dip a clean paper towel or napkin onto the top of the soup, absorbing any fat remaining on top. If the consommé is not to be used immediately, it can be cooled, covered, and refrigerated, after which congealed fat on the top can be removed.

Note: The *raft* that forms on the surface of the consommé as it simmers is created by the albumin in the egg whites and ground meat. The frequent stirring at the beginning of the process is *very important*. The egg whites—heavier than the stock—can drift to the bottom of the pot while the mix is still cold, and quickly burn, spoiling the entire dish. Once the brew heats past 110° F (43° C) or so, the egg whites begin to rise toward the top, slowly coagulating into what will become the raft. The slow coagulation of the raft, as the gently simmering stock moves through it, is the same phenomenon that occurs when an ordinary stock is made. As the liquid moves rhythmically through the slowly thickening albumin, the minute particles and impurities in the stock are trapped within the coagulating mass.

It is also of the utmost importance to cut into the raft very gently in order to remove the broth for straining. If it is shaken, particles that have been collected within the raft may dislodge, returning to the liquid.

Any stock can be clarified into a consommé. Simply substitute the chicken bones and ground chicken meat with bone and ground meat from beef, veal, lamb, or fish.

CELERY CONSOMMÉ

Rich beef consommé made with a liberal amount of celery, garnished with celery sticks.

FINE HERB CONSOMMÉ

Rich beef consommé made with a liberal amount of chives, parsley, tarragon, and thyme. (Can also be made with a different combination of four herbs, or with any single herb.)

LOVE APPLE JELLY

Rich chicken consommé made with a liberal amount of tomato purée, finished with Marsala wine.

MADRILÈNE CONSOMMÉ

Rich chicken consommé made with a liberal amount of tomato purée, garnished with blanched diced or julienned red bell peppers.

PORTUGUESE CONSOMMÉ

Rich chicken consommé made with a liberal amount of tomato purée.

TRUFFLE CONSOMMÉ

Rich beef or chicken consommé made with the addition of truffle peelings, garnished with a paper-thin slice of truffle.

MADEIRA CONSOMMÉ

Rich chicken consommé made with the addition of Madeira wine and finished with a little Madeira wine at service. Variations include Port Consommé (*au Porto*), Sherried Consommé (*au Xérès*), and Armagnac Consommé (*au Armagnac*).

141

WILD MUSHROOM CONSOMMÉ

Rich beef consommé made with the stems of wild mushrooms, garnished with julienned cèpes, chanterelles, morels, shiitakes, or other additions.

CREAMED PURÉED SOUPS

Although creamed soup is traditionally thickened with béchamel sauce and finished with heavy cream, a more sensible and cost-effective approach is to use a velouté instead of a béchamel. Béchamel sauce is made with milk, making it more expensive than velouté, which is made with stock (chicken or fish). The velouté is not only less expensive (stock is often made with secondary use of poultry and fish bones) but also more flavorful than the milk-based béchamel.

Virtually any creamed soup can be served cold (asparagus, broccoli, cauliflower, celery, fennel, leek, zucchini, for example). The following recipe can be adapted to the traditional varieties, which appear after this one.

CREAM OF CALIFORNIA LETTUCE

4 tablespoons (60 mL) unsalted butter
1 shallot, minced
1 bunch parsley stems, rinsed, trimmed, and minced
outside leaves of 2 large heads of romaine lettuce, coarsely chopped
3 tablespoons (45 mL) flour
salt and pepper to taste

1 quart (960 mL) rich chicken stock, hot
¾ cup (180 mL) heavy cream
4 slices of baguette, toasted
4 tablespoons (60 mL) sour cream or crème fraîche
½ cup (120 mL) romaine lettuce, cut into very fine julienne

- Sauté the shallot in the butter for several minutes, without browning. Add the lettuce and parsley, cover, and sweat for 5 minutes. Add the flour, blend thoroughly, and cook for about 5 minutes, stirring continuously.
- Add the chicken stock and blend thoroughly. Season to taste with salt and pepper. Simmer for 30 minutes.

- Transfer to a blender or food processor, and purée. Return to the fire, add the cream, and bring to a simmer. Season to taste with salt and pepper.
- Spread each of the croutons (baguette slices) with a tablespoon of sour cream. Ladle the soup into soup plates or bowls, and top with a crouton, sprinkled with the julienned lettuce.

CREAM OF CHICKEN

Rich chicken stock flavored with a liberal amount of herbs, thickened with roux, cooled, strained, and finished with cream.

CREAM OF CHICKEN, SULTAN

Rich chicken stock thickened with roux, simmered with a liberal amount of herbs; cooled, strained, and finished with cream; garnished liberally with ground toasted hazelnuts and pistachios.

CREAM OF CRAYFISH

Rich fish or chicken stock thickened with roux, simmered with crayfish shells, mirepoix, herbs, and tomato purée; cooled, strained, finished with brandy, cream, and paprika, and garnished with diced crayfish. (This dish is prepared in the same manner as *Lobster Américaine* and can be substituted with lobster as well.)

CREAM OF DUCK

Rich duck stock thickened with roux, finished with dry sherry and cream.

DUQUINHA CREAM

Five parts rich chicken stock thickened with roux, strained and cooled, finished with 1 part tomato purée and 1 part red pepper purée.

MARGOT CREAM

Rich chicken stock thickened with roux, seasoned with almond milk (sliced almonds steeped in hot milk, then strained), and finished with heavy cream.

CREAM OF MUSHROOM

Rich veal stock made with mushroom trimmings, thickened with roux, finished with cream, and garnished with diced or julienned mushrooms cooked in butter.

PORTUGUESE CREAM OF CHICKEN

Three parts rich chicken stock flavored with a liberal amount of herbs, thickened with roux, cooled, strained, and finished with 1 part tomato purée and cream.

SPECIAL REGIONAL COLD SOUPS

AVOCADO SOUP, CHAMPAGNE

2 cups (480 mL) milk
1 cup (240 mL) fresh white
   bread crumbs
4 large ripe Haas avocados,
   peeled and seeded
1 quart (960 mL) dry champagne

juice of 1 lemon
salt to taste
½ teaspoon mace
1 cup (240 mL) heavy
   cream, whipped
4 sprigs of mint

- Soak the bread in the milk for 1 hour. Place in a blender or food processor with 1 avocado and 1 cup of champagne, and purée. Transfer to another bowl.
- Purée the remaining avocados, interspersing the champagne and lemon juice. Blend all, and season with salt and mace. Fold in half the whipped cream, then serve garnished with a dollop of whipped cream and a sprig of mint.

GAZPACHO, ADALUSIAN STYLE

¼ cup (60 mL) olive oil
4 garlic cloves

1 small cucumber, peeled
   and seeded

1 medium green pepper

1 quart (960 mL) diced tomato

2 fresh vine-ripened tomatoes, peeled and cut into fine dice

2 tablespoons (30 mL) Worcestershire sauce

¼ teaspoon (1.25 mL) ground cumin

salt and cayenne pepper to taste

1 small, stale hard roll, finely chopped and soaked in 1 cup (240 mL) water and ½ cup (120 mL) white wine vinegar

1 pint (480 mL) half-and-half cream

2 egg yolks

1 cup (240 mL) plain croutons

2 tablespoons (30 mL) chopped parsley

- Cut a portion of the cucumber and the green pepper into fine dice, enough to yield ¼ cup (60 mL) each.
- Purée all of the remaining ingredients (except the croutons) in a blender or food processor. Adjust seasoning, and garnish with the croutons and chopped parsley.

GAZPACHO, DUTCHESS VALLEY STYLE

2 cups (480 mL) vine-ripened tomatoes, peeled, cored, seeded, and coarsely chopped

½ cup (120 mL) green pepper, seeded and coarsely chopped

½ cup (120 mL) cucumber, peeled, seeded, and coarsely chopped

½ cup (120 mL) onion, peeled and coarsely chopped

2 stalks celery, peeled and coarsely chopped

4 garlic cloves, coarsely chopped

½ cup (120 mL) tomato purée

¼ cup (60 mL) tarragon vinegar

½ cup (120 mL) rich beef stock or consommé

2 tablespoons (30 mL) olive oil

½ cup (120 mL) tomato juice

salt and white pepper to taste

¼ cup (60 mL) each, finely diced red bell pepper, green bell pepper, avocado, and cucumber (for the garnish)

¼ cup (60 mL) small, plain white bread croutons

2 tablespoons (30 mL) minced chives

- Place all of the ingredients, except the garnish, croutons, and chives, in a blender or food processor and purée. Season to taste with salt and pepper. Marinate at least 12 hours.

- Serve in individual chilled bowls, garnished with the diced vegetables, croutons, and chives.

Kænemælkskolskål (pronounced: canner-mal-**skole**-skal), Swedish buttermilk soup, is translated as follows: Kæne—*to churn from butter;* mælk—*made from milk;* skol—*cold;* skål—*bowl.*

KÆNEMÆLKSKOLSKÅL

3 egg yolks
½ cup (120 mL) sugar
juice of 1 lemon
1 quart (960 mL) buttermilk
zest of 1 orange and 1 lemon
1 cup (240 mL) fresh white bread croutons

2 tablespoons (30 mL) sugar
4 tablespoons (120 g) unsalted butter
4 sprigs fresh mint

- Whip the eggs and sugar until thick and lemon yellow. Beat in the lemon juice, then blend in the buttermilk.
- Blanch the zest briefly in boiling water, drain, then add to the buttermilk mixture. Chill until ready to serve.
- Toss the croutons in the sugar, then sauté in butter until golden brown. Refrigerate until well chilled.
- Serve in chilled cups, garnished with croutons and mint.

KESÄKEITTO

(FINNISH VEGETABLE SOUP)

½ cup (120 mL) string beans, cut into ¼-inch (6-mm) dice
½ cup (120 mL) carrots, cut into ¼-inch (6-mm) dice
½ cup (120 mL) cauliflower, cut into small buds
½ cup (120 mL) potatoes, cut into ¼-inch (6-mm) dice
½ cup (120 mL) radishes, cut into ¼-inch (6-mm) dice
½ pound (227 g) fresh spinach, cut into 1-inch (25-mm) pieces

3 tablespoons (45 mL) unsalted butter, kneaded together with 4 tablespoons (60 mL) flour
1 cup (240 mL) heavy cream
1 egg yolk
½ pound (227 g) titi shrimp
salt and white pepper to taste
2 tablespoons (30 mL) chopped dill

146

- Bring 3 cups of lightly salted water to a boil. Blanch the string beans, carrots, cauliflower, and potatoes, separately, until each is al dente (the potatoes should be cooked until tender). Reserve this liquid.
- Beat the flour and butter paste into the reserved liquid, and simmer 10 minutes. Strain, and return to the fire. Add the blanched vegetables, radishes, spinach, and shrimp, and simmer briefly.
- Beat the cream and egg, then temper into the soup by slowly adding the hot soup to the cream and beating in. Return this to the soup, and simmer for 3 minutes.
- Adjust the seasoning, then serve garnished with the dill.

VICHYSSOISE

4 medium leeks, coarsely chopped, and well rinsed
2 tablespoons (30 mL) unsalted butter
3 cups (720 mL) chicken stock
2 cups (480 mL) potatoes, coarsely chopped

salt and white pepper to taste
1 cup (240 mL) heavy cream
¼ cup (60 mL) sour cream
2 tablespoons (30 mL) chives, minced

- Sauté the leeks in the butter until tender. Add the stock and potatoes, and simmer until the potatoes are soft. Purée in a blender or food processor, return to the fire, add the cream, and bring to a boil. Season to taste with salt and white pepper, and set aside to cool.
- When chilled, check for seasoning (a squeeze of lemon juice can sometimes bring up the flavor if it is a little flat). Serve in a supreme dish or in a well-chilled bowl. Top with a tablespoon of sour cream, and sprinkle with chives.

CHAPTER 4

CANAPÉS

A *canapé* is a slice of bread cut into any of various shapes and garnished. Cold canapés are served at buffets or lunches or with cocktails and aperitifs; hot canapés are served as entrées or used as foundations for various dishes. These dainty slices of bread, cut into assorted shapes, usually toasted, and decorated to be visually appealing, are designed to be eaten with one's fingers or a small utensil.

Traditional European canapés, primarily French in origin and under the heading of *classical cuisine,* are awkward in style by today's standards. Many classical canapés, for example, are traditionally glazed with aspic, a crystal-clear highly gelatinous meat jelly. The function of aspic is to add flavor, to help prevent drying, and to add an attractive sheen. Aspic has not found common acceptance in North American cookery, as we are accustomed to clear jelly having a sweet flavor (as in Jell-O), rather than a savory taste. Nevertheless, classical canapés are important because they form the body of work from which today's genre has evolved. In the real world of foodservice production, their use is limited, yet a knowledge of classical canapés is essential to understanding this area of hors d'oeuvres.

Canapés represent a unique means of expression for the culinary practitioner. They are miniature, visually creative, edible works, requiring meticulous attention to detail and design and, thus, great patience and exact timing to produce. One may consider these bite-sized, open-faced decorative sandwiches as "art on a cracker."

The crunch of a canapé is important. Foods that crunch when bitten into *stimulate* the appetite, whereas soft foods *satiate.* The crunch should be the dominant texture, the softness a secondary texture. The function of a canapé is to stimulate appetites; thus it is acceptable to run out of canapés before dining guests' appetites are satisfied. In essence, their design should be simple and elegant—visually attractive but not overcomplex—and their flavor and color should be harmonious and pleasing to the eye. In the creation of a canapé menu, with the intent to fulfill a client's expectations, we consider the socioeconomics of the client's group: where they live geographically, the kind of work they perform, their social customs and dress, the reason for their assembling.

Consider a sit-down dinner once given for 8,500 conventioneers, representing an American automobile dealership association. The first course consisted of a shellfish terrine with tomato coulis, each garnished with a crayfish from the Louisiana delta. Virtually every plate came back to the kitchen with the crayfish untouched—a perfect example of an upscale dish served to a clientele better acquainted with more common and easily recognized fare. And although a group hailing from a cosmopolitan city would understand and recognize beluga caviar and salmon tartar, a group of midwestern American ranchers would better understand steak tartar. Hence, we must consider the tastes, styles, and preferences of any given dining group.

COMPONENTS OF A CANAPÉ

A canapé typically consists of four components: *base, adhesive, body,* and *garnish.*

BASE MATERIALS

Classical canapés are virtually all prepared on a base of toasted white, brioche, rye, or pumpernickel bread. It is essential that they be crunchy when bitten into. In contemporary practice, other bases are often innovated, made of polenta, wonton skin, small Red Bliss potatoes, phyllo, tortilla, small socles, and even mushrooms, snow peas, zucchini, crookneck squash, cucumber, jicama, and daikon.

ADHESIVES

Used as adhesives, butter and compound butters are important, because they act as a *moisture barrier* between the body of the canapé and the base. This prevents moisture from the body ingredients from seeping into the crouton and making it soggy. In actual practice, cream cheese is sometimes blended with butter, making it more palatable to contemporary tastes.

BODY

The body of a canapé consists of various ingredients, including fish (herring, salmon), shellfish (lobster, shrimp), eggs (hard-boiled: sliced or sieved), meat (roasted beef fillet, sausages), poultry (grilled or poached chicken), game (venison, pheasant, quail), and vegetables (broccoli, bell pepper, radish). In actual practice, odds and ends of food items are often used, but they *must* be made from premium products.

152

GARNISH

A garnish adds a final touch of color, shape, and focal point to the finished piece. The garnish may also function as an additional crunchy element, such as a toasted nut, slice of radish, or pâte à choux filigree. Most herbs do not hold up well as a garnish, with the exception of parsley and chives. Typical garnishes include asparagus, bell pepper, capers, caviar, cornichon, olive, and sieved hard-boiled egg.

CANAPÉ PRODUCTION

In commercial kitchens, canapé production for banquets and cocktail receptions can number several dozen, several hundred, or as many as a thousand or more per event. For this reason it is essential that an efficient and well-organized *mise-en-place* be set up to expedite the production of these miniature artworks. The following guidelines can facilitate an efficient operation:

- The bread used for canapé bases should ideally be purchased in *pullman* form, that is, unsliced. This bread can then be sliced into fairly large sheets, using a serrated knife (a serrated knife is engineered to cut bread and pastry, and is never sharpened). Though it is difficult to cut evenly at first, with practice one can achieve a level of expertise in slicing these sheets uniformly (*see Figure 4.1*).
- When toasting bread, timing is critical. The bread should be dry enough to have lost its pliability, though not so dry that it cracks when spread with an adhesive and cut into individual bases.
- After the bread has been toasted and cooled, it should be spread with the appropriate paste. It can then be cut into individual bases. Because these pieces are so small, uniformity is extremely important, and any variation in size and shape is easy to perceive.
- All of the components of a given canapé should be fully prepared and ready to set in place before production is begun. These include the toasted bread sheets, the adhesive paste, the individual body components, and all garnishes.
- Although there are specific names and ingredients for canapés of the classical mode, there are no hard-and-fast rules in terms of their design. This is where individual style and creativity come into play.
- In all of the classical canapés described in this chapter, the croutons are toasted. This is what will give the canapés their appetite-stimulating crunch.

153

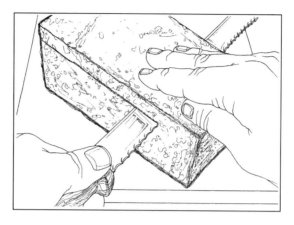

Hold the pullman loaf securely with one hand and, using a serrated blade, cut it into ⅙–¼-inch-thick slices.

Figure 4.1
Slicing the Pullman Loaf

- Sometimes a canapé is "edged" in minced parsley, sieved egg yolk, or egg white. This is accomplished by spreading the edges of a crouton lightly with butter (or with the same paste that is spread on its surface) and dipping it into a minced herb or sieved egg before it is completed.
- For a cucumber base, an English cucumber (also called a *hothouse* cucumber) is preferred because of its excellent crunch and absence of seeds.

PERCEPTUAL ATTRIBUTES OF A CANAPÉ

Size. Canapés should be small enough to be consumed in one to two bites (1½ to 2 inches/37 to 50 mm); the base should be thick enough to grasp easily (⅙ inch/4 mm).

Shape. Classical hors d'oeuvre bases come in the following shapes: square, diamond (also called *lozenge*), rectangle, circle, half circle, oval, and triangle. Other shapes, such as a crescent or a star, are sometimes innovated using a variety of cutters.

Color. Ideally, a canapé should be limited to four colors that harmonize well.

Texture. The base or one other component should be crisp, giving a resilient crunch (not soggy) when bitten into; the body should be smooth and tender.

Taste. The taste of a canapé should be a balance of savory, spicy, and tart, including salt, pepper, herbs, and spices.

154

COMPOUND BUTTERS AND PASTES

Compound butters and pastes are used both as adhesives for canapés and as flavoring components. Compound butters primarily consist of butter combined with herbs and/or spices; pastes are more complex preparations, often including cream cheese in addition to herbs and spices (the addition of cream cheese makes a paste a bit more palatable to contemporary tastes). Compound butters also have two other functions: they are used to fortify the flavor of sauces by mounting (*mounting* is the colloquial term for beating pieces of plain or compound butter into a simmering sauce just before it is to be served), and they are also used in place of sauces on certain grilled and fried foods—sliced from a wrapped cylinder of a particular butter preparation and placed on top of the grilled or fried item.

In canapé production, a compound butter or a paste is used as the *primary* adhesive, because it acts as a *moisture barrier*, preventing the crisp crouton from becoming soggy. There is no limit to the number of compound butters and pastes that can be innovated. For instance, compound butters can be made with ingredients such as basil, blue cheese, caviar, chives, coriander, curry, edible flowers, roasted garlic, green vegetables, horseradish, lemon (juice and zest), mustard, paprika, pistachios, red bell pepper, saffron, salmon or shrimp (fresh or smoked), tarragon, thyme, tomato, truffles, walnuts, and wild mushrooms.

COMPOUND BUTTERS

In the recipes that follow, ingredients should be whipped together thoroughly, either by hand or with an electric mixing bowl using a paddle attachment. Unsalted butter and cream cheese left out at room temperature will become soft enough to blend easily. Though some proportions of ingredients are included, they are not critical inasmuch only a small amount is used for each canapé. And, as with most cooking, the proper seasoning and flavoring are determined by the palate of the one who prepares it.

When a butter is blended, shape it, on baking parchment paper or wax paper, into a cylinder measuring approximately 1½ inches (37 mm) in diameter. Roll up the cylinder, wrap in plastic wrap, label it, and refrigerate (or freeze) it until needed.

ALMOND BUTTER

Unsalted butter blended with finely ground toasted slivered almonds, moistened with a little cold water, seasoned with salt and white pepper.

ANCHOVY BUTTER

Unsalted butter blended with mashed anchovy fillets (or anchovy paste), flavored with a little lemon juice, and seasoned with white pepper.

BASIL BUTTER

Unsalted butter blended with fresh basil leaves minced very fine, flavored with garlic, and seasoned with salt and white pepper.

Note: Basil butter is also excellent tossed with pasta.

BLUE CHEESE BUTTER

Unsalted butter blended with mashed blue cheese, seasoned with salt and white pepper.

CAVIAR BUTTER

Unsalted butter blended with mashed caviar, moistened with a little lemon juice, and seasoned with white pepper.

Note: Any good quality fish roe can be used to make this butter; it does not have to be beluga and osetra, the two best quality sturgeon varieties. Sevruga or the roe from salmon, trout, or whitefish works just as well.

Within India (a nation of 15 major languages and 1,600 dialects) curry blends vary as much as tomato sauces among the families of Sicily or barbecue marinades in regions of the southeastern United States. Among the herbs and spices used in curry blends are anise, cardamom, chili pepper, cinnamon, clove, coriander, cumin, fennel, fenugreek, garlic, ginger, lemon grass, mace, mustard, nutmeg, onion, saffron, tamarind, and turmeric.

CURRY BUTTER

2 shallots, minced
½ cup (120 mL) dry white wine

juice of 1 lemon
2 tablespoons (30 mL) curry powder

½ pound (227 g) unsalted
  butter, soft
2 tablespoons (30 mL)

cilantro, minced
salt and white pepper to
  taste

- Simmer the shallots, white wine, lemon juice, and curry powder until nearly dry. Set aside to cool. Whip the shallots and all of the other ingredients together until thoroughly blended, then wrap and store as described.

GREEN BUTTER

Unsalted butter blended with finely minced parsley leaves, seasoned with salt and white pepper.

HORSERADISH BUTTER

¼ cup (60 mL) grated fresh
  horseradish root (or prepared horseradish
  squeezed dry)
¼ cup dry white wine

½ pound unsalted butter,
  soft
salt and white pepper to
  taste

- Simmer the horseradish and wine until nearly dry. Whip this and all other ingredients together until thoroughly blended, then wrap and store.

LEMON BUTTER

Unsalted butter blended with the juice and zest (blanched in boiling salted water) of 1 lemon, seasoned with salt and white pepper.

MAÎTRE D'HÔTEL BUTTER

Unsalted butter blended with finely minced parsley, flavored with lemon juice, and seasoned with salt and white pepper.

MUSTARD-THYME BUTTER

Unsalted butter blended with minced fresh thyme leaves, flavored with Dijon-style mustard, and seasoned with salt and white pepper.

PIEDMONT BUTTER

Unsalted butter blended with grated Parmesan cheese, flavored with lemon zest, and seasoned with fresh grated nutmeg, salt, and white pepper.

ROASTED GARLIC AND HERB BUTTER

3 garlic bulbs, cloves separated
olive oil as needed
unsalted butter
⅓ cup (80 mL) minced fine herbs (basil, tarragon, parsley, cilantro, oregano, and/or thyme)
salt and white pepper to taste

- Preheat an oven to 375° F (190° C). Lightly coat the garlic cloves with olive oil. Place on a roasting pan, and roast for 45 minutes to 1 hour. Remove and allow to cool.
- Squeeze the garlic from the roasted cloves into a bowl. Whip this, along with the remaining ingredients until thoroughly blended, then wrap and store.

SAFFRON BUTTER

1 shallot, minced
1 garlic clove, minced
1 cup (240 mL) dry white wine
½ teaspoon (2.5 mL) saffron
1 bay leaf
1 sprig thyme
salt and white pepper to taste
¾ cup (180 mL) unsalted butter, soft

- Place all the ingredients, except the butter, into a saucepan. Simmer until reduced to approximately 3 tablespoons (45 mL). Remove the bay leaf and the thyme and discard. Whip the reduction along with the remaining ingredients until thoroughly blended, then wrap and store as described.

SARDINE BUTTER

Unsalted butter blended with mashed skinless, boneless sardines (drained of their oil) and seasoned with salt and white pepper.

TOMATO-CORIANDER BUTTER

Unsalted butter blended with peeled, seeded, and small-diced tomato and minced fresh cilantro leaves, moistened with a little dry white wine, and seasoned with salt and white pepper.

TUNA BUTTER

Unsalted butter blended with finely minced poached fresh tuna.

WINE MERCHANT BUTTER

1 shallot, minced
1 cup (240 mL) dry red wine
1 cup (240 mL) rich brown beef or veal stock, or consommé

1 tablespoon (15 mL) parsley, minced
unsalted butter
salt and white pepper to taste

- Simmer the shallot and wine until reduced by half. Add the stock or consommé, and continue reducing until two tablespoons of liquid remain. Whip the reduction along with the remaining ingredients until thoroughly blended, then wrap and store as described.

PASTES

ASIAN-STYLE PASTE

Cream cheese blended with powdered wasabi dissolved in a little soy sauce, flavored with grated gingerroot and a little oyster sauce.

CHEDDAR CHEESE PASTE

Equal parts of cream cheese and unsalted butter blended with grated sharp Cheddar cheese, flavored with prepared horseradish (squeezed dry) and a little beer, and seasoned with dry mustard dissolved in white Worcestershire sauce, salt, and white pepper.

CHICKEN LIVER PASTE

½ pound (227 g) chicken livers, trimmed of connecting membranes and coarsely chopped
¼ pound (113 g) unsalted butter
1 medium onion, coarsely chopped
3 cloves garlic, crushed
¾ cup (180 mL) mushrooms, coarsely chopped
¼ cup (60 mL) brandy
pinch of nutmeg
salt and pepper to taste
¼ pound (113 g) unsalted butter

- Sauté the livers in half the butter until pink in the center. Remove with a slotted spoon and set aside. Sauté the onions over medium heat, stirring continuously for 10 minutes, without coloring. Add the garlic and mushrooms, and sauté another 5 minutes. Add the brandy and deglaze, then add the nutmeg.
- Transfer the livers, onion, garlic, mushrooms, and remaining butter to a food processor, and purée. Press through a screen sieve, using a rubber spatula. Season to taste with salt and pepper. Allow to cool, then blend thoroughly with the remaining butter. Cover and refrigerate until ready to use.

EGG PASTE

Equal parts of cream cheese and unsalted butter blended with sieved hard-cooked egg yolks, moistened with a little mayonnaise smoothed with white Worcestershire sauce, flavored with Dijon-style mustard and a little Tabasco sauce, and seasoned with salt and white pepper.

EGGPLANT PASTE
(MOCK CAVIAR)

2 eggplants, about 1 pound
   (450 g) each
6 large garlic cloves, skin on
juice of 2 lemons
3 tablespoons (45 mL) olive
   oil

3 tablespoons (45 mL)
   chopped flat-leaf parsley
salt and pepper to taste

- Preheat an oven to 425° F (218° C).
- Split the eggplants lengthwise, coat the cut surfaces with olive oil, place on a baking sheet along with the garlic, and bake for 30 to 40 minutes or until tender. Remove and allow to cool.
- Scoop out the pulp and place in a food processor. Squeeze out the garlic and add, along with the remaining ingredients. Pulse until smooth.

JALAPEÑO PASTE

Cream cheese blended with seeded and finely minced jalapeño peppers, seasoned with salt and white pepper.

OLIVE AND ANCHOVY PASTE, PROVENCE STYLE

2 cups (480 mL) calamata
   olives, pitted
¼ cup (60 mL) anchovy fillets, with packing oil

6 garlic cloves
¼ cup (60 mL) brandy
¼ cup (60 mL) olive oil

161

2 tablespoons (30 mL)
   Worcestershire sauce
¼ teaspoon black pepper
2 tablespoons (30 mL)

chopped parsley
1 teaspoon (5 mL) thyme
   leaves, minced

- Purée all ingredients in a food processor, or pound with a mortar and pestle. Cover and refrigerate until ready to use.

OLIVE PASTE

1 cup (240 mL) calamata
   olives, pitted
2 garlic cloves
½ teaspoon (2.5 mL) grated
   lemon zest

1 tablespoon (15 mL) lemon
   juice
¼ cup (60 mL) olive oil
black pepper to taste

- Purée all ingredients in a food processor, or mince very finely with a knife and press through a fine sieve. Refrigerate until needed.

ROASTED GARLIC PASTE

1 garlic bulb
2 tablespoons (30 mL) olive
   oil
¼ pound (113 g) unsalted
   butter, soft

½ cup (120 mL) cream
   cheese
salt and white pepper to
   taste

- Preheat an oven to 375° F (190° C).
- Break the garlic bulb into cloves, discarding excess skin. Toss the cloves in the olive oil, place in a roasting pan, and roast for 30 to 40 minutes. Remove and set aside to cool.
- Squeeze out the soft garlic from the cloves. Mash thoroughly with a fork, and add the cream cheese and butter, blending thoroughly. Season to taste with salt and white pepper.

SALSA VERDE PASTE

4 tomatillos, skin removed,
   roughly chopped

2 jalapeño peppers
1 cup (240 mL) cilantro

162

leaves, roughly chopped
½ teaspoon (2.5 mL) ground
    cumin
½ cup (120 mL) water

1 cup (240 mL) goat cheese
salt and white pepper to
    taste

- Simmer all ingredients, except the goat cheese, in a small noncorrosive saucepan until soft. Continue simmering until the mixture yields a fairly dry paste.
- Allow to cool, then combine with the goat cheese and blend thoroughly. Season to taste with salt and pepper.

SARDINE PASTE

Equal parts of cream cheese and unsalted butter blended with drained and mashed boneless, skinless sardines, flavored with Tabasco, and seasoned with salt and pepper.

TUNA PASTE

Equal parts of cream cheese and unsalted butter blended with finely ground poached fresh tuna, flavored with Tabasco, and seasoned with salt and pepper.

COLD CANAPÉS

ADMIRAL CANAPÉS

Oval crouton spread with shrimp butter, topped with a poached shrimp, and garnished with lobster coral.

ALBERTA CANAPÉS

Square crouton spread with anchovy butter, crisscrossed with sliced smoked salmon, and garnished with beets and Maître D'hôtel Butter.

ALLADIN CANAPÉS

Half-circle-shaped crouton spread with stockfish paste, garnished with mango chutney.

ALSACIAN CANAPÉS

Round crouton spread with butter, topped with a slice of goose liver (or goose liver mousse), garnished with a slice of truffle, and glazed with Madeira aspic.

Truffles are members of the botanical family *Fungi,* which includes mushrooms, morels, and truffles. They are unique in that they produce their fruiting bodies underground and have a symbiotic relationship with trees such as beech, hazelnut, oak, poplar, and willow. The white truffle (Alba truffle) is found in the Piedmont and Emilia regions of Italy. The black truffle (Périgord truffle) is found primarily in the Dordogne region of southwestern France and in parts of Spain, Germany, and Italy. The French production of truffles today is about one-tenth of what it was a century ago, resulting from the loss of forest lands and overharvesting. The scarcity of truffles, combined with the labor required to locate them, explains their exorbitant cost.

ANCHOVY TOASTS

Crouton spread with dry mustard-cayenne pepper butter, topped with a crisscross of anchovy fillets, garnished with sieved hard-boiled egg, chopped parsley, and lemon.

ANDALOUSIAN CANAPÉS

Crouton spread with butter, topped with thin-sliced shrimp and anchovy fillets, coated with mayonnaise collée, and garnished with green pepper.

AURORA CANAPÉS

Round crouton cut from sliced brioche, spread with butter paste, topped with thin-sliced smoked salmon, garnished with a small circle of cooked beet, and sprinkled with sieved egg yolk.

BEATRICE CANAPÉS

Oval crouton spread with chervil butter, topped with two very thin slices of dried sausage with a thin slice of hard-boiled egg in between, garnished with dots of tomato butter.

BEAULIEU CANAPÉS

Round crouton spread with butter or basic paste, topped with a small wedge of seeded and skinned tomato, seasoned with salt and pepper, and garnished with a half black olive.

BELLE DE LAURIS CANAPÉS

Square crouton spread with asparagus butter, topped with a thin slice of poached chicken breast, coated with asparagus collée, and decorated with asparagus tips.

BORDEAUX CANAPÉS

Oval crouton spread with shallot butter, topped with two thin slices of shiitake mushrooms with a thin slice of ham in between.

BRILLAT-SAVARIN CANAPÉS

Oval crouton spread with crayfish butter, topped with poached crayfish tails split in half, and garnished with a small piece of truffle.

BUTTERCUP CANAPÉS

Round crouton spread with watercress butter, topped with watercress leaves, and garnished with egg yolk paste piped in a lattice pattern.

CAMBACÉRÈS CANAPÉS

Rectangular crouton spread with butter or basic paste, topped with thin-sliced seeded and peeled cucumber marinated in lemon vinaigrette (drained).

CAPUCHIN CANAPÉS

Round rye bread crouton spread with mayonnaise, one-half covered with chopped hard-boiled eggs, the other half covered with caviar, garnished with a small shrimp in the center.

CARDINAL CANAPÉS

Round crouton spread with mayonnaise, topped with a slice of lobster tail, and garnished with a slice of truffle.

Truffles are an intriguing food, fabled for centuries for their mystical and aphrodisiac qualities. In the first century A.D., the Roman satirist Juvenal told the Libyans, "Keep your wheat, and send us your truffles." Brillat-Savarin called them "the diamonds of cookery," and in Italy they are called *perle dela cucina*—"pearls of the kitchen."

CHANTEREINE CANAPÉS

Triangular crouton spread with butter, half spread with ham mousse and garnished with a small circle of hard-boiled egg, the other half spread with chicken mousse and garnished with a small round of truffle.

CLAIRE CANAPÉS

Rectangular pumpernickel crouton spread with lemon butter, topped with alternating thinly sliced strips of smoked salmon and caviar.

Collioure is a small village on the Mediterranean coast, near Spain, known for a dry, full-bodied red wine made from Grenache Noir grapes.

COLLIOURE CANAPÉS

Diamond-shaped crouton spread with anchovy butter, topped with anchovy fillets (crisscross or lattice pattern), and garnished with miniature tomato balls.

166

COQUELIN CANAPÉS

Crouton spread with anchovy and Parmesan cheese butter, garnished with chopped gherkins and capers.

CREOLE CANAPÉS

Rectangular crouton spread with butter, topped with a thin slice of Gruyère cheese, garnished with two thin slices of banana.

DANISH CANAPÉS

Square rye bread croutons spread with horseradish butter, topped with alternating strips of sliced smoked salmon and herring, and garnished with chives and caviar.

DERBY CANAPÉS

Crouton spread with ham paste and garnished with chopped toasted walnuts.

DOMINO CANAPÉS

Rectangular crouton spread with butter or plain paste, topped with a thin slice of poached chicken breast, glazed with mayonnaise collée, and decorated with small dots of truffle to resemble a domino.

The word *truffle* is derived from the Spanish *trufa* or the Italian *treffere*, both meaning "deceit," probably a reference to the fact that this variety of wild mushroom grows just under the surface of the ground and is thus difficult to locate. Because humans do not possess a keen olfactory sense, we must elicit help. In Sardinia goats are employed to track down truffles, bear cubs have been used in Russia, and pigs and specially trained dogs in Europe. Pigs are the true experts, however. German researchers recently discovered in truffles a musky chemical that is also secreted in the male pig's saliva, which prompts mating behavior. When the pig's sharp nose detects that aroma from under the ground (both pigs and dogs can detect it from as far away as 50 yards), it sends the creature into a lustful frenzy and it must be held back to prevent it from eating the truffle.

DOUARNEN CANAPÉS

Rectangular pumpernickel croutons spread with basic butter paste, topped with skinless and boneless sardines, and garnished with a small seedless and skinless lemon segment.

DUTCH CANAPÉS

Square or rectangular crouton spread with caviar butter, topped with thinly sliced pickled herring, and garnished with sieved egg yolks and minced chives.

FRENCH CANAPÉS

Rectangular crouton spread with anchovy butter, topped with a sardine (slightly flattened), coated with Rémoulade collée, and edged with chopped parsley.

GÂTINE CANAPÉS

Triangular crouton spread with butter and chicken liver pâté, garnished with tarragon leaves, and glazed with aspic.

GEDEON CANAPÉS

Rectangular crouton spread with butter or basic paste, spread with liver paste, and topped with crisscrossed strips of roasted duck breast.

GOURMET CANAPÉS

Oval crouton spread with goose liver butter, topped with a thin slice of poached chicken breast, garnished with chopped truffles, and glazed with Madeira aspic.

GRENOBLE CANAPÉS

Round crouton spread with walnut butter, topped with a thin slice of Gruyère cheese, and garnished with a toasted walnut.

HAMBURG CANAPÉS

Rectangular rye bread crouton spread with butter, topped with a thin slice of smoked meat, and garnished with a small gherkin fan.

HARLEQUIN CANAPÉS

A general term for a style of croutons cut into diamonds or rectangles, spread with horseradish, mustard, paprika, tomato, or watercress butter, topped with finely chopped ham, chicken, smoked or pickled tongue, edged with minced parsley, and attractively garnished with hard-boiled eggs, radishes, truffles, olives, or other decorative additions.

HELVETIAN CANAPÉS

Rectangular pumpernickel crouton spread with a paste made of ½ cup (120 mL) butter, ½ cup (120 mL) grated Gruyère or Emmentaler cheese, 2 sieved hard-boiled egg yolks, 1 tablespoon (15 mL) grated celery root, 3 tablespoons (45 mL) heavy cream, salt, and white pepper.

HUNGARIAN CANAPÉS

Round or oval crouton spread with paprika butter, topped with chicken paste, and garnished with strips of red and green bell peppers.

169

IMPERIAL CANAPÉS

Rectangular crouton spread with anchovy butter, topped with a thin slice of grilled tuna, and garnished with anchovy butter.

INDIAN CANAPÉS

Crouton spread with curry butter, topped with chopped hard-boiled egg yolks, and garnished with mango chutney.

JODLER CANAPÉS

Round pumpernickel crouton spread with butter or basic paste, covered with grated radish, topped with a square of Swiss cheese, and garnished with finely chopped toasted peanuts.

JOINVILLE CANAPÉS

Round crouton spread with shrimp butter, edged with minced hard-boiled egg, topped with titi shrimp, and garnished with a small (unsalted) butter curl.

LA FAYETTE CANAPÉS

Rectangular crouton spread with butter or basic paste, topped with a slice of boiled lobster, coated with lobster col-lée, garnished with truffle, and glazed with aspic.

LAGUIPIÈRE CANAPÉS

Diamond-shaped brioche crouton spread with truffle butter, edged with minced truffle and minced smoked tongue, and topped with thinly sliced chicken breast.

170

LILY-OF-THE-VALLEY CANAPÉS

Oval crouton spread with tarragon butter, topped with a lengthwise slice of hard-boiled egg, decorated with tarragon leaves and tiny, round cutouts of egg white, and glazed with aspic.

LIVONIAN CANAPÉS

Rectangular pumpernickel crouton spread with horseradish butter, edged in chopped chives, topped with slivers of pickled herring alternating with thin julienne of tart apple rinsed in lemon juice, and then drained (to prevent browning).

LOTHRINGIAN CANAPÉS

Square crouton spread with butter, topped with chicken paste blended with minced beef tongue, and glazed with aspic.

LUCCA CANAPÉS

Oval crouton spread with butter, topped with a raw or poached oyster, and garnished with caviar.

LUCILLE CANAPÉS

Oval crouton spread with butter, topped with minced beef tongue, garnished with a thin slice of poached chicken breast, and glazed with aspic.

LUCULLUS CANAPÉS

Round crouton spread with butter, topped with finely chopped raw beef tenderloin (tartar), a raw oyster in the center, and garnished with caviar and a segment of seedless and skinless lemon.

LULLI CANAPÉS

Square crouton spread with butter or basic paste, then spread with chicken mousse, garnished with truffle or pâte à choux filigree in the shape of a G clef sign (musical notation).

LUTETIA CANAPÉS

Round crouton spread with mustard butter, topped with lettuce chiffonade, and garnished with a small slice of tomato seasoned with salt and pepper.

MASCOT CANAPÉS

Rectangular crouton spread with green herb butter, topped with thin slices of artichoke bottom marinated in vinaigrette, and garnished with a small noisette (ball) of cooked potato.

MEXICAN CANAPÉS

Crouton spread with butter, topped with minced sardines and anchovies, followed by a slice of hard-boiled egg, and garnished with red bell pepper.

MONSELET CANAPÉS

Oval crouton spread with egg yolk paste, edged with minced truffle, topped alternately with thinly sliced poached chicken breast and smoked tongue, and garnished with a small thin slice of truffle.

Charles Pierre Monselet (1825–1888), journalist and author, was known for his witty style in writing on gastronomic matters. He collaborated with many well-known writers of his day (including Alexandre Dumas) on *La Cuisinière Poétique,* published in 1859. He also published a gastronomic newsletter—*Le Gourmet,* later changed to *Almanach des Gourmands*—off and on between 1861 and 1870. A gourmand of some distinction, Monselet was known to many of the finest restaurants of his day and had many dishes named after him, nearly all including some form of truffle.

Mont-Bry was a pseudonym used by Prosper Montagné, and denotes dishes created by or for him. His best-known work, first published in 1938, is the still-published *Larousse Gastronomique* (no relation to this author).

MONT-BRY CANAPÉS

Rectangular brioche crouton spread with herring butter, edged with chopped egg yolk, and garnished with alternating strips of herring, cooked beet, and gherkins.

MONTE-CARLO CANAPÉS

Crouton spread with goose liver paste, garnished with chopped hard-boiled egg.

MOSCOW CANAPÉS

Square pumpernickel crouton spread with horseradish butter, decorated with a border of lobster butter, filled with caviar, and garnished with a poached shrimp.

NANTES CANAPÉS

Oval crouton spread with sardine butter, topped with skinless and boneless sardines, and garnished with sardine butter.

NETHERLANDS CANAPÉS

Oval crouton spread with mustard butter, topped with a large mussel poached in white wine, and garnished with finely diced celery marinated in mustard vinaigrette.

NICE CANAPÉS

Round crouton spread with anchovy butter, topped with a thin slice of tomato, a split anchovy fillet placed crisscross on top, a slice of olive in each of the four sections, and garnished with chopped parsley.

NINON CANAPÉS

Oval crouton spread with green vegetable butter, topped with alternating thinly sliced poached chicken breast and ham, and garnished with a small thin slice of truffle.

NORWEGIAN CANAPÉS

Rectangular rye bread crouton spread with butter, topped with strips of anchovy fillets, and garnished with horseradish butter.

Ogourzi (or Agoursi) is also a dish made of the same ingredients (see Chapter 6, page 262).

OGOURZI CANAPÉS

Rectangular rye bread crouton spread with butter or basic paste, topped with a drained salad of paper-thin sliced seedless and skinless cucumber marinated in dill and sour cream, and garnished with a sprig of dill.

ONDINE CANAPÉS

Diamond-shaped crouton spread with tarragon butter, topped with a piece of sole poached in white wine, coated with tarragon-and-fish-flavored mayonnaise collée, and garnished with tarragon leaves.

ORIENTAL CANAPÉS

Triangular crouton, spread with butter or basic paste, topped with a thin slice of poached chicken breast, coated with tomato and saffron flavored collée, and garnished with roasted red bell pepper (or pimento) cut into a crescent and a star.

OTERO CANAPÉS

Round crouton spread with butter, topped with caviar and a raw or poached oyster, and coated with Rémoulade collée.

Henri Paul Pellaprat (1869–1950), a chef and pâtissier of considerable repute, worked under Casimir Moisson at the celebrated Maison Dorée in Paris (1840–1902), eventually taking over as chef. He is the author of *L'Art Culinarie Moderne,* first published in 1935, then published in 1966 and 1971 under the title *The Great Book of French Cuisine.*

Phileas Gilbert (1857–1942), worked with many great chefs, notably Auguste Escoffier and Prosper Montagné. He penned numerous books and articles, assisted Escoffier in writing his *Guide Culinaire,* and contributed a short preface to *Larousse Gastronomique* (removed from the 1988 edition).

Phocaea was an ancient city in what was known as Ionia, circa 1100 B.C., located in a group of islands situated between southern Italy and western Greece.
Salpicon is a fairly broad term, referring to any meat, fish, poultry, game, or vegetable, cut into fairly small dice and cooked by stewing or braising.

Paris Canapés

Rectangular crouton, spread with chervil butter, topped with thinly sliced poached chicken breast, coated with mayonnaise collée, and garnished with a small slice of truffle and tarragon leaves.

Pellaprat Canapés

Round crouton spread with watercress butter, edged with watercress butter, and spread with salmon mousse.

Phileas Gilbert Canapés

Round crouton spread with shrimp-cayenne butter, topped with a slice of poached turbot fillet, glazed with fish collée, garnished with truffle, and glazed with aspic.

Turbot is a large white-fleshed fish, similar in appearance to a large flounder, found in the North Atlantic and the Mediterranean. That it has been gastronomically prized for centuries is indicated by the fact that there exists a large poaching vessel fabricated in the shape of the turbot, known as a *turbotière.* Its gastronomic importance is also indicated by a considerable body of elaborate recipes for its preparation. Any variety of flounder is the best substitute for turbot.

Phocaean Canapés

Round crouton spread with lemon butter, topped with red mullet salpicon (baked in olive oil and lemon), and garnished with tomato concassé.

Pompadour Canapés

Oval or round crouton spread with butter or basic paste, topped with a thin slice of poached chicken breast, coated with tomato collée, and garnished with a sprig of chervil (or parsley) and miniature circles of tomato.

Numerous dishes, designated "Pompadour style" are named after Jeanne Antoinette Poisson (1721–1764), mistress of Louis XV, king of France, who conferred on her the title of Marquise de Pompadour. She was influential in promoting the artists of her time, and numerous dishes were named after her, notably a grilled lamb or beef medallion, accompanied by Choron and Périgueux Sauces, and an artichoke heart filled with sautéed noisette potatoes.

PRINCESS CANAPÉS

Round crouton spread with butter, topped with a slice of poached chicken breast, then crisscrossed with anchovy fillets, garnished with a slice of hard-boiled egg, and sprinkled with minced chives.

PROSPER MONTAGNÉ CANAPÉS

Oval crouton spread with tomato butter, topped with a thin slice of roasted turkey breast, and garnished with roasted red bell pepper or pimento.

RADISH CANAPÉS

Slice of fresh baguette (untoasted) spread with butter, topped with sliced radishes, and lightly seasoned with salt.

REFORM CANAPÉS

Crouton spread with anchovy butter, topped with minced smoked tongue and hard-boiled egg, garnished with a gherkin, and glazed with aspic.

SHRIMP, NEWEST STYLE

Poached, shelled, and deveined shrimp served on top of a half lemon, garnished with a sprig of parsley (*see color plate, Classic Caviar Service*).

SOUVAROFF CANAPÉS

Square pumpernickel crouton, spread with goose liver paste, topped with a thin slice of roast pheasant, garnished with truffle, and glazed with aspic.

SPANISH CANAPÉS

Rectangular or oval crouton spread with cayenne butter, topped with a sheet of cooked egg, and garnished with a little finely diced tomato concassé in the center.

To prepare an egg sheet: Beat very well 2 eggs and a little salt and pepper. Pour into a hot pan with some oil, and cook on both sides until light brown. Drain on absorbent paper, then cut to the exact size of the croutons.

SPRING CANAPÉS

Slice of baguette or white bread (untoasted) spread with parsley butter, topped with chopped watercress, and garnished with a slice of hard-boiled egg.

SULTAN CANAPÉS

Crouton spread with anchovy butter, topped with chopped lobster meat, coated with mayonnaise collée blended with minced lettuce, and garnished with chopped red bell peppers.

SWEDISH CANAPÉS

A general term for rye bread canapés, toasted and untoasted, spread with anchovy butter, topped with various ingredients—anchovies, smoked salmon, herring, eggs, lobster, shrimp, oysters, ham, and so forth—and attractively decorated.

TARTAR CANAPÉS

Square or rectangular rye bread (untoasted) spread with butter, topped with ground lean beef seasoned with salt and pepper, and garnished with chopped onions and gherkins.

TURBIGO CANAPÉS

Crouton spread with butter, topped with chopped shrimp, coated with seasoned tomato purée, and garnished with diced pickles and diced cooked celery root.

VÉRON CANAPÉS

Square pumpernickel crouton spread with horseradish butter, edged with a mixture of chopped egg yolks and chopped parsley, and topped with very thin slices of Bayonne ham.

WESTPHALIAN HAM CANAPÉS

Crouton spread with horseradish butter, topped with a thin slice of dry-cured ham, and glazed with aspic.

Simple ham and sausage canapés can be made from any variety of ham, and they then take on the name of the ham or sausage used. Typical variations include Ardennes, Arlesian, Bayonne, Berry, Parma, Virginia, or York ham; Arles, Calabrese, Chipolata, Cognac, or Lyons sausage, and so on.

WINDSOR CANAPÉS

Crouton spread with chicken paste mixed with chopped tongue, ham, and dry mustard, garnished with gherkins and capers, and glazed with aspic.

CONTEMPORARY CANAPÉ INNOVATIONS

The examples of contemporary canapés that follow here can be used as inspiration for individual variations. An example of innovations can also be seen in the color plate, Contemporary Canapés.

BASIC CRACKER RECIPE

2¼ cups (540 mL) flour
2 tablespoons (30 mL)
  sugar
2 teaspoons (10 mL) baking
  powder
1 teaspoon (5 mL) salt
¼ cup (60 mL) vegetable oil
¼ cup (60 mL) milk

1 egg, beaten
2 teaspoons (10 mL) finely
  minced herbs or ground
  spices, as needed (fennel,
  caraway seed, cracked
  black pepper, paprika,
  saffron, or other vari-
  eties)

- Blend the dry ingredients together. Add the oil, milk, egg, and herbs or spices. Knead together until smooth, and allow to rest 30 minutes.
- Preheat an oven to 350° F (176° C).
- Roll out the dough on a floured board, and cut into various shapes. Bake for 15 minutes, or until the edges brown.

Homemade crackers are excellent bases for canapés, both because of their crunch, and because of the option to season them and cut them in any way desired. They can also be made a day or two ahead.

BOUCHÉES

Bouchées are small pastry cases, generally round, 3 to 4 inches in diameter, though they can be cut into different shapes (such as diamond, oval, square, and rectangle). They are always made from puff pastry (pâte feuilletée), and can be prepared two different ways: first, puff pastry may be rolled out to a thickness of ¼ inch (6 mm), cut into a circle, and scored ½ inch (12 mm) inside the outside edge (creating a border ½-inch/6-mm wide). When the pastry is baked, a lid can be lifted out where it was scored. A second and more efficient way is to roll the pastry out to a thickness of ¼ inch (6 mm), cut the shape desired, brush with egg wash, then place a second piece of dough the same size and shape, with a center area cut out. When baked, a concave center area is automatically created.

Note: Bake bouchées on a lightly buttered pan, in a preheated 375° F (190° C) oven until puffed up and golden brown. There are dozens of different fillings for bouchées, which can be served as small dishes, luncheon main courses, or as a specified garnish for a larger dish.

ARTICHOKE BOTTOMS WITH GARDEN VEGETABLES

Trim canned artichoke bottoms into uniform circles, using a round pastry cutter, and flatten the bottoms. Drop into boiling lemon water for 15 seconds, drain, and cool. Pipe in ½ teaspoon (2.5 mL) cream cheese blended with chopped herbs (for instance, parsley, cilantro, tarragon), and garnish with four different varieties of blanched vegetables, such as a broccoli flowerette, carrot noisette, a half slice of radish, and a yellow turnip noisette.

ASIAN BIRD'S NESTS

1 cup (240 mL) titi shrimp
¼ cup (60 mL) celery cut into very fine dice
¼ cup (60 mL) scallion, finely minced
½ cup (120 mL) rice wine vinegar

2 tablespoons (30 mL) grated gingerroot
2 tablespoons (30 mL) minced cilantro leaves
2 tablespoons (30 mL) soy sauce

48 2-inch-square pieces of
    wonton skin
peanut oil as needed

½ cup (120 mL) chopped
    roasted peanuts
24 cilantro leaves

- Marinate the shrimp, celery, scallion, vinegar, ginger, minced cilantro, and soy sauce for 2 hours.
- Brush the insides of a miniature muffin pan with oil. Preheat an oven to 375° F (190° C).
- Brush one square of wonton with water, and press a second square on top, so that the corners do not line up. Press this square into an oiled muffin pan opening, and brush the top of the wonton with oil. Repeat with all the wontons, bake until golden brown, then set aside to cool.
- Drain the marinated shrimp, and divide up among the wonton bases. Garnish each with chopped peanuts and a cilantro leaf.

BEEF JANNA

Rectangular crouton, spread with horseradish butter, topped with a slice of roasted beef tenderloin, and garnished with a rosette of blue cheese and cream cheese paste, a cornichon fan, and a watercress leaf.

BROCCOLI ON ONION CRACKER

Prepare a basic cracker recipe, with the addition of finely minced onion lightly sautéed and drained. Spread the cracker with jalapeño cream cheese, top with a small broccoli flowerette lightly blanched in boiling salted water, and garnish with pâte à choux filigree.

Pâte à Choux Filigree
½ cup (120 mL) milk
½ cup (120 mL) water
pinch of salt
¼ pound (113 g) unsalted
    butter, cut up

1½ cups (360 mL) all-
    purpose flour, sieved
6 eggs

- Bring the milk, water, salt, and butter to a simmer in a noncaustic pan. When the butter is melted, add the flour and stir until completely blended. Continue stirring over medium heat until the paste comes away from the side of the pan. Remove from the fire.

- Add the eggs, one at a time, blending in each one completely before adding the next. Allow to cool, then fill a small pastry bag or parchment cone fitted with a No. 1 round tube. Pipe out in small filigree designs, no longer than 1 inch (25 mm), on a baking sheet covered with parchment paper. Bake at 350° F (176° C) 10 to 15 minutes, or until golden brown. Remove and set aside to cool.

BRUSCHETTA MEDITERRANEAN STYLE

1 large ripe tomato
1 medium green bell pepper
3 garlic cloves, pressed
3 tablespoons (45 mL) olive oil
2 tablespoons (30 mL) parsley, minced
salt and pepper to taste

1 sweet baguette, sliced ¼-inch (6-mm) thick on a sharp bias
unsalted butter as needed
thinly sliced Virginia or Bayonne ham
calamata olives

- Peel the tomato and cut into small dice, discarding excess seeds. Cut the green pepper into small dice. Combine the tomato, pepper, garlic, oil, parsley, salt, and pepper, toss thoroughly, and marinate several hours.
- Brush the baguette slices with olive oil, toast on both sides, and allow to cool. Spread each crouton lightly with butter, and top each with a slice of ham, trimmed to fit the crouton.
- Drain the tomato/pepper mixture of excess moisture, and place ½ teaspoonful (2.5 mL) on top of the ham. Garnish with a slice of black olive.

CAJUN SHRIMP CANAPÉS

Round cayenne pepper cracker, spread with jalapeño cream cheese paste. Dust a peeled deveined shrimp with Cajun spice blend, sauté briefly in a hot pan, cool, then place on top of the jalapeño spread. Garnish with cream cheese and a cilantro leaf.

CAMEMBERT AND APPLE CANAPÉ

Round crouton spread with butter, topped with a large rosette made with 2 parts Camembert cheese mashed with 1 part cream cheese, and garnished with a half red grape and a small wedge of apple dipped in lemon juice.

CHEDDAR AND CHICKEN LIVER CANAPÉS

Prepare a basic cracker recipe with the addition of grated Cheddar cheese. Spread cracker with cashew butter mixed with a little minced onion sautéed in oil until lightly caramelized then seasoned with a little basalmic vinegar. Pipe out a rosette of chicken liver paste blended with cream cheese on top of this, add a dollop of sour cream, and garnish with a toasted cashew nut.

CROSTINI WITH PROSCIUTTO AND FIGS

Rectangular crouton spread with herb butter, topped with a paper-thin slice of prosciutto, garnished with a small dollop of marscapone cheese and two wedges of fresh figs (Calmyra or Black Mission).

FOIE GRAS PARFAIT

A round crouton spread with butter, topped with a large rosette of cooked fresh or canned goose liver mashed into a smooth paste with cream cheese and seasoned with fresh herbs, and garnished with a dot of cream cheese and a slice of cornichon.

GAUFRETTE POTATO, RUSSIAN STYLE

Using a potato mandolin, slice peeled potatoes into ¼-inch (6-mm) thick gaufrettes. Deep-fry until golden brown and drain well. Place on top of round cracker spread with cream cheese paste, and top with a mixture of minced shallots caramelized in olive oil, cooled, and blended with sour cream, cream cheese, salt, and white pepper. Garnish with caviar and a chive spear.

GORGONZOLA BOUCHÉES

Pâte à choux bouchée filled with a mixture of equal parts Gorgonzola cheese, cream cheese, and butter, blended into a smooth paste. Garnish with a half slice of seedless grape and a toasted walnut.

GRECIAN MORSELS

Diamond-shaped crouton spread with a thin layer of olive tapenade, garnished with a half cherry tomato that is scooped out and filled with feta cheese blended into a paste with garlic, oregano, and black pepper.

GREEK TOMATO CANAPÉS

Round crouton spread with goat cheese, topped with a slice of Roma tomato, then a mixture of crumbled feta cheese, goat cheese, basil, olive oil, and garlic, garnished with a small wedge of calamata olive.

GRILLED CHICKEN ON FRIED WONTONS

Wonton skin brushed lightly with water, folded diagonally twice into a triangle, then deep-fried and drained. Spread with a thin layer of wasabi-flavored cream cheese, top with a slice of grilled chicken breast, and garnish with pickled ginger-root and a cilantro leaf.

HAM CORNETS

Cut thinly sliced ham into 1½-inch (37-mm) circles and make an incision from the center to the edge. Roll into a cone shape, and fill with cream cheese flavored with Dijon-style mustard and tarragon. Spread a round crouton with a thin layer of the same spread, place the cornet on top, and garnish with a small wedge of pineapple.

JICAMA AND CHORIZO CANAPÉS

Spread a ¼-inch (6-mm) thick slice of jicama, cut into a star, with a paste made from goat cheese and salsa verde (see recipe earlier in this chapter). Top with a slice of chorizo and garnish with a red pepper spear.

MEXICAN MEDALLIONS

A dill-flavored round cracker, spread with cream cheese blended with tequila and minced cilantro, topped with a slice of Mexican-style Gravlax rolled into a rose, and garnished with a dollop of sour cream and a cilantro leaf.

MUSHROOM AND CHICKEN LIVER CANAPÉS

Remove the stems of medium mushrooms (about 1½-inch/ 37-mm wide caps), and blanch the caps in white wine and lemon juice. Drain and cool. Stuff with basic chicken liver paste, and garnish with an asparagus tip blanched al dente, and a sprig of chervil or parsley.

POLENTA BOUCHÉE SOUTHWEST STYLE

Prepare a seasoned polenta (3 parts water to 1 part corn meal, salt and white pepper), and pour into a ¾-inch (18-mm) deep half sheet pan to slightly overflowing. Even off the top, using a ruler or straightedge. Refrigerate until cold, then cut into small rounds, and scoop out the center of each using a Parisienne scoop. Place on a cracker spread with adhesive, fill with guacamole (ripe avocado mashed with minced garlic, tomato, jalapeño, and salt), and garnish with two strips of smoked duck, a dab of sour cream, and a sprig of cilantro (*see Figure 4.2*).

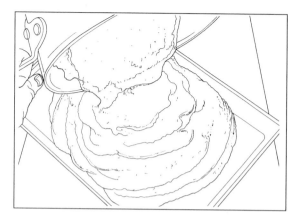

Rinse a baking pan with cold water, leaving it slightly wet, and then pour in the hot cooked polenta.

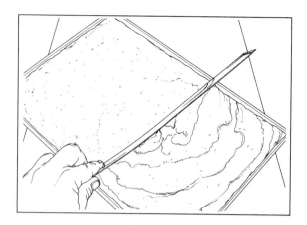

Even off the polenta by sliding a straight edge across the top edge of the pan (some of the polenta may spill over the sides of the pan).

Figure 4.2
Filling a Pan with Polenta

POLENTA SQUARES WITH SUN-DRIED TOMATO

Prepare a seasoned polenta (3 parts water to 1 part corn meal, salt, white pepper, and minced herbs), and pour into a ¾-inch (18-mm) deep half sheet pan to slightly overflowing. Even off the top, using a ruler or straightedge. Refrigerate until cold, then cut into 1½-inch (37-mm) squares. Scoop out each square, using a small Parisienne scoop, sauté the squares in hot olive oil or butter until golden brown on the bottom, then allow to cool. Fill each square with a paste made of cream cheese and minced sun-dried tomatoes, and garnish with a small dot of basil pesto.

POLISH PIECES

Square pumpernickel crouton, spread with a paste made of cream cheese, drained sauerkraut, and caraway seed. Top with a slice of grilled or sautéed keilbasa (Polish-style sausage) and a dot of the cream cheese, and garnish with a diamond-shaped piece of red onion.

186

Chilled Soups *Avocado Soup, Champagne (contemporary, p. 89) and Consommé Madrilene (classical, p. 275)*

Contemporary Canapés from top to bottom: *Olive Paste with Egg Yolk (p. 162); Ham Cornets with Watercress Cream Cheese (p. 184); Smoked Salmon with Asparagus; Gorgonzola with Almond and Grape; Shrimp with Caper and Chive*

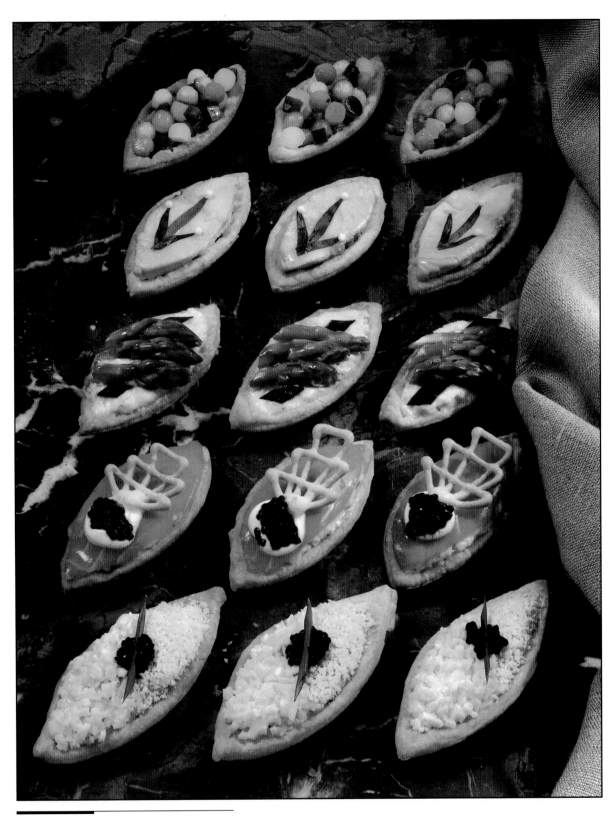

Barquettes (Cold) from top to bottom: *Greek (p. 204); Bigorre (p. 203); Northern (p. 205); Romanoff (p. 205); Norma (p. 205)*

Croustades and Puffs (Cold)   clockwise from bottom left: *Murat Puffs* (p. 209); *Rosamond Croustades* (p. 212); *Pompadour Puffs* (p. 214); *Sultan Puffs* (p. 210), followed by second *Rosamond Croustade; Queen Puffs* (p. 214); *rutabaga mukimono rose* (center)

Traditional Salads clockwise from bottom center: *Alexander* (p. 253); *Paris* (p. 241); *Hearts of Palm, Carnelian* (p. 229); *Bagration* (p. 249); *Pretty Helen* (Belle Hélène) (p. 231); *Dutch* (p. 238)

Crudité clockwise from bottom left (*indicates vegetables briefly blanched in boiling salted water): *daikon, cherry tomatoes, asparagus*, herb mayonnaise sauce* (in red cabbage) *(p. 265), celery, yellow bell pepper, zucchini, radishes, string beans*, dill and herb mayonnaise sauce* (in green cabbage) *(p. 122); cauliflower*, carrots, broccoli**

Fish and Vegetable Hors d'Oeuvres (Cold)   clockwise from bottom left (2 servings each): *lobster cocktail (p. 239); Fennel Root Italian Style (p. 267); Cucumber Cocktail, Swedish Style (p. 266); Alligator Pear* (avocado) *Cocktail (p. 262)*

Antipasti from left to right: *Asparagus wrapped in prosciutto (p. 82); calamata olives; sliced Roma tomatoes with anchovies; Broiled Eggplant; Roasted Red Onions (p. 93); Marinated Artichoke Hearts (p. 80); Fennel Root and grilled yellow squash (p. 93); buffalo mozzarella and roasted red bell pepper with basil leaves and Nafplion olives; Garbanzo and Red Kidney Beans; toasted foccacia (upper right)*

Vegetable Hors d'Oeuvres (Cold) clockwise from top left: *California Apples (p. 263); Vegetables Vinaigrette (p. 268); Celery Stuffed with Roquefort (p. 264); Beetroot Squares (p. 264); Cucumbers, Danish Style (p. 266); Leeks Vinaigrette (center) (p. 268)*

Hors d'Oeuvres, Greek Style front tray, clockwise from bottom corner: *zucchini spaghetti (p. 271); poached shrimp; poached octopus with vinaigrette (p. 83); poached shrimp; artichoke hearts with dried tomato vinaigrette (pp. 80 and 126); mushrooms with lemon;* rear tray: *mixed California olives; roasted Spanish onions (p. 193); dolmades (grapes leaves stuffed with rice pilaf); Agoursi (p. 262),* small container at left: *taramasalata (Greek-style fish roe paste)*

Seasonal Fruit Arrangement   Centerpiece: *watermelon with rose and leaf motif; carved half papaya*, center: *watermelon rind "bowl" filled with golden bing cherries, blackberries, blueberries, and sliced strawberries;* left to right: *orange honeydew melon wedges, sliced green honeydew melon, sliced watermelon, sliced pineapple, sliced peaches, apricot halves with strawberry and blueberry*

Vegetable Bounty   Centerpieces: *Two cauliflowers scooped out, poached in boiling salted water, and filled with mixed baby tomatoes* — sweet 100's (red), sungold (orange), yellow plum, and green grape — *seasoned with olive oil, vinegar, salt, pepper, garlic, and basil chiffonade; salad* (upper right): *bread croustade filled with warm diced potatoes, pearl onions, and red onion, all roasted, then seasoned with olive oil, salt, pepper, and minced herbs;* garnishes: *wonton socles with vegetable paupiettes* ("little packages") *bound with strips of blanched leek* (red, orange, yellow, and green bell pepper, celery, green and yellow string bean, and zucchini); *yellow patty pan squash filled with herbed goat cheese, garnished with purple Bolivian hot pepper*

Salmon Chaud-Froid Dishes   from top right down: *Salmon Cutlet, Green Meadow Style (p. 28);*
Salmon Cutlet, Royal Style (p. 282); Salmon Cutlet, Italian Style (p. 281)

Tomatoes (Cold, Stuffed)   left to right: *Oysters Borchardt Style* (p. 254); *Tomatoes Polish Style* (p. 257); *Tomatoes, Lucullus Style* (p. 256); *Tomatoes, Monaco Style* (p. 256); *Tomatoes, Waldorf Style* (p. 257)

PROSCIUTTO AND FENNEL POINTS

Triangular crouton, spread with garlic and basalmic vinegar cream cheese paste, topped with a paper-thin slice of prosciutto, garnished with a dot of the paste and a piece of paper-thin shaved and briefly blanched fennel root.

PROSCIUTTO AND MELON CANAPÉS

Baguette crouton spread with pistachio butter, topped with paper-thin prosciutto folded into a small fan, topped with a dot of cream cheese, and garnished with a melon ball.

RADISH AND NASTURTIUM CANAPÉS

Round crouton, spread with mustard butter, topped with very thinly sliced radishes, and garnished with a nasturtium leaf.

Nasturtium vegetable soup, a favorite of President Dwight D. Eisenhower, contains an herbal type of penicillin and a considerable amount of vitamin C. Flowers used in the kitchen should be purchased at a market where they are certain to have been grown specifically for consumption. *Never* use flowers for cooking unless they are specified for such use, because they may have been chemically sprayed. Moreover, some flowers are poisonous (for example, azalea, daffodil, oleander, poinsettia, and wisteria). Edible varieties include apple blossoms, chrysanthemums, marigolds, pansies, tulips, and violets.

In Japan and China, chrysanthemums are believed to increase longevity, make teeth grow again, and turn white hair black. In France, pansy oil is still rubbed on the eyelids to induce love at first sight. And medieval philosopher Albertus Magnus wrote that gathering violets during the final quarter of the moon would cause all one's wishes to come true.

ROAST DUCK CANAPÉS

Round crouton spread with orange butter, topped with a slice of roasted duck breast, garnished with an orange segment, and sprinkled with chopped toasted pistachios.

ROQUEFORT CHEESE BOUCHÉES

Fill a small bouchée with a paste made of 1 part Roquefort cheese mashed with 1 part butter, garnish with sliced radish and a sprig of parsley (*see Figure 4.3*).

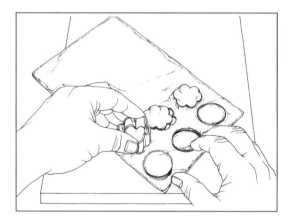

Punch out small rounds of puff pastry, using round or floral-shaped cutters.

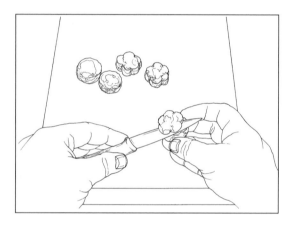

After baking, slice off the tops.

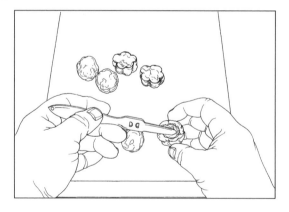

Press down the interior of each bouchée and then fill as required.

Figure 4.3
Making a Miniature Puff Pastry Bouchée

SALMON TARTAR CANAPÉS

Spread a large slice of toasted pullman pumpernickel with butter. Top with a layer of finely minced raw salmon, seasoned with lemon juice, salt, white pepper, and dill. Cut into squares or diamonds, and garnish each with a red onion triangle and poached lemon zest.

SHRIMP IN HEAT

Cucumber bouchée cut on a vertical bias, filled with wasabi-flavored cocktail sauce, filled with a shrimp poached on a bamboo skewer (so that it remains straight), tail left on, and garnish with radish sprouts.

SMOKE AND PUFF

Cucumber bouchée filled with a paste made of smoked salmon, dill, and cream cheese, garnished with a salmon egg and sprig of dill (*see Figure 4.4*).

SMOKED SALMON ROULADES

Lay very thin slices of smoked salmon, slightly overlapping, onto a sheet of plastic wrap or parchment paper. Place a sheet of nori on top of this, and spread a very thin layer of dill cream cheese, allowing a ½-inch (13-mm) border. Roll tightly, wrap in plastic, and freeze. Slice ¼-inch (6-mm) thick, place on a round crouton spread with butter, and garnish with a sprig of dill.

SMOKED CHICKEN MOUSSE BOUCHÉES

Prepare a mousse with finely chopped or ground smoked chicken, cream cheese, and Dijon-style mustard. Pipe into a puff pastry bouchée, and garnish with a wedge of quail egg, toasted walnut, and sprig of chervil (*see Figure 4.3*).

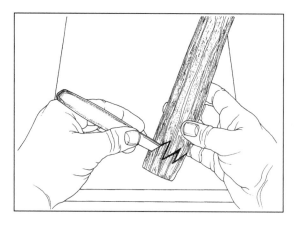

Cut a zigzag into a hothouse (English) cucumber and then cut it into approximately 1-inch segments.

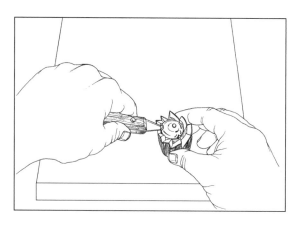

Scoop out the interior, using the small end of a Parisienne scoop, and fill as required.

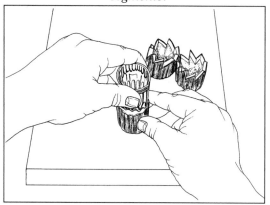

Punch out the interior of a cucumber segment, using a floral cutter (discard the skin).

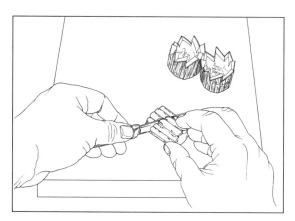

Cut each segment in half, on the bias (see first variety shown for comparison).

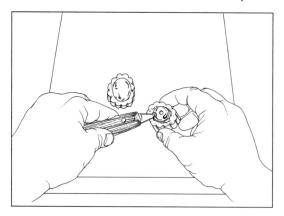

Scoop out each segment and fill as required.

Figure 4.4
Cutting Two Varieties of Cucumber Bouchée

SNOW PEAS STUFFED WITH ROQUEFORT CHEESE

Remove the very ends of snow peas, removing the thin strand of fiber from each side as you snap off the ends. Carefully open one side of each snow pea, and pipe in a paste of Roquefort cheese mashed with cream cheese. Garnish with carrot curls.

SOUTHWEST STARBURST

Remove and discard the tops from miniature patty pan squash. Scoop out, blanch briefly in boiling salted water, drain, and cool. Spread a round crouton with cayenne pepper paste, top with the squash, and fill with salsa fresca (tomato, green pepper, red onion, cilantro, and lime juice).

SPICY SHRIMP ON A CHIP

Cut flour tortillas into 1½-inch (37-mm) circles, sauté or deep fry until golden brown, drain, and cool. Spread with jalapeño cream cheese paste (jalapeño is roasted, seeded, and peeled, then mashed into a paste), top each with a small grilled shrimp, and garnish with the cream cheese paste, a cilantro leaf, and a red pepper spear.

SWEDISH CUCUMBER CANAPÉS

Small skinless English cucumber bouchée, filled with a little mustard-dill sauce, topped with a rolled rosette of Gravlax, and garnished with a sprig of dill.

THAI-STYLE CHICKEN ON WONTON BOUCHÉES

2 8-ounce (225-g) chicken breasts, pounded thin
2 tablespoons (30 mL) curry powder

¼ cup (60 mL) coconut milk
2 garlic cloves, pressed
2 tablespoons (30 mL) hot chili oil

salt to taste
24 wonton skins
oil as needed
1½ cups (360 mL) peanut
   butter

¼ cup (60 mL) coconut milk
3 tablespoons (45 mL) hot
   chili oil
2 scallions

- Marinate the chicken in the curry powder, ¼ cup (60 mL) coconut milk, garlic, 2 tablespoons (30 mL) hot chili oil, and salt for several hours.

- Brush the wonton skins with water, fold in half, and cut each into 2 triangles. Sauté or deep-fry until golden brown, drain, and cool.

- Drain the chicken and grill or sauté.

- Make a paste with the peanut butter, ¼ cup (60 mL) coconut milk, and 2 tablespoons (30 mL) hot chili oil. Spread a little of this paste on each wonton, and top with a slice of the grilled chicken. Top the chicken with a rosette of the peanut butter mixture, and garnish with a slice of scallion cut on the bias.

TUNA CARPACCIO ON TOAST POINTS

6 ounces (170 g) fresh,
   boneless ahi tuna, sliced
   paper thin
¼ cup (60 mL) Kimberly
   champagne vinegar
1 tablespoon (15 mL) sherry
   vinegar
2 tablespoons (30 mL) olive
   oil
1 tablespoon (15 mL) fresh
   tarragon leaves, minced

salt and pepper to taste
4 large slices white bread
unsalted butter as needed
1 head bibb lettuce, separated into 16 leaf cups
1 small red bell pepper, cut
   into very fine, uniform
   julienne

- Combine the vinegars, oil, tarragon, salt, and pepper. Add the sliced tuna, cover, and marinate in the refrigerator for 3 hours.

- Toast the bread, allow to cool, then spread with a light coating of butter. Trim the crusts and cut into 16 uniform triangles.

- Place a lettuce cup on each triangle. Top with a piece of sliced tuna, and garnish with the julienned pepper.

CAVIAR

Caviar, the salted roe (eggs) of sturgeon and other varieties of fish, is commonly served in canapé form. We know from the writings of Aristotle that it was known as far back as ancient Greece, and Shakespeare made reference to it in *Hamlet:* "T'was caviare to the general [populace]." This delicacy was introduced in France in the 1920s by exiled Russian nobility, and Charles Ritz promoted its popularity by putting it permanently on his hotel menu. Around the turn of this century, sturgeon was plentiful not only in the Caspian Sea, but in the Black Sea, the Baltic, the North Sea, the Gironde River (France), and in the rivers of North America. Overfishing and pollution has destroyed most of these habitats, leaving the Caspian as the primary source, providing 98% of the world's output. The Soviet Union, once the sole producer of caviar, produces about 1,800 tons a year. In 1953, Iran began processing caviar along its part of the Caspian coast and have added another 180 tons to annual production.

The ancestors of Christian Petrossian began processing sturgeon roe into caviar in the Russian town of Baku, long before the Russian revolution. Today, his company (Petrossian, Inc.) is the sole exporter of Russian caviar to the world's markets. The technique of processing the roe into caviar has evolved over hundreds of years and is considered a great skill. After the roe are removed, they are sieved, washed, graded, and salted. The less salt used in processing, the younger the roe, and the better quality the caviar. *Malossol,* meaning "little salt," is the finest of this kind. There are three sturgeon species from the Caspian used in the production of caviar:

- *Beluga:* The most expensive, produced from the largest sturgeon, weighing as much as 1,750 pounds (800 kg). The eggs are dark gray, firm, and well separated.
- *Osetra:* Smaller, more even-sized eggs, golden yellow to brown, from sturgeon weighing from 200 to 300 pounds.
- *Sevruga:* Very small, light to dark gray eggs from sturgeon weighing 50 to 100 pounds.

Of course, one could test the quality of caviar the way one gourmet did in Paris in the 1930s. According to Ludwig Bemelman, who began working in the Ritz-Carlton in 1914, the gentleman had the jeweler Cartier construct a little gold ball, which he wore on the other end of his watch chain. He would go to one of the good restaurants, have his plate heaped with caviar, and then drop the golden sphere from about a foot above the plate. If it passed through the caviar without effort, he pronounced the dish first rate. If the ball got stuck in its passage and did not reach the bottom of the plate, he sent the plate and the black stuff back to the kitchen.

TYPES OF CAVIAR

Grade 1 caviar is processed as fresh, whole eggs, then shipped and stored under continuous refrigeration at 28° to 32°F (–2.2 to 0°C). If properly stored, fresh whole (and fresh pressed) eggs have a shelf life of 6 months.

Grade 2 roe is processed as *fresh pressed* and *pressed pasteurized*. It is literally pressed, losing about 80% of its volume. Pasteurized caviar, which is vacuum packed, has a shelf life of one year.

American Caviar: Though not caviar in the traditional sense, some varieties have an excellent flavor. (See "Specialty Suppliers" toward the end of this book.)

HOW TO EAT CAVIAR

Purists maintain that the proper way to enjoy very fine caviar is that the roe be well chilled, eaten with only a bland cracker or a small Russian-style buckwheat pancake known as a blini, accompanied by iced vodka or well-chilled champagne. "The caviar may improve the oyster, but the oyster does nothing for the caviar" (Christian Petrossian). In canapé production, since it is used as a garnish combined with other ingredients (sour cream, buttered croutons, smoked and cured fish, hard-boiled eggs, and so forth) it is best to use the pressed variety, because it is much stronger flavored. In any case, the use of lemon or lemon juice with any caviar is considered inappropriate.

CAVIAR FAN

One of the most spectacular ways of serving caviar is to arrange it in the form of a fan. This is made by cutting large slices of pullman bread (a rectangular, unsliced loaf of white bread) into the shape of a fan, ultimately cutting it up into individual croutons. This is not as complicated as it appears, but it is labor-intensive. The template used for the caviar fan pictured in this book measures 17 inches (425 mm) at its

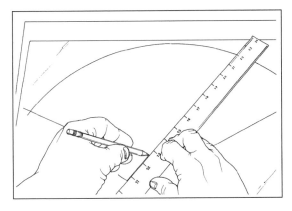

On a piece of bristol board (or other medium-weight paper), draw the outline of a fan.

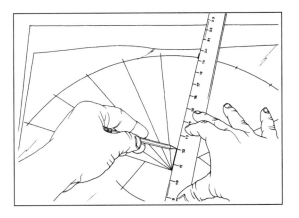

Divide the fan outline radially into 8 equal sections.

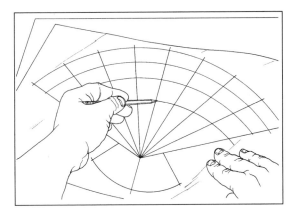

Divide the fan outline horizontally, as shown, into five sections. Cut the form out at the outside edge, discarding the trim. Place toasted sheets of pullman bread, spread with plain butter, on top of the template, and cut into 40 individual segments. Each segment is then topped with the appropriate caviar, garnished, and then reassembled onto a platter for service.

Figure 4.5
Cutting a Template for the Caviar Fan

widest point; top to bottom it is not quite 11 inches (280 mm). A template was cut from a medium-weight sheet of paper, known as bristol board (available at art supply stores). The fan was then penciled in, yielding 8 sections vertically, more or less, since it fans out from the bottom point; and 5 sections horizontally, more or less, on a convex curve. The pullman loaf was sliced in half, trimmed of exterior crust, then cut into

195

¼-inch-thick sheets. These sheets were then toasted light brown on both sides. It is important not to overtoast the bread, because it will break up indiscriminately when cut into the smaller croutons.

Once cooled, the sheets were placed on top of the template and cut to shape the eight vertically fanned-out sections. These long triangular forms were then spread with plain, unsalted, softened butter. Each triangle was returned to the template and cut into five individual croutons. Five varieties of caviar were then spread on each crouton, one variety for each of the horizontal curves. The varieties selected were also arranged in a specific order of color: lobster roe (red, Maine), Chinook salmon roe (orange, Great Lakes), whitefish roe (light yellow), Tobiko (light green, flying fish flavored with wasabi), Choupique (black, bowfin).

A central area, running across four of the horizontal sections, and three of the vertical sections, was covered with minced hard-boiled egg white. A template representing a Japanese calligraphic character (Harmony), was cut from a sheet of tracing paper. Once the fan was assembled, the paper template was placed over the egg-covered croutons and filled with whitefish roe, then highlighted with Choupique roe (it was piped out with a pastry bag, fitted with a No. 2 round tip). Finally, crêpes were rolled up around a filling of softened cream cheese, sliced on the bias, garnished with a dot of lobster roe and small pieces of blanched leek, and set at the bottom of the fan (*see color plate, Caviar Fan, and Figure 4.5*).

POTATO PANCAKES I

1 pound (450 g) Red Bliss
   or all-purpose potatoes
4 large eggs
¾ cup (180 mL) half-and-
   half
3 tablespoons (45 mL)
   unsalted butter

salt and white pepper to
   taste
cornstarch as needed
1 cup (240 mL) clarified
   butter

- Peel the potatoes and cut into 2-inch (50-mm) chunks. Boil in lightly salted water until tender. Drain, and mash, using a mashing tool or a food mill. Add the eggs, half-and-half, and 3 tablespoons (45 mL) butter, and beat in by hand or with an electric mixer.

- When the potatoes are cool enough to handle, portion out into 2-inch (50-mm) round pieces. Press down into round, flattened cakes, about ⅓ inch (8 mm) thick. Dust with the cornstarch, and sauté in hot clarified butter until golden brown on both sides.

POTATO PANCAKES II

4 large Red Bliss or all-purpose potatoes, peeled and grated
1 cup (240 mL) Quick Cream of Wheat cereal
4 eggs, beaten

1 cup (240 mL) flour
2 tablespoons (30 mL) parsley, minced
salt and white pepper to taste
clarified butter as needed

- Combine all ingredients except the butter, and blend thoroughly. Shape into 2-inch (50-mm) circles about ⅓ inch (8 mm) thick, and sauté in clarified butter.

BLINIS

½ pound (225 g) buckwheat flour
½ pound (225 g) all-purpose flour
1 cup (240 mL) warm milk
¾ ounce (21 g) granulated yeast

¼ teaspoon (1.2 mL) salt
¼ teaspoon (1.2 mL) sugar
¼ cup (15 mL) sour cream
2 small eggs, beaten
¼ cup (15 mL) heavy cream
butter as needed

- Sift the flours into a large bowl. Dissolve the yeast, salt, and sugar in the milk. Make a well in the flour, add the yeast mixture, and blend thoroughly with the flour. Let sit 30 minutes in a warm place.

- Add the remaining ingredients, and blend thoroughly into a smooth batter. Ladle into 2-inch (50-mm) round pancakes on a pan or griddle greased with butter, and cook on both sides until golden brown. Serve with caviar and sour cream.

BUCKWHEAT CAVIAR CONES

2 cups (480 mL) buckwheat
  flour
2 large eggs
1 large egg yolk
2 cups (480 mL) milk
2 tablespoons (30 mL)
  melted butter

salt and pepper to taste
½ cup (120 mL) sour cream
½ cup (120 mL) scallions,
  sliced very thin
1 ounce (28 g) caviar

- Whip the flour, eggs, and yolk together until smooth. Add the milk, butter, salt, and pepper, and blend thoroughly. Cover, and allow to rest 1 hour.

- Lightly butter a small nonstick sauté pan, and heat over medium flame. Pour in enough batter to just coat the bottom of the pan. When small holes form on the top surface, flip over and cook another 30 seconds. Remove the pancake, and repeat this process until all the batter is used.

- Place a dollop of sour cream and some scallions on the pancake, slightly off center. Roll the pancake up into a cone, and add a ½ teaspoon (2.5 mL) of caviar on top.

CHAPTER 5

SAVORY PASTRIES

BARQUETTES AND TARTLETS

A barquette is a small open pastry in the shape of a boat. A tartlet is a small open pie, filled with various fillings.

Like canapés, tartlets and barquettes provide the chef an opportunity to create miniature works of edible art. There are a considerable number of bite-sized pastries in the hors d'oeuvres arena which bear the name of persons, places, events, or styles of creation. Tartlets and barquettes may also be specific garnishes for a larger dish (for example, Chicken Nantua—barquettes filled with hot crayfish tail ragout; Chicken Demi-Deuil—barquettes filled with hot sweetbread, mushroom, and truffle salpicon; Fillet of Beef, Colbert—tartlets filled with baby vegetables, glazed with aspic).

The forms for baking tartlets and barquettes vary considerably in size, and come with straight or fluted sides. The author's preference for tartlets is the fluted variety, measuring 4 inches (100 mm) in diameter at the top and 3 inches (75 mm) at the bottom; for barquettes, straight sides, 4 inches (100 mm) long at the top and 2¾ inches (70 mm) on the bottom. There are also sets of small pastry forms with many special shapes (diamond, elliptical, square, triangular, and so forth). Although a classical barquette is oval and pointed at both ends, and a tartlet is usually round, these other shapes can be used innovatively as inspiration and creativity warrant.

After the tartlet and barquette forms are filled with short pastry, they are generally baked blind (empty) before being filled. When the filling is savory, they are served hot or cold, as hors d'oeuvres or as a garnish to a larger dish. When the filling is sweet (for dessert), they are generally served cold. Unless a dish specifies a particular filling, there is no limit to the kinds of fillings one can innovate.

DOUGH I

1¼ cups (300 mL) all-purpose flour
½ cup (120 mL/1 stick) unsalted butter, cut into ¼-inch (6-mm) pieces

pinch of salt
4 tablespoons (60 mL) ice water

- Combine the flour, butter, and salt together in a bowl, and rub together until the mixture has the consistency of coarse meal. Add the water, and press into a large ball. (Add additional water or flour if necessary; avoid overworking.) Wrap airtight, and allow to rest 30 minutes.

- Preheat an oven to 400° F (205° C).
- Roll the dough out on a lightly floured board to a thickness of approximately ⅛ inch (3 mm). Cut out a piece of dough about ½ inch (12 mm) larger than the form it will fill. Brush the interior of the form lightly with oil or clarified butter. Brush off excess flour from the underside of the dough, and set into the form. Trim the dough even with the edges of the form. Dock the entire bottom surface of the dough by piercing it all over with the tines of a fork. Take a second form, exactly the same as the first, and press it down onto the dough. Bake for 10 to 15 minutes, or until golden brown.
- Allow the pastries to cool for 10 minutes. Remove the top form, then invert the bottom form and carefully remove the pastry. Set aside until needed, or fill with appropriate filling, and reheat or refrigerate, depending on the recipe.

Note: The second tartlet/barquette form pressed into the dough of the first, helps to make an even pastry and to inhibit the dough from puffing up. Dried beans can be placed into this second form to add weight, though this is commonly done with larger tart and pie shells (the dried beans are often placed directly on top of the dough and can be used repeatedly).

In actual practice, because they are used daily, baking forms are not washed after every use. They are simply wiped out. In this way, they become *seasoned* and do not have to be greased every time they are used.

DOUGH II

1 cup (240 mL) all-purpose flour	1 egg yolk
¼ teaspoon (1.2 mL) salt	¼ cup (60 mL) sour cream
4 tablespoons (60 mL/½ stick) unsalted butter, cut into ¼-inch (6-mm) pieces	ice water as needed (about 3 tablespoons/45 mL)

- Combine the flour, butter, and salt together in a bowl, and rub together until the mixture has the consistency of coarse meal. Add yolk, sour cream, and the water, and press into a large ball. (Add additional water or flour if necessary; avoid overworking.) Wrap airtight, and allow to rest for 30 minutes until ready to use.
- Follow directions for baking as described for Dough I.

202

BARQUETTE RECIPES

AURORA BARQUETTES

½ cup (120 mL) mayonnaise
1 tablespoon (15 mL)
  tomato paste
3 tablespoons (45 mL)
  champagne vinegar
1 teaspoon (5 mL) anchovy
  paste
¼ cup (60 mL) carrots, cut
  into fine dice
¼ cup (60 mL) green beans,
  cut into fine dice
¼ cup (60 mL) potatoes, cut
  into fine dice
¼ cup (60 mL) rutabagas,
  cut into fine dice

¼ cup (60 mL) black olives,
  cut into fine dice
¼ cup (60 mL) capers,
  drained
1 teaspoon (5 mL) basil,
  minced
1 teaspoon (5 mL) oregano,
  minced
1 teaspoon (5 mL) parsley,
  minced
salt and pepper to taste
12 baked barquette shells
2 hard-boiled eggs, yolks
  and white sieved sepa-
  rately

- Blanch the vegetables separately, in boiling salted water, until al dente. Set aside to cool.
- Blend the mayonnaise, tomato paste, vinegar, and anchovy paste together until smooth. Add the vegetables, olives, and herbs, blend thoroughly, and season with salt and pepper. Marinate at least 2 hours.
- Fill the barquette shells with the salad and garnish with the sieved hard-boiled egg.

BIGORRE BARQUETTES

Barquette shells, baked, spread with tarragon butter, topped with a slice of poached salmon (cut to size), decorated with tarragon leaves, and glazed with aspic [*see color plate, Barquettes (Cold)*].

CALEDONIAN BARQUETTES

Barquette shells, baked, filled cone-shaped with ham mousse, covered with a thin slice of ham, decorated with blanched leek leaves and small diamond-shaped slices of truffle and hard-boiled egg white, and glazed with aspic.

203

DANISH BARQUETTES

Cut small rectangular boats, approximately 2 inches long and 1 inch wide, from a hothouse cucumber. Prepare a mousse with finely ground smoked salmon and smoked herring, minced hard-boiled eggs, cream cheese, and seasoned with prepared horseradish, squeezed dry. Fill the boats with the mousse and garnish with chopped egg whites, sieved yolks, and a cucumber loop (optional). *(See color plate, Vegetable Hors d'Oeuvres, Cucumbers, Danish Style; also see Figure 5.1.)*

GREEK BARQUETTES

Barquette shells, baked, filled with a salad consisting of assorted vegetables (shown in photo: carrot, red bell pepper, rutabaga, zucchini, white turnip) cut out with a pea scoop (noisette) or cut into small dice (brunoise), blanched al dente, and marinated in a Greek-style vinaigrette [*see color plate, Barquettes, (Cold)*].

INDIAN BARQUETTES

Barquette shells, baked, filled with a little rice pilaf, followed by ground or finely minced chicken and ham bound in curry

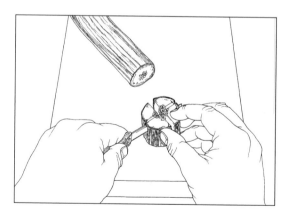

Cut a hothouse or standard cucumber into 1½-inch segments. Cut each segment lengthwise into quarters.

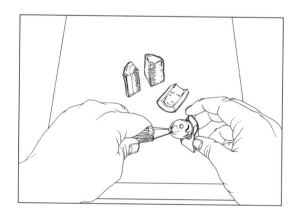

Scoop out the interior of each quarter, using a spoon or Parisienne scoop.

Figure 5.1
Cutting a Cucumber for Danish Cucumbers

mayonnaise, and garnished with sliced hard-boiled egg and chopped parsley.

MIRABEAU BARQUETTES

Barquette shells, baked, filled with chopped hard-boiled egg bound with anchovy butter, and garnished with anchovy fillets.

NORMA BARQUETTES

Barquette shells, baked, filled with finely ground tuna salad, garnished with sieved hard-boiled egg, caviar, chives, and lemon (lemon omitted from photo) [*see color plate, Barquettes (Cold)*].

NORTHERN BARQUETTES

Barquette shells, baked, filled with finely diced chicken salad, and garnished with asparagus tips and a small slice of truffle [*see color plate, Barquettes (Cold)*].

ROMANOFF BARQUETTES

Barquette shells, baked, filled with a finely diced egg salad, covered with a slice of smoked salmon, and garnished with sour cream and caviar. (The filigree trellis shown in the photo is a creative addition.) [*see color plate, Barquettes (Cold) and also Figure 5.2*].

RUSSIAN BARQUETTES

For the Dough

3 ounces (85 g) cream
   cheese, soft
4 ounces (113 g) unsalted
   butter, soft

1 cup (240 mL) flour
pinch of salt

Filling

2 tablespoons (30 mL)
   unsalted butter
2 shallots, minced
1 cup (240 mL) sour cream
salt and white pepper to taste

2 ounces (57 g) osetra or
   sevruga caviar
12 pâte à choux trellises
12 chive sprigs

205

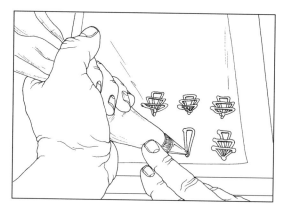

*Fit a pastry bag with a No. 1 round tip and
fill the bag with pâte à choux (puff paste).*

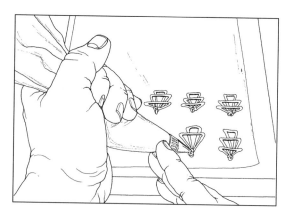

*Pipe out small geometric patterns onto
parchment paper, building up the filigree
trellises in three stages.*

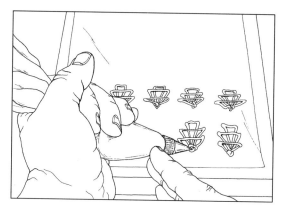

*Bake until golden brown, gently remove from
the paper, set aside, and use for garnishing
canapés, barquettes, tartlets, and so forth.*

Figure 5.2
Piping Filigree Trellises

- Combine the dough ingredients together until they form a
  smooth paste. Allow to rest 30 minutes. Roll out, press into
  the shells, and bake, as described at the beginning of this
  chapter.

- Sauté the shallots in the butter. Remove from the fire, and
  allow to cool. Blend the shallots, sour cream, salt, and pepper together. Fill the barquette shells with this mixture. Garnish with a little caviar, a trellis, and a sprig of chive (*see
  Figure 5.2*).

VARSOVIAN BARQUETTES

Barquette shells, baked, filled with a salad composed of finely diced cooked beets, sour gherkins, and hard-boiled egg whites, and garnished with caviar and sieved egg yolks.

TARTLET RECIPES

ANCHOVY TARTLETS

2 small tins anchovy fillets
½ pound (227 g) cream cheese
2 tablespoons (30 mL) parsley, minced
2 tablespoons (30 mL) tarragon, minced
1 garlic clove, pressed

2 tablespoons (30 mL) lemon juice
4 hard-boiled eggs, yolks and white pressed separately through a sieve
8 baked tartlet shells
8 small parsley sprigs

- Drain the oil from the anchovies, and reserve for another use. Separate 8 well-shaped fillets, split them in half lengthwise, and set aside.
- Mash the remaining anchovies, using a fork, into a smooth paste. Add the cream cheese, herbs, garlic, and lemon juice, and blend thoroughly. Spread this paste into the 8 tartlet shells. Garnish with the sieved yolks and whites, then place a split anchovy criss cross on each, on top of the egg, and a small sprig of parsley in the center.

ROMANOFF TARTLETS

¼ cup (60 mL) unsalted butter
¼ cup (60 mL) cream cheese
3 tablespoons (45 mL) anchovy paste
2 tablespoons (30 mL) minced chives

½ cup (120 mL) bowfin or sturgeon caviar
½ cup (120 mL) salmon caviar
12 baked tartlet shells
4 ounces (113 g) smoked salmon, sliced very thin
¼ cup (60 mL) sour cream
12 chive spears

207

- Combine the butter, cream cheese, anchovy paste, and chives, and blend into a smooth paste. Spread this paste on the inside bottoms of the tartlet shells.
- Carefully place the bowfin (or sturgeon) caviar along one side of tart, covering one-third of the butter/anchovy paste. Repeat on the opposite side of the tart, using the salmon caviar. Cover the remaining one-third area (in the center of the tartlet) with a slice of smoked salmon. Garnish with a dollop of sour cream and a chive spear.

SPRING TARTLETS

Tartlet shells, baked, filled with an attractive composition of poached baby vegetables (such as squash, turnip, carrot, broccoli flowerettes, asparagus tips) and glazed with aspic.

CAROLINES AND DUCHESSES

Carolines and duchesses (eclairs and puffs), both prepared with *choux* paste (*pâte à choux*), are different in shape and size. Carolines are 3-inch-long miniature eclairs, bringing to mind the familiar 4- to 6-inch-long eclairs filled with pastry cream and glazed with chocolate. A duchesse is a 1- to 1½-inch-round miniature version of the cream puff, a 3-inch-round puff filled with pastry cream and dusted with powdered sugar. The basic recipe is as follows:

Choux is also the French term for cabbage, and its application to this pastry reflects its appearance when baked—it looks like a little cabbage.

PÂTE À CHOUX

1 cup (240 mL) water
1 cup (240 mL) milk
10 tablespoons (50 mL)
   unsalted butter, cut into
   1-inch (25-mm) pieces

pinch of salt
2¼ cups (540 mL) flour
6 eggs

- Bring the water, milk, butter, and salt to a boil in a noncorrosive pan. When the butter has melted, add the flour and blend thoroughly until the mixture forms a ball of paste that comes away from the side of the pan (add a little additional flour if necessary). Continue stirring and cooking for several minutes, without browning. Remove from the fire.
- When the paste has cooled slightly, add the eggs, one at a time, and stir until completely incorporated.

- Scoop the paste out of the pan with a rubber spatula, and place in a pastry bag fitted with a No. 5 or No. 6 round tip. Pipe out onto a lightly greased pan, with about 1½ inches between each piece, to allow for expansion. Bake in a preheated 350° F (176° C) oven for 15 minutes, or until golden brown.

CAROLINE AND DUCHESSE RECIPES

LOBSTER PUFFS

12 duchesse shells
¾ cup (180 mL) cooked
   lobster, small dice
¼ cup (60 mL) celery, small
   dice
¼ cup (60 mL) scallions,
   small dice
1 teaspoon (5 mL) tarragon,
   minced
1 teaspoon (5 mL) parsley,
   minced

¼ cup (60 mL) mayonnaise
2 tablespoons (30 mL)
   lemon juice
salt and white pepper to
   taste
½ cup (120 mL) mayonnaise
2 tablespoons (30 mL)
   tomato paste
warm liquid aspic as
   needed

- Combine the lobster, celery, scallions, herbs, ¼ cup (60 mL) mayonnaise, lemon juice, salt, and pepper.
- Slice the top off the duchesse shells, and scoop out the interiors. Fill with the lobster salad, then set aside.
- Blend ½ cup (120 mL) mayonnaise, tomato paste, and enough aspic to make a smooth, thick collée. Place the pastry tops on a wire rack, and coat with the collée. Refrigerate until set, and recoat if necessary.
- Place the tops onto the stuffed pastries, and serve (*see color plate, Croustades, Puffs, and Pastries*).

MURAT PUFFS

A duchesse shell, filled with a purée of artichoke bottoms blended with cream cheese and herbs, glazed with mayonnaise collée, decorated with herbs, and glazed with aspic.

209

ROSSINI PUFFS

A duchesse shell, filled with a purée of goose liver and minced truffles, and glazed with demi-glaze and aspic (*see color plate, Croustades, Puffs, and Pastries*).

SULTAN PUFFS

A duchesse shell filled with chicken mousse, glazed with chicken chaud-froid, and garnished with chopped pistachios (*see color plate, Croustades, Puffs, and Pastries*).

SWEDISH ANCHOVY PUFFS

A duchesse shell, top removed, filled with a paste made with anchovies, butter, cream cheese, chopped parsley, the top glazed with aspic and covered with sieved egg yolks.

CROUSTADES

A croustade consists of a thick slice of bread or small roll, hollowed out, brushed with butter (the butter can be eliminated), then baked until brown and crispy. (A hot croustade can also be a case made of puff pastry, phyllo dough, duchesse potatoes, pasta, polenta, or rice, baked, removed from the mold, then filled with any of a number of fillings, ranging from salpicons and stews to vegetables and purées of various sorts.) A very elegant way of presenting a cold dish is to serve it in cooled croustades, a variation that opens up many creative possibilities. The following are some traditional croustades (*see Figures 5.3 and 5.4*).

CASANOVA CROUSTADES

Croustades filled with celeriac (celery root) julienne, truffles, and hard-boiled egg, bound with mayonnaise.

GOOSE LIVER CROUSTADES

Croustades filled with goose liver purée, glazed with Madeira aspic.

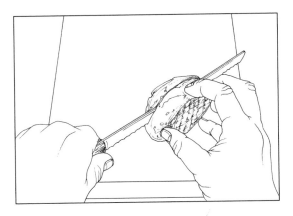

Slice the top off a small hard roll.

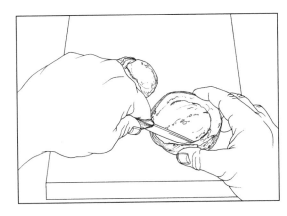

Score the inside of the roll with a paring knife.

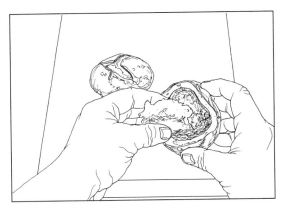

Pull out the dough from the interior of the roll.

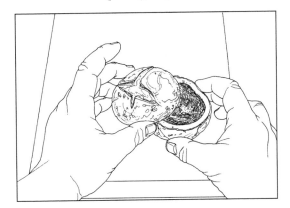

Brush the interior lightly with clarified butter, bake until golden brown, fill with appropriate filling, and set the top in place.

Figure 5.3
Creating a Croustade from a Roll

INDIAN CROUSTADES

Croustades filled with chilled curried rice pilaf mixed with diced shrimp, chutney, and parsley, and garnished with diced hard-boiled egg yolks and whites.

ROMANOV CROUSTADES

Croustades filled with a fine purée of tuna fish moistened with mayonnaise, and garnished with chopped pistachio nuts (*see color plate, Croustades, Puffs, and Pastries*).

211

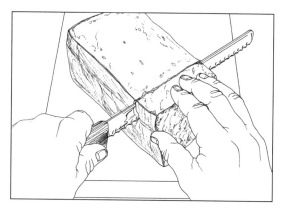

Cut a 1½–2-inch-thick slice of bread from a pullman loaf.

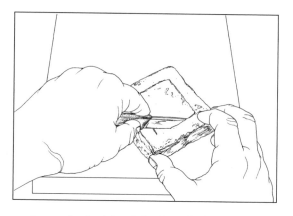

Score the inside of the bread slice, about halfway down, leaving a ½-inch wide border at the edges.

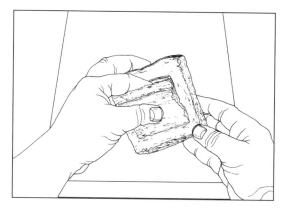

Carefully remove the interior bread, leaving a clean cavity. Brush it with clarified butter, bake until golden brown, and fill as required.

Figure 5.4
Creating a Croustade from a Thick Slice of Bread

ROSAMOND CROUSTADES

Croustades filled with tomato salad (diced peeled tomatoes, scallion, basil, olive oil, garlic, salt, and pepper), garnished with anchovy fillets and hard-boiled eggs (*see color plate, Croustades, Puffs, and Pastries*).

SPANISH CROUSTADES

Croustades spread with anchovy butter, filled with hard-boiled egg salad seasoned with anchovies and bound with tartar sauce, and garnished with green olives (*see color plate, Croustades, Puffs, and Pastries*).

TZARINA CROUSTADES

Croustades filled with onion paste (puréed onions and cream cooked down until thick, then cooled) seasoned with anchovy paste, filled with caviar.

VICTORIA ROLLS

A croustade made from a small dinner roll, filled with any shellfish (lobster, crab, crayfish), poultry (chicken, game) or meat (beef, pork, lamb) salad, bound with mayonnaise-based or vinaigrette sauce.

PUFF PASTRIES

A Napoleon, a dessert made with sheets of puff pastry, which are termed *mille-feuille* in French, which means "thousand leaves." By the repeated folding and rolling, folding and rolling of this dough, literally more than a thousand layers of flour and butter are created. (The recipe that follows yields 2,187 layers of butter and flour.) The final dough is rolled out to a thickness of ⅛ inch (3 mm), then baked. The butter in the dough melts; the water in the butter boils, producing steam; and that steam pushes up the minute layers of dough. This process renders an incredibly flaky and delectable pastry.

Puff pastry dough (*pâte feuilletée*, or *feuilletage*) is believed to have been invented in the seventeenth century by Feuillet, a pastry cook in service to the house of Condé. Another theory holds that it was developed in ancient Greece, which is quite possible, given the similarity of certain Greek dishes made with phyllo dough. Spanakopita and baklava, for example, though prepared differently, yield a product with a texture similar to those made with puff pastry. The French version is, however, unique, not only in the way in which it is created, but also in the inclusion of butter, not commonly prevalent in Mediterranean cookery.

Puff pastry is used to prepare hundreds of different dishes, both savory and sweet, ranging from pastry shells (*bouchées*) and cheese straws (*allumettes*) to Napoleons (*mille feuille*, both savory and sweet) and Elephant Ear cookies (*palmiers*).

213

PUFF PASTRY DOUGH

1 pound (450 g) flour
pinch of salt
1 cup (240 mL) cold water

1 pound (450 g) unsalted
  butter, soft
1 tablespoon (15 mL) flour

- Combine the flour (1 pound/450 g), salt, and water, and knead well into a smooth, elastic dough (adjust quantities as necessary). Set aside and allow to rest for 30 minutes.

- Knead the butter and flour (1 tablespoon/15 mL) into a smooth paste.

- Roll the dough out into a square, roughly 8 inches (200 mm) on each side, and of even thickness. Spread the butter in the center of the dough, allowing roughly a 2-inch (50-mm) border between the butter and the edge of the dough.

- Bring each corner up into the center of the butter, completely enclosing the butter. The edges of the dough, when the corners are brought up, should overlap each other slightly.

- Roll the dough out into a rectangular, measuring roughly 22 inches (560 mm) long, and 8 inches (200 mm) wide. Fold up the dough in thirds, and roll out again into this triangle. Fold up in thirds, make a small indentation in the top with two fingers, and refrigerate for 15 minutes.

- Roll the dough out again, fold up, mark with three fingers, and refrigerate.

- Repeat this process 3 more times, for a total of 6 turns. Refrigerate the dough until ready to use.

POMPADOUR PUFFS

A 3 × 12-inch (75 × 305-mm) sheet of baked puff pastry spread with cream cheese, topped with thinly sliced ham, topped with another sheet of baked puff pastry, a second layer of cheese and ham, and a third sheet of baked puff pastry. Trim all four edges square, slice widthwise at 1-inch (25-mm) intervals, and garnish with cream cheese and herbs (*see color plate, Croustades, Puffs, and Pastries*).

QUEEN PUFFS

A 3 × 12-inch (75 × 305-mm) sheet of baked puff pastry spread with a purée of finely minced cooked chicken breast blended

214

with cream cheese, topped with another sheet of baked puff pastry, a second layer of chicken paste, a third sheet of baked puff pastry. Trim all four edges square, slice widthwise at 1-inch (25-mm) intervals, and garnish with cream cheese and a toasted pecan (*see color plate, Croustades, Puffs, and Pastries*).

BLUE CHEESE NAPOLEON

1 pound (450 g) puff pastry
   (or 2 sheets frozen puff
   pastry)
2 eggs, beaten
1 pound (450 g) blue cheese
½ cup (120 mL) sour cream
¾ pound cream cheese, soft
2 ripe Bosc or d'Anjou pears
½ cup (120 mL) sour cream,
   beaten until runny
½ cup (120 mL) pistachio
   nuts, toasted and finely
   chopped
1 small bunch fresh mint

- Preheat an oven to 375° F (190° C).

- Roll out the pastry to a thickness of ⅛ inch (3 mm). Cut into three sheets, measuring approximately 4 × 10 inches (100 × 250 mm). Brush them with the beaten eggs, dock them (gently poke the dough with the tines of a fork), place on a lightly buttered baking sheet, and bake for 15 minutes or until golden brown. Remove and set aside.

- Beat the blue cheese with the cream cheese and sour cream until smooth.

- Peel the pears, cut in half lengthwise, cut out the core, and cut into ¼-inch (6-mm) thick slices.

- Spread one sheet of puff pastry with the cheese mixture, then top with a layer of pear. Coat another sheet with cheese, and place over the pears, cheese side down. Coat the top side of this second sheet with the cheese mixture, and top with pears. Spread a third sheet with the cheese mixture, and place on top of the pears, cheese side down. Press down gently.

- Trim the four edges of the pastry, using a serrated knife, then cut widthwise at 1-inch (25-mm) intervals. Drizzle the sour cream over the top, and garnish with the nuts and a sprig of mint (*see color plate, Croustades, Puffs, and Pastries*).

ASPARAGUS IN PUFF PASTRY, GREENSBORO STYLE

1 sheet puff pastry, 8 × 8 × ⅛ inches (200 × 200 × 4 mm)
2 eggs, beaten
1 cup (240 mL) rémoulade sauce

24 asparagus spears, trimmed to 5 inches (125 mm) and peeled
1 lemon, sliced very thin
4 sprigs parsley

- Preheat an oven to 375° F (190° C).
- Cut the puff pastry in eight 4 × 2 inch (100 × 50 mm) rectangles. Brush with egg wash, place on a baking pan, and bake 10 to 15 minutes, or until golden brown. Remove and set aside.
- Blanch the asparagus in boiling lightly salted water until al dente. Drain and cool.
- Spread a little rémoulade sauce on one side of each of the pastry pieces, and sandwich 6 asparagus spears between every two pieces. Place a dollop of the sauce on top, and garnish with the parsley and two twisted slices of lemon.

SANDWICHES

The sandwich was named after John Montagu, the fourth earl of Sandwich (1718–1792). These edible concoctions were prepared for him so that the inveterate gambler could remain at the gaming table without interruptions for meals. The Bookmaker Canapé described in this section is reportedly the original sandwich ordered by Montagu.

BAYONNE CANAPÉS

Two rectangular pieces of white bread, spread with parsley butter and filled with very thin slices of Bayonne-style ham.

BOOKMAKER CANAPÉS

Two rectangular croutons spread with butter, with a thin slice of rare beef tenderloin, seasoned with prepared mustard and prepared horseradish, placed between them.

CALIFORNIA SANDWICH

8 slices 9-grain bread,
  toasted
½ cup (120 mL) mayonnaise
¾ cup (180 mL) low-fat
  yogurt
12 thin slices Monterey
  Jack cheese
1 large ripe Haas avocado,
  peeled and cut into 16
  wedges

1 cup (240 mL) alfalfa
  sprouts
2 large vine-ripened tomatoes, sliced thin
8 raw carrot sticks
8 raw celery sticks
8 raw cucumber sticks,
  peeled and seeded

- Blend the mayonnaise and yogurt together. Spread on one side of each of the toasted bread slices.
- Divide the remaining ingredients among four slices of bread. Top with the second slice of bread and cut in half. Serve with carrot, celery, and cucumber sticks.

CROQUE MONSIEUR

8 ½-inch (12-mm) thick
  slices fresh white bread
unsalted butter (soft) as
  needed
12 ounces (340 g) Gruyère
  cheese, sliced very thin

12 ounces (340 g) ham,
  sliced very thin
6 eggs, well beaten
2 cups (480 mL) clarified
  butter
8 sprigs watercress

- Preheat an oven to 350° F (176° C).
- Spread a light coating of butter on one side of each slice of bread. Top four slices with 1½ ounces (42 g) of cheese, then 3 ounces (85 g) of ham, followed by 1½ ounces (42 g) of cheese. Place the remaining slices of bread, butter side down, on top of this.
- Trim the crusts from each sandwich, and place into the egg wash for 2 or 3 minutes, coating the bread thoroughly. Wipe off excess egg.
- Place about ½ inch (12 mm) of butter in a heavy-gauge sauté pan or cast-iron skillet, and heat over a medium flame. Sauté the sandwiches in the butter until golden brown on both sides. Transfer to the oven, and bake for 5 minutes. Cut the sandwiches in half, and serve garnished with the watercress and a side dish of cole slaw or another marinated salad.

Although the Croque Monsieur sandwich (as well as the Mozzarella en Carozza and the Reuben Grill) is served hot, it is often prepared in the garde manger and then sent to a hot station for cooking and serving. The word *croque* simply means "crunch," and variations include Croque à la Brandade, made with Brandade de Morue—a paste fashioned from salt cod, oil, garlic, and lemon—and sliced tomato; Croque Jeune-Fille, substituting the ham with sliced chicken breast, and the Gruyère with Gouda; Croque Madame, a Croque Monsieur served with a baked egg on top; Croque Marin, substituting the ham with thinly-sliced shellfish; and Croque Monte Cristo, a triple-decker sandwich made with turkey, ham, and cheese.

217

MOZZARELLA EN CAROZZA

For the Sauce

2 tablespoons (30 mL)
  unsalted butter
½ small tin anchovy fillets,
  minced
2 tablespoons (30 mL) parsley, minced

¼ cup (60 mL) capers,
  drained
juice of 1 lemon

For the Sandwich

1 fat loaf Italian bread
  (minimum 3½ inches/
  90 mm in diameter)
1 pound (450 g) mozzarella
  cheese, sliced ¼-inch
  (6-mm) thick

5 eggs, beaten with ¼ cup
  (60 mL) milk
1 cup (240 mL) milk
dry bread crumbs as needed
vegetable oil as needed

- Combine the sauce ingredients, and simmer for 3 minutes. Set aside, keeping warm.

- Slice the bread into ½-inch (12-mm) thick slices and, using a cookie cutter, cut them into 3-inch (75-mm) circles. Cut the sliced mozzarella into 2½-inch (63-mm) circles.

- Place a slice of cheese between 2 slices of bread. Dip the edges in milk, and pinch together securely. Dip the entire sandwich in the beaten egg, brush off excess egg, then dip the edge in bread crumbs. Refrigerate for a half hour.

- Heat ½-inch (12-mm) deep oil to a temperature of 375° F (190° C). Fry the sandwiches to golden brown on both sides. Place on absorbent paper, and place in the oven until all the sandwiches are fried. Serve accompanied by the anchovy sauce.

PEANUT BUTTER AND JELLY CLUB SANDWICH

12 slices whole wheat
  bread, toasted
unsalted butter as needed
2 cups (480 mL) chunky
  peanut butter
1 cup (240 mL) Zinfandel
  grape jelly

1 large banana, peeled and
  sliced very thin
1 cup (240 mL) low-fat
  yogurt
¾ cup (180 mL) dried cur-
  rants, soaked in hot water
6 green seedless grapes
6 red seedless grapes

1 Granny Smith apple,
cut into 12 wedges and
sprinkled with lemon
juice

8 large sprigs of mint

- Spread one side of the bread lightly with the butter. Spread the peanut butter onto four slices of bread. Top with the jelly, then place another slice of bread, butter side down, on top of this.
- Spread the yogurt on the second slice of bread. Top with the drained currants and the sliced banana. Take the final slice of bread and place on top of the banana, buttered side down.
- Trim the crusts on all four sides. Run a toothpick through a grape, and place four of these into each sandwich. Cut each sandwich into quarters, stand up each quarter on its outside edge, and serve garnished with fresh mint and sliced apple.

REUBEN GRILL

2 slices rye bread
¼ cup (60 mL) Thousand
Island dressing
4 ounces (113 g) corned
beef, sliced

2 slices Swiss cheese
¼ cup (60 mL) sauerkraut
½ cup (120 mL) clarified
butter

- Brush one side of both slices of rye bread with clarified butter. Spread the dressing on the other side. Top one slice with the corned beef, the sauerkraut, and the cheese. Top with the other slice of bread, dressing side down.
- In a sauté pan, or on a hot griddle top, brown the sandwich on both sides in the remaining clarified butter. Place in a preheated 375° F (190° C) oven for 10 minutes. Remove from the oven, cut in half, and serve garnished appropriately.

SPINACH AND CUCUMBER PITA SANDWICH

¼ cup (60 mL) olive oil
6 garlic cloves, pressed
1 bunch spinach, stemmed
and well rinsed
juice of 1 lemon

¼ cup (60 mL) fresh mint,
cut into a fine julienne
12 ounces (340 g) low-fat
plain yogurt

1 small cucumber, peeled,
   seeded, and sliced thin
salt, pepper, and ground
   cumin to taste

4 pitas
¼ cup (60 mL) sesame
   seeds, toasted

- Sauté the garlic briefly in the olive oil, without browning. Set aside.
- Blanch the spinach in a small amount of boiling salted water for several minutes. Drain, squeeze dry, and finely chop.
- Combine the oil, garlic, spinach, lemon juice, mint, yogurt, salt, pepper, and cumin, and blend thoroughly.
- Cut the pitas in half and toast in a moderate oven for 10 minutes. Stuff the pitas with the filling and some of the cucumber, and sprinkle with the sesame seeds.

CHAPTER 6

SALADS AND VEGETABLES

SALADS

A salad is a dish of raw or cooked food items, seasoned and dressed with a sauce. The linguistic origin of the word *salad* comes from the Latin *sal*, meaning "salt," a simple indication of how this food item was seasoned in its early days. A formal body of specific salads is a fairly modern innovation, because even basic salad vegetables such as peppers, potato, tomato, and squash were unknown outside of South America until the sixteenth century. In their most basic form, salads are made up of plant foods (vegetables), and only since the seventeenth century have such a wide variety of cultivated foods been available on a large scale in any given culture.

Salads are divided into the following general categories, although the boundaries between these categories are not absolute:

- *Tossed Green.* For example, Caesar Salad; Salade de Laitue (Lettuce Salad); Tossed Garden Salad, Vinaigrette.
- *Marinated.* For example, Celery Root Rémoulade; Mushrooms à la Greque; Leeks Vinaigrette, Potato/Pasta Salad; Cole Slaw; Waldorf Salad.
- *Composed.* For example, Salade Niçoise; Cobb Salad; Shrimp/Crab Louis; Chef's Salad.

SALAD SAUCES

Salad sauces are derived from two *mother* sauces: vinaigrette and mayonnaise. A true basic vinaigrette, also referred to as *French* dressing, consists of two parts oil, one part vinegar, salt, and pepper. The type of oil used in a salad sauce depends on the dish, as well as the culinary practitioner's style. Olive oil is the most commonly chosen, both for its unique flavor and for its nutritional advantages—it is high in mono-unsaturated acids, which have been found to help regulate both harmful and beneficial cholesterol levels. *Extra virgin* olive oil, the first pressing of the olive, is the strongest in flavor and color (some varieties will coagulate under refrigeration). Because it is strong (and more expensive than other grades), extra virgin is recommended for use in its uncooked state—in salad sauces, drizzled over a finished dish, or as an accompaniment to bread served at the beginning of a meal. Subsequent pressings are lighter, thus better suited for cooking, and are bottled as *virgin* and *pure*. Other oils used in salads include almond, avocado, corn, grape seed, hazelnut, peanut, poppy seed, safflower, sunflower, and walnut.

Vinegar dates back to the early days of the Roman Empire. Diluted with water, it was a common drink among Roman legionnaires. The word *vinaigre,* literally "sour wine," is a combination of *vin* (meaning "wine," from the Latin *vinum*), and *aigre* ("sour," from the Latin *acer,* meaning "sharp"). A vinegar merchants corporation was formed in Orléans in 1394 and became the center of wine production in France. More than sour wine, vinegar is a fermented product requiring nearly as much care as wine fermentation, though less time. White or red wine is fermented in oak barrels, using a "mother," a strain of bacteria that consumes the alcohol in the wine and excretes acetic acid. This fermentation, which requires roughly six months, is followed by a careful filtering of the vinegar, then adjusting the acid content (roughly 6% in the finished product) by adding water and/or wine. The *Orléans method* is the name applied to the careful fermentation process, whereas the *German method* refers to industrially produced vinegar, a short distillation method requiring one to three days. The differences in flavor, character, and aroma between the two, of course, are significant.

Vinaigrette

Basic vinaigrette can be augmented in innumerable ways to create an infinite number of variations. Although specific sauce variations with specific names do exist, there is no limit to innovations. For example, a vinaigrette intended for a salad having an Asian bent may include ginger and oyster sauce; New England-style salad may include dried cranberries; and a salad with a Cajun character may include an abundance of cayenne pepper. Mayonnaise-based sauces may also be varied to complement a vast array of culinary styles. *(For mayonnaise and vinaigrette derivations, see Chapter 2, "Cold Sauces and Marinades.")*

BASIC VINAIGRETTE (FRENCH DRESSING)

1 cup (240 mL) olive oil
⅓ cup (80 mL) red or white
    wine vinegar

⅛ teaspoon (.6 mL) salt
⅛ teaspoon (.6 mL) white
    pepper

- Combine all ingredients in a bowl and blend thoroughly with a wire whip.

EMULSIFIED VINAIGRETTE

3 cups (720 mL) olive oil
1 cup (240 mL) champagne
  vinegar
2 garlic cloves, peeled
1 small shallot, peeled and
  chopped
1 tablespoon (15 mL) Dijon-
  style mustard

½ teaspoon (2.5 mL) salt
¼ teaspoon (1.2 mL) pepper
½ cup (120 mL) parsley
  leaves, well rinsed
½ cup (120 mL) water

- Place all ingredients in a blender and purée. Adjust seasoning with salt and pepper.

Mayonnaise

BASIC MAYONNAISE

3 egg yolks
½ teaspoon (2.5 mL) dry
  mustard
3 tablespoons (45 mL)
  lemon juice

1 pint (480 mL) olive oil
salt and white pepper to
  taste

- Beat the yolks, mustard, and 1 tablespoon (15 mL) of the
  lemon juice in a stainless steel bowl, using a wire whip.
- Add the oil in a slow, steady stream, whipping continuously.
  Alternate the oil with the remaining lemon juice as the
  sauce thickens.
- Season to taste with salt and white pepper.

SELF-SERVICE SALADS

Although there are traditional salads with specific nomencla-
tures, a buffet can also offer a salad bar with one or two varieties of mixed greens and a dozen or more accompaniments,
from which guests can create their own salads. Salad mixes,
depending on price and availability, may include all or some
of the following greens: arugula, butter lettuce, shredded red
or green cabbage, frisée, Joseph's coat, mâche (Danish or
French), olorosa, radicchio, spinach (American, Indian Sum-

mer, Melody, Savoy, Tyee) red and green oak, red and green romaine, Mizuno, Tango, Tat Soy, and so on. Garnishes may include alfalfa sprouts, artichoke hearts, diced avocado, crumbled cooked bacon, beans (black, garbanzo, kidney), pickled beets, broccoli and cauliflower flowerettes, grated Cheddar cheese, crumbled blue or feta cheese, whole kernel corn, seasoned croutons, cucumbers, pickled ginger, julienned jicama, hard-cooked eggs, raw or marinated mushrooms, olives (calamata, nafplion, niçoise, Sicilian), green peas, bell peppers, sliced red onion, scallions, sunflower seeds, cooked shrimp, cherry or sliced tomatoes, sliced zucchini, and so on.

VEGETABLE SALADS

ALBERT SALAD

A mix of chicory, escarole, and romaine lettuces, sprinkled with crisp chopped bacon and minced herbs, seasoned with salt and pepper, and dressed with oil and vinegar.

AMERICAN SALAD

Sliced tomatoes and potatoes on a bed of lettuce, topped with celery and whole kernel corn tossed in emulsified tomato vinaigrette, and garnished with sliced onion rings and hard-boiled egg halves (*see color plate, Contemporary Salads*).

ARIZONA SALAD

1 head butter lettuce
1 heart romaine lettuce, cut into chiffonade
2 Red Bliss potatoes, boiled al dente, peeled, and sliced ¼-inch (6-mm) thick
1 cup (240 mL) scallions, sliced very thin on the bias

1 cup (240 mL) diced tomatoes
3 hard-boiled eggs, quartered
1 cup (240 mL) mayonnaise
¼ cup (60 mL) lemon juice
¼ cup (60 mL) chopped parsley

- Arrange a base of butter lettuce, and top with the romaine. Arrange the potatoes, scallions, and tomatoes on top of this. Blend the mayonnaise and lemon juice together thoroughly, and nap over the salad. Garnish with the eggs and parsley.

BLACKSMITH SALAD

3 pints mesclun salad mix (may include arugula, butter, frisée, limestone, mâche, radicchio, and so on)
1 cup (240 mL) shaved Pecorino cheese

1 cup (240 mL) olive oil
½ cup (120 mL) balsamic vinegar
salt and pepper to taste

- Toss the greens, cheese, oil, and vinegar together. Season to taste with salt and pepper.

CALIFORNIA SALAD

4 butter lettuce hearts, quartered
2 Belgian endive, bottom removed and quartered lengthwise
12 fat asparagus, cut to 4-inch (100-mm) lengths, peeled and blanched al dente

1 large Ruby Red grapefruit, segments separated from skin and seeds
1 orange, peeled, sliced, and seeded
8 sprigs mustard blossoms
1 cup (240 mL) olive oil
½ cup (120 mL) champagne vinegar
salt and pepper to taste

- Arrange a bed of lettuce hearts and two endive quarters, then arrange the remaining salad components on top. Beat oil, vinegar, salt, and pepper, and drizzle over the top.

DAKOTA SALAD

1 head butter lettuce
2 cups (480 mL) cabbage, shredded very thin

½ cup (120 mL) minced parsley, tarragon, and mint

227

½ cup (120 mL) mayonnaise
½ cup (120 mL) sour cream
½ cup (120 mL) low-fat
  yogurt
¼ cup (60 mL) white wine
  vinegar

salt and white pepper to
  taste
½ cup (120 mL) carrot, cut
  into very fine julienne
1 cucumber, peeled, seeded,
  and sliced very thin

- Combine the cabbage, herbs, mayonnaise, sour cream, yogurt, and vinegar and blend thoroughly. Season to taste with salt and white pepper, and allow to marinate 4 hours.
- Prepare a bed of butter lettuce leaves. Top with the cabbage, and garnish with carrot and cucumber.

DANTICHEFF SALAD

Medium-diced celeriac and potatoes bound in lemon mayonnaise and chopped chervil, served in artichoke bottoms, garnished with asparagus tips, sliced truffle, and chopped chervil.

EQUITAINE SALAD

Ripe avocado halves, set on a base of lettuce leaves (or chiffonade), stuffed with sliced figs and kumquats, and dressed lightly with herb mayonnaise thinned with lime juice.

GERTRUDE SALAD

Hearts of endive cut lengthwise in half, set on a base of watercress, topped with mushrooms cut in julienne and tossed in tomato vinaigrette.

GREENSBORO SALAD

1 head green leaf lettuce,
  rinsed and torn into bite-
  size pieces
1 English cucumber, 5
  inches (125 mm) long,
  sliced paper thin

1 cup (240 mL) mush-
  rooms, medium dice
1 cup (240 mL) vidalia
  onions, sliced paper thin
1 cup (240 mL) olive oil
½ cup (120 mL) red wine
  vinegar

2 tablespoons (30 mL)
  chopped parsley
salt and pepper to taste

1 cup (240 mL) feta cheese,
  crumbled

- Beat the olive oil, vinegar, parsley, salt, and pepper together. Pour over the mushrooms and onions, and marinate 1 hour.
- Toss the greens, cucumbers, and marinating mix together. Arrange on chilled plates, and top with the feta.

GUILLAUME SALAD

Diced cooked potatoes and diced artichoke bottoms moistened with paprika vinaigrette, set on a base of watercress, and garnished with thin slices of radish.

HEARTS OF PALM, CARNELIAN

1 head butter lettuce
4 palm hearts
1 grapefruit, sections separated from skin and seeds
1 ripe Haas avocado, peeled, seeded, and cut into 8 wedges, using a serrated knife

8 strips pimento, 2 × ¼ inches (50 × 6 mm)
1 cup (240 mL) olive oil
½ cup (120 mL) champagne vinegar
salt and pepper to taste

- Wash the palm hearts, and cut in half lengthwise. Beat the oil, vinegar, salt, and pepper together, and marinate the palm in this mixture for 1 hour.
- Remove the outer leaves of the butter lettuce, and arrange a bed of lettuce leaves on each of four plates. Place the palm hearts side by side in the center. Place 2 grapefruit sections in the center of the palm halves, and top with a cross of pimento strips. Place two wedges of avocado along the outside of the palm halves, and drizzle with the vinaigrette (*see color plate, Traditional Salads*).

ISABELLA SALAD

¼ cup (60 mL) olive oil
2 cups (480 mL) eggplant, large dice

1 cup (240 mL) red bell pepper, medium dice

229

½ cup (120 mL) dry white wine.

2 cups (480 mL) cooked rice

2 medium zucchini, medium diced and blanched al dente

½ cup (120 mL) cooked lima beans

1 cup (240 mL) diced tomatoes

1 cup (240 mL) cucumber, peeled, seeded, and medium diced

½ cup (120 mL) olive oil

juice of 1 lemon

1 tablespoon (15 mL) chopped oregano

1 tablespoon (15 mL) chopped basil

2 garlic cloves, crushed

salt and pepper to taste

- Sauté the eggplant and pepper in the olive oil, covered, about 5 minutes or until the eggplant is soft. Add the white wine, simmer another few minutes, then remove from the fire, drain, and set aside.

- Beat the oil, lemon juice, herbs, garlic, salt, and pepper together. Combine all ingredients, and adjust the seasoning. Cover and marinate overnight before serving.

JASPER SALAD

3 medium pears, ripe, but firm

pinch of salt

black pepper to taste

2 teaspoons (10 mL) sugar

¼ cup (60 mL) champagne vinegar

¼ cup (60 mL) peanut oil

2 cups (480 mL) celeriac, cut into fine julienne

juice of 2 lemons

3 tablespoons (45 mL) mayonnaise

2 tablespoons (30 mL) champagne vinegar

salt and white pepper to taste

1 large (or 2 small) head red leaf lettuce, rinsed, dried, and torn into bite-size pieces

- Peel and core the pears. Toss with the salt, pepper, sugar, ¼ cup (60 mL) of vinegar, and oil, and marinate 1 hour, refrigerated.

- Pour the lemon juice and 2 cups (480 mL) of boiling water over the celeriac. Allow to sit 10 minutes, then drain and cool.

- Add the mayonnaise, 2 tablespoons (30 mL) of vinegar, salt, and pepper to the celeriac, and blend thoroughly.

- Drain the liquid from the pears onto the lettuce, and toss. Arrange the lettuce on each of four plates. Top with the pears and the celeriac.

JERSEY SALAD

1 head romaine lettuce
1 head escarole
1 cucumber, peeled, seeded, and cut into fine julienne
1 green bell pepper, cut into fine julienne
4 scallions, cut into fine julienne

4 large radishes, sliced paper thin
12 calamata olives
1 cup (240 mL) emulsified vinaigrette
½ cup (120 mL) ketchup

- Discard the outer leaves of both lettuces. Separate the romaine into very large leaves and the escarole into smaller pieces, rinse, dry, and chill. Prepare a base of romaine leaves, and arrange the escarole on top.

- Blend the vinaigrette and ketchup together, and add enough to the cucumber, bell pepper, and scallions to lightly coat. Place these vegetables in the center of the lettuce, garnish with radishes and olives, and drizzle additional sauce as needed.

KENTUCKY SALAD

Hollowed-out green bell peppers filled with grapefruit, diced apple, and walnuts, bound lightly with mayonnaise.

MATHILDE SALAD

Sliced avocado, apple, and cucumber, arranged on a bed of romaine lettuce, garnished with toasted chopped walnuts, accompanied by a sauce of mayonnaise thinned with lemon juice, and blanched lemon zest added.

PRETTY HELEN SALAD

A mound of blanched celery root cut into julienne, bound with a little mayonnaise, surrounded by a circle of baked beets sliced and cut into crescents, slices of calamata olives, sprinkled with toasted walnuts, and garnished with watercress or parsley (see color plate, *Traditional Salads*).

RICHMOND SALAD

1 small head romaine lettuce
1 heart of escarole
1 heart of butter lettuce
1 cup (240 mL) string
  beans, frenched,
  blanched al dente
1 large beet, boiled in the
  skin until tender, peeled,
  and sliced ⅛-inch (3-mm)
  thick

3 hard-boiled eggs, whites
  minced and yolks sieved
½ cup (120 mL) scallions,
  sliced paper thin
1 cup (240 mL) olive oil
½ cup (120 mL) red wine
  vinegar
salt and pepper to taste

- Tear the greens into bite-size pieces. Rinse, drain, and chill.
- Arrange the lettuce in a bed. Toss the string beans and sliced beets in the oil, vinegar, salt, and pepper, and place on top of the lettuce. Garnish with the eggs and scallion.

Note: *Frenching* string beans refers to cutting them lengthwise into 2 or 3 pieces.

ROYAL SALAD

Sliced tomato set on a bed of romaine and watercress, garnished with celery julienne tossed in basic vinaigrette.

SERENA SALAD

Sliced avocado and tomato set on a bed of romaine, garnished with celery julienne, and drizzled with mayonnaise thinned with cream and tinted with paprika.

SOUTHERN CROSS SALAD

1 head romaine lettuce
2 Belgian endives
1 bunch watercress
1 ripe Haas avocado
4 palm hearts

1 cup (240 mL) olive oil
½ cup (120 mL) white wine
  vinegar
salt and pepper to taste

- Remove the outer leaves of the romaine and discard (or save for Cream of Lettuce Soup). Cut the remaining lettuce into ½-inch (12-mm) pieces. Remove and discard the bottoms of the endives, and cut the leaves into ½-inch pieces. Remove the leaves of the watercress. Wash all the three varieties of in cold water, drain, and chill.

- Peel the avocado, and cut into 12 wedges.

- Rinse the palm hearts well, and drain. Cut in quarters lengthwise.

- Toss the romaine, endive, and watercress in the oil and vinegar, and season with salt and pepper. Arrange on four individual chilled plates. Place the palm hearts in the center of the base, and garnish with the wedges of avocado. Drizzle with additional oil and vinegar, and top with freshly ground pepper.

TABBOULEH

2 cups (480 mL) bulgur wheat
3 bunches parsley, leaves only, rinsed, and minced
1 bunch mint, leaves only, rinsed, and minced

2 large vine-ripened tomatoes, peeled, seeded, and diced
½ cup (120 mL) olive oil
½ cup (120 mL) lemon juice
salt and white pepper to taste

- Cover the wheat with 2 quarts cold water and allow to soak 3 hours. Drain, and add the remaining ingredients. Marinate overnight, refrigerated. Serve with roasted pita bread wedges (*see color plate, Vegetable Pâté en Croûte*).

Note: Reserve the parsley and mint stems for use in stock, sauce, or soup.

THERESA SALAD

Celery, apples, and cooked potatoes, cut into julienne, set on a bed of romaine lettuce, and drizzled with mayonnaise thinned with cream.

TRIANON SALAD

Sliced, drained pickled beets on a bed of lettuce chiffonade, topped with orange segments, drizzled with Lorenzo vinaigrette (oil, vinegar, ketchup, and minced hard-cooked eggs), and garnished with toasted chopped walnuts (*see Figure 6.1*).

VALENTINA SALAD

An arrangement of sliced, poached leek and sliced hearts of palm on a bed of green leaf lettuce, Belgian endive, and radicchio leaves, garnished with baby corn, enoki mushrooms, and tomato wedges; oil and vinegar served separately (*see color plate, Contemporary Salads*).

SALADS WITH FISH

There are more than 20,000 known varieties of fish—the oldest living vertebrates on earth, as well as the earliest source of human food, second in importance to cereals (grains and rice). They are an excellent source of protein in the human diet, and rich in minerals: phosphorus, magnesium, copper,

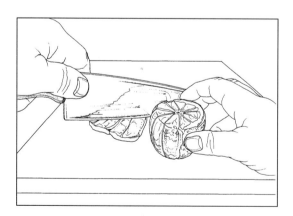

Slice and remove the ends of an orange (lime, lemon, or grapefruit). Slice and remove the skin and pith.

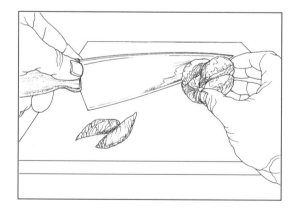

Remove the segments by cutting between the membranes that separate the segments. (Squeeze and reserve the juice from the remaining membranes.)

Figure 6.1
Cutting Segments from Citrus Fruit

iron, iodine, and B-complex vitamins. *Oily* fish also contain vitamins A and D; eel ranks highest in fat content (26%), followed by moray and lamprey (13–17%), tuna (6–12%), and salmon (8–12%). *Semi-oily* fish, which contain 4–10% fat, include herring, mackerel, sardine, and trout. *Lean fish*, with 0.5–4% fat, include the cod species (haddock, hake, pollack, and whiting), flatfish (dab, flounder, and sole), and bass (sea bass, mullet, perch, and skate).

Before modern forms of transport and processing, fish was preserved by drying, smoking, or salting. In our time, however, with a worldwide commercial harvest estimated at 70 million tons per annum, fresh fish is more widely available in more locales and at more times of the year. Still, when selecting fish to buy, freshness is most important and can be determined by the following criteria:

- *Odor.* Fresh and mild, not overfishy
- *Head.* Clear, bulging eyes; pink, slime-free gills
- *Body.* Firm and slightly resilient to the touch
- *Skin.* Slightly moist, slimy, and shiny

Although the availability of fish has increased, its future as a source of food is in jeopardy. The bays, lakes, oceans, and rivers of the world continue to be polluted with garbage and industrial waste; modern deep-sea trawlers, which carry their own processing plants on board, overfish in international waters; and modern engineering projects, such as draining marshes for housing developments, and damming up and changing the flow of rivers, alter an often delicate ecosystem, spelling disaster for the fish and shellfish living in these waters. The effect of these human endeavors is to diminish and often eliminate valuable species. We believe that an awareness and understanding of these problems can lead to solutions. Because culinarians are significant users of raw materials, including fish, they are in a key position to make choices in menu design that will benefit all.

AVOCADO GOURMET SALAD

1 head romaine lettuce	½ cup (120 mL) mayonnaise
2 ripe Haas avocados	½ cup (120 mL) Dijon-style
2 cups (480 mL) titi shrimp	mustard
1 large ripe tomato, cored and cut into 8 wedges	¼ cup (120 mL) half-and-half cream
8 parsley sprigs	

- Remove the outer leaves of the lettuce, remove the core, and cut the remaining lettuce into chiffonade.
- Cut the avocados in half, and remove peel and seed.
- Blend the mayonnaise, mustard, and cream until smooth.
- Place a bed of lettuce on each of 4 chilled plates. Press the shrimp into a 4-ounce (113-g) scoop, and place on top of the cut side of each avocado half. Place the avocados on the bed of lettuce. Garnish with 2 tomato wedges, nap the shrimp with the sauce, and garnish with parsley.

BANKER'S WELCOME SALAD

2 celery hearts, 4 inches (100 mm) long
1 cup (240 mL) white wine vinegar
1 cup (240 mL) dry white wine
2 cups (480 mL) water
1 bay leaf
1 teaspoon (5 mL) salt
1 teaspoon (5 mL) peppercorns
1 ripe tomato, cut into 8 wedges

½ ripe Haas avocado, peeled, cut widthwise using a serrated knife
1 cup (240 mL) titi shrimp
12 Dungeness crab claws, shells removed
8 parsley sprigs
1 cup (240 mL) olive oil
½ cup (120 mL) white wine vinegar
salt and pepper to taste

- Poach the celery hearts in the vinegar, wine, water, bay leaf, salt, and pepper until tender. Remove from the fire, and allow to cool.
- Place the chilled celery hearts in the center of each of 4 chilled plates. Arrange the tomato, avocado, shrimp, and crab in individual arrangements around the celery and garnish with the parsley. Beat the vinaigrette together, and drizzle over the salad.

CAESAR SALAD

1 garlic clove, crushed
3 garlic cloves, pressed
1 teaspoon (5 mL) Dijon-style mustard
4 anchovy fillets

juice of half a lemon
2 tablespoons (30 mL) wine vinegar
1 teaspoon (5 mL) white Worcestershire sauce

pinch of salt
pinch of pepper
1 large egg, immersed in a
    cup of warm water (cod-
    dled)
1 cup (240 mL) olive oil

1 large head romaine let-
    tuce
1 cup (240 mL) garlic crou-
    tons
½ cup (120 mL) grated
    Parmesan cheese

- Remove the exterior leaves of the romaine; cut and remove the base. Split the remaining leaves lengthwise, then cut into 1-inch (25-mm) pieces. Rinse well in cold water, drain, dry, and chill.
- Rub the interior of a wooden salad bowl with the crushed garlic clove. Discard.
- Place the pressed garlic, mustard, anchovy, lemon juice, Worcestershire, salt, and pepper into the bowl. Mash thoroughly, using the tines of a fork. Crack the egg, discard the white, and add the yolk to this mixture. Add the olive oil in a slow, steady stream, and blend thoroughly. Add the vinegar and blend.
- Add the romaine, croutons, and cheese, and toss thoroughly. Transfer to serving plates, and top with fresh ground black pepper.

CAFÉ ANGLAIS SALAD

Sliced morels blanched in white wine, drained and cooled, and poached shrimp bound in mayonnaise, served on a bed of lettuce, and garnished with shaved truffle.

DUNGENESS CRAB COCKTAIL, CALIFORNIA STYLE

Drop the crab into boiling salted water, return to a boil, cover, remove from the fire, and allow to sit 20 minutes. Remove the crab from the water, and when cool enough, separate the claws and legs of the creature and crack with the heel of a knife. Tear off the top shell, and save (scrape off the furry part on the underside of the shell, boil the shell in water with a little vinegar, and save for serving *Crab Cardinale*). Cut the body into 6 pieces, and serve all with mustard mayonnaise, parsley, and lobster forks (for removing the meat).

The Café Anglais was originally established in Paris in 1802, named in honor of the peace treaty of Amiens between England and France. In 1822, Paul Chevreuil purchased the café and made it into a very fashionable restaurant. Adolphe Dugléré (1805–1884) took over the kitchens in 1866 and brought it to the gastronomic heights that made it one of the most enduring establishments until the early twentieth century. His Dinner for Three Emperors was served to Russian Emperor Alexander II; his son, Alexander III; Wilhelm I, emperor of Prussia; and Otto Von Bismarck, chancellor of Germany. It remains an excellent example of the style of haute cuisine of that era. Among the dishes Dugléré created, which remain well known today, were *Anna Potatoes, Filet de Sole Dugléré,* and *Soufflé à l'Anglaise.*

237

DUMAS SALAD

Mussels poached in white wine, served on a bed of diced potatoes dressed with simple vinaigrette, and garnished with truffle.

DUTCH SALAD

Flaked cooked salmon, diced potatoes, and sliced (or diced) gherkins on a bed of lettuce, garnished with hard-boiled eggs and asparagus, seasoned with oil and lemon juice, and sometimes garnished with a little caviar (*see color plate, Traditional Salads*).

EMPIRE SALAD

A composed salad consisting of sliced poached sturgeon, sliced tomatoes and cucumbers, green beans, cauliflower flowerettes, diced artichoke bottoms, green peas, asparagus tips, dressed with a simple vinaigrette.

ESCABECIA

12 whole small fish (such as smelt, herring, anchovy)
salt, pepper, flour, and vegetable oil to taste
1 cup (240 mL) olive oil
½ cup (120 mL) lime juice
¼ cup (60 mL) orange juice
1 small carrot, peeled, trimmed, and sliced thin on the bias

1 small onion, peeled and sliced thin widthwise
2 garlic cloves, crushed
1 bay leaf
2 sprigs dill
1 bunch parsley stems, trimmed and rinsed
¼ cup (60 mL) cilantro leaves, roughly chopped
1 tablespoon (15 mL) black peppercorns

- Season the fish with salt and pepper, dust with flour, and sauté in the oil until golden brown. Transfer to absorbent paper, then place in a glass bowl.
- Bring the remaining ingredients to a boil, and pour over the fish. Marinate for 24 hours, and serve chilled on a bed of lettuce leaves or chiffonade.

Another sauce that can be served with chilled shellfish (clams, crab, lobster, mussels, or oysters) is *Raspberry Mignonette:* 1 cup (240 mL) raspberry vinegar, ¼ cup (60 mL) dry white wine, 1 teaspoon (5 mL) coarsely ground black pepper, 1 shallot minced, 1 teaspoon (5 mL) minced basil leaves, and salt to taste.

GRAND DUCHESS SALAD

Mixed diced vegetable salad bound in a simple vinaigrette, garnished with strips of poached sole fillet, shrimp, anchovies, and cucumbers.

LOBSTER COCKTAIL

For the Cocktail

2 1½-pound (680-g) lobsters
8 fat asparagus

8 butter lettuce leaves

For the Sauce

½ cup (120 mL) onion, coarsely chopped
2 garlic cloves
1 tablespoon (15 mL) apple juice concentrate
1 cup (240 mL) ketchup
1 tablespoon (15 mL) tomato paste
juice of 2 lemons

2 tablespoons (30 mL) white Worcestershire sauce
2 tablespoons (30 mL) champagne vinegar
¼ cup (60 mL) prepared horseradish
salt and cayenne pepper to taste

- Purée all of the sauce ingredients in a food processor or blender. Refrigerate until ready to serve.
- Drop the lobsters into boiling salted water, return to a boil, cover, remove from the fire, and allow to sit 20 minutes. Remove the lobsters, and when cool enough to handle, remove the claw and tail meat (reserve the bodies for use in other dishes).
- Arrange the lettuce in four champagne saucers. Divide the lobster meat among the glasses, top with some of the sauce, and garnish with asparagus and 2 slices of lemon (*see color plate, Hors d'Oeuvres, Greek Style*).

LOBSTER SALAD, EAST BAY LODGE

2 1½-pound (680-g) live lobsters
16 asparagus spears
½ cup (120 mL) scallions, finely sliced

½ cup (120 mL) celery, small dice
½ cup (120 mL) leeks, cut in small dice and cooked in boiling salted water until tender

juice of 3 lemons
1 cup (240 mL) mayonnaise
¼ cup (60 mL) chili sauce
2 tablespoons (30 mL) prepared horseradish,
squeezed dry
2 tablespoons (30 mL)
minced tarragon
2 tablespoons (30 mL)
minced parsley

salt and white pepper as
needed
1 head butter lettuce, rinsed
and separated into leaves
4 hard-boiled eggs, cut in
quarters lengthwise
12 golden cherry tomatoes
4 sprigs flat-leaf parsley

- Immerse the lobsters in boiling water. Bring to a full boil, cover, remove from the fire, and allow to sit 20 minutes.
- Remove the top 2 inches (50 mm) of each asparagus spear, peel, and set aside. Cut the remaining stalks into ¼-inch (6-mm) pieces, only as far as the beginning of the woody part of the spear. Blanch the asparagus, spears and dice, in boiling salted water, until al dente. Drain and set aside.
- Remove the lobsters and drain. Crack the shells, arms, and tails, and remove the meat. Cut this into ¼-inch (6-mm) dice.
- Combine all the ingredients, except the asparagus spears, eggs, tomatoes, and parsley sprigs, and blend thoroughly. Season to taste with salt and white pepper.
- Arrange a base of lettuce leaves on four chilled plates. Divide the salad among the four plates. Garnish with the asparagus spears, egg quarters, tomatoes, and parsley.

MARYLAND SALAD

1 head butter lettuce
1 cup (240 mL) crab meat
claws, shell off
1 cup (240 mL) 20–24 count
cooked shrimp, split
lengthwise

1 cup (240 mL) diced
tomatoes
1 cup (240 mL) green bell
pepper, cut into fine julienne (1 inch/25 mm)
1½ cups (360 mL) Thousand
Island dressing

- Arrange a base of butter lettuce, top with the crab, shrimp, tomatoes, and green peppers, and nap with the dressing.

MONACO SALAD

A bed of sliced potatoes, topped with flaked poached white-fish, garnished with diced artichoke bottoms and tomatoes, and niçoise olives, dressed with mustard-anchovy vinaigrette.

240

MUSHROOM SALAD, GOURMET STYLE

1 cup (240 mL) olive oil
½ cup (120 mL) white wine vinegar
salt and pepper to taste
1 cup (240 mL) crimini mushrooms, washed and sliced
1 cup (240 mL) oyster mushrooms, medium diced
1 cup (240 mL) chanterelles, washed and medium diced
12 artichoke hearts, blanched and halved
1 cup (240 mL) celery, cut into fine julienne
4 Roma tomatoes, cored and quartered

16 24–30 count shrimp, peeled, deveined, and poached
1 head butter lettuce, rinsed and leaves separated
2 radicchio leaf cups
1 cup (240 mL) mayonnaise
juice of 2 lemons
1 tablespoon (15 mL) minced parsley
1 tablespoon (15 mL) minced tarragon
1 tablespoon (15 mL) minced cilantro
1 tablespoon (15 mL) minced chives

- Whip the oil, vinegar, salt, and pepper together, add the mushrooms, and marinate 1 hour.
- Combine the mayonnaise, lemon juice, and herbs, and blend.
- Place a bed of lettuce on 4 individual serving plates. Drain the mushrooms, and place in the center of the lettuce inside a radicchio cup. Arrange the artichokes, celery, tomatoes, and shrimp around the mushrooms, in concentric circles, and serve with a side of the herb mayonnaise.

NIÇOISE SALAD

Poached or grilled tuna fish, on a bed of sliced boiled potatoes, blanched string beans, and capers tossed in basic vinaigrette with garlic, garnished with tomato wedges, sliced or wedged hard-cooked eggs, anchovy fillets, and black Nice olives, with a little vinaigrette drizzled on top.

PARISIAN SALAD

A half tomato, topped with a slice of hard-boiled egg, topped with a dollop of mayonnaise, garnished with cooked string beans, some peas and carrots blanched and tossed in a little vinaigrette, a heart of butter lettuce, and a little cooked diced lobster (*see color plate, Traditional Salads*).

ROMAN RICE SALAD

1½ cups (360 mL) long grain white rice

2½ cups (600 mL) water

1 cup (240 mL) white navy beans, soaked in water overnight

1 tablespoon (15 mL) chopped basil leaves

1 tablespoon (15 mL) chopped marjoram leaves

2 tablespoons (30 mL) chopped parsley

½ cup (120 mL) dried bread crumbs

4 garlic cloves

1 teaspoon (5 mL) red chili pepper flakes

1 cup (240 mL) olive oil

½ cup (120 mL) red wine vinegar

1 head butter lettuce

12 green olives

12 anchovy fillets

- Cook the rice in the water until all the water has been absorbed. Boil the beans in 1 quart (960 mL) water until tender (about 1 hour). Drain the beans and blend with the rice, along with the bread crumbs and the herbs.

- Combine the garlic, pepper flakes, oil, and vinegar in a blender, and purée. Pour this over the rice, and blend. Season to taste with salt.

- Serve the rice on a bed of lettuce leaves, garnished with green olives wrapped with anchovy.

RUSSIAN SALAD

A mixture of various vegetables and meats, cut in a uniform medium dice (macédoine), lightly bound with mayonnaise, and served alone on a bed of lettuce as a salad dish, stuffed into hollowed-out tomatoes, or in conjunction with numerous dishes "Russian style." There are no strict guidelines on the exact ingredients, but they typically include artichoke bottoms, carrots, green beans, mushrooms, peas, potatoes, and turnips. The meat ingredient consists of ham and tongue, and the salad is garnished with anchovies, cooked beets (set in place at the last minute to avoid bleeding), capers, hard-cooked eggs, and caviar.

SACHA SALAD

1 head butter lettuce, rinsed and separated into leaves
12 1-ounce (28-g) slices fresh salmon
1 English cucumber, 3 inches (75 mm) long, sliced very thin
1 cup (240 mL) snow peas, ends trimmed, blanched briefly in boiling salted water
1 cup (240 mL) olive oil
¼ cup (60 mL) red wine vinegar
¼ cup (60 mL) lemon juice

salt and white pepper to taste
½ cup (120 mL) carrots, cut into ¼-inch (6-mm) spheres (using a small noisette scoop), and blanched al dente
½ cup (120 mL) garbanzo beans, cooked
½ cup (120 mL) fresh green peas, blanched briefly in boiling salted water
½ cup (120 mL) sunflower seeds, toasted
½ cup (120 mL) ¼-inch (6-mm) square croutons

- Season the salmon with salt and pepper, and grill or sauté briefly on both sides. Set aside.
- Beat the oil, vinegar, lemon, salt, and pepper together. Pour over the carrots and beans, and marinate 1 hour.
- Arrange a bed of lettuce on each of four chilled serving plates. Arrange the fresh salmon, cucumber, snow peas, carrots, and beans on top of the lettuce in individual sections. Top with the green peas, sunflower seeds, and croutons.

SALMON TARTAR, GARNI

1 pound (450 g) fresh salmon fillet, boneless and skinless
¼ cup (120 mL) olive oil
1 shallot, minced
1 garlic clove, pressed
1 anchovy fillet, minced
1 teaspoon (5 mL) capers
2 tablespoons (30 mL) lemon juice
1 tablespoon (15 mL) minced dill

½ teaspoon (2.5 mL) green peppercorns, mashed
8 radicchio leaves
1 lemon, cut into 8 wedges, seeds removed
¼ cup (120 mL) salmon caviar
4 scallions, sliced very thin
4 sprigs flat-leaf parsley
1 small brioche, sliced ¼-inch (6-mm) thick, and toasted

- Mince the salmon very fine. Add the oil, shallot, garlic, anchovy, capers, lemon juice, dill, and mashed peppercorns, and blend. Refrigerate for 2 hours.

- Shape the tartar into four individual round or oval portions, and serve on a bed of radicchio. Garnish with lemon, caviar, scallion, parsley, and brioche.

SEVICHE, PACIFIC COAST STYLE

1 pound (450 g) sea scallops
¼ cup (120 mL) lime juice
2 tablespoons (30 mL)
  lemon juice
4 blood oranges
¼ cup (120 mL) red bell
  pepper, medium dice
¼ cup (120 mL) green bell
  pepper, medium dice
1 green jalapeño pepper,
  minced

¼ cup (120 mL) red onion,
  sliced paper thin
2 tablespoons (30 mL)
  cilantro leaves, minced
salt and white pepper to
  taste
8 butter lettuce leaves
3 tablespoons (45 mL)
  chives, minced

A blood orange is a small, sweet variety of orange with a rough-textured skin and bright red flesh and juice.

- Slice the scallops widthwise into three rounds each, and marinate in the lemon and lime juice overnight.
- Peel the blood oranges, and separate the segments from between the skin. Squeeze out the juice from the remaining pulp. Drain the scallops, and combine with the orange segments, orange juice, bell peppers, jalapeños, onion, and cilantro. Season to taste with salt and pepper. Marinate 2 hours, then arrange on the lettuce leaves, and top with the chopped chives (*see Figure 6.1*).

SHRIMP IN BEER

1 pound (450 g) 12–16
  count shrimp, shells on
2 bottles beer
1 to 2 cups (240 to 480 mL)
  water
1 teaspoon (5 mL) salt
2 garlic cloves, crushed
1 small onion, thinly sliced
1 bay leaf
½ cup (120 mL) olive oil

½ cup (120 mL) champagne
  vinegar
½ cup (120 mL) beer
1 shallot, minced
salt, pepper, and Tabasco to
  taste
1 cup (240 mL) mayonnaise
1 tablespoon (15 mL) curry
  powder

1 tablespoon (15 mL) lemon juice
2 tablespoons (30 mL) water

1 head butter lettuce
6 sprigs parsley
1 lemon, cut into 8 wedges

- Combine the shrimp, 2 bottles of beer, 1 to 2 cups (240 to 480 mL) of water, 1 teaspoon (5 mL) of salt, garlic, onion, and bay leaf in a saucepan. Bring to a boil, then turn off and allow to sit 30 minutes. Drain, reserving the shrimp. Peel, devein, and set aside.

- Combine the oil, vinegar, ½ cup (120 mL) beer, shallot, salt, pepper, and Tabasco in a bowl, and blend. Add the shrimp, and marinate refrigerated for 3 hours.

- Combine the curry, lemon juice, and 2 tablespoons (30 mL) of water, and blend into a smooth paste. Add to the mayonnaise, and blend thoroughly.

- Serve the shrimp on lettuce leaves, with the curry mayonnaise on the side, and garnish with parsley and lemon wedges.

SHRIMP DORIA STYLE

For the Shrimp Salad
½ pound (227 g) shrimp meat, ¼-inch (6-mm) dice
¼ cup (120 mL) scallions, finely sliced
¼ cup (120 mL) celery, small dice
¼ cup (120 mL) leeks, cut in small dice and cooked in boiling salted water until tender
juice of 2 lemons
¾ cup (180 mL) mayonnaise

¼ cup (60 mL) chili sauce (or ketchup)
2 tablespoons (30 mL) prepared horseradish, squeezed dry
1 tablespoon (15 mL) minced tarragon
1 tablespoon (15 mL) minced parsley
salt and white pepper to taste
4 large ripe tomatoes

For the Cucumbers
one-half hothouse cucumber, sliced very thin
½ cup (120 mL) olive oil
¼ cup (60 mL) champagne vinegar

1 shallot, minced
1 tablespoon (15 mL) dill, minced
salt and pepper to taste

- Combine all of the salad ingredients, blend thoroughly, and season to taste with salt and white pepper. Cover and refrigerate.
- Combine the oil, vinegar, shallot, dill, salt, and pepper, and blend thoroughly. Pour over the cucumber, and marinate for several hours.
- Remove the core and a slice from the bottom of each tomato. Cut in half widthwise, and scoop out the interior (save for another use). Fill the tomatoes with the salad, and garnish with the marinated cucumber.

SHRIMP MODERN STYLE

Blend medium-diced cooked shrimp and mayonnaise together, and season with salt and white pepper. Line champagne saucers with a bed of lettuce, top with the shrimp salad, and garnish with a whole shrimp, sliced hard-boiled egg, and sliced lemon.

SMOKED SALMON SALAD, LAS VEGAS STYLE

An arrangement of thin-sliced smoked salmon, garnished with boiled carrot slices, croutons, sliced boiled eggs, scallions, Belgian endive, and cream cheese balls (*see color plate, Contemporary Salads*).

SQUID SALAD, CAPRI STYLE

½ cup (120 mL) scallion, very finely sliced

¼ cup (120 mL) celery, medium dice

¼ cup (120 mL) carrot, medium dice

¼ cup (120 mL) red bell pepper, medium dice

1½ cups (360 mL) olive oil

½ cup (120 mL) lemon juice

2 tablespoons (30 mL) water

6 garlic cloves, pressed

2 tablespoons (30 mL) basil, minced

salt and white pepper to taste

1 pound (450 g) squid

1 bunch curly endive

2 lemons, cut into 8 wedges each

- Blanch the diced carrot in boiling salted water for several minutes, until tender but firm.

- Remove the cartilage from the squid body, and the inner part of the tentacles. Slice the body into ¼-inch (6-mm) thick slices, and cut the tentacles into ½-inch (12-mm) pieces. Blanch in boiling salted water, with a little white wine, until fully cooked. Drain, cool, and set aside.
- Beat the olive oil, lemon juice, water, garlic, basil, salt, and pepper in a bowl.
- Marinate the squid and vegetables in the marinade, and refrigerate overnight.
- Cut the endive into 1-inch (25-mm) pieces, and arrange as a bed on one large plate or on 4 individual serving plates. Place the marinated salad on top, and garnish with lemon wedges.

TARPON SPRINGS GREEK SALAD

For the Hummus

1 cup (240 mL) garbanzo beans, soaked in water overnight

1 cup (240 mL) sesame tahini

6 garlic cloves, pressed

½ cup (120 mL) olive oil

1 teaspoon (5 mL) salt

¼ teaspoon (1.2 mL) white pepper

For the Salad

1 head iceberg lettuce

2 cups potatoes, sliced ¼-inch (6-mm) thick, and boiled al dente

2 ripe tomatoes, cored and cut into 6 wedges each

1 cucumber, peeled, seeded, and cut into large julienne

1 ripe Haas avocado, cut into 8 wedges

1 cup (240 mL) feta cheese, crumbled

1 green bell pepper, cut into rings

1 medium beet, boiled skin on, until tender

4 anchovy fillets

12 calamata olives

4 scallions, cut into 2-inch (50-mm) lengths, and quartered lengthwise

1½ cups (360 mL) olive oil

¾ cup (180 mL) white wine vinegar

salt and pepper to taste

To Prepare the Hummus

- Boil the beans in 2 quarts (2 L) lightly salted water until tender. Drain and cool.
- Place the beans and remaining ingredients into a food processor and purée. Adjust seasoning with salt and pepper.

To Prepare the Salad

- Remove the outer leaves of the lettuce, and arrange in a bed on a large platter. Cut the remaining lettuce into chiffonade, and place this on top of the bed. Arrange the remaining ingredients (including the hummus), in individual sections, on top of the lettuce. Drizzle with oil and vinegar, and season with salt and pepper.

TUNA AND GRILLED EGGPLANT SALAD, PACIFIC RIM STYLE

8 1-ounce (28-g) slices ahi tuna

2 tablespoons (30 mL) sesame oil

¼ cup (120 mL) rice wine vinegar

¼ cup (120 mL) soy sauce

3 dried red Thai chili peppers, coarsely chopped

¼ cup (120 mL) lemon grass, minced

4 Japanese eggplants

peanut oil, salt, and pepper as needed

2 cups (480 mL) daikon radish, peeled and cut into long ¹⁄₁₆-inch (2-mm) strands

½ cup minced cilantro leaves

- Combine the oil, vinegar, soy sauce, peppers, and lemon grass, and blend well. Coat the slices of tuna, and marinate 3 hours.
- Cut the eggplant into ¼-inch (6-mm) thick slices, on a *very sharp* bias. Brush with peanut oil, sprinkle with salt and pepper, and grill or sauté until golden brown.
- Arrange a bed of the daikon strands on each of four individual plates. Arrange the eggplant slices around this bed, top with two slices of tuna, and sprinkle with the chopped cilantro.

SALADS WITH POULTRY

AMAGANSETT DUCK SALAD, CORNBREAD CROUTONS

4 boneless duck breasts (preferably Long Island duck)

¼ teaspoon (1.2 mL) parsley, finely minced

¼ teaspoon (1.2 mL) ground sage

¼ teaspoon (1.2 mL) ground thyme

¼ teaspoon (1.2 mL) cayenne

¼ teaspoon (1.2 mL) cumin

¼ teaspoon (1.2 mL) paprika

¼ teaspoon (1.2 mL) black pepper

2 tablespoons (30 mL) vegetable oil

1 cup (240 mL) stale cornbread, cut into ¼-inch cubes, toasted until brown and crispy

1 bunch arugula

1 head green leaf lettuce

1 head curly endive

¾ cup (180 mL) olive oil

¼ cup (60 mL) red wine vinegar

½ teaspoon (2.5 mL) Dijonstyle mustard

salt and pepper to taste

- Preheat an oven to 375° F (190° C).
- Combine the herbs and spices, and dredge the duck breasts in the mixture. Heat the vegetable oil in a hot sauté pan and brown the breasts on both sides. Place on a baking sheet and roast for 8 minutes.
- Tear the greens into bite-size pieces, rinse well, drain, and pat dry.
- Combine the olive oil, vinegar, mustard, salt, and pepper, and blend well. Toss the greens in this vinaigrette, and arrange on individual serving plates. Cut the duck breasts very thin across the grain, on an angle, place on top of the greens, and top with the cornbread croutons.

BAGRATION SALAD

Two artichoke bottoms filled with blanched celery and ditalini (or other small pasta) cooked al dente, bound with a little mayonnaise, accompanied by sliced poached chicken breast, garnished with hard-boiled eggs and watercress or parsley, drizzled with mayonnaise thinned with a little vinegar or lemon juice (*see color plate, Traditional Salads*).

CALIFORNIA GRILLED CHICKEN AND ARUGULA SALAD

12 chicken tenderloins, trimmed of connecting membranes

salt, pepper, and olive oil as needed

5 ounces (142 g) goat cheese

1 tablespoon (15 mL)
  minced parsley
1 tablespoon (15 mL)
  minced tarragon
1 tablespoon (15 mL)
  minced cilantro
8 slices of baguette, toasted
1 shallot, minced

1 cup (240 mL) orange juice
½ cup (120 mL) basalmic
  vinegar
2 tablespoons (30 mL)
  chicken glaze
2 bunches arugula, rinsed
  and dried, and stems
  trimmed

- Preheat an oven to 375° F (190° C).

- Coat the tenderloins lightly with olive oil, and season with salt and pepper. Place in a hot sauté pan, brown lightly on both sides, and place in the oven for 5 minutes. Remove and set aside.

- Mash the goat cheese with the herbs until smooth. Spread on the toasted baguette slices, and set aside.

- Simmer the shallot, orange juice, and vinegar until reduced by half. Add the chicken glaze, blend thoroughly, and set aside to cool.

- Divide the arugula among four serving plates. Slice the tenderloins on the bias into four pieces each, and arrange on top of the arugula. Drizzle the warm sauce over the salad, and garnish with the baguette slices (*see color plate, Contemporary Salads*).

CHICKEN SALAD, MEDITERRANEAN STYLE

2 6-ounce chicken breasts, boneless and skinless

For Poaching the Chicken

1 cup (240 mL) dry white
  wine
1 cup (240 mL) water
1 small onion, quartered

2 garlic cloves, crushed
2 sprigs thyme
1 bay leaf
salt and pepper to taste

For the Salad

1 cup (240 mL) string
  beans, ends trimmed, cut
  in half, and split
½ cup (120 mL) finely
  grated celery root

¼ cup (60 mL) capers,
  drained
2 tablespoons (30 mL)
  tarragon leaves, minced
½ cup (120 mL) mayonnaise

2 tablespoons (30 mL)
walnut oil
3 tablespoons (45 mL)
basalmic vinegar

pinch of saffron
salt and white pepper to
taste

For Serving

8 large butter lettuce leaf
cups
8 small radicchio lettuce
leaf cups
1 ripe tomato, cut into 8
wedges

2 hard-boiled eggs, cut into
4 wedges each
16 calamata olives

- Bring the poaching ingredients to a boil, add the chicken breasts, simmer for 5 minutes, then turn off the fire and set aside for 10 minutes. Drain, pat dry, and cut the chicken across the grain (widthwise) into ¼-inch (6-mm) strips.

- Blanch the string beans in boiling salted water until al dente. Drain, cool, and set aside.

- Bring the vinegar and saffron just to a boil, and set aside to cool.

- Combine the mayonnaise, oil, vinegar, salt, and pepper, and blend well. Add the chicken, string beans, celery root, capers, and tarragon, and blend thoroughly. Place a bed of butter lettuce, topped with the radicchio leaves, on four individual plates. Place a mound of the chicken salad in the center of each, and garnish with tomato, egg, and olives.

COBB SALAD

2 medium heads romaine
lettuce
2 8-ounce (227-g) chicken
breasts, skinless and
boneless
6 slices thick bacon
3 eggs, hard-boiled
2 large tomatoes

1 medium cucumber
1 cup (240 mL) crumbled
blue cheese
1½ cups (360 mL) olive oil
½ cup (120 mL) white wine
vinegar
salt and pepper to taste
¼ cup (60 mL) water

- Slice the romaine into 1-inch wide pieces. Rinse in cold water, drain, wrap in paper towels, and refrigerate until ready to use.

- Poach the chicken in lightly salted water. Drain, pat dry, and cut widthwise into a thin julienne.
- Roast or pan-fry the bacon until brown and crispy. Pat dry and mince.
- Press the egg yolks through a screen sieve, and finely mince the whites.
- Core the tomatoes, and cut into medium dice.
- Peel and seed the cucumber, and cut into medium dice.
- Divide the romaine lettuce among four clear glass bowls. Arrange the chicken, bacon, egg yolks, egg whites, tomatoes, cucumbers, and blue cheese in sections on top of the lettuce. Beat the olive oil, vinegar, salt, and pepper, and serve on the side (*see color plate, Contemporary Salads*).

IMPERIAL SALAD

Poached chicken cut into julienne strips, asparagus tips, and green beans, arranged on a bed of lettuce, garnished with truffle, and dressed with a simple vinaigrette.

SONOMA FOIE GRAS WITH MIXED GREENS

½ cup (120 mL) olive oil
¼ cup (60 mL) champagne
  vinegar
salt and pepper to taste
1 bunch arugula
1 head butter lettuce
1 head red leaf lettuce
1 small head radicchio

8 ½-inch (12-mm) thick
  wedges Brie cheese
¼ cup (60 mL) vegetable oil
8 1-ounce (28-g) slices
  Sonoma foie gras
12 ¼-inch (6-mm) thick
  slices of baguette, toasted

- Combine the oil, vinegar, salt, and pepper in a bowl, whip vigorously, and set aside.
- Preheat an oven to 350° F (176° C).
- Tear all of the salad greens into bite-size pieces. Rinse well in cold water, drain, wrap in paper towels, and refrigerate.
- Place the Brie wedges on a baking pan, and place in the oven for about 5 minutes.
- Heat the vegetable oil, and sauté the foie gras for about 10 seconds on each side, or until slightly browned. Remove to absorbent paper.

252

- Toss the salad greens in the vinaigrette, and arrange on salad plates. Place 2 slices of foie gras, and 2 wedges of cheese on top of each salad. Serve with the toasted baguette.

SALADS WITH MEAT

ALEXANDER SALAD

1 cup (240 mL) ham, cut into 1-inch (25-mm) long julienne
1 cup (240 mL) celeriac, cut into 1-inch (25-mm) long julienne
2 Belgian endives, cut widthwise into ¼-inch (6-mm) strips
1 cup (240 mL) olive oil
½ cup (120 mL) white wine vinegar
salt and pepper to taste
½ cup (120 mL) mushrooms, cut into ¼-inch (6-mm) dice, blanched in white wine, drained, and cooled

2 large chef's potatoes, peeled, sliced, and blanched until tender but firm
2 small Granny Smith apples, thinly sliced and immersed in lemon juice
2 large beets, baked, peeled, cut in half, and thinly sliced
½ cup (120 mL) mayonnaise (optional)

- Marinate the ham, celeriac, and endive in the oil, vinegar, salt, and pepper.
- Arrange the potatoes overlapping in a circle on each of four salad plates. Arrange a second circle of the apples (drained), followed by a circle of beets.
- Drain the ham, celeriac, and endive, add the mushrooms, and arrange in the center of each circle. Top with a dollop of mayonnaise (optional) (*see color plate, Traditional Salads*).

PRINCESS SALAD

Broiled or grilled veal kidneys, finely diced. Diced celery and red bell peppers, marinated in mustard vinaigrette and then drained. Served on a bed of lettuce, garnished with asparagus tips and sliced cucumber, seasoned with a sauce of mustard and mayonnaise thinned with lemon juice.

253

ROAST BEEF SALAD, THAI STYLE

¾ pound (340 g) medium-rare roasted beef tenderloin, cut into ¼ × 2-inch (6 × 50-mm) julienne

½ cup (120 mL) fish sauce (nam-pla)

½ cup (120 mL) lime juice

2 tablespoons (30 mL) sugar

4 garlic cloves, pressed

1 teaspoon (5 mL) dried red chili pepper flakes

1 head butter lettuce

2 limes, sliced very thin

- Combine the fish sauce, lime juice, sugar, garlic, and red pepper flakes, and marinate the beef in this mixture for 3 hours.
- Tear the lettuce into bite-size pieces, rinse in cold water, drain, pat dry, and refrigerate until ready to serve.
- Drain excess marinade from the beef. Arrange on a bed of lettuce and garnish with the sliced lime.

RUSSIAN SALAD

Cooked carrots, green beans, mushrooms, and turnips, medium diced and lightly bound in mayonnaise flavored with a little strained chili sauce; cornichons, ham, lobster, beef tongue, and truffles, either medium diced and added to the salad, or attractively cut and used as part of the garnish; also garnished with sliced cooked beets, capers, hard-cooked eggs, and caviar.

SWEDISH SALAD

A composed salad consisting of sliced boiled beef, cooked potatoes and beets, apples, herring fillets, and raw oyster arranged in sections, garnished with anchovies, gherkins, capers, and quartered hard-boiled eggs, and dressed with mustard-paprika vinaigrette.

STUFFED TOMATOES

OYSTERS BORCHARDT

A raw oyster served on a slice of tomato, topped with a dollop of sour cream, garnished with caviar and a chive spear [*see color plate Tomatoes (Cold, Stuffed)*].

TOMATOES, ANDALUSIAN STYLE

4 ripe medium tomatoes
3 tablespoons (45 mL) olive oil
¼ cup (60 mL) green pepper, finely diced
¼ cup (60 mL) onion, finely diced
1 cup (240 mL) cooked rice
salt and pepper to taste

¼ cup (60 mL) mayonnaise, thinned with 2 tablespoons (30 mL) lemon juice
4 ¼ × 2-inch (6 × 50-mm) julienne strips of green pepper
8 ¼-inch (6-mm) round circles of green pepper

- Slice the top from each of the tomatoes, and scoop out the pulp (reserve for another use). Sprinkle with salt and pepper, and invert on absorbent paper.

- Sauté the pepper and onion in the olive oil for several minutes, without browning. Remove from the fire and blend with the rice.

- Stuff the tomatoes with the rice, top with the mayonnaise, and garnish with a strip of green pepper down the center, and a green pepper circle on either side.

TOMATOES, BALTIC STYLE

Tomatoes stuffed with finely diced potatoes, herring, apples, onions, and gherkins bound with a little mayonnaise, garnished with a gherkin fan.

BARRET SALAD

Scooped-out tomatoes filled with diced celery, scallion, and pineapple bound with mayonnaise, topped with toasted walnuts, and garnished with watercress.

TOMATOES, GENOA STYLE

Sliced tomatoes, topped with green pepper julienne marinated in garlic vinaigrette, garnished with anchovy fillets.

255

TOMATOES, HOTEL PLAZA STYLE

Half tomatoes topped with mashed sardines flavored with a little ketchup and mayonnaise, garnished with finely diced green peppers and green olives.

TOMATOES, LUCULLUS STYLE

Tomatoes stuffed with finely diced chicken, celery, capers, and toasted chopped hazelnuts bound with a little mayonnaise, garnished with sliced hard-boiled eggs, anchovy fillets, and black olive (*see color plate, Tomatoes (Cold, Stuffed)*).

TOMATOES, MIRABEAU STYLE

Tomatoes stuffed with finely diced celery, anchovies, and minced truffles, bound with a little mayonnaise, and garnished with anchovy fillets.

TOMATOES, MONACO STYLE

6 large ripe tomatoes
½ cup (120 mL) celery, medium dice
½ cup (120 mL) carrots, medium dice
½ cup (120 mL) green peas
½ cup (120 mL) celery root, medium dice
½ cup (120 mL) cauliflower, cut into ¼-inch flowerettes

½ cup (120 mL) broccoli flowerettes, cut into ¼-inch flowerettes
1 cup (240 mL) mayonnaise
juice of one lemon
salt and white pepper to taste
1 8-ounce (227-g) piece of fresh tuna, blanched and chilled

- Blanch all of the vegetables, except the celery, in lightly salted boiling water, until al dente. Drain, and set aside to cool.
- Blend the mayonnaise with the lemon juice, then blend in with the blanched vegetables and the celery. Season to taste with salt and pepper.
- Remove the cores and slice the tops from the tomatoes, then scoop out the pulp (reserve the pulp for other uses). Fill each tomato with the salad, place the lid on, and top with a slice of tuna [*see color plate, Tomatoes (Cold, Stuffed)*].

TOMATOES, NANA STYLE

Tomatoes stuffed with finely diced chicken and toasted chopped walnuts, bound with a little mayonnaise, served on a bed of lettuce, and topped with a little mayonnaise thinned with vinegar.

TOMATOES, NORTHERN STYLE

Half tomatoes filled with caviar, topped with a slice of hard-boiled egg and a crisscross of anchovy fillet, garnished with a dollop of tartar sauce.

TOMATOES, PARIS STYLE

Sliced tomatoes on a bed of lettuce, topped with blanched diced celery root, flavored with minced anchovy, chervil, chives, and shallots marinated in a little vinaigrette.

TOMATOES, POLISH STYLE

Tomatoes stuffed with finely diced herring, celery, onion, and minced dill, bound in a little mayonnaise, and garnished with a piece of herring and a sprig of dill [*see color plate, Tomatoes (Cold, Stuffed)*].

TOMATOES, ROMANIAN STYLE

Tomatoes stuffed with rice pilaf mixed with diced tomatoes and green peppers stewed in olive oil and lemon, garnished with a thin slice of peeled and seeded lemon.

TOMATOES, WALDORF STYLE

Tomatoes stuffed with finely diced apple, celery, and toasted chopped walnuts, bound in a little mayonnaise, and garnished with sliced apple and a toasted walnut [*see color plate, Tomatoes (Cold, Stuffed)*].

PASTA SALADS

Pasta salad is a uniquely American innovation; thus, there are no strict guidelines as to ingredients. Because the history of pasta is an international one, and because pasta is sufficiently neutral in flavor to combine with any other ingredients, there is room for much inventiveness. Pasta salads also provide a cost-effective way to utilize extemporaneous ingredients, provided one adheres to a high standard of quality for such "leftovers." In searching for a theme around which to create a salad, innovators tend to draw inspiration from major geographic regions. For example, a "Mediterranean-style" pasta salad may incorporate ingredients such as anchovies, artichoke hearts, capers, garlic, olives, roasted onions, tomatoes, and zucchini; a "garden-style" salad, asparagus, beans, broccoli, green peas, bell peppers, and several fresh herbs; a "hunt-style" salad, roasted chicken, pheasant, or squab, along with roasted shallots, orange zest, and dried cranberries; an "Asian-style" variety, duck, water chestnuts, five-spice powder, soy sauce, and ginger; a "seashore" salad, flaked halibut, salmon, tuna, lobster, shrimp, or mussels, plus whole kernel corn or green peas, and thinly sliced cucumber. The choice of pasta is both a matter of preference and kinetics, based on the other ingredients selected. Fusilli is always a good choice, because it tends to hold on to other ingredients (in pieces) within a sauce; penne is attractive to the eye, but it is smooth, and other ingredients used with it tend to slip and slide; other varieties to consider include cavatappi, cavatelli, conchiglie, farfalle, funghini, gemelli, and gnocchi (the pasta, not the dumpling). Long pasta types, such as spaghetti, fettuccine, and vermicelli, are a bit sloppy for salad unless they are cut in halves or thirds.

When selecting and cooking a pasta, consider these important guidelines:

- A quality dried pasta made from durum semolina (the hard wheat that makes the best pasta) is generally superior. (Fresh pasta only requires as little as 1 minute of cooking time.)
- Pasta must be cooked in plenty of rapidly boiling, lightly salted water [2 gallons (7.5 L) per pound of pasta]. It should be stirred for the first couple of minutes, to prevent the pasta from sticking to itself, until the water returns to a boil.
- Olive oil is added to the water for cooking pasta, not to prevent the pasta from sticking together, but to prevent the

water from boiling over. This can also be prevented by using a pot large enough to allow sufficient space between the water and the top edge of the pot. (Olive oil may also be considered a *spiritual* ingredient, one of many enigmatic little tricks of the trade that add a certain indescribable something to a dish.)

- Pasta prepared for a salad should be cooked decidedly al dente, because it will absorb the accompanying sauce and moisture from other ingredients.

GARDEN PASTA SALAD

1 cup (240 mL) basil pesto
½ cup (120 mL) sun-dried tomatoes, medium dice
½ cup (120 mL) mayonnaise
2 pounds (907 kg) fusilli, cooked al dente
¾ cup (180 mL) green peas, lightly blanched

¾ cup (180 mL) red onions, finely diced
¾ cup (180 mL) zucchini, cut into medium julienne and lightly blanched
salt and white pepper to taste

- Combine the pesto, tomatoes, and mayonnaise, and blend thoroughly. Place all ingredients in a bowl, and blend thoroughly. Season to taste with salt and pepper.

PESTO AND PASTA SALAD

2 cloves garlic, pressed
¼ cup (60 mL) olive oil
2 pounds (907 kg) conchiglie (medium shells), cooked al dente
1½ cups (360 mL) cooked chicken breast, cut into julienne
1 cup (240 mL) basil pesto

½ cup (120 mL) Pecorino Romano, grated
½ cup (120 mL) pine nuts, toasted
2 tablespoons (30 mL) lemon zest, blanched in boiling salted water
salt and pepper to taste

- Sauté the garlic in the olive oil, until it just begins to brown. Combine the garlic, pasta, chicken, pesto, and cheese, and toss. Season to taste with salt and pepper. Serve topped with the pine nuts and the lemon zest.

PASTA SALAD, MEDITERRANEAN STYLE

1 large eggplant
½ cup (120 mL) olive oil
1 yellow or green bell pepper, cut into medium julienne
2 bunches scallions, cut on the bias in 1-inch (25-mm) lengths
4 garlic cloves, pressed
¼ cup (60 mL) dry red wine
¼ cup (60 mL) anchovies, minced

¼ cup (60 mL) balsamic vinegar
2 pounds (900 g) cavatappi, cooked al dente
¾ cup (180 mL) calamata olives
1 cup (240 mL) ham, fat trimmed, cut into julienne
¾ cup (180 mL) feta cheese, crumbled

- Cut the eggplant into 1-inch (25-mm) cubes, place in a colander, and sprinkle lightly with salt. Allow to sit 20 minutes.

- Heat the olive oil until just smoking, add the eggplant, and sauté. Add the bell pepper and scallion, and continue sautéing 5 minutes. Add the garlic, and cook another few minutes. Add the red wine and anchovies, remove from the fire, and allow to cool.

- Combine the vegetables, vinegar, pasta, and olives, and blend thoroughly. Garnish with the ham and feta cheese.

PASTA SALAD, MIDDLE EASTERN STYLE

⅓ cup (80 mL) peanut oil
1 large strip of orange zest, roughly chopped
1 tablespoon (15 mL) fenugreek seed, cracked
1 tablespoon (15 mL) coriander seeds, cracked
2 dried hot red chili peppers
2 garlic cloves, crushed
1 teaspoon (5 mL) ground cumin
¼ teaspoon (1.2 mL) ground cinnamon

2 pounds (900 g) ditalini, cooked al dente
½ cup (120 mL) salted toasted peanuts
½ cup (120 mL) salted cashew pieces
½ cup (120 mL) dried currants
¼ cup (60 mL) dried bananas, crumbled
1 cup (240 mL) plain yogurt
¼ cup (60 mL) mint leaves, cut in fine chiffonade
juice of 2 limes

- Sauté the orange zest and spices in the oil over very low heat, for about 10 minutes. Remove the zest and spices and discard, reserving the oil. Sprinkle the cumin and cinnamon onto the oil, blend thoroughly, and set aside to cool.

- Combine the oil, yogurt, mint, and lime juice and blend thoroughly. Combine the sauce with the remaining ingredients in a large bowl, and blend thoroughly. Season to taste if necessary

PASTA SALAD, ASIAN STYLE

1 cup (240 mL) mayonnaise
½ cup (120 mL) rice wine vinegar
1 tablespoon (15 mL) gingerroot, grated
2 tablespoons (30 mL) hot chili oil
2 tablespoons (30 mL) toasted sesame oil
3 tablespoons (45 mL) soy sauce
1 teaspoon (5 mL) cumin
2 pounds (900 g) penne, cooked al dente
½ cup (120 mL) fresh snow peas, cut lengthwise into a fine julienne

½ cup (120 mL) celery, cut into fine julienne
½ cup (120 mL) bamboo shoots, well rinsed and cut into fine julienne
1 bunch scallions, sliced on the bias very thin
½ cup (120 mL) cilantro leaves, minced
cilantro sprigs as needed
1 fat carrot (for carving flower garnishes)
½ cup (120 mL) salted toasted peanuts, roughly chopped

- Combine the mayonnaise, vinegar, ginger, oils, soy sauce, and cumin, and blend thoroughly.
- Combine the sauce with the remaining ingredients (except peanuts), and blend thoroughly. Sprinkle the top with the peanuts, and garnish with cilantro leaves and carrot flowers.

VEGETABLE DISHES

Vegetables are divided botanically into six groups:

Fungi	Mushrooms, morels, and truffles
Roots	Beet; radish and turnip; carrot and parsnip
Tubers	Potato, sweet potato, water chestnut, and yam
Leaves and Stems	Asparagus, leek, and onion; cabbage and Brussels sprout; lettuce, endive, and dandelion; bamboo shoot; celery; rhubarb; spinach; watercress

261

Flowers	Broccoli and cauliflower; artichoke
Fruits	Botanical fruits considered culinary vegetables

The squash family	Cucumber, pumpkin, and squash
The legume family	Beans and peas
The nightshade family	Eggplant, pepper, tomato, avocado, corn, okra, and olive

VEGETABLE RECIPES

AGOURSI (ALSO OGOURZI)

Peeled cucumber sliced very thin, sprinkled with salt, allowed to drain, rinsed and dried, blended with sour cream and minced dill (*see color plate, Hors d'Oeuvres, Greek Style*).

ALLIGATOR PEAR COCKTAIL

(AVOCADO COCKTAIL)

1 cup (240 mL) ketchup
3 tablespoons (45 mL)
   white Worcestershire
   sauce
¼ cup (60 mL) mayonnaise
3 tablespoons (45 mL)
   heavy cream

juice of 1 lemon
salt and white pepper to
   taste
2 ripe Haas avocados
8 butter lettuce leaves

- Combine the ketchup, Worcestershire, mayonnaise, cream, lemon juice, salt, pepper and blend thoroughly. Cover and refrigerate until ready to use.
- Peel and seed the avocados, and cut into ½-inch dice.
- Place 2 lettuce leaves in each of four champagne saucers. Divide the avocado among the four, top with the sauce, and garnish with a twisted lemon slice (*see color plate, Hors d'Oeuvres, Greek Style*).

ARTICHOKE BOTTOMS, DIEPPE STYLE

Artichoke bottoms filled with a mound of finely diced poached mussels and shrimp bound with a little mayonnaise, and garnished with chopped parsley.

262

ARTICHOKE BOTTOMS, DUBARRY

Artichoke bottoms filled with a mound of small cauliflower flowerettes blanched in boiling salted water until al dente, coated with mayonnaise thinned with a little vinegar, and garnished with chopped parsley.

ARTICHOKE BOTTOMS, PRESIDENT STYLE

Artichoke bottoms filled with a mound of finely diced chicken bound with mayonnaise, topped with a slice of hard-boiled egg and a thin slice of truffle, and glazed with aspic.

BEETROOT SQUARES

Roast some large beets in a preheated 400° F (205° C) oven, with a little water in the pan, for about 1 hour, or until tender when pierced with a fork. Remove and allow to cool. Cut the beets into uniform 1-inch (25-mm) cubes, and marinate 1 hour in vinegar. Using a Parisienne scoop, scoop out the top of each beet cube and fill with a salad consisting of finely diced capers, gherkins, egg whites, and anchovies, marinated in mustard vinaigrette. Sprinkle the tops with sieved egg yolks [*see color plate, Vegetable Hors d'Oeuvres (Cold)*].

CALIFORNIA APPLES

Remove the tops and scoop out the interiors of medium Gravenstein or Granny Smith apples (or any preferred variety). Douse in a lemon bath, drain well, then fill with finely diced chicken and celery bound with mayonnaise, seasoned with lemon juice, fresh herbs, salt, and white pepper. Set the tops back in place, and pipe out a rosette of butter, mashed into a smooth paste with finely minced herbs, onto each top, and serve well chilled [*see color plate, Vegetable Hors d'Oeuvres (Cold)*].

Celeriac, also called German, or turnip-rooted, celery has a starch-storing root, with long green stems and minimal development of leaves. The best known varieties are Verona and Alabaster.

CELERY ROOT RÉMOULADE

2 medium celery roots
juice of 4 lemons
1 cup (240 mL) rémoulade
  sauce

salt and white pepper to
  taste

- Bring about 1 quart (960 mL) of lightly salted water to a boil.
- Peel the celery, then cut into a long fine julienne, using a Japanese mandolin. Place the celery in a bowl, pour over the lemon juice, and pour in enough boiling water to cover. Allow to sit 15 minutes. Drain thoroughly and allow to cool.
- Blend the rémoulade sauce with the celery, and allow to marinate overnight. Serve on a bed of lettuce, garnished with parsley sprigs.

Note: This very simple and elegant dish can be prepared with any variety of mayonnaise-based sauce.

CELERY HOUSEWIFE STYLE

Peeled celery sliced very thin on the bias, combined with sliced potatoes, bound with mustard-mayonnaise.

CELERY STUFFED WITH ROQUEFORT

Peeled celery cut on a sharp bias, into 1-inch (25-mm) long diamond-shaped pieces, then stuffed with a paste made with Roquefort cheese, cream cheese, and butter, seasoned with white Worcestershire sauce and paprika [*see color plate, Vegetable Hors d'Oeuvres (Cold)*].

CHILLED ASPARAGUS, AURORA

Peel 24 fat asparagus, and blanch in boiling salted water until al dente. Thin some mayonnaise with a little lemon juice, and ladle onto 4 serving plates, or a serving platter. Thin some tomato paste with some of the water used to blanch the asparagus, transfer to a plastic squeeze bottle, and squeeze out a spiral. Run a toothpick out from the center in eight equidistant lines, then run the toothpick in toward the center, between the other lines. Arrange the asparagus on top of the sauce (*see Figure 6.2*).

CRUDITÉS, HERB MAYONNAISE

An assortment of raw vegetables attractively arranged and served with an herb mayonnaise. Some of the vegetables are improved by brief blanching in boiling salted water: broccoli, cauliflower, string beans, yellow squash, and zucchini. Other varieties are better left raw: bell peppers, celery, cucumber, radishes, and scallion.

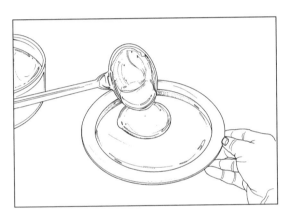

Ladle the thinned mayonnaise onto a serving platter.

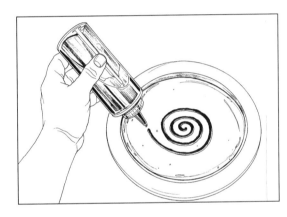

Carefully squeeze out a spiral line of the tomato paste.

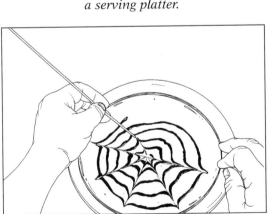

Run a toothpick or skewer from the center out, in eight equidistant radial lines.

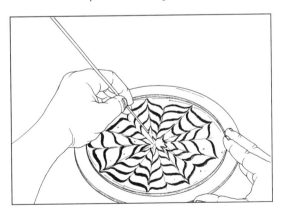

Run the toothpick from the outside in, through the center of each section. Place the prepared asparagus on top and serve.

Figure 6.2
Sauce Painting

CUCUMBERS, DANISH STYLE

Scooped-out cucumber boats, 2 inches (50 mm) long, filled with a paste made of smoked salmon and cream cheese, seasoned with horseradish, and garnished with hard-boiled egg [*see color plate, Vegetable Hors d'Oeuvres (Cold)*].

CUCUMBERS, SWEDISH STYLE

1 large hothouse cucumber
1 cup (240 mL) marinated
   herring fillets, drained
¼ cup (60 mL) red onion,
   finely diced
¼ cup (60 mL) celery, finely
   diced

¼ cup (120 mL) mayonnaise
juice of 1 lemon
1 teaspoon (5 mL) dill,
   minced
salt and white pepper to
   taste
12 sprigs dill

- Combine the herring, onion, celery, mayonnaise, lemon, dill, salt, and pepper, and blend thoroughly. Set aside.
- Cut the cucumber widthwise into 1½-inch (37-mm) lengths. With a Parisienne scoop, scoop out the cucumber, about 1 inch (25 mm) deep, and within a ¼ inch (6 mm) of the outside edge. Fill the cucumbers with the salad, and garnish with a dill sprig (*see color plate, Hors d'Oeuvres, Greek Style*).

EGGPLANT CAVIAR

2 eggplants, about 1 pound
   (450 g) each
6 large garlic cloves, skin on
juice of 2 lemons

3 tablespoons (45 mL) olive
   oil
3 tablespoons (45 mL)
   chopped flat-leaf parsley
salt and pepper to taste

- Preheat an oven to 425° F (218° C).
- Split the eggplants lengthwise, coat the cut surfaces with olive oil, place on a baking sheet along with the garlic, and bake for 30 to 40 minutes, or until tender. Remove and allow to cool.
- Scoop out the pulp and place it in a food processor. Squeeze out the garlic and add, along with the remaining ingredients. Pulse until smooth and refrigerate. Serve with toasted croutons.

Cheese Platter   from left to right: *Maytag blue* (from Iowa; remaining varieties from Wisconsin); *dill havarti; Cheddar; smoked Swiss; provolone; gouda; camembert*

Chicken Chaud-Froid Dishes from top to bottom: *Chicken Breast Chaud-Froid, Aurora (p. 282); Chicken Breast Chaud-Froid with Tarragon (p. 283); Chicken Breast Chaud-Froid, Vincent (p. 283)*

Salmon Trout in Aspic   *Poached salmon trout fillets decorated with cucumber, glazed with aspic, and accompanied by a vegetable timbale in aspic and Genoa mayonnaise (p. 111)*

Classic Caviar Service *Sturgeon caviar* (center) *accompanied by* (clockwise from lower right) *blinis (p. 197), Northern Style Pancakes, and Shrimp Newest Style (p. 177).* (Also shown: mother-of-pearl spoon and luncheon menu from *S.S. George Washington,* June 14, 1922)

Caviar Fan (p. 194) (from top to bottom of fan): *Lobster roe (Maine), Chinook salmon roe (Great Lakes), whitefish roe, Tobiko (flying fish, flavored with wasabi), choupique (bowfin), northern style pancakes (crêpes filled with cream cheese, sliced on the bias, garnished with lobster roe and leek); Japanese graphic* (Harmony) *done in whitefish and choupique roe, on a bed of minced egg white*

Gravlax *Sliced dry-cured salmon (p. 344); California mukimono flower bouquet made from rutabaga, white turnip, butternut squash, and carrot; sliced cucumbers marinated in dill vinaigrette, served in scooped-out acorn squash; mustard-dill mayonnaise sauce; sliced whole grain rye bread*

Cold Roast Pork Loin, Scandinavian Style   Centerpiece: *Wizard's hat* (fashioned from weaver's dough) *with assorted dried fruit and nuts; roasted pork loin stuffed with prunes, with edges dipped in aspic and then minced herbs, glazed with aspic;* garnishes: *wonton socles filled with wild rice and almond salad; apples stuffed with apricot/onion compote;* flow salad: *leaf socle* (made from wonton dough) *filled with red cabbage and peanut salad*

Ham Platter, American Style Centerpiece: *Wisconsin applewood-smoked ham* (whole, bone in), *coated with mayonnaise collée, decorated with leek leaf, red onion* (boiled), *and flat-leaf parsley;* garnish: *apple socles filled with cranberry relish (p. 345), marked with small orange triangle and sprig of parsley;* flow salad: *fennel root, orange segments, and red onion in vinaigrette*

Sausage and Charcuterie   clockwise from bottom left: *Sausages: smoked venison and whiskey fennel on a bed of braised red cabbage; smoked andouille on a bed of Jasmine blend rice; Burmese brand curried chicken and turkey on a bed of sautéed bok choy; New Mexico brand smoked chicken and turkey on a bed of braised leeks; smoked chicken and apple on a bed of sauerkraut (p. 270);* center tray, left to right: *smoked duck legs and breasts; Canandian-style bacon* (smoked pork loin); *smoked Cajun tasso* (smoked pork butt coated with hot spice blend)

Cold Roast Leg of Lamb, Jardinière   Centerpiece: *lamb saddle with rib bones wrapped in blanched leek leaves, topped with two rows of sliced boneless lamb leg and a row of sliced lamb loin* (wrapped in nori); main item: *sliced boneless lamb leg;* garnishes: *barquettes filled with arrangement of blanched vegetables, and tartlets filled with onion chutney;* flow salad: *broccoli, carrot, celery, radish, and zucchini in vinaigrette; marble slab backed with Wild Stallions* (tallow sculpture created by Bread Effects Culinart)

Chicken Legs in Aspic (Jambonneaux) (p. 276)   *Chicken legs with thigh bone removed and stuffed with veal and pork farce, wrapped in bacon, trussed, roasted on a rack until golden brown, chilled, and coated with aspic. Served accompanied by julienned vegetables* (from top to bottom: radish, carrot, yellow squash, celery, zucchini, and beet) *and dressed with vinaigrette in onion flower cups, garnished with diced aspic*

Chicken Roulade, Veronique *Chicken breasts rolled around chicken and basil mousse, wrapped tightly, and poached in chicken stock; drained, chilled overnight, then sliced, and arranged over the breast of a whole chicken, poached and coated with mayonnaise collée. Chicken and slices of roulade coated with aspic; carved pumpkins holding pickled green and red seedless grapes*

Duck Liver Terrine (Foie Gras de Canard) (p. 369)   *Slice of liver terrine accompanied with brioche toast, garnished with nasturtium flowers, accompanied by a glass of French sauterne* (book pictured is facsimile edition of *The Epicurean*, published in 1893, by Charles Ranhoffer, acclaimed chef of Delmonico's, New York City's first significant restaurant)

Duck Pâté with Green Peppercorns (Pâté de Canard au Poivre Vert)   Centerpiece: *Whole pâté trimmed and the top spread with cream cheese, decorated with pickled yellow banana peppers (güreos) and cornichons; sliced pâté garnished with cream cheese star, scallion, and caper; tartlets filled with Chicken Liver Mousse with Armagnac and Truffles, garnished with pastry trellis (p. 206)*

EGGPLANT, NÎMES STYLE

2 large eggplants
salt, white pepper, and olive
 oil as needed
½ cup (120 mL) lemon juice
½ cup (120 mL) red bell
 pepper, small dice
4 garlic cloves, pressed

½ cup (120 mL) tomatoes,
 medium dice
1 tablespoon (15 mL) parsley, minced
1 tablespoon (15 mL)
 cilantro leaves, minced
1 tablespoon (15 mL) tar-
 ragon leaves, minced

- Preheat an oven to 325° F (163° C).
- Slice the eggplants widthwise, into 1-inch (25-mm) thick slices. Brush with olive oil, sprinkle both sides with salt and pepper, drizzle with half the lemon juice, and place on a baking sheet. Bake for 30 to 40 minutes, turning once or twice, until tender. Remove from the oven and allow to cool.
- Sauté the pepper and garlic in a little olive oil. Add the tomatoes, herbs, salt, pepper, and the remaining lemon juice, and simmer about 10 minutes. Remove from the fire, spoon over the eggplant, and set aside to cool.
- Allow the eggplant to marinate in the refrigerator overnight, and serve chilled or at room temperature.

FENNEL ROOT, ITALIAN STYLE

4 fennel bulbs, trimmed of
 stalks, bottoms, and any
 dark spots, and cut in
 half
¼ cup (60 mL) olive oil
1 cup (240 mL) dry white
 wine
1 medium onion, peeled
 and thinly sliced

4 garlic cloves, thinly sliced
1 cup (240 mL) tomatoes,
 diced
4 sprigs thyme
salt and white pepper to
 taste
2 tablespoons (30 mL) parsley, minced

- Preheat an oven to 375° F (190° C).
- Blanch the fennel bulbs in boiling salted water for 2 minutes. Drain and place cut side down in an oiled casserole dish. Drizzle with the olive oil, and sprinkle with salt and pepper. Add the remaining ingredients, except the parsley, cover, and bake 30 to 40 minutes, or until tender. Remove from the oven, allow to cool, and refrigerate overnight.

- Serve the fennel chilled or at room temperature, sprinkled with the parsley (*see color plate, Hors d'Oeuvres, Greek Style*).

HUMMUS

2 cups (480 mL) cooked garbanzo beans
¾ cup (180 mL) sesame tahini
juice of 3 lemons

6 garlic cloves, pressed
¼ cup (60 mL) olive oil
1 teaspoon (5 mL) salt
¼ teaspoon (1.2 mL) white pepper

- Purée all ingredients in a food processor, using the pulse switch. Serve with vegetable crudités, with toasted pita bread slices, or as part of another appetizer (*see color plate, Vegetable Pâté en Croûte*).

LEEKS VINAIGRETTE

This is a good all-purpose cold sauce, because it is made to one's taste—and because the parsley emulsifies the sauce, which will stay that way up to 12 hours. To reemulsify, simply place in a covered jar and shake well.

4 medium leeks, white part only
1½ cups (360 mL) olive oil
½ cup (120 mL) champagne vinegar
2 garlic cloves

2 tablespoons (30 mL) Dijon-style mustard
½ cup (120 mL) parsley leaves, roughly chopped
water as needed
salt and black pepper to taste

- Place all the ingredients except the leeks in a blender, and purée. Adjust seasoning, and set aside.
- Remove the roots from the leeks, and discard. Split the leeks lengthwise, into quarters, up to 1 inch (25 mm) from the root end, leaving them attached. Rinse the leeks well in cold water, then blanch in boiling salted water until tender. Drain, cool, and set aside.
- Complete the two cuts in each of the leeks, dividing each leek into quarters. Arrange on a serving plate, and coat with the vinaigrette [*see color plate, Vegetable Hors d'Oeuvres (Cold)*].

The Vegetables Vinaigrette pictured in the same photo with the leeks is prepared with the same vinaigrette. Select some seasonal vegetables, such as broccoli, carrots, cauliflower, white turnip, yellow bell pepper, or zucchini, and blanch lightly (firmly al dente), drain, cool, and toss in the vinaigrette.

MARINATED MUSHROOMS, GREEK STYLE

1 cup (240 mL) button mushrooms
1 cup (240 mL) shiitake mushrooms

1 cup (240 mL) chanterelle mushrooms
the juice of one lemon

1 package of fresh enoki
   mushrooms
1 cup (240 mL) olive oil
1 cup (240 mL) white wine
   vinegar
1 cup (240 mL) water
salt and white pepper to
   taste
4 garlic cloves, crushed
1 shallot, thinly sliced

2 sprigs rosemary
2 sprigs thyme
2 sprigs oregano
1 bay leaf
8 Boston lettuce cups
4 red cabbage leaf cups
16 Belgian endive leaves
¼ cup (60 mL) chopped
   parsley

- Trim the very bottom portion of the stems of the button, shiitake, and chanterelle mushrooms, and discard. Rinse the mushrooms in cold water and lemon juice. Pat dry. Cut the shiitakes into julienne, and the chanterelles into ½-inch (12-mm) pieces.

- Combine all of the marinade ingredients in a saucepan, and bring to a boil. Add the prepared mushrooms, simmer for 1 minute, then turn off the fire and allow to cool to room temperature. Cover and refrigerate overnight.

- Arrange the butter lettuce leaves on four individual plates, place a cabbage leaf in the center, and four endive leaves on each plate. Place the marinated mushrooms on the cabbage leaves, and garnish with the enoki mushrooms and chopped parsley.

Note: This marinade can be used to marinate numerous other vegetables: artichoke bottoms and hearts, celery, fennel, bell peppers, summer squash, zucchini, etc.

PICKLED GARDEN VEGETABLES

2 cups (480 mL) assorted
   vegetables, cut into an
   variety of shapes (e.g.,
   bell peppers, cucumbers,
   pearl onions, baby zucchini, yellow squash,
   patty pan squash, carrots,
   cauliflower, Brussels
   sprouts, and broccoli, cut
   in round slices, half circles, on the bias, spheres,
   squares, triangles, julienne, etc.)

salt as needed
3 cups (720 mL) champagne vinegar
1 cup (240 mL) water
1 teaspoon (5 mL) salt
½ cup (120 mL) sugar
¼ teaspoon whole cloves
1 teaspoon (5 mL) mustard
   seeds
1 teaspoon (5 mL) coriander seeds
1 teaspoon (5 mL) black
   peppercorns

| 1 bay leaf | 4 garlic cloves, crushed |
| 2 sprigs oregano | |

- Place the vegetables in a colander, sprinkle with salt, and allow to sit for 3 hours.
- Combine the remaining pickling ingredients in a saucepan, bring to a boil, and simmer for 5 minutes. Rinse the salted vegetables in cold water, and drain. Place the brine over the vegetables, allow to cool, then cover and refrigerate. Marinate 24 hours before serving.

SAUERKRAUT

Sauerkraut (literally, "bitter herb") is an extremely healthful dish. It can be eaten as is or used in numerous Alsatian and German dishes. Typically served with pork, smoked pork, or sausages, and apples, sauerkraut is also cooked with Alsatian wine and accompanied by smoked salmon, salt cod, monkfish, or fish sausages.

| 2 heads white cabbage | salt as needed |

- Cut the cabbages in half, removing and saving the outer green leaves, and removing the cores. Slice as thinly as possible, rinse, and drain.
- Line the bottom of a stone crock (ok to substitute a stainless steel or glass container) with the outer cabbage leaves. Place a 1-inch (25-mm) deep layer of cabbage on top of this, and sprinkle lightly with the salt. Repeat this, with layers of cabbage alternating with the salt, until the container is full. Cover with a final layer of cabbage leaves, and set a wood board or plate on top of the cabbage. Press down firmly until the juice that has drained from the cabbage rises above the plate. Place a heavy weight (a stone is the usual choice) on top, so that the plate remains below the level of the juice. Place in a cool spot (basement) for 3 months. At the end of 3 months, remove any moldy cabbage from the top, and refrigerate the sauerkraut until needed.

STUFFED GRAPE LEAVES
(DOLMADES)

1 cup (240 mL) long grain white rice	½ cup (120 mL) dried currants (or raisins)
1 tablespoon (5 mL) olive oil	¼ cup (60 mL) pine nuts
1 medium onion, finely chopped	2 cups (480 mL) chicken stock (or water)
3 garlic cloves, minced	2 tablespoons (30 mL) chopped parsley

270

2 tablespoons (30 mL)
   chopped mint
salt and pepper to taste

1 jar grape leaves
lemon juice and zest

- Rinse the rice thoroughly in cold water. Sauté the onion in the olive oil, over medium heat, until transparent. Add the garlic, currants, and pine nuts, and sauté briefly. Add the chicken stock, herbs, salt, and pepper. Blend well, cover, and simmer for 15 minutes. Set aside and allow to cool.

- Lay out one or two grape leaves, and place a tablespoon of the rice in the center. Roll up firmly (like a burrito), and place in a saucepan or casserole. Pour over the olive oil and lemon juice, cover, bake for 20 minutes in a 350° F (176° C) oven, and serve hot or cold (*see color plate, Hors d'Oeuvres, Greek Style*).

ZUCCHINI SPAGHETTI

This is not actually a pasta dish, but zucchini cut to resemble spaghetti. Cut and discard the ends of the zucchini. Set the fine blade into a Japanese mandolin, and slice each zucchini three times along each of four sides (discard the remaining rectangular center piece). Drop into boiling lightly salted water for 1 to 2 minutes, drain, cool, and dress with emulsified vinaigrette (*see color plate, Hors d'Oeuvres, Greek Style*).

CHAPTER 7

ASPIC, CHAUD-FROID, AND TIMBALES

ASPIC

Aspic is a crystal clear, gelatinous meat, game, poultry, or fish-flavored jelly, used in various applications in buffet presentations. The gelatin is derived from the bones used in the preparation of the stock, which is then clarified (in the same fashion as consommé), then either reduced to concentrate the gelatin content or fortified with the addition of unflavored gelatin (powdered gelatin is dissolved in cold water, brought to a boil, and strained). Because this process is rather labor-intensive, a packaged granulated aspic powder is generally used. Two brands imported from Switzerland are quite good—designated as light or heavy, in reference to color. They can be reconstituted using white wine, sherry, port, or even gin, giving them a very fine flavor. (For information on how to obtain these products, see "Specialty Suppliers," at the end of this book.)

Aspic provides a very fine and savory taste experience, although in a culture more familiar with Jell-O, a dessert of sweetened and flavored gelatin, adaptation to the savory taste is required. Visually, as well as gustatorily, there is nothing quite as fine as a delicate consommé madrilène (a chilled, gelatinous, tomato-flavored clear soup, *see color plate, Chilled Soups*) or a roasted duck or duck breast stuffed with prunes and coated with a Madeira or Port-flavored aspic.

To prepare powdered aspic for coating cold dishes, heat some water and sherry, port, Madeira, or dry white wine—depending on the dish—then sprinkle in the powder while stirring continuously [a plastic spoon and instructions are usually packaged within the can; roughly 1 teaspoon (5 mL) of powdered aspic is used per cup of hot liquid]. Bring to a boil, then strain through a fine sieve into a clean bowl. Set the bowl in an ice water bath, and stir until it cools to a temperature of roughly 90° F (32° C). Take the bowl out of the bath, and use the liquid to coat chaud-froid dishes, canapés, and other pastry appetizers. If the aspic cools to a point at which it begins to jell, return the bowl to a hot water bath, stir until liquefied, then cool again in the ice water bath. For cutting into geometric shapes, dicing, or mincing for use as a garnish, pour enough warm aspic into a pan so that it is ½ inch (12 mm) deep. Allow the aspic to set in the refrigerator, then cut out or dice as needed.

There are some traditional dishes that are prepared and served with a thick coating of aspic jelly, examples of which follow.

CHICKEN IN ASPIC, ITALIAN STYLE

A large, round, fluted mold, lined with a good layer of aspic, topped with sliced tongue and poached chicken breast, and truffles, sealed with aspic, and served with Italian salad.

CHICKEN LEGS IN ASPIC

Boneless chicken legs stuffed with a veal and pork farce, wrapped in bacon, skewered securely, and roasted on a rack until golden brown. (As a hot dish, this is served with a pan sauce finished with cream.) Allow to cool, then cover and refrigerate. Coat with aspic, then decorate as desired and serve with an appropriate salad.

Note: In French this dish is referred to as *jambonneau,* meaning "little ham."

CHICKEN AND HAM IN ASPIC, MERCÉDÈS

A large, round, fluted mold, lined with a good layer of aspic, topped with sliced poached chicken breast and ham, followed by chicken mousse garnished with diced ham, and sealed with aspic. It is then unmolded and decorated with aspic cutouts.

DUCK IN ASPIC WITH PRUNES

1 5-pound (2,250-g) duck, well rinsed
juice of 1 lemon
salt and pepper to taste
3 cups (720 mL) pitted prunes
2 cups (480 mL) Madeira
½ cup (120 mL) bacon, medium dice

2 shallots, minced
1 cup (240 mL) duck (or chicken) livers, well rinsed, trimmed of connecting membranes, and cut into medium dice
6 chestnuts, roasted and shelled, and cut into medium dice

2 cups (480 mL) plain
  cooked rice
1 teaspoon (5 mL) thyme
  leaves
½ teaspoon (2.5 mL) ground
  poultry seasoning

salt and pepper to taste
2 cups (480 mL) liquefied
  aspic
2 bunches watercress

- Preheat an oven to 400° F (205° C).
- Barrel-bone the duck by carefully cutting around the inner bone structure, beginning at the cavity opening and working inward. Leave the wings and legs intact. (If necessary, this boning step can be performed at a butcher shop upon request.) Season inside the cavity with lemon juice, salt, and pepper, and set aside.
- Heat the Madeira, and pour over the prunes. Set aside to macerate and plump.
- Render the bacon until golden brown. Add the shallot and cook briefly. Add the livers and cook until done. Moisten with a half cup of the Madeira, and remove from the fire.
- Discard the rest of the Madeira, and cut half of the prunes into medium dice. Place them in a large bowl, along with the livers, chestnuts, rice, thyme, and poultry seasoning. Season to taste with salt and pepper.
- Fill the duck with the stuffing mixture, and tie or skewer the two ends of the duck closed. Roast for 15 minutes on its breast, then 15 minutes on its back. Turn the heat down to 350° F (176° C), and continue roasting for another 30 to 40 minutes, or until the juices run clear when pierced with a fork. Remove from the oven, allow to cool, remove trussing string or skewers, and refrigerate overnight.
- Place the duck on a rack over a pan, and coat with the aspic. Refrigerate until the aspic sets, then nap with another coat. Continue this process until there is a good coating of aspic over the bird (about ⅛ inch/3 mm). Serve on a large platter, garnished with the remaining plumped prunes and watercress.

DUCK AND ORANGES IN ASPIC

Roast 2 ducks, cool, and separate the thighs (bone in) and the breasts (boneless). Slice the breasts thin and on the bias, and set aside. Remove the segments from 3 or 4 oranges, poach briefly in a little white wine or sherry, drain well, and set aside. Remove the skin from the thighs and separate the meat from the bones, being sure to take out all cartilage and bones. Cut into a fine dice, blend with some finely diced or julienned carrots and minced scallion, bind lightly with mayonnaise, and season with salt, pepper, and minced tarragon.

Line a large, round mold with aspic, then arrange orange segments radially, in a circle about 1 inch (25 mm) from the edge of the mold. Coat with a thin layer of aspic and allow to set. Arrange the sliced duck breast, also in a radial pattern, on top of this. Coat with a thin layer of aspic and allow to set. Place the duck leg salad on top of this, gently add enough aspic to rise to the top of the salad, and refrigerate until set. Fill up the rest of the mold with aspic, and refrigerate until set.

CHAUD-FROID

Literally, "hot-cold sauce," *chaud-froid* (pronounced "show-fwa") refers to a brown, green, red, ivory-tinted, or white sauce, so named because it is prepared hot and served cold. The white version is the most commonly used, inasmuch as it provides a food "canvas" that can be decorated. It consists of a cream sauce (béchamel) combined with aspic or gelatin, which, when cold, provides a gelatinous covering for roasted or poached meat, game, poultry, or fish. It is possible that long before the advent of modern refrigeration, chaud-froid was used as a protective cover for foods served on a buffet—a flap of the elastic coating could have been pulled back, exposing the meat, poultry, or fish beneath, then replaced to prevent exposure to the air. However, according to Philéas Gilbert (1857–1942), notable chef and author, it was created at the Château de Montmorency in 1759:

> One evening, the Marshall of Luxembourg had invited a large number of illustrious guests to his château. Occupying a place of honor on the menu was a fricassée of chicken in white sauce. When it was time to sit down at table, a messenger arrived; the Marshall was summoned without delay to the King's Council. The Marshall gave orders that his absence should not delay the serving of the food. Returning late, and desiring only one dish, he was served with the cold chicken fricassée, congealed in the ivory-colored sauce. He found this food succulent, and a few days later expressed a wish to have it served again. Presented under the name of *refroidi* (rechilled), this term displeased the marshal, who insisted on the name of *chaud-froid*.

In the garde manger department, chaud-froid is used to coat individual portions of specific cold dishes, as well as roasted whole chickens and turkeys, hams, and poached

278

salmon, placed on large platters, around which are arranged items of the same food cut into individual portions. The creamy-white background of the chilled sauce then becomes an excellent surface on which to place various geometric and floral designs. This provides one of the most exciting opportunities to work creatively.

I myself have always preferred mayonnaise collée to the milk-based white sauce; it performs the same function, is much easier and faster to prepare, and has a superior taste. This collée is made by beating liquefied tepid aspic into mayonnaise, straining, and then coating. On rare occasions, chaud-froid sauces of other colors are used. These are made by mixing aspic with a specific sauce: for brown, demi-glaze; for light brown or tan, chicken velouté; for green, mayonnaise collée mixed with juice squeezed from minced parsley or watercress; for red, tomato paste thinned with stock or water.

The decoration of the chaud-froid-coated item is done with shapes and forms cut out directly from vegetables or from what are known as color sheets. Color sheets consist of a food item puréed with stock, combined with aspic or gelatin, then poured into a small clean pan, and refrigerated. Foods typically used are tomato paste for red; pimento for orange; hard-cooked egg yolks for yellow; and spinach for green. A variety of shapes are cut out using aspic cutters; these cutouts are dipped in liquefied aspic (the aspic acts as an adhesive), then set onto the chaud-froid surface. However, the cutouts from color sheets are time-consuming to prepare, and their color is not as brilliant as cutouts directly from vegetables. To save time, the use of very thinly-sliced pimento, carrot, yellow squash, leek leaves, hard-cooked egg white, and truffle (or mock truffle) is preferable.

Chaud-froid and mayonnaise collée, either on a centerpiece for a large platter or for an individual dish (cold egg and pastry dishes), are not as frequently seen on buffets or menus in recent years, for two reasons: restraints of time and labor costs, and a dining public that is unaccustomed to or does not understand these dishes. Yet there are instances when such dishes have a place—for the inspired garde manger who feels challenged to create a platter with a large, visually riveting, chaud-froid-coated centerpiece for a buffet, or in preparing a fine meal for a dining clientele that understands and appreciates the dish when it is served as a small appetizer. In such cases, these specialties can be worth the time and effort needed to create them.

INDIVIDUAL CHAUD-FROID DISHES, SERVED AS APPETIZERS

Cold Salmon Dishes

Cold fish dishes are made from any number of saltwater and freshwater species (carp, cod, eel, herring, mackerel, perch, pike, sole, trout, and turbot), but salmon is one of the most familiar because of its appeal and its availability. The high fat content of salmon, as well as its unique flavor and color, identify it with elegance and fine dining. Salmon is one fish universally accepted when served cold.

Individual portions of salmon cut from a whole boneless, skinless fillet, can be decorated in a number of different ways. The cutlets are first cut, then poached slightly rare to prevent their drying out and breaking up when transferred to a rack for decorating.

A design should be determined before preparation, so that the necessary *mise-en-place* can be set up to execute the design. Decorating can be done with vegetables, such as bell pepper, carrot, cucumber, radish, and scallion, as well as cooked egg white, sieved egg yolk, and truffle. All (except the egg yolk) should be sliced very thin, cut into geometric shapes, placed into a shallow dish filled with tempered aspic, then set in place on the salmon cutlets (bell pepper, carrot, and scallion cutouts are all briefly blanched to heighten their color and make them maleable for placement). Such decoration can be placed directly on the surface of the salmon, or onto the mayonnaise collée or other colored collée that coats the salmon (the application of such coating depends on the recipe). After the decorated salmon has set in the refrigerator, it is coated with a layer of aspic and allowed to set again under refrigeration. Repeat as needed until sufficiently coated.

SALMON CUTLET, GARDEN STYLE

Decorated as desired (generally a floral motif), coated with aspic, served on a bed of vegetable salad bound lightly with mayonnaise, garnished with cutout, diced, or minced aspic jelly.

SALMON CUTLET, GISMONDA

One-half coated with mayonnaise collée, the other half coated with collée mixed with puréed crayfish (shrimp or lobster may be substituted), decorated with a line of caviar between the two collées, glazed with aspic, served with Russian salad, and garnished with watercress.

*SALMON CUTLET, GREEN MEADOW STYLE

Coated with green herb collée, served on a base of vegetable salad bound lightly with mayonnaise, and garnished with cutout, diced, or minced aspic jelly (*see color plate, Salmon Chaud-Froid Dishes*).

*SALMON CUTLET, ITALIAN STYLE

Coated with tomato collée, decorated with truffle and finely chopped pistachios, glazed with aspic, and served on a base of Italian salad (*see color plate, Salmon Chaud-Froid Dishes*).

SALMON CUTLET, MOSCOW STYLE

Coated with mayonnaise collée with the addition of minced chives, garnished with small pastry barquettes filled with caviar, and served with Russian sauce (dressing).

*SALMON CUTLET, OSTEND STYLE

Decorated with slices of truffle, served with a side salad of shrimp and oysters.

*SALMON CUTLET, PARIS STYLE

Coated with mayonnaise collée, garnished with a slice of truffle, served on a bed of asparagus, carrot noisettes, and diced string beans bound lightly with mayonnaise, set inside a large scallop shell (or similar ceramic dish).

---

* Indicates dishes that were originally designed to be served in a puréed form (mousse), formed in timbale or dariole molds lined with aspic jelly, some then lined with collée, mousse added, and then sealed with aspic. They are modified here to conform with a commonsense style.

SALMON CUTLET, ROYAL STYLE

Coated with mayonnaise collée, decorated with truffle, egg yolk, and herb leaves (chervil, tarragon), glazed with aspic, and served with cutout, diced, or minced aspic jelly (*see color plate, Salmon Chaud-Froid Dishes*).

SALMON CUTLET, RUSSIAN STYLE

Coated with mayonnaise collée, served on a base of lettuce chiffonade moistened lightly with oil and vinegar, accompanied by butter lettuce hearts, hard-cooked eggs, olives, capers, and anchovies; Russian sauce (dressing) served separately.

Cold Meat and Poultry Dishes

VENISON LOIN CHAUD-FROID

Roasted, chilled venison tenderloin, sliced on the bias, coated with brown chaud-froid, decorated, glazed with aspic, served on an oval tartlet filled with goose liver or venison pâté, and accompanied by Cumberland sauce.

CHICKEN BREAST CHAUD-FROID, AURORA

Poached or roasted chicken breast, coated with mayonnaise collée blended with tomato paste, decorated as desired, and glazed with aspic (*see color plate, Chicken Chaud-Froid Dishes*).

CHICKEN BREAST CHAUD-FROID, ROSSINI

Poached or roasted chicken breast, coated with mayonnaise collée, decorated with truffle, glazed with aspic, and served on a slice of poached goose liver.

CHICKEN BREAST CHAUD-FROID, SCOTCH STYLE

Poached or roasted chicken breast, coated with mayonnaise collée mixed with finely minced truffle, beef tongue, hard-cooked eggs, and cornichons; decorated with a slice of beef tongue and glazed with aspic; served on a bed of diced cooked green beans bound with mayonnaise.

CHICKEN BREAST CHAUD-FROID, SPRING STYLE

Poached or roasted chicken breast, coated with green herb mayonnaise collée, decorated, and glazed with aspic; served with artichoke bottoms filled with mixed vegetable salad bound with mayonnaise, and glazed with aspic.

CHICKEN BREAST CHAUD-FROID WITH TARRAGON

Poached or roasted chicken breast, coated with mayonnaise collée, decorated with tarragon leaves, glazed with aspic, and served with asparagus napped with tomato vinaigrette (*see color plate, Chicken Chaud-Froid Dishes*).

CHICKEN BREAST CHAUD-FROID, VINCENT

Poached or roasted chicken breast, coated with green herb mayonnaise collée, glazed with aspic; served with tartlets filled with celery and hard-cooked egg salad, and a side dish of Agoursi (also *Ogourzi*), made of peeled cucumber sliced very thin, sprinkled with salt, allowed to drain, rinsed and dried, blended with sour cream and minced dill, and seasoned with salt and pepper (*see color plate, Chicken Chaud-Froid Dishes*).

DUCK CHAUD-FROID, MONTMORENCY

For the Mousse

½ pound (225 g) duck (or chicken) livers, well rinsed and trimmed of connecting membranes

1 small onion, finely chopped

2 garlic cloves, pressed

¼ teaspoon (1.2 mL) ground cumin

¼ teaspoon (1.2 mL) allspice

3 tablespoons (45 mL) Cognac

3 ounces (85 g) unsalted butter, soft

salt and white pepper to taste

For the Duck

4 large individual airline duck breasts (airline breast has upper wing joint intact)

2 cups (480 mL) fresh Bing cherries, pitted (or canned, pitted variety)

2 cups (480 mL) Madeira wine

24 whole almonds, toasted

3 cups (720 mL) duck demi-glaze, flavored with kirsch

1 cup (240 mL) liquefied aspic

8 sprigs watercress

To Prepare the Mousse

- Sauté the livers, onion, and garlic in the butter, until the livers are cooked but still slightly pink (8 to 10 minutes). Add the spices and Cognac, blend, then set aside to cool.

- Place the liver mixture in a food processor, along with the 3 ounces (85 g) of butter, pulse until smooth. Season to taste with salt and pepper and set aside.

To Prepare the Duck

- Season the duck breasts with salt and pepper, and roast or grill. Remove and set aside to cool.

- Pit the cherries (using the end of an ordinary pencil, eraser removed). Simmer the cherries in the Madeira until tender (if using canned cherries, simply marinate them in the Madeira for about an hour). Drain and set aside. When cool, stuff each of 24 cherries with a toasted almond. Mince the remaining cherries.

- Butterfly the duck breasts by slicing them in half horizontally (leave them attached at the wing tip end). Spread a layer of liver pâté on the bottom portion of each breast, sprinkle with some of the minced cherries, fold over the top half of the breast, and gently press.

• Place the chilled duck breasts on a wire rack over a pan. Combine the demi-glaze and the aspic, and nap the breasts with this sauce. Refrigerate until the sauce sets, then coat again. Continue this process (applying three or four coats, depending on the thickness of the sauce) until the breasts are well coated with the sauce. Add two or three coats of aspic in the same fashion, and chill until ready to serve. Serve with the stuffed cherries, garnished with watercress.

CREATING DECORATIVE CHAUD-FROID CENTERPIECES

In contemporary garde manger practice, items typically used for centerpieces include whole capon, chicken, ham, salmon, and turkey. It is best to begin with a common item, such as a turkey, ham, or salmon, in order to learn how the technique is employed. The item to be covered with chaud-froid sauce or collée, then decorated and used as a decorative centerpiece on a platter, will reflect similar small individual items arranged around it on the platter:

Centerpiece	Accompanying Items
Turkey	Sliced roasted or poached turkey; diced or julienned turkey salad
Capon, chicken, Rock Cornish game hen	Cut-up roasted capon/chicken/hen; sliced or breast of capon/chicken; sliced capon/chicken roulade; capon/chicken/hen mousse (molded)
Ham (bone-in)	Any sliced similar charcuterie items derived from pork: Virginia-style ham, prosciutto, Westphalian or Bayonne ham; large and small sausages and wursts made from ham, pork, liver or a combination; head cheese, salami and other dried sausages; coppa, roasted or smoked pork loin

With the exception of ham and other charcuterie items that are already smoked, cured, or dried, the centerpiece to be decorated must be cooked. Poultry items can be either poached or roasted—poaching is preferred because it leaves the flesh moister than roasting. If a portion of the bird is to be left exposed, such as the legs, then it should be roasted. The breast can be coated with chaud-froid or collée and decorated; or the breasts can be removed intact, the remaining cavity filled with a mousse, then carefully cut slices of breast can be arranged in a cascading manner over the mousse and down the front of the bird. In such a case, the breast is sometimes removed, and the legs and sides of the bird are coated with chaud-froid or collée and coated with aspic. Then the sliced breast is set into place (cascading down from the carcass and onto the platter or mirror).

Salmon is always poached, in either a flat or curved position, with the underbelly of the fish as the bottom, so that after cooking it remains in the position it will later take on the platter. To render the salmon flat, it is held in position in two possible ways: it can be tied onto a plywood board on its belly, or it can be tied to the perforated metal plate with long vertical handles that is part of a pochière. A *pochière* is a long, narrow vessel with a lid and a metal insert, specifically designed to poach fish (similar to a *turbotière*, a large diamond-shaped vessel in which turbot, brill, or skate is poached). To render the salmon curved, the salmon ends are pulled together to create a curve. A length of butcher's cord is tied around the gills at one end, the fish is pulled into a semicircular shape, and the other end of the cord is tied around the thinnest part of the tail. It is then poached in a large braisiere. After poaching, the fish retains this shape, giving it a lively appearance, as in a *frozen moment of action*. As with poultry items, the fish can be either completely coated with chaud-froid, or partially coated—only the head and tail. I prefer the latter style, because it allows the skin to be carefully scraped off on one side, exposing the pink salmon flesh.

All centerpieces to be coated are placed on a rack over a pan, so that excess chaud-froid sauce or collée and, later, aspic will drain down into the pan. The sauce should be at a temperature of approximately 80° F (27° C), thick enough to coat, but viscous enough to flow over the centerpiece. Achieving the right temperature is something of a balancing act, inasmuch as the centerpiece must be refrigerated to allow each coat to set up, leaving the sauce to cool further and gel. A solution is to set the sauce in a warm-water bath while the centerpiece sets up. An ice bath can also be used to cool the sauce if necessary.

When sufficient coats of chaud-froid have been applied, leaving an undisturbed surface, one can begin the decoration. It is important to have the design firmly decided before applying it to the centerpiece. A sketch can be made on paper, preferably in colored pencil. For the inexperienced, however, it is wise to practice the design on a mock surface well before the actual execution (this is *always* done when preparing for sanctioned competition). Simply coat a dinner plate, pie pan, or half sheet pan, with a thin layer of chaud-froid or collée (to a thickness of ⅛ inch/4 mm), allow it to set in the refrigerator, then execute the design. When the design is completed, it is coated with a final thin layer of aspic. It is also a good idea to photograph the results for future reference.

As for the design itself, there are few restrictions. The centerpiece is essentially an artist's canvas, where one is free to create a tasteful and visually appealing rendering, executed in a medium of multicolored vegetables, and/or egg white, and/or mock truffle. Floral motifs, fairly simple to create, are common designs. For competition or very important dinners, however, images tend to be more involved: sailing ships and landscapes, outlined figures from Maxfield Parrish paintings, and profiles of U.S. presidents; a Japanese No actor's theater mask, an M. C. Escher geometric pattern, or a lattice-patterned basket filled with flowers. In actual practice, such complex renderings done in vegetables, hard-cooked egg white, or the paper-thin shaved lines of mock truffle, are rarely found in daily buffet productions—they are just too labor-intensive. Yet it is essential for the garde manger practitioner to know of such work and to explore these venues when they are called for. The demand for such meticulously detailed and elaborate work, however infrequent, by an appreciative clientele will, it is hoped, continue.

Three-Dimensional Diamond Motif

The three-dimensional diamond motif is a classic design, made from diamond-shaped cutouts fashioned from items of three different shades: one is always white—cut from cooked egg whites; a second is always black—cut from truffle or faux truffle; and the third is a color an intensity somewhere between black and white—such as cut from pimento, carrot, or ham. The diamonds are arranged to give an illusion of depth, appearing as a three-dimensional pattern. Though time-consuming to create, this motif is well worth the effort in the appropriate situation (*see color plate, Salmon Trout in Aspic*).

In the daily buffets in hotels throughout North America and elsewhere in the world, the trend is to present cold buffet items made visually beautiful by the actual food that is offered on a platter. This means fewer farces and more charcuterie; fewer elaborate centerpieces and a more direct and simple arrangement of foods. This trend, reflecting efforts to keep labor costs in line, has resulted in platters being assembled faster and more of the food components actually being consumed.

TIMBALES

The word *timbale* is derived from an Arabic word, *tahbal*, meaning "drum," referring to a small drinking cup. Traditionally, a guest entering a host's home was offered such a cup filled with an aperitif beverage. In contemporary culinary parlance, a timbale is specifically a 3-inch (75-mm) tall, sloping-sided cylinder, in which numerous small dishes, both hot and cold, are prepared. It is similar in shape to a charlotte mold, though a bit smaller in size and without the handles. In actual practice, however, a timbale is any dish prepared inside a timbale mold. Sometimes the mold is lined with a farinacious layer, such as crêpes, sliced bread, bread or pastry dough, mashed potatoes, pasta, or pasta dough, filled with a farce or filling, and served hot. In other cases, the timbale is filled directly with a farce or filling of some kind, cooked (baked or steamed), then chilled and served coated with aspic. Essentially, this genre opens up endless creative possibilities.

Variations to the tall, sloping-sided timbale form include ramekins (round, ceramic, with the same shape as soufflé molds); darioles (oval metal, 2 × 3 inches/50 mm × 75 mm wide, 1¾ inches/44 mm deep); and minature bombe molds. In practice, however, any ovenproof bowl or cup can be used with excellent results.

Timbale and dariole molds are used to prepare scores of savory or sweet dishes, served both hot and cold, including aspics, custards, mousses, pastries, puddings, and salpicons. The following are classical savory examples, all served hot.

AGNÈS SOREL TIMBALE

A buttered mold sprinkled with minced truffle, half-filled with an indented layer of chicken farce; center filled with minced chicken and truffle bound with Madeira sauce; filled with remaining farce, covered, poached, and served hot with Madeira sauce.

ALEXANDRA TIMBALE

A buttered mold lined with short pastry, baked blind; filled with a salpicon of chicken, asparagus, and truffles lightly bound with Mornay sauce; inverted, topped with a little Mornay sauce, sprinkled with Parmesan cheese, and glazed.

AMBASSADRESS TIMBALE

A buttered mold lined with sliced beef tongue, a slice of truffle on the bottom; half-filled with an indented layer of chicken farce, filled with a salpicon of cooked pasta (such as ditalini), cooked mushrooms, truffles, chicken livers, and lamb sweetbreads bound lightly with Madeira sauce; filled with remaining farce, covered, baked in a water bath, and served hot with Madeira sauce.

BADISH TIMBALE

A buttered mold lined with noodle (or wonton) dough, baked blind, filled with sweetbreads and ham lightly bound with Financier's sauce (Madeira finished with chicken glaze, garnished with mushrooms and truffles), and served hot with additional sauce.

BAGRATION TIMBALE

A buttered mold lined with sliced beef tongue and truffle, half-filled with an indented layer of chicken farce; center filled with a salpicon of cooked pasta (such as ditalini), truffle, and beef tongue bound lightly with Suprême sauce; filled with remaining farce, covered, baked in a water bath, and served hot with additional sauce.

BEAUMARCHAIS TIMBALE

A buttered mold lined with truffle slices, half-filled with an indented layer of game farce; center filled with diced goose liver and cooked mushrooms bound lightly with Madeira sauce; filled with remaining farce, covered, baked in a water bath, and served hot with Madeira sauce.

BEAUVILLIER TIMBALE

Brioche dough baked in a dariole mold, cooled, top removed and scooped out; filled with a salpicon of chicken bound lightly with Allemande sauce (mushroom and nutmeg-flavored chicken velouté, finished with yolk and cream liaison), served hot, garnished with asparagus tips cooked in butter, and served with additional sauce.

BECKENDORF TIMBALE

A buttered mold well lined with very finely ground dry bread crumbs; filled with cooked small pasta (ditalini) seasoned with a little tomato sauce and mixed with flaked salmon, diced cooked mushrooms, and egg yolks; covered, baked in a water bath, and served with tomato sauce.

CALAIS TIMBALE

A buttered mold lined with short dough, baked blind; filled with a salpicon of lobster, mussels, shrimps, and mushrooms bound lightly with Normandy sauce (mushroom and oyster-flavored fish velouté beaten with yolks, cream, and butter), and served with additional sauce.

CAVOUR TIMBALE

A buttered mold lined with short dough, baked blind, and filled with a salpicon of lamb sweetbreads, mushrooms, olives, and truffles bound lightly with Madeira sauce; inverted, garnished with slices of sautéed goose liver on top, and served with additional sauce.

COURTISANE TIMBALE

A buttered mold lined with crêpes (cut to shape), filled with ground cooked chicken bound with béchamel and egg yolks;

covered, baked in a water bath, and served hot with soubise sauce (béchamel flavored with cayenne and onion purée).

DUCHESS TIMBALE

A buttered mold lined with short dough, baked blind; filled with a chicken mousse made with cooked ground chicken, mushrooms, and truffles lightly bound with béchamel; covered, baked in a water bath, and served hot with additional sauce.

FLORENTINE TIMBALE

1 pound (450 g) spinach, rinsed and stemmed
2 eggs, beaten
3 tablespoons (45 mL) grated Parmesan cheese
1 cup (240 mL) cream
salt, pepper, and nutmeg to taste
unsalted butter as needed

- Blanch the spinach in a small amount of lightly salted water. Drain, squeeze dry, and mince. Add the beaten eggs and grated cheese, and blend.
- Preheat an oven to 375° F (190° C).
- Simmer the cream until reduced by about half, and set aside to cool to room temperature. Strain, add to the spinach, blend thoroughly, and season to taste with salt, pepper, and nutmeg.
- Butter 4 to 6 ramekins or timbale molds. Fill them with the spinach mixture, cover each with a small circle of buttered parchment paper, then place in a baking pan filled with boiling water. Bake for 15 minutes, then remove and allow to sit 10 minutes. Run a knife around the inside edge of each timbale, invert, and serve with melted or brown butter.

MILANESE TIMBALE

A buttered mold lined with short pastry or noodle dough, baked blind; filled with a mixture of cooked small pasta (ditalini), cooked mushrooms, diced ham and tongue lightly bound with tomato sauce; served hot with additional tomato sauce.

PRINCESS TIMBALE

A buttered mold lined with duchess potatoes, filled with a salpicon of chicken breasts and asparagus tips lightly bound with Allemande sauce, covered, baked in a water bath, and served hot with additional sauce.

RACHEL TIMBALE

A buttered mold lined with short dough, baked blind, filled with a salpicon of sweetbreads, artichoke bottoms, and blanched bone marrow lightly bound with Bordeaux sauce; covered, baked in a water bath, and served hot with additional sauce.

REGINA TIMBALE

A buttered mold lined with minced shrimp, half-filled with an indented layer of white fish farce (such as halibut, pike, or sole); center filled with minced shrimp and mussels bound with shrimp sauce (fish velouté beaten with shrimp butter), filled with remaining farce, covered, baked in a water bath, and served hot with additional sauce.

ROTHSCHILD TIMBALE

A buttered mold with a thin slice of truffle placed in the bottom, half-filled with an indented layer of pheasant farce; center filled with a salpicon of diced goose liver bound lightly with Madeira sauce, filled with remaining farce, covered, baked in a water bath, and served hot with additional sauce.

SAINT-HUBERT TIMBALE

A buttered mold lined with minced beef tongue and truffle, half-filled with an indented layer of game farce; center filled with a salpicon of game, truffles, and mushrooms bound with poivrade sauce (a pepper-flavored game demi-glaze), filled with remaining farce, covered, baked in a water bath, and served hot with additional sauce.

292

TALLEYRAND TIMBALE

A buttered mold, half-filled with an indented layer of chicken farce; center filled with a salpicon of cooked pasta, chicken, goose liver, and truffles lightly bound with Périgord sauce (brown truffle sauce), filled with remaining farce, covered, baked in a water bath, and served hot with additional Périgord sauce.

Some of the simpler varieties of both hot and cold timbales can on occasion be found in small, unheralded European bistros and restaurants. They are rarely seen, however, in standard restaurant fare, because they are labor-intensive and so antiquated in style that the time required to produce them would not be appreciated. A knowledge of such dishes is important, however, since they are still served at gastronomic dinners and in international culinary competition, even if infrequently and with little fanfare.

Cold timbales are not organized in the same specified manner as the hot varieties, which makes the genre open to innovation. They can be prepared individually, or in larger forms, and decorated as one sees fit. Fillings typically consist of eggs, goose liver, various mousses (fish, ham, poultry, for instance), poached fish (eel, sole, and salmon), or vegetables. For the garde manger practitioner, such small dishes are delightful to prepare for a clientele who appreciate the beauty of a poached egg, shellfish, or mousse, encased in amber-tinted aspic, simply decorated, and accompanied by a green leaf or marinated vegetable salad.

LINING A MOLD WITH ASPIC

To line a mold with aspic, place the ramekins, darioles, timbales, or large mold into an ice water bath. The top edge of the mold *must* be nearly even with the top of the ice water, so that it will set at that point, but it must not be allowed to fall below the level of water—for obvious reasons. Fill the forms to the top with liquid aspic—about 80° F (26° C)—and allow it to sit in the water 5 to 6 minutes. Carefully remove the forms from the bath, then pour out (and reserve) any liquid aspic remaining. There should remain about a ¼-inch (6-mm) thick layer of jellied aspic on the bottom and sides of the forms (it will be much thicker at the bottom corners). If this layer is not thick enough, repeat the process. If the layer is too thick, melt the aspic, and repeat the steps. It takes practice to keep the forms steady while they are in the ice bath and to remove them when just the right amount of aspic has jelled on the inside surfaces.

DECORATING THE ASPIC

Once the first layer of aspic is set in place, there are two approaches to decorating. The first is to set a design in place on the thin layer of aspic; this is then coated with mayonnaise collée in the same way the first layer of aspic is applied: the form is filled completely with liquefied collée and set into an ice bath for several minutes; the excess is then poured out, leaving a coating of the collée. A mousse or salad is carefully placed into the cavity, covered with another layer of collée, followed by a layer of aspic. The second approach is to place a design on the initial aspic layer, which is followed by another layer of aspic, then by a mousse or salad and, finally, sealed in a final layer of aspic.

Designs are fashioned from the same materials used to decorate a chaud-froid or mayonnaise collée-coated center-piece—various vegetables, egg white, truffle (or mock truffle)—all cut very thin and in various geometric shapes. Backed with the off-white collée, or held suspended in the shimmering aspic, these designs stand out beautifully.

Generally, the outer design should harmonize in some fashion with the contents of the interior. If the interior of the mold is to be filled with an egg, ham can be used as the decoration around the egg; if the interior is to be filled with chicken mousse, finely sliced poached chicken breast may be used; with vegetable salad, an arrangement of vegetables is appropriate. In practice, there are few specific rules governing the components of the decoration, leaving it open to innovation. Consider, for instance, a large vegetable timbale prepared in a flat-bottomed 9-inch (225-mm) round, 3-inch (75-mm) deep baking form. After the initial layer of aspic is set in place, a fluted, poached mushroom is set into the center. This is followed by concentric circles of vegetables: cherry tomatoes, carrot spheres, yellow squash triangles, diced celery, halved Brussels sprouts, and broccoli flowerettes (all of the vegetables are blanched, with the exception of the tomatoes). The sides of the form are covered with asparagus tips, or another vegetable cut into julienne (zucchini, celery, string beans), placed vertically around and covering the sides. After a second coat of aspic, to hold the design in place, a vegetable salad is set into the center, then sealed with aspic.

CHAPTER 8

CHEESE AND EGGS

CHEESE

Modern archeological evidence indicates that dairying dates from 4000 B.C., and the earliest evidence of cheese was found in an Egyptian tomb dating back to 2300 B.C. It is likely that the value of cheese as a food was discovered by accident, perhaps by a wandering tribal nomad carrying milk within a sack fashioned from the stomach lining of a livestock animal. Traces of rennet and salt interacted with the milk, and in the heat of the desert, the milk curdled, leaving the equivalent of cottage cheese floating in milky whey. The nomad found it tasty and eventually realized that he had stumbled onto a method of preserving an important food, until then quite perishable.

Historically, dairy products were important throughout Eurasia, though more significantly in the cold North, where long, sunless winters made such foods essential sources of vitamins A and D, calcium, phosphorus, and trace minerals. In these regions, not just cheese, but all dairy products—milk, cream, butter and its by-products—were an important part of diet. The ancient Romans and Greeks, as well as other cultures closer to the warm Mediterranean, disliked fresh milk and cream, preferring to turn these raw materials into cheese, while using olive and walnut oils for other culinary uses. A Greek poet, mocking a fourth-century Thracian wedding, referred to the guests as "butterophagous gentry"; Herodotus, a fifth-century Greek historian referred to barbarian inhabitants of the Caucasus disdainfully as "milk-drinkers;" and the Roman Pliny commented on "barbarous nations, who live on milk, [who] do not know or disdain the value of cheese." "Cheese," Clifton Fadiman once said, "is milk's leap towards immortality." The ancient Romans were, for their time, masters of the art of cheese manufacturing, and some of their most favored cheeses came from provinces that are now parts of France and Switzerland; the British Isles and other parts of Europe also owe the birth of their cheese-making expertise to the occupation of the Romans.

Throughout history, there are scores of poignant tales related to cheese and cheese making. From Einhard, a monk at the monastery of Saint Gall, who penned *The Life of Charlemagne* in the mid-ninth century, comes the oft-told tale of Charlemagne's unannounced visit to the monastery at Rueruit in 774. Unable to provide a meal of fish on what was a Lenten day, the bishop served a white cheese to the emperor. "He picked up his knife, threw away the skin, which, so he thought, was not edible, and began to eat the white cheese. Then the bishop . . . asked: 'Why do you do that, my Lord Emperor? You are throwing away the best part.' " Charlemagne subsequently ordered "two cart-loads" per year of the cheese sent to his palace in Aachen. On a second occasion the emperor was served a blue-veined ewe's milk cheese at the monastery in Aveyron, and here attempted to scrape away the blue-veined portion, until the bishop educated him otherwise. In both cases, Charlemagne's favorable regard for these cheeses had a significant bearing on their popularity; both cheeses are extremely popular and well-known around the world. Roquefort—the blue-veined one—was legally protected on August 31, 1666, through government decree in Toulouse. And at the Congress of Vienna in 1815, where European national boundaries were being redrawn following Napoleon's defeat at Waterloo, politicos discussed the merits of 60 varieties of cheese at a dinner affair. The Duc de Talleyrand-Périgord (1754–1838) had added a French Brie to the table, and it was subsequently voted the "king of cheeses."

Many cheeses throughout the world are made at family farms on a small scale and do not reach every commercial market. The Vella Cheese Company, in Sonoma, California, is one such small producer, operated by Ignatius Vella, third generation of his family to operate the company. Monterey Jack cheese, first produced by Scottish immigrants to Monterey Bay in the mid-nineteenth century, became an important staple for the burgeoning state. During World War II, Monterey Jack became a substitute for the Parmigiano, Romano, and other hard grating cheeses that were unavailable from Italy and Europe at this time. When the war ended, and the traditional cheeses became available again, there was suddenly a huge surplus of Jack cheese. Ignatius's father, Thomas Vella, constructed storage rooms for this surplus, hoping that demand might reach previous levels. It never did, at least for the fresh cheese. In the process, however, he discovered that aging Monterey Jack created a hard and very flavorful grating cheese, similar to those of Italy. The process for drying was improved, and dried Monterey Jack now represents a significant market share and a unique market niche—there is no other cheese quite like it.

HOW CHEESE IS MADE

The transformation of milk into cheese consists essentially of removing the greater part of the water that makes up the bulk of the milk, while retaining the dry matter—proteins, milk fat, and milk sugar. (In a semihard cheese, ten parts milk yields one part cheese.)

The cheese-making process can be divided into six basic steps (the order of steps can change, depending on the variety of cheese):

1. Curdling
2. Breaking up the curd
3. Molding or shaping the cheese
4. Salting, rubbing with salt, or dipping in brine
5. Draining and drying to remove the remaining whey
6. Curing

The curdling is done with a starter culture of lactic bacteria, transforming lactose into lactic acid. Then rennet—an extract found in the stomach of calves—coagulates the casein, the part of cheese protein that coagulates. Following this step, the curd is broken up, and the finer it is cut, the more whey is released and the drier and harder the final cheese. (In some cases, the curd is heated to further remove whey, making it denser.) The remaining steps—molding, salting or brining, drying, and curing—vary according to the kind of cheese being made and are significant in giving each cheese its unique flavor and characteristics.

The Milk

The origin and type of milk used is important to the type of cheese produced. The milk of cows, goats, ewes (sheep), mares, and water buffalo is made into cheese, with milk-fat content ranging from that of skimmed, to whole, to enriched milk. The resulting cheese is loosely classified as follows: low fat: 20% or less; medium fat: 20–40%; high fat: 40–45%; extra-high fat: 45% +; double-cream: 60% +; and triple-cream: 75% +.

The diet of the animals whose milk is used is also significant. In our age of techno-homogenization, many of the mass-produced cheeses lack the unique characteristics of small, home cheese makers, whose cheeses vary from year to year as their animals' forage and grazing habits change. When animals feed on newly sprouted grass, meadows in full flower, or late summer foliage, the flavor of the milk that is transformed into cheese is duly affected. Cheeses produced from milk obtained during the winter tends to be lighter in color and flavor; during the summer, more yellow and flavorful. The fat content of the milk also affects flavor; the lower the fat content, the blander the flavor. Pasteurization of milk, a relatively modern innovation, and an important one in safe mass production of cheese for human consumption, has also contributed to a milder and more consistent flavor in the cheese and other foods produced from this milk. Like the finest foods in the world, a cheese is at its best when it reflects the character of the place from which it comes. On a smaller scale, in remote agricultural regions, this is still the case; time-honored techniques are still in practice. It is up to the student of culinary excellence to seek out such foods, in order to develop a full understanding of the differences between the mundane and the bland, the exceptional and the time-honored.

STYLES OF SERVICE

The most elegant manner of serving cheese is also the least ostentatious and the least labor-intensive from the point of view of the kitchen: a carefully chosen selection of five to eight cheeses, placed on a wooden cutting board on a wheeled cart, is rolled up to each table of dining clientele near the end of a meal (as the last or next-to-last course, before dessert). Each guest makes his or her selection, whereupon the food server cuts or slices the selected cheeses, places them on a serving plate, and sets it before the patron. A basket of sliced fresh or toasted bread accompanies this serving, which may or may not include cut fruit (usually apples or pears), inasmuch as a final dessert course may conflict with this offering. A light to medium-bodied red wine is also recommended as an accompaniment. Sometimes an individual portion of cheeses is offered on a menu, plated in the kitchen when ordered, and delivered to the table.

At the other end of the spectrum is a buffet, serving as few as 50 or as many as 10,000 guests. At a buffet given some years ago, which served 8,500 guests over a period of six days in a huge banquet hall, in which ten different food stations made up the buffet, one station offered only cheeses, fruits, and breads. To expedite the flow of guests through the various stations, the cheese is often cut or sliced and arranged in an attractive manner. This kind of service offers an excellent opportunity for creative layout, perhaps using a large piece of each cheese variety, in front of which flows a visually attractive line of cut cheese. Complementary garnishing is generally added, for instance, cut fruit—apples and pears (always dipped in a lemon-water bath to inhibit discoloration); nectarines, peaches, and plums; kiwis, mangos, and melon—whole blueberries, cherries, raspberries, and strawberries;

dried apples, apricots, cranberries ("craisins"), and figs; toasted almonds and/or walnuts (sometimes caramelized with sugar), and shelled pistachios. The addition of fresh rosemary sprigs, which hold up well on a buffet, adds color and an aromatic "outdoorsy" bouquet.

Personal style and preference of the restaurant operation, as well as the demographics of the dining guests, are significant in the choice of cheeses and accompaniments. A buffet presentation of cheese on a large wooden board, slab of marble, or ceramic platter, with herbs, fruit, and nuts, is quite different from the simple and unpretentious individual tableside offering. Although a large buffet layout adds color and excitement, as well as a sense of abundance, each is fitting in the appropriate place. (*See color plate, Cheese Platter.*)

CHEESE VARIETIES

There are more than 2,000 documented varieties of cheese worldwide, but classification is difficult because of many varieties with overlapping criteria—origin of the milk, type of rind, consistency, length of aging, culinary use, and so on. The best way to understand cheese, if one has such interest, is to participate in cheese tastings, visit production facilities in as many locations and as often as possible, and keep a journal to record these experiences. The following paragraphs give a fairly broad view of cheese types.

Fresh

In the production of fresh cheeses, coagulation is accomplished with lactic acid only (rennet is sometimes added in large productions to speed the process). Most contain no salt, allowing a relatively short shelf life; some are lightly salted and briefly cured. Examples include: boursin, Boursault, Brillat-Savarin (bloomless) (French); Marscapone and ricotta (Italian); cottage and farmer (from North America and elsewhere).

Natural-Rind Goat

Natural-rind goat cheeses are more or less soft cheeses, depending on how the curd is handled. They come in fresh forms—sometimes dipped in herbs or volcanic ash—as well as in aged forms. There are two types in this category: farmer's—develops a blue rind that forms naturally while drying in cellars; and commercial—*Penicillium candidum* is added to develop bloomy rind while drying. Examples include: Chevrect de Bellay, Bucheron, Chabichou, Chevrotin, Montrachet, Valençay (French).

Soft Ripening

Soft-ripening cheeses are so-called because of the texture and appearance of the rind, which is covered with white fuzz caused by the spraying of *Penicillium candidum* mold in the curing stage. To help retain their moisture, the curds are carefully placed in molds to prevent additional breakdown. If the curds are broken down too much, the growth of the rind will be inhibited. Examples include: (all French, unless otherwise noted) Bellétoile, Brie, Camembert, Caprice des Dieux, Creama Dania (Danish), Coulommiers, l'Explorateur, St. Andre, and Valcuvia.

Washed Rind

Similar in texture to the soft-ripened cheeses, the washed-rind cheeses are slightly drier. The curd is broken down more than in the soft-ripening types, so they are incapable of growing surface mold. The cheese is washed periodically with brine, whey, beer, cider, wine, brandy, or oil (depending on the type of cheese), in order to maintain internal moisture needed for proper aging. The result is a smooth rind with a varnished look. Examples include: Bel Paese (Italian), Esrom (Danish), Livarot, Pont l'Évêque, Port Salut (French), Muenster (German), oka (Canadian), and Tallagio (Italian).

Cheddar Types

During a ripening period following curdling, color is added to some Cheddar-type cheeses. Traditionally, grated carrots or crushed marigolds were used for color; today, *annatto* is used—a tasteless coloring extracted from the seeds of the Central American tree by the same name. The settled curds are sliced into slabs and stacked to further remove whey, after which they are placed in cloth-lined metal hoops and pressed for up to 24 hours. Aging takes between 2 and 12 months.

Examples include: Vermont, Wisconsin, and New York Cheddars, Coon, and Colby (North American); Mimolette and Cantal (French); Cheshire, Gloucester, Leicester, Wensleydale, and Derby (English).

Dutch Types

Similar to Cheddars as to pressing and coloring, Dutch cheeses are of a little softer consistency and require less curing time (2 to 6 months). Manufactured not only in Holland, but in Scandinavia and other parts of Europe as well, they are often flavored with herbs and/or spices (such as caraway, clove, cumin, dill, pepper, and sage). Examples of Dutch-style cheeses include: Edam, Gouda, and Leydan (Dutch); Kuminost and Nögelost (Norwegian); and Tilsit (German).

Stretched Curd

The elasticity of stretched curd cheese results from the addition of hot whey (115° F/46° C) after the initial coagulation and draining process, making it tough and pliable. Hotter water (180° F/82° C) is then added, and the curd is kneaded, either manually or by machine. The resulting "ropes" are then hand- or mold-shaped, chilled in cold water, brined, and cured up to 4 months. Examples include: mozzarella, Provale, Provatura, provolone, Scarmorze, Caciocavallo (Italian).

Hard/Cooked

Some hard cheeses get their texture by being cooked in whey after the curd has been broken up, then wrapped in cloth before being placed in molds, where the curd is pressed as much as possible. They are then moved to a fermentation cellar, where a temperature of roughly 73° F (23° C) and relative humidity of approximately 85% are maintained. The cheeses are washed several times a week in a salt brine, and over a period of roughly 2 months, carbon dioxide gas, trying to escape from within, creates the characteristic holes of this variety. The rind is natural; it is brushed and lightly washed throughout the curing periods and brushed with oil before being shipped to prevent further drying. Examples include: Alpsberg (Austrian), Comté (French), Emmenthal and Gruyère

(Swiss), Fontina Val d'Aosta (Italian—probably the finest, though Denmark and Sweden also produce an excellent Fontina); Jarlsberg (Norwegian); Lappi (Finnish) Samsoe (Danish).

Hard-Grating

Hard-grating cheeses are prepared similarly to the Swiss-style cheeses mentioned in the preceding paragraph, yet with subtle differences that yield a completely different product. Fermented whey, for example, is used in place of a lactic acid starter—the whey is left over from a preceding batch of cheese. The rinds are natural (except for Dried Monterey Jack, which is coated with cocoa and olive before being aged), and curing time is a minimum of 2 years. Examples include: Asiago, Parmesan, Pecorino, Romano (Italian); Dried Monterey Jack (Californian); sapsago (Swiss).

Internal Mold

Like soft cheeses, cheeses with internal mold are neither pressed nor cooked. Most frequently they are made from crumbled curd that is sprinkled with *Penicillium glaucum*. This mold is made from bread that is burnt in an oven. The best of these cheeses are those whose veining is evenly and widely distributed. These cheeses ripen from the inside out. The bronze-green mold growth depends on perforation and aeration of the cheese with special large needles during the curing process, which is done in very humid cellars. Examples include: Blue d'Auvergne and Roquefort (French); Danish Blue, Dolcelatte, and Gorgonzola (Italian); Maytag Blue (North American), and Stilton (English).

Processed

Processed cheeses come in many different formats and varieties. They are usually made with hard cheeses, which go through the six manufacturing steps and are then shredded, melted down, remolded, and packaged. Some are fairly respectable, such as Gourmandise and Laughing Cow; others can be rather offensive, such as Velveeta and Cheez Whiz. Budget and demographics have a bearing on the selection of such cheeses.

SELECTING, HANDLING, AND STORING

Whether serving a sit-down dinner for a party of four or setting up a buffet station for service to 4,000, it is wise to select one or several cheeses from each classification—the larger the event, the larger the selection and quantity. This is where personal knowledge of market varieties is essential. The following is a suggested appropriate offering:

- *Soft Ripening.* Brie, Camembert, l'Explorateur, or St. Andre
- *Natural Rind Goat.* Chevret de Bellay, Bucheron, Chabichou, Chevrotin, Montrachet, or Valençay
- *Washed Rind.* Bel Paese or Esrom
- *Cheddar.* Vermont (white) Cheddar, or Chesire
- *Dutch.* Edam, Gouda, or Kuminost
- *Hard/Cooked* (*Swiss*-style). Comté, Emmenthal, or Jarlsberg, plus a Fontina (Italian Val d'Aosta, or another variety)
- *Hard-Grating.* Parmesan, Pecorino, Romano, or Dried Monterey Jack
- *Internal Mold.* Gorgonzola, Maytag Blue, or Stilton.

Opened cheeses require tight closure, limiting exposure to air for two reasons: to prevent drying and to prevent them from absorbing flavors and aromas from other items in cold storage. This means wrapping well in plastic wrap or storing in secure plastic containers with tight-fitting lids.

Cheeses that have appeared on the cheese tray in the dining room and have been sliced into, can be trimmed squarely, wrapped, and reused. Cheeses that are to appear on a buffet station, partially sliced, should include one large piece, in front of which is arranged a flowing line of the same cheese, cut: soft-ripening cheeses, such as Brie and Camembert, should be cut in radial wedges, roughly ½-inch (12-mm) wide at the wide end, leaving a larger piece of the same cheese for presentation; goat cheeses can be dipped in minced herbs, then sliced with a thin-bladed knife dipped in very hot water; washed-rind and Dutch-style cheeses should be sliced in wedges, radially, also using a knife dipped into very hot water; large blocks of cheese, such as Cheddar, Jack (including the dried version), and Swiss-style varieties, can be sliced on an electric slicer in uniform, ¼-inch (6-mm) thick slices, then cut into smaller rectangular or triangular shapes; hard-grating and internal mold cheeses should be presented in large pieces, accompanied by a cheese knife so that guests can help themselves.

When the buffet is over, any presliced cheese remaining should be gathered up and recycled into other dishes. Separating cheeses according to their possible secondary uses—

fondues, gratinées, omelets, sauces, soufflés, and so on—will help expedite their future use.

EGGS

Eggs are among the most important foods in the human diet, and people consume a large variety, including those from ducks, ostriches, partridges, peacocks (popular among the ancient Romans), pelicans, quails, and turtles. Hen's eggs, the variety consumed most today, date back to the domestication of wild jungle fowl in India, circa 2000 B.C. In spite of the recent clamor over saturated fat in the human diet, eggs are a very healthful food, containing all the amino acids, all vitamins except vitamin C, and most essential minerals. It is estimated that as many as 250 billion eggs are consumed each year, and, like all other foods, they are an acceptable part of a diet as long as they are eaten in moderation and properly prepared. The method of cooking is significant, inasmuch as overcooking or excessively browning them in butter or oil makes eggs difficult to digest. Poached and soft-boiled eggs are easiest to digest. The ability to cook an egg properly is a skill taken lightly by some, yet, surprisingly, one not commonly found among culinary practitioners.

In culinary uses, eggs are indispensable and are used in all areas of the kitchen. They are used as an emulsifier for cold sauces and a liaison for hot sauces; in pasta, shortbread, and cakes; in bread crumb toppings and as a leavener for soufflés; in certain bread doughs and batters; to coat and seal pastries; and in certain drinks. The freshness of an egg is extremely important. Because the shell is porous, in its first week of existence an egg begins to lose moisture, its cohesiveness begins to break down, and its flavor diminishes. The older the egg, the less its binding and leavening ability, and the less its nutritional value. For the commercial consumer of eggs, it is best to know a local producer so as to be sure that eggs are received within a week of their gathering. As an Italian proverb tells it, "Eggs of an hour, bread of a day, wine of a year, a friend of thirty years."

There has been justifiable concern in recent years over the presence of salmonella in mass-produced eggs. The crowded and unsanitary conditions in vast egg-producing facilities breeds the kind of environment where this bacterium thrives. The best precaution is to know your producer, even if it is a wholesale producer catering to the food service industry. As the buyer, you can insist on documentation that the eggs you purchase are produced from hens raised in modern and sanitary facilities, and, consequently, be certain that they will be fairly safe from salmonella contamination.

COOKING EGGS

Approximately half of the dishes that follow require boiling the eggs so that they are either fully cooked—what is commonly known as "hard-boiled"—or nearly fully cooked—sometimes referred to as *mollet,* meaning "soft." The latter is referred to in the recipes as "medium-cooked." The remaining dishes call for poached eggs, of which two specify fried eggs.

The advantage of medium-cooked eggs is that the yolk remains moist and slightly runny in the center, making it easy to digest. It is akin to a medium-rare cooked piece of beef or lamb, or a salmon or tuna fillet that is slightly translucent in the center. To cook eggs to a medium state, immerse them in cold water with about one-half teaspoon of salt per egg. Bring to a boil, and continue boiling for 7–8 minutes. Remove from the fire, drain, drop into ice water, and peel immediately. For hard-cooked eggs, follow the same procedure, adjusting the boiling time to 10 minutes. The cooking time will vary according to the age of the eggs (the older the egg, the shorter the cooking time will be), their size, and their temperature at the time of cooking. An hour spent experimenting with different methods is the best way to develop one's own technique. The most important dictum is to avoid overcooking, which makes them hard to digest and their texture dry.

For poached eggs, bring some water to a simmer, about 2 inches (50 mm) deep and acidulated with a little plain or white wine vinegar. Freshness of the egg is important: the older the egg, the more the albumen will spread in the water before setting. The vinegar helps the egg set, although it should be a very small amount so that it does not affect the taste. Immerse the eggs in the water, cook 4–5 minutes, then drain well. When cool, trim the edges of the egg whites, using a pair of scissors.

Fried eggs are easiest to prepare in a nonstick frying pan, with a small amount of oil or butter. They should be cooked a minute or so on one side, then flipped, cooked another 10 seconds, flipped over again, and slid out onto absorbent paper. When cool, they are trimmed with a knife or round pastry cutter.

EGGS ALEXANDRA

Poached eggs, served on pastry tartlets filled with lobster mousse, decorated with truffles, glazed with aspic, and garnished with caviar (around the edge of the eggs).

EGGS AMBASSADRESS

Medium-cooked eggs, coated with mayonnaise collée, decorated with tarragon leaves, glazed with aspic, served on pastry tartlets, and garnished with minced aspic jelly (around the base of the eggs).

EGGS IN ASPIC, PARMA STYLE

6 medium eggs, hard-boiled, peeled
¼ pound (113 g) Parma ham, thinly sliced
4 large sprigs dill
1 quart (960 mL) liquid aspic

- Place four medium ramekins or dariole molds into an ice bath and fill with aspic. Allow to sit 5 to 6 minutes, remove from the bath, then pour out (and reserve) any liquid aspic remaining.
- Cut the ham into long triangles (1½ × ½ inch/38 × 12 mm), dip into liquid aspic, and arrange on the set aspic inside each ramekin, with the short side of each triangle up on the edges, and the point down toward the bottom center. Place a sprig of dill on the bottom, then fill with enough aspic to cover the dill. Place the ramekins in the refrigerator to set.
- Carefully place an egg in each ramekin, fill to the top with aspic, and place in the refrigerator to set. Place the remaining aspic in a small, clean tray (about ¼ inch/6mm deep), and allow to set in the refrigerator.
- When the aspic in the pan has set, carefully lift out, place on a clean cutting board, and cut into fine dice.
- Invert the molded eggs onto a chilled plate or platter. Wrap each in a warm cloth for several seconds, or until the aspic slides out. Return them to the refrigerator once again.
- Serve with a mayonnaise-based sauce, and accompanied by salad greens or vegetables dressed in vinaigrette [*see color plate, Eggs (Cold)*].

Eggs Balzac

Poached eggs, coated with mayonnaise collée, decorated with celery leaves, glazed with aspic, and served on pastry tartlets filled with a finely diced celery root salad garnished with minced aspic jelly (around the base of the eggs).

Eggs Baroda

Hard-cooked eggs, cut in half lengthwise, stuffed with yolks mashed into a paste with anchovies, butter, and curry powder, drizzled with mayonnaise sauce flavored with curry, and garnished with minced aspic jelly (around the base of the eggs).

Eggs Berlin

Poached eggs, coated with mayonnaise sauce flavored with smoked salmon paste, served on pastry tartlets filled with smoked salmon paste or a finely diced smoked salmon salad.

Eggs Beyram Ali

6 large eggs, poached
8 medium shrimp, poached and split
¼ cup (60 mL) asparagus, ¼-inch (6-mm) dice
¼ cup (60 mL) carrots, ¼-inch (6-mm) dice
¼ cup (60 mL) cauliflower, ¼-inch (6-mm) flowerettes
¼ cup (60 mL) celery, ¼-inch (6-mm) dice
¼ cup (60 mL) green peas
¼ cup (60 mL) yellow bell pepper, ¼-inch (6-mm) dice
¼ cup (60 mL) scallions, sliced very thin
1 large vine-ripened tomato
1 pint (480 mL) mayonnaise
salt and white pepper to taste
juice of 1 lemon
1 tablespoon (15 mL) dill, minced
1 tablespoon (15 mL) tarragon, minced
1 tablespoon (15 mL) parsley, minced
1 small head butter lettuce, leaves separated, rinsed, and dried.

• Blanch the vegetables individually in boiling salted water until al dente. Remove, cool in cold water, drain thoroughly, and set aside.

- Combine the vegetables with enough mayonnaise to bind lightly. Season to taste with salt and pepper.
- Add the minced herbs to the remaining mayonnaise, and blend. Thin with a little lemon juice (or vinegar).
- Arrange the vegetable salad, on four individual plates, on a base of lettuce leaves. Set an egg on top of each, and nap with the green mayonnaise. Garnish with four shrimp halves each.

Note: This recipe calls for six eggs, in the event that the yolks of one or two break during cooking. The two eggs that remain unused, broken or not, should be reserved and utilized in another dish.

The blanched diced vegetables that are bound with mayonnaise are also known as a vegetable macedoine—referring to their fine uniform dice. Any vegetable variety specified in the recipe can be substituted based on season and availability.

EGGS CARÊME

Fried eggs trimmed round, slice of truffle on the center, caviar sprinkled on the white, garnished with small aspic triangles, and placed on a pastry tartlet filled with flaked salmon bound with mayonnaise.

EGGS CARMEN

Coat medium-cooked eggs with mayonnaise collée, decorate with finely cut green and red bell peppers, and coat with aspic. Place a lettuce leaf base in the center of a platter, and top with some very finely sliced bell peppers macerated in vinaigrette. Arrange the eggs around this salad, and some minced aspic around the eggs.

EGGS CASINO

6 eggs, medium-cooked
½ cup (120 mL) tomato paste
2 cups (480 mL) liquid aspic (lukewarm)
salt and white pepper to taste
liquid aspic as needed
4 large barquette shells, baked
½ cup (120 mL) chicken mousse or finely chopped chicken salad
12 fat asparagus spears

The undersides of the eggs sometimes do not take to the tomato collée, because it does not have any fat (mayonnaise) in it. Although the addition of mayonnaise will solve this problem, it will also significantly lighten the color of the collée, which is sometimes adjusted with red food coloring. We prefer to avoid the use of food coloring and allow the undersides to remain a bit uncoated.

- Blend the tomato paste, 2 cups (480 mL) liquid aspic, salt, and pepper together, until smooth. Place four of the eggs on a screen over a pan, nap with the tomato mixture, and refrigerate until it sets. Repeat until the eggs are well coated with the tomato mixture.

- Slice the egg white from the remaining eggs, and cut out into geometric shapes. Place in a dish with a little liquid aspic, then decorate the eggs. Nap the eggs with two additional coats of aspic, and refrigerate until ready to serve.

- Peel the asparagus, and blanch in boiling water until al dente. Drain, cool, and set aside.

- Spread a little of the mousse or salad on the bottom of each barquette shell. Place a coated egg on top, and serve garnished with the asparagus [*see color plate, Eggs (Cold)*].

EGGS CHARTERHOUSE

Dariole molds lined with aspic, decorated with mixed vegetable julienne, a poached egg set inside, filled with aspic, and set. Turned out on a bed of vegetable macédoine (see Eggs Beyram Ali), with mayonnaise served on the side.

EGGS COLINETTE (SINGLE SERVING)

Poached eggs set inside dariole molds, lined with aspic, decorated in a chequered pattern with squares of truffle and egg white, served on a bed of Rachel Salad (celery, artichoke bottom, potato, and asparagus tips cut into fine julienne, bound with mayonnaise, garnished with truffle), and garnished with minced aspic jelly.

EGGS CHRISTOPHER COLUMBUS

Hard-cooked eggs cut in half lengthwise, filled with minced cooked chicken breast, decorated with anchovy-flavored egg yolk paste, garnished with capers, pickled cucumbers, and sliced radishes, and served on a bed of lettuce chiffonade, accompanied by mustard mayonnaise (Alexandra or Rougemont).

EGGS COLINETTE (SERVICE FOR SIX)

Line a savarin mold (hollow in the center) with aspic, then set 6 thin slices of truffle (not artificial), equidistant, around the bottom of the form. Coat 6 medium-poached eggs with mayonnaise collée, allow to set, then place on top of the truffles. Set 2 poached, deveined shrimp in between the eggs, and fill the form with aspic. Allow to set, then turn out onto a plate or platter. Fill the center with Rachel Salad (celery, artichoke bottom, potato, and asparagus tips cut into fine julienne, bound with mayonnaise, garnished with truffle).

EGGS COLUMBUS

Medium-cooked eggs served on pastry tartlets filled with puréed goose or duck liver (foie gras), napped with mayonnaise, garnished with chopped tomato aspic.

EGGS DENMARK

Hard-cooked eggs cut in half lengthwise, stuffed with egg yolk and smoked salmon paste, napped with mayonnaise, and garnished with dill.

EGGS ESTERHAZY

Poached eggs served on toasted and buttered oval croutons, topped with an oval slice of beef tongue, napped with ravigote sauce (olive oil, white wine vinegar, Dijon mustard, tarragon, chives, parsley, chervil, onion, and capers), garnished with minced aspic jelly.

EGGS FROU-FROU

Poached eggs coated with light yellow mayonnaise collée (color derived from chopped egg yolks), served on a string bean, green pea, and asparagus salad lightly bound with mayonnaise, and garnished with minced truffle sprinkled around the edges of the eggs, and chopped aspic jelly.

EGGS GABRIELLE

Poached eggs set inside dariole molds lined with aspic, decorated with lobster coral, served on pastry barquettes filled with puréed white fish (such as sole, halibut, or swordfish).

EGGS GENTLEMAN

Hard-cooked eggs, stuffed with a paste made of egg yolk and pheasant purée, coated with a natural demi-glaze (brown chaud-froid), topped with a thin slice of truffle, and glazed with aspic.

EGGS GERMAINE

Poached eggs set inside dariole molds lined with tomato aspic, served on oval bread croustades filled with finely diced lobster lightly bound with mayonnaise.

EGGS HARLEQUIN

Medium-cooked eggs, coated with various flavors of mayonnaise collée (chef's choice), decorated attractively, glazed with aspic, served on pastry tartlets filled with mixed vegetable macédoine lightly bound with mayonnaise (see Eggs Beyram Ali).

EGGS HUNGARIAN

Hard-cooked eggs sliced, served on a bed of mixed vegetable macédoine lightly bound with mayonnaise (see Eggs Beyram Ali), garnished with lettuce leave cups filled with cucumber and tomatoes seasoned with simple vinaigrette (oil, vinegar, salt, black pepper).

EGGS HUSSARDE

Medium-cooked eggs served on crayfish mousse, napped with mayonnaise thinned with cream and flavored with horseradish, and garnished with green peppers cut into fine julienne and lightly blanched.

EGGS IMPERIAL

Poached eggs served on artichoke bottoms filled with vegetable macédoine with beef tongue and tomato, napped with rémoulade sauce (mayonnaise, Dijon mustard, anchovy, tarragon, parsley, gherkins, and capers).

EGGS JEANETTE

Coat medium-poached eggs with mayonnaise collée, allow to set, then place in a medium ramekin half filled with liquid aspic. When the aspic has set, pipe in a border of goose or duck liver paste blended with butter, around the eggs. Fill with aspic, and garnish with flat-leaf parsley.

EGGS JOANNA

Poached eggs glazed with aspic, served on pastry tartlets filled with ham mousse.

EGGS MARGOT

Medium-cooked eggs served on oval bread croustades stuffed with beef tongue, anchovies, and cornichons bound lightly with mayonnaise, napped with mayonnaise.

EGGS MAUPASSANT

Poached eggs coated with Sailor Sauce (also known as *Sauce Matelote*, demi-glaze simmered with fish trimming and red wine) and garnished with fish aspic jelly.

EGGS MIRABEAU

Fried eggs trimmed round, glazed with aspic, served on round croutons spread with anchovy butter, garnished with anchovy fillets and pitted olives.

EGGS MODERN

Medium cooked plover's eggs served on pastry tartlets filled with mixed vegetable macédoine (see Eggs Beyram Ali) lightly bound with mayonnaise.

EGGS MONTE CHRISTO

Poached eggs set inside dariole molds lined with aspic, filled with aspic, and when set, served on a bed of mixed vegetable macédoine (see Eggs Beyram Ali) lightly bound with mayonnaise.

EGGS MORTIMER

Hard-cooked eggs cut in half widthwise, with ends trimmed so they stand on end, yolk removed, filled with caviar, served in artichoke bottoms, garnished with anchovy fillets, sliced truffle, and chopped aspic jelly.

EGGS NICE STYLE

Poached eggs coated with tomato-flavored mayonnaise collée, served in pastry tartlets filled with diced potato, green bean, and tomato salad bound lightly with mayonnaise and tomato purée.

EGGS NORWEGIAN STYLE

Poached eggs served on a bed of shrimp salad flavored with minced anchovies.

EGGS OLÉA

Hard-cooked eggs cut in half lengthwise, stuffed with a paste made of the yolks mashed with butter, minced olives, and cayenne pepper, and garnished with aspic jelly.

EGGS OLGA

Hard-cooked eggs cut in half lengthwise, stuffed with a paste made of the yolks mashed with butter, minced olives, and cooked diced celery root, napped with thinned mayonnaise, and garnished with caviar.

EGGS PAGANINI

Medium-cooked eggs served in puff pastry shells (bouchée) filled with diced tomato bound lightly with mayonnaise, napped with thinned mayonnaise, and garnished with a slice of truffle (*see Figure 8.1*).

EGGS PRETENDER STYLE

Poached eggs served on puff pastry tartlets filled with diced mushrooms marinated in vinaigrette, garnished with white asparagus tips napped with green (herb) mayonnaise.

EGGS PRINCE OF WALES

Medium-cooked eggs cut in half widthwise, served in a half tomato scooped out, seasoned with vinaigrette, and filled with diced celery, napped with thinned mayonnaise.

EGGS QUEEN STYLE

Medium-cooked eggs served in small hollowed-out brioches filled with chicken salad, napped with thinned mayonnaise, garnished with a slice of truffle, and glazed with aspic.

EGGS ROMANOV

Poached eggs served on marinated artichoke bottoms filled with caviar, garnished with pitted olives and green peppers.

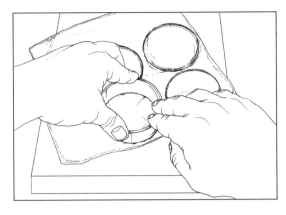

Cut out 3–4-inch circles of puff paste.

Cut out a smaller interior circle, leaving an approximately ¼-inch wide circle.

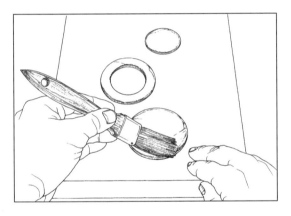

Brush the larger circle with egg wash.

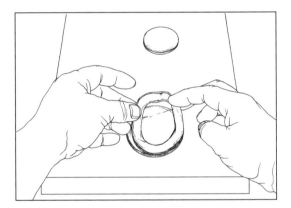

Place the cut-out circle around the edge of the full circle, brush with egg wash, and bake until golden brown.

Figure 8.1
Preparing a Large Bouchée (Puff Pastry Shell)

EGGS ROSITA

Poached eggs served on a bed of chopped aspic jelly, coated with mayonnaise collée, garnished with sliced truffle, and accompanied by cherry tomatoes stuffed with tuna fish paste.

EGGS RUSSIAN STYLE

Poached eggs served on puff pastry tartlets filled with Russian salad, garnished with smoked salmon, caviar, and cornichons.

EGGS SEVILLE STYLE

Medium-cooked eggs cut in half lengthwise, one-half served on an oval crouton spread with anchovy butter, garnished with stuffed green olives.

EGGS SKOBELEFF

Poached eggs served coated with tomato-mayonnaise collée, garnished with strips of smoked salmon, served on pastry tartlets filled with diced crayfish (or shrimp or lobster) tails, bound lightly with mayonnaise and anchovy paste.

EGGS SPRING STYLE

Poached eggs glazed with aspic, served on puff pastry tartlets filled with vegetable macédoine bound lightly with mayonnaise.

EGGS TARTAR STYLE I

Poached eggs coated with sour cream, sprinkled with paprika and minced chives, and served on a bed of steak tartar.

EGGS TARTAR STYLE II

Hard-cooked eggs cut in half lengthwise, stuffed with egg yolk paste made with minced anchovies, cornichons, and mayonnaise, garnished with caviar, and accompanied by tartar sauce.

EGGS TZARINA STYLE

Medium-cooked eggs coated with pink mayonnaise collée (using a little tomato paste), served on puff pastry tartlets filled with Russian salad, garnished with strips of smoked salmon, caviar, and minced aspic jelly.

EGGS VALENCIA STYLE

Poached eggs napped with mayonnaise seasoned with mustard and garlic, served on artichoke bottoms, accompanied by tomato salad.

EGGS WLADIMIR

Medium-cooked eggs, served on a bed of asparagus salad, napped with thinned green (herb) mayonnaise.

MARBLE TEA EGGS

1 quart (960 mL) water
10 eggs
2 tablespoons (30 mL) black
  tea leaves
2 star anise
1 teaspoon (5 mL) Szech-
  wan peppercorns
1 tablespoon (15 mL) sliced
  gingerroot
¼ cup (60 mL) soy sauce

- Combine all the ingredients in a pot, and bring to a boil (the eggs should be immersed in the liquid). Turn the fire off. Lift out the eggs, one by one, using a slotted spoon, and place on a cutting board. Tap an egg gently with the back of the spoon, making random cracks all around the shell. Repeat with the rest of the eggs.
- Return the eggs to the liquid, boil another 5 minutes, then remove from the fire. Allow to cool, then refrigerate as is, overnight.
- Remove the eggs from the liquid, remove the shells, and use as desired (stuffed or as a garnish). They should all have a brown-lined mottled appearance, similar to marble.

STUFFED EGGS, CALIFORNIA

4 large eggs, hard-cooked
¼ cup (60 mL) cilantro
  leaves, minced
mayonnaise as needed
salt and white pepper to
  taste
alfalfa sprouts as needed
2 radishes, cut in half and
  sliced very thin
8 very thin green bell pepper spears, about 2
  inches (50 mm) long

8 very thin yellow bell pep-
    per spears, about 2
    inches (50 mm) long
8 slices calamata olives

2 cups (480 mL) mixed
    salad greens
½ cup (120 mL) vinaigrette

- Cut the eggs in half widthwise, and remove the yolks. Mash the yolks and cilantro with mayonnaise, salt, and pepper into a smooth thick paste.
- Place some alfalfa sprouts into the cavity of each egg half, so that the tops of the sprouts stick out slightly over the edge of the cavity. Fill the egg halves with the paste, using a pastry bag fitted with a round tip. Garnish with a fan of radish slices, 2 pepper spears, and a slice of olive, and serve on a bed of mesclun salad mix (mixed California salad greens) tossed in the vinaigrette [see color plate, Eggs (Cold)].

STUFFED EGGS, FELIX

6 medium eggs, hard-boiled
mayonnaise as needed
salt and white pepper to
    taste
1 tablespoon (15 mL) ham,
    minced
1 tablespoon (15 mL)
    gherkins, minced
1 teaspoon (5 mL) shallot,
    minced

1 tablespoon (15 mL) tar-
    ragon, minced
1 tablespoon (15 mL) pars-
    ley, minced
1 thin slice of ham
4 paper-thin slices of truffle
2 cups (480 mL) light aspic,
    warm

- Cut the eggs in half lengthwise and remove the yolks. Mash the yolks with mayonnaise, salt, and pepper into a smooth, thick paste. Add the minced ham, gherkins, shallot, and herbs, and blend in. Fill 8 egg halves with this paste, using a knife dipped in hot water to shape each into a smooth mound.
- Cut the ham, truffle, and remaining egg white into ⅓-inch (9-mm) long diamond shapes (lozenge). Place on a saucer with a little of the aspic.
- Ladle a line of the truffle cut-outs, end to end, across the top of each egg, slightly off-center. Set the egg and ham cutouts next to the truffle cutouts, on the wider side. Repeat a second row if desired. Ladle a coat of aspic over each egg, and place in the refrigerator to set. Ladle a second coat of aspic,

refrigerate, and serve on lettuce leaf cups [*see color plate, Eggs (Cold)*].

STUFFED EGGS, FLORIST STYLE

4 medium eggs, hard-boiled
mayonnaise as needed
salt and white pepper to
    taste
2 carrots, cut into 1 × ⅛
    inch (25 × 4 mm) julienne
1 red bell pepper, cut into
    1 × ⅛ inch (25 × 4 mm)
    julienne

1 medium rutabaga, cut
    into 1 × ⅛ inch (25 × 4
    mm) julienne
1 cup (240 mL) green string
    beans, 1 × ⅛ inch (25 × 4
    mm) julienne
4 Roma tomatoes

- Remove a thin slice from each end of the tomatoes (so they will stand upright). Cut them in half widthwise, and scoop out the interior pulp (save for another use). Invert and set aside.

- Cut the eggs in half widthwise, and remove the yolks. Mash the yolks with mayonnaise, salt, and pepper, into a smooth, thick paste.

- Lightly blanch the vegetables in boiling salted water. Drain, cool, and set aside.

- Place the egg halves in the tomato halves, and fill the eggs with the paste, using a pastry bag fitted with a plain round tube. Insert 4 or 5 julienne strips of each vegetable into the paste, so that they fan out from the center [*see color plate, Eggs (Cold)*].

CHAPTER 9

CHARCUTERIE, CURING, AND SMOKING

CHARCUTERIE

The pig population of the world is estimated at 400 million, part of reason that pork is the butcher's single most important product. China is the leading pork-consuming nation in modern times, and roughly 70% of the pigs in the world reside in China—in part due to Mao Tse-tung's revolution, which led to a fivefold increase in China's pig population. Although the intent was to increase availability of fertilizer for crops (the average pig produces more than 8,000 pounds/3,600 kg of manure in a single year), the increase in the pig population ultimately solved other problems as well. As a relatively efficient transmuting machine (20 pounds/9 kg of pork meat is produced for every 100 pounds/45 kg of feed, as compared with 7 pounds/31.5 kg for cattle and 10 pounds/4.5 kg for chickens), during Mao's revolution pigs subsisted on leftover products such as cotton leaves, corn stalks, rice husks, and peanut shells. Pigs have always been scavengers, able to forage for themselves or survive on virtually any form of leftover edible substance. The ancient Romans, who were responsible for fine-tuning the manufacture of numerous foodstuffs still in production today, innovated an early form of foie gras by force-feeding pigs with dried figs and honey. Centuries later, in what is now Europe, the wild pigs that lived on acorns, in what was primarily fully wooded forest, were considered to have the best-tasting flesh.

In ancient Rome and Greece (where the animal was sacrificed to appease the gods), in London and Paris during medieval times, and in New York City and Naples as late as the nineteenth century, pigs were permitted to roam municipal streets scavenging for food. These were times when public thoroughfares had yet to be cleaned by the local governments, though at various times and places throughout history the authorities would attempt to rid a town or city of wandering pigs. When, for example, early in the twelfth century, French Prince Philip died from a fractured skull as a result of falling from his horse after it was frightened by a street pig running between its legs, in Paris pigs were banned from the public streets, as they were in nineteenth-century New York City. But the residents always prevailed—pigs, after all, were often the only source of protein food for a town's poorest citizens.

Not only is a pig economical and efficient in its dietary requirements, but most of the animal is used in some fashion: its skin is transformed into leather, the glands provide important essences in pharmaceutical manufacturing, inedible parts of the fat are used for lubrication, and the hair is used in upholstery and insulation. The meat itself is also well disposed for preservation: legs and belly brined, then smoked, salted, and/or dried to create ham, bacon, and salt pork; other parts are cooked in their own fat and preserved in the same manner as duck confit; the intestines are stuffed to form sausages.

We tend to think of ethnic and religious taboos against eating pork as a natural outgrowth of early hygienic practices. But in the Islamic and Judaic cultures that forbade the consumption of pork, the mutton that often replaced it was just as perishable, and all ancient peoples developed methods of preservation. The evolution of these taboos probably stem from the pig's incompatibility with nomadic societies. Raising pigs requires geographic stability, which may lead to a relatively sedentary life-style, but wandering tribes needed to maintain mobility. They had to follow shifting sources of food, and they had to be able to mobilize quickly when their survival was threatened by another warring tribe. Settling down to tend herds meant a potential loss of available manpower required for a quickly assembled army; thus the consumption of pork came under a negative religious mandate as being "unclean."

Traditionally, *charcuterie* refers to all products made from pork, both meat and offal; in modern times, it refers to any meat product—beef, veal, lamb, pork, poultry, or game—slated, cured, or smoked, including meat that is fashioned into sausage.

The etymology of the word *charcuterie* is derived from *chair* (old French), meaning "flesh," and *cuit*, meaning "cooked." Pork butchery dates back to ancient Greece and Rome. During the early centuries of the Roman Empire, mutton and goat were the most commonly consumed animal foods; during the later centuries, the emphasis shifted to pork. A "porcella law" was established, which governed the rearing, feeding, slaughtering, and preparation of pork. Pork butchers were housed separately from beef and mutton butchers, a practice that was renewed in Paris in 1475, when a special edict created a new job classification for *"maîtres charcutiers-saucissier-boudiniers."* This edict differentiated pork butchers from the trade organizations of strictly butchers and roasters, permitting them to purchase pork meat directly from the producers and to sell and serve the cooked items made from pork flesh and offal.

The word *sausage* is derived from the Latin *salsicia* and *salsus,* meaning "salted." This product consists of a mixture of ground, seasoned meat stuffed into pig, sheep, or lamb casings (small intestines), or enclosed in caul fat (a thin membrane, veined with fat, that encloses the stomach of a pig and is used to wrap a farce to create a *crépinette*). Sausage mixtures can be coarsely ground or finely puréed (emulsified). Fresh sausages can be prepared by grilling, broiling, pan-frying, deep-frying, or braising; other varieties are preserved by smoking or drying. Much like Italian pasta or Chinese dim sum, shapes, sizes, and nomenclature vary widely, from town to town, region to region, country to country. Lengths vary from 2 inches (50 mm) to 3 feet (1 meter); diameter ranges from small: 1 to 2 inches (25 to 50 mm); to medium: 2 to 3 inches (50 to 75 mm); to large: 4 to 6 inches (102 to 152 mm). Inasmuch as sausage is a form of farce (forcemeat), charcuterie overlaps into pâtés, terrines, galantines, and other dishes made with a meat stuffing, but, generally speaking, the latter are more refined and specialized than meats simply made into sausages, whether fresh, smoked, or dried.

There are innumerable varieties of sausages, found in all regions of the world where pork is a part of the local diet. Certain varieties, well known and typical to a particular region, are passed on from generation to generation by the butchers of that region. And any butcher worth his salt, anywhere, generally prepares his own unique varieties, which are consumed by his clientele and will probably never get any recognition outside that particular market neighborhood. In the case of certain specialty suppliers in North America, however, "regional" sausages are becoming big business, and varieties beyond the usual pork, beef, and lamb can be shipped anywhere. One can find any number of chicken, turkey, and seafood sausages, with garnishes and flavors well beyond the typical varieties. As for the typical traditional varieties, a number of examples are described in the following paragraphs.

GERMAN SAUSAGES

Germany has the greatest variety of sausages, which include the following:

- *Bierwurst.* Large pork sausage, typically served with beer
- *Brägenwurst.* Long, thin, pork fat and brain, oatmeal, and onion sausage, lightly smoked
- *Bratwurst.* Several small-to-medium varieties, served fried

327

- *Frankfurter.* Medium emulsified pork sausage, sometimes smoked, served poached
- *Nuremberg.* Long, thin herb sausage, served grilled
- *Plockwurst.* Small, shiny brown beef and pork sausage, served poached
- *Presskopf.* Medium pork, veal, and beef sausage
- *Schinkenwurst.* Large beef and pork sausage, smoked and served poached
- *Zungenwurst.* Lean pork, tongue, and blood sausage, garnished with pieces of tongue wrapped in bacon and arranged geometrically in the casing

FRENCH SAUSAGES (SAUCISSE, SAUCISSON)

There are numerous French varieties of sausage. *Saucisse* is usually small and fresh; *saucisson* is usually large, and smoked or dried. French sausages are often served with pickled cabbage, (sauerkraut) in a dish unique to Alsace (*Choucroute à l'Alsacienne*). Varieties include:

- *Saucisse d'Alsace.* Small, emulsified veal sausages, served deep-fried.
- *Saucisson d'Arles.* Coarse, lean beef and fat pork sausage, dried; traditionally also contains lean donkey or horse meat.
- *Saucisse de Bordeaux.* Small pork sausage, grilled and served with white wine and oysters.
- *Boudin Blanc (white pudding).* An emulsified poultry, veal, pork, or rabbit sausage, of endless variations, traditionally sold in France during Christmas time. Varieties include *à la Richelieu* (primarily chicken, cooked in small individual molds); *Le Havre* (pork fat, milk, eggs, bread, and rice flour); *Avranches* (chicken breast, veal sweetbreads, fish fillets, and cream); *Le Mans* (pork fat, lean pork meat, eggs, onions, and milk).
- *Boudin Noir (blood pudding).* Fine-grained sausages made from seasoned pig's, cow's, or sheep's blood and fat. Variations are endless, including the addition of cooked onions (Paris), onions marinated in brandy and herbs (Lyon), milk (Nancy), pork cracklings and bread soaked in milk (Strasbourg), apples (Normandy), prunes (Brittany), raisins (Flanders), and chestnuts (Auvergne).
- *Bougnette de Castres (also d'Albi, de Cévennes, and l'Auvergne).* Flat sausage made from pork belly, bread, and eggs, served fried or baked in fat, and eaten cold.

328

- *Coudenou de Mazamet. Boudin Blanc* made with equal quantities of ground pork rind and a paste of egg and bread crumbs, and served poached in water.
- *Crépinette.* Flat pork and chopped parsley, wrapped in caul fat (*crépine,* a thin, fat-veined membrane that surrounds an animal's stomach). *Crépinettes* are generally brushed with butter, sometimes coated with fresh white bread crumbs, then grilled, broiled, sautéed, or baked.
- *Francfort.* Medium beef, veal, and pork sausage, smoked and dried, served poached.
- *Galabart.* A large black pudding sausage, consisting of pig's head, skin, tongue, lungs, heart, and blood, mixed with bread. Unique to southwestern France, and measuring 3½ to 4 inches (90 to 100 mm) in diameter, it is eaten cold.
- *Gogue.* Blood sausage originating from Anjou, consisting of vegetables, bacon, cream, and blood; poached in water, then sliced and fried.
- *Saucisson de langue.* Numerous varieties of sausage containing tongue and pistachio nuts.
- *Cervelas de Lyon.* Pork sausage with pistachios or truffles, served poached.
- *Saucisson de Montagne.* A small 2 to 3-inch (50 to 75-mm) long, very coarse, semidried or dried pork sausage.
- *Saucisson Princesse.* Medium pork and veal sausage, garnished with diced beef tongue.
- *Saucisse de Toulouse.* A long, thin pork sausage served pan-fried or braised.
- *Tripotcha.* Mutton blood pudding, sometimes with veal lungs and blood, unique to the Basque region, sometimes eaten with apple purée.

OTHER REGIONAL VARIETIES

- *Boutifar.* Large black pudding sausage, 3⅓ to 4 inches (90 to 100 mm) in diameter, made with blood and pieces of fat and meat. Unique to Catalonia and North Africa, it is eaten cold.
- *Chorizo.* A long, thin, dry pork or pork and beef sausage (horse, donkey, or mule may also be used), flavored with red chili pepper and garlic. Of Iberian origin, it is used in Paella and the Spanish stew *cocido* (similar to the French *pot-au-feu*).
- *Coppa.* Italian or Corsican salted, fatty pork loin, marinated in red wine and garlic, tied and dried. (*Coppa* means "nape of the neck," in reference to the part of loin closest to the neck that is used.)

329

- *Gendarme.* Dry, smoked sausage unique to Austria and Switzerland, often served as an ingredient in a stew.
- Madrid. A veal, pork fat, and sardine sausage.
- *Merguez.* A small beef, mutton, and red pepper sausage, originating in North Africa and Spain. It became popular in France in the 1950s. This sausage, ¾ inches in diameter, is served fried, grilled, or broiled and is often used in couscous.
- *Salami.* A dried sausage produced in Austria, Denmark, France, Germany, Hungary, Italy, and Switzerland. Salamis are made with pork and other meats, including beef, goose, and wild boar, and are often flavored with red wine, fennel, basil, parsley, paprika, and other herbs. Among Italian regions, Milan and Bologna are particularly well known for their salami, which comes in various forms: *Salame Milanaise, Fiorentino, de Felino, di Fabriano, di Secondigliano, Calabrese,* and so on.

PREPARING SAUSAGE

A vast number of sausages are now available wholesale to the food service industry, but some garde manger kitchens enjoy the challenge of producing their own unique varieties to offer their clientele. Customarily, the form that makes sausage what it is, is created by the pork, lamb, or beef casings into which it is stuffed. These casings are the cleaned intestines of a given animal, a fact that some may find distasteful. There are also synthetic casings, such as the plastic casings used in the commercial production of hot dogs, knockwurst, and keilbasa, which must be removed before consumption, but sausage is typically a food product derived from animal ingredients, and the casing just happens to come from the innards of the creature. Casings come in two forms: packed in salt, which requires soaking in water for 24 hours to rehydrate; and fresh, stored in a salt solution. An additional form of casing is "caul fat," the inner lining of the animal's stomach, which is a thin membrane mottled with bits of fat. Five-inch (125-mm) square pieces of caul fat are wrapped around certain farces, dusted with flour or cornstarch, and sautéed in oil or butter.

The following guide offers an overview of sausage production.

- Be certain that all grinding and/or emulsifying utensils are clean and dry.
- All ingredients and grinding/emulsifying utensils must be well chilled in order to facilitate a clean grinding and pre-

vent separation of meat and fat. This is usually accomplished by placing the metal parts (bowl, blade, separator, and cover) of a horizontal rotating food chopper (commonly referred to as a "buffalo chopper") into the refrigerator or freezer for 30 minutes. Do the same with the six metal parts of a food grinder (housing, screw, blade, plat[s], cover, and feeder pan), as well as with the parts of a food processor.

- In the event a grinder is not available, the meat intended for grinding can be cut up, then placed into the freezer for 1 hour. In such a semifrozen state, it can then be ground in a food processor using the pulse switch.
- The herbs and spices used to season sausage are often mixed ahead of time—each mix is used for a different variety. (See the spice blends in Chapter 10 "Farces.")
- Have ready at hand all of the meat, fat (meat and fat must be fresh! they must also be cut into ½-inch/12-mm pieces before grinding), spices, garnish, and binding agents, according to the recipe to be prepared.
- Set the parts of the food grinder into place (be sure the blade is kept sharp and the screw-on cover is securely in place).
- Run the meat, fat, and seasoning through the grinder twice—once through the large or medium-holed plate, and a second time through the small-holed plate.
- Set the parts of the buffalo chopper into place, and place the binding agents (cream, eggs, bread) and one-third (or more, depending on the recipe) of the ground meat mixture into the metal bowl. Add crushed ice (1 quart/960 mL per 12 pounds/5.4 kg of meat), and emulsify. (This step can also be accomplished using a food processor; be sure the bowl, blade, and cover are chilled beforehand. Some sausage varieties are fully emulsified, others part emulsified–part ground, and still others ground only—first through the medium-holed plate, then through the fine-holed plate.) Combine the emulsified mixture with the ground mixture, and blend manually until fully blended.
- Take a teaspoon of the farce, and poach in a little salted water until cooked. Remove and taste for seasoning balance, then correct seasoning in the rest of the farce as needed.
- Place into a sausage stuffer (a large pastry bag can also be used to stuff the mixture into the casings), load the casing onto the spout, and carefully fill the casing. (Be careful not to stuff too tightly, which can cause the sausage to burst during cooking.)
- Twist the stuffed casing at even intervals to create links. The size of the links depends on one's preference, or is specified

in the recipe (some varieties are rolled into individual coils instead of being twisted into links).

- Sausage can be poached after stuffing, in either boiling lightly salted water, court bouillon, or an appropriate stock. The internal temperature should always reach a minimum of 150° F (65° C), and the sausage must be allowed to cool before refrigerating.
- Under refrigeration, uncooked sausages will last up to five days; poached sausages up to one week. Freezing is recommended *only* for cooked sausage (be sure it is well wrapped).
- Fresh sausages can also be smoked. Be sure that the internal temperature reaches at least 150° F (65° C).

SAUSAGE RECIPES

In the recipes that follow, ingredients and methods of preparation are only guidelines. Proportions of ground to emulsified farce can be modified according to the texture desired. Grinding gives a coarser texture; emulsifying yields a finer texture. Seasonings can be adjusted as well, according to one's taste.

Seafood

OCEAN SAUSAGE WITH FINE HERBS

1 pound (450 g) fresh white fish (cod, sole, halibut, etc., or a combination), boneless and skinless and cut into ½-inch (12-mm) pieces

½ pound (225 g) salmon fillet, boneless and skinless, and cut into ½-inch (12-mm) pieces

½ pound (225 g) ocean scallops

1 teaspoon (5 mL) salt

½ teaspoon (2.5 mL) white pepper

¼ teaspoon (1.2 mL) cayenne pepper

1 tablespoon (5 mL) dill, minced

1 tablespoon (5 mL) tarragon, minced

1 tablespoon (5 mL) cilantro, minced

1 tablespoon (5 mL) parsley, minced

whites of 4 large eggs

1 cup (240 mL) heavy cream

sausage casings as needed

- Coarsely grind the fish, seasoning, and herbs. Emulsify in a food processor along with the egg whites and cream, then pipe into the sausage casings.

SEAFOOD SAUSAGE, MEXICAN STYLE

3 pounds (1.3 kg) fresh red snapper (or rock cod) fillet, boneless and skinless, and cut into ½-inch (13-mm) pieces
1 teaspoon (5 mL) salt
½ teaspoon (2.5 mL) white pepper
½ teaspoon (2.5 mL) jalapeño peppers, minced
¼ teaspoon (1.2 mL) cayenne pepper
¼ cup (60 mL) tequila

1 tablespoon (15 mL) lime zest
whites of 4 large eggs
½ cup (120 mL) heavy cream
¾ pound (340 g) shrimp, shelled, deveined, poached, and finely diced
½ pound (225 g) squid, cleaned and finely diced
½ cup (120 mL) cilantro, minced
sausage casings as needed

- Coarsely grind the fish, seasoning, tequila, and zest. Emulsify in a food processor along with the egg whites and cream. Combine with the shrimp, squid, and cilantro and blend, then pipe into the sausage casings.

SEAFOOD SAUSAGES WITH MUSTARD SAUCE

1 shallot, minced
½ cup (120 mL) dry white wine
6 ounces (170 g) boneless, skinless cod, cut into ½-inch (12-mm) pieces
6 ounces (170 g) boneless, skinless salmon, cut into ½-inch (12-mm) pieces
8 ounces (225 g) sea or bay scallops

1 tablespoon (15 mL) dill, minced
1 tablespoon (15 mL) parsley, minced
salt and pepper to taste
½ cup (120 mL) heavy cream
24 inches (600 mm) fresh lamb sausage casings

- Place the fish and scallops in the freezer for 30 minutes. Simmer the shallot and wine until nearly dry. Place the fish and scallops, herbs, salt, pepper, and shallots in a food processor and purée, using the pulse switch. Incorporate the cream, using the pulse switch.

- Fill a pastry bag fitted with a large (No. 6) round tube with the fish farce. Slide one end of the sausage casing over the tube, and carefully pipe in the farce. When it is filled, twist the casing at roughly 4-inch (100-mm) intervals. Poach the sausage in barely simmering court bouillon for 10 minutes. Remove and set aside, keeping warm.

Note: To prepare the sauce, simmer 1 minced shallot, ½ cup (120 mL) fish stock, and 1 cup (240 mL) dry vermouth, until reduced by three-fourths. Add 1 cup (240 mL) heavy cream, and reduce until it reaches the desired thickness. Add 2 tablespoons (30 mL) grainy Dijon-style mustard, 1 tablespoon (15 mL) minced chives, and season to taste with salt and white pepper.

SCALLOP AND SALMON SAUSAGE

2 pounds (900 g) fresh white fish (cod, sole, halibut, etc., or a combination), boneless and skinless, and cut into ½-inch (12-mm) pieces
1 pound (450 g) fresh sea scallops
1 teaspoon (5 mL) salt
½ teaspoon (2.5 mL) white pepper
¼ cup (60 mL) brandy
1 tablespoon (15 mL) lemon zest

whites of 6 large eggs
½ cup (120 mL) heavy cream
1 pound (450 g) salmon fillet, poached and finely diced
2 stalks celery, finely diced and sautéed in butter until tender
¼ cup (60 mL) tarragon leaves, minced
sausage casings as needed

- Coarsely grind the fish, scallops, seasoning, brandy, and zest. Emulsify in a food processor along with the egg whites and cream. Combine with the salmon, celery, and tarragon and blend, then pipe into the sausage casings.

Poultry

CHICKEN SAUSAGE

1 pound (450 g) chicken breast meat, boneless and

skinless, cut into ½-inch (12-mm) pieces

8 ounces (225 g) chicken fat, cut into ½-inch (12-mm) pieces
1 teaspoon (5 mL) salt
½ teaspoon (2.5 mL) white pepper
2 pounds (900 g) chicken thigh meat, boneless and skinless, cut into ½-inch (12-mm) pieces
1 tablespoon (15 mL) lemon zest

1 cup (240 mL) Spanish onions, finely diced and sautéed in butter until transparent
1 cup (240 mL) leeks, finely diced and blanched al dente in boiling lightly salted water
¼ cup (60 mL) finely chopped parsley
sausage casings as needed

- Coarsely grind the chicken breast, fat, salt, and white pepper, and set aside. Repeat this grind with the thigh meat and zest. Emulsify the ground breast meat in a food processor, then combine all ingredients, blend, and fill the sausage casings.

CHICKEN AND SPINACH SAUSAGE

2 pounds (900 g) breast and thigh meat, cut into ½-inch (12-mm) pieces
¾ pound (340 g) fatback
1 bunch spinach, well rinsed, stemmed, and blanched briefly in boiling salted water
1 cup (240 mL) Spanish onion, finely diced and sautéed
1 tablespoon (15 mL) quatre épices (2 parts cloves, 2 parts black pepper, 1 part nutmeg, 1 part ginger)

1½ tablespoons (23 mL) salt
1 cup (240 mL) bread crumbs, soaked in ½ cup (120 mL) heavy cream
1 egg, beaten
1 cup (240 mL) coarsely chopped pistachios, toasted
sausage casings as needed

- Coarsely grind the chicken breast and thigh, fatback, sautéed onion, spices, and salt. Add the bread crumbs soaked in cream and the egg, and emulsify in a food processor. Fold in the spinach and pistachos, and fill sausage casings.

CHICKEN SAUSAGE, PARIS STYLE

2 pounds (900 g) chicken breast meat, cut into ½-inch (12-mm) pieces

1 pound (450 g) pork butt, cut into ½-inch (12-mm) pieces

¾ pound (340 g) fatback, cut into ½-inch (12-mm) pieces

2 teaspoons salt

1 teaspoon (5 mL) white pepper

1 teaspoon (5 mL) *quatre épices* (2 parts cloves, 2 parts black pepper, 1 part nutmeg, 1 part ginger)

2 shallots, minced and reduced in 1 cup (240 mL) dry white wine (2 tablespoons/30 mL should remain)

1 cup (240 mL) bread crumbs, soaked in 1 cup (240 mL) heavy cream

2 eggs, beaten

1½ cups (360 mL) Granny Smith apples, peeled, cored, finely diced, and held in lemon water

sausage casings as needed

- Coarsely grind the chicken, pork, fatback, salt, white pepper, spices, and shallot reduction. Place in a food processor, along with all remaining ingredients (except the apples), and emulsify (can be done in small batches if necessary). Blend in the apples and stuff into sausage casings.

DUCK AND CRANBERRY SAUSAGE

1 pound (450 g) duck breast meat, boneless and skinless, cut into ½-inch (12-mm) pieces

½ pound (225 g) duck thigh meat, boneless and skinless, cut into ½-inch (12-mm) pieces

½ pound (225 g) coarsely ground pork butt

½ cup (120 mL) craisins (dried cranberries), rehydrated in a little brandy

2 tablespoons (30 mL) mint leaves, roughly chopped

1 teaspoon (5 mL) salt

½ teaspoon (2.5 mL) white pepper

½ teaspoon (2.5 mL) ground cumin

½ cup (120 mL) heavy cream

8 pieces pork caul, approximately 5 × 5 inches (125 × 125 mm)

cornstarch and vegetable oil as needed

336

- Place the duck and the pork in the freezer for 1 hour, then place in a food processor along with the craisins (drained of brandy), mint, salt, pepper, cumin, and cream. Emulsify, using the pulse switch. Shape the ground meat into 8 equal patties, and wrap in the pork caul. Dust with cornstarch and sauté in vegetable oil on both sides until golden brown. Place on absorbent paper, and hold in the oven.

Note: This sausage is ideally served with warm rhubarb or dried fruit compote.

Spicy Duck Sausage

1 pound (450 g) skinless, boneless duck breast, cut into ½-inch (12-mm) pieces
½ pound (225 g) pork butt, cut into ½-inch (12-mm) pieces
¼ pound (113 g) duck livers, trimmed and roughly chopped
½ cup (120 mL) dry sherry
1 shallot, minced
3 garlic cloves, pressed
2 bay leaves
1 teaspoon (5 mL) marjoram (or oregano) leaves, minced
1 teaspoon (5 mL) thyme leaves, minced
1 teaspoon (5 mL) red chili pepper, minced
1 teaspoon (5 mL) mustard seeds, crushed
½ teaspoon (2.5 mL) cumin
1 teaspoon (5 mL) salt
sausage casings as needed

- Combine all ingredients in a bowl, blend well, cover, and allow to marinate at room temperature for 2 hours.
- Remove and discard the bay leaves, and pour off excess liquid. Grind the mixture first through a medium-holed plate, followed by a second grinding through a fine-holed plate.
- Pipe the farce into sausage casings, and twist or tie at 4-inch (100-mm) intervals. Poach the sausages in simmering salted water for 5 minutes. Remove, allow to cool, and set aside. Serve grilled or sautéed, with appropriate accompaniments.

Pork

Chorizo

1 pound (450 g) lean pork, cut into ½-inch (12-mm) pieces
½ pound (225 g) fatback, cut into ½-inch (12-mm) pieces

¼ cup (60 mL) red wine, reduced by half with 2 crushed garlic cloves and ½ teaspoon (2.5 mL) chili powder

1½ teaspoons (7.5 mL) salt

¼ teaspoon (1.2 mL) sugar

1 red bell pepper, roasted, peel and seeds removed

½ teaspoon (2.5 mL) cayenne pepper

1 tablespoon (15 mL) tomato paste

sausage casings as needed

- Grind all ingredients once through a large-holed plate, and a second time through a fine-holed plate, then pipe into casings.

GARLIC AND SAGE SAUSAGE

2 pounds (900 g) pork butt, cut into ½-inch (12-mm) pieces

1 pound (450 g) fatback, cut into ½-inch (12-mm) pieces

1 shallot, minced, and sim- mered in 1 cup (240 mL) gin, until reduced by three-fourths

1 bulb garlic, cloves peeled, and simmered in ½ cup (120 mL) Cointreau until reduced by half

2 teaspoons (10 mL) salt

1 teaspoon (5 mL) white pepper

2 tablespoons (30 mL) fresh sage leaves, minced

sausage casings as needed

- Grind all ingredients twice, then pipe into casings.

Lamb and Veal

LAMB SAUSAGE, MEDITERRANEAN STYLE

2 pounds (900 g) lean lamb, cut into ½-inch (12-mm) pieces

¾ pound fatback (340 g), cut into ½-inch (12-mm) pieces

2 tablespoons (30 mL) olive oil

¼ cup (60 mL) onion, minced

1 tablespoon (15 mL) tomato paste

2 tablespoons (30 mL) gar- lic, minced

1 egg, beaten

½ cup (120 mL) cilantro, minced

¼ teaspoon (1.2 mL) mint, minced

½ teaspoon (2.5 mL) quatre épices

1 teaspoon (5 mL) coriander

1 teaspoon (5 mL) cumin

¼ cup (60 mL) lemon juice

1 teaspoon (5 mL) black pepper
2 tablespoons (30 mL) salt
¼ cup (60 mL) sun-dried tomatoes, small dice
¼ cup (60 mL) red bell pepper, small dice, sautéed in olive oil

¼ cup (60 mL) pine nuts, lightly toasted
sausage casings as needed

- Grind all ingredients (except tomatoes, bell pepper, and pine nuts) twice. Combine with the tomatoes, pepper, and pine nuts, blend, and pipe into casings.

Spicy Lamb Sausage

1 pound (450 g) lean lamb, trimmed of sinew and cut into ½-inch (12-mm) pieces
¼ pound pancetta (113 g), cut into ½-inch (12-mm) pieces
¼ pound fatback (113 g), cut into ½-inch (12-mm) pieces
1 teaspoon (5 mL) salt
½ teaspoon (2.5 mL) black pepper

¼ teaspoon (1.2 mL) ground cinnamon
¼ teaspoon (1.2 mL) ground cumin
¼ teaspoon (1.2 mL) ground cardamom
½ teaspoon (2.5 mL) grated ginger
3 tablespoons (45 mL) chopped parsley
3 tablespoons (45 mL) chopped cilantro
sausage casings as needed

- Combine the lamb, pancetta, fatback, salt, pepper, and spices. Blend well, and allow to marinate 2 hours.
- Place a third of this mixture in a food processor, along with ½ cup (120 mL) of crushed ice. Pulse until finely chopped. Set aside, and repeat with another third of the mix. Process the final third, leaving it a bit chunkier. Combine the three batches, along with the herbs, and stuff into pork casings.

Veal Sausage

3 pounds (1.3 kg) veal shoulder, well trimmed and cut into ½-inch (12-mm) pieces

1 pound (450 g) pork butt, cut into ½-inch (12-mm) pieces

½ pound (225 g) fatback,
    cut into ½-inch (12-mm)
    pieces
2 ounces (60 g) salt
1 ounce (30 g) pepper
½ cup (120 mL) beer

⅓ cup (60 mL) Cognac
1 tablespoon (15 mL) sugar
1 cup (240 mL) leeks, finely
    diced and sautéed in but-
    ter until tender
sausage casings as needed

- Grind all ingredients (except leeks) twice. Combine with the leeks, blend, and pipe into casings.

CURING AND SMOKING

Before the advent of modern refrigeration, curing and smoking were the primary and traditional means of preserving fresh fish, poultry, game, and meat. By packing these foods with salt and sugar, and then treating them with controlled heated smoke within an enclosed area, surface bacteria were eliminated and moisture removed, rendering the treated food relatively protected from spoilage. (Curing, by the way, is both a separate means of preservation and, in some cases, a prestep to smoking.)

Smoking is not an exact science, and the techniques, devices, and nomenclature vary considerably. The information given here is a basic guideline, from which one can develop one's own style and technique. Some foods are dry-cured only, some are dry-cured and subsequently smoked, and others are marinated in a brine and then smoked. Recipes for cures and brines, as well as types of wood, vary immensely. Smoking devices range from state-of-the-art electrically controlled units to oil drums cut in half, scrubbed clean, top hinged, and the interiors fitted with grates. Temperature also plays a part in smoking, depending on whether an item is *cold* smoked or *hot* smoked. Smoked foods have come into vogue because of the flavor imparted, and we recommend that one practice with different cures, brines, and techniques until one's own unique style is developed. We also recommend that a limited number of such items be included on a menu, because the flavor of smoked foods is so dominant.

SODIUM NITRITE

Potassium nitrate (saltpeter) and sodium nitrite are compounds that have been used in the commercial processing of meat (such as bacon, ham, hot dogs, and bologna) since roughly the seventeenth century. In the early twentieth century, scientists discovered that sodium nitrite was the active ingredient that inhibited the growth of bacteria, particularly *Clostridium botulinum,* which produces a deadly toxin—botulism—in an airless environment. Sodium nitrite also maintains the pink color of the meat, improves flavor (it is a form of salt), and lengthens shelf life by virtue of its antibacterial action. That sodium nitrite is also used in the manufacture of explosives, matches, rocket propellants, and fertilizers may be little news to those aware of nitrite's reputation as a carcinogen. In a 1956 study in the United States, sodium nitrite was found to create nitrosamines in the human body, which are known to be carcinogenic in animals. Because this study concluded that cured meats accounted for about 20% of the available nitrite needed for the creation of nitrosamines in the human body, it was not considered dangerous enough to be banned. Then, in 1978, a study at the Massachusetts Institute of Technology indicated that nitrite itself could be carcinogenic, when it was found to produce lymph cancer in laboratory rats. A battle ensued, during which the FDA investigated the situation, the industry representatives argued for nitrite's importance as a preservative that protected the consumer against the botulism bacterium, and consumer groups argued that because it was primarily a color-preserving agent in preserved meats that were cooked— such as bacon and hot dogs—nitrite could be eliminated. The U.S. Department of Agriculture nevertheless directed meat processors to lower the levels of residual nitrite in their products from 200 to 40 parts per million. Then, in 1980, a review of the 1978 MIT study found fault with its methods, and the FDA took no further action.

In our time, nitrate and nitrite usage is 10 to 50 times less than before the advent of modern refrigeration and a scientific understanding of their functions. The U.S. Department of Agriculture requires 6.1 grams of sodium nitrite to cure 100 pounds (45 kg) of meat. A curing salt blend is available, made up of 94% ordinary salt combined with 6% sodium nitrite. *Curing salt* should be used in cures or brines when an item is *intended for cold smoking in excess of three hours.* Hot smoking, or curing fish only (such as Gravlax), does not require curing salt. The proper quantity of curing salt is 4 ounces (113.4 g) per 100 pounds (45 kg) of meat.

THE SMOKING STEP

Whether you use a small home smoker (which looks like a tall barbecue grill with a domed top), a large commercial smoker

341

(both of these are accompanied by instructions on use), or one innovated from an oil drum or metal trash can, all contain roughly the following interior parts: a basin for burning chips and sawdust (may include a gas or electric-fired heating element); a pan to catch drippings (or to be filled with water for *steam-smoking*); a rack on which food, such as fish or cheese, is placed; and hooks from which larger pieces of meat, poultry, or game are hung.

In preparing a food item for smoking, it is first exposed to one of two presteps: it is either dry cured or marinated in a brine. Both dry cures and brines consist of coarse salt, sugar, and aromatics (herbs and spices). In curing, the mixture is rubbed into the flesh, the food is allowed to sit for a period and is then smoked. In using brine, ingredients are brought to a boil, cooled to room temperature, then used as a marinating medium. Sometimes brine is injected directly into the food to be smoked, with the use of a brine pump or injection needle.

A *cold smoke* is one in which the temperature ranges between 70° and 85° F (21° and 29° C); a *hot smoke* runs at temperatures of 140° to 175° F (60° to 79° C). Cold smoking is generally applied to small fish and shellfish, such as blue fish, cod, eel, herring, mackerel, sea bass, trout, white fish, clams, mussels, oysters, and shrimp, and to subordinate items such as dried beans, cheese, eggs (hard-cooked and peeled first), nuts, pasta, salt (smoked salt is a unique and lively seasoning for other dishes), seeds, and vegetables (such as corn, eggplant, garlic, onion, summer and winter squash, and tomato). Hot smoking can be applied to larger, high-fat fish, such as halibut, sable, salmon, shad, sturgeon, and tuna, as well as meat, poultry, and game—boar, chicken, goose, lamb, pheasant, pork belly, leg, and loin (bacon, ham, Canadian bacon), turkey, and venison. There are, however, no hard-and-fast rules on what is cold smoked and what is hot smoked—the choice is a matter of preference. Cold smoking is slower and thus takes a bit longer; hot smoking actually cooks the items and produces a drier exterior. (Kippered fish, by the way, are fish that have been hot smoked, thus cooked.)

The types of wood and aromatics vary as well. Common varieties of wood used include alder, apple, beech, chestnut, grape vine, hickory, mesquite, and oak. Aromatics can be added during the smoking period for additional flavor. There is no limit here—choices are based on preference. A cost-conscious kitchen uses herb leaves for culinary purposes and saves stems for smoking. Suggestions for herbs include bay leaf, marjoram, mint, rosemary, sage, oregano, tarragon, and thyme; spices include anise, celery seed, caraway seed, cinnamon, clove, dill seed, fennel seed, garlic, ginger, juniper, lemon and orange rind, and peppercorns.

To further appreciate the imprecision of smoking, consider the following recipe for Tea-Smoked Duck, prepared right on the kitchen stove, using a covered wok.

TEA-SMOKED DUCK

1 5-pound (22.5-kg) duck
¾ cup (180 mL) soy sauce
3 cups (720 mL) water
2 cinnamon sticks
6 star anise
1 cup (240 mL) plain white rice

1 cup (240 mL) black tea leaves
¼ cup (60 mL) brown sugar
2 tablespoons (30 mL) toasted sesame oil

- Cut extraneous fat from the duck, then wash and pat dry. Over a wok or stock pot, rub the duck inside and out with the soy sauce. Place the water and spices in a wok (or heavy-gauge pan with domed lid), and set the duck in, on top of a rack (4 chopsticks spaced equally at right angles in the bottom of the wok can act as a rack). Bring the liquid to a simmer, cover, and allow to steam for 45 minutes. Remove the duck, pour off and discard the liquid, and allow the duck to dry.
- Place the rice, tea, and sugar in the wok. Rub the exterior of the duck with the sesame oil, and place on top of the rack again. Cover, and heat over a medium fire until the wok starts to smoke. Turn the fire down to medium/low, and allow to smoke for about 30 minutes. Adjust the heat as needed, so as to maintain a slow, even smoke. Remove the duck, cut into bite-size pieces, and serve as an appetizer with a flavored soy sauce (soy sauce plus scallion, grated ginger, hoisan sauce, and rice wine).

CURES

Cures consist of salt, sugar, herbs, and spices. These ingredients are blended together and rubbed into meat, fish, or poultry, which is then allowed to sit for several days. For salmon, the cure is the preparation, creating a Scandinavian specialty known as *Gravlax*, an appetizer that has become quite popular. It is sliced very thin on a low horizontal angle, served with small rectangles of rye bread and some form of dill-flavored mustard or mayonnaise. For other food items, curing is a prestep to smoking.

GRAVLAX

(BASIC RECIPE)

2 boneless salmon fillets, scaled, skin on
¼ cup (60 mL) brandy
juice of 1 lemon
1½ cups (360 mL) kosher salt

1½ cups (360 mL) sugar
3 tablespoons (45 mL) black peppercorns, cracked
½ cup (120 mL) fresh dill, roughly chopped

- Rinse the fillets with cold water and pat dry. Cut several shallow slits in the skin (to allow the cure to penetrate that side).

- Rub the brandy and lemon juice into the flesh of the fillets, and sprinkle with the pepper. Blend the sugar, salt, and dill together, and pack about half the mixture onto the flesh of the salmon fillets.

- Place two fillets, flesh side down, in a hotel pan. Sprinkle the remaining sugar/salt/dill mix over the skin. Cover with plastic wrap, then set a second hotel pan on top, and weight down (three No. 10 cans work well). Allow to cure 2 to 3 days refrigerated, pouring off excess juice once daily. (Additional sugar/salt/dill mix may have to be added.)

- Rinse the fillets thoroughly in cold water and pat dry. Press a small amount of additional cracked pepper and minced dill onto the salmon, wrap and refrigerate until ready to use (*see color plate, Gravlax*).

Gravlax should be sliced very thin, on a very low angle (about 25°). It can be used for individual canapés or laid out on a mirror or platter. It is generally accompanied by a mayonnaise-based mustard and dill sauce, or a horseradish sauce: 1 cup (240 mL) cream, 1 cup (240 mL) fresh white bread crumbs, 1 cup (240 mL) sour cream, 1 pint (480 mL) prepared horseradish squeezed dry, the juice of 1 lemon, salt, and white pepper to taste.

The proportion of salt to sugar varies considerably among culinarians. The preceding recipe includes equal amounts, but they can be adjusted to suit one's taste. The function of the salt is to draw out moisture, effectively curing the fish; the function of the sugar is to sweeten. In the Norwegian style (*Gravlax*), the ratio is 5 parts sugar to 4 parts salt, along with white peppercorns, brandy, lemon juice, and dill; the Swedish style (*Gravadlax*) consists of nearly all salt, a sprinkling of sugar and white pepper, plenty of dill, and no brandy or lemon. Equal proportions of salt and sugar work well, but experimentation with other proportions is encouraged.

Contemporary innovations to traditional Gravlax include a Tex-Mex version, made by substituting the brandy with tequila, dill with cilantro, and pepper with chopped jalapeño peppers; and an Asian or Pan-Pacific version made with brandy, grated ginger, and soy sauce (both are excellent!).

DRY CURED SALMON, NEW ENGLAND STYLE

1 3 to 4-pound (1,350 to 1,800-g) side of fresh salmon, skin on, pin bones removed
1 cup (240 mL) gin
½ cup (120 mL) salt
¾ cup (360 mL) sugar
1½ tablespoons (22 mL) black peppercorns, crushed
1½ teaspoons (7.5 mL) mustard seeds, crushed
1 cup (240 mL) fresh whole cranberries, mashed
1 orange, sliced very thin
zest of 1 orange, blanched in boiling salted water

- Combine the salt, sugar, peppercorns, and mustard seeds. Place the salmon, skin side down, in a shallow glass casserole dish. Rub ¼ cup (60 mL) of the gin into the salmon flesh, then sprinkle on half of the spice mix. Press the mashed cranberries onto this, and cover with a layer of the orange slices. Top with the remaining spice mix, and pour on the remaining gin. (The blanched orange zest is for garnish.)
- Lay a sheet of plastic or wax paper over the salmon, and place another pan, slightly smaller than the first, on top. Weigh down, using cans or other heavy objects. Place this in the refrigerator for 3 days, pouring off excess liquid once each day.

This dish is designed to be served with a cranberry relish and sauce. For the relish: Simmer together 6 tablespoons (90 mL) sugar, 1 cup (240 mL) dry sherry, 1 cup (240 mL) dry white wine, ½ cup (120 mL) orange juice, and the zest of 1 orange, until reduced by half. Add 2 cups (480 mL) whole cranberries (fresh or frozen), and simmer until thick and smooth and the cranberries have all opened. Allow to cool, then cover and refrigerate at least 24 hours before serving. For the sauce: Simmer ¾ cup (360 mL) gin and ¼ cup (60 mL) crushed juniper berries for about 10 minutes; remove from the fire and allow to cool. Press the gin mixture in a sieve, squeezing the juice into a bowl. Add 1½ cups (360 mL) mayonnaise, ½ cup (120 mL) half-and-half, 2 tablespoons (30 mL) white wine vinegar, ¼ cup (60 mL) prepared horseradish, and salt and white pepper to taste. Blend thoroughly, then cover and refrigerate at least 24 hours before serving.

PEPPER CURE

(FOR HIGH-FAT FISH, SUCH AS BLUE FISH, MACKEREL, SHAD, SWORDFISH, OR TUNA)

½ cup (120 mL) brandy
3 cups (720 mL) coarse salt
1 cup (240 mL) light brown
  sugar

¼ cup (60 mL) cracked
  black pepper
3 tablespoons (45 mL)
  ground cumin

- Brush fish steaks on both sides with brandy. Combine the remaining ingredients, and rub into the flesh. Place in a pan on a bed of the cure, and sprinkle remaining cure on top. Cover and refrigerate overnight.

- Rinse the steaks in cold water and pat dry. Place on a smoking rack, and smoke as desired.

NORTH AFRICAN CURE

(FOR CHICKEN)

¼ cup (60 mL) ground car-
  away seed
2 tablespoons (30 mL)
  cayenne pepper
¼ cup (60 mL) ground
  cumin

¼ cup (60 mL) garlic
  powder
¼ cup (60 mL) paprika
2 tablespoons (30 mL)
  ground black pepper
¼ cup (60 mL) coarse salt

- Rub a whole chicken or a cut-up chicken with a mixture of the cure ingredients, place in a pan on a bed of the same, and sprinkle remaining cure on top. Cover and refrigerate overnight.

- Rinse the chicken in cold water and pat dry. Place on a smoking rack, and smoke as desired.

Virtually any variety of meat, game, or poultry (including buffalo, deer, elk, and moose) can be turned into jerky, a native North American staple. The meat used should have little fat—which can turn rancid later—and should be cut into strips, with the grain, for hot smoking.

JERKY CURE

3 cups (720 mL) coarse salt
1 cup (240 mL) sugar
2 tablespoons (30 mL) garlic powder
2 tablespoons (30 mL) onion powder
1 teaspoon (5 mL) ground dill seed
1 teaspoon (5 mL) ground celery seed

1 teaspoon (5 mL) ground mustard seed
1 teaspoon (5 mL) ground allspice
1 teaspoon (5 mL) cracked black pepper
1 teaspoon (5 mL) ground cumin

- Combine the ingredients, rub vigorously into meat strips, then cover and refrigerate overnight. The next day, rinse the meat, and hot smoke.

Cure for Vegetables

Vegetables do not have the connective membranes that meat, poultry, and game have, thus for curing they need only to be brushed with oil, seasoned with salt, pepper, herbs, and spices. In the case of winter squash, such as acorn or butternut squash, drizzling a little maple syrup or sprinkling a little brown sugar adds an excellent flavor.

BRINES

The use of a brine is the beginning of a process of preserving food: the high salinity destroys undesirable bacteria, the addition of aromatics adds flavor, and the use of acid (vinegar and wine) cuts the strong "gamey" flavor (in the case of game) and begins to break down connective tissue. The aromatics used can vary depending on one's personal tastes. In the following recipes, the brines should be brought to a boil, the dry ingredients dissolved, then cooled to room temperature (the ratios of salt and sugar to liquid are roughly 12% and 2 to 3%, respectively). The length of time for brining is calculated by weight—1 hour per pound. After brining, food items should be rinsed in fresh water, patted dry, then placed in a smoker.

During smoking the brine can also be used to baste the items being smoked, to add additional flavor.

BASIC FISH BRINE

2 gallons (7.6 L) water
4 cups (960 mL) coarse salt
1 cup (240 mL) sugar
1 teaspoon (5 mL) white
   peppercorns

1 bunch dill stems
zest of two lemons
3 bay leaves

FISH BRINE II

1 cup (240 mL) olive oil
1 cup (240 mL) water
juice of 3 lemons
¼ tablespoon (1.2 mL) parsley, minced
¼ tablespoon (1.2 mL)
   thyme leaves, minced

¼ tablespoon (1.2 mL) dill,
   minced
¼ tablespoon (1.2 mL)
   cilantro, minced
2 tablespoons (30 mL) salt
2 tablespoons (30 mL)
   white pepper

FISH BRINE III

1 cup (240 mL) peanut oil
1 cup (240 mL) water
juice of 3 limes
8 garlic cloves, pressed
½ cup (120 mL) cilantro,
   minced

2 tablespoons (30 mL) salt
2 tablespoons (30 mL)
   white pepper

SALMON BRINE

6 tablespoons (90 mL)
   coarse salt
2 tablespoons (30 mL) sugar
2 cups (480 mL) water

1 cup (240 mL) dry white
   wine
2 lemons, sliced
2 oranges, sliced

After brining, and before cold smoking, the salmon is coated with a paste consisting of ½ cup (120 mL) Dijon-style mustard, ½ cup (120 mL) brown sugar, 2 cups (480 mL) finely chopped pecans, ¼ cup (60 mL) light brown sugar, and 1 tablespoon (15 mL) cayenne pepper.

POULTRY BRINE I
(FOR CHICKEN, DUCK, OR TURKEY)

2 gallons (7,680 mL) water
4 cups (960 mL) coarse salt
1 cup (240 mL) sugar

2 cups (480 mL) Madeira wine

POULTRY BRINE II
(FOR CHICKEN OR DUCK, WITH AN ASIAN FLAVOR)

1½ gallons water (5.7 L)
1 quart (960 mL) sake or marin (rice wine and sweetened rice wine, respectively)
1 cup (240 mL) soy sauce
½ cup (120 mL) sesame oil
3 cups (720 mL) coarse salt

1 cup (240 mL) sugar
¼ cup (60 mL) five-spice powder (anise, clove, cinnamon, fennel, and pepper)
4 garlic cloves, crushed
2 tablespoons (30 mL) gingerroot, sliced very thin

POULTRY BRINE III
(FOR CHICKEN, DUCK, OR GAME BIRDS)

1 gallon water (3.8 L)
1 quart (960 mL) dry vermouth
2 cups (480 mL) maple syrup
2 cups (480 mL) coarse salt

1 medium onion, finely sliced
3 garlic cloves, crushed
1 small fennel bulb, finely sliced
3 bay leaves

POULTRY BRINE IV

(FOR CHICKEN OR DUCK)

1 gallon water (3.8 L)
1 pint (480 mL) pineapple juice
1 cup (240 mL) coconut milk
2 tablespoons (30 mL) coarse salt
2 tablespoons (30 mL) coconut sugar

1 tablespoon (15 mL) poultry seasoning
2 bay leaves
1 cup (240 mL) plain yogurt (add after brine is cooked and cooled)

POULTRY BRINE V

(FOR RABBIT)

1 gallon water (3.8 L)
1 quart (960 mL) dry vermouth
1 bunch tarragon, roughly chopped
2 cups (480 mL) coarse salt
1 onion, finely sliced

2 bay leaves
2 tablespoons (30 mL) crushed black pepper
1 tablespoon (15 mL) juniper berries
1 teaspoon (5 mL) freshly ground nutmeg

PORK BRINE I

(FOR LEG, LOIN, SHOULDER, OR BUTT)

4 gallons (15.2 L) water
1 cup (240 mL) dry white wine
3 cup (720 mL) coarse salt
1½ cups (360 mL) sugar

2 tablespoons (30 mL) whole cloves
3 star anise
½ cup (120 mL) sliced gingerroot

PORK BRINE II

(FOR LEG, LOIN, SHOULDER, OR BUTT)

3 gallons (11.4 L) water
1 cup (240 mL) dry sherry

3 cups (720 mL) coarse salt

2 quarts (1.9 L) apple cider (or juice)
3 Granny Smith apples, cored and roughly sliced
2 tablespoons (30 mL) whole cloves
1 teaspoon (5 mL) cinnamon, ground
1 teaspoon (5 mL) allspice, ground
½ cup (120 mL) gingerroot, sliced very thin

LAMB BRINE

(FOR LEG, LOIN, OR SHOULDER)

1 quart (960 mL) water
1 quart (960 mL) dry red wine
½ cup (120 mL) olive oil
2 tablespoons (30 mL) Dijon-style mustard
¼ cup (60 mL) coarse salt
2 tablespoons (30 mL) black peppercorns, crushed
6 garlic cloves, crushed
4 stalks rosemary
1 bunch parsley stems
2 bay leaves

GAME BRINE I

(FOR LIGHT GAME, SUCH AS DUCK, GOOSE, PHEASANT, QUAIL, OR SQUAB)

2 gallons (7.6 L) water
1 cup (240 mL) dry white wine
½ cup (120 mL) white wine vinegar
2 cups (480 mL) coarse salt
½ cup (120 mL) sugar
1 tablespoon (15 mL) black peppercorns
1 tablespoon (15 mL) juniper berries
2 garlic cloves, crushed
1 bunch parsley stems
2 bay leaves

GAME BRINE II

(FOR HEAVY GAME, SUCH AS BOAR, MUTTON, OR VENISON)

2 gallons (7.6 L) water
1 quart (960 mL) dry red wine
1 pint (480 mL) red wine vinegar
2 cups (480 mL) coarse salt

½ cup (120 mL) sugar
2 garlic cloves, crushed
1 jalapeño pepper, minced
½ bunch thyme
1 bunch parsley stems
2 bay leaves
peel of 1 orange, cut into
  rough strips

peel of 1 lemon, cut into
  rough strips
1 tablespoon (15 mL) black
  peppercorns
1 tablespoon (15 mL)
  juniper berries
2 tablespoons (30 mL) mustard seed

CHAPTER 10

FARCES

The word *farce* comes from the Latin *farcire*, and its meaning may have originated in third-century Rome, when dining and entertaining were of excessive proportions. In "Trimalchio's Dinner," a chapter in Gaius Petronius's *Satyricon*, we read of servants bringing a large platter into the dining room, upon which rests an enormous roasted wild sow. She is adorned with a "freedom cap" (a hat worn by former slaves who had earned their freedom) on her head, hard pastry piglets at her teats, and two baskets of dates hanging from her tusks. When the carver arrives, he whips out a knife and slashes through the sow's flank, freeing several dozen thrushes which came whirring out into the room. The guests are supposed to respond with shock and/or surprise at such a "farcical" display, a good-natured teasing preplanned by their host.

A farce, or forcemeat, is a ground, seasoned mixture of meat, game, poultry, fish, or vegetables, prepared as a dish on its own or used to stuff numerous other dishes, including eggs, fish, poultry, game, meat, vegetables, pastry shells, or pasta. Such dishes, with the exception of those that are served hot, are typically prepared in the garde manger department. As for most things of a culinary nature, nomenclature for the different dishes under this heading varies considerably among kitchens and practitioners, as well as among regions and cultures. The guidelines in one kitchen that designate a specific hot *timbale a pâté*, or a *pâté en croûte* baked in an earthenware vessel as a *terrine*, may well be incorrect in another kitchen. This can be very confusing; for example, consider the *Pâté de Faisan, Périgourdine*, once served by my mentor, Peter Van Erp. It was an exquisite pheasant farce (a "parfait," because it was emulsified), steamed in a minaiture bombe form (about the size of a small orange), napped with a very fine brown truffle sauce. It seemed to me that it should have been termed a mousse, albeit a hot one, and so I queried the chef on the subject. He informed me this that was the way he had learned it some years ago, and there was no need to correct the nomenclature. He qualified his response with the same point I make here: There are no absolutes in the culinary universe, and one learns by doing, weeding out the inaccurate, eventually developing a repertoire that is both unique and based on individual common sense. Nevertheless, the basic guidelines for various farces are given in the following paragraphs.

PÂTÉ (FROM OLD FRENCH, *PASTÉ*, MEANING "PASTE")

Pâté can also be translated as a "block (of buildings)," in reference to the rectangular shape of a typical pâté (this is the author's deduction). This block is created by baking a farce in a metal form, usually rectangular—roughly $12 \times 3 \times 3$ inches ($30 \times 75 \times 75$ mm)—and typically designed with four panels attached to the bottom plate with hinges. After baking, these panels can be swung down in order to remove the pâté. If the form is lined with dough, the dish is designated as "en croûte." If the texture of the farce is coarse (two grindings, no sieving) and no "lightening" ingredients (cream, eggs, egg whites) are added, it is considered to be "peasant" or "country" style; if it is finely ground (two grindings, emulsification in a buffalo chopper or food processor, plus sieving), it is sometimes referred to as a *parfait* (literally, "perfect").

Terrine (from the Latin *terra*, meaning "earth")

The term *terrine* refers to both the farce and the earthenware vessel in which it is baked, nearly always within a water bath. A terrine is essentially a pâté prepared in an earthenware (ceramic, cast-iron, or terra-cotta) vessel. Although a pâté is always removed from the form in which it is baked, a terrine is often served directly from the vessel in which it is prepared. Pâté and terrine forms are traditionally lined with fatback before filling to prevent loss of moisture from the farce and to add flavor. And though purists may scoff, contemporary innovations include terrines made of layered potatoes (the starch therein is a binding agent) with poultry or fish, without the fatback lining. After cooling, the top of the terrine is decorated with herbs and/or flower forms cut out from vegetables and coated with a layer of aspic.

Galantine (from Old French *galant*, meaning "gorgeous" or "showy")

A galantine is most commonly a boneless—or partially boned—chicken, duck, pheasant, or other poultry bird, filled with a forcemeat, rolled into a more-or-less cylindrical shape (imitating the original shape of the bird), wrapped in muslin, and poached in stock or court bouillon. Galantines can also be fashioned from fish (such as salmon, pike, and trout), as well as veal breast, boar's head, pig's feet, and goose neck. When chilled, they are sometimes coated with chaud-froid or collée and decorated (for a centerpiece) or sliced and coated with aspic. (If two or more galantines are to be prepared, one can be coated and decorated and used as a centerpiece, and the other(s) can be sliced, glazed in aspic, and laid out on the platter in front of the centerpiece.)

BALLOTINE (FROM THE ITALIAN *BALLA*, MEANING "BALL")

A ballotine is a single portion of boneless poultry, stuffed with a farce, roasted, and served hot with an appropriate sauce.

QUENELLE (FROM THE ALSACIAN FRENCH *KNÖDEL*, MEANING "DUMPLING")

A quenelle is seasoned puréed fish, veal, or poultry, shaped into an oval dumpling in the palm of a (clean) hand, using a spoon and a little cold water. It is generally 2 to 3 inches (50 to 75 mm) in length, poached in stock or court bouillon, and served hot with an appropriate sauce. (Although a quenelle is a type of farce, because it is served hot, the uncooked farce is sometimes prepared in the garde manger kitchen, then passed on to the hot kitchen for preparation.)

ROULADE (FROM THE FRENCH *ROULER*, MEANING "TO ROLL")

A roulade is any farce, usually made of game, poultry, or fish, rolled in plastic wrap or parchment paper and poached. It is chilled, unwrapped, sliced, and then either glazed with aspic for inclusion on an appropriate platter presentation or used as an hors d'oeuvre on a crouton base with a garnish (*see color plate, Chicken Roulade, Veronique*).

MOUSSE (FROM THE FRENCH, MEANING "FROTH")

A mousse is a light, soft preparation, either savory or sweet, in which ingredients—either cooked or raw, depending on the recipe—are finely ground, blended with whipped cream, and/or beaten egg whites and/or egg yolks and/or cream sauce folded in, then served hot or cold. (Dessert mousses are a creation of different kind, usually created from a base of egg yolk cooked over steaming water, mixed with a chocolate or fruit-flavor base, and folded into whipped cream.) Classically, a savory mousse is made from a primary ingredient that has already been cooked, an indicator that this dish evolved as a way to use food items that had already cooked. These mousses are most commonly served hot or warm, and less frequently cold. The choice of sauce in either cases is strictly a matter of taste and style: when served hot, any sauce derivative from the family of mother sauces (demi-glaze, velouté, béchamel, hollandaise, beurre blanc, tomato); when served cold, any derivative of mayonnaise or vinaigrette.

It is important to note that the mixtures for preparing a quenelle, roulade, or mousse, are often quite interchangeable, depending on the form in which the dish is cooked or the manner in which it is served. Quenelles are shaped into 2 to 3 inch (50 to 75 mm) long ovals formed in the palm of a (clean) hand; roulades are rolled into long cylinders; and mousses are set into ramekins, timbales, darioles, or larger forms, and then baked or steamed.

BASIC GUIDELINES FOR THE CREATION OF A FARCE

Both the meat, poultry, or fish components of a farce, as well as the meat grinder and food processor or buffalo chopper, if used, *must* be well chilled. Such chilling is essential, because it facilitates the clean grinding of the farce, as opposed to tearing—which inhibits the release of proteins that later bind the farce and results in a pasty texture. A sharp cutting blade is also essential; if the blade to be used is not sharp, it should be sharpened or replaced.

The process of grinding these food items is similar to the process used in creating sausage: First, the ingredients are coarsely ground through a medium-holed plate, then ground through a small-holed plate. If the farce is to be further ground (emulsified, to create a fine-textured farce), it is emulsified in a buffalo chopper or food processor. A small amount of crushed ice can be added (roughly 1 quart/960 mL per 12 pounds/5.4 kg of meat) and emulsified. Finally, the farce is pressed through a screen drum sieve (the utensil used to sift flour), with a flexible plastic pastry scraper. This last step is performed to remove any remaining vestige of sinew or skin in the farce.

There are times when a food grinder is not available. In this case, the primary ingredient can be placed in the freezer for a period of 30 to 60 minutes, rendering it partially frozen. This is done so that when it is placed in a food processor, the interaction of the blade against the partially firmed meat, poultry, or fish results in its being cut up, much the way it would if put through a meat grinder. It is important to be aware of this option if one needs to create a farce and possesses only a food processor. (Because fish has so little connective tissue, in actual practice it is often puréed, without freezing, in a chilled food processor using the pulse switch.)

Traditional meat farces for pâtés, terrines, galantines, ballotines, and quenelles are made up of four parts:

1. *The Primary Ingredient:*   Veal, game, poultry, or fish, which provides the dominant flavor. These ingredients must be fresh and of the best quality. All bones (except in some galantines), skin, sinew, and gristle are removed, and the flesh is cut up into ½-inch (12-mm) pieces before grinding.

2. *Pork and Pork Fat:*   Pork is included (except in fish farces) for flavor and smoothness, as well as its binding qualities.

3. *Binding Agents:*   To lighten the farce and give it a finer texture, binding agents are added. These are typically used in poultry, fish, and vegetable farces. They can consist of egg yolks and/or egg whites; fresh bread soaked in milk, cream, or stock; thick béchamel sauce (cream sauce); beurre manié (raw flour and butter paste); or cooked rice.

4. *Seasoning and Garnish:*   Seasoning tends to be extravagant, perhaps because of a former practice of covering up ingredients of less than top quality. This trend continues, and often a specific blend of herbs and spices is created ahead of time to apply to a dish as needed.

    The garnish is related to the farce to which it is added. A central garnish—lamb loin in a lamb farce, strips of ham in a pork farce, or a piece of goose liver in a game farce—provides a visual focal point when the farce is sliced. Garnishes interspersed throughout the farce include pistachios nuts, diced truffle, capers, toasted nuts, mushrooms, and other additions.

HERB AND SPICE SEASONING BLENDS

Garde manger practitioners develop their own standard blends of herbs and spices in varying degrees of strength for different applications, ready for use as needed: a light blend for fish roulade perhaps, a medium blend for a pork and veal terrine, a heavy blend for game pâté. They should be made of fresh ingredients (very finely minced fresh herbs and freshly ground spices), and finely ground so that they blend into a farce. A mortar and pestle or small electric coffee grinder, used solely for this purpose, is the appropriate tool for grinding spices. Once blended, they should be shaken through a screen sieve. Not all of the farce recipes that follow include a spice blend, because such inclusion is a matter of personal choice. Spices are simply applied to a dish as one sees fit. The following are suggested blends:

SEASONING BLEND 1

(AN ALL-PURPOSE BLEND FROM AUGUSTE ESCOFFIER'S *LE GUIDE CULINAIRE*)

5 parts bay leaf
4 parts clove
4 parts cinnamon
3 parts coriander
3 parts gingerroot
3 parts mace

6 parts nutmeg
5 parts black pepper
5 parts white pepper
1 part cayenne pepper
3 parts thyme

SEASONING BLEND 2

(GOOD FOR FISH FARCES)

7 parts thyme
6 parts white pepper
4 parts nutmeg
3 parts dill seed

3 parts bay leaf
3 parts clove
3 parts coriander
3 parts cumin

SEASONING BLEND 3

(FOR COUNTRY-STYLE MEAT AND POULTRY PÂTÉS)

3 parts white pepper
2 parts clove
2 parts tarragon
1 part allspice
1 part ground nutmeg

1 part paprika
1 part cumin
1 part thyme
1 part marjoram

SEASONING BLEND 4

(GOOD FOR HEAVY MEAT AND GAME PÂTÉS)

7 parts juniper berries
4 parts cumin
3 parts basil
3 parts bay leaf
3 parts clove
3 parts garlic

3 parts gingerroot
3 parts nutmeg
3 parts black pepper
3 parts white pepper
2 parts marjoram

LINING AND FILLING A PÂTÉ EN CROÛTE

- Allow the pâté dough to sit at room temperature for an hour, then roll out in a rectangular shape to a thickness of ⅛ inch (3 mm) (two strips of pine molding, ⅛-inch thick × 1-inch wide × 2-feet long/3 × 25 × 600 mm, is an excellent aid in rolling out the dough). Lay the mold gently on the dough, close to one edge, and lightly mark the shape of the four sides and bottom of the mold into the dough, using a paring knife. Allow about an inch of additional dough at the outside edge, to later overlap the top. Cut out the dough in one piece: it should appear as a central rectangle (for the interior bottom of the mold), with two rectangular pieces on each side (for the sides), and two small square pieces at the two ends (for the inside ends). Cut an additional rectangle, slightly thinner than the other pieces, to serve as the lid.

- Lightly butter the inside of the mold.

- Fold the four outer flaps inward, and set the dough down into the mold. Lift up the four flaps and, using a small ball of dough, press the dough into the sides of the form. With a pastry brush dipped in water, lightly brush the edges of dough at the four corners of the mold, then press together to form a tight seal. (It is important to seal the dough securely, in order to prevent seepage of fat and juices during baking.) Allow excess dough at the top edge of the mold to hang over the side.

- Fill a large pastry bag (without tip) with the farce, and pipe an even layer of farce into the dough-lined mold. Smooth the top with a spoon or spatula. Set the central garnish in place, then fill up the rest of the mold with farce to within roughly a quarter-inch of the top of the mold. Tap the mold on a counter to tamp down the farce securely into the mold.

- Fold the excess dough overlapping the edges onto the top of the farce, so that they almost cover the top of the farce. Add another strip of dough to fill in the remaining space down the center. Brush the top with egg wash, and lay the lid over the top. Using a paring knife, press the edges of this dough down and over the edges of the dough at the top of the sides, sealing this top edge. Cut out flowers, flower petals, or geometric designs; brush the top again with egg wash, arrange a decoration with the cutouts, then brush the design pieces with egg.

- Cut two ½-inch (12-mm) wide holes in the top of the dough, roughly equidistant across the length of the form. Fashion two small "chimneys"—small cylinders, ½ inch (12 mm) in diameter, 2 inches (50 mm) long—using a double thickness of aluminum foil, and press them into the holes, about ½ inch (12 mm) down into the farce.

- Bake the pâté in a preheated 350° F (175° C) oven, for 1 to 2 hours (depending on the size). As the pâté is nearing completion, check the internal temperature by sliding a meat thermometer into the center of the pâté near one end. The internal temperature should reach 140° F (60° C) for rare (in the event a center garnish consists of a meat fillet), or 160° F (72° C) for fully cooked.

- Remove the pâté from the oven and allow to cool. Carefully remove the pâté from the form, sliding a paring knife down between the sides of the form and the dough, then carefully dropping the hinged sides. Allow to cool to room temperature, then wrap and refrigerate until ready to serve; or if the pâté is to be filled with aspic, allow it to cool to room temperature and fill the form with liquified aspic by pouring carefully through the chimneys. Refrigerate the pâté overnight, to allow the aspic time to set, before removing it from the mold.

FILLING AND PREPARING A TERRINE

- Line a terrine with thin sheets of fatback, or rub the interior liberally with butter or olive oil.

- Fill a large pastry bag (without tip) and fill the terrine with a layer of farce. Place the garnish (or garnishes) in place, and continue filling with layers of farce and garnish. Cover the top with thin sheets of fatback or a piece of parchment paper cut to size, and seal with a sheet of aluminum foil (this step can be omitted if the terrine comes with a lid).

- Bake in a preheated 300° to 350° F (150° to 175° C) oven, for 1 to 2 hours (depending on the size), or until internal temperature reaches 160° F (72° C).

PÂTÉ AND TERRINE RECIPES

CHICKEN LIVER PÂTÉ

1 pound (450 g) chicken livers, trimmed of connecting membranes
½ cup (120 mL) dry white wine
¼ cup (60 mL) brandy

salt and pepper to taste
pinch of nutmeg
6 tablespoons (90 mL) unsalted butter, cut into about 12 pieces

1 cup (240 mL) heavy
  cream
unsalted butter as needed

1 bunch watercress
1 cup (240 mL) Madeira or
  Cumberland sauce

- Marinate the livers in the wine for 1 hour, then drain.

- Coarsely purée the livers, brandy, salt, pepper, and nutmeg in a food processor. Using the pulse switch, add the 6 tablespoons (90 mL) of butter, a few pieces at a time, and purée. Add the cream in a steady stream until fully incorporated.

- Butter 8 ramekins, timbales, or dariole molds. Divide the mousse mixture among the molds, cover each with a piece of lightly buttered parchment paper, and set on a rack in a large saucepan or roasting pan. Fill the bottom with about ½ inch (12 mm) water, cover the pan, and steam the molds for 10 minutes. Turn the fire off, and allow to sit for 15 minutes.

- Using a paring knife, carefully loosen the mousses, and invert onto serving plates. Serve with Madeira sauce, or a side of Cumberland sauce, and garnish with fresh watercress.

PÂTÉ DOUGH

1 pound, 2 ounces (507 g)
  all-purpose flour
½ teaspoon (2.5 mL) salt
5 ounces (150 g) unsalted
  butter, cut into ½-inch
  (12-mm) pieces

3 ounces (85 g) lard, chilled
  and cut into ½-inch
  (12-mm) pieces
1 egg, beaten
⅓ to ½ cup (80 to 120 mL)
  ice water

- Place the flour, salt, butter, and lard in a large bowl, and rub between the hands until it resembles coarse meal.

- Add the egg and ⅓ cup of water, and press together, kneading only as much as necessary to press the dough into a smooth mass. (Add more water if needed.) Avoid overworking the dough, which can make it tough and chewy when baked. Wrap the dough in plastic and refrigerate overnight.

PORK PÂTÉ EN CROÛTE

1 cup (240 mL) brandy
2 sprigs of thyme
2 strips of orange zest
8 juniper berries, crushed

2 garlic cloves, crushed
2 pounds (900 g) pork butt,
  cut into ½-inch (12-mm)
  pieces

¾ pound (675 g) fatback, cut into ½-inch (12-mm) pieces

1 large pork tenderloin, trimmed of skin and fat

½ pound (225 g) pork tenderloin, cut into ¼-inch (6-mm) dice

salt and white pepper to taste

olive oil as needed

½ cup (120 mL) pistachio nuts, skinless and halved

unsalted butter as needed

a double batch of pâté dough

1 egg, beaten

2 cups (480 mL) sherry aspic, liquified

- Place the brandy in a bowl, and over it rub the thyme vigorously between the hands, then drop into the brandy. Squeeze the orange zest over the brandy, and drop that in as well. Add the juniper and garlic.
- Season all the meat with salt and pepper, then add to the brandy mixture. Cover and refrigerate overnight.
- Remove the meat from the marinade (leave all the herbs and spices in the bowl) and pat dry. Grind the pork butt and fatback twice, blend with the diced pork and pistachios, and set aside in the refrigerator.
- Sear the pork tenderloin in olive oil in a hot pan. Remove and pat dry.
- Butter the interior of a pâté mold and line with dough. Fill half full with the farce. Set the seared tenderloin down in the center, and press down firmly. Fill the rest of the form with the farce.
- Fold over the flaps of dough, top with a dough lid, then cut chimneys and decorate as desired. Brush with egg wash and bake in a preheated 350° F (175° C) oven for about 1 hour, or until the internal temperature reaches 160° F (72° C). Allow to cool to room temperature, then fill with the aspic.

VENISON PÂTÉ

1 pound (450 g) pork belly, cut into ½-inch (12-mm) pieces

1 pound (450 g) pork neck meat, cut into ½-inch (12-mm) pieces

1 pound (450 g) lean venison, cut into ½-inch (12-mm) pieces

1 pork tenderloin, well trimmed and cut in half lengthwise

4 slices bacon, cut into 1-inch (25-mm) pieces

½ cup (120 mL) chicken livers, trimmed of membranes

½ teaspoon (2.5 mL) white pepper
1 teaspoon (5 mL) salt
1 teaspoon (5 mL) paprika
½ teaspoon (2.5 mL) ground cloves
1 sprig thyme
½ cup (120 mL) brandy

½ cup (120 mL) Madeira
3 eggs
½ cup (120 mL) mango chutney
2 pounds (900 g) sliced fatback
½ pound (225 g) thinly sliced ham

- Marinate the pork belly, neck, meat, and venison in the spices, brandy, and Madeira for 24 hours.

- Discard the marinade, pat the meat dry, and set aside. Season the tenderloin pieces with salt and pepper, then grill, sauté, or broil until almost fully cooked. When cool, wrap both pieces with the ham into a long cylinder and set aside.

- Drain off excess liquid and put the marinated meats, bacon, and chicken livers through the large-holed plate of a meat grinder. Add the eggs and chutney, and grind again through the fine-holed plate.

- Preheat an oven to 350° (175° C).

- Line a pâté mold with fatback, and fill nearly half full with the farce. Place the wrapped tenderloin lengthwise down the center of the mold, fill with the remaining farce, and cover with fatback. Bake for 1 hour or until internal temperature reaches 160° F (72° C).

- Remove from the oven and allow to cool. Refrigerate overnight. When ready to serve, wrap the mold with a towel dipped into hot water, invert, and remove the pâté. Slice, serve with cornichons, a plain lettuce salad, toasted sliced baguette, and Cumberland sauce.

CHICKEN TERRINE WITH WILD MUSHROOMS

For the Sauce
1 bunch watercress leaves (stems removed), minced

1 cup (240 mL) mayonnaise
juice of 1 lemon

For the Farce
2 tablespoons (30 mL) unsalted butter
1 shallot, minced

½ pound (225 g) shiitake mushrooms, stems removed, cut into small dice

½ cup (120 mL) dry ver-
  mouth
1 pound (450 g) boneless,
  skinless chicken breasts,
  cut into ½-inch (12-mm)
  pieces
2 eggs
1 tablespoon (15 mL) thyme
  leaves, minced

1 cup (240 mL) heavy
  cream
salt and white pepper to
  taste
butter as needed
4 sheets dried nori
8 sprigs watercress
24 baguette slices, toasted

- Combine the watercress, mayonnaise, and lemon juice, and blend thoroughly. Cover and refrigerate until ready to serve.
- Place the chicken in the freezer for 1 hour.
- Sauté the shallot and mushrooms in the butter for several minutes. Add the vermouth, and reduce until nearly dry. Set aside to cool.
- Place the chicken, eggs, thyme, salt, and pepper in a food processor and purée, using the pulse switch. Pour in the cream in a slow, steady stream and incorporate, using the pulse switch. Fold in the mushrooms, poach a small test dumpling, and adjust seasoning as required.
- Preheat an oven to 300° F (149° C).
- Liberally butter a 1-quart (960-mL) terrine form. Brush the sheets of nori lightly with water, and line the inside of the mold with the nori (where the nori is pieced together, over-lap the seams). Fill the mold with the farce, cover with nori, and then with buttered parchment paper, and finally seal with aluminum foil. Place in a hot water bath and bake 50 minutes. Allow to cool, then refrigerate overnight.
- Dip the terrine mold into very hot water, invert the mold on a plate, and remove the terrine. Serve with the baguette slices, a side of sauce, and garnish with the watercress sprigs.

Note: Nori, a dried seaweed used for wrapping sushi, can be found in most Asian grocery stores.

COUNTRY-STYLE DUCK TERRINE

1 large fresh duck
1 pound (450 g) pork butt,
  cut into ½-inch (12-mm)
  pieces

½ pound fatback, cut into
  ½-inch (12-mm) pieces
½ pound of duck foie gras
1 cup (240 mL) brandy

½ cup (120 mL) orange juice
2 tablespoons (30 mL)
  orange zest
3 teaspoons (15 mL)
  country-style seasoning
  (blend No. 3)
1 cup (240 mL) mirepoix,
  finely chopped

2 sprigs thyme
2 cloves garlic, crushed
salt and white pepper to
  taste
2 eggs
1½ pounds (680 g) fatback,
  sliced very thin
white wine aspic as needed

- Completely bone the duck, leaving the two breast halves intact, and the leg meat cut up into pieces. Place in a bowl with the pork butt and the foie gras, and macerate with brandy, orange juice, zest, and 1 teaspoon (5 mL) of the seasoning. Cover and set aside.

- Cut up the duck carcass, and along with the other bones, cover with cold water, bring to a simmer, and skim. Add the mirepoix, thyme, and garlic, and allow to simmer several hours. Strain and simmer until reduced to ¼ cup (60 mL) of liquid. Set aside to cool.

- Add the marinade to the simmering stock, then pat dry the duck breasts, pork, and foie gras. Sear the duck breasts in olive oil in a hot pan. Twice grind the pork, fat back, eggs, and remaining seasoning. Cut the foie gras into medium dice, blend with the farce along with the stock reduction, then set aside.

- Line a terrine mold with the fatback, and wrap the duck breasts in any remaining fatback. Place half of the farce in the terrine, then top with the duck breasts, and press gently into the farce. Add the remaining farce, press down, then cover the top with sliced fatback. Prepare a decorative arrangement of thinly sliced oranges and herbs on top of the fat, and cover with the lid.

- Bake in a preheated 300° F (149° C) oven for 1½ hours. Remove from the oven and allow to cool to room temperature. Cover the top with a layer of aspic, and chill until ready to serve.

FOIE GRAS

Foie gras is an important ingredient in pâtés and terrines, both as a farce and as a garnish within the farce. The production of foie gras is a tradition that dates back to the ancient

Romans, who used figs and honey for fattening their foul. As a result, the goose or duck being fattened developed an enlarged liver, which has come to be considered a great gastronomic specialty. The average weight of fattened goose liver (*foie gras d'oie*) or duck liver (*foie gras de canard*) is 500 to 600 grams (1 to 1¼ pounds); many quality-conscious producers will not allow livers to become larger than 650 grams (about 1.35 pounds). The record size for goose liver is 2 kilograms (4½ pounds); for duck liver, 400 grams (14 ounces).

In the United States, the technique of overfeeding is thought to be barbaric, but in other cultures such treatment is considered an honor for the bird. In actual practice, the birds are treated with great respect and are neither penned up nor physically abused in any way. Charles Gérard, in *L'Ancienne Alsace à Table*, wrote: "The goose is nothing, but man has made of it an instrument for the output of a marvelous product, a kind of living hothouse in which there grows the supreme fruit of gastronomy." Foie gras is also produced in Austria, Czechoslovakia, Hungary, Israel, and Luxembourg. Until recently fresh foie gras was unavailable in the United States, because the Department of Agriculture prohibits the import of raw foie gras. Now, however, it is available in the United States, supplied by several domestic producers (see "Specialty Suppliers," toward the end of this book).

The following describes the process ducks go through in the creation of foie gras:

Stage	Duration	Comments
Breeding (*accouvage*)		Athletic ducks, with strong hearts and lungs are preferred.
Raising (*élevage*)	12 weeks	The birds live outdoors, where they grow strong enough to handle the rigors that come with ingesting copious quantities of corn. The ducks are fed once daily, and they eat aggressively until satiated. During this process, they develop a *jabot*, a pocket in the throat, which facilitates force-feeding.

Force-feeding (*gavage*)	2 weeks	Ducks are fed twice daily, a total of 9 kilos of corn. They are carefully tended to, because they are extremely sensitive to stress during this period. The sound of a barking dog within earshot of the birds can literally kill 30 of them in a matter of minutes.
Slaughter (*abbatage*)		

The method of culinary preparation is crucial to maintaining a good yield, because when heat is applied, cell membranes break, releasing the fat and depleting the yield of the product served. The amount of fat lost ranges from 10 to 40%, depending on the size and age of the liver and the way it is handled in the kitchen. Palmilord, a producer near the Loire Valley (which produced 1,000 metric tons in 1995), has worked hard at finding ways of keeping fat loss down to a minimum of 10%. The company has done this in two ways: first, through strict quality control—its duck livers weigh an average of 500 to 650 grams, never exceeding 650 grams, and the product reaches the end users no later than 48 hours following processing. When livers are allowed to fatten beyond 650 grams, or are delivered later than 48 hours after processing, the cell membranes begin to break down, which facilitates fat loss during cooking. Second, the producer works closely with local consumers, educating them on the importance of proper handling: avoiding sautéing at a too high temperature or overpoaching; and dusting sliced foie gras (*escalope*) with flour before sautéing (helps seal the exterior, keeping fat intact).

FOIE GRAS TERRINE WITH FIGS

3 pounds (1,350 g) fattened fresh goose or duck liver
salt and white pepper to taste
1 cup (240 mL) brandy

1 cup (240 mL) plum wine (or ordinary port)
½ pound (225 g) dried calymyra figs, stemmed and cut into eighths

- Remove any membranes and blood vessels remaining on the liver. Season with salt and pepper, set it in a bowl along with the brandy and wine, and knead the liver, breaking it up into smaller pieces. Add the figs, cover, and refrigerate overnight.
- Drain the marinade, and pat the liver pieces dry. Press the pieces of liver into a terrine form (preferably equipped with a lid), along with the figs, pressing each piece down firmly into the form. When the form is full, set the cover in place and bake in a water bath in a preheated 275° F (135° C) oven for 45 minutes. Allow to cool before refrigerating. Serve with minced port wine aspic and toasted sliced brioche, accompanied by a glass of sauterne wine (*see color plate, Duck Liver Terrine*).

SALMON AND SUN-DRIED TOMATO TERRINE

For the Pesto

1½ cups (360 mL) sun-dried tomatoes, packed in olive oil
½ cup (120 mL) olive paste
3 garlic cloves, crushed

6 tablespoons (90 mL) olive oil (drained from the tomatoes)
¼ cup (60 mL) grated Romano cheese

For the Terrine

1 pound (450 g) all-purpose potatoes
1½ pounds salmon fillet, boneless and skinless, cut into 6 pieces

1 cup (240 mL) dry white wine
1 cup (240 mL) water
1 shallot, minced
1 sprig dill
1 bay leaf

For the Vinaigrette

1½ cups (360 mL) olive oil
½ cup (120 mL) champagne wine vinegar
1 tablespoon (15 mL) Dijon-style mustard
3 tablespoons (45 mL) water

salt and white pepper to taste
2 heads butter lettuce, separated into individual leaves, rinsed, and dried

To Prepare the Pesto

- Drain the oil from the tomatoes, and set the oil aside. Combine all the ingredients in a food processor and blend until puréed. Cover and refrigerate until needed.

370

To Prepare the Terrine
- Peel the potatoes, then cook in boiling salted water until tender. Drain, cool, then cut into ¼-inch-thick slices.
- Bring the wine, water, shallot, and herbs to a boil. Poach the salmon in this liquid, about 10 minutes. Drain, cool, then break up into small flakes.
- Lightly coat the inside of a terrine mold or bread pan with the olive oil remaining from the tomatoes. Cut a piece of parchment paper to fit the inside bottom of the mold, and set inside. Brush the parchment paper with olive oil.
- Press a layer of salmon onto the parchment paper, about ½ inch deep. Spoon a layer of the tomato pesto onto the salmon. Then press a layer of the potatoes on top of this, so that the potatoes completely cover the previous layer. Repeat this process two additional times, pressing each layer firmly on top of the preceding one. Cover with plastic wrap and refrigerate overnight.

To Prepare the Vinaigrette
- Whip the oil, vinegar, mustard, water, salt, and pepper together.

To Serve
- Arrange a bed of butter lettuce leaves on 8 serving plates.
- Run a knife around the inside of the terrine or bread pan. Set the pan in an inch of hot water for 3 seconds, then invert onto a large plate. Tap the top of the mold so that the terrine falls from the form. Dip a knife in hot water, and carefully slice the terrine into 8 slices. Place each on a lettuce bed and drizzle with the vinaigrette.

A BASIC GALANTINE RECIPE

CHICKEN GALANTINE

1 large roasting chicken (about 3½ pounds/1,575 g)
1 8-ounce (225 g) chicken breast, boneless and skinless, cut into ½-inch (12-mm) pieces
1 pound (450 g) pork butt, cut into ½-inch (12-mm) pieces
¼ pound (113 g) fatback, cut into ½-inch (12-mm) pieces

salt and white pepper to taste
1 teaspoon (5 mL) poultry seasoning
¼ cup (60 mL) ground cumin
⅓ cup (80 mL) ham, medium dice
⅓ cup (80 mL) pistachios, peeled and halved

371

- Using a sharp boning knife, cut a line through the skin on the center of the back of the chicken, running the length of the bird. Lift up one side of the skin, and begin cutting around the carcass of the bird, removing the flesh from the bones. Continue cutting around the carcass, leaving the legs and wings intact. (Be sure to leave as much flesh as possible in place, and be careful not to cut through the skin.) When the chicken is removed from the carcass, as far as the breast bone, repeat the process from the center of the back, down the opposite side.

- Remove the carcass, and reserve for preparing a future stock. Season the interior of the chicken lightly with salt and pepper and set aside.

- Season the chicken breast, pork, and fatback with salt, pepper, poultry seasoning, and cumin. Grind twice, then take half the mixture and emulsify in a food processor along with a little ice (1 quart/960 mL per 12 pounds/5.4 kg of meat; or, in this case, about ¼ cup/60 mL of ice). Combine the ground mixture, emulsified mixture, ham, and pistachios, and blend thoroughly.

- Open up the boned chicken, and place the farce in the center so that it occupies roughly the same area where the carcass had been. Wrap the chicken around the farce, pulling the skin back up and around it, and stitch up the skin using an upholstery or trussing needle and heavy white cotton thread (any other than white cotton may melt or run color).

- Shape the chicken back to roughly its original shape, slightly lengthened and well rounded. Truss the legs together and wrap the butcher cord down and around the lower back of the bird, then around the wings.

- Poach the galantine in chicken stock, barely simmering (about 175° F/79° C), for 1 hour, 15 minutes. Remove from the fire, place a weight (such as a plate topped by a heavy can) on the chicken, and allow to cool to room temperature. Refrigerate overnight.

- Remove the galantine from the broth and wipe off any excess fat or jelly. Remove the trussing cord and the thread from the back of the bird, and trim any extruding pieces of skin. Coat the bird with chaud-froid or collée, or partially slice, coating each slice with aspic. Serve accompanied by minced aspic and a mayonnaise-based sauce; add other garnishes as deemed appropriate (a plain lettuce salad, Belgian endive leaves, and croutons; or celery root rémoulade, leeks vinaigrette, and zucchini spaghetti.)

QUENELLE RECIPES

PIKE QUENELLES

1 cup (240 mL) dry white wine
2 shallots, minced
¼ pound (113 g) unsalted butter, soft
½ cup (120 mL) flour
1 pound (450 g) fresh pike, boneless and skinless, cut into 1-inch (25-mm) pieces

1 pint (480 mL) heavy cream
4 large eggs
salt and white pepper to taste
fish stock as needed
½ pound (225 g) puff pastry dough

- Simmer the wine and shallots until reduced to about ¼ cup.
- Place the pike in the freezer for 30 minutes. In the meantime, roll out the puff pastry dough to a thickness of ⅛ inch (3 mm). Using a 3-inch (75-mm) round or fluted pastry cutter, cut crescent-shaped pieces of dough ("fleurons") roughly 1-inch (25-mm) wide. Place on a baking sheet, and bake in a preheated 375° F (190° C) oven until puffed up and golden brown. Remove and set aside.
- Place the pike and shallots in a food processor and purée roughly, using the pulse switch.
- Knead the butter and flour together. Place this paste, along with the cream, eggs, salt, and pepper into the processor, and purée until smooth. Bring the fish stock to a bare simmer.
- Dip a tablespoon into cold water, and scoop out a heaping spoonful of the mousse. Wet the palm of the opposite hand, and shape successive spoonfuls of the mousse into smooth ovals. Drop the quenelles gently into the stock, and poach about 10 minutes or until fully cooked.
- Remove the quenelles from the stock and drain on absorbent paper. Place on serving plates, accompanied by an appropriate sauce (lobster sauce, *Sauce Américain*), and garnish with the pastry fleurons.

Lobster base is a commercial form of concentrated lobster stock (*glace de homard*), generally rather salty. Some versions are available without MSG or other preservatives, and it is an acceptable source of lobster flavor.

LOBSTER QUENELLES

1 pound (450 g) fresh sole or flounder, cut into 1-inch (25-mm) pieces
1 quart (960 mL) heavy cream
2 eggs

2 tablespoons (30 mL) lobster base
2 tablespoons (30 mL) brandy
1½ pounds (680 g) lobster meat, finely chopped
salt and white pepper to taste

- Place all ingredients into a food processor and purée, using the pulse switch. (Be careful not to overwhip.) Season to taste with salt and pepper.

- Dip a large serving spoon or tablespoon into cold water, and moisten the palm of one hand. Scoop out 1 to 2 ounces (28 to 57 g) of the farce, and using the spoon, shape the quenelles in the palm of other hand. They should be nicely shaped ovals, with no creases or rough spots. Ease them into barely simmering court bouillon, poach 6 to 8 minutes (depending on their size), and serve with an appropriate small sauce (*beurre blanc*, velouté, cream sauce, tomato sauce, or another sauce).

CHICKEN QUENELLES

2 shallots, minced
1 cup (240 mL) dry white wine
2 teaspoons (10 mL) seasoning blend No. 3 (for country-style meat and poultry pâtés)
1 pound (450 g) chicken breast, boneless and skinless, cut into 1-inch (25-mm) pieces

2 tablespoons (30 mL) butter
2 tablespoons (30 mL) flour
3 eggs
1 cup (240 mL) heavy cream, very cold
salt and white pepper to taste
chicken stock as needed

- Sprinkle the chicken with 2 teaspoons (10 mL) of seasoning blend No. 3, and place the chicken in the freezer for 30 to 60 minutes or until it is "half frozen." Simmer the shallots and wine until reduced to ¼ cup (60 mL) of liquid. Strain and allow to cool.

- Place the chicken, reduction, butter, and flour in a food processor and purée, using the pulse switch.

- Add the eggs, one at a time, and incorporate, still using the pulse switch. Add the cream in a slow, steady stream, again using the pulse switch. When it is fully blended, take a small portion of the farce and poach in the court bouillon, then taste for seasoning.

- Moisten a tablespoon and the (clean) palm of one hand with cold water. Scoop out heaping tablespoons of the farce and shape into smooth ovals in the moistened palm. Place in barely simmering chicken stock, about 8 minutes, or until fully cooked. Remove the quenelles, drain thoroughly, and serve topped with an appropriate sauce (such as beurre blanc—plain, or with ginger or herbs).

ROULADE AND MOUSSE RECIPES

SALMON AND SCALLOP ROULADE

1 large skinless, boneless salmon fillet

3 tablespoons (45 mL) brandy

salt and white pepper to taste

1 cup (240 mL) dry white wine

2 shallots, minced

½ teaspoon (2.5 mL) thyme, finely minced

1½ pounds (6.8 kg) fresh (or fresh frozen) scallops

½ cup (120 mL) heavy cream

1 egg, beaten

½ cup (120 mL) clarified unsalted butter

- Cut the salmon fillet in half, across the width. Carefully slice the salmon horizontally into 4 thin slices. Rub the brandy into the flesh, and season with salt and pepper.

- Simmer the wine and shallot until reduced to about 3 tablespoons (45 mL) of liquid. Add the thyme, simmer briefly, remove from the fire, strain, and set aside to cool.

- Place the scallops, cream, egg, and cooled reduction in a food processor, and purée, using the pulse switch. Season to taste with salt and pepper. Scoop out a teaspoonful of the farce, poach in lightly salted water, and taste for seasoning (adjust seasoning with salt and pepper). Remove the farce, and set aside.

- Lightly brush a large sheet of plastic wrap with the butter, then arrange two of the salmon pieces into a square. Spread an even layer of the farce over the salmon, within a half-inch of all four sides. Carefully and tightly roll up, using a ruler or other straightedge to make the roll tight and even. Twist the ends shut, and refrigerate 1 hour. Repeat this procedure with the remaining ingredients.

- Poach the roulades in a simple court bouillon for 20 minutes, or until a toothpick comes out clean when pushed into the center of the farce (do this at one end).

CLASSICAL MOUSSE RECIPE

1 pound (450 g) primary
protein item (see the note
following this recipe),
roughly cut into ½-inch
(12-mm) pieces
2 egg whites
1 egg

2 cups (480 mL) heavy
cream
salt and pepper to taste
additional seasoning as
desired (see the note following this recipe)

- Purée the primary item in a (chilled) food processor. Add one egg white at a time, and process. Cover the processor bowl and refrigerate 1 hour.

- Using the pulse switch, incorporate the cream in a slow, steady stream. Adjust seasoning, then fill buttered ramekins, timbales, or darioles. Cover each with a small circle of buttered parchment paper, and bake in a hot water bath in a preheated 375° F (190° C) oven for 25 minutes. Serve hot or cold with an appropriate sauce.

Note: Suggested fish varieties include halibut, salmon, sole, trout, lobster, and shrimp; poultry items include chicken and duck breast; other items include foie gras, chicken liver, and ham.

Additional seasoning can include any herbs or spices deemed to be harmonious with the primary item—dill with salmon, tarragon with chicken, ginger with duck, sage with ham, and so on.

LOBSTER AND SCALLOP MOUSSE

1 tablespoon (15 mL) butter
1 shallot, minced
8 ounces (225 g) fresh scallops (ocean or bay)
¼ cup (60 mL) dry white
wine
2 tablespoons (30 mL)
lemon juice
salt and white pepper to
taste

1 slice fresh white bread,
crusts trimmed
1 egg white
2 tablespoons (30 mL)
unsalted butter, coarsely
chopped
pinch of nutmeg
1 cup (240 mL) heavy cream
1 cup (240 mL) lobster
meat, finely diced

- Sauté the shallot and scallops in 1 tablespoon (15 mL) of butter for 3 minutes. Remove the scallops with a slotted spoon and set aside. Add the wine, lemon juice, salt, and pepper, and simmer until reduced by half.

- Place the bread in a food processor, and pulse until it is well shredded. Add the scallops, wine reduction, egg white, 2 tablespoons (30 mL) of chopped butter, and nutmeg, and pulse until fairly smooth. Add the cream in a steady stream, and continue pulsing until well blended. Add the lobster meat and fold in.
- Butter a mold large enough to accommodate the mousse, cover with plastic wrap, and refrigerate overnight. To unmold, dip the mold into very hot water, then invert onto a flat cutting surface. Slice, and serve with an appropriate sauce.

SCALLOP MOUSSE

1 pound (450 g) sea scallops
½ pound (225 g) sole fillet, cut into 1-inch (25-mm) pieces
3 eggs
1 pint (480 mL) heavy cream

salt and white pepper to taste
1 tablespoon (15 mL) clam base

- Place the scallops and sole in a food processor and purée coarsely, using the pulse switch. Add the eggs, a little salt and pepper, the clam base and, while pouring the cream in slowly, purée, again using the pulse switch. Scrape down the sides of the processor, and pulse again, until the mixture is smooth. (Test the mousse by poaching a tablespoon of it in a little simmering water, and adjust seasoning to taste.)

Note: This basic fish mousse recipe can be used to stuff ravioli or other fish (such as trout), or it can be poached as for quenelles or prepared in a small mold.

SWEETBREAD MOUSSE

1 pound (450 g) sweet-breads
¼ cup (60 mL) Cognac
¼ cup (60 mL) dry vermouth
2 tablespoons (30 mL) minced basil
¼ teaspoon (1.2 mL) salt

¼ teaspoon (1.2 mL) white pepper
pinch of nutmeg
1 teaspoon (5 mL) lemon juice
2 egg whites
1 cup (240 mL) heavy cream

Madeira is a fortified wine originating on the island of the same name, off the coast of Portugal. Madeiras are named after the grapes from which they are produced: Sercial is the driest, Verdelho is nutty and mellow, Boal and Malmsey are sweet and full-bodied. In exceptional vintage years, a Madeira can last a century or more in the bottle.

- Break the sweetbreads into small pieces, removing most of the connective membranes. Marinate in the Cognac, vermouth, and basil for 3 hours.
- Remove the sweetbreads from the marinade, and purée in a food processor with the salt, pepper, nutmeg, and lemon juice. Add the egg whites and pulse, while adding the cream. Continue pulsing until smooth and completely purréed.
- Butter four or five ramekins, timbales, or dariole molds, and fill with the mousse. Cover each form with plastic wrap, wax paper, or buttered parchment paper, place on a rack over simmering water, and steam for 15 minutes. Allow to sit for another 10 minutes, then remove. Slide a paring knife around the mousse inside each mold, invert, and place on a serving plate. Serve hot with a rich brown sauce (such as Madeira, Périgordine, or Zingara), garnished with fresh watercress.

CHICKEN LIVER MOUSSE

2 pounds (900 g) chicken livers, trimmed of connecting membranes
1 small onion, finely chopped
2 garlic cloves, pressed
4 ounces (120 g) unsalted butter
¼ teaspoon (1.2 mL) ground cumin
¼ teaspoon (1.2 mL) allspice
1 tablespoon (15 grams) anchovies, mashed

6 ounces (180 g) unsalted butter, soft
¼ cup (60 mL) Madeira wine
salt and white pepper to taste
unsalted butter as needed
1 cup (240 mL) light aspic
1 bunch watercress
1 baguette, sliced and toasted

- Sauté the livers, onion, and garlic in 4 ounces (120 g) of butter, for 7 minutes. Set aside and allow to cool.
- Place the liver mixture in a food processor, along with the spices, anchovies, 6 ounces (180 g) of soft butter, and wine, and pulse until smooth. Season to taste with salt and pepper.
- Lightly coat the inside of a fancy domed mold (such as a bombe mold) with butter, then fill with the mousse. Cover and chill overnight.
- Dip the mold in very hot water for about 10 seconds, then invert onto a rack over a pan. Coat with aspic, and serve garnished with watercress and toasted baguette slices.

Aspic is a crystal clear, highly gelatinous meat jelly, used to coat various appetizer items both for flavor and to prevent drying. A fairly good powdered version is available in gourmet markets, which can be improved by using sherry, Madeira, or brandy instead of water. After the aspic has been heated to liquid form, it is *tempered* by placing it into a bowl, set into ice water, and stirred until it is just barely tepid. It should be slightly viscous, though liquid enough to flow freely over the mousse. After each coating, it is placed in the refrigerator, allowing that coat to gel. Repeat the coats until a thin layer of aspic has formed over the mousse.

CHICKEN LIVER AND MUSHROOM MOUSSE

½ pound (225 g) chicken livers, trimmed of connecting membranes and coarsely chopped
¼ pound (113 g) unsalted butter
1 medium onion, coarsely chopped
3 cloves garlic, crushed
¾ cup (180 mL) mushrooms, coarsely chopped
¼ cup (60 mL) brandy
pinch of nutmeg
salt and white pepper to taste

- Sauté the livers, onion, garlic, and mushrooms in the butter until the livers are fully cooked. Set aside and allow to cool.

- Place this mixture in a food processor, along with the brandy, nutmeg, salt, and pepper, and pulse until smooth. Adjust seasoning.

- Lightly coat the inside of a domed mold (such as a bombe mold) with butter, then fill with the mousse. Cover and chill overnight.

CRAB MOUSSE

1 pound (450 g) sole fillet, coarsely chopped
pinch of cayenne
1 egg
salt and white pepper to taste
pinch of nutmeg
1 cup (240 mL) heavy cream
1 pound (450 g) crab claw meat, cut into ¼-inch (6-mm) dice
butter as needed
1 cup (240 mL) ginger *beurre blanc*

- Place the sole, cayenne, egg, salt, pepper, and nutmeg into a food processor and purée. Add the cream in a steady stream, and continue processing until smooth and emulsified.

- Remove the mousse to a large bowl, and fold in the diced crab. Butter 8 ramekins, timbales, or dariole molds, and divide the mixture among the molds. Cover each mold with a piece of lightly buttered parchment paper and set on a rack in a large saucepan or roasting pan. Fill the bottom with about ½ inch (12 mm) of water, cover the pan, and steam the molds for 10 minutes. Turn the fire off, and allow to sit for 5 minutes.

- Using a paring knife, carefully loosen the mousses, invert onto serving plates, and serve hot with *beurre blanc,* or chilled with a mayonnaise sauce.

CARROT MOUSSE

1½ pounds (680 g) carrots, peel and tops removed, cut into ¼-inch (6-mm) thick slices
1 cup (240 mL) chicken (or vegetable) stock
½ teaspoon (2.5 mL) sugar
salt, white pepper, and nutmeg to taste
2 tablespoons (30 mL) unsalted butter, soft
4 eggs
⅓ cup (80 mL) heavy cream
butter as needed

- Simmer the carrots, stock, sugar, and seasoning until the carrots are tender and completely cooked. Set aside to cool.

- Place the carrots (with stock) into a food processor and purée. Press through a sieve, then add the butter, eggs, and cream, and blend thoroughly.

- Butter 4 6-ounce (113 to 170-g) ramekins, timbales, or darioles, and fill with the purée. Cover each with a small circle of buttered parchment paper. Place in a hot water bath, in a 375° F (190° C) oven, and bake about 25 minutes or until a toothpick inserted into the mousse comes out clean.

- Remove from the oven and allow to cool. Run a paring knife carefully around the inside edge of each form and invert so that the mousse comes out. Serve hot with an appropriate sauce (such as Walnut Cream, herb *beurre blanc,* or a hollandaise derivative), or cold, coated with aspic and accompanied by a mayonnaise sauce.

SPINACH MOUSSE

1 pound (450 g) spinach
½ cup (120 mL) chicken (or
  vegetable) stock
2 tablespoons (30 mL)
  unsalted butter, soft
salt, white pepper, and
  nutmeg to taste

3 large eggs
⅓ cup (80 mL) heavy cream
butter as needed

- Remove the stems from the spinach leaves and rinse several times, making sure that all silt is removed. Simmer the spinach and chicken stock, covered, for several minutes. Remove the stock and spinach from the cooking vessel and set aside to cool.

- Place the spinach (with stock) in a food processor, along with the butter, seasoning, eggs, and cream, and purée, scraping down the sides to make sure the mixture is completely puréed.

- Butter 4 6-ounce (113 to 170-g) ramekins, timbales, or darioles, and fill with the purée. Cover each with a small circle of buttered parchment paper. Place in a hot water bath, in a 375° F (190° C) oven, and bake about 25 minutes, or until a toothpick inserted into the mousse comes out clean.

- Remove from the oven and allow to cool. Run a paring knife carefully around the inside edge of each form, and invert so that the mousse comes out. Serve hot with an appropriate sauce (such as Walnut Cream, herb *beurre blanc*, a hollandaise derivative), or cold, coated with aspic and accompanied by a mayonnaise sauce.

Note: Any number of vegetables can be substituted in this recipe, including asparagus, broccoli, cauliflower, celery, and so on. Spinach cooks in a matter of minutes; if another vegetable is used, be sure to cook it fully before puréeing.

ZUCCHINI MOUSSE

5 slices fresh white bread
⅓ cup (80 mL) heavy cream
¼ cup (60 mL) olive oil
5 large zucchini
2 large eggs plus one egg
  yolk

1 teaspoon (5 mL) cilantro,
  minced
salt and white pepper to
  taste

- Remove and discard the crusts from the bread. Tear or cut the bread into small pieces, combine with the cream, and set aside.

- Remove and discard the ends of the zucchini. Cut them into quarters lengthwise, and cut off and discard the inside edge of each quarter (to remove the seeds). Grate the remaining zucchini, and sauté in the olive oil about 3 minutes, or until tender. Remove from the fire and set aside.

- Purée the soaked bread, zucchini, eggs, cilantro, salt, and pepper in a food processor. Shape into individual quenelles and poach, or set into timbale or dariole molds and steam until fully cooked.

CHAPTER 11

SCULPTED CENTERPIECES

Pièce montée, the French term for "centerpiece," historically refers to large, multileveled creations fashioned primarily from dessert ingredients—sponge cake, chocolate, candied fruit, marzipan, meringue, nougatine, pastillage, spun and pulled sugar, and so on. But *pièce montée* is translated literally to mean "lifted piece," in reference to its placement up high, on or near a buffet, and thus refers to sculpted forms fashioned out of dough (weaver's, or dead, dough), salt dough, ice, tallow, and fruits and vegetables. These various sculpting mediums are introduced to students in the second year of two-year culinary programs, with the intention that some will expand their knowledge following training. Hotel operations in which large banquet productions are fairly frequent offer a venue for such work and often lead recent graduates to discover an inner creative bent that extends beyond their interest in food production. Some may go on to apply their sculpting skills in the major and minor culinary and ice-carving competitions around the world, including the international Culinary Olympics held in Frankfurt, Germany, every four years.

The history of grand pastry centerpieces dates back to the sixteenth century, and this art form reached a peak in the creations of Antoine Carême. Sent off into the world at the age of ten by his father, a poor handyman with a brood of 24 to support, Carême was ultimately led to Bailly, a celebrated Parisian caterer. Bailly recognized exceptional talents in the 17-year-old boy and encouraged their development. Carême wrote, "This good master showed a lively interest in me. He allowed me to leave work in order to draw in the print room. When I had shown him that I had a particular vocation for his art he confided to me the task of executing *pièces montées* for the Consul's [Napoleon's] table."*

The "print room" of which Carême wrote was in the National Library, which contained architectural renderings of the monuments in Paris. As a result of this experience, Carême designated confectionery as a branch of architecture: "The fine arts are five in number, to wit: painting, sculpture, poetry, music, architecture—whose main branch is confectionery."

Carême was one of the most celebrated chefs of his time. His employers included Charles-Maurice de Talleyrand-Périgord, England's prince regent (the future King George IV), Czar Alexander I, the Viennese Court, the British Embassy in Paris, the household of Princess Bagration, and

* The quote is from Carême's writings, as found in Larousse, *Larousse Gastronomique* (New York: Crown Publishers, 1961).

the Baron de Rothschild. And although he possessed something of an acerbic personality, his innovations have had a major influence on the profession. "Few . . . escaped the sting of his bitter pen [yet] Carême's . . . pièces montées, created from pastries, puff paste, preserved fruits, creams, and sherbets, have influenced centuries of pâtissiers" (Christian Guy, *An Illustrated History of French Cuisine*, 1962). He is also credited with several innovations: modifying the design of saucepans so that they could pour sugar; designing molds; updating the design of a chef's toque (hat); and inventing the vol-au-vent and large meringues. Carême died on January 12, 1833, at the age of 49, according to Laurent Tailhade, "burnt out by the flame of his genius and the heat of the ovens."

THE TRANSIENCE OF THE CULINARY MEDIUM

My own interest in culinary sculpture lies principally in fruit and vegetable carving, initially sparked upon my first perceiving an apple bird, a fairly simple garnish learned in second-year garde manger class. I appreciated both its simplicity—no toothpicks or adhesive required—and the curved lines created by straight cuts into a spherical object. I came to call my work in this genre *California mukimono*—the locale of my birth combined with a Japanese term meaning "to slice things." As I developed a *mukimono* repertoire, I considered all elements of the "art" in culinary arts and came to ponder the question, "Is food really art?" based on a foundation of hands-on experience in nearly three dozen kitchens and teaching in nearly as many sites over a period of more than two decades. One particular experience, during my work in a competition in the autumn of 1984, brought the transient nature of the medium (food) into poignant view. As an instructor at Johnson & Wales University, I joined a team of fellow instructors in a competition sanctioned by the Société de l'Art Culinaire in New York City. I entered both a vegetable pâté mirror and a large bouquet of vegetable flowers (a *mukimono* bouquet). The bouquet was initially scoffed at by my teammates—something that provoked discussion over that question: "Is it art?" Yet to my great satisfaction, it became *the* centerpiece for a two-tiered banquet table, on which was displayed our 30 classical dish entries for the show. The original centerpiece—a deer sculpted from salt dough—had been damaged beyond repair during transport. After two days of being exposed to the open air, however, the vegetable flowers, in spite of being well coated with aspic, were wilted and shrunk, a sad end to a work that required 24 hours over three days' time and a dozen student assistants to produce. (In addition, quite tragically, the Sociétés' judges, for some still unknown reason, neglected to judge our table, which profoundly distressed and discouraged all participants in the effort.) That experience led me eventually to accept the transience of this so-called art medium and to consider it in a different light. First of all, culinary competitions, which have reached greater importance since the initiation of several international competitions, do not represent the epitome of artistic expression in the culinary arts. They are merely a periodic gathering of practitioners, creating a vehicle to focus on developments in food preparation and presentation as demonstrated by a cadre of chefs from the hotel and restaurant trade around the world. This is not meant to diminish such competitions in any way, but to point out that these brief intersections of culinary practitioners showing off their work, provide a way of seeing what is happening in the food world, concentrated in one place every two to four years. Rather, it is the culinary experiences (dining) that take place day after day, in restaurants all over the world, in which the art or the craft of the profession is revealed. It is in such settings that the question, "Is this art?" should be considered.

I initially found the transient aspect of working artistically in a food medium to be a negative. One spends years perfecting a repertoire, and then, on any given evening, toiling behind the range in a dining establishment, one creates delicious and visually gorgeous expressions, the results of those years of work and practice. The negative element of this endeavor becomes apparent with the realization that in the space of an hour or two, the beneficiaries of that toil and effort will have consumed all of the creative results, paid the tab, and gone home to bed. In the evolution of an artist it is important to understand his or her own place in the world of artistic expression, this world that outsiders perceive only as words—"culinary art"—without understanding the time and toil it demands. That Carême, the ultimate tormented artist, had deemed confectionery (pastry work) the "main branch" of a discipline within the arts (architecture), is a great boon to those of us who today perceive ourselves as artists. Unfortunately, Carême remained angry and bitter to the end of his days.

For the artist working with food, the frustration of constantly seeing one's work disappear could be devastating if he or she failed to understand the function of artistic expression in a transient medium. I watched the heartbreak suffered by some of my elder mentors, passionate artists struggling for creative breath after years of striving for excellence. I saw grown men weep for the pent-up creative passion, who could find only a hot production line filled with self-satisfied and ego-driven personnel, or a hot broiler lined up with steaks and chops, as their only outlet. I knew I had to be careful in the world of kitchens, else I would go the way of some of my instructors.

I cannot say that through my years of work in this field I emerged completely unscathed, but becoming aware of where I was headed and developing an appropriate philosophy provided some consolation. I concluded, then, that a culinary creation was more a performance piece than a "thing" to be perceived (and consumed). Of course, art forms such as dance, theater, and opera are also experiential—and just as transient as culinary art. But the culinary experience includes a very private and personal ingestion of the art: One actually puts the fruit of the chef-artist's work onto one's palate and ingests it; and it becomes part of one's physical being. This makes dining unique. There is no other "art experience" that invokes the visual, olfactory, gustatory, tactile, and auditory senses. Yet, the question persists: "Is it art?" That consumption of food is consumption of fuel for the body further complicates the question. Ultimately, the answer rests with the beholder. If the support elements of a dining experience—room ambiance, service, table accessories, timing, and so on—are all properly in place, and if the dining patrons are receptive to the demonstrated skill of the kitchen, then the scene is set for an appreciation of food as an expression of art. As for the culinary practitioners whose hearts and hands are filled with the passion of an artist, they must forge their own philosophies, adhere to the standards they have created for themselves, and not be affected by the audience that is simply consuming fuel for their bodies.

ICE CARVING

Among culinary sculpting mediums, nothing is more clearly transient than ice. Initially, the mere thought of sculpting a hard, cold object that begins to dissipate immediately may seem utterly absurd, as well as self-defeating. On closer inspection, however, one may find considerable more to it than meets the eye.

First of all, ice is water, which is composed of hydrogen and oxygen, elements essential to life. It is no coincidence that the human body is made up of 65% water and 70% of the earth's surface is covered with water. And although one can wave a hand through water or splash it on one's face, water is, in fact, the strongest material on the planet. Consider Lao-tze's classic commentary: "Nothing under heaven is softer, more yielding than water. But when it attacks things hard and resistant, there is not one of them that can prevail—for they can find no way of altering it. That the yielding conquers the resistant, and soft conquers the hard is a fact known by all men, yet utilized by none." With this understanding in mind, one can gaze into a block of ice and begin to sense both its beauty and its power. And in its solid form, shimmering and transparent, it can be sculpted and shaped into artistic expressions of indescribable beauty.

Ice sculpting was introduced in Japan by Tokuzo Akiyama, chef of the Imperial Household (1912–1926) following a trip to France during which he witnessed carved ice being used as dishes for food. On his return to Japan he began to imitate these sculptures, and this skill eventually evolved into a very high art form. The training program in Japan involves a formal five-year apprenticeship divided more or less into the following progression: first year, moving ice; second, sharpening tools; third, assembling blocks; fourth, cutting; and fifth, carving. Japanese carvers have taken ice carving to incredible heights, executing innovative designs both realistic and impressionistic (with titles such as Poseidon's Dream Mission, Triangle of Hope, Howling Wind, and Simplicity), utilizing lighting for both color and drama, color dyeing (inserting colored water into a block, then freezing), and leaving certain parts of a sculpture disproportionately large so that when it melts it becomes proportionate to the whole. (Japan is not the only nation where ice carving is an art form; but we have learned of their work in this area both from books on the subject published in Japan, and from a cultural exchange between France and Japan that began in the early twentieth century. At about the same time as Tokuzo Akiyama's visit to France, Auguste Escoffier traveled to Japan, where he was considered the Western world's greatest chef.)

In a sense, ice carving represents the supreme expression of beauty within the fleeting transience and impermanence of life. It is almost as if the artist is inviting the viewer with the following sentiment: *I will create a gorgeous, shimmering sculpture from this block of frozen matter. It will be more beautiful than anything you have ever seen. Come and see this frozen moment of creative expression, but come quickly—in a matter of hours, it will be gone.*

The execution of an ice carving also embodies a physical expression of the Grand Terminus—the yin and yang—an

389

understanding that all things within the realm of the physical universe contain within them polar opposites. This concept relates to ice sculpture, because it requires a *patient interior* and a *swiftly moving exterior.*

Considerations in Preparing to Carve Ice

Preplanning is essential to a successful execution and display of carved ice, and certain elements must be determined before carving is executed:

Design. What is the nature of the function? Has the design been fully developed and communicated so that it meets the client's expectations?

Display Area. There is an unwritten law that the sculptor is responsible for the safety of all people around the displayed ice. Thus, are the proportions of size, weight, and (ice) supports sufficient? Is there sufficient drainage during display?

Selection. The age (fresh), clarity (minimal "snow"—opaque white areas caused by air bubbles), and size (there are two basic block sizes) of the ice must be considered.

Tools. A basic tool set should include a flat chisel, a V-chisel, a six-prong chipper, a small Japanese handsaw, tongs, and a chain saw—double insulated with a ground plug. (*Warning:* Tying off a chain saw cord to a stationary object can precipitate a carving mishap. If movement of the saw strains the length of the cord, the plug should be allowed to come out of the wall.)

Transportation. How and when is the ice to be transported to the execution area? If the display area is separate from the execution area, how is the ice to be transported when completed?

Tips and Other Considerations
- Protective gear for the sculptor is important: this should include a jacket (if working in a refrigerated area), gloves, rubber boots, safety goggles, and a plastic apron (chaps style).
- Sharpen flat chisels at a 17° angle, using a 6,000 grit stone; sharpen gouge chisels (½ moon and ¼ moon) with four swipes in one rotation, four swipes in the opposite direction.
- Work as an assistant for a practicing carver, and take copious notes on the work executed. When developing an ice

carving repertoire, get in the habit of creating templates—cut to actual size from parchment paper—that can be dried and reused. Begin with basic forms: ball, pedestal, scallop shell, flower vase, and so on. Then move on to more complex and multiblock forms.

- There is a mental aspect to sculpting ice, in that once the work begins, time is of the essence. Therefore, if the sculptor can develop a vivid mental picture of the finished work, the execution will unfold more smoothly. (Maku Yoshi, a well-known competitor, works very swiftly with his tools once he begins—although if the work space is cold enough, he always stops to break for tea.)
- Average melting speed is 1 inch per hour. Air circulation affects melting time, and blocks can melt at different rates, which affects the safety of the structure. (An ice carving should be pulled down if it melts to a dangerous shape.)
- Cutting and shaping are always executed from the top down.
- A hand grip cut into the base of the sculpture allows ease of transportation.
- Ice that is too cold will crack. After manufacturing, ice blocks should be kept for 24 hours at a temperature of 25° F (–4° C).
- If the execution area is too warm, when the ice is moved there, the dramatic change in temperature can cause the ice to crack. Tempering—allowing the ice to adjust slowly within a slightly warmer environment for 1–2 hours—will prevent this. At no time should the ice be subjected to sunlight.
- Water used for ice is *not* sanitary. Food served in a carved ice vessel should be placed on a bed of cubed or crushed ice, with a hole cut through the vessel to allow drainage.
- Ice block weights and dimensions are as follows: 40 × 20 × 10 inches (100 × 55 × 25 cm), 300 pounds (135 km); and 60 × 20 × 10 inches (150 × 50 × 25 cm), 425 pounds (190 km).
- A completed carving, on average, weighs half the original weight of the ice.

Dough Sculpting

Weaver's Dough

Weaver's dough—sometimes referred to as "dead dough"—is simply a bread dough without a leavener and containing enough fat to minimize elasticity. Elasticity is created when water is combined with flour and then kneaded, which activates the gluten. This is what gives a dough its strength and is much desired in crusty and chewy breads such as baguette and pizza (hence the preference for "hard" wheat flour or durum semolina, both of which contain more gluten than other flours). Yet too much gluten in this dough can make it difficult to work with, hence the inclusion of margarine to lessen gluten development.

There is no limit to the types of forms that can be created using weaver's dough. The most obvious are bread baskets (*see color plate, Ham Platter, American Style*), made by rolling out pieces of the dough into long tubular strands and then weaving them on a solid form into a basket. Forms that work well include metal bowls, croquembouche molds (*see "wizard's hat" sculpture in color plate, Cold Roast Pork Loin, Scandinavian Style*), strainers, and china caps. Forms can also be shaped and fashioned from aluminum foil, folded, crumpled up, and patched together into the intended shape; for larger pieces, use chicken wire manipulated into a desired shape, then cover with aluminum foil. There are no specific guidelines for sculpting themes; the culinary sculptor is free to try anything, from cornucopias to flying saucers, animal figurines to abstract forms, woven baskets to miniature fruits and vegetables (*see color plate, Vegetable Pâté en Croûte*). This area is completely open for exploration for those who enjoy working with dough. There are, however, a few guidelines and pointers to be aware of:

- Generally, a sculpture should be built onto a metal form in such a way that the baked sculpture can be removed from the form (oiling the form liberally is one way of assuring easy removal). In some cases, particularly with larger pieces, the form can remain within the baked piece, provided that the dough fully covers the infrastructure so that it is out of sight.
- Be careful not to overbake a sculpture—over baking will render it brittle.
- Sculptures can be coated with a nontoxic, glossy glaze that will preserve them for as long as three years (periodic recoating may be necessary). For information on how to obtain this glaze (or completed bread sculptures), contact Bread Effects Culinart in Cincinnati, Ohio (see "Specialty Suppliers" toward the end of this book).
- If you are not planning to coat a sculpture with the long-lasting glaze, brush the dough with egg wash before baking to render the exterior visually appealing.
- Be careful about size. Avoid creating sculptures so large that they dominate the work they accompany.
- Because weaver's dough is elastic, it is difficult to form fine detail with this medium. Thus, designs should be simple.

RECIPE FOR WEAVER'S DOUGH

7 pounds (3.15 kg) bread flour
1 egg
1½ pounds (680 g) margarine
2 pounds (1 quart/960 mL) water

1 tablespoon egg shade (optional yellow food color)
1 tablespoon (15 mL) salt
1 ounce (30 mL) vinegar

- Combine the first four ingredients, and work manually into cornmeal consistency.
- Combine the last three ingredients, blend, and then combine with the dry ingredients. Knead until smooth and elastic (use a dough hook if using a mechanical mixer). Cover, and allow to rest overnight before sculpting.

Salt Dough and Tallow Sculpting

Two sculpting mediums that have a bit more permanence than others are salt dough and tallow. Their advantages, as compared with sculpted ice or fruit and vegetables, include the following:

- Can be stored at room temperature (do not require refrigeration).
- If handled carefully, can be used repeatedly.
- Both varieties can be repaired; tallow can also be reworked into new sculptures.
- Considerably lighter and more durable than ice carvings.
- Can be worked on over a period of time.
- Can be worked on by a designated team (good team-building exercise).

Infrastructures

Infrastructures are essential in giving stability and form to large pieces fashioned from tallow or salt dough. There are two types of infrastructure: metal armature and Styrofoam core.

Note: When working with salt dough or tallow, Styrofoam can be added to a metal armature to fill up space and to reduce the final weight of the piece.

The Metal Armature   An armature is fashioned from two to four primary metal rods bolted to a piece of plywood. A lighter, flexible wire is bent firmly in place around the heavier rods, then secured with floral or duct tape. The shape and form of both the infrastructure and the base plywood board will be determined by the desired shape and form of the completed sculpture. A preliminary pencil sketch of the proposed sculpture to actual scale will assist in making this determination.

Once the overall shape is determined, a piece of ½ to ¾-inch (12–20 mm) thick plywood should be cut into an appropriate shape—square, rectangular, round, or oval—depending on the intended shape of the final sculpture. (Remember that the height and weight of the finished sculpture will have a bearing on the size of the base board—something best learned by doing.) An aluminum or galvanized steel rod, with roughly 1½ inches (38 mm) of threading at one end, is attached to the board using two lock washers and nuts on the threaded part of the rod, to be tightened against both sides of the board. The rod fits into a hole, drilled into the board, that is of the same diameter as the rod. The board should also be sanded down to a sufficient smoothness, so that it will not be obtrusive to the viewer once the sculpture is set in place. Both the armature and the base board should be spray painted with glossy white paint. This is particularly important when using an àrmature as the infrastructure for a tallow sculpture, so as to avoid the possibility of armature parts being seen through the translucent tallow.

Another concern is the nut and bolt that extend beyond the bottom plane of the base board. In some cases, the hole in the bottom plane can be drilled out using a countersink, so that the nut can be screwed in tightly enough to set inside this bottom board (in such a case, ¾-inch (20 mm) thick plywood is essential). Another solution is to attach a small square block of wood to each of the four corners of the base board. This should be done carefully, so that the corner edges of the blocks and the corner edges of the base board are flush, and all exposed surfaces should be properly sanded.

The Styrofoam Core   The use of a Styrofoam core permits the construction of larger display pieces, inasmuch as it lowers the overall weight of the finished piece. This core piece should be cut into a shape representative of the finished sculpture's form, and like the metal armature, is best cut following a full-scale rendering of the intended piece. Cutting can be done with a mat knife or fine-toothed saw. (Be sure to use genuine Styrofoam, and not "beadboard," a less expensive version.)

This form should then be attached to a plywood base, which can be done using a common adhesive (such as Elmer's glue). The base board should be sanded and then painted white or a different color, depending on its ultimate use.

When Styrofoam is used as an infrastructure, it must first be covered with an initial layer of tallow. The tallow is softened in the hands, then either applied by hand directly onto the Styrofoam, or softened and layered between two sheets of parchment paper and then applied. If the remaining details of the tallow sculpture are to be *added* (modeled), the Styrofoam should be fully covered with tallow to a minimum thickness of ¼ inch (25 mm); if the details are to be *subtracted* (carved), the Styrofoam should be fully covered with tallow to a minimum thickness of ½ inch (12 mm).

Salt Dough

Salt dough is a sculpting paste consisting of equal parts of cornstarch, water, and very finely ground salt (popcorn salt). As a sculpting medium it has distinct advantages over tallow, both in ease of use and durability. It is the longest-lasting and cleanest material to work with in this genre. Salt dough has a number of desirable qualities:

- Accepts color readily, adding tremendous dimension to the medium
- Has a consistency similar to "play dough," allowing it to be worked into small, delicate shapes
- Permits considerable detail in a design
- Dries opaque, allowing detail and color to be clearly seen
- Dries rock hard, after which it can be sanded and painted
- Is strong enough to withstand the rigors of repeated appearances on a buffet

RECIPE FOR SALT DOUGH

1 part cornstarch   1 part popcorn salt
1 part cold water

- Combine the water and cornstarch, and blend until smooth. Transfer to a heavy-gauge (thick-bottomed) stainless steel pan (aluminum can discolor the dough) and, over low to medium heat, stir with a whip until the blend begins to thicken. Continue stirring, using a heavy wooden spoon or wooden paddle (must be very clean!) and continue working it until the mixture pulls away from the sides of the pan and becomes nearly impossible to stir. (This process usually requires two people—one to stir and one to hold onto the pot.)

- Transfer to a large mixing bowl (very clean!) and, using a dough hook, incorporate all of the salt. (Be sure to scrape the salt down from the sides.)
- Shape the dough into smooth bricks of approximately 1 pound each, and double wrap in plastic to seal out the air. If wrapped airtight, the bricks will last indefinitely.

Note: If the cornstarch and water mixture is not cooked sufficiently, the salt will absorb excess water, leaving the dough slightly sticky. In such a case, the entire batch can be returned to the stove, and heated and stirred until enough water evaporates, eliminating stickiness.

Adding Color to Salt Dough   Coloring the dough before application yields better results than adding color externally to the finished form; it renders a superior depth of color and a more natural appearance. Because salt dough is a food-related product, the pigments used to color it should originate from food items. Such colors will be more pastel than brilliant and will harmonize when used on a buffet table. Liquid food coloring can also be used, although this type of coloring yields bright hues that may give a sculpture a surreal or artificial quality. We recommend experimenting with different pigments to add color according to one's taste.

There are 2 methods of adding color to salt dough: the *Dry Method* and the *wet method*. For the dry method, add ground spices (pigments) into the completed dough. Some examples include:

Coloring Material	Color
paprika	orange
turmeric	yellow
cocoa powder	brown

For the wet method, add ground spices or designated liquids to the water before combining with the cornstarch. Some examples include:

Coloring Material	Color
red cabbage water (made by soaking shredded red cabbage in cold water)*	blue

* If any acid comes in contact with this water, it will immediately turn purple.

saffron tea (saffron steeped in hot water, then strained)	yellow
beet juice, port or red wine	red
squid ink	gray to black*

Applying Salt Dough to an Infrastructure There are two basic ways of applying salt dough to an infrastructure: blocking and sheeting (often used together on a single piece).

Blocking is similar to working with clay. Pieces of dough are broken off from the wrapped blocks, moistened with water, and pressed firmly onto the armature.

Sheeting involves breaking off pieces of dough and rolling them out into sheets of various thickness (dusting with cornstarch to prevent sticking). Areas that will include detail (such as feathers, leaves, and scales) should be covered with sheets thick enough to handle the detail embellishments. The portion where a sheet is to be placed should be brushed with water to create an adhesive surface. Large sheets can also be draped to resemble cloth or clothing and can be fringed to imitate the texture of a thatched roof or the fur of an animal.

Tallow

Tallow is a sculpting medium traditionally fashioned from one part animal fat, one part beeswax, and one part paraffin. The practice of sculpting tallow, estimated to be roughly a century old, has its roots in butter sculpting, which dates back to the sixteenth century. The animal fat was obtained by rendering the fat tissue of beef, lamb, or pork at a temperature no higher than 275° F (135° C), straining it, then blending it with beeswax and paraffin (candle wax). The problem with traditional tallow is that the animal fat is where most of the chemicals and toxins in the animal are stored. Even when rendered and strained, these impurities remain, and in a short time the fat turns rancid, making it sticky and emitting an unpleasant odor. The beeswax and paraffin also present problems, since neither is uniform in hardness, color, or melting point; in addition, when exposed to light, beeswax turns yellow, and eventually brown. Add to this an unpleasant stickiness (even when recently made) and the dust and dirt that were retained

---

* Depending on the quantity used.

on that sticky surface; it is not surprising that sometime during the late 1970s tallow centerpieces virtually vanished from buffet tables.

Fortunately for the dedicated artisans of the culinary world, one culinary-graduate-turned-entrepreneur mourned the decline of tallow sculpture. After two years of research, Dominic Palazzo arrived at a formula for a purified, deodorized beef fat, combined it with modern waxes (not available a century ago), and, essentially, single-handedly revived an entire sculpting genre. His company, Bread Effects Culinart (see "Specialty Suppliers," toward the end of this book), supplies both tallow sculptures and the raw materials for other sculptors. (Because there are now several suppliers of purified tallow for the foodservice industry, use of the traditional variety is not recommended.)

This tallow is fairly hard, which allows finished sculptures to stand up to the rigors of a commercial foodservice environment. In working with the tallow, the warmth of the sculptor's hands is sufficient to make it malleable, and at room temperature it simply returns to its former hardness. Softening the tallow can be accomplished by first scraping shavings from it with a putty knife. Held in the hands and manipulated, the shavings will soften in a matter of minutes.

Softening can be expedited in one of two ways (these steps are intended only to presoften the tallow; overheating will render the tallow liquid):

- Place a small piece of tallow on a pan and place in an oven at 130° F (54° C), until slightly softened, or
- Place a small piece of tallow on a plate in a microwave oven and apply a low frequency (half or three-quarters power is usually sufficient) for 2 minutes. Check the softness, and repeat if necessary.

Tallow comes in three forms:

Modeling	Manually manipulated, modeling tallow will soften to the consistency of soft artist's clay. After being applied to an armature, it firms up and can be detailed with carving tools.
Carving	Slightly harder than modeling tallow, carving tallow is designed for direct sculpting.
Casting	Slightly harder than carving tallow, casting tallow is designed to be melted down and carefully poured into molds; its hardness makes it ideal for unmolding from one-piece rubber molds.

Tips for Carving and Maintaining Tallow Sculptures

- Make certain that infrastructures are completely covered with a base coat of tallow.
- Allow the base coat to cool to room temperature before adding or subtracting details.
- For cutting and detailing tallow, keep knives and tools in very warm water.
- A hair dryer or heat gun (similar to a hair dryer, but with much higher heat) can be used to direct a stream of hot air onto a finished tallow sculpture. By moving the gun in a circular manner from a distance of approximately 12 inches (310 mm), the intense heat briefly softens the outer surface, leaving a hard, glossy exterior skin. (Be very careful *not* to overheat and melt the tallow.)
- To remove dust or fingerprints and restore a luster to the surface, tallow sculptures can be washed, using plain warm water no warmer than 120° F (49° C).
- Between appearances on a buffet table, cover tallow sculptures with a large plastic trash bag and store in a clean, cool area.

MUKIMONO

The importance of garnishing food was repeatedly reinforced during my culinary training, based on the simple premise that *people eat with their eyes first*. I perceived some of the garnishes I learned at school as miniature works of art. Apple birds and tomato roses were among the most popular items, and it seemed at the time that they were a considerable improvement over sprigs of parsley, wedges of lemon, and slices of orange.

In the years since, garnishes like tomato roses have fallen from fashion, with the realization that a rolled up strip of *tomato skin*, no matter how beautiful to the eye, is not exactly an edible item. Other garnishes, such as apple birds, hard-boiled-egg snowmen, and crookneck squash swans, are also clearly out of place on a plate or platter of fine food.

Mukimono is a Japanese word that means "to slice things." I am not aware of a separate study of carving within Japanese or other Asian cooking disciplines—in these cooking realms, garnishing is simply an integral part of food preparation and presentation. An example of this can be found by watching the action behind the counter at any sushi bar, where garnishing is simple and 100 percent functional— *what you get* is *what you eat*. My own style of garnishing has developed over a period of more than two decades, and it represents an amalgam of techniques that has evolved into a personal style of sculpting fruits and vegetables, and applications thereof. In this approach, simplicity is as important as frequency of appearance. M.F.K. Fisher once wrote (in *Serve It Forth*), "Recipes in my book will be there like birds in a tree—if there is a comfortable branch." I prefer to approach garnishing with a similar philosophy of economy and to avoid sculptures that look like a familiar item or "thing." With the exception of flowers and flower forms, I seek forms that simply highlight the beauty of both the sculpting medium and the prepared dish with which it is served.

Garnishes can be sculpted out of virtually every variety of fruit and vegetable, although root vegetables—carrot, daikon, radish, white and yellow turnip—are among the best vegetable sculpting mediums (due to their texture and ability to hold up immersed in water), while melons and apples are among the best fruit-sculpting mediums.

Note: Sculpted garnishes can be found in the following color plates: Croustades and Puffs (rutabaga rose); Crudité (radish crowns); Fish and Vegetable Hors d'Oeuvres (twisted lemon and cucumber slice in *Alligator Pear Cocktail*); Vegetable Hors d'Oeuvres (three separate small flowers carved from daikon, carrot, and rutabaga); Seasonal Fruit Arrangement (several carved pieces including a rose motif on the watermelon, a layered pattern on a half papaya and eight orange honeydew wedges); Cheese Platter (apple fan and apple feather); Classic Caviar Service (*Northern Pancakes* wrapped in scallion leaves; Gravlax (mukimono flower bouquet made from rutabaga, white turnip, butternut squash, and carrot; sliced cucumbers topped with cucumber); Vegetable Pâté en Croûte (carrot and daikon sticks [batonnets] in cucumber socles; mukimono flower bouquet similar to same in Gravlax photo); Chicken Legs in Aspic (Jambonneaux) (radishes, carrots, yellow squash, celery, zucchini, and beets dressed with vinaigrette, and served in onion flower cups); Chicken Roulade, Veronique (two small pumpkins decoratively carved).

GLOSSARY

aiguillettes: Long, thin slices of poultry or game breast, or fish fillet, cut on the bias.

al dente: Literally, "to the tooth" or "to the bite," this term is used to describe pasta and vegetables cooked until they are tender but not mushy. They should be somewhat firm and resilient when bitten into.

aspic: An ultraclarified, strong-flavored stock made from meat, poultry, game, fish, or shellfish, with a high gelatin content, giving it a translucent quality when chilled. Aspic is used to coat numerous dishes prepared in the garde manger department, including canapés, centerpieces, and a variety of sliced items arranged on mirrors for buffet service. It is also a medium in which various *timbales* are prepared (such as *oeufs en gelée*) and can be cut into numerous shapes and used as a garnish for buffet items.

barquette: A small boat-shaped mold, measuring from 2 to 4 inches in length, used to bake a pastry shell for use as a canapé base.

batonnet: A large julienne, measuring ¼ × ¼ × 2½ to 3 inches (from the French *bâton*, meaning "stick").

blanch: To place a food in boiling salted water, stock, or other liquid, in order to cook it partially, set its color, or facilitate peeling.

boil: To cook a food in water or other liquid at 212° F. A full rolling boil is essential for cooking some foods (such as pasta), but undesirable for cooking others (such as stocks).

bouchée: A small bite-size pastry case made from *pâte feuilleté* (puff pastry), into which various fillings are placed, then served as an hors d'oeuvre or as a garnish to a larger dish. Attributed to Marie Leszcynska, queen to Louis XV. In contemporary times, bouchées are also fashioned from numerous farinaceous foods, such as wonton skins and tortillas.

bouquet garni: A collection of herbs and spices, tied together in a bundle with cotton twine and added to a stock, soup, sauce, or stew, to impart the flavor of those herbs and spices to the dish it is simmered with. A standard bouquet garni consists of parsley stems, bay leaf, thyme, and peppercorns. Variations are limitless, depending on an individual's style and the dish in which it is used. Loose herbs and spices can be added within a tea ball, or can be tied up in a large leek leaf.

brunoise: French term for a very small dice, measuring approximately ⅛-inch square.

caramelize: To cook sugar or another food in a sauté pan or saucepan over direct heat long enough to allow the sugar, or the sugar in the food, to begin to brown. Caramelizing imparts a brown color and a nutty flavor to the finished dish.

chaud-froid (pronounced "show-fwa"; literally, "hot-cold sauce"): A brown, green (herb), red (tomato), or white colored

401

sauce that is prepared hot and served cold. It is typically used as a base coating for pieces of meat, poultry, fish, or game, which are then decorated in elaborate fashion, coated with aspic, and served on a buffet table with other cold food items.

chiffonade: A leafy vegetable (such as lettuce, basil leaves, radicchio, etc.) cut into shreds, approximately ⅛-inch wide, and used as a salad base or as a garnish.

china cap (chinoise): A cone-shaped strainer, with a single handle extending from the wide end of the strainer. China caps come in three basic varieties, designated by the size of their perforations: large (*chinoise gros*), small (*chinoise fin*), and very fine (bouillon strainer, or *chinois mousseline*).

court bouillon: A liquid medium used for poaching various forms of meat, fish, poultry, quenelles, and vegetables. The ingredients vary, depending on the item poached, but generally include water, wine, and aromatics (mirepoix, herbs, and spices).

croustade: A small farinaceous vessel, made from hollowed-out bread, pastry, mashed potato (Duchess potato mixture), or rice. The vessel is usually deep-fried or baked, then filled with a stew, soup, purée, or other viscous dish.

crouton: A small, crisp piece of toasted or fried bread, used as a base for canapés or as a garnish for various soups (from the Old French *crouste*, and Latin *crusta,* meaning "crust.")

crudité: Raw vegetables (can also be fruit), cut into interesting and uniform pieces, served with a sauce as an hors d'oeuvre.

deep-fry: To cook a food item by immersing it in hot fat.

dock: To puncture a rolled-out pie, tart, or puff pastry dough, using the tines of a fork (or a special rolling tool), to prevent the dough from rising during baking.

drum sieve: A circular metal frame, open on one side and covered with a screen on the other. Used for sifting flour and other dry ingredients, as well as pressing mousses and various farces through, with the help of a rubber spatula, as a final step in puréeing. Pressing mousses, pâtés, and other finely puréed preparations through a sieve eliminates remnants of sinew or elements not fully puréed.

egg wash: Beaten whole egg, sometimes with water or milk added, that is brushed onto a pastry exterior. When the pastry is baked, the egg browns slightly, resulting in a glossy, golden-brown veneer.

fine herbs: A mixture of finely minced fresh herbs, traditionally parsley, chervil, tarragon, and chives. In actual practice, it may consist of any assemblage of herbs—parsley plus three others.

fleuron: A small crescent-shaped savory pastry, cut from puff pastry dough (*pâte feuilleté*), used as a garnish for certain fish dishes (when accompanied by a sauce) or as a decorative element on a pastry-covered pie, tarte, pâté, or terrine.

flowerettes: Cauliflower or broccoli, cut into ¼ to ½-inch pieces.

foie gras: Literally, "fat liver," the fattened liver of goose or duck, prepared in various ways.

food mill: A straight-sided or conical container with a perforated bottom and a curved flange attached to a crank, which rests in the center of a perforated plate at the bottom. The crank is manually rotated, pressing a soup or sauce through one of three different sizes of perforated plates. With the advent of food processors, this ingeniously simple device has fallen on hard times, but it can still be a tremendous aid in puréeing soups and sauces.

grosse pièce: Literally, "large piece," a centerpiece on a buffet mirror or platter, from which slices are removed and arranged.

hors d'oeuvre: Literally, "outside of the main piece." This is a small course served before the main course.

julienne: A designated rectangularly shaped vegetable cut, generally used for garnishes, measuring from ⅛ × ⅛ × 1 inch to ¼ × ¼ × 2 or 3 inches, or any food cut into strips. A large julienne is also referred to as *bâtonnet* (little stick).

large dice (jardinière): A designated vegetable cut, measuring approximately ⅓ to ½-inch square.

lozenge: Diamond-shaped cut, often used for canapé bases, but also for meat, fish, poultry, game, and vegetables.

medium dice (macédoine): A size of vegetable cut, measuring approximately ¼-inch square.

mince: To chop a spice, herb, or vegetable very fine.

mirepoix: A mixture of celery, carrot, and onion, commonly used for flavoring a stock or sauce.

mise-en-place: From the verb *mettre*, "to place." In culinary parlance this phrase is translated to mean "a place for everything, and everything in its place." It refers to the importance of being well organized and well prepped, so that kitchen production can move smoothly and all problems can be handled in the heat of peak production.

mother sauce (sauce de mère): One of five foundation sauces, originally formulated by Antoine Carême and later revised by Auguste Escoffier. Also called *leading*, or *foundation* sauce.

nap: To coat a food with a hot or cold sauce.

offal: Edible internal organs (and some external parts) of an animal, considered by some to be gastronomically superior to other edible parts. They include bone marrow, brains, ears, feet, heart, kidneys, liver, sweetbreads (thymus gland), tongue, and tripe (stomach lining).

Parisienne scoop: Commonly known as a melon baller, this tool creates spherical garnishes from fruits and vegetables.

paupiette: Literally, "little package," referring to a rolled fish fillet, bundle of julienned vegetables tied together with scallion greens, and so forth.

peasant style (paysanne): A common term for both a style of cooking and a method of cutting food ingredients. As a cooking style, it is characterized by a robust and spontaneous approach, based on available ingredients and/or refashioned leftovers, often including root vegetables (potatoes, carrots, and turnips) and cabbage. As a cutting technique, it refers to *mirepoix* cut into approximately 1-inch, uneven pieces, then used as an aromatic, as well as an integral ingredient in various dishes.

pièce montée: A sculpted centerpiece fashioned from ice, tallow, butter, salt dough, weaver's dough, pastiage, pulled sugar, or other mediums, and elevated on or near the buffet table. *Montée* is the past participle of the French verb *monter,* meaning "to lift."

poach: To cook very gently in simmering liquid, at a temperature between 180° F (82° C) and 200° F (93° C).

ramekin: An oven-proof, round, ceramic dish, in which individual custards, shirred eggs, and soufflés are prepared. Side portions of cold sauces, compotes, salsas, and so forth, are also served in ramekins. Their size varies with the application: smaller ones (about 2 ounces/57 g) are used for side dishes; medium ones (4 to 6 ounces/113 to 170 g) for egg dishes and custards; and larger ones (6 to 8 ounces/170 to 227 g) for soufflés.

roasting pan (plaque à rôtir): A large rectangular metal pan, deeper and heavier than a baking (sheet) pan, used for roasting meats and poultry.

sachet: A small piece of cheesecloth (muslin) tied into a small bag, containing herbs and/or spices for flavoring a stock or court bouillon.

salpicon: A small dice of one or more ingredients, bound with any number of sauces: cold (mayonnaise); brown (Bordelaise, Madeira, Perigordine, etc.); white (Lyonnaise, Mousseline, Newburg, etc.); or tomato (Amatricianna, Bolognese, Napolitana, etc.); cooked or served in a bread, pasta, pastry, or polenta case.

scallop: Though most often associated with the connector muscle of one variety of bivalve mollusk, the term also refers to a slice of meat, game, poultry, or fish, pounded very thin, then cooked. The French word for this is *escalope;* the Italian, *scallopine.*

shallot (eschallote): a unique aromatic vegetable, a separate variety of the onion family, and an essential ingredient in finished sauces. The name is derived from Ascalon, an ancient Palestinian port, and it is believed that shallots were cultivated as early as the middle of the eighth century. Their flavor is subtler than onion, with a hint of garlic. They are also served raw in salads and grilled or roasted as an accompaniment to scores of dishes. Because of their ancient and Middle Eastern origins, shallots are also used frequently in Vietnamese, Chinese, Indian, and Creole cookery.

skillet: A heavy-gauge cast-iron pan with a single handle. Sometimes called a Griswold pan, it can be placed in the oven, thus doubling as a roasting pan.

small dice (brunoise): A designated vegetable cut, measuring approximately ⅛-inch (3 mm) square.

socle: A container for food made out of food. Examples are cucumbers scooped out for use as canapés, apples and tomatoes scooped out and filled with salad, and small rolls scooped out for use as croustades.

temper: To combine two liquids, one hot and the other cold, by slowly blending the hot liquid into the cold one. By gradually raising the temperature of the cold liquid, the two can be combined without adversely affecting either liquid. Applies to the incorporation of final liaisons, in the making of chaud-froid and mayonnaise collée, crème anglaise, pastry cream, as well as to melting chocolate.

turned (tourné): A potato or other vegetable cut into a seven-sided oval or an olive-shaped oval, measuring 1 to 3 inches (25 to 75 mm) long.

whip (fouet): Sometimes referred to as a *whisk*, a whip consists of several strands of stainless steel wire, in various thicknesses, bent into loops and held in place with a metal handle. The very heavy, stiff wire whips are commonly called "French whips," the lighter, more flexible ones are "piano wire whips," and the even lighter, large, bulbous ones are known as "balloon whips." All are indispensible in a well-equipped kitchen, used for beating liaisons into sauces, blending baking batters, and whipping air into various foods (such as heavy cream and egg whites).

white pepper: Black pepper that has been soaked in water, then rubbed to remove the skin and thin outer pulp. White pepper is preferred over black pepper in some dishes because of its lighter color. Dedicated cooks often keep two pepper mills, one filled with black pepper, the other with white, and each labeled accordingly.

zest: The outermost skin of a citrus fruit, excluding the pith (the underlying white part of the skin). It is shaved off with a zester, a five-holed tool specifically engineered for that purpose, or with a sharp paring knife or vegetable peeler. Zest contains the essential oils of the fruit and is used as both a flavoring agent and a garnish.

SPECIALTY SUPPLIERS

For information on specialty food items mentioned or used in this text, contact the following organizations.

Asian Ingredients: Epicurean International, Inc., P.O. Box 13242, Berkeley, California 94701; (510) 268-0209. Distributors of premium imported Thai and other Asian cooking ingredients. Seth Jacobsen, contact person.

Aspic: Haller Foods, P.O. Box 422483, San Francisco, California 94142; (415) 588-3192. Wholesale supplier of powdered aspic and other specialty items. Hans Haller, contact person.

Berries: The Oregon Caneberry Commission, 712 NW 4th Street, Corvalis, Oregon 97330; (503) 758-4043. For recipes using blackberries, boysenberries, caneberries, loganberries, marionberries, and information on their availability in various forms. Jan Marie Schroeder, contact person.

Oregon Department of Agriculture, 121 SW Salmon Street, Suite 240, Portland, Oregon 97204-2987; (503) 229-6734. For information on other unique products, write for a catalog.

Books and Tools: Pro Chef International, 12656 Mengibar Avenue, San Diego, California 92129; (619) 484-6423. Carries some of the finest and most difficult to find ice and mukimono carving tools, as well as books. Write for current catalog.

J. B. Prince, 29 West 38th Street, New York, New York 10018. Suppliers of unique culinary tools, books, and small wares. Write for current catalog.

Dover Publications, Inc., 31 East 2nd Street, Mineola, New York 11501. Publishes facsimile edition of *The Epicurean*, published in 1893, by Charles Ranhoffer, acclaimed chef of Delmonico's, New York City's first continental restaurant [seen in color plate, *Duck Liver (Foie Gras de Canard) Terrine*].

Bread: Boudin Bakery, 132 Hawthorne Street, San Francisco, California 94107; (415) 882-1808. One of San Francisco's oldest bakeries and home of Fernando Padilla, a production baker who can create out of bread, from a picture, virtually any animal or structure. Debbie Smith, Director of Marketing, contact person.

Buffet and Dining Tableware: Robert King Associates, 11 Tillman Place, San Francisco, California 94108; (415) 989-5866. Distributors of several lines of exquisite dinnerware, table linens, and accessories from some of the finest manufacturers in the world. Robert King, contact person.

Le Creuset of America, Inc., Yemassee, South Carolina 29945; (803) 589-6211. Manufacturers of exceptional, high-quality cast iron cook-and-serve-ware.

B.I.A. Cordon Bleu, Inc., 1135 Industrial Road, San Carlos, California 94070; (415) 595-2400. Northern California distributors of a line of porcelain and ceramic serviceware. Ulrich Honigausen, contact person.

Gourmet Display, 309 South Cloverdale Street, D-14, Seattle, Washington 98108; (800) 767-4711. Suppliers of an innovative and expansive line of faux marble and acrylic platters in a wide assortment of colors, designs, sizes, and shapes. Tim Ecker and Ernie Gilmer, contact persons.

Towle Silversmiths, P.O. Box 9115, East Boston, Massachusetts 02128; (617) 568-1300. Manufacturers, for more than 300 years, of classical sterling and silverplated flatware, holloware, and giftware. For information, contact Robert J. McAniff, Vice President of Sales, or Sue McCarthy, National Bridal Director.

Caviar: Carolyn Collins Caviar, P.O. Box 662, Crystal Lake, Illinois 60014; (312) 226-0342. Producer of a line of North American caviars. Carolyn Collins, contact person.

Centerpieces: Bread Effects Culinart, 5677 Rapid Run Road, Cincinnati, Ohio 45238; (800) 333-5678; (513) 922-5329. Suppliers of extraordinary tallow and bread sculptures, and sculpting supplies, including a modern tallow sculpting medium. Dominic Palazzolo, Chef/Owner, contact person.

Cheese: Laura Chenel's Chevre, 1550 Ridley Avenue, Santa Rosa, California 95401; (707) 575-8888. Producer of an exceptionally fine line of goat cheeses. Laura Chenel, contact person.

Wisconsin Milk Marketing Board, 8418 Excelsior Drive, Madison, Wisconsin 53717; (800) 373-9662. Primary marketing organization for Wisconsin dairy products. Offers information on cheese, including the *Cheesecyclopedia Study Course,* a comprehensive self-directed study course on how cheese is manufactured. Linda Funk, Director, National Product Communications, contact person.

Maytag Dairy Farms, P.O. Box 806, Newton, Iowa 50208; (800) 247-2458. Producers of one of the first blue-veined cheeses produced in North America (1941), and descendants of F. L. Maytag, early innovator of the washing machine. Jim Stevens, President and contact person.

Duck Liver (Foie Gras de Canard): Sonoma Foie Gras, P.O. Box 2007, Sonoma, California 95476; (707) 938-1229. Guillermo and Junny Gonzalez, contact persons.

Commonwealth Enterprises, Ltd., P.O. Box 49, Airport Road, Mongaup Valley, New York 12762; (914) 583-6630.

Eau de Vie: Clear Creek Distillery, 1430 Northwest 23rd Avenue, Portland, Oregon 97210; (503) 248-9470. Producer of several fruit brandies, including an exceptional pear brandy. Stephen R. McCarthy, contact person.

Equipment: Hobart Corporation, Inc., 890 Cowan Road, Burlingame, California 94011; (415) 697-9122. Charles Canny and Dave Browing, contact persons.

Grains: Indian Harvest Specialtifoods, Inc., P.O. Box 428, Bemidji, Minnesota 56601; (800) 346-7032. Call for complimentary samples of unique side dishes featuring rice, grains, pasta, and beans.

Ice Carving: For information on national and international competitions, tips and developments in the industry, contact the National Ice Carving Association (NICA), P.O. Box 3593, Oak Brook, Illinois 60522-3593; (708) 871-8431. Alice Connelly, contact person.

Meat and Charcuterie: Adiells Sausage Company, 1625 Alvarado Street, San Leandro, California 94577; (510) 614-5450. One of northern California's best-known producers of sausage.

Marcel & Henri, Charcuterie Française, 415 Browning Way, South San Francisco, California 94080; outside California: (800) 227-6436; within California: (800) 542-4230. One of San Francisco's best-known producers of pâtés and terrines; also ships nationwide. Henri Lapuyade or Joyce Smith, contact persons.

Nueske Hillcrest Farms, Wittenberg, Wisconsin 54499; (800) 382-2266. Producers of an exquisite apple-smoked country ham and related charcuterie. Jim Neuske and Gilbert Thompson, contact persons.

Southland/Superior Farms, 3163 E. Vernon Avenue, Vernon, California 90058; (213) 582-4868. Wholesale distributors of North American produced lamb and other meat products, and innovators of a precooked and seasoned boneless lamb leg. Dan Wallace, contact person.

Olive Oil, Olives, Vinegars: Nick Sciabia & Sons, P.O. Box 1246, Modesto, California 95353; (209) 577-5067. Second-generation, family-operated olive vineyard, producing an exceptional line of olives, olive oil, and vinegars. Daniel Sciabia, contact person.

Kimberly Wine Vinegar Works, 290 Pierce Street, Daly City, California 94015; (415) 755-0306. Produces several varieties of exceptionally fine vinegars and olive oils. Ruth Robinson, contact person.

B. R. Cohn Olive Oil, 15140 Sonoma Highway, Glen Ellen, California 95442; (707) 938-4064. (415) 593-9468, Ron Morris, Director of Marketing and contact person.

For information on Mediterranean-produced olive oil, telephone the Olive Oil Council at 800-232 OLIVE.

Smoked Salmon: The Cambridge House, 133 East De la Guerra, #6, Santa Barbara, California 93101; (805) 684-2082. Patrick A. Martin, contact person.

RECIPE
INDEX

SUBJECT INDEX

Worcester College of Technology

0143297

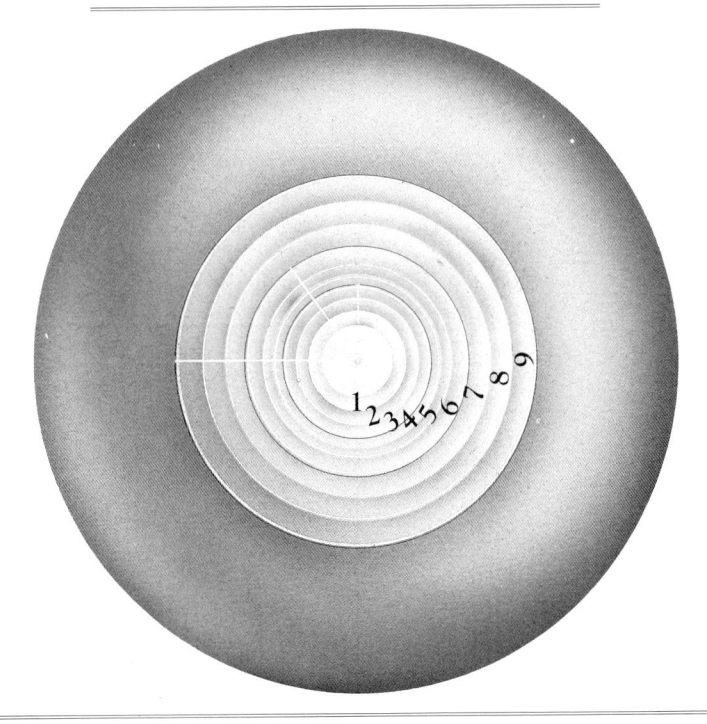

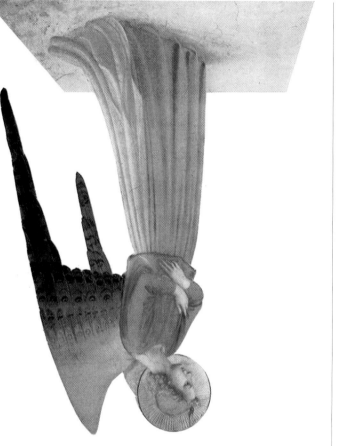

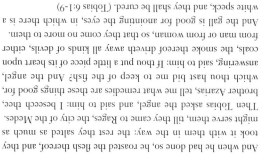

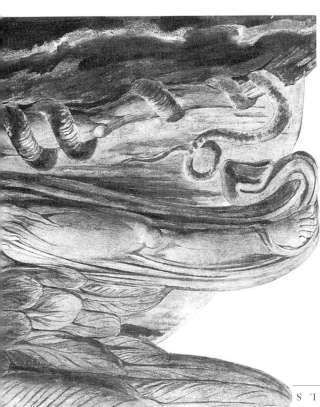

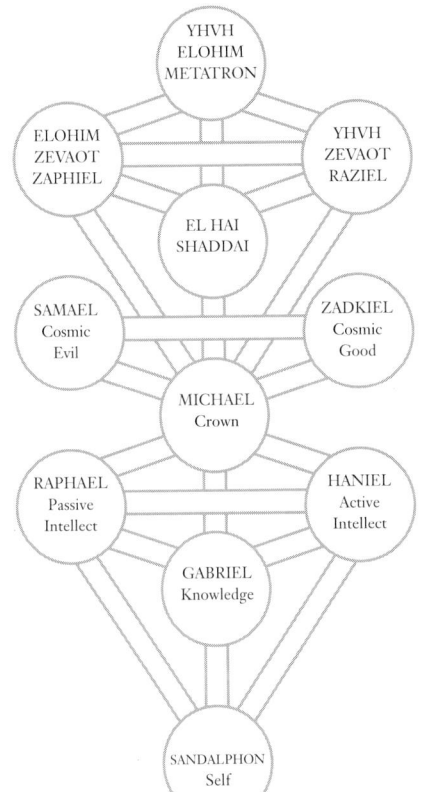

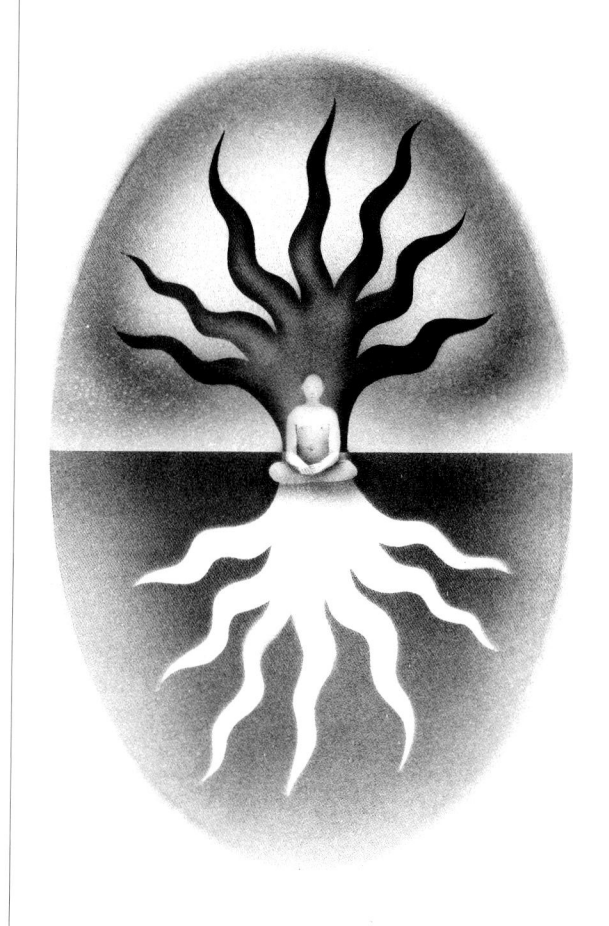

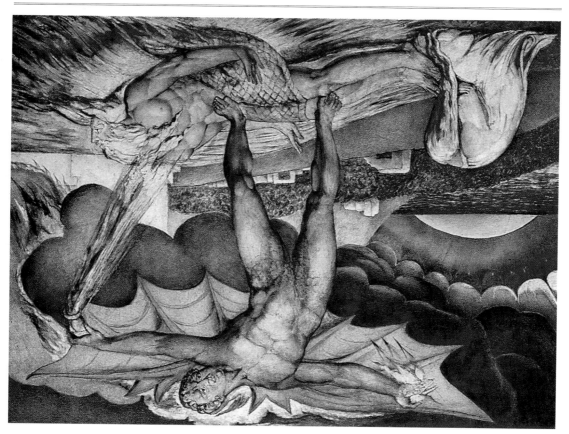

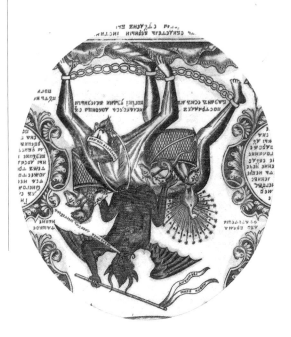

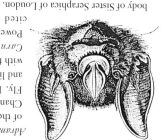

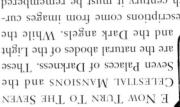

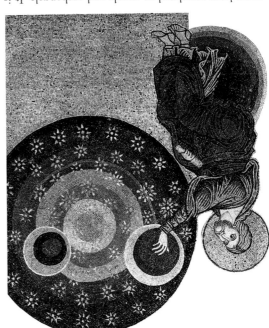

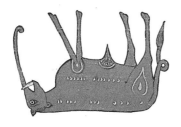

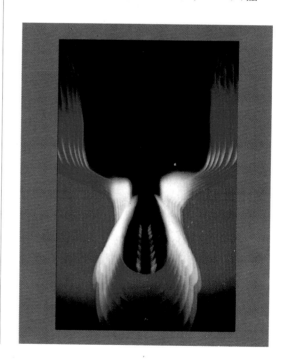

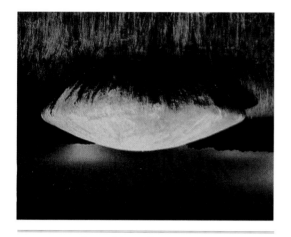

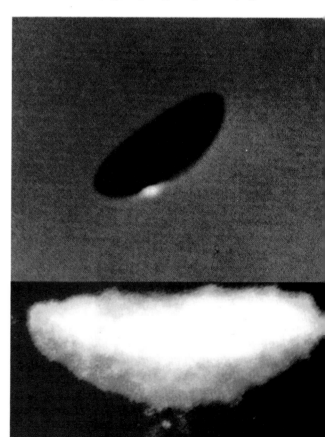

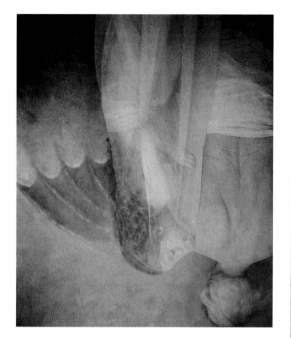

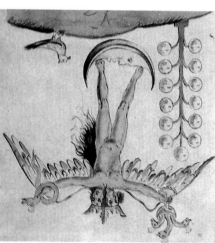

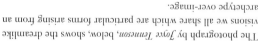

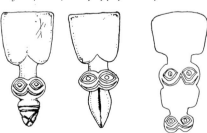

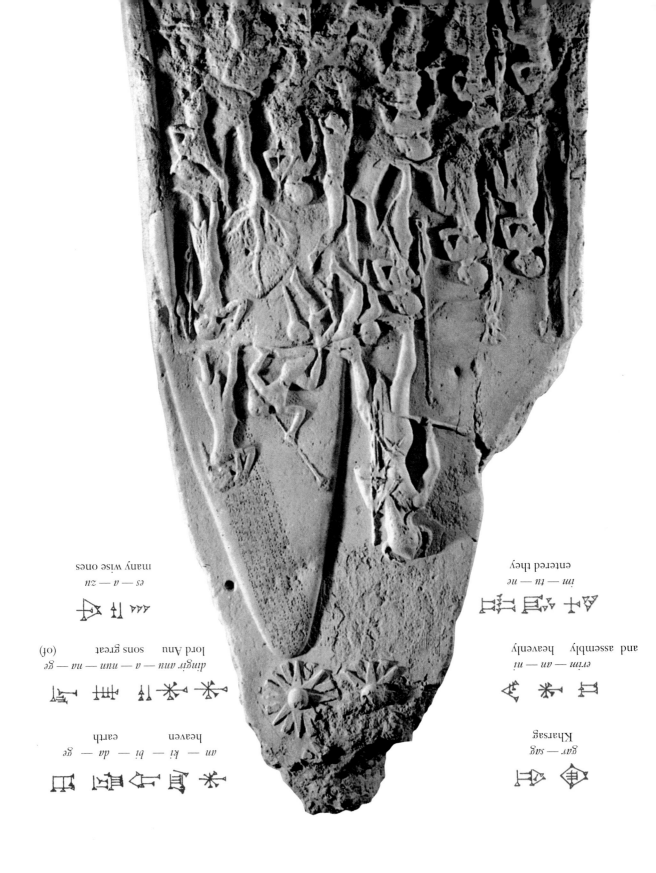

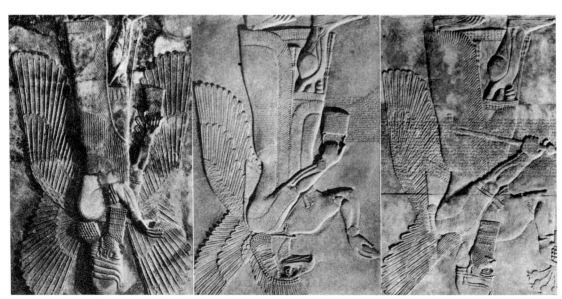

open. Feeble-minded or not, Joseph could fly. It first occurred in the middle of mass: the monk could not restrain his ecstatic mood and drifted up from his seat to land on the high altar twenty feet away. Such zeal did not escape the Pope who ordered him to Rome. Joseph was so ecstatic in the Pontiff's presence that he floated off the ground for all to see. So high did he go that it was commented that he even showed due propriety by having on underwear for the occasion. In Assisi he was so overcome by the enthusiastic reception of the crowd that he sailed over the onlookers to land on the altar and embrace the statue of the Virgin. Once he flew into the topmost branches of a tree on overhearing a fellow monk remark on the beauties of the day. He demonstrated his bizarre power too many times for it to be dismissed as a mass hallucination. He could even help others to fly, as he demonstrated when he healed a demented aristocrat by seizing him by the hair and taking off. This time he flew for a record fifteen minutes. The Church is often a little embarrassed by such miraculous displays. But before they decided to canonize this rather awkward saint, the authorities examined the sworn testimonies of hundreds of witnesses including a Pope, two Kings, the Duke of Brunswick and his philosopher friend Leibnitz, who was certainly no credulous fool. Even when the doctor was cauterizing Joseph's leg just before he died, the surgeon was shocked to find that the friar was floating six inches above the chair.

It is certainly difficult to know quite what to make of this story. The sworn depositions of so many intelligent people suggest that Joseph could, indeed, fly. If a simpleton like this monk could do so, then surely it is not beyond others to use a human capacity which, for some reason or another, apparently lies idle. The Shining Ones of the Middle East could

have discovered the magical secret by stumbling on one of our inherent potentials.

Illumination

If it is difficult to unearth concrete evidence as far as flight is concerned, what of the second "advanced" technology? In the case of electric light there is at last real and substantial evidence of its use as far back as five thousand years ago. There are, for instance, actual examples of efficient electrical batteries which have been unearthed in Egypt and Baghdad. Many of these devices were actually used to electro-plate metals with gold and silver. There is, however, one example of a huge device depicted in a wall carving in Egypt, dating from 2500 B.C. which clearly resembles an electric light bulb.

Returning to the settlement for a moment we read in the earliest tablet:

"At the House of Joy and Life, the bright dwelling, Where the destiny of Man was established; The splendid place of Flaming Brightness".

Another reference was to a "Brilliant, glowing House" which was obviously very different from the mud walled dwellings of the lowlands lit by either oil lamps or rush torches.

In Enoch's later account of the same house it is difficult to know whether his awed description is the genuine response of a simple country man who lived at the edge of pre-history and who had never seen brilliant light at night time, or a case of the "chair transformed to a throne." But Enoch was known as a writer of truth and most of his descriptions are remarkably free of religious or supernatural trappings. He enters a building with glistening white stone walls which was brilliantly lit. The floor

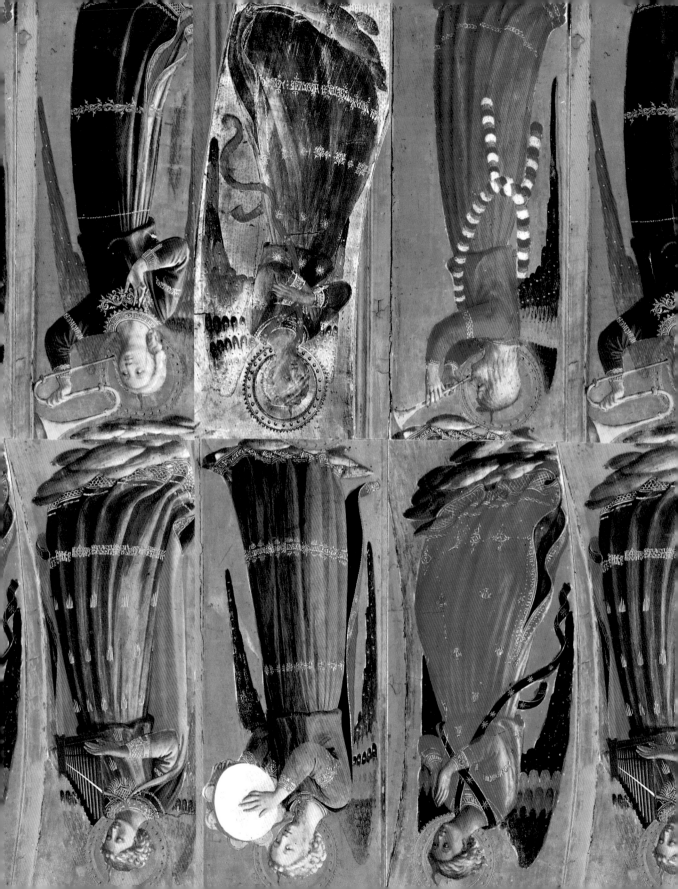

A N G E L S

An Endangered Species

by
Malcolm Godwin

■ newleaf

A LABYRINTH BOOK

First published in Great Britain in 1993 by Boxtree Limited
First published in 1990 in the United States of America
by Simon & Schuster

Text © Malcolm Godwin 1990
Illustrations © Yatri 1990

The right of Malcolm Godwin to be identified as Author of this
Work has been asserted by him in accordance with the
Copyright, Designs and Patents Act 1988

3   5   7   9   10   8   6   4   2

Edited by Deborah Bergman
Designed by Malcolm Godwin
Typeset by Simonetta Castelli
Printed and bound in Spain by Graficromo, S.A. - CORDOBA
for Labyrinth Publishing (UK) Ltd

Boxtree Limited, Broadwall House,
21 Broadwall, London SE1 9PL

A CIP catalogue entry for this book is available from the British Library

ISBN 1 85283 506 0

CONTENTS

INTRODUCTION

No-one on earth could feel like this,
I'm thrown and overblown with bliss
There must be an angel
Playing with my heart
I walk into an empty room,
and suddenly my heart goes "Boom"!
Its an orchestra of angels
And they're playing with my heart.
(Must be talking to an angel)
And when I think that I'm alone,
It seems as if there's more of us at home
Its a multitude of angels
And they're playing with my heart.
(Annie Lennox and David. A. Stewart)

This is a typical lyric by the Eurythmics. No-one could accuse this modern group of being overly sentimental, yet their lines are still typical of the genre of the eighties. It is no exaggeration to say that over the last thirty years *one in every ten* pop songs mentions an angel.

It is likely that at least half of the listeners don't belong to any of the religions which gave rise to these beings, yet still know what an angel is supposed to be. Whatever this symbol means to anyone, its power remains extraordinarily alive and magically potent, otherwise the song would lose its whole significance. Opposite page: *Poster by Mouse and Kelly for the group Led Zeppelin.*

[† Newsweek, June 26th 1978 p.32]

HE Angel is one of those Articles of Faith as unshakable as our belief in the existence of God, an atom, or the ill luck of the number 13. One in every ten popular songs invokes angels in some form. They appear on Christmas cards and wedding invitations, they abound as souvenirs, jewelry and religious or semi-religious bric-a-brac. Every museum is packed full of paintings and sculptures of these winged beings and even artists and writers depict them to this very day.

But ask anyone if they really believe in the existence of the angel and suddenly a profound conflict arises between the unthinking certitude of a faith and the sophisticated realism of the 20th century.

In a Gallup poll conducted in the United States during 1978[†], over half the subjects questioned about their belief in angels and demons answered positively. For those who did not share the belief, it might be assumed that they felt angels or devils were an outdated Gothic superstition, for which there must be some simple scientific or psychological explanation.

Such unexamined assumptions from believers or non-believers tell us far more about the blurred nature of the belief systems which underpin our particular culture than about the truth of the actual angels.

It doesn't seem to matter whether the opinions come from the scientific community, the orthodox Churches or the New Age thinkers – on one level angels still manage to retain their magical popularity and power, while on another no one quite believes in them any more.

So, what or who are angels? And why do they seem to persist in the popular mind even today? Such seemingly simple and straightforward questions will lead us into an extraordinary, unexpected and often bizarre world. It is a landscape in which reality, myth, fantasy, legend, dreams and supernatural visions all appear hopelessly entangled.

Throughout history, religions, both primitive and sophisticated, have held beliefs of spiritual beings, powers and principles that mediate between the One transcendental realm of the sacred and the profane dualistic world of space and time. These convictions range from belief in the power of ancestors, spirits of nature or fairy beings from the "other world" to the spiritual beings called angels by the four Western "Religions of the Book."

Our particular concern is with the genus *Angelus Occidentalis*. This is a general term for a number of species and sub-species to be found in the monotheistic religions of Judaism, Zoroastrianism, Christianity and Islam. What is especially significant is that these four religions share the view of a tripartite universe. That is to say, they believe that the cosmos is divided into Heaven, Earth and Hell and is populated accordingly with angels, humans and demons.

This contrasts with the monistic cosmos of the Hindus, the Jains and the Buddhists; the East gene-

rally has no belief in angels as revealers of the truth. This function is left to other beings, often reincarnations of holy sages or incarnations of the deities. But in Western traditions, which are based on prayer rather than meditation, the angel is an essential ingredient. There is even a special group of angels who fall silent at dawn in order to listen to the prayers and praises of Israel.

In Western tradition, in order to reveal the purpose and destiny of humankind, God's Word is communicated through celestial messengers whose primary function was to praise and serve the Almighty and do His Will. Before modern science appeared in the 16th and 17th centuries, and with it the newly discovered Laws and Forces of Nature, angels were supposed to have moved the stars and the elements. Gravity was not a law of nature but an active angelic intelligence.

The term angel derives from a Greek translation of the original Hebrew *mal'akh*, which originally meant the "Shadow side of God," but later came to mean messenger. This derivation may offer a clue as to why we all feel a certain vagueness when attempting to describe the nature of an angel. For a "messenger" implies a function or status within a cosmic hierarchy, rather than an essence.

The primary significance of angels lies not in who or what they are, but rather in what they do. Their inherent nature cannot be separated from their relationship with the Prime mover, the God or Ultimate Source.

Thus we find the Iranian messenger-angel Vohu Manah (Good Mind), revealing God's message to Zoroaster two thousand five hundred years ago, and the Archangel Gabriel dictating the Qur'an to Mohammed over a millennium later. In both cases the role of these spirits of God is far more important than their identity, their nature or "being."

Not only are angels inseparable from God, they are also indivisible from their witnesses.

The Swedish mystic Swedenburg once said: "I am well aware that many will say that no-one can possibly speak with spirits and angels so long as he is living in the body; many say it is all fancy, others that I recount such things to win credence, while others will make other kinds of objection. But I am deterred by none of these: for I have seen, I have heard, I have felt."

It is impossible to argue with a statement like this and we will discover that most of the witnesses to be found within this volume will be as sincere as Swedenburg in their belief that they encountered a real angel with a real message. In the majority of the cases we shall examine this might well be true. However, the simple fact is that it is impossible to separate the observer from the observed. To question the truth of the angel is also to question the truthfulness of the witness. Most of the available evidence of the existence of a real heavenly host would hardly stand up in a court of Law. Substantial facts are hard to come by. Angels, like the Extra-Terrestrials which followed them, don't leave footprints.

* ¹ **The Apocrypha.** Material found within the Old Testament was gradually gathered over a period lasting about a millennium. Most of its scriptures were actually compiled during, or shortly after, the period of Exile in Babylonia (586 to 538 B.C.). In the second century B.C. these Hebrew scriptures were translated into Greek (called the Septuagint) to form the Old Testament but some texts were subsequently rejected from the canon by the later Church Fathers. These are now known as the *apocrypha* or the "hidden books". They are not to be confused with the *pseudepigrapha* or the "false writing" which was never included in the original canon at any time. The latter appeared in great profusion during the apocalyptic phase of writing which commenced about 200 years B.C. and ended about one hundred years after Christ's death. The end of the world had failed to arrive, the New Golden Age had failed to materialize and apocalyptic revelations went out of fashion.

The Hidden Books

It's reasonable to assume that everything one would want to know about angels; their names, attributes and duties would be found in the Christian Bible. Surprisingly this is just about the last place to discover such information. The Old Testament actually only mentions three angels by name, if we count the Catholic Book of Tobit. So where do we find the more intimate details of angelic life – who they were, or are, what they are called, what they do and how they interact with humankind?

Virtually all the information that we possess comes from *outside* the orthodox scriptures and canons of the four religions that believe in the existence of angels. Indeed most of these particular texts have been declared heretical, pseudepigraphical or apochryphal.*¹ And yet it is largely these heretical texts which form the basis of our present, if hazy ideas of the host, and on which a large portion of this present volume is based.

Typical of such texts are the three great Chronicles of Enoch, compiled around the 2nd century B.C. from much earlier sources. The pages simply teem with angelic life, names, duties, characteristics and the most intimate descriptions of the host of angels. St. Jerome declared these chronicles to be apocryphal in the 4th century A.D., but up until then they had been deemed an inspired canonical scripture by all the earliest Fathers. In it the scribe Enoch described his journey to the ten Heavens in which he saw gigantic angels in a penal and punishment area. Now this was hardly consistent with the later view of the Church of a separate Heaven and Hell. So Enoch's texts fell into disrepute and virtually disappeared until the 18th century.

Yet Enoch was known as "the man who spoke truth" and the text is remarkably free of all the usual

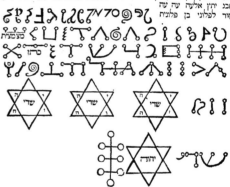

religious extravaganzas. Although it is unacceptable to orthodox Doctrine, nevertheless much of Enoch's apocryphal material found its way into the New Testament without anyone suspecting. He will be the most important guide to the "Seven Heavens" and the dark caverns of the underworld of Sheol, Gehenna, Hell and the Bottomless Abyss.

God and Devil

This volume is not limited to the benevolent host of Heaven but includes the rebel angels led by Lucifer, once named the" Morning Star," and "The Bringer of Light." Such titles for the Prince of Darkness reveal the difficulty of discovering exactly

which side any particular angel is on – God's or the Devil's. For instance, in the Old Testament, there is no reference to the fallen angels at all. There is nothing to suggest that Satan was evil. We read of *ha-satan*, the "Adversary," but this appears to stand for an office, and by no means a wicked one, rather than being the name of an angel. Whoever held the office was the being most beloved by God and certainly not the Satan who appears in the New Testament. *Any concept of good and malevolent angels seems to be completely lacking in Old Testament writings.* But by the time the New Testament was compiled one third of the heavenly host, led by Satan, had fallen into the Abyss. And there are at least seven conflicting accounts of their fall which took nine days to reach the Pit. There is even one Gnostic version in which the Jewish God, Yahweh, is shown to be Satan, Prince of Darkness, who created our universe and rules it with his dark and evil angels.

It is only by studying the apocrypha, the apocalyptic scriptures and the pseudepigrapha, that the rich and multi-colored picture of the angelic and demonic legions can be pieced together. This is not a static and consistent mosaic. Rather we find a dynamic and constantly evolving panorama of the warring forces of Righteousness and Malevolence. In one early account, for instance, the supposedly "Good" Almighty is seen to possess a disturbingly ambivalent nature: in a moment of pure pique He annihilates an entire "globe" of his angelic choir for failing to sing His praise on cue. We also find the same ambiguity as to what is good and what is wicked in the behavior of many of the Heavenly Father's favorites. These often seem to lead double lives, appearing as Dukes of Hell one moment and singing Hallelujahs around the Celestial throne the next, without a trace of tarnish to their shining haloes.

By the 3rd century A.D. this essentially Jewish

Opposite: **Siren Bird of Heaven** *Russian Lubok of the 18th century, Historical Museum, Moscow.* The Siren bird was very popular in Russia. The text explains the creature appears in the land of India. The Hindu Apsaras were the dispensers of bliss and delight on the heavenly plane. It is said that they wrapped the deceased in their voluptuous arms, carrying the fortunate soul in ecstasy to paradise. The Sirens were a little naughtier but equally effective in their promised delights. Like the Faeries of the Celts, the power of Sirens is the power of the female. This is the opposite pole to the world of the angels of the Religions of the Book.
Above: **Winged Artemis**, *Greece 5th Century B.C.*

ambivalence had disappeared and two very distinct and opposing species had emerged.

Themes of Two Volumes

Even theologians found the concepts of angels and demons to be an anachronism when viewed alongside scientific observations of the nature of the cosmos. The astronomical findings of the 16th century demolished the last vestiges of a world at the center of the universe. Angels could not survive the fact that Earth was a very minor planet circling a mediocre star on the outer arm of a relatively inconspicuous galaxy. However, with the emergence of 20th century Western psychology, the principles, underlying the belief in angel and demon took on a new significance. Many theologians have re-mythologized the tripartite cosmos into a three layered structure of the personality (the superego, the ego and the libido) or the later concept of the three brain layers (Reptilian, Neo-Mammalian and Neo-Cortex). The Freudian and Jungian "myths" of the human personality have initiated an entirely new dimension in the study of both angels and their fallen brothers. It is just such themes as these which will be explored in this volume.

In fact this book is really two volumes within one cover. In order to examine all the possible explanations of the host it is necessary to have a clear reference as to what the traditional and orthodox view of the angelic host might be. However, we find that today there simply isn't a unified and consistent vision. For instance, when the Catholic Encyclopedia, published in 1967, maintains that "Theology has purified the obscurity and error contained in traditional views about angels, " they promptly confuse us further by assuring the faithful that angels are "completely spiritual and no longer merely a very fine material, fire-like and vaporous." And so the ambiguities remain. Conservative Catholics, including the present Pope, also argue for an actual angelic spirit called the devil, while skeptics within the same Church believe that there is only individual sin by the choice inherent in exercising our free will. There are Bishops who insist on angels and others who declare that they don't exist.

Protestant theology is no less ambivalent. Martin Luther swept aside the entire elaborate angelic superstructure in a contemptuous gesture, but curiously and grimly held on to his belief in Satan and his dark hordes. But, as he pointed out, if there was no sin and no Devil what need of Christ as a redeemer?

So as there is a real confusion today over the nature of the angel a complete Treasury of Angelic Lore has been compiled from the period when the angels were in Heaven and all was clear in the world. Part One is a time-sealed treasure house in which we can view the angels at the very peak of their power and authority. This Golden Age abruptly came to an end during the apocalyptic Black Death which decimated the population of Europe in a few short years. Only a decade after the plague had swept by, the Church, under the merciless pressure of new ways of thinking about man and the cosmos, was beginning to disown the elaborate angelic hierarchy. The once teeming streets of the Heavenly City were suddenly silent and deserted.

But where did the angels go? This is the subject of the second part of the book.

Fact and Faith

There seem to be two basic methods to approach a subject like that of angels. One fruitful approach appears to be historical. This can be summarized as the method in which *facts outweigh faith*. It has the added advantage of allowing us to examine the various genealogical family trees of the angelic host. Each separate species can be traced back to its particular cultural origins. In many cases

there is blatant evidence of wholesale borrowings from earlier bloodlines. We see how scribes from one religious group simply absorbed into their writings the juicier myths of those tribes they conquered or were conquered by. This is most evident in the eclectic borrowings of the Hebrews. With some justification they can claim to be the first to introduce angels on a truly heavenly scale. The great temptation, in applying a strictly historical method, is to conclude that angels are simply the collected and exaggerated fantasies of holy scholars. And it appears that it is true in many cases.

There is, however, another method which might be labeled the supernatural. In this *faith outweighs fact*. This is actually the one most of us apply to a subject like angels without really thinking. We have been handed down a number of assumptions, based on a continuing tradition of popular piety which seems to have archetypal roots far deeper than many of the religions which pass in the night. These archaic images, which are far older than Christianity, Islam or Judaism, seem almost to be passed down in the genes, or at least have a powerful connection with a collective memory field.

The last approach is that of scientific method. Here the equation is more subtle. One might say that *faith is created by fact*, or that by observing a phenomenon scientifically an observer can build up an idea of how it works and what it is. But modern scientists are discovering that the world is not quite so simple and that often *fact is created by faith*. Quantum physicists know, that if they expect a particle to act like a wave, it does. If they expect it to act like a point, it likewise accommodates their idea. This is partially due to the fact that any method of observing the world necessarily changes our perception of it. More fundamental is the notion that we cannot step outside of the universe

to observe it. We are part of our own experiment. This has far reaching significance when trying to observe angels. Remember that the angel cannot be separated from the witness. There is no substantial and concrete evidence save for what the witness saw and felt. The rest is the stuff of myth, legend and speculation.

Reasonable Intuition

The purpose of Part Two of Angels is to offer a number of classic cases of both encounters and speculations of angelic nature.

In the following pages, you will see that *something* really has happened to those who have experienced angels or demons. Many witnesses have been transformed beyond recognition by the encounter. It is my hope that in some way this may happen to the reader.

For, as far as angels are concerned, Samuel Butler was right when he said, "all reason is against it, and all healthy instinct is for it." And that seems as true now as it was in the bible lands ten thousand years ago.

Adoration of the Lamb *Jan Van Eyck 15th Century Flanders*

PART ONE

THE TREASURY

Angelic Lore

THE TREASURY

Angels surrounding Christ and the four Apostles. *Illuminated manuscript 1109 A.D. British Museum MS 11695.*

HE FIRST PART OF THIS VOLUME is really a separate, miniature reference manual. It inventories the entire Angelic Host as it was known at the peak of its most dazzling Golden Epoch, during the late Middle Ages in Europe. It coincided with the new vision of the Renaissance and the rise of Humanism, and ended abruptly in the middle of the 14th century during the apocalyptic horrors of the Black Death. The images of the Angelic Host as known in that era, are the ones that have been passed down to us, almost intact, by the lore of popular piety. It is fascinating to discover that the image of the angel has hardly altered from this epoch, almost as if time had not touched the species' golden youth. Somehow the angel has been sealed in a time-proof capsule. And it is this 'eternally' young form which we all respond to and vaguely acknowledge when the subject arises.

After this blaze of glory, quite suddenly, angels ceased to have the full doctrinal blessings of the Church. During the Inquisition of the following two hundred years the authorities turned their undivided attentions to the fallen host of devils and demons. However, through popular piety and an almost pagan worship of the celestial spirits, angels retained a powerful emotional hold upon most believers.

The evolution of the idea of a unique angelic species can be viewed from countless angles. Historically speaking, for instance, they are clearly the hybrid result of an extraordinary Hebrew program of cross-breeding original Egyptian, Sumerian, Babylonian and Persian supernatural beings. This genetic interaction of ideas produced the outward appearance of the winged messenger of God which we know of today. By the 1st century after Christ this essentially Jewish creation was adopted, almost wholesale, by the new religion, and six centuries later by the Muslims. Since then that fundamental angelic form has undergone no radical alterations.

In a way, this Treasury of Angelic Lore is somewhat like a time-sealed museum; a rare collection of old and precious things. However a true treasure house does not necessarily imply either classification or meaning. It is simply a place to display the elaborate gems of a lore which spans a historical period of over four thousand years. Whether the collection still retains a significance in this century, or is merely shelves of paper angels which are the creation of scholars and priests, is a question reserved for the second half of the volume.

Either way, belief in angels has persisted in popular lore, while the Church from which they sprang almost seems embarrassed by references to them. It is as if the beliefs of their Golden Age had been caught in the years of perpetual youth by some medieval camera or fixed in polished amber like exotic archaic flies. We will now examine some of those unique portraits.

Above: **Cherubim guarding the Ark of the Covenant.** *French miniature 14th Century.* Compare this image with the **Sphinxes** below *from 8th Century Persia.* The two golden Cherubim who were the guardians of the Ark of the Covenant were far more likely to resemble these bizarre figures than either the French version or the later sugary creatures which decorate baroque walls. Our present day concepts of angels hardly includes such monsters.

Right: **Jacob's dream of the ladder** with angels ascending and descending. *Hayley, 18th Century.*

THE FIRST WING : Heavenly Hierarchy

TALIAN BUREAUCRACY is claimed to be the closest to that of Heaven; it works solely by Divine Intervention and takes Eternity for anything to happen. One glimpse into the celestial archives certainly makes anyone wonder just what might occur in an emergency. The observer can get quickly lost in the unbelievable complexity of the various orders and departments, the changing number of Heavens, the conflicting hierarchies and the duplication of department heads. It seems obvious, in such a heavenly muddle, why the dark forces have such an easy and unopposed life on earth.

But much of the apparent confusion actually arises from the conflicting accounts of our authoritative sources. St. Ambrose differs with St. Jerome, who disagrees with St. Thomas Aquinas, who says that St. Paul must have been wrong. The theologians are even worse than the saints. Few even agree on the nature of the celestial hierarchies, let alone on what their various duties and missions might be.

For instance, no two authorities see eye to eye on who the Archangels are. While it is generally thought that there are seven, Islam only recognizes four. Often an Archangel appears as a member of an entirely different angelic order, far higher up the celestial league table. That same Archangel might also

appear as warden of more than one heavenly domain, while simultaneously operating as the angel of death and a terrible Duke of Hell.

The Nine Choirs

In order to make some sense of what first appears to be an unholy mess, we will adopt the most standard and orthodox hierarchy of the angels. According to both the two foundational texts, the *Celestial Hierarchies* of Dionysius and the *Summa Theologica* by Thomas Aquinas, there are nine celestial orders orbiting the Throne of Glory, rather like that of our own planetary system. The nine angelic orders surrounding the Divine Core, appear within the following three distinct groups:

Highest Triad:
1. Seraphim 2. Cherubim 3. Thrones
Middle Triad:
4. Dominations 5. Virtues 6. Powers
Lowest Triad:
7. Principalities 8. Archangels 9. Angels

We can now enter a mysterious landscape where few have been for many centuries.

Details from the Last Judgment *by Giotto, Campo Santo, Italy, 15th Century.*

The Upper Triad

According to the Hebrews the universe is a hierarchy. The Christians adopted this Jewish model of the Cosmos in which God is both at the center of the cosmos and at the highest point of the hierarchy. Entities radiate outwards from His Presence, some being close to the center while others move further and further away from the Divine source of Light and Love.

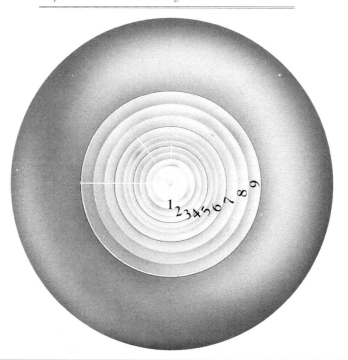

It is a dynamic and ever shifting scenario. Angels are arranged on three descending levels. Each level has three ranks or Orders. The highest Triad is made up of the Seraphim, the Cherubim and the Thrones. These are in direct communion with the Divine Unity and receive God's unfiltered Illumination. The next triad orbiting God is composed of the Dominations, Virtues and Powers who receive the Divine Illumination from the first Triad and then in turn, transmit it to the lowest triad – the Principalities, Archangels and Angels. These then convey that illumination to us mortal humans.

Right: This diagram shows the inner orders of the Primary Triad resonating Love (the Seraphim) and Knowledge (the Cherubim). These subtle vibrations issue from the beat of their wings and the sound of their voices and yet remains essentially immaterial and insubstantial. However the subsequent "orbit" of the Ofanim is a region where form and substance begin to materialize. It shows the outward movement from the central Divinity which is pure Thought. Thought slows down as it moves from the source and becomes Light, which in turn decelerates to become Heat which condenses into matter.

Virtus est Donum Dei.

The entire hierarchy of angels can best be described as an endlessly vast sphere of beings who surround an unknowable center-point which is called God. The Divine Core is described as an emanation of pure thought of the highest vibration, whose subtle rays appear to change frequency the further they travel from the center. As the vibrations slow down, they first become an orbiting region of pure light. As this light slows down even further from the source it begins to condense into matter. Thus the image would appear as a vast sun surrounded by a thin skin of dark matter.

The first Triad of angelic presences are known as the Seraphim, the Cherubim and the Thrones and they are clustered around that central core of purity. A Seraph vibrates at the highest angelic frequency. The Cherub, on the next orbiting ring around the source, has a vibration rate which is a little lower, while the Thrones of the third ring mark the point at which matter begins to appear.

The First Choir: Seraphim.

Seraphs are generally accepted to be the highest order of God's Angelic Servants. It is they who ceaselessly chant in Hebrew the Trisagion – *Kadosh, Kadosh, Kadosh* –" Holy, Holy, Holy is the Lord of Hosts, the whole earth is full of His Glory" while they circle the Throne. One beautiful explanation for this otherwise seemingly monotonous activity is that it is actually a song of creation, a song of cele-

bration. It is the primary vibration of Love. It is a creative, resonating field of Life. The Seraphim are in direct communion with God and as such are beings of pure light and thought who resonate with the Fire of Love. However, when they appear to humans in their angelic form it is as six-winged and four-headed beings. The prophet Isaiah saw flaming angels above the Throne of God: "Each had six wings: two covered the face, two covered the feet and two were used for flying."

Serpent Fire of Love

Popularly known as the "fiery, flying serpents of lightning," who "roar like lions" when aroused, the Seraphim are more identified with the serpent or dragon than any other angelic order. Their name actually suggests a blend of the Hebrew term רפא *rapha*, meaning "healer," "Doctor" or "surgeon" and שר *ser*, meaning "higher being" or "guardian angel." The *Ser*pent or dragon has long been a symbol for the healing arts, being sacred to Aesculapius. Two snakes curl around the legendary "caduceus," our present-day symbol of the medical profession, which originally appeared as a wand in the hand of the universal Indo-European God Hermes. It will be discovered later that the Greek Hermes was the self-same Deity as the Egyptian Thoth, the Roman God Mercury and the later Archangel Michael who was also a Seraph. The serpent image of this angelic order symbolizes rejuvenation through its ability to shed its skin and reappear in a brilliant and youthful form, much as we see in the myth of the fiery phoenix.

According to Enoch, there were only four Seraphim, corresponding to the four winds or directions. This is in accord with their four-headed aspect. Later commentators amended this to mean there were four major Princes who ruled over the Se-raphim. Their chief is said to be either Metatron or Satan, while the others are given as Kemuel, Nathanael and Gabri-el.

Confusion in the Ranks

Even in this brief account of the hi-ghest angelic presence ambiguities show through the seams. It can be obser-ved in the diagram that, although Arch-angels rank six orders *below* that of the Seraphim, appearing on the outer, more mate-rial, rings of the sphere, some ruling Seraph Princes of the innermost core have been called Ar-changels. And one likely candidate is none other than the arch-fiend – Satan. To add to the theologi-cal confusion, Metatron, who is also named as the leader of the fiery serpent angels, in some occult cir-cles is known as Satan, Prince of Darkness, or that "old dragon." In his whiter, Seraphic mode Meta-tron is claimed to be the mightiest of all the hea-venly hierarchs and is specifically charged with the welfare and sustenance of humankind. He is reputed to possess not six but six times six wings, thirty-six wings in all and countless eyes.

This type of heavenly paradox is all too common, but having alerted the reader to potential confusion, in future we will try to list such ambiva-lent attributes without comment.

The Second Choir: Cherubim

In both Judaic and Christian lore, God is said to have stationed "East of Eden the Cherubim and the Ever Tur-ning Sword to guard the way to the Tree of Life."

Although in this famous passage they are the first angels to be encountered in the Bible, the Cherubim are actually late comers to the cele-stial hierarchy. Even so they mana-ged to secure the second place around the Throne of the Almighty by the time Dionysius drew up his fundamental work. The Hebrew word was כרוב *Kerub*, transla-ted by some scholars as meaning "one who in-tercedes", and by others as "Knowledge." The original *Ka-ri-bu* were the terrible and monstrous guardians of temples and palaces in Sumer and Babylon. During their captivity in Babylon the He-brews must have become familiar with these multi-ple-bodied, fabulous, winged beasts at the entrances to holy places. Similar guardian genii were to be found throughout the whole of the Near East, and

---

Above and opposite page: **Seraphim** *8th century Spain.* The se-raphim once referred to the mighty Chaldean, earth-fertilizing, lightning snakes. These later became the inter-twining serpent spirits of the caduceus carried by Mercury. Mercury is associated with Archangel Michael who is said to have the wings of a pea-cock. The "eyes" on the peacock wings are all seeing. These se-raphim are illustrations of the encounter of Ezekiel which describes the myriad eyes on the wings of the celestial being.

tacular accounts of a Cherub from an encounter with one at the river Chebar. The Hebrew prophet, Ezekiel, witnessed at close hand four Cherubim, each with four faces and four wings (see chapter 2, Part 2). John of Patmos insists in *Revelations* that they had six wings and many eyes, but in the heat and excitement of the Apocalypse he can be forgiven his haste in identifying a Seraph by mistake. As vindication of the Cherub's old role as a guardian spirit two can be found as golden sculptures covering the Ark of the Covenant.

As already seen when Seraphim ceaselessly intone the Trisagion, the vibrations created by that Holy, Holy, Holy give rise to the Fire of Love. By contrast, the subtle vibration emanating from the Cherubim is one of Knowledge and Wisdom.

How such magnificent and awesome beings shrunk to the size of tubby little winged babies, fluttering prettily in the corners of Baroque ceilings, remains one of the mysteries of existence.

The Third Choir: Thrones (Ophanim or Galgallin)

In Jewish Merkabah lore these angels are described as the great "wheels" or the "many eyed ones." The Hebrew *Galgal* has the double meaning of wheels and "pupil of the eye." Strangely, while the Cherubim appear to be God's charioteers, the Ophanim seem to be the actual chariots.

Without doubt the most detailed account of their appearance is from Ezekiel (1:13-19) "and their appearance was like burning coals of fire. Something like the appearance of torches was moving back and forth between the living creatures, and the fire was bright, and out of the fire there was lightning going forth... As I kept seeing the living creatures, why look! There was one wheel on the Earth beside the

winged, eagle-headed deities already guarded an Assyrian Tree of Everlasting Life.

It was a simple step for the awe-struck Hebrew scribe to borrow both the Tree and its guardian and transplant them into the Jewish Garden of Eden. By the time Theodorus, the Christian Bishop of Heraclea, speaks of the Cherubim as being "Beasts, which might terrify Adam from the entrance of Paradise," the transformation is complete.

So much for their historical pedigree. In the original Hebrew form they have four wings, four faces and are often depicted as being the Bearers of God's Throne and His charioteers. In *Psalm 18* God rides a Cherub, although the actual chariot seems to have been an angel of the next order down – namely a Throne or Ophanim.

We are fortunate to have one of the most spec-

creatures, by the four faces of each. As for the appearance of the wheels and their structure, it was like the glow of chrysolite; and the four of them had one likeness. And their appearance and their structure were just as when a wheel proved to be in the midst of a wheel... And as for their rims, they had such height that they caused fearfulness; and their rims were full of eyes all around the four of them. And when the living creatures went, the wheels

---

Left: Toomes conception of a **Cherubim** *from Heywards, The Hierarchy of the Blessed Angels.* Here we see a seventeenth century illustration of a Cherubim. This is seen as a four winged, single headed being. In the background we can make out the biblical Cherubim who guards the Tree of Life with an ever turning flaming sword.

Above: **A Cherubim charioteer** with the distinctive wheels of an Ophanim. *From a carving, 10th century.*

---

would go beside them, and when the living creatures were lifted up from earth, the wheels would be lifted up."

We find echoes from Elijah who was born up in a luminous whirlwind and from Enoch who calls these angels as "of the fiery coals."

The descriptions of the thrones have caught the imagination of many a UFO buff. They do tally very closely to observations of present-day encounters with so called alien spacecraft. Of all the angelic forms the "wheels" are certainly the most puzzling. Perhaps it is the simple fact that they do resemble images of our own technology but at the same time they were described in an era when even the wheel itself was hi-tech.

The Thrones are variously said to reside in the third or the fourth heaven. Some confusion may have arisen because those borders have some very bizarre properties. So far we have been exploring the *immaterial* universe of the Seraphim and Cherubim who inhabit the innermost spheres around the central core. Both these angelic principles are said to express His Divine Will as constantly flowing waves

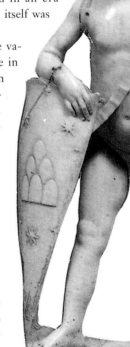

Originally the Cherubim were mighty guardian figures which appeared throughout the Near and Middle East. The earliest Sumerian term is six thousand years old. This is found in the archaic pictogram of Ka-ri-bu. In this Ka is a head crying out, ri is a winged form which also suggests protection while bu is a sharp spear or sword like image which is associated with an armed man. Thus the overall portrait is that of a winged and armed guardian. This certainly corresponds to the huge Assyrian creatures with winged bodies of lions, bulls, sphinxes or eagles with faces of men who often flanked the portals of the temples. The sweet Italian cherub by *Rosso Fiorentino* demonstrates the gulf between the original angel and the sentimental product which has come down to us.

of creativity. But they are still insubstantial, or more accurately, immaterial manifestations of those creative forces. The Ophanim, however, inhabit a region of Heaven *which begins to take on form and substance* much as we know it. It is at this point that Heaven meets Earth and takes on the substance of the flesh and thus becomes exposed to the possibility of corruption. Rudolph Steiner goes so far as to say that, in a gesture of love, the Ophanim offered matter as a basis for our material existence

The ruling Prince of this order is commonly thought to be Raphael. According to rabbinic writings all the Hebrew patriarchs promptly became angels of this order upon arrival in heaven. Understandably, Christian theologians do not subscribe to this point of view.

Right: **Expulsion from the Garden.** Top: *Hildesheim 1015.* Center: *Lorenzo Maitani 1310.* Bottom: *Basilica di San Zeno, Verona.* As can be seen, the central image shows a six-winged Cherub guarding the Tree of Life. As the depictions of angels became more realistic artists found it increasingly difficult to express these multiple-winged beings so this little panel is a rare little masterpiece of invention.

The Second Triad

The second group of three orders is composed of the Dominions, the Virtues and the Powers. The theme of an ultimate unification with "God the Source" epitomizes the whole endeavor of the Second Triad of angels. Because of this there is a constant dualistic tension arising between the polarities of good and bad, matter and spirit, higher and lower. All of the Orders within the Triad strive to balance or reconcile such opposites, and all are prone to the risk of corruption in doing so.

The Fourth Choir : Dominions

Variously described as Dominations, Lords, Kuriotetes, or by Hebrew lore as the Hashmallim (Hamshallim), this order, according to Dionysius "regulate angels' duties." Other authorities maintain that the Dominions are channels of mercy living within the second heaven. Supposedly this holy sphere has the celestial letters of the Holy Name suspended within its realm. The ruling Lords are said to be Zadkiel, Hashmal, Yahriel and Muriel. Hasmal, or Chasmal, is known as the "fire speaking angel."

The Fifth Choir : Virtues

Variously known as the Malakim, the Dunamis or the Tarshishim, these angels of grace bestow Blessings from on high, usually in the form of miracles. They are most often associated with heroes and with those who struggle for good. It is said that they instill courage when it is needed most. They appeared in the Ascension of Christ where two provided his escort to Heaven. It is recorded in the *Book of Adam and Eve* that two Virtues acted like midwives at the birth of Cain. Known as "The Brilliant or Shining Ones" their ruling princes are said

to be Micha-el, Gabri-el, Rapha-el, Bari-el, Tarshish and, before the great rebellion, Satan-el.

The Sixth Choir : Powers

Variously named Dynamis, Potentiates and Authorities, they were supposedly the first angels created by God. The Powers inhabit the perilous border region between the first and second heavens. Dionysius accredits them with resisting the efforts of Demons to take over the World. They appear to act as a kind of border guard who patrol the Heavenly Pathways on the lookout for devilish infiltration. These patrols are obviously a risky business and St. Paul sternly warned his various flocks that Powers can be both good and evil. In Romans 13:1 it is revealed that "The Soul is subject to the Powers," and it is in their efforts to keep a balance within our souls that some are known to become over-identified with the darker side of human beings and thus to fall. Even so the Powers find their true vocation in balancing or reconciling opposites.

As chief of the order, Cama-el does deserve close scrutiny for he exemplifies that wavering path between good and evil which is such a pronounced characteristic of the entire Order. His name means "he who sees God" and the *Magus* suggests he is one of the favored seven angels who stand in the Presence of God. Some say it was Chamuel who wrestled with Jacob and who later appeared to Jesus in the Garden of Gethsemane. But in the darker mode Cama-el is identified as a Duke of Hell, appearing with the body of a leopard, and in the occult he is known as the ruler of the evil planet of war, Mars. Even the Druids, hardly noted for their interest in the Angelic Host, have Camael as their

God of war. He is commander of 144,000 angels of Destruction, Punishment, Vengeance and Death. Whether these are in the service of God or the Devil remains uncertain. As Kemu-el, this Prince acts as mediator between the prayers of Israel and the Hierarchs of the seventh heaven.

According to one legend it was Cama-el who was blasted by Moses when he tried to prevent the Lawgiver from receiving the *Torah* from God. This apparent contradiction of motives gives the great clue to the major attraction of the Powers. In Christian lore the soul is considered the great battleground of the forces of good and evil. Being in charge of our souls gives the Powers an intriguing, far-ranging, and often capricious, territory. Their demanding task is to transform the duality of our everyday understanding into a unity with the Divine source. In esoteric terms they are the spirit guides who assist those who have left the body and have lost their way in the astral plane. If the deceased are unbalanced by the experience, their fears can magnify to such an extent that they become insane and it is the spirit guides who help at this moment.

A Power from Toome's engraving in Heywards, *Hierarchy of the Blessed Angels.*

Of all the fallen angels, the greatest defection seems to have come from the ranks of the Powers. Of their once powerful Princes, Beleth is now a Duke of Hell commanding 85 legions of devils, Carniveau is a greater Demon invoked in many witches sabbaths. Carreau is claimed to have been one of the devils which possessed the body of Sister Seraphina of Loudon and Crocell is now a Duke of Hell with 48 legions at his command. Even the angel companion of Michael, Sensiner rebelled as did Uvall who became a Duke of Hell and appears to be the demon pimp as his speciality is to procure the love of women for his supplicants.

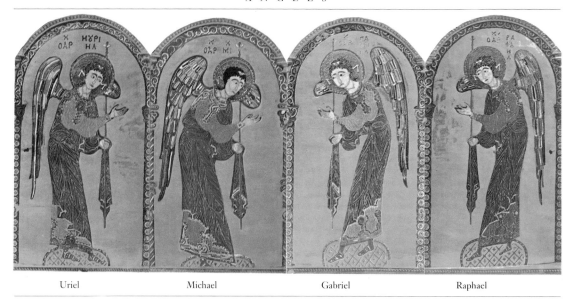

| Uriel | Michael | Gabriel | Raphael |

The Third Triad

The third triad of Principalities, Archangels and Angels, is firmly rooted within the realm of the first heaven and its borders with our temporal and material universe. This means that all three orders are the most exposed and vulnerable to any corrosion of the flesh. It might also account for the fact that individual angels from these orders are most well known to us simply because they are most like us.

The Seventh Choir : Principalities

Originally the Princedoms were seen as an order which was in charge of nations and great cities on Earth. Later these boundaries expanded, but in so doing the borders became very vague. The Principalities extended their dominion and became the protectors of religion (a difficult assignment if all four major religions are involved), tending to take a rather orthodox view of good and evil. This said, it must be added that one contender for chief of the Princedoms is Nisrock. Originally an Assyrian deity he is considered, at least in occult writings, to be the chief chef to the Demon Princes of Hell. A more likely candidate as chief is Ana-el who is named one of the seven angels of creation, which might account for his association with human sexuality. He is also governor of the second heaven, and is held to control all the kingdoms and leaders on earth with a Dominion stretching to encompass the Moon. Another prince is Hami-el who was said to have transported Enoch to Heaven although he is more well known as the Chaldean deity Ishtar.

The great Prince of Strength, Cervill, is claimed to have aided David in his bid to slay Goliath.

Above: **The four Archangels** *from the altarpiece, San Marco, Rome.* Opposite page: **The Archangel Micha-el,** *13th Century Istanbul.*

The Eighth Choir : The Magnificent Seven

Most people can name at least two or three Archangels. Of all the angelic orders these justifiably have the greatest claim to fame. The seven angels who stand before God in Revelations are usually interpreted as the Archangels. The *Koran* of Islam only recognizes four and actually names but two – Jibril (Gabriel) and Michael. While Christian and Jewish sources agree on the number seven, there is an unholy debate as to who they might actually be. Four names which do however appear regularly are: Michael, Gabriel, Rapha-el and Uri-el. The other three candidates are traditionally chosen from Metatron, Remi-el, Sari-el, Ana-el, Ragu-el and Razi-el.

Dionysius tells us that Archangels are "Messengers which carry Divine Decrees." They are considered the most important intercessionaries between God and humans and it is they who command the legions of Heaven in their constant battle with the Sons of Darkness.

Archangel Micha-el

His name means "who is as God." In most Christian lore he is the" Greatest." In fact he and Gabriel

The singular-EL is an ancient word with a long and complex etymological history which has a common origin with many other ancient words in other languages.

Sumerian	EL	"brightness" or "shining"
Akkadian	ILU	"radiant one"
Babylonian	ELLU	"the shining one"
Old Welsh	ELLU	"a shining being"
Old Irish	AILLIL	"shining"
English	ELF	"shining being"
Anglo-Saxon	AELF	"radiant being"

are the only two actually mentioned in the Old Testament at all, save for Raphael who introduces himself in the Catholic *Book of Tobit*. Originally Michael was a Chaldean deity but since those ancient days his exploits have captured the popular imagination far more than any other angel. Many of his deeds are also attributed to the other Archangels. It is a measure of Micha-el's popularity that this should occur.

In one account he is said to have wiped out, single-handed and overnight, a hundred and eighty-five thousand men from the army of the Assyrian king, Sennercherib, who was threatening Jerusalem in 701 B.C.. Michael is said to have stayed the hand of Abraham who was about to sacrifice his son Isaac. According to Jewish lore it is Michael who appeared to Moses in the midst of a burning bush and who appears again in the burial episode, where he disputes the possession of the body of the old patriarch with Satan. It is Michael who will descend from heaven with "the key of the abyss and a great chain in his hand" and will bind the Satanic dragon for 1000 years (Revelation: 20:1).

He assuredly remains the undisputed hero in the first war against Satan: in single combat he defeated the arch-fiend and hurled him down from heaven. Another, more popular version of this is of course the one in which he subdues the dragon-Satan, although now St. George has monopoly on these great serpents.

Michael is usually shown with an unsheathed sword which signifies his role as God's great champion. In a curious passage in Daniel, God speaks in a uncharacteristically humble fashion, admitting

that He had been unavoidably delayed in keeping a promised appointment with the prophet. The reason He gives is that Cyrus, the Prince of Persia, had successfully resisted Him for twenty-one days. He tells Daniel "but Michael, one of the leading Princes, has come to my assistance." He confesses that "In all this there is no one to lend me support except Michael, your Prince, on whom I rely to give me support and re-inforce me." From this we can deduce that Michael was the guardian angel of Israel, but it also appears he is the only one who backed up the Throne when the chips were really down.

There are Muslim traditions which describe Michael in wondrous form. "Wings the color of green emerald...covered with saffron hairs, each of them containing a million faces and mouths and as many tongues which, in a million dialects, implore the pardon of Allah." In the Koran it is said that from the tears shed by this great angel over the sins of the faithful, cherubim are formed.

In earlier Persian legends Michael is identified with Beshter, "the one who provides sustenance for mankind." In one Dead Sea Scroll, *The War of the Sons of Light Against the Sons of Darkness*, Michael is named the "Prince of Light," who leads a host against the dark legions of Belial, Prince of Darkness. In this role Michael is Viceroy of Heaven which, oddly enough, was the title of the Prince of Darkness before the fall.

Michael is also known as the angel of the Last Judgement and, as the "weigher of souls," has a pedigree dating from when the tribes of Israel were in captivity in Egypt. There, the weigher of hearts of the deceased was Anubis. This Dog, or jackal-headed deity was identified with the most important star in the Egyptian sky, Sirius, the dog star. In Persia the star is known as Tistar, the "Chief," and

the earlier Akkadian term was Kasista, which denotes a Prince or leader. Add a pinch of Hebrew (*saris* commander or Prince) and we come very close to the "Prince and Commander of the Stars(angels) who is Michael." His peacock decorated wings recall the eye of the Egyptian Goddess, Maat, whose feather was weighed against a mortal's heart which lay in the balance of Anubis.

In the Middle Ages Michael was also held to be the "Psychopomp," the conductor of souls to the other world. As the Church was anxious to attract the old pagan worshipers of Roman Gaul, who remained faithful to the God Mercury, they endowed Michael with many of the attributes of that under-

(continued on page 43)

The Weighing of the Heart *from the Papyrus of Anhai.* Anubis, the jackal-headed God of the Egyptian underworld was identified with the Indo-European god Hermes in his role as Psychopomp, Conductor of Souls. Hermes was also one of the Aegean serpent-consorts of the Great Mother. His caduceus, as that of the Roman god Mercury, remains the great alchemical and healing symbol. In its dragon form it represents the Serpent which is overcome by the other angel of death Michael. Many of the temples and shrines dedicated to Mercury-Hermes were sited on top of hills. On their ruins were built the chapels and churches dedicated to Michael. Hermes ascended to Heaven in the form of Sirius, the Dog or Jackal headed Star. Opposite page. **Micha-el** *Detail from the Last Judgment by Hans Memlinc.*

Michael and the Dragon Left: *Engraving by Martin Schongauer, 1470.* Below: *Lubok, 19th Century Russia.* Right: *Painting by Giambono, Rome.* Michael has many competitors for the title of Dragon Slayer. St. George is the most famous rival although the story of the Assyrian hermit St. David provides a fascinating variation.

This saintly hermit who loved nature found to his horror that many of the animals nearby were being ravaged by a "large and fearsome dragon with bloodshot eyes and a horn growing out of his forehead, and a great mane on his neck."

When St. David threatened to make mincemeat of this terrible descendant of the Evil Tiamat unless it left the area in peace, the dragon admitted that it dared not venture forth because of its terror of thunderbolts. Agreeing to leave on the sole condition that the weather was clear and that the Saint would promise not to take his eyes from the Dragon for one second until they had reached the safety of a great river, the two of them set out. As they almost reached the river the weather suddenly worsened and David heard the voice of the archangel Michael call from behind him, 'David!' Startled he forgot his promise and looked around. Thereupon the poor dragon's worst fears were realized as he was struck by a lightning bolt and incinerated. The gentle hearted David was deeply saddened and asked the reason for the trick. Michael told him that if the dragon had entered the water it would have grown so vast it would have destroyed ships and have ravaged the coasts. (9th century legend of St. David)

(continued from page 39)

world God. Chapels dedicated to Michael sprang up over the ruins of the earlier temples which invariably had been built on hills or mounds. Thus Michael became, like Mercury, the guide for the dead. The many "Michael's Mounts" to be found throughout Europe and Britain attest to the power of that ancient archetype – the mound of the dead. Many of the sites were, in more ancient times, the focal points of Earth Forces known as Dragon Power so it is hardly a coincidence that Micha-el's fame should be connected with destroying the Dragon. Yet another curious link is to be found with the God-magician, Hermes, who

in many cases is interchangeable with Mercury. The Greeks also called Hermes the Psychopomp, and his phallic spirit in the form of standing stones protected crossroads throughout the Greco-Roman world. While the Church banished all the earlier pagan deities to hell, in the case of Micha-el the various powers of all these Gods were absorbed within the Archangel's attributes.

It is foretold in Daniel that when the world is once again in real trouble Micha-el will reappear. Many scholars point to this century as being the one in which he will reveal himself once more in all his glory.

Archangel Gabri-el

The Sumerian root of the word Gabri is *GBR*, gu-bernator, or governor. Some argue that it means *Gibor*, power or hero. Gabri-el is the Governor of Eden and ruler of the Cherubim. But Gabri-el is unique amongst an otherwise male or androgynous host, for it is almost certain that this great Archangel is the only female in the higher echelons.

She is also the only angel mentioned in the Old Testament by name, except for Micha-el, and is said to sit on the left hand side of God which is further evidence of her being female. To Mohammedans, Jibril/Gabriel dictated the entire Koran to Mohammed and is considered the angel of Truth (although devout Moslems will hardly agree to her female gender). Gabri-el is described as possessing 140 pairs of wings and in Judeo-Christian lore she is the Angel of the Annunciation, Resurrection, Mercy, Revelation and Death. As ruler of the first heaven, she is closest to Man. According to the testimony of Joan of Arc it was Gabri-el who persuaded the Maid of Orleans to help the Dauphin.

Gabri-el appears to Daniel in order to explain the prophet's awesome vision of the fight between the ram and the he-goat (the oracle of the Persians being overthrown by the Greeks). She appears again to Daniel to tell him of the coming of a messiah, a message which half a millennium later she repeats to Mary in the Annunciation. It is curious that she should appear at so many conceptions. Before Mary she had just announced to Zacharias the coming of John the Baptist.

The essentially female character of this remarkable Archangel is once again revealed in popular lore, which tells of how she takes the invariably protesting soul from paradise, and instructs it for the nine months while it remains in the womb of its mother.

Christien O'Brien, in *The Chosen Few* has put forward an interesting and closely argued case which supports Gabri-el's apparent interest in conception and birth. He suggests that she was once a real being in the biblical lands who experimented with the genes of early man and that Adam and Eve were amongst her first experiments. This real, down-to-earth being was then given supernatural powers by those inveterate deifiers, the Sumerians. There is a strange parallel with this hypothesis in the conflicting accounts of Matthew and Luke over the conception of Christ. In Matthew (1:20) the notably male Holy Ghost " begets Mary with child" while in Luke (1:26) it is Gabri-el who "came in unto her." As this can also be translated as "placing something within her" and as she then tells Mary that the conception is successful within her womb, it does raise a few questions if not a few eyebrows. Could such an otherwise primitive world have really had expertise in artificial insemination? Such an idea is much favored by those who believe that human beings are the outcome of experiments by extra terrestrials. But for the skeptics and those fundamentalists who remain unconvinced that female angels are possible, there is comfort in discovering that "Gabri-el" also can mean "Divine Husband."

St. Jerome tells us that when the archangel appeared to the Virgin she was mistaken for a man.

Mary "was filled with terror and consternation and could not reply; for she had never been greeted by a man before." When she learned that it was an angel (or a female) she could converse freely for there was no longer anything for her to fear, or we might add, desire.

Like the great female angel Pistis-Sophia before her, Gabri-el once fell from grace for some unspecified misdemeanor. The angel Dobiel took her place for the period she was an outcast.

Previous page: **Gabriel.** *Detail from the Annunciation by Simone Martini.* Gabriel is best known in her role as the Angel of the Annunciation. Her emblem is the lily. Originally the lily was the flower of Lilith, the first of Adam's wives. As Gabriel is also associated with the Sumerian deity Ninkharsag who is in turn identified with Lilith we seem to have some corroboration. Since Lilith had scornfully rejected both her chauvinistic husband and his God, scholars and priests sent her plunging into the depths of the abyss to become one of Satan's feisty mates. However the virginal aspect of this triple goddess lingered on in the symbolism of the lily, *lilu* or *lotus* of her vagina. Thus it was used to symbolize the impregnation of the Virgin Mary. However, the later Christian contempt of the flesh masked the earlier pagan origins. The lily in Gabriel's hand now filters the seed of God which is transformed into the seminal words of the annunciation which somewhat coyly enter now through the Virgin's ear.

We find a similar theme in the legend of the Blessed Virgin Juno who conceived her own son Mars through a magical Lily and without any male intervention. The three lobes of the Fleur-de-lis represents the triple aspect of the goddess.

Tobias and the Angels. In this 15th century painting of Tobias and three angels, the painter, *Botticini*, has taken considerable artistic license by adding both Michael and Gabriel to the scene. He also takes the liberty of giving Raphael the peacocks feathers usually attributed to Michael. In the smaller version by a disciple of Verrocchio the artist sticks to the original story of the one angel who only reveals his identity at the end of a journey with the young Tobias. St. Paul often warned his congregations that any of them might meet an angel on the road and not recognize him so to be careful to treat everyone as a potential messenger from God (or the Devil!)

Archangel Rapha-el

"The Shining One who heals" was originally known as Labbi-el in Chaldea. The Hebrew term רפא *rapha* meant "healer," "doctor" or "surgeon". As angel of healing he is often associated with the image of a serpent. He is known to be the chief ruling prince of the second heaven, chief of the Order of Virtues, guardian of the Tree of Life in Eden and by his own admission one of the seven angels of the Throne. This he reveals to Tobias in the book of Tobit.

In this account he travels with Tobit's son in disguise without letting on who he is until the journey's end. He shows Tobias, who has caught a huge

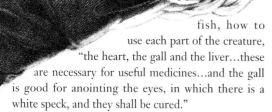

fish, how to use each part of the creature, "the heart, the gall and the liver...these are necessary for useful medicines...and the gall is good for anointing the eyes, in which there is a white speck, and they shall be cured."

He is declared to be "one of the four presences set over all the diseases and all the wounds of the children of men" (Enoch 1), and in the *Zohar* is "charged to heal the earth...the earth which furnishes a place for man, whom he also heals of his illnesses."

He heals Abraham of the pain of circumcision since the patriarch had skillfully avoided this rite until old age, and cures Jacob of his disjointed thigh which he managed to get while wrestling with one of Rapha-el's colleagues.

Although officially a Virtue, he is said to have the six wings of a Seraph but at the same time belongs to the Cherubim, the Dominions and the Powers. He is said to be both the chummiest and funniest of all the angelic flock and is often depicted chatting merrily with some unsuspecting mortal. His sunny disposition is possibly due to his being Regent, or Angel of the Sun.

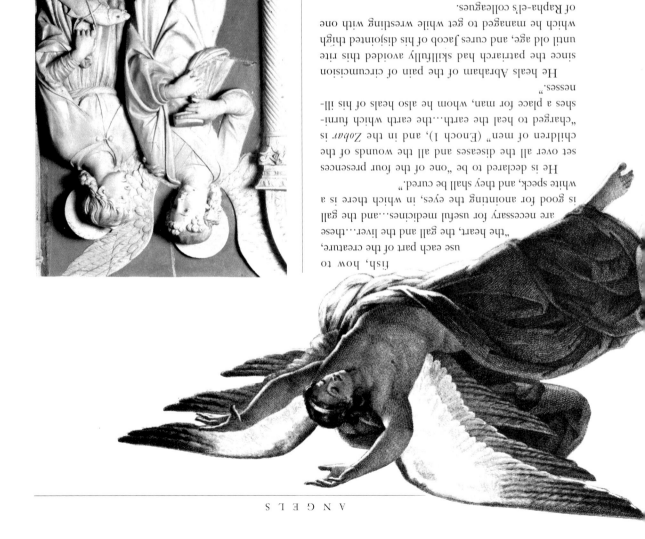

Raphael descending to earth. In this illustration for *Paradise Lost* the artist, *Hayley*, seems to have intuited that Raphael is the Regent of the Sun.

Amongst other friendly acts he presented Noah with a medical book which could have been the mysterious *Book of the Angel Raziel*. It is said that this book gave Noah the knowledge he needed to build the Ark.

This story would seem to fit Rapha-el's status as the Angel of Science and Knowledge.

But strangely this Archangel is also a guide of Sheol, the Hebrew "Pit," or the womb of the underworld, and as a demon of earth he manifests in monstrous beast-form.

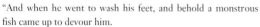

"And when he went to wash his feet, and behold a monstrous fish came up to devour him.

And Tobias being afraid of him, cried out with a loud voice, saying: Sir, he cometh upon me.

And the angel said to him: Take him by the gill, and draw him to thee.

And when he had done so, he drew him out upon the land, and he began to pant before his feet.

Then the angel said to him: Take out the entrails of this fish and lay up his heart, and his gall, and his liver for thee: for these are necessary for useful medicines.

And when he had done so, he roasted the flesh thereof, and they took it with them in the way: the rest they salted as much as might serve them, till they came to Rages, the city of the Medes.

Then Tobias asked the angel, and said to him: I beseech thee, brother Azarias, tell me what remedies are these things good for, which thou hast bid me to keep of the fish? And the angel, answering, said to him: If thou put a little piece of its heart upon coals, the smoke thereof driveth away all kinds of devils, either from man or from woman, so that they come no more to them.

And the gall is good for anointing the eyes, in which there is a white speck, and they shall be cured. (Tobias 6:1-9)

Archangel Sari-el

Also known as Suriel, Suriyel, Zerachiel and Sara-quel, his name means "God's command." This would fit the description of his duties as given by Enoch who says that it is "Sariel who is responsible for the fate of those angels who transgress the Laws."

While there are many worthy contenders for the dubious honor of being the Angel of Death, Sari-el has always been the most likely candidate. Although it is commonly believed to have been Zagzagel who taught Moses all his knowledge, many authorities credit Sari-el with the task. Certainly he is known to have been almost Swiss in matters of hygiene, instructing Rabbi Ishmael in many sanitizing details of righteous behavior.

Sari-el is also claimed to be a healer like Rapha-el, a Seraphim and a Prince of the Presence. Yet, with what we are beginning to recognize as an angelic pattern of behavior he is also listed by Enoch as one of the fallen rebels. This is difficult to reconcile with the fact that in *The Wars of the Sons of Light Against the Sons of Darkness* his name appears on the shields of one of the fighting units of the Sons of Light. Presumably his double agent character had been cleared by the 1st century.

The Triumph of Death *ascribed to Franscesco Traini in the Campo Santo, Pisa.* Here we see an unsuspecting group of peaceful revelers who are about to be scythed down by the Angel of Death. The fact that he is depicted with demonic wings would attest to Sariel as being listed amongst the fallen rebels. It would seem that his role as the "Grim Reaper" did not fit comfortably with the idea of luminous beings of good in Heaven.

Angels and Devils are shown in a wild aerial battle for the possession of the souls of the blessed and the damned. Seraphim are seen cradling the righteous in their arms while the sinners appear to receive less gentle treatment from the demons.

Archangel Uri-el

Said to be one of the four angels of the Presence, Uri-el, meaning "Fire of God," is identified in later scriptures with Phanuel "Face of God." He presides over Tartarus (or Hell) being both a

Seraphim and a Cherubim. In the wrathful and hellish *Apocalypse of St. Peter*, Uri-el appears as the Angel of Repentance who is graphically depicted as being about as pitiless as any demon you wouldn't want to meet in Hell. "Uri-el, the angel of God, will bring forth in order, according to their transgression, the souls of those sinners... They will burn them in their dwelling places in everlasting fire. And after all of them are destroyed with their dwelling-places, they will be punished eternally...

Those who have blasphemed the way of righteousness will be hung up by their tongues. Spread under them is unquenchable fire so they cannot escape it." For those readers who still fondly imagine that angels are all sticky and sweet, this description must come as a warning. Righteous angels are as unswerving in the pursuit of their duty as a forty-ton truck traveling ninety miles an hour, with roughly the same effect.

Often identified as the Cherub who stands "at the Gate of Eden with a fiery sword," or as the angel who "watches over thunder and terror," Uri-el appears to be a pretty heavy dude, and as such his Presidency of Hell seems most appropriate.

The claim that he was the angel who gave the magical *Kabbalah* to man is curiously at odds with what we know of his fanatical righteousness. Yet there is a certain poetic justice in the fact that it was just this stickler to the rules who was so sternly reprobated in the 8th century by a Church Council. Later the Church relented and Uri-el was reinstated, but transformed into a saint whose holy symbol was an open hand holding a flame.

The most intriguing extra-canonical account of this Archangel comes from the *Prayer of Joseph*. In the incident when Jacob wrestled with a dark angel (and Uri-el has always been a strong candidate for that celestial strong arm), somehow there was a mysterious merging of the two beings. For Uri-el says,

"I have come down to earth to make my dwelling among men, and I am called Jacob by name." Now we know quite a few of the patriarchs supposedly have become angels, the most notable case being Enoch who was transformed into Metatron (more of this later). But Uriel's is the first recorded instance of an angel becoming a man. In this he is the herald of the shape of things to come.

Uri-el is also known for being the sharpest eyed angel of all. He was the messenger sent to warn Noah of the forthcoming floods and is also known as the Angel of the month of September.

He was not always as helpful to the patriarchs as he was to Noah. In the *Midrash Aggada Exodus* he appears as a fiery serpent and attacks Moses for failing to observe the rite of circumcision for his son. According to the *Sibylline Oracles* Uri-el is the immortal angel who, on the Day of Judgment, will "break the monstrous bars framed of unyielding and unbroken adamant of the brazen gates of Hades, and cast them down straightway." It seems a little melodramatic considering that as president of Hades he already holds the keys to those self-same gates. But the stage management of heaven sometimes resembles Italian Grand Opera and maybe this flamboyant bit of theatre is needed to set the scene before he brings on all the souls and arranges them before the Judgment Seat.

Three versions of the incident when Jacob wrestles with the angel. In the painting by *Paul Gauguin*, above, we experience the sheer earthiness of the encounter. "And there wrestled a man with him until the breaking of the day. And when he saw that he prevailed not against him, he touched the hollow of his thigh; and the hollow of Jacob's thigh was out of joint, as he wrestled with him."

The illustration by *Gustave Doré* on the opposite page shows Uriel and Jacob fighting in a place which Jacob afterwards called Peniel. One of Uriel's names is Pheniel and another is Jacob-Israel. In the center the encounter as pictured by the 19th Century painter, *Eugène Delacroix*.

Archangel Ragu-el

Traditionally known as Rasuil, Rufael, Akrasiel, and "Friend of God," Ragu-el, according to Enoch, "takes vengeance upon the world of luminaries." This is also interpreted as one "who watches over the good behavior of the angels." As we will discover this is probably the most overworked office in the whole celestial bureaucracy! Angels are a particularly vulnerable breed when it comes to corruption. And even this angel who is supposed to be judging the behavior of his peers was, by a wonderful twist of fate, himself reprobated by the Church in 745 A.D., along with Uri-el. Both Archangels suffered the indignity of being excluded from the lists in the prestigious Saintly Calendar. This was the infamous Church council held by Pope Zachary which conducted a sort of angelic witch-hunt amongst the higher echelons of the celestial beings. He condemned Raguel as being a demon "who passed himself off as a Saint." How on earth Zachary managed to acquire evidence for this is beyond imagining and must have been a source of puzzlement and speculation even at that time.

In happier moments this angel was mentioned in part of the manuscript of the apocryphal *Revelation of John*. It reads" Then shall He send the angel Raguel saying: go sound the trumpet for the angels of cold and snow and ice and bring together every kind of wrath upon them that stand on the left."

It was Raguel who transported Enoch to heaven. Amongst his other duties he is said to have been an angel of Earth and a guardian of the second heaven.

Archangel Remi-el

In early records he is known as Jeremiel or Yerahmeel – "Mercy of God." This name identifies him as the "Lord of Souls awaiting Resurrection." He is the one "Whom God sets up" in order to lead the souls to Judgment. Certainly he should know about such matters of the soul for he is clearly listed in the Enoch writings as a leader of the apostates and one of the fallen. Simultaneously he appears as one of the seven Archangels who stand before God. According to Enoch, this hierarch was "responsible for spreading the instructions of the Seven Archangels". Earlier in his career it was he, and not Michael, who is said to have been the angel who destroyed the army of Sennacherib. As he is the angel who presides over true visions and it was through the "true vision" of Baruch that Remiel appears as the victor over Sennacherib, he certainly appears to have an unfair advantage over Michael in claiming the deed.

In this encounter he is said to have overcome Nisroch "the Great Eagle" who was ruler of the order of Principalities until his defeat as the champion of the Assyrians.

These are the orthodox portraits of the Seven Archangels according to Enoch and tradition. However, there are many alternative listings of this Sacred Seven which include Chama-el, Jophi-el, Zadki-el, Baruchi-el, Jeduhi-el, Sima-el, Zaphi-el and Ani-el. In this century Georges Gurdjieff further complicated the matter by adding many more in his *Beelzebub's Tales to his Grandson*. In this we discover

that His End-lessness's Most High Commission to the Planet Earth includes "Chief Common-Universal-*Arch*-Chemist-Physicist *Angel* Looisos, The Most-Great-*Arch-Seraph* Sevohtartra and The Most Great *Archangel* Sakaki" who we learn was one of the four "Quarter-Maintainers of the Whole Universe."

Notwithstanding such ingenious inventions there are two quite remarkable candidates who are far more likely to oust Remi-el, Suri-el or Ragu-el from the roll call of the Magnificent Seven. The first of these, Metatron, is claimed to be the "all time Greatest." But this supreme title is tossed back and forth between rabbi and priest, in an energetic game of angelic one-upmanship.

If the story of the two Egyptian wizards is anything to go by, then Metatron is clearly more powerful than Michael and Gabriel put together. Somehow the two great and wily magicians, *Jannes* and *Jambres*, managed to infiltrate heaven and were a considerable embarrassment to the Almighty for they refused to leave. He sent Michael and Gabriel against them, but our two champions were no match for the dynamic duo of the Nile. Finally Metatron drove them out and "was appointed (so saith the *Yalkut Hadash*) over Michael and Gabriel."

The other powerful angel who attracts especial attention as being one of the most likely members of the Seven is Razi-el.

Archangel Razi-el

Also known as Ratziel, Gallizur, Saraquel and Akrasiel, Razi-el has the intriguing title of the "Angel of the Secret Regions and of the Supreme Mysteries." Author of the legendary *Book of the Angel Raziel*, "wherein all celestial and earthly knowledge is set down," Razi-el is supposed to have presented it to Adam. After a long and convoluted history it passed into the hands of Enoch, who is said to have incorporated much of it in the *Book of Enoch*. It then was given to Noah who modeled the Ark on information he discovered in its pages. Then it seems to have disappeared after a brief spell with Solomon. It resurfaced under the authorship of one Eleazer of Worms, a medieval writer. It is said that within this volume Razi-el revealed the 1,500 keys to the mysteries of the Universe. Unfortunately, these are in a secret writing which is not even understood by the greatest of angels.

We do know, however, from *Targum Ecclesiastes*, that "each day the great angel Razi-el stands upon the peak of Mount Horeb, proclaims the secrets of men to all mankind." According to Moses Maimonides, Razi-el is the chief of the Erelim, or Thrones, and is identified with a brilliant white fire which is one of the characteristics of that order. One strange attribute, recorded by the *Pirke Rabbi* is that Razi-el "spreads his wings over the Hayyoth lest their fiery breath consume the ministering angels." The Hayyoth, or heavenly beasts, are equated with the Cherubim. Heaven might not always be as comfortable to its workers as is fondly imagined.

Above: **Angelic writing** *from the Book of Raziel, Netherlands 17th Century.* Taking compassion on Adam, God sent Raziel to give him a book so that he might look into the mirror of existence and so see the Divine Face and himself so illuminated as an image of God. It is reported that an oral version still exists within the traditions of the Kabalah.

Archangel Metatron

We now come to an entity who, we are assured by many rabbis, is *really* the greatest angel of all. It must be remembered that there are many contenders for this heavyweight throne and any confusion probably arises from their over enthusiastic supporters. Metatron certainly has substantial claims which are favored by the rabbis, although as a Christian angel he is more of an enigma than most. Variously called Prince of the Divine Face, Angel of the Covenant, King of Angels and the Lesser YHWH (tetragrammaton), he is charged with the sustenance of the world. In this and on many other occasions he absorbs territory usually claimed by the other Archangels, especially Micha-el with whom he is mostly identified. This could simply be explained by differences in the Jewish and Christian lore. In *Talmud* and *Targum* he is the direct link between God and humanity.

In terms of seniority Metatron is actually the most junior in the heavenly host. In one version of his history he was once the patriarch Enoch who was transformed into a fiery angel with 36 wings (6x6) and countless eyes. This would only make him about 8500 years old. While this is doubtless impressive by mortal standards, it hardly registers on the angelic scale if we are to believe that the angels were created at the same time as the universe, fifteen billion years ago.

There is a beautiful passage early in the *Chronicles of Enoch* when the scribe first visited heaven before his death and transformation. From the perspective of our century, the scene is like a rehearsal for what was to come. "Then the Lord said to Michael: 'Go and strip Enoch of his own clothes; anoint him with oil, and dress him like ourselves' and Michael did as he was told. He stripped me of my clothes, and rubbed me over with a wonderful oil like dew; with the scent of myrrh; which shone like a sunbeam. And I looked at myself, and I was like one of the other (angels); there was no difference and all my fear and trembling left me."

Enoch had been chosen by the Lord as a writer of truth, the greatest scribe of the land, so it is hardly surprising that in that quantum leap into angelic form, as Metatron, his previous abilities

The angel Metatron staying the hand of Abraham who is about to sacrifice his beloved son Isaac. *Filippo Brunelleschi, 1401, Florence.*

should follow him. For Metatron is known as the heavenly scribe who records everything which happens in the etheric archives.

This mighty angel has another more sinister side, being identified with Satan or with the earlier office of ha-satan, the Adversary. There is a passage in Exodus which refers to Metatron. "Behold I send an angel before thee, to keep thee in the way and bring thee unto the place which I have prepared." This is clearly a reference to the angel of God, or as some maintain God Himself, who led the children of Israel through the wilderness. Further evidence that it was Metatron in his role as the lesser Yahweh, rather than God in person, is that he appears "as a pillar of fire, his face more dazzling than the sun."

If anyone has the stomach to read Exodus (which must rank as the ugliest and least spiritual of all religious texts), they can witness what sort of an angry, jealous, spiteful, pathological killer this lesser YHWH must have been. As he orders horrendous atrocities upon his chosen peoples, any intelligent reader will be more able to see the hand of radical evil rather than that of the Lord of Light.

By the size of his tent (Tabernacle) as described in Exodus and Numbers, and from descriptions of YHWH, it would appear he was an impossibly tall being. If we use a standard .53 meters as being an ancient cubit this angel was recorded to have been anything from 8 to 13 feet in height. Such evidence points to Metatron, for he is said to be the tallest angel in the hierarchy. He has also been named the Demiurge, the Creator of the Universe. In gnostic scriptures this is decidedly Satan, the Prince of Darkness.

All in all, Metatron is indeed a strange and discomforting figure. On the one hand he is set above Micha-el and Gabri-el for being able to

defeat the wizards of Egypt, while on the other, in one particularly gruesome episode, he is a bloodthirsty angel who delights in impaling hundreds of his own disobedient people and leaving them in the desert to die in agony.

Duet in the Mirror

But Metatron's portrait is not complete without a last, mysterious connection; the Shekinah. This is the Hebrew version of the Hindu Shakti, which can be understood as the female principle of God in man. The creation of the world was, according to the *Zohar*, the work of the Shekinah. The male aspect is of course the Creator, or Demiurge, one of Metatron's roles. The Shekinah was exiled after the Fall of Adam and Eve and rabbis claim that "to lead the Shekinah back to God and to unite Her with Him is the true purpose of the Torah." In other words the whole purpose of life is to re-unite the female and the male into one Whole. According to some, angels naturally manifest such a union by being androgynous. What an extraordinary and wondrous richness of imagery encapsulated within one angelic entity!

Elohim Creating Adam. *Color printed drawing by William Blake, 1795.* This mystic artist saw the act of creation by the Demiurge as a colossal Error, or Fall. In his vision, before Creation there was Unity and Eternity. Creation brought division and the dualities of good and bad, body and soul, man and woman. Above: **Metatron carries the Patriarch Enoch to Heaven** on the backs of a white and a black eagle. The Hebrew version maintains the Enoch was transformed into Metatron but the Christian legends are notoriously muddled and eclectic by comparison. Above left: **YAHWEH, IAWAH.** *Four seals showing YAHWEH as a serpent deity, 1st century A.D..* These images of a warlike god were popular during the early Christian era. One theory suggests that they are the seals of Metatron in his guise as the Tetragrammaton.

Angel on the Horizon

This set of miniature portraits appears to complete our brief survey of the Archangels. But it is one of the great attractions of angels that the tantalizing mystery of their existence always seems *about to unfold*. We are always poised on the brink of understanding them, yet at the very moment of revelation a veil descends revealing another, entirely new and equally kaleidoscopic viewpoint: another new horizon to strive for and never reach.

To illustrate how easy it is to be seduced by such a new archangelic horizon we take a brief diversionary path to look at a science of sevens as practiced by the Essenes over four thousand years ago.

Angelology and the Tree of Life

The Essene Brotherhood really dates from Moses. Their understanding of the Law was very different from the ten commandments given by the patriarch. The forces with which they communed were positive and were seen as angels corresponding to the good *Ahuras* and *Fravashis* of the Persian angelic host. Central to their belief was the Tree of Life which had seven branches reaching to the heavens and seven roots deep in the earth. These were related to the seven mornings and seven nights of the week and correspond to the seven Archangels of the Christian hierarchy. In a complex cosmology, which is both macrocosmic and microcosmic, man is situated within the middle of the tree suspended

---

The Creation and the Expulsion from Paradise *Lubok 1820, Moscow.* This popular depiction of the walled garden of Eden with its exotic and curious animals also shows the legendary Siren Bird or Indian Apsara and the six winged, flaming red Cherub guarding the gates of Paradise.

Heaven

Heavenly Father
Angel of Eternal Life
Angel of Creative Work
Angel of Peace
Angel of Power
Angel of Love
Angel of Wisdom

Earth.

Earthly Mother
Angel of Earth
Angel of Life
Angel of Joy
Angel of the Sun
Angel of Water
Angel of Air

between heaven and earth. The tremendous forces which flow around him are supposed to create "magnetic" fields which are grouped in harmonious couples of:

The Essenes believed that these heavenly and earthly angels of the invisible and visible world were mistakenly "personified" in the Hebrew, Christian and Moslem worlds, becoming the Seven Archangels of Light and Seven Archangels of Darkness, with names like Michael, Gabriel and Raphael.

The "personified" archangels can, however, be assigned to the seven days of the Essene system. This is best seen in the Morning Communion.

Saturday : "The Earthly Mother and I are one.
(Cassiel)   She gives the food of life to my whole body."

Sunday : "Angel of Earth, enter my generative
(Michael)   organs and regenerate my whole body."

Monday   : "Angel of Life, enter my limbs
(Gabriel)   and give strength to my whole
               body."

Tuesday   : "Angel of Joy, descend upon the
(Camael)   earth and give beauty to all things."

Wednesday :   "Angel of Sun, enter my solar
(Raphael)   center and give the fire of Life to
               my whole body."

Thursday   : "Angel of Water, enter my blood
(Sachiel)   and give the water of life to my
               whole body."

Friday   : "Angel of Air, enter my lungs and
(Anael)   give the air of life to my whole
               body."

In a surprising number of cultures throughout the world there
are legends of paradise gardens with a magical tree of eternal life
at its center. This Tree of Life invariably has a guardian to pro-
tect it from the uninitiated or the unworthy. In the spiritual crucible of the Near and Middle East this particular archetype has
become the Tree guarded by the Cherub, the Jewish Sefiroth,
the seven branched candlestick and the Tree of the Freemasons.
The purest teaching is acknowledged to be that of the ancient
Essenes. Their vision closely parallels that of the mystical Indian
and Tantric Tree of Man which corresponds to the seven chakras
of the body which flower from the crown off the head.

Far left: **Tree of Life** *from the Apocalypse of Liebana, 975.* Left:
The archangels of the Holy Sefiroth. Above left: **Tree of
Knowledge,** *Russia, 1830.* Above: **Essene Tree of Life.**

The Ninth Choir : Angels

This is the last order of the celestial hierarchy and the one closest to humankind. The actual Hebrew term for angel is *mal'akh*, meaning "a messenger." In Sanskrit it is *Angeres*, a divine or celestial spirit which becomes the Persian *angaros* meaning "courier," which appears in Greek as *angelos*. It is through such routes that we finally arrive at the modern concept of an angel as being an intermediary or intercessionary between the Almighty and human mortals, between Eternity and our Universe of Time.

As we have already seen the greatest single early source of names and angelic functions comes from the three Chronicles of the Hebrew patriarch, Enoch. Even though declared apocryphal the Chronicles are so packed with such a wealth of detail that by the 13th century, at the height of angel fever, Enoch and many other non-canonical writers were very much back in vogue (a full version of the Chronicle didn't actually turn up until the 18th century when an original copy was discovered which had been preserved by the Ethiopic Church). By the Middle Ages the relatively modest count by Enoch of a few hundred angels had soared to precisely 301,655,722, that is if we are to trust the words of the Kabbalists.

The Stuff of Angels

Many early Hebrew sources recognized angels as substantial and material beings created every morning like the dew "through every breath that the Almighty takes." In the *Talmud*, however, we learn that having been created they sing a Hymn of praise

Three Angels *detail from the Adoration of the Virgin by Perugino, 15th Century.*

to God and promptly expire only to be reborn anew the following day.

The early Catholic Church claimed that angels existed even before the Creation or at the very latest on the second day of that event. They were supposedly created all at the same moment and are immortal (that is to say, until the last trump). The official stance of the Catholic Church today is that angels are purely spiritual and non-substantial.

Guardian Angels

One of the many separate orders within the angelic host is that of the ministering angels who teach the seventy nations "that sprang from the loins of Noah." This places them, historically, as appearing no earlier than eight thousand years before Christ. The earliest record tells of seventy administering angels led by Michael, but later this number shot up to several hundreds of thousands.

One of the sub-classes of ministering angels is that of the Guardian angels, usually accepted as having Michael, Raphael, Gabriel and Uriel at their head. These are the angels which are in charge of nations, states and cities. It turns out that this is the really high risk country. Angels have little resistance to corruption when they over-identify with their national charges. This is evident even in the early scriptures. Rabbis only actually mention four nations with their angel guardians by name. But from those we are left in no doubt as to where the Jewish writers stood and where those angels fell. Michael, in charge of Israel, remains unimpeachable, but his fellow tutors seem to have been very much changed by their very charges, who of course are all arch-enemies of Israel anyway. Dubbiel (the Bear Deity) was guardian angel of Persia, Rahab (Violence and Prince of the Primordial Sea) was angel for Egypt, and Samael (the

Adversary, Prince of Darkness) was the guardian of Rome. They were all corrupted by their wards and fell. The Egyptian guardian, Rahab, even has the distinction of having been slaughtered by the Lord for refusing to separate the upper from the lower waters at the time of the Creation.

He is then somehow resurrected, only to be destroyed a second time for attempting to stop the Hebrews from escaping across the Red Sea. So of all the seventy tutelary angels only Michael managed to stay uncorrupted. It is perhaps uncharitable

to ascribe this to the fact that his charges were God's chosen people.

Sheer Numbers

Such regrettable transgressions do not seem so prevalent at the individual level although there is much evidence to show that angels are still eminently corruptible. We find in Job 4:18 that God appears "to put no trust in his servants" and later "His angels He charged with folly." Folly or not, the *Talmud* speaks of every Jew being assigned eleven thousand guardian angels at birth. Christians have no official policy as far as guardian spirits are concerned, although there are records which suggest two are entrusted to guide each Christian: one for the right hand, which inspires him to good, and one on the left, which nudges him towards evil. A 19th century children's poem expands this number to four. "Four angels to my bed, Four angels round my head. One to watch and one to pray, and two to bear my soul away."

In our New Age the traditional guardian angel has taken on a new flavor and is now equated with the spirit guides of the psychics, or the "entities" of the channellers.

A Flaw in the Sons of God

Enoch mentions in very detailed and fascinating passages the role of the mysterious Grigori or "Sons of God." It is these angels who, in one version, precipitated the "fall." These gigantic beings were called the "Watchers" and appear to constitute an almost separate Order, although they are generally grouped under the angelic wing. Amongst the ranks of this particular group we find such infamous names as Shemjaza, Arakiba, Ramiel, Kokabiel, Tamiel, Ramial, Asael, Armaros, Batanel, Ananel, Zaquiel, Daniel, Ezequeel, Bariqijael, Samsapiel, Turiel, Jomjael and Sariel.

The term Watcher or Grigori can mean "those who watch, "those who are awake" or "the ones who never sleep." Satanail was the leader of one group of seven Watchers who first disobeyed the Lord and were punished. These were held in a penal area within the fifth heaven which is described as reeking of sulfur.

It was some of the Watchers who first cohabited with the women of the lowlands which lay below Eden. In doing so they produced monsters which later became identified with the Babylonian legend of Tiamat's terrible brood. Enoch was the grandfather of Noah and so could record, in detail, the flood which was meant to destroy these mutant and ravaging giants.

Lust and the Choirboys of the Tenth

The later Church fluctuated for many centuries as to whether the fall of the rebel angels had happened through pride, lust or both. Lucifer is said to have fallen through *hubris*, which is a Greek combination of lechery and pride. This was associated with phallic erections and as Barbara Walker points out, "Patriarchal Gods especially punished hubris, the sin of any upstart who became – in both senses – " too big for his breeches."

As angels really were considered sexless, and therefore above reproach, a typical compromise adopted was one given by the Bishop of Paris in the 13th century. According to this theory there were nine orders of angels but it was a separate one, the tenth that fell. It was these Sons of God who were held to be of a separate essence, who saw the Daughters of Man and who, we are told in Genesis 6, lusted after their seductive flesh and "took themselves wives from among them." The Watchers had become the "Voyeurs."

This was a neat solution to a decidedly discomforting theological double-bind. For it was difficult to reconcile a theology which insisted that angels were sexless, and therefore sinless, with the damning evidence from sacred scriptures that showed these lusty celestials were enthusiastically demonstrating just the opposite.

So it appears there were three distinct orders of angels in the lower echelons. At the top were the seven Archangel chiefs, who were known as the aristocratic two-eyed serpents. Each commanded

496,000 myriads of ministering angels who were known as the one-eyed serpents. Last came the real working class Watchers or guardian angels.

That Crucial Nine-Tenths

Neither archangel nor angel was supposed to be able to reproduce (only demons can do this, but fortunately for us they are reported to have relatively short lives). It does appear the Grigori, however, are nearer in form, genes and sexual enthusiasm to humankind. As we shall later discover, their association with the daughters of Eve ended in disaster. As far as can be ascertained, mixing the genes was totally against the Law and those angels guilty of the act were severely punished. One can understand how such a scripture sits uncomfortably with any orthodox Christian idea. The rabbis had no such qualms, although Simeon ben Yohai, the fanatic author of the *Zohar*, forbade his disciples, on pain of curse, to ever speak of the Sons of God having the mechanics to cohabitate. Nevertheless it is these Grigori who are later punished for "bringing sin unto earth."

In His punishment of these Watchers, God ignores the fact that these angels appeared to have mixed motives ranging from lusty appetites to a genuine friendship and a desire to teach humans the secrets of heaven. Early commentators insist that nine-tenths of the Watchers fell, which left only one-tenth in Heaven. Later theologians reversed the proportions when it was seen that such an imbalance gave a decided edge to the Satanic forces. The ten leaders, all once illustrious angels, were listed as fallen by the 4th century A.D..

Angelogia

It was during the era of Angel Fever, in the 12th and 13th centuries, that the occult and esoteric embellishments reached truly exotic heights. By this time angels not only governed the seven planets, the four seasons, the months of the year, the days of the week, but also the hours of the day and the night. Spells and incantations abounded to conjure up both benign and bedeviled entities. By the 14th century there were said to be 301,655,722 of the host hovering at the

borders of our temporal universe. 133,306,668 of these were of questionable help to the faithful as they were supposedly those who had fallen. Others insisted that the nine choirs or orders each had 6,666 legions, with each legion having 6,666 angels. Add to this, according to rabbinical lore, the fact that every blade of grass had its guardian angel coaxing it to grow, and we have quite a population explosion on the "other side". We have no way of knowing whether the plague which decimated Europe about this time had any direct effect upon these numbers, although by the witch hunts which followed we might deduce the dark third was at least immune.

Opposite page: **Ithuriel and Zephon hunting Satan in the Garden of Eden.** *An illustration by Gustave Doré for Paradise Lost IV.* The Evil One is about to tempt Eve in the form of a Toad. Milton's version does not fit well with that accorded by the apocryphal texts. In these it is Zephon who was tempted by the Prince of Deceit. He left the orthodox choirs to join the rebels who were delighted because of his reputation of being the most ingenious of all the angelic minds. He immediately came up with a plan to set fire to Heaven but before this could be accomplished all the conspirators found themselves hurled to the bottom of the bottomless abyss. Zephon, now a second rank demon, has to fan the embers of the furnaces of Hell. No doubt he has invented an ingenious solution to do so by now. Even the orthodox scenario gives devils a definite edge over their brothers "upstairs" when it comes to creative intelligence.

Above: **Angel Musicians** *by Melozzo da Forlì, 1480, Rome.*

Nun Mem Lamed Caph Iod Theth Cheth

Zaïn Vau He Daleth Gimel Beth Aleph

Res Kuff Zade Pe Aïn Samech Samech Shin Tau

Right: **Musician Angels** *by Hans Memlinc.* The Angel of Music is often given as being Uriel. In Islam we find this is Israfel. The rabbis give the title of the "Master of Heavenly Song" to Metatron or Shemiel.

Above: Examples of angelic script with variations of the Hebrew Alphabet from *La Kabbale Pratique.* While we are not told whether all angels are literate, it is evident that they are superb linguists, considering the messages they bring are always in the native tongue of the witness. Rabbis, of course, maintain that the official angelic tongue is Hebrew, although, understandably the Catholic Church insists it is Latin, or, in exceptional cases, Greek.

Who's Who and Who does What?

There are angels who have very specific functions which are named and invoked in many situations. Here are just a few angels found in occult, mystic and alchemical lore.

Angel of: Abortion (Kasdaye), Alchemy (Och), Anger (Af), Aquarius (Ausiel), Barrenness (Akriel), Birds (Arael), Calculations (Butator), Chance (Barakiel), Conception (Laila), Dawn (Lucifer), Day (Shamsiel), Dreams (Gabriel), Earthquakes (Rashiel), Embryo (Sandalphon, twin brother of Metatron), Fear (Yroul), Fish (Gagiel), Food (Manna), Forests (Zulphas), Forgetfulness (Poteh), Free Will (Tabris), Future (Teiaiel), Greece (Javan), Hail (Bardiel), Health (Mumiah), Hope (Phanuel), Immortality (Zethar), Insomnia (Michael), Inventions (Liwet), Lust (Priapus), Memory (Zad-kiel), Morals (Mehabiah), Mountains (Rampel), Music (Israfel), Night (Leliel), Patience (Achaiah), Plants (Sachluph), Poetry (Uriel), Precipices (Zarobi), Pride (Rahab), Prostitution (Ei-

sheth Zenunim), Rain (Matriel), Rivers (Dara), Showers (Zaa'fdiel), Silence (Shateiel), Sky (Sahaquiel), Snow (Shalgiel), Strength (Zeruel), Thunder (Ramiel), Treasure (Parasiel), Vegetables (Sofiel), Water Insects (Shakziel), Womb (Armisael).

This list just skims the surface of vast warehouses of records but it does show the incredible scholarship which decides who does what and where and how many times. One can understand the unsuccessful attempt by the Church to put a curb on this celestial supermarket of angels all jostling for a place in the Holy Who's Who.

The list is given to show the sheer ingenuity of the scribes and Kabbalists who juggled with names and numbers, often adding –el to rather dull ideas which suddenly gave a sparkle and authentic flutter to a new angelic presence.

Space doesn't permit any further examination of the angelic host loyal to the Almighty for we must now pass on to their dark brethren who rebelled and were to become Hell's Angels.

Above: **Alkanost and Sirin, the Birds of Paradise** *Lubok, Russia, 19th century.* These two birds of Paradise were favorite subjects in Russian folk art. The Sirin was a symbol of beauty, happiness and a reward for a pure life. Alkanost, who has the same face of a young girl, is the bird of death, temptation and sorrow who bestows pleasure for which the price is death. While the Sirins correspond to the Indian Apsaras, the dispensers of bliss to the worthy souls, the Alkanosts are more like the Valkyries of the Norsemen. These Angels of Death flew over the battlefields to take the brave warrior souls to Odin's Heaven, Valhalla. In the illustration by Gustave Doré on the right the angels seem more like the Saxon "walcyries," the dreaded corpse eaters, the Northern counterparts of the vulture priestesses of Egypt. Valhalla was originally the realm of death in Hel, but in no way suggested punishment or even the slightest whiff of sulfur.

The Second Wing : Hell's Angels

"And no wonder for Satan himself keeps transforming himself into an angel of light."
St. Paul speaking of deceit
(2 COR 11:14)

form the Light and create Darkness; I make Peace *and create Evil* (our italics)." But gradually, from the 2nd century B.C. onwards, the Hebrews turned from this belief in an ambivalent God, to one who is *only good*. Although there were many variations on this monist theme, a belief in the existence of a separate Evil One gradually developed. This malevolent principle had a completely distinct life of its own, being totally opposed and alien to the benevolent nature of the Good Almighty.

This created an obvious dilemma, for how could a totally benign Divinity who had created all and everything, include in His Creation an equally powerful opponent who sought at all times to overthrow Him? The result was a paradoxical tension between the essentially monist concept of a single divine principle underlying the cosmos and a dualistic idea of a separate principle for Good and a separate principle for Evil.

Whilst the rabbis have managed to extricate Judaism from those earlier conflicts, to this day the doctrine of the Christian Church remains hampered by the confusion arising from the two essentially incompatible ideas. And standing like a

Opposite page: **Lucifer, Bearer of the Light** by *William Blake.* Satan in his original glory outshone all the other angels and was the most beloved of God.

Elvis Presley
Oh yes you are!
You're like the Devil in disguise!
But my, oh my
You talk like an angel,
You walk like an angel,

The Evolution of Evil

AMUEL BUTLER ONCE SAID that no one heard the Devil's side of any story, because God wrote all the books. The following portraits of the Dark Host may in some way break up this monopoly.

The Fall of the rebel Angels is a subject which priests and theologians have been at considerable pains to explain away. The whole legendary story has a long and very convoluted history.

The early Hebrews attributed everything which happened everywhere, whether in Heaven or on Earth, to the One God. The evolution of a single separate force for evil which opposed the One Good God only began two hundred years before the birth of Christ. The Old Testament God did not live in such dualistic times. He was always the One held responsible for what happened in the entire Universe and thus, like the Indian deity, Shiva, encapsulated creativity and destruction in one indissoluble principle. This is clearly stated in Isaiah 45:7 when God says "I

shadow in the center of the ensuing cyclone is the dark angel. The idea of separate evil or that of the fallen Angels does not appear at all in the Old Testament. Instead we find *ba-satan*, "the Adversary." Yet this was only a common noun which simply meant "an opponent." It was possibly the title of an office like that of the prosecution in present day law, rather than the name of any particular diabolic personality.

The earliest account of any Angels who actually were known to have rebelled and were punished for it appears in the apocryphal *Book of the Secrets of Enoch*. It is therefore exists outside of the canon. But by the time the New Testament was compiled Enoch's influence had been quietly absorbed along with the dualistic ideas of the Persian Zoroaster. The notion of the fallen host had become a cornerstone of in Christian dogma. In Revelations John of Patmos points an unwavering finger at Satan, that old Dragon, "And his tail drew the third part of the stars (Angels) of heaven and did cast them to earth ...and Satan, which deceiveth the whole world; he was cast out into the earth and his Angels were cast out with him."

John here names a specific individual as Satan, who by this time is clearly synonymous with the old office of the Adversary. Whereas in the Old Testament story of Job this office was neither good nor wicked, by the 2nd century AD it had become the symbol of Evil.

During the following two millennia this separate Prince of Darkness was variously identified as Azazel, Mastema, Beelzebub, Beliel, Duma, Sier, Salmael, Gadreel, The Angel of Rome, Samael, Asmodeus, Mephistopholes, Lucifer and in the Islamic traditions as Iblis. He also attracted a number of popular titles which offer comic relief from the usual terror he is supposed to evoke. Amongst such

names were: Old Horney, Lusty Dick, The Gentleman, Monsignor, Black Bogey, Old Nick, Old Scratch and the Old Lad Himself.

A Necessary Evil

The Devil is, of course, an essential ingredient in any religion which preaches Redemption. To overcome evil, in the first place one must have evil to overcome. Even a Church reformer like Martin Luther insists that without the Devil and the threat of damnation there is little need for either Christ or his Church. Luther's whole life was a constant "war against Satan." So much so that it is said that the Devil slept more with him than Luther did with his own wife, Katie.

There are at least seven conflicting versions of how Satan appeared and how he managed to gather such a huge following. While Enoch only numbers two hundred rebels, by the 13th century this number had soared, according at least to the pen of the Cardinal Bishop of Tusculum, to a diabolic 133, 306, 668. If Satan did indeed take one third of the heavenly host with him this would still leave a substantial 266, 613, 336 Angels loyal to the Throne. And yet despite the reassurances of Isador of Seville that "the rest were confirmed in the perseverance of eternal beatitude," this does not seem to be borne out by our researches into subsequent angelic behavior.

It really is a blatant bit of wishful thinking on the part of the medieval writer, for we discover that even long after the fall the Almighty was heard muttering about "the folly and untrustworthiness" of His servants.

Sin of Sins

All the evidence points to the incontrovertible fact that Angels really are extremely vulnerable to corruption when in the company of human beings. It is difficult to make out whether it is the wanton nature of the manifest, material world which corrodes their armor of righteousness, or whether there is some magnetic field within the flesh that plays havoc with their virtuous compasses. Whatever the cause, Angels are unquestionably susceptible to "a friendship of the thighs" and in being so always run a high risk of falling flat on their faces when encountering a pretty woman. The Hebrews apparently had a soft spot for the sins of the flesh and were far more liberal in their views on the subject of lust than their Christian brothers. However, to the Jew, the sin of disobedience was an altogether different matter. Their God, Yahweh, exhibited an almost obsessive worry about it. Disobedience, especially amongst those He had created, touched a very sensitive spot on His Divine person, if we can judge by His often rash reactions when someone actually said "No." Even if later He publicly repented of His haste, considerable and often irreparable damage was usually done.

Disobedience was adopted by the Christians as the Original Sin and was of course the reason for the fall of Adam and Eve. It is also listed as one of the seven possible reasons that the Angels fell. We will now, briefly, examine seven of the legends of the Fall.

Legend One: The Shadow of God

Originally the Devil was the dark aspect of God. Mal'ak represented the side of God which was turned towards humanity. This concept was oddly translated into Greek as angelos or "messenger." This emissary was actually the "shadow" side of God which was able to communicate with mortals, the bright side being too fierce for humans to bear.

As the Hebrew religion developed, so the Shadow evolved; first into the Word, the Voice or Touch

Reptiles and creatures of the night appear to be enduring and fearful archetypes. It is difficult to determine whether we have been conditioned to identify scales and membranes with evil or whether these life forms are just alien to human beings. The fox bat of India, shown above, is in reality a timid and gentle vegetarian and most snakes are harmless and were revered in ancient cultures as the wisest of creatures.

of God and then into a separate entity having its own free will. However, with separation, the dark, destructive aspect became predominant. By the time the New Testament was compiled the Shadow had passed through the intermediate stage of *ba-satan*, the neutral Adversary, to become Satan, the evil opponent of the Good God.

We see the change clearly when comparing early biblical accounts with later versions and translations. In the Old Testament God Himself slays the first born of Egypt and personally tests Abraham by demanding that he sacrifice his beloved son, Isaac.

Hardly a century later, in the *Book of Jubilees*, God has been replaced by His separated Shadow in the form of *Mastema*, Prince of the Evil Spirits. From this moment it is this Accusing angel, the Tempter and Condemner, who does all the nastier things once imputed to the Good God. The separation of the good side from the bad is now established and the fall is complete.

Legend Two: Free Will

The second version of the fall is equally "cosmic" in its scope and themes. It comes from one of the most influential theologians of the early Greek Church. Origen of Alexandria maintained that God created a number of angelic intelligences who were equal and free. Through their free will they chose to leave the Divine Unity and gradually drifted away from the Source. Those who drifted the least remained in the ethereal regions nearest God. Those who moved further out fell into the lower air. All these aerial beings are the Angels. Those who fell away further from the center took on human bodies, while those who drifted out farthest of all became demons. By orbiting so far away from the central hub of All

Quetzalcoatl *Aztec stone figure, back and front.* The Plumed or Feathered serpent of Central America, Quetzalcoatl was another of the great hero figures to be found throughout the world who was born of a virgin, was voluntarily sacrificed, descended into hell and was reborn again from the dead. From the sacrifice of his blood humans were created. Like the Indian deity, Shiva, the Egyptian, Horus and Set or the Greek Apollo and Python, Quetzalcoatl was the two faced Creator/Destroyer. In the sculpture above, the front is shown in his benevolent aspect as Lord of Life while the back reveals the malevolent Lord of Death. The concept of two distinct and separate principles of Good and Evil coexisting in the universe was the unique invention of the Persian prophet, Zoroaster who lived in the 5th century B.C.. His dualistic idea found its richest soil in the two centuries surrounding the birth of Christ. While the Hebrews deftly stepped aside from the implications of a universe created by a Good God which included a separate principle of Radical Evil, the Pauline Christians grasped the thorn in both hands. The ensuing juggling with such a hot ember has created a confusion which remains unresolved up to this day.

Being these damned beings move into the territory
of non-being and purposelessness.

When Angels fall through their own free will
they then walk upon earth as humans. If they continue in their impure and evil ways they ultimately
become demons with "cold and obscure bodies." In
one bold speculation Origen claims that men can
become Angels just as easily as Angels become men.
This is also true for demons, who can regain their
angelic intelligences.

Origen explains his cosmic principle with disar-
ming simplicity.

"When intended for the more imperfect spirits,
it becomes solidified, thickens, and forms the bodies
of this visible world. If it is serving higher intelligences, it shines with the brightness of the celestial
bodies, and serves as a garb for the Angels of God."

Legend Three : Lust

The third account of the fall comes from Enoch the
Scribe. He lists two hundred *bene ha Elohim* (Watchers or Sons of God), who descended onto Mt.
Hermon about 12,000 years ago. Originally they
were assisting the Archangels in the creation of
Eden. At the same time they began teaching men
some of the arts of civilization. The trouble was that
their extra-curricular activities included the unexpected seduction of the daughters of Adam. Rabbi
Elkiezer, in the 8th century, with typical patriarchal
zeal put the blame squarely upon the women. "The
Angels who fell from Heaven saw the daughters of
Cain perambulating and displaying their private
parts, their eyes painted with antimony in the
manner of harlots, and, being seduced, took wives
from among them."

It is difficult to believe the Angels were entirely
innocent bystanders but they did prove to be highly

Above: **Charon the Etruscan God of the Dead** *Tomb of Orca
– Tarquinia 5th century B.C..* Charon had a huge hooked nose
like the beak of a bird which overhung bestial features. He has
wings and serpents growing from his blue-gray colored body.
He pre-dated the Devil by four hundred years. Yet the Etru-
scans did not appear to see him as a force for evil but the deity
who presided over the huge cities of the dead which were built
alongside of those of the living.

the gigantic Grigori.

vulnerable. These Angels of fire were transformed on contact with earth and the fire changed to flesh.

According to official Papal authority these apostate Angels actually came from a separate tenth order of Angels. As we have already seen these were

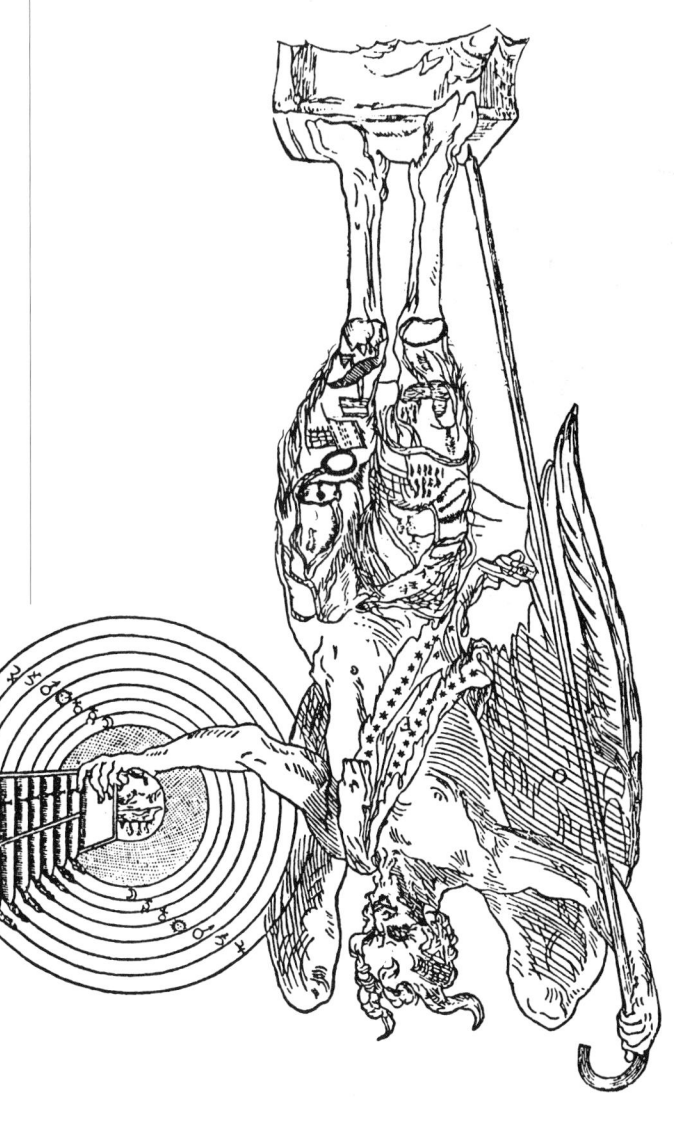

Presumably these Angels were the only order which possessed the physical wherewithall to couple with the daughters of man, since it is held by the Church that the rest of the Angels, being of the spirit, cannot reproduce. But there are heretical accounts which suggest that when Angels sin they "clothe themselves with the corruptibility of the flesh." In the case of the lusty tenth order this was obviously unnecessary.

One further piece of evidence shows that the Watchers possibly came from an entirely separate stock from that of the Angels. A description of the four Archangels found in Enoch XL:1-10 speaks of the four Archangels as being "Four presences different from those who sleep not." This latter term was given to mean the Watchers, so it appears they may have been physically completely unlike the other angelic orders. It is certainly known that by the human standards of the area the Grigori appeared to be giants.

Not only had these Sons of God cohabited with the mortals but they began teaching them many of the deeper secrets of heaven such as making weapons from metal or creating perfumes and cosmetics so that women could become even more desirable. However benign were their intentions to educate the lowlanders, these gigantic Angels managed, at the same time, to spawn some pretty horrendous and very unruly monsters. These mutant hoodlums began to ravage the lands and finally, regretfully it seems, had to be dispatched by Angels loyal to the Throne.

The Lord then bound the angelic fathers and hurled them into everlasting hell. However, since that time they have somehow managed to escape to both tempt and be tempted by the all too corruptible flesh.

Above: **Satan smiting Job with Sore Boils** *by William Blake 1826* Opposite: **Pan** *Illustration from Kitcher's Oedipus Aegyptiacus.* Here we see the occult and composite winged goat, with the pipes symbolizing the harmonies of the seven spheres. Christians had a blanket disapproval of all deities or legends which were not mentioned in the bible. It did mean that Hell quickly filled with the very best of characters of the Middle and Near East. Pan was one of the most ancient pagan deities and the one which the Church fathers most feared. And whosoever they feared always ended up demonic.

Originally Pan was the lusty son of Hermes. He epitomized the spirit of nature, fertility and sexuality. As such he was wild and loved freedom above all else. His redoubtable sexual exploits hardly recommended him to the ascetics of the early Church. Being so much part of the great cycle of fecundity, rebirth and death, he was an obvious denizen of the Underworld.

His outsized phallus symbolized that aspect of man which was untameable by any organization and thus became, in the Church father's eyes the ultimate in depravity and sin. Supposedly the oracles of Greece were silenced at the birth of Christ, having given one last utterance, "Great Pan is dead!" In fabricating the story the early fathers might have added, "Great Satan is now alive!"

Above: **The Lecherous Demons** *by Gustave Doré.* Right:
Lilith, Goddess of Death *Bas relief from Sumer, c. 2000 B.C..*
Here we see the "Eye" or "Owl" Goddess who was known
throughout the Middle East and Old Europe. She is identified
with the original Great Mother, or Triple Goddess. She is depicted as Bird, Serpent and human and holds in her hand the
key of Life.

To the Romans the owl, or *strix*, meant a witch and according
to Christian legend the owl was one of three disobedient sisters who defied God and was promptly turned into the bird
which cannot look directly into the Light or the Sun.
The owl was known to monks as the "night hag" and was
feared by the celibate who believed them to be Lilith's daughters, the Lilim.

Lust and the Female Angel

It must have been noticed that all the seducable Grigori have been male so far. What of their female angelic counterparts? Both Hebrew and Christian sources are notably reticent on the subject and there is no mention of fallen females from the original rebels.

There was, however, one powerful exception who openly sneered at all attempts to quietly dispose of her embarrassing legend. This was the mysterious Lilith, Satan's favorite bride of Hell who the clergy have attempted to ignore as having been Adam's first wife. Hebrew traditions tell of God creating Lilith as a mate for the first man. But she proved far too lively and wild for her husband. Adam tried to force her to lie beneath him in the approved patriarchal style of the "missionary posture." Now male Jews and Christians are not alone in their insistence of sexually "being on top." Moslems even state "Accursed be the man that maketh woman heaven and himself earth." Catholic authorities went so far as to say that any other position is sinful.

Lilith didn't appear to share this male thesis and laughed at Adam for his crudity. She then promptly left him for the doubtless more enjoyable delights to be had with demons, begetting the prodigious number of one hundred offspring each day from their attentions.

As the Great Serpent's bride she is identified with the Triple Mother goddess of the earlier matriarchal and agricultural tribes of Canaan, who resisted the warlike herdsmen of Adam.

While Lilith was somewhat obscured by the Church, her daughters, the *Lilim*, were famous as a major hazard to monastic life. Variously depicted as the Harlots of Hell, Succubae or Night Hags, these beautiful she-demons were much given to copulating with men in their sleep. Like their brazen mother they favored squatting over their dreaming lovers, reversing the male-superior position required by Divine Law. The horrified celibate monks had no defenses and tried to prevent the dread orgy by tying crucifixes to their genitals before going to sleep. However every time one of them succumbed and had a wet dream Lilith's "filthy laugh" was heard down the monastery corridors.

By some heretical accounts she appears to have been too much for the Lord Himself, who was not entirely immune to her abandoned charms. However, He seemed to think better of any ideas which may have passed through the Purity of His Mind and quickly presented her to Satan.

Legend Four : Pride

Enoch himself gives a rather conflicting alternative account of the fall in the second of his Chronicles. In the *Book of Secrets* he describes how, "One of the Order of Angels having turned away with the order that was under him, conceived of an impossible thought, to place his throne higher than the clouds above the earth."

It is now known that this is one of many variations on a very popular and well loved theme current throughout the Middle East. The guardian angel of Edom (Rome) also boasts that he will do the same. In the New Testament Jesus sees Satan, a Son of God, plunging towards earth as a stroke of lightning. It is the original story of the fall of Lucifer, the "Bringer of Light." Lucifer's other title is "The Morning Star," the star which heralds the rising sun, and we discover that this story is a borrowing from the even earlier legend of Shaher. This Canaanite deity of the Dawn was born out of the womb or "Pit" of the great Mother Goddess. Shaher, like Lucifer, was The Morning Star who was the last light to proudly defy the rising sun. He attempted to storm the solar throne of light, but was cast down from heaven for his impudence. This ancient epic was recorded seven centuries before Christ in a Canaanite scripture. Five centuries later a Hebrew scribe copied it almost verbatim, but borrowed the words to put into the mouth of the prophet Isaiah. The comparison is instructive for those readers who still maintain the Bible came from one source. The original Canaanite version is in italics.

> *How hast thou fallen from heaven, Helel's son Shaher!*
> How hast thou fallen from heaven, O Lucifer, Son of the morning!
> *Thou didst say in thy heart, I will ascend to Heaven.*

Below: **Satan Falling** *From the Divine Comedy by Dante. Illustration by Gustave Doré.*

Dante picked up the theme of the lightning serpent falling to earth in the Divine Comedy. In his account Satan, once again, had been the mightiest of the seraphim but through "hubris" fell like lightning from heaven. He plunged through the sphe-

res to crash on earth. So pregnant was he and heavy with sin that he plummeted through creation like hot lead in soft butter.

His explosive fall created a vast tomb that became hell. And there he remains stuck at the dead center of the cosmos with his huge horned head facing Jerusalem in the north.

His buttocks and genitals are frozen in the dread ice and his huge hairy Pan-like legs rear up towards purgatory. But he is compressed by the sheer brutal weight of the entire cosmos. This Lucifer has lost all trace of his earlier magnificence and is just a mountainous mass of emptiness and non-being.

Opposite: Lucifer, Star of the Morning contemplates the rising Sun.

Legend Five: War

At the beginning of the world, some say on the second day of creation, there was a tremendous battle in heaven. God had created the Angels with free will but He observed they were fallible. The Almighty was uncomfortable with the idea that his creations could sin and probably would, given half the chance. So he strengthened many of them in their pursuit of Goodness by an act of Grace. According to St.Augustine this confirmation gave them a profound understanding of the workings of the cosmos and their unique place within it.

Then God created a second group but withheld His Grace and so gave them the opportunity to sin. True to God's suspicions they embraced sin with enthusiasm. A war broke out between the two factions and Michael, who of course had the advantage of God's Grace, managed to cast the legions of sinners from out of heaven. Considering the minor inconvenience this seems to have caused the Devilish forces, this great battle must, at best, be considered a pyrrhic victory. Theologians assure us that the final conflict will eventually be an overwhelming victory for the Angels of Good. Yet even in this bitter pre-knowledge Satan's hordes still prefer to try the impossible, rather than turn to the Light. Which confirms they are either stupid, proud, stubborn or just courageously following their own dark, inner light.

War in Heaven. *From a series of illustrations by Gustave Doré,* culminating in the defeat of Satan by the Archangel Michael (below right). The estimated size of the rebel army was over 133 million while Michael led twice that number of God's troops.

Legend Six: The Passion of the Redeemer

This scenario is more subtle and more difficult to grasp than any of the others. This play opens with the Devil and his Angels already separated from God. They have already committed the sin of pride and their Love of Self is above their Love of God. The Devil has an obsessive hatred of humans and has already managed to seduce Eve, and for this God has cursed him. But the real fall of the forces of Darkness comes with the birth and passion of Christ.

Up until this point God has given the Devil and his legions of Angels the power to tempt, to test and finally to punish humankind. God could have left us mortals in this perilous and unrewarding state, but St. Augustine comes up with an original proposal. He says that instead of abandoning us, God took on human nature in order to make a full reconciliation with His creation. He was to feel as we feel and to suffer as we suffer under the Devil's reign. So, in the form of Christ He delivered himself, like the rest of us, to Lucifer.

The Prince of Darkness, out of a blind hatred of Adam's line, greedily took what St. Augustine calls "a bait and hook." What Satan did not recognize as he grabbed at the prize was that Christ was both divine and sinless. So the Devil transgressed the terms of

the contract he had with God. For the agreement was that he only had dominion over sinners and so by breaking the contract he was damned.

In his unsuccessful temptation of Christ, the second Adam, Satan was puzzled and could not decide whether Christ was divine or not. A medieval mystery play shows the Devil's dilemma perfectly:
"What he is I cannot see;
whether he be God or Man
I can tell in no degree:
In sorrow I let a fart."
In this particular plot, typical of Passion plays created by the clergy in order to bring a complex message home to a simple audience, the Devil and his demons make a terrible series of blunders. They are portrayed as being buffoons who cannot make up their minds whether to kill Christ or not.

Lucifer has suspicions that if their quarry really is the Incarnation, to seize him will bring ruin upon them all. When Satan finally tries to seize Christ's soul the trap is sprung. For, instead of grabbing an unfortunate sinner, they find God instead. So God did not leave us all in the Devil's power. Although He had allowed us to fall into the Evil One's hands, He then chose to allow the same to happen to Himself in order to save us.

Musical Inferno *by Hieronymus Bosch.*

When God as Christ harrows Hell to release those souls who had not enjoyed the benefit of the same redemption, Satan is furious and swears to renew his efforts to corrupt the world. At this Christ hurls him down and Michael binds him fast in Hell. Here is the real fall of the dark Angels. Trapped in Hell all they have left is power to punish those humans who refuse to participate in Christ's sacrifice.

Legend Seven: Disobedience

This brings us to the last variation of the Fall in which Disobedience and Pride are the combined cause.

When Adam was first presented to the hierarchs by God, Satan, who was at that time the greatest of the Seraphim and Regent of Heaven, refused to bow before the new creation. "How can a Son of Fire bow to a Son of Clay?" was his response. The Divine sculptor was not amused at such a poor critical response to His masterpiece and His reaction was characteristically swift. As He flung His ex-regent into the Abyss, one third of the Angels chose to follow Satan.

But there is a far more poignant Sufi version of this story. In this, Satan is seen as the angel who loved God the most. When God created the Angels He told them to bow to no one but Himself. Then He created Adam whom He considered higher than the Angels. He commanded them to bow before the new figure, forgetting his previous commandment. Satan refused, partly because he couldn't disobey the first commandment, but also because he would only bow to his Beloved God. God, who has a long record of being a hasty judge of character or motive, didn't understand Satan's dilemma and cast him from heaven. The worst pain of Hell for Satan was the absence of the Beloved. All Satan has left is the eternal echo of God's angry last words and the merest lingering trace of His passing. Hell is the terrible loneliness of separation from love. In this story Satan becomes the jealous lover, who loathes Man as the new object of God's love and the one which has replaced himself.

The North American Indian Sun-Dancers have a similar understanding of the fall. They believe that each person is a Living Medicine Wheel, powerful and limitless. Each of us is in reality a Power which possesses boundless, unimaginable energy but we have chosen to learn the lessons of limitation through being encapsulated in a body with finite boundaries. This created a new experience of separateness and loneliness. Only by understanding the illusory nature of this experience can a sense of being One with the divine be reawakened. This is also the significance of the parable of the Prodigal Son who had to leave his father's house in order to realize what he had lost. This is one of the more poignant underlying themes of the fall and one which puts Satan in a very different light.

Above: **Satan contemplates the Fall:** This shows the transformation of Satan from a radiant being to one of darkness. The wings are now reptilian and bat-like, the feet are cloven and the hair is serpentine. This engraving and those on the previous four pages are by *Gustave Doré*.

Left: **Popular 18th century view of the Devil,** *from Cheshire, England.*

This illustration shows the "foul fiend" flying off with Over Church, which is supposed to have once occupied a different location.

It was believed that evil spirits fear the sound of church bells and in this particular legend, it was the pious ringing of the local abbey bells that caused Satan so much pain and anguish that he was forced to drop his sacred burden. Protected by prayer, the church landed unharmed on a new site, far from its original home.

Although also allegedly protected by prayers, hymns and holy relics, it would seem that German churches were not so fortunate during the same century. For Lucifer, as Prince of the Power of Air, appeared to have been exceptionally active with his lightning bolts. In the short space of thirty years he managed to hit 400 church towers, killing no less than 120 bell-ringers. Curiously, with the invention of a "device of the Devil" – the lightning conductor – lightning is no longer under the control of Satan but is now "an Act of God."

The Invention of Hell

The whole idea of a *demonic* form of a fallen angel was very far from Enoch's experience of the gigantic Grigori. The entire demonic and devilish super-structure, with its Hell located far from the Pearly Gates of Heaven, is a relatively late Christian invention. While the concept of monstrous fiends and ghoulish demons was not entirely the creation of the Middle Ages, the writers of that time certainly managed to embellish the idea until little remained of the original Jewish images. The dark collective unconscious of medieval Europe was an extraordinary field of imaginative energy. It was an era of magic and a new preoccupation with the mysteries of alchemy, the Kabbalah and those areas of knowledge which were later to become the proto-sciences. In such an atmosphere both Angels and demons were summoned by Holy or diabolic practitioners. Their secret pentacles opened to reveal nightmare legions of Angels and Devils from a dark collective unconscious which spewed forth in majestic and towering heavens and hideous depths.

In order to understand the nature of the Angels who are said to inhabit those Realms of Darkness, it is best to examine the portrait of the entity who is the most enigmatic and surprising angel of all – Satan. Hell is inseparable from the Evil One. This dark entity is the complete antithesis of the archangel Michael. In some traditions the Prince of Evil looks through a dark mirror at his reflection as the twin brother of the Logos, or Christ. It is no coincidence for without the Arch-fiend there would be no Christ needed to defeat him.

Fall of the Rebel Angels *by Pieter Breughel the Elder, Brussels.*

ATAN-EL

(Alias Lucifer, Sammael, Mastema, Beliel, Azazel, Beelzebub, Duma, Gadreel, Sier, Samael, Mephistopheles and Asmodeus). Most authorities agree that he was once the mightiest of the Seraphim, Viceroy or Regent of God. In this original form he is depicted as having twelve wings. Gregory of Nazianus says of him that before his fall he had worn the rest of the Angels "as a garment, transcending all in glory and knowledge." Even St. Jerome tells us that this mighty angel will one day be reinstated in that primal splendor and in his prior rank.

It seems only appropriate that this Prince of Lies and Deception should hide behind so many aliases. Yet Satan in all his multi-various aspects combines many ancient deities. He has the horns, the hairy legs, the hoofs and the formidable phallus of the ancient and lusty woodland deity, Pan. He has the fearsome lightning trident of the God of the Underworld; the serpent form of the Leviathan (Apollyon) and the six wings of the awesome Babylonian Guardian spirits.

He is the *Evil One* and the *One Evil* who encapsulates all the seven deadly sins in one being: 1.The Pride of Lucifer; 2.The Avarice of Mammon; 3.The Anger of Satan; 4.The Lechery of Asmodeus; 5.The Gluttony of Beelzebub; 6.The Envy of Leviathan and 7.The Sloth of Belphegor. He is also to be found behind other masks and aliases. Here are just a few taken from the heavenly police files.

baddon-Satan

This was the Hebrew name for Apollyon, the angel of the Bottomless Pit. The hebrews borrowed the seven-layered model of the underworld from the Babylonians to create Gehenna, whose Dark Prince is also named Arsiel. This means the "Black Sun," the negative sun of anti-matter. Within the central pit in the bottom layer lives the serpent angel Apollyon, the fallen Greek Sun God Apollo, King of the Demonic Locusts. This is much to be expected for most of the more powerful pagan deities are to be found in Hell. As far as the Church was concerned anyone not mentioned in the Bible was bad. It does mean that most of the really interesting characters are to be found in the Infernal regions.

ammael-Satan

This alias is Sumerian in origin (Sam means poison, thus Sammael is the "bright and poisonous One" or the "Angel of Poison"). He is also the Angel of Death. One title specifically gives him as Chief of the Satans. One explanation for this can be found in Enoch I, where the scribe records his first eye witness account of a meeting with the Lord (En XL:6). At this meeting Uriel is "arguing against the satans and refusing them permission to come before the Lord to accuse those from the Earth." In the context of this passage Enoch seems to be referring to the satans as some sort of enforcers of the Law. From their role as a kind of angelic police force in the early version they seem to have become the worst of the Gestapo in a later account in which Enoch calls Sammael the "Chief of Demons."

Known as the great serpent with twelve wings who drew after him the solar system, he is also accused of being the self-same serpent who tempted Eve. In one account he not only tempted our pliable ancestor but managed to father Cain into the bargain. Isaiah in his visit to heaven saw the hosts of

Sammael squabbling and envying one another. Dogs howl in the night when Sammael" flies like a bird" and "takes through the town his flight."

eliel-Satan

The Ruling Prince of Sheol (part of the infernal regions). Beliar means "worthless." Beliar himself tells us in the Gospel of Bartholomew that "At first I was called Satanel, which is interpreted as messenger of God, but when I rejected the image of God my name was called Satanas, that is an angel that keepeth Hell." He cannot resist the temptation to boast, "I was formed the first angel." Michael supposedly was the second, Gabriel third, Uriel fourth, and Raphael the fifth. And there may be some truth to the boast, for these are also named as the Angels of Vengeance.

eelzebub-Satan

Originally Beelzebub was a Canaanite deity. His name meant "Lord of the House." In many ancient religions flies bore the souls and there was a popular belief that women would conceive by swallowing them. The Greek *psyche* actually signifies a butterfly. As "Lord of the Flies", Beelzebub was actually a psychopomp or Lord of the Souls. Notwithstanding the distinction, he was confirmed as the incarnate evil, "Lord of Chaos" and chief Demon by no less than three of the Apostles. Christ is supposed to have given Beelzebub dominion over Hell for helping in the evacuation of Adam and the other saints during the harrowing of the underworld. Satan had refused to let them go but it might be that our Prince of Deception, who must have realized the hopelessness of opposing the Savior, at least could save face by see-

ming to help in the disguise of the Lord of Flies.

Georges Gurdjieff makes Beelzebub an extraterrestrial who is languishing in a tedious exile, far from the Presence of His beloved Endlessness, and makes Earth his particular study.

Johann Weyer in his *Pseudographica Demoniaca* makes him the Supreme Overlord of the Underworld and founding father of the Great Order of the Fly.

zazel-Satan

According to Enoch, Azazel was another of the fallen Watchers. Other sources give him as the chief of the Grigori. In the occult lore he is a demon with seven serpent heads, each with two faces. He is also said to have twelve wings. According to both rabbinical and Islamic lore it was Azazel (Iblis in Islam) who refused to acknowledge and bow before Adam when this first human was presented to the other hierarchs of heaven. It was he who originally voiced the famous question, "Why should a Son of Fire bow to a Son of Clay?" As we know, predictably, God was swift in His reply.

astema-Satan

Mastema is a Hebrew word for "animosity," "inimicable" or "adverse." This is the Accusing Angel, the tempter and executioner, and it is in this capacity that he tried an unsuccessful attempt on the life of Moses. It was he who hardened the Pharoah's heart and was instrumental in assisting the Egyptian wizards against the Israelites. He slaughtered the first born of Egypt and appeared as the first named separation of the *mal'ak*, or Shadow of God.

The Seven Deadly Sins *Popular print, Russia 1830.* The Evil One encapsulates all the seven sins in one being. (See page 102)

ucifer-Satan

We now come to the most fascinating alias of all. Lucifer, Bearer of Light, Son of the Morning, Dragon of Dawn, Prince of the Power of Air was once held to be the greatest of the Angels and favorite of God the Father, Lord of Light. But he was also the first to separate himself from the Divine source.

The painting on the opposite page by the mystic artist William Blake illustrates the following quotation from the Old Testament (Ezekiel XXVIII 13-15) and shows Lucifer in his full splendor and light before his fall. It has been argued that this passage is actually addressed to Nebuchadrezzar, King of Babylon, but as St. Jerome assures us that it is di-

rected at the greatest of the fallen Angels, we will take his word for it.

"Thou hast been in Eden the Garden of God; every precious stone was thy covering, the sardius, topaz, and the diamond, the beryl, the onyx, and the jasper, the sapphire, the emerald, and the carbuncle, and gold: the workmanship of thy tabrets and of thy pipes was prepared in thee in the day thou wast created.

Thou art the anointed cherub that covereth; and I have set thee so: thou wast upon the holy mountain of God; thou hast walked up and down in the midst of the stones of fire.

Thou wast perfect in thy ways from the day that thou wast created, till iniquity was found in thee."

Lucifer, Son of the Morning, according to one further interpretation of the fall, is maddened by jealousy when God the Father proclaims Lucifer's brother, Jesual, the Son. From his head he gives birth to Sin and, copulating with her, fathers Death. He is cast out of heaven and is renamed Satan-el – the Adversary.

In the painting, the many winged figure has his right foot forward, denoting his spiritual aspect (it is interesting that in the East the left foot invariably is the spiritual leader). His outstretched hands hold the orb and scepter, symbols of earthly domain. Part of his wing disguises his original androgynous nature. He is surrounded by a retinue including the pipes and tabrets. The pipes are associated with the music of the spheres.

Lucifer, as both the Evening and the Morning star, is seen as the dying and reborn light of the air. He shares with the serpent the ability to shed the old dead skin and arise as if newborn.

His lightning fall into the Abyss reminds us that the Hebrews were long in Egypt, for there is an

Egyptian serpent God, Sata, who is father of lightning and who likewise fell to earth. The Babylonian
Zu was also a lightning god who fell as a fiery flying
serpent and this recalls the fact that Lucifer was
once a Seraph.

   Lucifer, like his twin brother Christ, is the son
who defies the Old Father (Christ accuses the Jews
of worshipping the wrong God). And as he falls
his phallic lightning bolt pierces the bottomless pit
of the Mother Goddess Hel. Hel was once a ute-
rine shrine, a womb or a sacred cave of rebirth.
Christ as God is the lover-son of the Virgin Mary,
his mother. Brunnhilde was the leader of the Valkyries, the northern Angels of death. Her name
means "Burning Hell." As can be observed, things
in the underworld are not what they at first appear
to be.

Encounter with Evil

We now turn to what are claimed to be first hand accounts of meetings with the Enemy. During the five centuries after Christ many Christian hermits and monks withdrew into the wilderness in order to leave worldly temptations. Legions of demons seemed to follow them with enthusiasm, if the contemporary monastic diabology is anything to go by. This diabology was a new type of writing which gave instructions as to how to resist temptation and cope with the threat of demonic attacks. It also gave the writers an opportunity to give the most lurid accounts of the arch-enemy himself.

The most influential of these visionary, yet practical, manuals of how to deal with both angel and Devil was the classic *Life of Anthony*, composed by the Bishop of Alexandria in 360. In it we read of the constant struggle of the hermit Anthony (and thus all his monastic brethren) with the Devil and his demons. "The Devil's eyes are like the morning star. In his mouth gape burning lamps and hearthfuls of fire are cast forth. The smoke of a furnace blazing with the fire of coals flares from his nostrils. His breath is of coals, and from his mouth issues flames."

In spite of Christ's passion to redeem sinners and destroy Satan's power, the Devil and his hordes seemed to have suffered only a minor inconvenience. In composing his *Life of Anthony*, Bishop Athanasius is at considerable pains to assure the monks that Christ really had pulled Old Nick's teeth. However threatening the demons appeared the Bishop tells us, all they could actually do was to tempt or to accuse. So the next meeting with the Evil One reveals a complaining Devil, stripped of power and almost unrecognizable from his earlier image, yet very perceptive of the monkish habits.

"Someone knocked at the door of my cell, and opening it I saw a person of great size and tallness. I inquired, "Who are you?" and he replied "Satan." When I asked, "Why are you here?" he answered, "Why do monks and other Christians blame me so undeservedly? Why do they curse me every hour?" I answered, "Why do you trouble them?" He replied, "I don't trouble them, for I am become weak: they trouble themselves. Haven't they read that 'the swords of the enemy are finished and the cities destroyed for him'? I no longer have a weapon or a city. The Christians are spread everywhere, and even the desert is now filled with monks. Let them

take care of themselves and cease cursing me." I marveled at God's grace and said to Satan, "Although you are a liar and never speak the truth, you have spoken the truth here, albeit against your will. For the coming of Christ has weakened you, and He has cast you down and stripped you."

Gradually such "do it yourself" manuals gave way in popularity to more visionary works of Heaven and Hell. While the diabologies had an almost exclusive readership within monastic walls, the new Visions of Paradise and the spectacular and often grisly scenes of the Inferno held the secular public in thrall.

The following account of one such Vision was written in 1149 by an Irish monk and was enormously popular in the Middle Ages, being translated into no less than fifteen different languages and being the subject of many paintings. Part of its popularity was that the witness was an unabashed sinner, an Irish knight who was well on the burning road to Hell before he had this transforming vision. One day he collapsed, having eaten something poisonous or drugged, and had every appearance of being dead. Only a mysterious warmth on his left side prevented his immediate burial. He lay in this state for three days during which time his soul was met by a guardian angel who took him on an educational tour of both Heaven and Hell. Even the celebrated Dante or Milton cannot excel this graphic description of the Prince of Hell.

The Irish knight was called Tundale. His guardian angel, having led him through some of the more harrowing scenes of the underworld, now invites him to see the greatest adversary of the human race.

"Drawing near, Tundale's soul saw the depths of hell, and he would not be able to repeat in any way how many, how great and what inexpressible torments he saw there if he had a hundred heads and in each head a hundred tongues. I do not think it would be useful to omit the few details that he did bring back for us.

He saw the Prince of Shadows, the enemy of humanity, the Devil whose size overshadowed every kind of beast that Tundale saw before. Tundale was not able to compare the size of the body to anything, nor would we dare to presume to say what we did not draw from his mouth, but such a story as we did hear we ought not to omit.

This beast was very black, like a raven, with a body of human shape from its feet to its head,

except that it had many hands and a tail. This horrible monster had no less than a thousand hands, and each hand was a thousand cubits long and ten cubits wide. Each hand had twenty fingers connected to it; they had very long claws with a thousand points, and they were iron, and his feet were just as many claws. Moreover, he had a very long and great beak, and his tail was very long and sharp and ready to injure souls with its sharp points. The horrible stooping spectacle was seated on a forged iron wickerwork placed over coals inflamed by the inflated bellows of an innumerable number of demons. Such a multitude of demons and souls circled above him that no one can believe how many there were, because the world has produced all these souls from the beginning. This host of humanity was attached through each member and at their joints with very large and flaming iron bonds. Moreover, when this beast was turned to coal and then burned, he turned himself from one side to the other in very great wrath, and he stretched out all his hands into the multitude of souls and then compressed them when they were all replenished. This thirsty boor pressed out the clusters so that there was no soul able to avoid him who was not either dismembered or deprived of head, feet or hands.

Then by just breathing, he inhaled and exhaled all the souls into different parts of hell. Immediately the Pit belched, from which, as we said before, there was a fetid flame. When the dreadful beast drew his breath again he sucked back to him all the souls that

Lucifer, detail of Hell *from the Last Judgment by Giotto*. The enormously popular visionary account of Hell by the Irish knight Tundale had been translated into thirteen languages by the time this image was painted. It is obvious from the details that Giotto was familiar with Tundale's version.

he dispersed before, and he devoured those who fell into his mouth with the smoke and sulfur. But whoever fled from his hand he struck down with his tail; and the miserable beast, always striking hard, was struck hard, and the burning tormentor was tormented in the punishment with the souls.

Seeing this Tundale's soul said to the angel of the Lord, "My Lord, what is this monster's name?" Answering, the angel said, "This beast whom you see is called Lucifer, and he is the prince of the creatures of God who took part in the pleasures of paradise. He was so perfect that he would throw heaven and earth and even hell into total disorder."

THE HORDES OF HELL
Who's Who of the Underworld

Predictably the hell as depicted in the Middle Ages is very medieval in concept, being founded on a strictly feudal basis. Although the bonds of allegiance and loyalty are none too reliable in an infernal region where it's every demon for himself, most descriptions still keep to the typical Lordship-retainer structure well known to Teutonic Barons. The most complete hierarchy ever published of the Infernal pecking order was Johann Weyer's *Pseudo Monarchia Daemonium*, which appeared in the 16th century. It later turned out that this definitive work, which was quoted by every aspiring alchemist, kabbalist, occultist and demonophile, was actually an elaborate spoof. It caricatured the hated hierarchy of the Church and probably is a better mirror of European kingdoms of the time than of the Infernal realms.

However Weyer did use much occult material which is no longer accessible to us and offers insights into the constitution of the nether regions along with their principal characters.

He gives the Talmudic figure of 7,405,926 demons who were divided into 72 companies. In his version it is Beelzebub who was the Supreme Overlord of the Dark Empire. He is the founder of the Order of the Fly and this reflects his Philistine and Canaanite origins as Baal-ze-Bub, Lord of the Flies. His great captains were: Satan, Prince of Darkness and The Adversary; Pluto, Prince of Fire and Hades; Molech, Prince of the Land of Tears; Baal, General of the Diabolic Hordes; Lucifer as, curiously, the Chief Justice; Baal-beryth as the Minister of Devilish Pacts and Treaties; Nergal as Chief of the Secret Police; Proserpine, the Arch She-Devil as Princess of Demonic Spirits; Astarte, who was masculinized as Astaroth, Duke and Treasurer of Hell.

Weyer's entire superstructure was a beautiful deception within the best traditions of the Lord of Lies.

The following diagrams of Hell have been compiled from less questionable sources although it must be admitted the veracity of many of those sources might be in question.

There are two quite distinct species to be found in the nether world which have completely different genealogical trees.

Demons

Demons originally derived from the personal familiar spirits which were a respected and common species throughout the Near East. *Daimon* is Greek for "soul." These were the invisible spirits who occupied the ethereal spaces between God and humanity. But by the time of the first translation of the *Septuagint*, these pagan demons were interchangeable with Devils.

As the usual practice of both the Jewish scribes and those of the early and medieval Church was to relegate to Hell any deity or spirit not actually mentioned in the Bible most of the earlier pagan *daimones* found themselves serving the Devil. St. Thomas Aquinas reveals a healthy respect for their pagan aspect by stating: "It is a dogma of faith that demons can produce wind, storms and a rain of fire from heaven." It was also an assumed dogma of faith that Devils existed. In reality to believe otherwise was heresy.

St. Augustine vehemently denied that there was any connection between the fallen Angels and any pagan demons. He even denied that the dark Angels had any sex while of course everyone knew that the pagan deities were, if anything, over endowed.

Devils

Compared with Demons, Devils have a far more distinguished pedigree. The word comes from the Greek *diabolos* which means a "slanderer," "perjurer" or "adversary." When the Old Testament was translated into Greek (2nd century B.C.) *diabolos* was used as an equivalent to the Hebrew Satan. Some claim that the meaning of "Devil" is arrived at through another route, which is the Indo-European *devi*, "goddess," or the Persian *daeva* meaning "evil spirit," although this argument is open to questioning.

While Demons and Devils constitute two quite separate diabolic species, there are also two very distinct types of fallen angel, each having a unique family tree. One tree traces the descent from the tenth order of bene Elohim, the Grigori or Watchers, and the other from the *Ma'lakim*, which includes all the other nine angelic orders. It is important to distinguish the gigantic Grigori, who fell through lust and who spawned some of the less savory monsters of hell, from the more aristocratic two-eyed serpents who fell through rebellion or pride.

The Sons of God

As we have already seen, the Watchers, known also as the bene-ha-Elohim or the Sons of God, were sent from heaven to teach human beings, but they succumbed to the highly seductive flesh of the daughters of Cain. Nine tenths of them are said to have yielded to the temptation and either dwell in the third heaven or in hell.

There seem to have been two leaders of the Grigori, Azazel and Shemjaza. Of the two Shemjaza appears to have been the one who repented of his actions. It is a little unclear as to whether he was of a different species to the Watchers. Some traditions maintain that he was a mighty Seraph who was seduced into revealing God's name to the beautiful but deadly Ishtarah. One version shows him so mortified by the consequences of his lust when he sees his gigantic mutant sons being destroyed by the Angels of Vengeance, that he voluntarily hurls himself into the constellation of Orion and this is where he can still be seen hanging upside down. This

Satan and Belzebuth. *Illustration for Paradise Lost by John Milton by Hayley.*

perhaps is a later piece of propaganda from the clergy for most versions assure us that he is alive, lusty and very much in action.

Certainly this story of Azazel is one of the possible origins of the Hanging Man in the Tarot Deck.

There is certainly no doubt of Azazel's alignment, although from descriptions it would seem he also comes from a higher species. Said to have seven serpent heads, fourteen faces and twelve wings, he also is named the "Lord of Hell" and the "Seducer of Mankind."

In his identification with Satan it was supposedly Azazel who refused to bow to Adam. Whereupon the Divine Sculptor cast Azazel from Heaven and changed his name to Eblis, which fits neatly into Islamic traditions. He is Satan's standard bearer and is said once to have been a Cherub but his nature seems far more like the bene-ha-Elim. For it was this Watcher who first showed women how to use cosmetics, perfumes and fine silks to inflame a man's passions. This is why God has an especial loathing for this "Son," for it was the Angels who were seduced by the seductive finery rather than the men.

Each year a "scapegoat" for Azazel fell to its death on the Day of Atonement having been thrown off the desert cliff at Haradan. This goat was believed to transfer the sins of Israel to their instigator, Azazel, who supposedly lay imprisoned beneath a huge pile of rocks at the foot of the cliff. Other apocrypha, however, inform us that he was free and up to mischief and didn't even seem to know of this annual sacrifice.

A complete list of the most notable Watchers is listed below:

Agniel: Taught the peoples of earth the enchantments of roots and the secrets of conjury, as well as using those arts to seduce one of the daughters.

Anmael: Like Shemjaza he made a sexual pact with a mortal woman to reveal the secret name of God.

Araquiel (Saraqael): Taught the signs and secrets of earth (geography) but is still said to lead souls to Judgement.

Araziel (Arazyael): "God is my noon," but lust seems to have been his midnight.

Asael: "Made by God."

Asbeel: "God's Deserter," Asbeel was the one who really sowed the seeds of dissention and who led the other Watchers astray.

Azael: "Whom God Strengthens," Obviously not enough for he was one of two Angels who succumbed to the all too delicious flesh of Lamech's daughter, Naamah. She gave birth to *Azza:* "The Strong One."

Azza further got himself into trouble with the Almighty by objecting to the transformation of Enoch the scribe into the most powerful angel of all – Metatron. It was also Azza who revealed the heavenly arcana to Solomon, thus making him the wisest man on earth.

Baraqijal: A lusty demon who taught men astrology.

Exael: One of the Watchers who according to Enoch, "taught men how to fabricate engines of war, works in silver and gold, the uses of gems and perfumes."

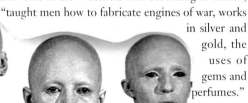

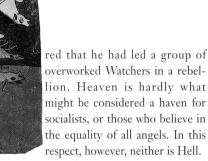

Ezeqeel: Taught meteorology to the early tribes.

Gadreel: "God is my Helper." Enoch names Gadreel as the angel who led Eve astray. Eve protested loudly that she had copulated "with no false beguiling serpent," but as we have learnt Eve's word is not always to be trusted. Gadreel is also known for having taught men how to make tools and weapons.

Kasdaye: He taught women the art of abortion.

Kashdejan: Taught men cures for various diseases, including those of the mind (Celtic Diyan Cecht) considered one of the worst sins.

Kokabel: Taught astronomy and the science of the constellations.

Penemuel: Who taught the art of writing "although through this many went astray until this day, for Men were not created for such a purpose to confirm their good intentions with pen and ink." (Ouch!)

Penemue: The Watcher who taught men writing. Strangely, for an evil angel he is a curer of stupidity. This seems at variance with Church doctrine which holds that demons are stupid. In fact the evidence shows that the nether regions are on the whole far better read, can quote scriptures and obscure ramifications of the Law far more accurately than their brethren "upstairs." The official reason given for this is that a demon needs to be intelligent and cunning in order to be able to tempt the wisest of men.

Pharmoros: Taught pharmacy, herbal lore, practical medicine and diagnosis of illness.

Satanail: Also known as Salamiel. He is a great prince of the Grigori. According to Enoch he and a small group of his followers were already being punished for some serious offense even before the "fall through lust." The angel with Enoch never elaborated upon his particular crime, although it was inferred that he had led a group of overworked Watchers in a rebellion. Heaven is hardly what might be considered a haven for socialists, or those who believe in the equality of all angels. In this respect, however, neither is Hell.

Talmaiel: A descendant of the Grigori who managed to escape both the flood and the swords of the avenging Angels.

Tamiel: "Perfection of God." *Turel:* "Rock of God." *Usiel:* "Strength of God."

Below: *A still from Wim Wender's classic film, "Wings of Desire."* Set in Berlin, this movie tells of an administering angel who, having fallen in love with a mortal trapeze artist, chooses to take on the flesh. He leaves his good, yet monotone world, in order to experience the universe of dualities. Immediately he discovers the sensuous pleasures and suffering of the flesh, heat and cold and the entire spectrum of colors along with the range of emotions with which we are all too familiar. The story suggests that the world of the good angel does lack the contrast which is only fully appreciated by those who have fallen. It does raise the question that if one only knows good, how could one recognize evil?

The Aristocrats of Hell

The second roll-call is from the separate Devilish tree of the "Shadows of God." These dark Angels originally come from the other nine angelic orders. The cause of their fall into darkness was either the sin of *hubris* or overweening Pride. In this group the higher the original position in heaven, the deeper their subsequent fall. In the following diagrams we find the most prominent of the diabolic personalities.

The Seven Princes of Hell

Baal-beryth: An Ex-prince of the cherubim and now the Grand Pontiff and Master of all Infernal Ceremonies. He always appears as the counter-signatory in the pacts made by mortals and demons.

Dumah: This angel of the "Silence of Death" is, according to the *Zohar,* the chief of all the demon princes in Gehenna and guardian of Egypt during the Hebrew escape from Egypt.

Sariel: Claimed to be an archangel of heaven but most authorities agree he spends a lot of time in Hell. His expulsion came from an over enthusiasm with the subject of the moon. He taught the Canaanite priestesses the tides and courses of the moon which helped them enchant the land. The moon and the priestesses of Canaan are not popular subjects with the jealous Hebrew God of the Sun so before Sariel was hurled from heaven he quietly and gracefully departed.

Mephistopheles: "He who hates the light" or the "deceitful" destroyer. Once this great Prince was an archangel in heaven and even in his fallen and evil state is sometimes unaccountably admitted to the Holy Presence. Sometimes mistakenly identified with Satan probably because he has, on occasion, stood in for his Unholy Lord. He is said to have urbane and impeccable manners, a smooth and glib tongue and a philosophic view of life tinged, it is said, with regret.

Rofocale: According to the *Grande Grimoire* Lucifer Rofocale is the prime minister of the whole Infernal Region. He has complete control over all the treasure and wealth of our world.

Meririm: Prince of the Power of Air, the title he proudly shares with Lucifer. This has been given by no less an authority than St. Paul, who seems to have known his demonic Who's Who better than most. If the identity is correct then Meririm is the angel of the apocalypse who is charged with "hurting the earth and the oceans" (Revelations)

Rahab: "The Violent One." Originally he was the Prince of the Primordial Oceans. This mighty angel has caused the Almighty a great deal of inconvenience. Early in the Creation He ordered Rahab to separate the Waters. When Rahab refused God destroyed him. Somehow he was resurrected for he appeared again when helping the Egyptian Pharoah in his attempt to stop the Hebrews from crossing the Red Sea. Once again the Almighty showed His displeasure and destroyed him for a second time. But either the witnesses were mistaken or angels are a very hardy breed, for Rahab is claimed by Christians to be alive and well as the Angel of Insolence and Pride.

Angels of Punishment

Dumah: (as above).

Ksiel: "Rigid one of God" who punishes the nations with a whip of fire.

Lahatiel: "The flaming One." An Angel of Punishment who presides over the gates of death.

Shaftiel: Lord of the Shadow of Death and judge of God.

S OF GOD

Makkiel: The "Plague of God." *Chitriel:* The "Rod of God." *Puriel:* The "Fiery and Pitiless Angel of God" who is said to probe and torment the soul.

Arch-She-Demons

Astarte: Originally the Creating and Destroying Goddess of the Indo-Europeans she was known to the Egyptians as *Ath-ur,* "Venus in the Morning," in Aramaic she is "The Morning Star of Heaven." As *Astroarche,* "Queen of the Stars" she ruled all the spirits of the dead whose "astral" bodies could be seen as the stars. *Astarte-Astaroth* was transformed by Christians into a male Duke of Hell. (See Astaroth)

Proserpine: Originally the Greek "Queen of the Underworld" she is the destroying Kali of India. In Christian traditions she is "Queen of the She-Demons".

Barbelo: The daughter of the female aeon, Pistis-Sophia who according to the gnostics was the pro-creator of the superior angels. Barbelo was so perfect in glory that it was rumored that she even outshone the Father in Heaven, which hardly seems any reason to find her on the fallen lists. Her particular crime is unknown although her mother, Sophia, had a few, but very unkind, words to say to Yahweh when he boasted of being the Creator. Perhaps it is enough to believe like mother, like daughter.

Leviathan: The coiled chaos she-dragon whose fins say the *Talmud* radiate such a brilliant light that they obscure the rays of the sun. Often identified with the great serpent who dwells in the bottomless abyss, Leviathan is later masculinized by medieval writers becoming "king" over all the children of pride. Manifests as the great Crocodile or the crooked snake.

Satan's Brides.

Agrat-bat-Mahlaht and *Eiseth Zenunim:* Both angels of prostitutes.

Lilith: The feisty, wild, first wife of Adam, who spurned both God and his male creation is said to be Satan's favorite. While demons do live long they are not immortal but Lilith has the distinction, according to the *Zohar,* of continuing " to exist and plague man until the Messianic day."

Naamah: "Pleasurable," the most sensual and sexual of Satan's four wives. She was once the sister of Tubal-Cain and Noah. She became the mother of the great *Asmodeus.* She is the fourth angel of prostitution and is the greatest seductress of both men and demons. Far from being jealous or possessive Satan is said to be relieved at the respite offered by being cuckolded.

Arch-Demons or Archangels of Hell

Adrameleck: "King of Fire" One of the angels of the Throne and Chancellor of the Order of the Fly. Is bearded, eagle-winged and lion-bodied and is identified with fire sacrifices.

Carniveau: Once a Prince of Powers, was one of the demons cited as having possessed the body of Sister Seraphica of Loudon.

Python: Is the monster serpent who has extraordinary oracular talents yet who is called the "prince of the lying spirits."

Sut: One of the sons of Eblis and Demon of Flies.

Kesef: An angel of wrath who overstepped his authority and attacked Moses at Horeb. It was Kezef who was imprisoned by Aaron.

Moloch: Once known as a Canaanite God who was worshipped by the early Semites. It was to this fearsome God that the tribes offered their first born, sacrificed in the fires of his awful shrine outside of Jerusalem.

Dubbiel: Once the guardian angel of Persia who stood in for Gabriel when she was in temporary disgrace. As we know by now virtually all the tutelary angels of nations ended up in the nether regions. Whether this is through over-identification with the national pride of their charges, or whether the Israelites had a lot of enemies is debatable.

Mammon: The prince of Tempters. Listed as an arch-demon Mammon appears to be the devil of Avarice and Greed. Continental Infernal Encyclopedias list Mammon as the diabolic ambassador to England which all goes to show what Europe thought of British enterprise.

Rimmon: Once an archangel of heaven who commanded lightning and storms which his name the "roarer" implies.

Dukes of Hell

Agares: This duke of Hell appears as an old man astride a crocodile and carrying on his arm a goshawk.

Aniquiel: One of the nine grand dukes who is specifically named as the serpent in the Garden of Paradise.

Ashmedai: An ex-Cherubim who is more of a philosopher than thoroughly evil. He is considered fairly harmless but his legions are said to be an unruly lot even by hell's standards.

Asmodeus: "Being of Judgment." Originally a Persian deity, a raging fiend. It was he who killed the seven bridegrooms of Sarah and fought the archangel Raphael almost to a standstill," before that archangel managed to banish him to Upper Egypt from where he made his way to Hell.

Astaroth: Supposedly he manifests as "a beautiful angel astride a dragon and carrying a viper in his hand." This could be because Astaroth suffered a sex change at the instigation of the medieval Church authorities. Originally better known, at least in Hell as Astarte.

Balam: Once belonging to the Order of Dominations he is now a terrible demon with the heads of a man, a bull and a ram with the tail of a serpent.

Byleth: Once a great Prince of Powers now rides, like death, a pale horse.

Belphegor: Once a Prince of the order of Principalities his impeccable pedigree of evil can be traced to the Moabite God of Licentiousness. It would seem that with credentials like this he was the obvious choice for demonic ambassador to France. He is also known as the guardian demon of Paris.

Furcalor: Once of the order of Thrones, he is the great slayer of men who apparently takes especial delight in sinking warships. Is unique in the demonic regions as manifesting as a man with griffin wings.

Isis: Another curious slip by the medieval Church. Originally Isis was the Egyptian deity born from the union of the earth and the sky. This great Mother Goddess suffered the fate of any figure who was not mentioned in the bible. If not mentioned then it must be a demon. Which is all to the advantage of Hell.

Kakabel: Once an angelic prince who was a great astrologer and astronomer. He still exercises dominion over stars and constellations and commands an impressive 365,000 spirits.

Salmael: Once of the Order of Angels he has an obsessive loathing for the chosen tribes of Israel and their God, Yahweh. Each year he calls for their annihilation.

Haroth: Once of the order of Angels Haroth remains a great teacher of magic and sorcery and rules the North. In his younger days he fell in love with Zorba, a mortal woman and revealed the hidden name of God to her.

Forneus: Once of the mighty Order of Thrones now a Marquis. He has the strange yet useful attribute of causing love in his enemies.

Raym: Once of the order of Thrones he now commands 30 legions which he uses in his especial mission to destroy all cities, which he loathes. He is seen in the form of a black crow perched amongst the ruins.

Lahash: Once led 184 myriad spirits to stop the prayers of Moses from reaching God. For this he received 70 blows of fire as punishment and was expelled from the presence.

Gazarniel: An angel of fire who attacked Moses but was turned aside by the Lawgiver. Chose to enter the nether regions voluntarily and has formed an alliance with Lahash.

The Nephillim

Helel: Son of the Canaanite Shaher who is often identified with Lucifer himself. But he is really the leader of the Nephillim, those gigantic offspring who were sired by the angels upon the daughters of Cain. These Nephillim were the builders of the Tower of Babel. Hell also shelters the other monstrous progeny; the *enim* "Terrifying," the *naphaim* or the "weakeners" and the *gibborim*, "giants" who were rescued by the dark angels from the flood.

Spies, Double-Agents and Shady Characters

Angels of Destruction: There is a split amongst rabbinical scholars as to whether these awesome "*malache Habbalah*" are in the service of God or Satan. Certainly they spend most of their time meting out the most horrendous punishments to sinners with a diabolic enthusiasm. The handsome figure of 90,000 of such beings is given by Jewish lore. Each wields a "Sword of God" as an instrument of destruction, which would suggest they serve the Almighty. But sometimes it is difficult to know which side He is on! At the same time they helped the two Egyptian wizards to enter heaven on one occasion so it does suggest the whiff of double dealing. *Kemuel, Simbiel, Azriel, Harborah, Za'afiel, Af* and *Kolazanta* are given as leaders and even *Uriel* is supposed to be their general.

Cammael: Also known as *Quemel* was once the chief of the Order of Powers and now as a Count Palantine commands as *Kemuel* 12,000 angels of destruction. Many commentators cite him as the angel who supported Christ in his Agony in the

Garden of Gethsemane although this was under the pseudonym of *Chamuel*, "He who seeks God." It was Kemuel who supposedly tried to prevent Moses from receiving the Torah. For this misdeed he was destroyed by an infuriated Law Giver. Cabbalists insist that he survived the blast.

Biqa: At the very moment of being created on the second day he turned away from his Creator. For this he was promptly dropped into the Abyss where he sank like a stone. When he reached the bottom his name had been changed to Kazbeel, "One who deceives God." In this role he tried to trick the archangel Michael into revealing the hidden name of God but he really had picked the wrong guy.

Cahor: The Genius of Deception. Hebrews did not consider this as necessarily evil but Christian theologians were adamant in listing him in hell.

Malach-Re: Like Cahor this angel of Evil is somewhat of a paradox. for while personifying Evil he is not actually Evil himself.

Tartaruchus: "The Keeper of Hell" It is difficult to discover whether this is a God appointed office or whether this gruesome angel actually enjoys overseeing the torments of hell. As Christians believed that part of the enjoyment of the righteous in heaven was to view the torments of even their beloveds in hell maybe the dividing line between righteous and damned wavers some.

Iniaes: One of the seven angels reprobated by the Church council; at Rome in 745. Reportedly he was so incensed at the tromped up charges and the sheer stupidity of the clergy that he voluntarily defected to the Lower regions. He has not regretted his decision and has great fun with the more pompous and sanctimonious clergy by loudly farting whenever they make a profound remark.

Nergal: The Angel of Pestilence and said to be the Chief of the Secret Police of Hell.

Zophiel: Quite specifically named "God's Spy" this angel actually is a double agent who once reported to his heavenly contact that that the rebel army was about to attack. Since then he has regretted this deed and was welcomed by the rebels as a Herald of Hell.

Xaphan: An apostate angel who was particularly welcomed by hell as he had the most inventive mind of all the angels. He had an ingenious plan to set fire to heaven but before he could carry it out the conspirators were discovered. Now he fans the embers of the infernal furnaces at the bottom of the abyss.

Melchi Dael: A huge black angelic prince of pimps, who, like Mephistopoles in Faustian lore, can provide a man with any woman of his choice. The usual price of course is the pact of one's soul. It always seems odd that devils are really likely to get their sinners anyway but perhaps they are aware of that redemption at the eleventh hour.

Baresches: This greater demon is said, on the unquestionable authority of the clergy, to be the very best procurer of women in hell. The usual price is asked.

Pharzuph: The Angel of Lust and Fornication. Hebrew for "two faced" or "a hypocrite." A great tempter of patriarchs, hermits and celibate monks.

Dommiel: This is St. Peter's mirror image as gatekeeper of Hell. He is the reverse of all that Peter stands for. He neither needs keys to enter as Hell is always open 24 hours a day nor is he a woman hater. He is a paragon of lechery although being also the prince of terror and trembling may give him problems.

Chief Chef of Hell

Nisroc: The great Eagle-headed deity who was once of the Order of Principalities. Was worshipped by Sennacherib, the despotic ruler of the Assyrians. After the slaughter of thousands of Sennacherib's troops during the night by one of the angels of God Nisroc was so disgusted that he joined the rebels. He was one of the winged guardians of the Tree of Immortality and is said , in his new job as chief chef to the Princes of Hell, he liberally spices their food with its fruit.

Jester of Hell

Nasr-ed-Din: One of the seven archangels of the Yezidics. It appears he is the famous Muslim wise-

acre, *Mulla Nasrudin*. He is also celebrated by Georges Gurdjieff as the incomparable teacher, *Mulla Nassr Eddin*.

The Third Wing
Heaven's Above and Earth's Below

E NOW TURN TO THE SEVEN CELESTIAL MANSIONS and the Seven Palaces of Darkness. These are the natural abodes of the Light and the Dark angels. While the descriptions come from images current in the 14th century it must be remembered that theologians of that period still envisioned the world as the center of the universe. Their belief in the existence of a flat earth had not been seriously challenged. So any journey across the actual angelic or demonic landscapes is bound to be a tightrope walk over many a metaphorical abyss.

The number seven is one of the more mysterious marvels of our universe. Virtually all religious and occult systems include the number somewhere close to their holiest of holy sanctums.

Many teachings of the Far East are founded upon hierarchies of seven. A recurring theme tells of the One, Transcendental Ground of All Being, slowly awakening to the awareness of existing. To do so "It" had to descend through seven tiers, planes or spheres ending in our material world of substance.

So it is hardly surprising to learn that the sacredness of the principle of seven was one of the most common religious insights which permeated the Middle and Near East during the early development of all the Western religions. It is easy to trace the rich mosaic of such fragmented spiritual ideas which make up the Judeo-Christian world. And while the overall picture has a breathtaking richness of imagery, it also has some very sloppy seams. It is around the joints of some really mismatched concepts of Heaven and Hell that confusion is most evident.

One of the first original models of a seven-layered Heaven comes from the ancient Sumerians. The Hebrews in captivity in Babylon must have been overawed by the impressive ruins of the Sumerian Ziggurats with their seven rising terraces signifying Heaven, with the highest temple-tower on top. The captives would have arrived in Babylon only a few years after the completion of the "Etemenanki," a huge terraced tower called the "House of the Creation of Heaven and Earth," which was indubitably the legendary Tower of Babel. Later they would have been introduced to the Persian belief in an Almighty "seated on a great white throne surrounded by winged cherubim" in the highest of seven heavens. The origin of this concept predates the Hebrew hierarchy by one thousand five hundred years and the Christian vision by over three millennia.

Jewish scribes were always eager to incorporate the juicier beliefs of their various conquerors. However, they also had another rich Hebrew tradition to draw upon, which predated even the earliest civilizations of Sumeria. For the patriarch Enoch was supposed to have lived almost nine thousand years ago and we are deeply indebted to the later copiers of his original chronicles for many of the more detailed descriptions of the various Heavens and Hells. This is held to be a first hand account which therefore owes little to the Sumerians or Babylonians who were to follow.

However, it is quite clear from his text that the heavens he described were actually firmly on the

earth. His account reads more like a tourist guide book of the Lebanon highlands than that of a supernatural Other World. Other early texts describing the heavens often seem to share with Enoch a strange sense of being actually set with feet firmly on real earth. The term Heaven can in many cases be translated as nothing more spectacular than "Highlands," while Earth can equally signify nothing more than "lowlands." Even the Sumerian word Edin or Eden actually means a "remote and uncultivated land."

It is tempting to see these detailed accounts of Enoch as being actual down-to-earth descriptions of a real visit to seven Havens or settlements. These descriptions could have been later borrowed and transformed into supernatural events by overzealous scribes who wanted to enliven their scriptures. The transformation of the secular into the sacred was one of the greatest pastimes of both Sumerian and Hebrew scholars as we shall see later. Anyway, according to the original story, these havens were the homes of the "Shining Beings," the (Elohim) who

the Upper Waters and is the home of two hundred astronomer-angels who watch over the stars. To complete the scene we find legions of guardian angels of snow, ice and dew living in the vicinity.

According to Enoch (En:III:1) "We landed in the first haven and there, they showed me a very great sea, much bigger than the inland sea where I lived." He describes it as being " a treasury of snow and ice and clouds and dew." The two angels took him "to the swiftly flowing river, and the fire of the west, which reflects every setting of the Sun. I came to the river of fire in which fire flows like water, and discharges itself into the Great Sea towards the west."

As can be seen, this description could have come from a rather poetic guide book. What is remarkable is that it would perfectly describe an actual view from Mount Hermon at sunset. Any observer would see the River Orontes flowing north, the Jordan towards the south and the long stretch of the River Leontes as it flowed into the Mediterranean to the west. To a man who only knew the lowlands the Leontes could well have looked like fire in the setting sun.

In the more visionary mode of the *Apocalypse of St. Paul*, Paul calls this the Land of Promise." Now every tree bore twelve harvests each year, and they had various and diverse fruits, and I saw the fashion of that place and all the work of God, and I saw there palm-trees of twenty cubits and others of ten cubits, and the land was seven times brighter than silver."

were later translated as angels and archangels. It is quite plausible that Enoch, who lived to see the Flood (6500 B.C.), actually visited the site of the paradise garden in Eden.

Whether this is so or not, Enoch will still accompany us on the tour of the seven Heavens, as he remains an excellent guide.

The Seven Heavens

FIRST HEAVEN (*Shamayim.*) This is the lowest heaven which borders our own world and is said to have been the abode of Adam and Eve. Its angel ruler is Gabriel. Rabbi Simon ben Laquish calls this first heaven, Wilon (curtain). All the other heavens vault over Earth, one above the other, but Wilon is the exception, in that it acts as a kind of shade for earth during the day, a shade which is then rolled back at night to reveal the Moon and the stars which are visible from the Second Heaven.

This lowest heaven contains clouds and winds,

SECOND HEAVEN (*Raquia*). The angel ruler is Raphael. This is where Enoch claims the fallen angels are imprisoned although, from what is known of their subsequent activities on earth it could hardly have been a top security establishment. Both Moses and Enoch visited this heaven which is also rumored to be the dwelling place of John the

Baptist. Complete darkness reigns over sinners who are chained there awaiting judgement. This rather inhospitable description may have been in part inspired by the timing of Enoch's visit. He recorded that he stopped there on his journey to the seventh heaven but that it was night and all he could make out was that it was in a valley where the stars shone brightly. This would be in accord with the name of this heaven being Raqui'a or the "firmament." St. Paul also confirms this: "The Angel brought me down from the third heaven and led me into the second heaven, and he led me again to the firmament."

THIRD HEAVEN (*Sagun or Shehaqim*). Anahel is the angel ruler of this Heaven. It is also the domain of Azrael, the Islamic angel of Death, which seems to accord with Enoch who places Hell within its northern boundaries. Other authorities also place Gehenna North of Eden, where dark volcanic fires burn continuously polluting the air with heavy sulfurous fumes, and a river of flame flows through a desolate land of cold and ice. Here the wicked are punished and tortured by the angels.

One can understand that the Church was chary of including such an account of heaven in their canon. From this description few would want to go there, and this is supposedly where the righteous get their reward. But we find a very different story in the paradise lands of the south, where it is reputed that divine bees store the manna-honey. A pair of vast millstones grind manna for the delight of the righteous, and it is from this image that we get the name of the heaven – Shehaqim meaning a "grindstone" or a "cloud." There is a certain confusion as to whether it is in this heaven or the next that the Garden of Eden is to be found. But certainly a vast orchard exists there, resplendent with thousands of fruit trees, including the Tree Of Life under which God takes a nap whenever He visits. Two rivers are supposed to issue from Eden: one flows with milk and honey, and the other with wine and oil. These descend and surround the earth. Three hundred angels of Light guard the garden to which all the perfect souls come after death.

St.Paul was taken up to the third heaven which had a gate with pillars of gold."When I had entered the gate of paradise an old man came there to meet me. His face shone like the sun and he embraced me." This was Enoch, the scribe, which all goes to show that the Christian heaven sometimes differs considerably from the Hebrew heaven. According to the rabbis, the patriarch had been successfully transformed into the angel Metatron a long time before. It would seem that Paul, quite independently, echoes Enoch's description of the Shining Ones.

The Last Judgment *by Nicolò and Giovanni, Roman School, 11th century.* The Medieval concept of the universe was round and layered. In the **Creation** on the opposite page which is from 12th century Sicily, God creates the spherical cosmos of time, space and matter.

Evidently Enoch applied the ointment so "his face shone like the Sun."

FOURTH HEAVEN (variously given as Zebhul or Machanon.) The ruling Prince is Michael. Here is the site of the heavenly Jerusalem, the holy. Temple and its altar. The 12th century bard, Cynewulf, says of it: "O vision of peace, Holy Jerusalem, best of royal thrones, City State of Christ, native seat of angels." St. Paul describes it in his Apocalyse: "It was all gold, and twelve walls encircled it, and there were twelve towers inside, and every wall had a furlong between them round about... There were twelve gates of great beauty in the circuit of the city, and four rivers encircled it. There was a river of honey and a river of milk and a river of wine and a river of oil. I said to the angel, 'What are these rivers that encircle this city?' He said to me, 'These are the four rivers that flow abundantly for those who are in this Land of Promise.. These are their names: the river of honey is called Phison, and the river of milk Euphrates, and the river of oil Geon, and the river of wine Tigris'."

Enoch insists that it is this heaven, and not the previous one, which houses the beautiful orchards and the great Trees of Life. (Enoch XXXII:3–6): "And I came to Paradise, the Garden of Righteousness and saw beyond the first trees, many large trees growing there. They were a glorious sight – large, beautiful and of a lovely fragrance – and among them was the Tree of Understanding, the fruit of which they eat and, thereby, obtain great purpose. The height of this tree is like unto a fir, and its leaves resemble the Carob. Its fruits hang in clusters like grapes on the vine and are very beautiful and its fragrance can be detected from a long way off."

Above: **Kudurru of King Melishpak,** *12th century B.C..* The Sumerians and Assyrians often inscribed path markers with the layered representations of their heavens. At the top can be seen the sun and the moon and a third mysterious globe which has variously been identified with a planet or even an aerial chariot.

"I commented on how beautiful and attractive the tree was and Raphael, the archangel who was with me said: This is the Tree of Understanding; your ancestral father and mother ate of it and it made them realize that they were naked; so they were expelled from the Garden." There was another tree which likewise attracted the attention of Enoch the scribe. This time Michael answered his curiosity: "And as for this fragrant tree, no human is allowed to touch it until the great selection; at that time he (The Great Lord of Judgments, the arbiter of the length of Life) will finally decide on the length of life to be granted."

In the fourth heaven great chariots ridden by the Sun and the Moon and many of the greatest stars circle the earth. The winds which draw the chariots are shaped like a phoenix and a brazen serpent, with faces like lions and lower parts like that of the Leviathan.

FIFTH HEAVEN (Machon or Ma'on). Seat of God, Aaron and the Avenging Angels. Apparently the early Hebrews were most suspicious of the north for once again it is these territories which are set aside for yet another penal settlement. This time it is for the gigantic Grigori who seem to be serving eternal imprisonment for what they did with the daughters of man. It is here that these gigantic fallen angels crouch in silent and everlasting despair.

While the ruling prince is Metatron's twin brother, Sandalphon, there are authorities who insist that Sammael is the Dark Angelic Ruler. It does make the fifth heaven a curious place altogether.

There is confirmation of dark goings on in the north from Enoch. "And I saw a deep rift in the earth with columns of flame and smoke: the fires rose to a great height and fell again into the depths. Beyond the rift, I saw a place where no sky could be seen above, and which had no firm ground below. There was no water on it, and no birds – it was a desolate and terrible place. (The archangel) Uriel said to me: This is the place where the angels who have cohabited with women will be imprisoned; those who, in many different ways, are corrupting Mankind, and leading men astray into making sacrifices to demons. They shall remain here until they come to trial."

One can imagine how the next passage could have acted as an inspiration to Christians bent upon the hell-fire and damnation aspect of their religion. "Still more horrible, I saw another fearful thing – a great fire which burnt and blazed in a place that was cleft down to the bottom of the ravine, full of great, falling columns of fire. I could neither see its size or its extent; nor could I even guess at them." Uriel told him: "This is the prison of the angels, and here they will be imprisoned for life."

In the more hospitable and beautiful south of this heaven, hosts of ministering angels chant ceaselessly the Trisagion all night, but are said to fall silent at dawn thus allowing God to hear His praises sung far below by Israel.

SIXTH HEAVEN (Zebul or Makhon). Domain of duality. Zebul rules by night and Sabbath rules by day. It is the dwelling place of seven Phoenixes and seven Cherubim who chant in praise of God, and a vast host of Shining Ones who study astronomy. There are other angels who study time, ecology, the seasons and humankind in a vast Building of Knowledge.

Enoch seems to be describing the campus of a vast Angelic University when he says: "And there I saw seven groups of Angels, very bright and won-

derful, with their faces shining brighter than the sun. They were brilliant and all dressed alike and looked alike.

"Some of these angels study the movement of the stars, the sun and the Moon and record the peaceful order of the world. Other angels, there, undertake teaching and give instruction in clear melodious voices. These are the archangels who are promoted over the other angels. They are responsible for recording the fauna and the flora of both heaven and earth. There are angels who record the seasons and the years; others who study the rivers and the seas; others who study the fruits of the Earth and the plants and herbs which give nourishment to men and beasts.

"And there Angels study Mankind and record the behavior of men, and how they live."

Makhon, which means residence, does have its disadvantages, however, for much of its climate is hardly what we usually associate with heaven. It is a major repository of snow, hailstones, dew and rain with chambers of storms and caves of fog. But we must remember that for Tibetans, living in the harsh and perpetual snows of the mountains, heaven is believed to be hot, while the Hindus in the sweltering valleys of India are assured that their heaven will be cold, or at least air conditioned.

SEVENTH HEAVEN (Araboth). The ruling prince is Cassiel. This is the abode of God on His Divine Throne, surrounded by Seraphim, Cherubim and Wheels all bathed in ineffable Light.

Enoch describes this holiest of holies in rather surprising terms. "Two angels conducted me to a place where those who were there were as bright as fire, but when they wished could appear as ordinary men. They had brought me to a place of darkness from a mountain whose summit reached to the heavens. There I saw lighted places, and heard thunderous noises; and in the deepest part, there were lights which looked like a fiery bow and arrows with their quiver, and moving lights like a fiery sword."

The Tower in the Void

14th century theologians conceived of the Seven Heavens and the Seven Earths as being intricately bound together by vast hooks which are attached to the rim of each heaven and connected to its corresponding Earth.

Each heaven is likewise hooked to its neighbor as is each earth. The whole structure resembles a colossal tower which is only prevented from collapsing into the Void by these hooks.

The Seven Heavens are balanced by their partners, the Seven Earths. These Earths are not seen as hells, although Arqa does include Gehenna and the seven hells on one of its continents. Each world is separated from its neighbor by "intervals of whirlwind," whatever that might mean. Our own world is supposedly the seventh and last. However, seven other worlds are named, so we will assume that our own planet marks the center of the heavens and the earths. The diagram shows the descending order as discovered in the Kabbalah.

The Seven Earths

Earth: *Heled* (World)

Seventh Earth: *Tebbel* (also means world) very like earth in its form of having hills and mountains, valleys and flatlands. It is however peopled by three hundred and sixty-five different types of very bizarre creatures. These weird monstrous beings with double heads or hybrid and multi-various bodies are actually considered perfectly splendid and righteous beings. They live on the aquatic life which abounds in the waters of their world and are considered superior to all other sentient beings. They have divided their planet into special zones for those inhabitants who differ too greatly from one another in both form and mind, to live harmoniously.

It seems that they are able to either prolong the life of their species or in some way bring the dead back to life. Their world is at a greater distance to their sun than we are to ours which presumably would make it a colder and darker place.

Sixth Earth: *Arqa* (an earth). A world whose seasons differ greatly from our own, being longer and with harvests and sowing at wider intervals. The inhabitants are able to cross the whirlwind spaces in order to visit all the other earths and can speak all the known languages. They have faces which are very different to ours. What is curious about Arqa is that it also contains, on one of its continents, Gehenna or in other terms, Hell. This includes the whole seven horrible layers of fire and darkness. The topmost layer of hell is called Sheol, while those that lie beneath it are called Perdition, The Gates of Death, The Gates of the Shadow of Death, Silence, The Bilge and The Lowest Pit.

Fifth Earth: *Yabbasha, Nesziah* (dryland). Here we find a tiny race of beings who appear to be very forgetful. Luckily it does not really seem to matter as they can easily live off the land. They have never been able to think consecutively long enough to build any towns or sow any crops. They just eat shrubs and small plants which grow in a very dry land which is dominated by a huge red sun. They have two holes in their heads instead of our noses in order to breathe the thin, dry air.

Fourth Earth: *Siyya* or *Tziah* meaning dryness. This world appears to be even drier than Yabbasha. Perhaps this is caused by the existence of two suns in their skies. The inhabitants are constantly looking for underground watercourses although it is reported that their cities and buildings are very rich and wondrous. The peoples are said to be very fair of feature and have more spiritual faith than all other beings.

Third Earth: *Harabha* or *Geh* (parched lands). It would seem that fertile and lush earths like our world are hard to come by. However, although Geh is a twilight planet of shadows it is a also world of woods and forests, jungles and orchards. The inhabitants live on the abundant fruits of the trees but know nothing of wheat or cereal.

Second Earth: *Adama* (earth). A world peopled by the descendants of Adam. They are cultivators and hunters but are afflicted with an almost continual melancholia. When not sad they make war upon one another. Visitors once traveled from the world of Thebel to Adama but these superior beings were often overcome by a strange malais which left them without any memory of who they were. The visits seem to have ceased.

First Earth: *Eres* (earth). The inhabitants of this world are supposedly descendants of Adam but little is known of the world itself except that Adam himself had complained that it was dull and cheerless.

ERES

ADAMA

HARRABA

SIYYA

YABBASHA

ARQUA

TEBBEL

The Seven Earths are joined to the Seven Heavens by vast
hooks attached at their rims. This colossal tower is only prevented from collapsing into the Void by these hooks. The
figure at the left, from Freiburg cathedral, shows the sevenfold
creation of the stars of Heaven.

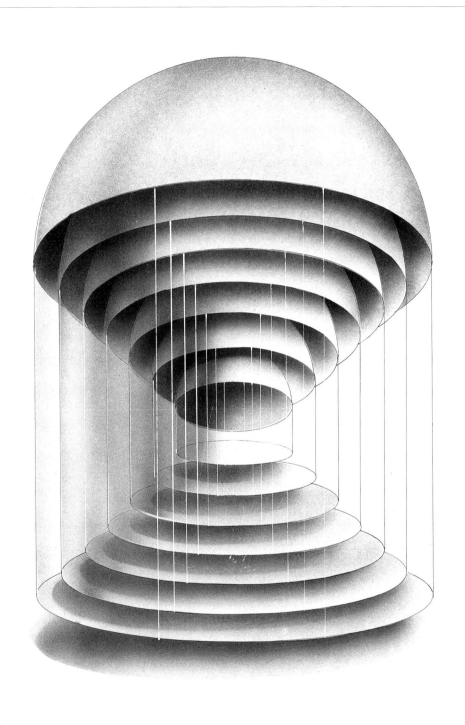

Ancient Planets of the Angels

A number of commentators have suggested that the seven earths or worlds are actually seven planets, and not even necessarily within our own solar system. There is a curious meeting in the *Zohar* between Rabbi Yosse and a mysterious stranger who had "a different face"and who asked the Rabbi the name of the world on which he had arrived. He described his own world, mentioning that the constellation of the stars in our night sky looked very different to his.

We might well ask the question whether the angels actually came from the seven planets rather than the seven heavens. The reader probably spotted the nice touch of the superior race of Thebel who forgot who they were when on Adama. There are many accounts of angels coming to earth and losing their angelic memory and superior intelligence by taking on the characteristics of mortals. Considering that these fragments from the Kabbalah can be traced to Rabbi Simon who lived almost two thousand years ago and who, even then, was continuing a tradition probably over four thousand years old, it appears that the biblical times were not so primitive as we have fondly imagined them.

The Regions of Hell

The conflicting nature of the Hebrew and Christian cosmologies is never more noticeable than when one tries to reconcile the location of Hell and its many layers.

The essentially Hebrew picture of seven heavens hooked to seven earths contrasts greatly with the later Christian version which locates Hell deep beneath our Earth, or the even earlier Hebrew version of various punishment sites spread throughout the seven Heavens.

The poet-historian, Robert Graves, suggests that it is a deliberate policy of the Church to leave a certain chaotic ambience when on the subject of the nether regions. He may be right. Anyway he quotes Amos (IX:2) to back his card. In this passage God tells us "Though they dig into hell, there shall Mine hand take them; though they climb up unto heaven, thence will I bring them down."

While it is impossible to reconcile the conflicting locations it is however possible to clear up some of the more blatant misconceptions about the home of the fallen angels.

In the version of Hell which is situated on the sixth earth there are seven layers of the infernal region of Gehenna. These are Sheol, Perdition, the Gates of the Shadow of Death, the Gates of Death Silence, the Bilge and the Lowest Pit.

Above: **Paradise** *Detail from painting by Fra' Angelico.* Right: **Paradise** *Detail of painting by Benozzo Gozzoli, 15th century.* During the Golden Era of Angels artists tended to envision Heaven as being a well kept garden. Yet at the very moment that these images were being created the Black Death was decimating Europe in, what seemed at the time, the apocalyptic scourge come true. So it is all the more remarkable that Benozzo Gozzoli tried to show that angels could actually smile or even giggle. In the group on the right the smile is a little forced but is none the less visible. For the pious clergy who commissioned the work, Heaven was obviously a serious business and certainly no laughing matter so it is an especially treasured sign that at least one artist thought that Heaven without laughter would be a dull place indeed.

The overall infernal name is Gehenna, which once referred to an actual historical fire-altar, dedicated to Molech, the deity worshipped by Solomon. The early Jews sacrificed their first born child at this shrine, which was in the valley of Hinnom, outside Jerusalem. Later Yahweh stopped the barbaric practice and the site was abandoned. It became a rubbish dump and a burning ground for the bodies of criminals and social pariahs. With such a foul background it is little wonder that the site became rooted in the Hebrew mind as being hell.

Gehenna is claimed to be sixty times as big as our earth. Each of its palaces has six thousand houses, each with six thousand vessels of fire and gall for the unfortunate sinner. The top layer is Sheol, which is Hebrew for "Pit," "Cavern", or "Womb." Strangely its equivalent in Tibet is a paradise garden called Shal-Mari. In the Middle East the name was identified with the Virgin Goddess's "walled garden." Only the sacred kings who were sacrificed on trees could enjoy this Other World of delights. There was a common practice, in Persia, of hanging human sacrifices to the deity Ishtar (Mari) on trees, and the name became Sheol-Mari.

Gehenna Moves to Hell

Although the Jews had perfected their hell centuries before the birth of Christ there was never any Hebrew concept of eternal punishment for even the worst of offenders. Even the horrors envisaged by the Persian Zoroastrians, who had especially gruesome punishments in store for women, did not go on forever. Those eternal and unremitting tortures were left to the Christians to invent.

The everlasting torments were supposed to be enthusiastically applied by a variety of Avenging Angels, Angels of Torment, Angels of Punishment, Angels of Wrath and Angels of Destruction.

With such righteous angels of the Lord hacking away at the wretched sinners, one marvels at the need of Devils at all. It is often difficult to understand whether a particularly nasty demon who tortures a victim is doing the Devil's work or that of the Almighty.

Even St. Paul, who is noted for a strong stomach when it comes to watching the punishment of sinners, recoils upon seeing a particularly revolting punishment when he visits Hell under the protection of a guardian angel. He blurts out: "It would be better for us if we were not born, since we are all sinners."

And because both Paul and the Archangel Michael have appealed to Christ, begging that some souls be given mercy, the Savior grants the souls a respite and refreshment of a day and a night from the eternal torments. At this rather modest act of mercy it is the devils who are infuriated. They scream at the sinners. "You had no mercy. This is the Judgement of God on those that did not have mercy. Yet you have received this great grace."

Satan Enthroned in Hell *by Gustave Doré.*

In Northern countries *Hel* was a pre-Christian underworld of death. This dark place was a huge prison of souls who would fight the Gods at Ragnarok. The palace of the Queen of Hel was called *Sleetcold* and this was where the Queen most tormented her unfortunate charges. Even so there was never any talk of such torments being forever.

These seem more the righteous words of a fundamentalist preacher than those of a demon. How a fallen angel can be so supportive about God's work is hard to fathom, but such double talk abounds in all the early visions of the infernal regions.

Perhaps one of the more disheartening aspects of Hell was that the "saved" were expected to enjoy watching the torments of the sinners from viewing platforms. These blessed souls were to find eternal pleasure in the sufferings of others, even if the damned who writhed in the eternal fires were their own beloved ones.

After reading some of the ecclesiastical advertisements for the righteous, sometimes one has more sympathy with the fallen.

Such a heretical point of view might well have been understood by some of the early critics of the orthodox vision. The Gnostics claimed a very different location for hell and an even more surprising chief suspect for the role of the Enemy of Man. This we can now explore in the fourth wing of the Treasury.

The Simoniac Pope *illustration by William Blake*. In the third trench of the eighth circle of Hell those who have bought or sell positions in the Church are held upside down in a well of fire. To Blake this symbolized the fallen state of man and angel.

Above: **Satan lost in the Abyss.** *Engraving by Gustave Doré.* In the Apocalypse of St. Paul an angel tells the saint, "The abyss has no boundary, for beneath it there follows also what is beneath; and so if someone strong took a stone and threw it into a very deep well, after many hours it would reach the bottom. this abyss is also like that. For when souls are thrown into it, they hardly come to the bottom after five hundred years." Gehenna, itself, has seven layers of which sheol is the highest. Below Sheol lie *Perdition*, the *Lowest Pit*, the *Bilge*, *Silence*, the *Gates of Death*, and the *Gates of the Shadow of Death*. The fire of each layer is sixty times fiercer than that immediately beneath.

The Fourth Wing
The Heresy

O FAR we have examined the orthodox part of the treasury with its elaborately bejeweled hierarchies of Heaven and Hell. This intricate superstructure was only seriously challenged once before the Middle Ages, when the Gnostics flung down the angelic gauntlet during the first four centuries after the death of Christ. According to them it is Satan-el who holds the key to the creation of our universe and all and everything it contains. The Gnostics were amongst the multi-various mystery cults and sects of the early Christian era who quickly ran afoul of their orthodox brethren. By the 4th century they had been denounced as heretics and a century later were virtually wiped out.

Their fundamental heresy was a belief in the existence of a female cosmic principle *prior* to that of the male Yahweh or Jehovah. They believed this to be a Primal Realm of Silence which then gave birth to the Great Mother Sophia (Wisdom), who then became simultaneously both the mother and the lover of God the Son. This is an archetypical "Goddess" theme, common throughout the ancient world and one which finds its recurring expression within the Christian Virgin Mary-Jesus relationship.

Another concept condemned as abhorrent by the patriarchal orthodoxy was the equality enjoyed

by women within the heretical hierarchy. Gnostics claimed that the true revelation of esoteric Christianity was channeled through Mary Magdalene, the whore who was so beloved by Christ. The highly charged Tantric mold of subsequent Gnostic teachings and meditation techniques had remarkable similarities to the Indian practice of having sacred temple prostitutes as channels for the Divine. The link with the teachings of the Far East could be most clearly discerned in the most popular Gnostic teacher of the times, Simon Magus.

His fame eclipsed all the orthodox apostles who were in the area at the time. He traveled with a sacred harlot from Babylon called Helen. His relationship with this reincarnation of Helen of Troy was said to parallel that of Christ and the prostitute, Mary Magdalene, who to gnostics was known as Pistis-Sophia-Prunikos (Faith-Wisdom-Whore).

It seems only fitting that it should be the despiser of women, St. Peter, of whom Magdalene once said "he hates the female race," who claimed to eventually have destroyed Simon. The encounter according to church records was in Rome. The Mage was rather theatrically showing off by flying over the Campus Martius in a chariot drawn by dark winged demons, when Peter spoke a magical spell and sent the heretic crashing to his doom. In one version the magician broke his arm in three

places and in another Simon promptly reincarnated into Menander, the "moon being." As we now know that Peter was never in Rome the whole incident probably reflected the rivalry between the Church which worshipped the Essenic Sun God and whose priests were called "Peter," and the Gnostics who worshipped the Luna Hero. We can add two further esoteric bonuses to the legend if we recall that Peter's original name was Simon, and that this story echoes the lightning descent of both Shaher and Lucifer.

One of the major detractors of the Gnostics was Irenaeus, who rather petulantly observed that "they sprout up like mushrooms and fight like hydras." It was the very diversity of their interpretations of Christ's teachings which infuriated the orthodox leaders who were already having so much trouble in giving some consistency to their own canons. Irenaeus goes on critically: "None of them is considered perfect unless he expounds something different in high sounding phrases." There is certainly some justification for his irritation with their incredibly convoluted interactions of good aeons and evil archons in an utterly bewildering cosmology. His scorn that "they

The Death of Simon the Magician *from the Nurenburg Chronicles.* The heretic, Simon flies through the air above Rome supported by demons. Peter orders them to drop Simon who in one story breaks his leg in three places. This victory was a

fabrication by the Church. Strangely, while Simon is an authenticated historical figure there is considerable doubt, even amongst Catholic theologians, that Peter ever existed. Even if he did it is sure he was never in Rome.

recount all their ludicrous genealogy as confidently as if they had been midwives at their (the angels) birth" might be better directed at the Church itself. It appears that there was a lively atmosphere of spiritual one-upmanship existing in those early days. But in spite of the parochial attitudes of most of the early fathers much of the Gnostic's material quietly found its way in through the backdoor, into the canon of the very Church which persecuted them. Even so, their basic beliefs remain diametrically opposed to those of the Church.

However, the reason for our particular interest in the Gnostic vision is that according to these heretics the role of the angel in the whole cosmic plan is far more essential and a great deal more awesome than so far shown. It could be said that the Christian view of angels is largely built upon the notion of function. Angels are seen as messengers, having a particular status within the cosmic hierarchy.

So these beings are significant in what they do rather than in what they are. In the Gnostic vision it is rather their essential nature which is of concern. In order to understand this it is best to summarize their teaching.

A New Beginning

According to the Gnostics the origin of all and everything firmly rests in a Supreme First Principle. The Hebrew God is replaced at the center of creation by a secret, hidden and *female* Divinity: one that is nameless, unknown and unknowable. Only silence can express this original Nothingness. For equally mysterious reasons a ripple moved in the Void. This wave is identified with Will, and arising from that Will, a Divine Self is revealed. So far this is almost precisely the cosmological model of the Hindus, the Buddhists, the Sufis: it can also be found in the traditions of both Yoga and Tantra. But the route chosen after this critical crossroads takes us along a uniquely Western highway.

By a unique manifestation which did not involve "creation" or any intermediary or evolutionary process, this Divine Self brought into existence a complex and highly paradoxical (at least to us) state of descending hierarchies of spiritual "beingness." The highest state of being was manifested in what might be called the "Divine Attributes". These can be considered abstract qualities or metaphysical concepts such as Love, Power, Compassion, Mercy, or Truth. Valentinus gives an eightfold version of the emanations which are Thought, Grace, Silence, Mind, Truth, Man, Church, and Sophia. From these sprang another fifteen pairs totaling 38 emanations in all.

At first these attributes were not aware of themselves, but gradually they became conscious of the unique separateness of their existence. They slowly became "hyperstatized" or personified as independent beings. These new entities are the Aeons – celestial beings who represent the multitude of divine forms and powers which we refer to as Angels. Every manifestation of God the Father is an angel.

Apparently they are formless, but when visiting human beings they often assume physical bodies in order not to cause unwarranted fear or disquiet.

The Aeonic, or Angelic, hierarchy is made up roughly as we have already seen it in the traditional view. The Gnostic bureaucracy however is divided into seven principalities of: the Ancient Ones, the Powers, Thrones, Dominions, Authorities, Lesser Gods and Rulers. Each of these divine bodies corresponds to each of the seven heavens.

God gave these newly self-aware angels free choice, knowing that they might even move away from His love and thereby possibly disobey. So, it is said, God withdrew His own will, and in that moment of supreme love gave them the gift of their own destinies. No longer were they robots, mere puppets of the Divine Will, but autonomous entities. This contraction of the divine will led directly to the fall. For in the sudden vacuum, the emptiness of the abyss, left by God's withdrawal, our own material universe came into being. But, and here comes the great heresy, GOD is not here!

Fundamental to the Gnostic teaching is that we abide in a place where *God is not*. Where His spirit is absent, matter appears; where love and goodness depart, evil appears; where light is absent, darkness prevails; and where once there was eternal life, time and death take their place.

However, traces of the divine light do remain like spoors, a scent or the mark of a footprint. It was from these scant traces that the great Aeon Lucifer, Prince of Light, but now Satan-el, Prince of Darkness, is said to have created our own universe.

The great contraction of God and the exercise of free will resulted in a rebellion by what is reputed to have been one third of the original Aeonic host, and these became what is known as the Archons or demons. These dark angels fell from the higher heavens of eternity to dwell in the lower heavens of time space and illusion.

The leader of the evil archons was of course Satan-el. And as we have just learnt, it was he, and not the supreme deity, who created our universe. The Gnostics, like Jesus before them, accuse the Jews (and by inference the Christians as well) of worshipping the wrong God. *Yahweh = Satanel* is the Gnostic equation which certainly gives all of us space for reflection.

Satanel had once been the most trusted and beloved angel of God. He had been the vice-regent of heaven, brother of the heavenly Jesus, Lucifer the bearer of light. He was not the only great angel to fall. Another of the great archangels was Sophia, who fell through curiosity and the jealousy of other aeons (no one is perfect in the Gnostic heaven). While she managed to redeem herself, Adamel, the third member of the company, did not. Satanel fell through pride (the greatest sin), while Adam fell through disobedience, (the sin that appears to infuriate the Almighty most).

It is generally accepted that the great Gnostic teacher, Basilides, was the best arithmetician when calculating how many other aeons fell. He numbers them as 365, which is both the number of days in the year and also the numerical product of the letters of the name Abraxas, (which is either the group as a whole or the name of the greatest aeon of all). The mightiest of the demon-archons rule the lower evil orders. They also control Time and its Division, Space and its various Dimensions, along with the workings of the stars and planets.

Perhaps the most refreshing aspect of Gnostic teachings, in an otherwise dominantly male arena, is the regard the sects had for the female. Many

powerful women were in controlling positions and they were considered the major channellers of divine visions. This view of women was very much influenced by what appears to be the greatest Gnostic Angel of all; Sophia.

The Virgin Sophia of the Rosicrucians. This occult figure is seen as the Heavenly & Earthly Mother from whose womb all things, both sacred and profane, were born.

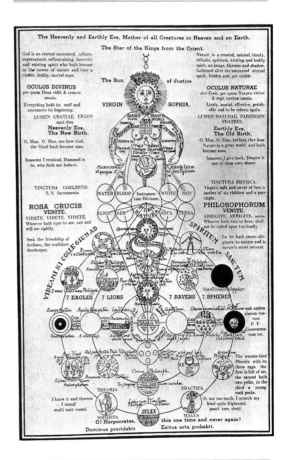

Sophia

She is the Angel-Aeon who gave birth to all the others. As both mother and lover of her progeny she caused a mass defection from the mysteries of Light. Her lover sons became seduced and obsessed by the mysteries of sexual union. It is said that out of their incestual yet angelic union sprang the demon-archons and lesser demons. But Sophia tired of this sensual pursuit and returned to her original fascination and thirst to discover the mystery of the Light of the Absolute. Her subsequent curiosity, and the jealousy of the sexually aroused and yet unsatisfied lovers, caused her great fall.

In one account, she desired to create without the male principle, which infuriated the chauvinist Angel-Aeons. In another version she is so curious that she mistakes a false reflection in the depths below and plunges down to meet it becoming enmeshed in our material world in the process. Her lover-angels spitefully conspired to imprison her in a body in which she is subjected to the deepest humiliations of rape and whoredom. In this aspect she is known to the Gnostics as "Our sister Sophia, who is a whore." In this role she is the lustful keeper of corrupt, carnal and profane knowledge. Many of the Gnostic visionaries were originally from the "oldest profession," which they see as a tradition stemming from Christ's liaison with Mary Magdalene. In Jewish lore Sophia is identified with the Shekinah, the female principle which was introduced in the first wing of the treasury.

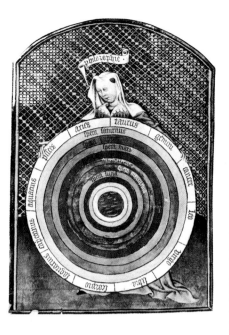

Sophia manages to endure these endless trials and gains a new understanding of the mysteries of the Light and Pistis, "faith." She is restored to heaven to become the greatest of all angels. She makes an appearance in the orthodox apocalypse of John. In Revelations (21:9) she has become the bride of Christ in a mystical marriage with the Logos. In her own words discovered in the Dead Sea scrolls of Nag Hammaddi she says, "I am the first and the last, the honored and the despised, the whore and the holy one, wife and virgin, barren and fertile."

The Heretic Angel: the Demiurge

The other mighty aeon which caught the Gnostic imagination is of course *ophiomorpus*, "serpent shaped," *diaboles*, "the slanderer" or *diabolos*, the devil.

Satan is the fiery archon, but because he is Prince of Darkness his fire is of the element of darkness too. To the Gnostic he is the Demiurge who created our universe which is, in essence, evil. He is identified with the detested Yahweh, God of the Israelites, and is scorned along with the Jewish

Right: **Unio Mystica** by *Johfra, 1973.* This represents the middle pillar of the Tree of Life and adam Kadmon, the Universal Man. Above: **Philosophie** *illustrated French manuscript.* Sophia, or Wisdom still exerted her influence amongst the Kabbalists of the 14th century.

patriarchs as being the epitome of falsehood. They point an accusing finger at the apparently schizophrenic actions of Jehovah who openly admits, "My name is Jealous and I am a jealous God," whilst maintaining the image that He is a loving deity. The Gnostics cite the legend of Moses who comes down from the mountain having been given the ten commandments. One of the commandments says not to kill and yet the Lawgiver promptly, following the orders of his God, slaughters three thousand men, women and children. Apparently, point out the Gnostics, neither he nor Jehovah see any ambiguity in the situation. Here, they insist, there is the singular proof that we are dealing with a merciless, wrathful, bloodthirsty monster who cannot possibly be the Father of Light. Instead this can only be Satan.

It is small wonder that the Gnostics were accused of anti-Semitism. They ceaselessly hammered all the beliefs and institutions of the Hebrews, condemning their scriptures as being trivial, exclusive, of only tribal interest and having no spiritual value for the rest of the world. In doing so, of course, they make quite a hole in our previous orthodox studies which are based on such material.

We begin to feel on even less firm ground when Jesus Christ himself accuses the Jews: "Ye are of your Father; the Devil." The New Testament is notable for its silence in mentioning Jehovah except in this passage.

The fundamental dualism which underpinned the Gnostic ideas was originally a Persian concept which developed around the middle of the last millennium before Christ. In this Persian belief our universe is seen as the battle ground between the Lord of Light (the Zoroastrian Ormazd) and the Prince of Darkness (Ahriman).

The further the demon-archons moved from the divine source the greater the darkness, ignorance, error and evil. The archons are identified with the seven deadly sins which are in turn equated with the seven planetary bodies, being the absolute antithesis of the seven archangels.

In the following list, however, the archons are set alongside our traditional archangels who supposedly control the seven planets. This shows how far away the Gnostics were from the orthodox Church by the 3rd century A.D..

Sins		Planet		Archangel
Pride	=	Jupiter	=	Zadkiel
Envy	=	Moon	=	Gabriel
Wrath	=	Mars	=	Sammael
Lust	=	Venus	=	Aniel
Sloth	=	Saturn	=	Kafziel
Greed	=	Sun	=	Raphael
Falsehood	=	Mercury	=	Michael

While the Zoroastrian idea of a constant battle being waged between the forces of good and evil was much embellished by the Gnostics, the final polish was left to the Christian Church. The passionate and intense series of apocalyptic visions which appeared at the time of the Messiah arose from a magnificent obsession with the nature of good and evil which had absorbed the Hebrew theologians for over two centuries. When the end of the world did not materialize in the century after Christ, many came to believe that the final battle of the angels had been re-scheduled to be fought sometime in the future. Many see that future as being here and now, within our lifetimes. The great battle with the anti-Christ and the forces of evil which support his enterprise is billed for the end of this millennium.

War Above and Below

One of the Dead Sea scrolls discovered in the first Qumran cave is a war scroll. There is no precedent for such a work. It is unique and unlike anything else so far uncovered. The scribe obviously felt that the "end of days" was just round the corner and he had to prepare his sect for the final victory over the Sons of Darkness. Two thousand years later we find ourselves at the end of an era which has been prophesied as the "Armageddon," "the end of days" when the Sons of both Light and Darkness must stick up their heads and be numbered.

In reading the scroll there is a sense of immediacy, as if at any moment the scribe just has to look up to see the archangel, "Michael stand up, the great prince that standeth for the children of Thy people."
It was probably one of the last texts written in the truly apocalyptic genre. But however much the writer might search the heavens for signs of the great armies of the heavenly hosts, the promised end of the forces of Beliel which he so passionately described was obviously a long time coming. Tiny communities like his were being ruthlessly destroyed by invaders who were in turn followed by more invaders. It is unlikely that

Above: **Angel with the Key of the Abyss** *wood engraving by Albrecht Dürer.* Left: **Michael driving out Lucifer from Heaven** *engraving by Gustave Doré.* The angel is Apollyon-Abaddon, the "destroyer." He is the Angel of the Bottomless Pit who is to bind the Satanic Dragon for 1000 years. The gnostics pointed out that many of the orthodox angels were in fact villains.

Abaddon is the Angel of Death and Destruction and chief of Demons according to the Kabbalists.
As the Greek Apollyon he is described in Bunyan's Pilgrims Progress as "clothed with scales like a fish, and wings like a dragon, feet like a bear, and out of his belly come fire and smoke."

the author survived long after he hid his precious manual of victory.

The text is a very detailed preparation for each battle between the forces of Light and the hordes of Darkness. The text meticulously describes which trumpets to blow for both advance and retreat, the inscriptions which must be on the trumpets and the precise sound which must issue forth. The battle is to take forty years and consists of seven Lots or major engagements with the dark forces of Beliel. Although Beliel will be victorious in three of the great engagements, God and His angels will finally carry the day in the seventh encounter. In fact the mortal armies, along with the hideous demonic hordes of the Evil One, will finally fall to the swords of Michael and his glorious angelic legions and not to those of men.

This whole battle is the culmination of thousands of years of preparation and minor skirmishes to test the opponent's strength. But according to the scroll the final outcome is already decided in favor of the author's peoples.

This type of apocalyptic vision had an enormous appeal to the religious sects who had been ceaselessly oppressed by the Babylonians and Persians in the East, the Egyptians in the South, the Philistines, Greeks and Romans in the West and the various marauding Kingdoms of the North. All these are

understandably seen as the forces of Belial or Satan.

Of course the most famous of the apocalyptic genre is to be found in the New Testament. In *The Revelations of John* the most powerful of images of those final days can be found. In a graphic description which could also be read as an account of the original fall, it is said, "And war broke out in heaven: Micha-el and his angels battled with the dragon and the dragon and his angels battled. But it did not prevail, neither was a place found for them any longer in heaven. So down the great dragon was hurled, the Original serpent, the one called Devil and Satan, who is misleading the entire inhabited world."

The Good and Evil Angels *two versions by William Blake.* They depict a child being held by the Good angel who prevents the shackled and fiery dark angel from reaching it. Above this design we find the following insight:
"The voice of the Devil
All Bibles or sacred codes have been the causes of the following Errors:
1. That Man has two real existing principles: Viz: a Body & a Soul.
2. That Energy, call'd Evil, is alone from the Body; and that Reason, call'd Good, is alone from the Soul.
3. That God will torment Man in Eternity for following his Energies.
But the following Contraries to these are True:
1. Man has no Body distinct from his Soul; for that call'd Body is a portion of Soul discerned by the five Senses, the chief inlets of Soul in this age.
2. Energy is the only life, and is from the Body; and Reason is bound or outward circumference of Energy.
3. Energy is Eternal Delight."

Elementals

At this culminating point as the angels of Light finally overcome the angels of Darkness let us take a break from the noise of battle to examine a little gem from *The Magus of Strovolos* by Kyrialos Markides. This is rich little book crammed full of the wiseacerings of a beautiful mystic healer in modern Greece. They are particularly relevant to those apocalyptic visions of twenty centuries ago, for in the following excerpt we find an unusual description which seems to unite both Christian and Gnostic concepts of the good and evil forces. According to the *Magus*, demons are far more human than angels. It appears that you can reason, argue or strike bargains with demons. An angel, on the other hand, being part of the Divine Will, cannot do anything but follow that will. An angel can only do good; whereas Lucifer, having his own free will, can follow any path he chooses, even when it is mostly for the bad. From this brief account it can be seen that demons seem completely in tune with human nature and all its frailties.

"Responding to my question on the difference between angels and demons, Daskalos (the Magus) went on to say that they are both emanations of angelic forces. In themselves neither demons nor angels are eternal beings. They are elementals of the archangelic force which projects them. Humans are capable of creating both demonic and angelic elementals.

"Demons are archangelic emanations in the opposite side of existence in order to create the realms of separateness. Archangel Lucifer in the noetic world is no different from all the other archangelic systems. But his work down here is to create the opposite side of energy and power in order to bring the balance. I believe this must be part of the Divine Plan. It is that which we call Evil. The purpose of this Evil is to create for us more sharply the meaning of the Good."

The questioner then asks how demons are different from the elementals (projected energy) that we create all the time. "The elementals that human beings create are either angelic or demonic. Man is allowed to create both kinds. An archangel, on the other hand, can only create angelic elementals, with the exception of Lucifer who can only emanate demons.

"'Demons,' said Daskalos, 'possess a form of subconsciousness that enables them to converse with humans. I am telling you,' he continued, 'you may reason with a demon but not with an angel because an angel is an unshakable law. An angel cannot deviate from his divine purpose. But, although a demon is something analogous to the angel, he opposes the work of the angel and can influence man. Once a demon attaches himself to a human being, he acts along with him, using the logic of man regardless of the fact that it may be a form of unreason. An angel cannot do that. He works monolithically within the realms of Creation. Do you understand now what is happening? An angel has no choice but to do good. A demon cooperates with man and therefore absorbs part of his experience, like the ability to logicalize. The angel expresses the love of his archangel uncolored. A demon expresses within the realm of separateness the love of his own archangel, which is sentimentality. It is very similar to human sentimentality. That is why a demon can more easily get attached to a human than an angel. The only work of the angel in the plant and animal kingdom and in man is to create blindly and beautifully through the Holy Spirit, cells and tissues and to assist in cures. The demon on the other hand does everything that man does. He lives fully with man's sentiments'."

There is a parallel to this experience found in the *Life of Anthony*, written over 1600 years ago. In it are listed the weapons which the hermit saint used to ward off constant demonic attacks. Demons seemed especially attached to all monks and hermits who were always trying to exorcize them, ignore them or even blow them away by hissing. Anthony maintains that, if a spirit approaches, the monk should boldly ask what it is. Sometimes the demon will appear as a beautiful woman or an angel. If it is a real angel it will fully reveal itself but if it is a demon it will flee in terror at such courage.

Such timidity on the part of the devil's legions does tend to suggest the final battle is going to be a real walkover for the Righteous, contrary to what advertisements of this event claim. For this final battle has been awaited thousands of years. After so many qualifying rounds and minor skirmishes to test the enemies' tactics and defenses, it is almost a disappointment to find the devil is a wimp. But it is pretty disheartening for the Enemy to know that however skillfully, courageously or brilliantly he deploys his diabolic forces, God has already decided on the outcome.

However, the devil also knows that without the permanent state of siege, without a constant tension between the opposing forces of the Good One and the Evil One, the whole hierarchy of both Heaven and Hell would topple. Without such ideas as obedience and disobedience, there would be no sense of sin. Without sin there is no need for Heaven and Hell. So here we see two co-existing themes. One is the dualistic conflict of good and evil; the other is the simple commerce of sin and righteousness with subsequent rewards in heaven or punishments in hell.

But rewards and punishments are not really such a simple matter, especially when one man's sin can be another's salvation. A devout Moslem who kills a Christian on a Holy Jihad is assured of a warrior's place in paradise with two beautiful and desirable angel maidens for his delight. Simultaneously this righteous hero has secured his everlasting torment in the Christian hell for killing a Christian, for not being a Christian and for the corruption of the flesh in even thinking about those two seductive Muslim maidens. Yet, historically speaking at least, there is virtually no real difference between the Semitic Allah and Jehovah, who even share the same angelic servants.

Above: The goat-headed, occult figure with the wings of an eagle, the body of a hermaphrodite and the caduceus of Hermes encompasses both principles of Good and Evil.

A Line down the Middle

The purpose of this brief heretical interlude is to highlight the ever present question of just where does one draw the line to show which is an angel of darkness and which is one of the light? Satan is one of the terrible scourging Angels of Vengeance, but so is the archangel Michael. The 90,000 Angels of Destruction are known to be the most enthusiastic punishers in Hell, and yet are given the "swords of God" with which to torment the sinners. No wonder theologians squabble over whether angels serve God or the devil. If they are God's loyal troops then they must be doing good and the eternal horrors they dish out to sinners must also be good. If they serve the Devil, then those self-same horrors must be evil. The paradoxes are, like heaven itself, eternal, and one begins to wonder which side even God is on.

There is a little known tradition which has never been encouraged by the Church. In this version of the war of the angels in heaven, one third is supposed to have sided with God, one third with the Devil and one third chose to be neutral. It was these angels who were not-very-bad yet not-very-good, who brought the Holy Grail to earth. The Grail represented the religious, mystical or spiritual way that passed between the polar extremes. It is the middle path chosen by Gautama the Buddha; it is the union of opposites.

The mysterious Grail held a passionate fascination for readers in the Middle Ages. Although strongly Christian in theme there is strangely not one mention of angels or demons in any of the many versions. The reason why this favorite legend managed to do without these celestial beings, at a time when they were immensely popular elsewhere, can be found in the opening line of one version. "Every

action has both good and evil results." Such an enlightened view cannot support angelic hosts who only know of one or the other.

Without the polar opposites of the righteous and the damned, there can be no devil and no angel of light. As the reader must have already noticed this Treasury has no example of neutral plumage.

END OF PART ONE

PART TWO
AN ENDANGERED SPECIES

CHAPTER ONE
Eye Witness

IN the course of the Dante-like jour-ney through each of the four wings of the Treasury it has probably become evident to the reader that many of the images of Paradise and the Underworld have simply arisen within a historical context. Yet the fact that a clear line of descent can be traced from the Cherubim to earlier Babylonian sources in no way invalidates the possible existence of an authentic angelic presence. However, the historical approach does help to iso-late some of the more obvious inventions of the scholars. Evidence of a real angelic phenomenon is not lessened merely because a few paper wings can be clipped by historical methodology. The ulti-mate enigma of the angel remains as fascinating as ever.

The second half of this volume is devoted to an exploration of what, or rather who, angels really are and why they remain such an evocative subject even in this century of scientific rationalization.

The golden picture described in the Treasury is one which has been painstakingly built up over thousands of years of scholarship, is a condensation of legends and angelic lore to be found in literally thousands of scripts, scrolls, books and documents; enough to fill a large library. In contrast, the scraps of evidence that might indicate that there really are such beings, would hardly fill a small brief case. And on examination, even these precious few re-cords would often seem to be the visions and imagi-nings typical of those found in any modern psy-chiatric ward. Often the mentally disturbed also experience the self-same wild visions and encoun-ters with bizarre beings that are to be found in ac-counts of meetings with angels. Yet the patients are

as adamant in their belief of the reality of what they have seen as any biblical prophet. Even under deep hypnosis the visionary will maintain that the phenomenon was real. A mys-tic like William Blake would have convinced any lie detector that he actually *saw* angels even when there were a number of impartial observers who saw nothing when he insisted that angels were pre-sent.

Seeing is Believing

Many psychologists would agree that the whole imaginative aspect of angel sightings might be neatly summed up as either "Seeing is believing" or "Believing is seeing." Both situations have *belief* as the bottom line. Simply put, anyone who, suppor-ted by a particular belief system, expects to expe-rience a particular phenomenon is all the more likely to have that experience. One psychologist put it neatly, "Demonic possession happens to those who believe in demonic possession."

There is a beautiful anecdote concerning the power of belief. It comes from the psychiatrist Ro-nald Laing and concerns a patient who always be-lieves what her husband told her. One evening, entering her lounge unexpectedly and finding her husband with a naked woman on the couch, she is stupefied and asks "Who is this woman?" Her hus-band, seemingly a resourceful man, answers: "It's not a woman, it's a waterfall." The wife is caught in a real bind. She has always believed her husband and yet her instincts and her eyes tell her something entirely different. This double-bind situation is one of the roots of the psychological distress found in many schizophrenics. This wife's senses, her total being cried one perception, while her habitual belief system calmly told her quite the opposite. When confronted by such a double-bind a person can simply block out the unacceptable part or the habitual response to it. A similar principle seems to be in operation when a witness blocks a memory of encounters with angels, spirit guides, demons or even extra-terrestrials. Sometimes such memories only surface under deep hypnosis. How many crucial messages from "above" may have been lost to humanity simply because the subject cannot acknowledge what appeared to be real simply because it didn't fit into his or her belief system.

The same dilemma surfaced in Europe at the dark edge of the Middle Ages on a massive, collective scale during the horrendous persecution of witches and heretics. In this case the double-bind was created by the vision of life dictated by a Church dogma. The infernal fires of demonic hysteria were constantly stoked by an Inquisition far more diabolic than any poor wretch they condemned. But somehow we forget that the magnificent churches of the Renaissance, the sudden flowering of such artists as Botticelli, Leonardo da Vinci, and Michelangelo was contemporaneous with the infamous *Malleus Maleficarum*, the Inquisitors' manual of the witch hunts. The weird and ambivalent nature of the whole Renaissance lay in the fact that in one single moment humanism flowered in a world infested with demons. Later, under the Inquisition, that old world attempted to crush the newly found and originally unhampered intellectual development of man and Europe became as tormented as any of the worst scenes of the Inferno to be found on the church walls.

Equally schizophrenic was the stark contrast between the priests' condemnation of the sins of the flesh and the exuberant celebration of that very same flesh which appeared in the works of art commissioned by the clergy. Popular piety chose the new earthly and earthy imagery, most probably because of a healthy pagan spirit which permeates popular worship and which manages to save most of us from the effects of religious fanaticism.

The Medium is the Messenger

The Church had long controlled virtually all the popular visual media. In many respects the Church took the place, in terms of visual stimulation, of our modern cinemas and television. Today, it is difficult to imagine what a profound effect the fleshy, realistic, angels and demons had upon the collective imagination of Renaissance Florence, Siena, and Venice. Meanwhile in northern Europe the first printed pages were beginning to run off the new printing presses. Early books were liberally illustrated with woodblocks and engravings of the most lurid demonic goings on. And by the late Renaissance these images had multiplied a thousand-fold. And so, tragically, had the torments of the Inquisition.

At first glance it seems an unjustified leap of imagination to blame the passionate outpourings of the artists for the sufferings of innocent witches. But the fascination with the diabolic that was a raging torrent during the late Renaissance was maintained at fever pitch by many of the graphic images circulating at the time. Even in our century, a film like *The Exorcist* brings in its wake a whole series of reports of unaccountable demonic happenings and a wave of exorcisms. Consider what any image of hell fire and demonic nastiness, found hanging in any church of the time, might do to a less sophisticated mind.

imagery, leaving much of the responsibility for expressing angelic form in the hands of artists. This had an unexpected side effect. The calling of the artist at the time of the Renaissance was to quite literally explore the world through a new perspective. The painters and sculptors of this unique era were a vanguard who challenged all the time honored ways of perceiving life, time and space long before the philosophers and theologians ever got around to it. By the time the Church recognized that the earthy, solid and realistic images which had appeared on their walls were instrumental in bringing down the old traditional order, it was too late.

Previous page: **Adoration of the Magi**, *detail from a painting by Ghirlandaio, 1485.*

Above: **Virgin and Child** *on the left by Lorenzo Monaco, 1416, and on the right by Hans Memline in 1490. Although only seven decades separate these two works, we can see how the infant Christ has been transformed from being a purely spiritual embodiment of the flesh, as sexless as any of the angelic host, to a realistic and male, human child.*

So it is relevant to ask ourselves, today, to what extent do our present visions and ideas, of both the light and the dark angels, depend upon all the visual and literary imaginings of the past? To attempt an answer to this question, let's return to the original equation of "believing = seeing." We'll demonstrate the power of this equation by examining the unfolding visual evolution of the Angel from the 7th century until its culminating expression during the late Renaissance, which has come down to us almost untouched by the intervening five centuries. Interestingly enough, while the outward appearance of the whole angelic species has hardly changed since 1450, it was in this very epoch that they underwent their greatest inner transformation.

Angels in Perspective

The second council of Nicaea in the year 787 decreed that it was lawful to depict angels in both paintings and sculpture. This decision of the early Church altered the entire evolution of Christian

Yet if we look back to the 8th century, when the original foundations of the angelic host were being laid down, we discover that the original inspirational sources were not Christian at all but Pagan. The two major and available images which caught the fancy of the artists of the time were the classic Greek examples of Nike, the Winged Victory, and the various renderings of the winged Eros. It is fitting that Eros as Love, or the later Roman version, Cupid, should form the image of the later angels of mercy and love. Curious, too, is the link between Venus with Cupid on her lap and the image of the Virgin Mary with Jesus on her lap. It took another six centuries before the Greek influence was again to find new winds for its flame in the Renaissance as angels lost much of their numinous and ethereal quality to become more fleshy and down-to-earth embodiments of the spirit.

The Renaissance was packed jam full of paradoxes. One which quickly becomes apparent is that the less substantial angels became in the eyes of the theologians and humanitarian thinkers the more solid and real they were when appearing on church walls. So much so that in Michelangelo's great masterpiece of the Last Judgment in the Sistine chapel their wings have disappeared altogether. But Michelangelo was far ahead of his times in convincingly clothing his angelic host in the flesh. The Church was unconvinced that angels were sexual and that the male phallus was redeemable. The clergy still hotly denied that angels had anything between their

The Annunciation, *detail from the painting by Leonardo da Vinci.* Inset: **Gabriel** *by Jacopo Bellini, Brescia.* Only twenty years separate these works yet the Leonardo is revolutionary by comparison with the earlier work. There is a new sense of spacious perspective.

Top: **Kairos of Tragir,** *300 B.C.* This winged God of Luck or Coincidence, who predates any Christian depiction by over one thousand years, holds the scales of chance on a razor's edge. Above: **Demon,** *an Etruscan tomb painting 500 B.C.* Long before the Christian Church decreed that it was lawful to depict images of angels, paintings such as this, were appearing on the walls of the tombs of Tuscany.

thighs at all. Playing safe, the Curia had all sex removed from the Sistine's naked figures by painting little bits of blue to conceal what was underneath. We can hardly blame them, for quite clearly these angels were revolutionary. They were of flesh and blood and real like us which should have made the authorities even more suspicious than they were.

But such ideas even find an echo in our our enlightened century. The novelist D.H. Lawrence was understandably outraged when his own exhibition of nude paintings was closed down by the police in England. He vented his frustration in verse.

"Fig trees don't grow in my native land,
There's never a fig leaf near at hand
when I want one. So I did without.
And that's what all the row's about."

The solution was as unacceptable to a rebel like Lawrence as it was to Michelangelo, and he wrily adds,

"A fig leaf, or if you cannot find it,
a wreath of English mist with nothing
behind it!"

Even so the ecclesiastic horror of the flesh was subtly being eroded by the new humanistic atmosphere of the 15th century. As the insubstantial angelic host and the complex hierarchies of heaven were seriously challenged by the new philosophers, even the infant Christ was assuming a very real human flesh on the canvases.

As Christ became more identified with the suffering of human beings in the midst of the Black Death, he became more a real Man. It took theologians another century to see that Christ needed no hierarchy of angels to back him up. He was enough unto himself as a human being. Artists had felt this more immediately and by the end of the plague were even giving him a real sex. Up until this point Christ had appeared as primly androgynous as any

of the angelic host. He now appears in portraits with the Virgin Mother, sporting a proud little penis. Only fifty years before such ideas would never have been permitted for the highest ideal in those times was to be as sexless as the angels. And that had included the Savior and the fanatic Christian saints and hermits.

Top: **Nemesis,** *votif relief at Brindisi, 300 A. D.* The Greeks understood this Queen of Heaven as Fate. Winged victories attend her.

Below: **Nike,** *450 B.C.* Victory makes all things obey her tune on the lyre and the sculpture from Samothrace on the right is one of the pagan images which had the greatest impact and influence upon the later painters of angels.

Eros Restored

During this extraordinary period in Europe, and especially in the courts of the new trading and banking Princes, as exemplified by the Medicis of Florence, the Church and the secular powers came to an uneasy truce over the new republican and humanitarian ideas. In works of art for the courts, interest in angels gave way to a fascination with classical heroes and Gods. The old pagans once again were restored to their place on the walls replacing the angelic host who had somehow got lost. Eros reappeared as if a cycle was complete. By then the form of the angel which had been based on these pagan originals was fixed in the popular imagination. Since the Renaissance the continuing evolution of the angel has simply and abruptly been arrested. It is as if specimens have been inadvertently sealed up forever at the peak of their power in an eternal golden age. Seldom has an entire species been wiped out at the height of its youthful glory. But perhaps only the good angels die beautiful. And that is a lot more than can be said of the bad ones who managed to live on, consuming the fearful attention of the whole of Europe for at least another two centuries.

Dark Shadows on the Wall

The fascination and belief in the devil and his hordes long outlasted any corresponding belief in angels. In the demonic atmosphere of Europe it was a matter of survival. There were too many instances of what could happen to anyone who claimed to have met with an angel. When even a national heroine like Joan of Arc was burnt at the stake by the Inquisition for having claimed that she had seen the Archangel Gabriel, what chance had any normal citizen. Even if someone actually encountered a Son of Light few would have had the courage or stupidity to admit it. No one could ever be quite sure that it wasn't a devil in disguise. However, you could be sure that the Inquisition would know. And who better equipped to recognize the Enemy? So it is hardly a wonder that angels got a very bad reputation. At least the devil you know is better than an angel you don't.

The early renderings of both the devil and his demons were meant to be expressions of the monstrous. Lucifer, who was once the most beautiful angel in heaven, had to become his own antithesis in hell. While good angels had been modeled upon the Greek Eros, or Love, the devil took his shape from Pan, the God of nature and the wilderness, of fertility and above all of lust. As we watch the evolution of the Devil's image, this wild goat God is never far from the surface. As soon as Pan had been re-established on the Renaissance palace walls, the shape of the devil correspondingly changed until he became the suave and urbane Mephistopheles in the drama of Faust.

Adoration of the Shepherds, *detail from a Triptych by H. Van der Goes, Uffizi*. This northern vision depicts the angels as being the "little people," who seem far more like the celtic faeries than their substantial Mediterranean counterparts. The northern el-f, like the ang-el, derives from the original root word meaning a shining one. The faerie Queen described her realm as "the land of the ever-living, a place where there is neither death, nor sin, nor transgression," which could equally describe Heaven. Celtic Christians claimed the fairies were offspring of the fallen angels.

These four images of the Archangel Gabriel span thirty-five years. The one above, on the left, is by *Lorenzo Monaco* and was completed in 1420. Here, Gabriel is seen to luminously float against a solid golden background. The figure is delicately modeled but seems ethereal and insubstantial. The decorative wings remain essentially two dimensional. Fifteen years later the Gabriel of *Fra Angelico* is placed in an enclosed almost cage-like setting. Both the figure and its robe have taken on a more substantial appearance, although the wings remain a little flat and awkward, as if belonging to the earlier epoch.

Masolino, painting around the same time (1435), gives a soft, full roundness to the figure by the use of a subtle play of light and shadow. In the last painting by *Piero della Francesca*, in 1455, we find Gabriel's transformation into a real being of flesh and blood, firmly kneeling on the ground, as if gravity has at last anchored the spirit. The luminous angel of light now has a face almost hidden in shadows. Clothed in the flesh, the angel obeys the laws of the material world. The inner illumination can no longer be seen for the angel has become like man.

1420

1432

The Angel comes to Ground

The persuasive visual fantasies of the Renaissance artists have largely shaped our internal ideas of what the devil or the angel looks like. For instance, in the early painting on this page, by Lorenzo Monaco, Gabriel is both luminous and numinous. The painting of the Archangel expresses an unearthly and mystical being. The original, solid gold background against which the angel floats, symbolizes the Light;

the natural spiritual home of the angel. By the time Piero della Francesca created Gabriel, the Archangel has become a creature of flesh and blood, kneeling in a setting of solid and substantial architecture. Even the face is obscured and darkened by shadows cast by natural, earthly light. She is no longer illuminated from within by the supernatural light of the Divine flame and is a long way from being the original "fiery, flying serpent of Love." Likewise, in the last picture of the evolutionary sequence on

1435

1455

page 167, all the unique signs which symbolize angelic illumination, including the halo, are gone. We are left with a human being, essentially no different from the figure of the Virgin: that is save for the wings. Could it be that artists of that era instinctively felt the transformation of the angelic host long before philosophers, reformists and theologians began to challenge the old orthodox beliefs in the Heavenly Hierarchy? Or are we back to the original equation of seeing is believing? For it must be remembered that these images inspired an entirely new way of envisioning space, time and matter and the natural laws of the Cosmos. As this, of course, also included the angels, they had to become human-like in order to fit the new belief in a Supreme Law of Nature.

Yet if seeing is believing then what of believing is seeing? To understand how we begin to only see what we believe it is necessary to expose that what we all accept as real might be nothing more than the effect of an artistic device; perspective. Perspective is actually an illusory visual trick to make the observer believe he or she is looking through a window upon a scene which has an imaginary vanishing point on the horizon. It is cetainly one way of looking at the world but is very limiting. Most of our everyday world is made up of a mosaic of constantly changing and moving images. But the painters of the Renaissance offered a static and unchanging viewpoint which was a play of light and shadow giving the illusion of an arrested moment of time. Our present day cameras are no more than a mechanical version of this principle. We have been conditioned to this way of seeing by a constant barrage of images which surround us today, often forgetting that when we see a picture of a movie star or actually watch a movie the images are only light reflecting from a flat surface, giving an illusion of a live person. Many fresco painters of the late Renaissance attempted to trick the observer into thinking there were real windows with scenes behind them when in fact they were looking at a wall or a ceiling. Trompe l'oeil, or "deception of the eye," became a rage in many courts. The same principle holds with the images of angels which we collectively share today. As we look at a photograph of our beloved and she or he seems to be staring back at us, it is difficult to make the visual jump and just see the piece of photographic paper as just a collection of colors on a flat surface. Internally we all have the same problem when visualizing an angel. The Renaissance artist did us the questionable favor of making them "real" and bring the original fiery messengers of Light and Love, down to earth.

A Question of Wings

From the latter part of the Renaissance until today artists and their patrons gradually lost interest in angels, save for the chubby, little cherubs so useful to decorate the odd empty corner or ceiling. But during the 12th to the 15th centuries angels appeared everywhere. For those artists who were thrilled with the challenge of representing these powerful winged messengers of God the dilemma was to fit wings onto the bodies of human-like angels and yet still give the impression that the mechanics of actual flight were possible.

Largely speaking, the wings chosen to be most befitting for an angelic body were of course modeled upon the largest and most beautiful birds which were available to the artists for study. Thus it was that the wings of swans, eagles and geese that adorned the shoulders of the celestial bodies in the great masterpieces of Leonardo, Botticelli and Caravaggio. The hideous denizens of the abyss, by contrast,

were given the wings of reptiles or bats, these being associated with the dragon, the serpent or unknown and fearful creatures of the night.

The Renaissance artists, in their attempt to create a feasible connection between the human form and wings, used as their models the winged figures of Hellenic Greece. If we examine the anatomical reality of welding wings to the earthly form, we find that none of these renderings could possibly fly, yet somehow we have all suspended our disbelief in accepting their possible reality.

The visual trick which has been offered is that they *look* real and yet, without divine and supernatural intervention profoundly adjusting the laws of gravity, we all intuit that these beings could never lift off the ground.

Above: **Creation of Adam,** *detail from The Last Judgment by Michelangelo.* In many ways artists became God-like in their creation of angels. In the artistic evolution of the angelic form pictured below, we see the complete transformation from 1315 to 1515. While the 12th century angels appear plausible due to the symbolic nature of the paintings, the later, more realistic versions suffered, inevitably, from the awkward feeling that their tiny wings could never lift a real body to the sky. One of the drawbacks of the new perspective was that in order

objects obeying natural and mathematical laws of space, light and gravity. Shadows are cast and color depends upon reflected light in contrast to the earlier paintings which seemed to have an internal light and color of their own. Angels who entered within the new framework had to abide by the very same laws. They cast shadows, they had weight and form and were illuminated by natural earthly light. In fact, they looked exactly the same as humans, except for their wings. Michelangelo even dispenses with these, preferring a whirlwind of figures and billowing drapes. This naturalism coincided with the rise of the new humanistic philosophies and the early proto-sciences. Belief in a universe which was moved by angels gave way to a cosmos which ran like a Divine clock mechanism. The Book of Nature supplanted the Book of the Angel. More than anything else, it was the paintings which anchored the celestial host so firmly to the ground; so firmly, that the tiny wings the artists gave them could no longer return them to the heavens.

for the scene to visually work, the artist had to suggest that the observer was looking through a window frame without being able to move his or her head. This "single view-pointed" vision of the world is the one we have inherited in the camera images which surround us today. However, in the mid 14th century this was a revolutionary step. It laid the ground for the later objective sciences and continued up until the middle of this century as our major perspective of the world. Such an image gives the impression of a moment, frozen in time, with

It'll never Fly!

Just suppose for a moment that the earthy-looking angel of Caravaggio on this page, which is one of the prototypes of the most popular versions appearing in our times, actually does manifest as a real being of flesh and bone with normal human reactions to the force of gravity. In fact, there is at least one incontrovertible reference in the Bible suggesting that angels do take on the full gravity of humans. Jacob wrestled with an angel all night in what seems to have been a close fight. When the angel saw "that he had not prevailed over him, then he touched the socket of his thigh joint; and the socket of Jacob's thigh got out of place during his grappling with him" (GEN 33:25). This is hardly the act of an insubstantial and weightless wimp pitted against a strong desert man!

So if angels did, on occasion, weigh in about 200lb., what would the size of their wings have to be in order to lift such a mass from the ground or allow them to hover in the air?

The largest birds on earth, like the white pelican or the mute swan, have a weight of about 25 to 30lb. They need a wingspan of about 13 feet to lift this bulk. The record for an efficient lift amongst the large birds is held by the Canadian goose which lifts about 4lb. for every square foot of wing. Most birds, however, manage little more than half a pound for every square foot of lifting feathers.

If we calculate an average lift power it will be found that a tall angel, having a full earthly weight of about 200 lb., would need a wing span of anything from 36 feet [12 meters] to 120 feet [40 meters]. This roughly corresponds to the size of a modern hang-glider, although those types of wings can only be used for gliding and soaring. It does indicate that the modest Renaissance wings have more than a flutter of poetic license.

Yet it is strangely such models as these which constitute our present-day hazy ideas of how an angel should be.

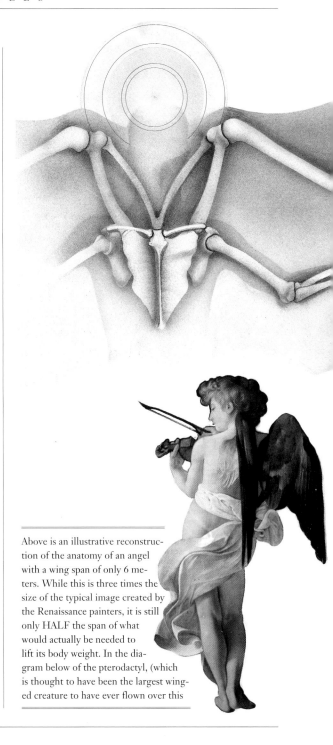

Above is an illustrative reconstruction of the anatomy of an angel with a wing span of only 6 meters. While this is three times the size of the typical image created by the Renaissance painters, it is still only HALF the span of what would actually be needed to lift its body weight. In the diagram below of the pterodactyl, (which is thought to have been the largest winged creature to have ever flown over this

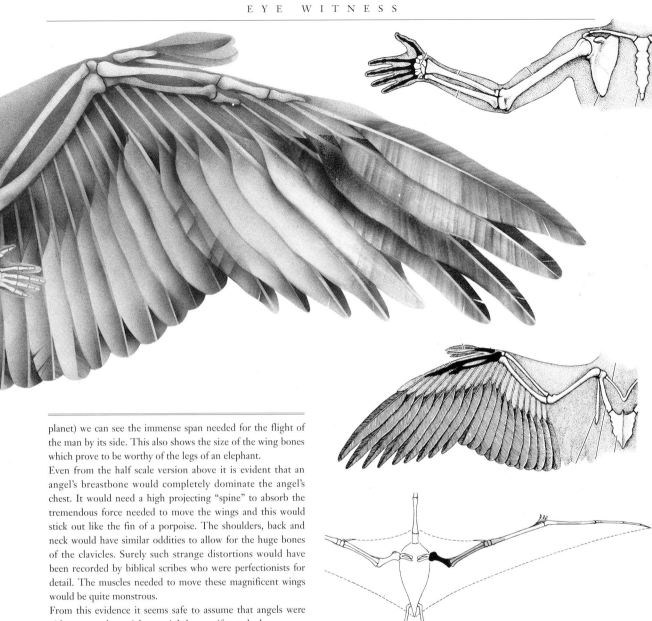

planet) we can see the immense span needed for the flight of the man by its side. This also shows the size of the wing bones which prove to be worthy of the legs of an elephant.

Even from the half scale version above it is evident that an angel's breastbone would completely dominate the angel's chest. It would need a high projecting "spine" to absorb the tremendous force needed to move the wings and this would stick out like the fin of a porpoise. The shoulders, back and neck would have similar oddities to allow for the huge bones of the clavicles. Surely such strange distortions would have been recorded by biblical scribes who were perfectionists for detail. The muscles needed to move these magnificent wings would be quite monstrous.

From this evidence it seems safe to assume that angels were either non-substantial or weightless or if not, had some un-known divine dispensation. If they actually obeyed the laws of gravity they would have been quite monstrous.

However beautiful, fascinating or real the images seem, like that on the left by *Caravaggio*, the angelic fictions by artists of the Renaissance must be considered amongst the most fanciful flights of imagination ever conceived.

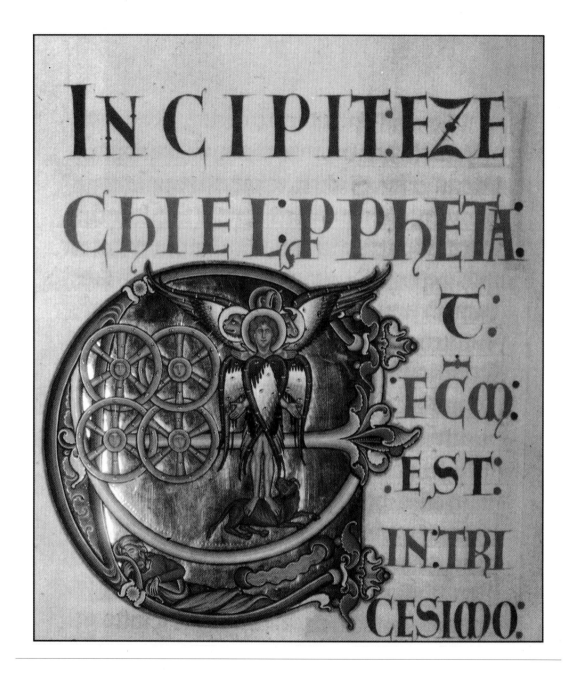

CHAPTER TWO

Ancient Encounters of a Luminous Kind

SO FAR WE STILL DON'T KNOW whether angels are ethereal beings of light without substance or if they take a solid human form with real wings which actually enable them to fly. Just how many people have actually had a close enough encounter with one to be able to tell us?

When my own grandmother was dying she became ecstatic on seeing angels awaiting her on the 'other shore.' Yet in that moment of supreme truth her detailed descriptions of the divine beings surrounding the deathbed had, even to my mind as a small child, a suspicious resemblance to one of her favorite Victorian Pre-Raphaelite paintings.

But who is in a position to judge whether her vision was real or not? Most visions of angels do seem to come when the witness is in a near death state or has an out of body experience on the so called astral plane. And who is to say that Gabriel or Michael don't resemble the sentimental renderings of a Burne-Jones or the earthiness of a Caravaggio? Maybe, in order not to alarm anyone by appearing in their true form (or formlessness), they assume the contemporary and fashionable ideals of the day. On the other hand artists could be privy to visions of worlds which are denied to the less sensitive among us.

In this century only the vaguest theories have been advanced as to the nature of angels. The official Church stance that angels are "insubstantial and spiritual" hardly constitutes a substantial theory. There are suggestions that angels might have something to do with electro-magnetism, collective hallucinations or morphological memory fields. When all else fails we can always fall back upon lumping the whole phenomenon under the heading, para-normal. Yet as we have seen in Part I, angels and devils have had, in earlier centuries, just as much a reality as the equally ethereal and invisible atoms and particles of our present technologies. Some prominent psychics and channellers of today go as far as to claim that it is we who are are the angels. It is both a comfortable and persuasive idea that we are beings of light and energy who have just forgotten our real identity. It is suggested that many of our dream images or near death experiences are actually glimpses of our true light nature when free of the restrictions of the body and of earth's gravitational forces. We will shortly explore such possibilities as angels being collective archetypes or reflections of our astral bodies of light, as the creators of the universe, messengers of God, spirit guides and even as extra-terrestrials. But before embarking on these delightful higher realms of speculation let us come to earth with some real hard facts and substantial evidence.

Witness for the Defense

Any cross-examination of witnesses who have claimed to have encountered an angel is impossible today because most of the most famous witnesses are dead. And as the entire case of whether angels exist or not rests with first hand accounts, the case for the reality of an angelic host rests on decidedly shaky foundations. It has already been seen that it is impossible to separate the witnessed from the witness. And even if it were feasible to establish the unimpeachable character of the observer, we are still left with the vague and confusing nature of the reports themselves. The dilemma facing any witness, and one common to all the records, is that the words used to describe the indescribable are obviously inadequate. Almost invariably the encounter is so overwhelming, being completely outside of any normal experience, that all the observer could do is to describe it in terms of *something else*. The phrase "has the appearance of…" all too frequently occurs. So, what might well have appeared as a radiating glow of light became "like wings of Fire." An unfamiliar style of boot is expressed as "feet like unto burnished gold." This poetic form of speaking and writing in symbols, metaphors and analogies, of course leaves a completely open field of speculation, which more often than not is exaggeratedly sensational in form.

As a demonstration of the pitfalls and difficulties likely to be encountered in building up a lucid image of what an angel might be, let us look at a classic encounter. We have already been introduced to part of the most spectacular account ever recorded of a meeting with an angelic presence in the Treasury. This is the one which has stirred the popular imagination the most. In it the ancient Hebrew prophet Ezekiel is transported from Chaldea to Jerusalem and back in an "aerial chariot of God," operated by angels.

Encounter with a Hebrew Angel

EZEKIEL 1:4

And I began to see, and look! There was a tempestuous wind coming from the north, a great cloud mass and quivering fire, and it had a brightness all around, and out of the midst of it there was something like the look of electrum, out of the midst of the fire.

5: And out of the midst of it there was a likeness of four living creatures, and this is how they looked: they had the likeness of earthling man.

6: And [each] one had four faces, and each one of them had four wings.

7: And their feet were straight feet, and the sole of their feet was like the sole of the foot of a calf; and they were gleaming as with the glow of burnished copper.

8: And there were the hands of a man under their wings on their four sides, and the four of them had their faces and their wings.

9: Their wings were joining one to the other. They would not turn when they went; they would go each one straight forward.

10: And as for the likeness of their faces, the four of them had a man's face with a lion's face to the right, and the four of them had a bull's face on the left; the four of them also had an eagle's face.

11: That is the way their faces were. And their wings were spreading out upward. Each one had two joining to each other, and two were covering their bodies.

12: And they would go each one straight forward. To wherever the spirit would incline to go, they would go. They would not turn as they went.

13: And as for the likeness of the living creatures, their appearance was like burning coals of fire. Something like the appearance of torches was moving back and forth between the living creatures, and the fire was bright, and out of the fire there was lightning going forth.

14: And on the part of the living creatures there was a going forth and a returning as with the appearance of the lightning.

15: As I kept seeing the living creatures, why look! There was one wheel on the earth beside the living creatures, by the four faces of each.

16: As for the appearance of the wheels and their structure, it was like the glow of chrysolite; and the four of them had one likeness. And their appearance and their structure were just as when a wheel proved to be in the midst of a wheel.

17: When they went they would go on their four respective sides. They would not turn another way when they went.

18: And as for their rims, they had such height that they caused fearfulness; and their rims were full of eyes all around the four of them.

19: And when the living creatures went, the wheels would go beside them, and when the living creatures were lifted up from the earth, the wheels would be lifted up.

20: Wherever the spirit inclined to go, they would go, the spirit [inclining] to go there; and the wheels themselves would be lifted up close alongside them, for the spirit of the living creatures was in the wheels.

21: When they went, these would go; when they stood still, these would stand still; and when they were lifted up from the earth, the wheels would be lifted up close alongside them, for the spirit of the living creature was in those wheels.

22: And over the heads of the living creatures there was the likeness of an expanse like the sparkle of awesome ice, stretched out over their heads up above.

23: And under the expanse their wings were straight, one to the other. Each had two wings covering on this side and one had two wings covering on that side their bodies.

24: And I got to hear the sound of their wings, a sound like that of vast waters, like the sound of the Almighty one, when they went, the sound of a tumult, like the sound of an encampment. When they stood still, they would let their wings down.

25: And there came to be a voice above the expanse that was over their head.

26: And above the expanse that was over their head there was something in appearance like sapphire stone, the likeness of a throne. And upon the likeness of a throne there was a likeness of someone in appearance like an earthling man upon it, up above.

27: And I got to see something like the glow of electrum, like the appearance of fire all around inside thereof, from the appearance of his hips and upward; and from the appearance of his hips and

downward I saw something like the appearance of fire, and he had a brightness all around.

28: There was something like the appearance of the bow that occurs in a cloud mass on the day of pouring rain. That is how the appearance was of the brightness round about."

Ezekiel was not the only witness of the biblical world to meet such wheeled vehicles, with their accompanying pillars of cloud and light, with an angel at the helm. Elijah also ascended in a fiery chariot and was gathered up "in a windstorm to the hea-

had access to technologies superior to those of the local tribes, or that they were a different human type. What is to be made of this description for instance? "...two very tall men different from any that I have seen in the Lowlands. Their faces shone like the sun and their eyes burned like lamps."

This quote is from the Chronicles of Enoch. This was a document copied or compiled from material believed to be some eight thousand years old. Even five thousand years after this meeting these mysterious peoples were still around if the account

vens" (2 KINGS 2:11). Enoch sees a luminous cloud: "and a mist summoned me, and the course of the stars and the lightning sped by me, and the winds caused me to fly and be lifted upward and bore me to heaven" (EN:XIV 8VB).

by the prophet Daniel is anything to go by. (Dan 10:4-6) "A man dressed in linen, with a girdle of pure gold round his waist; his face shone like lightning, his eyes were like fiery torches, his arms and legs had the gleam of burnished bronze, the sound of his voice was like the noise of a crowd."

The Shining Serpents

There were other encounters like that of the prophet Isaiah which bear remarkable similarities to the experience of Ezekiel. In fact so closely do some of the descriptions tally that we might even be tempted to imagine there really were people living in the biblical lands who did exhibit bizarre differences in appearance to the indigenous peoples of the area. Perhaps there were beings who were definitely taller, and who possessed a strange luminosity about their faces, especially around their eyes. It is not such a wild speculation as one might at first think to suppose they

Left: The Vision of John, *from the Apocalypse of Liebana*. The four compass points correspond to the four flags of the tribes of Israel. The Bull, the Eagle, the Lion and the Man. Originally these were in the multiple form of the winged temple guardians of the Sumerians and Assyrians. They appear in the vision of Ezekiel as the four headed aspect of the Cherubim. Later these were to become the symbols of the four Evangelists; Matthew as Man, Mark as the Lion, Luke as the Bull and John as the Eagle. These can be seen on the following pages from the Irish, *Book of Kells* and in the Christ of the Apocalypse from *Chartres Cathedral*.

In Chapter Five we will find that some researchers have gone so far as to suggest that these were the first great cultivators who lived in the highlands of Lebanon, located to the east of the modern town of Ehdin (Eden?). In a number of Sumerian and Babylonian tablets these peoples were specifically described as Shining or Radiant Ones or, more curiously as Serpents. It would certainly explain the origins of the later Chaldean seraphs who were the fiery, flying, lightning serpents. Obviously there were some very mysterious angelic goings on in the Middle East at that time, and it is unwise to dismiss even the most outlandish proposals as to what they might have been.

Illuminating Speculations

Of course, such fascinating passages can be interpreted in some pretty bizarre ways. There have been claims that Ezekiel actually saw an Adamran helicopter with an ancient luminous priest at the helm; that his was just one amongst many meetings with flying saucers whose glowing occupants were from another galaxy. More ingenuous is the 16th century illustration on this page which shows a literal bed of coals underneath a typical papal ceremonial throne. But perhaps higher technologies from Atlantis or the stars did exist six thousand years ago and the original angel was in fact an extra-terrestrial being. In any event, it might be instructive to imagine how

a primitive mind would attempt to describe the sight of an illuminated helicopter from our century. Any advanced technology need not have been that advanced to impress men like Enoch, Elijah or Ezekiel.

On examining the original Bible text, with its deeply evocative imagery, it is understandable that there have been so many seemingly plausible speculations as to what Ezekiel or other biblical witnesses actually saw. Some of these "scientific" explanations make those of the very unscientific world of esoteric symbolism and mysticism seem almost solid ground by comparison.

The alchemical symbolism of the Kabbalah and early Christian writing on the occult curiously offers a pragmatic interpretation of what the prophets really were indicating. According to such symbolism, the wheels supporting the throne represent the orbiting planets, while the whole chariot is the solar system. The four headed aspect of the angel is seen as the four directions of the compass. We find surprising historical evidence to support this view. When the twelve tribes of Israel encamped in the wilderness, the banners of Reuben (Man), Judah (Lion), Ephraim (Bull), and Dan (Eagle) were placed at the four corners. The encampment itself was a representation of the universe and this is clearly seen in the Rosicrucian illustration on this page.

Ezekiel himself would have been familiar with such concepts and would know that his readers knew the symbolism as well. And so his elaborate description of what at first appears to be an actual phe-nomenon could in reality have been a daring piece of symbo-lism which contained hidden meanings for the initiates. So in reconstructing the image of such an angel we have to be extremely wary of jumping to sensational conclusions too soon. The sub-ject, as we have already seen, is spectacular enough in itself.

The Christian Angel

The preceding texts were of course Hebrew accounts of Jewish angels as recorded over two thousand years be-fore Christ. Just over twelve hundred years after his death there is a new report. "On a certain morning about the feast of the Exaltation of the Cross, while Francis was praying on the mountainside, he saw a Seraph with six fiery and shining wings descend from the height of heaven. And when in swift flight the Seraph had reached the spot in the air near the man of God, there appeared between the wings the figure of a man crucified, with his hands and feet extended in the form of a cross and fastened to a cross." Here we have the highest angelic order, the seraphim, assuming the body of Christ rather than taking on normal human form. This signifies an en-tirely new angelic concept, for it implies that a man like Francis, who, at the time of this vision, receives the stigmata of Christ, can also be transformed into Christ Consciousness. St. Francis appears to have been one of the few enlightened beings who became a realized consciousness within the fra-mework of Christianity. He would have probably

felt far more at home in India where his liberation would have been instantly re-cognized. The Christian tradi-tion, according to most Eastern mystics, stops short at the stage of the saint. But on a spiritual ladder the saint is at the fourth level with three rungs still to climb to being one with the Divine Source. According to the same seers, angels are disembo-died spirits at the same level as the saint. So the great tran-sformation of Francis is one which soars high above his an-gelic peers. This was ac-tually the great turning point, when human-like angels became angel-like humans. This theme will be explored in the last chapter.

St. Teresa of Avila has a similar and parallel expe-rience three centuries later. "It pleased the Lord that I should sometimes see the following vision. I would see beside me, on my left hand, an angel in bodily form – a type of vision which I am not in the habit of seeing, except very rarely. Though I often see repre-sentations of angels, my visions of them are of the type which I first mentioned. It pleased the Lord that I should see this angel in the following way. He was not tall, but short, and very beautiful, his face so aflame that he appeared to be one of the highest types of angel who seem to be all afire. They must be those who are called cherubim: they do not tell me their names but I am well aware that there is a great difference between certain angels and others, and between these and others still, of a kind that I could not possibly explain. In his hands I saw a long golden spear and at the end of the iron tip I seemed to see a point of fire. With this he seemed to pierce my heart several times so that it penetrated to my entrails. When he drew it out, I thought he was drawing them out with it, and he left me completely afire with a great love of God. The pain was so sharp that it made me utter several moans; and so excessive was the sweetness caused me by this intense pain that one

can never wish to lose it, nor will one's soul be content with anything less than God. It is not bodily pain, but spiritual, though the body has a share in it – indeed a great share. So sweet are the colloquies of love which pass between the soul and God that if anyone thinks I am lying I beseech God, in His Goodness, to give him the same experience."

Amen!

Ecstasy of St. Teresa by Bernini, 1650

Angels, Hot and Cold

For all of their power and poetry, it can be seen that few of these reports could claim to be the best of the witness accounts. It can be argued that this hardly amounts to evidence at all. One might reasonably wonder how on earth with such slim pickings as these that the whole galaxy of angels managed to remain a Christian corner stone. It is significant that, compared with the handful of first-hand glimpses, which might altogether fill a single small file, the volumes of theoretical treatises upon the heavenly agents could fill a library. The following expansive rhetoric from Gregory of Nazianus, a 4th century Church Father, typifies the theoretical genre. "The angel is then called spirit and fire: spirit, as being a creature of the intellectual sphere; fire, as being of a purifying nature; for I know that the same names belong to the first nature. But, relatively to us at least, we must reckon the angelic nature incorporeal, or at any rate as nearly so as possible. Do you see how we get dizzy over this subject, and cannot advance to any point, unless it be as far as this, that we know there are angels and archangels, thrones, dominions, princedoms, powers, splendors, ascents, intelligent powers or intelligences, pure nature and unalloyed, immovable to evil, or scarcely movable; ever circling in chorus around the first cause (or how should we sing their praises?), illuminated thence with the purest illumination, or one in one degree and one in another proportionally to their nature and rank." Dizzy, yes, but any clearer? Hardly, for here is a classic example of the cool intellectual and *second-hand* knowledge so beloved by scholars. By contrast the first-hand accounts are passionately on fire with love. You can even feel the punch and the power of the episode of the seraph and St. Francis through the writings of his biographer, Bonaventure. A real first hand experience carries its own authentic ring of truth.

Forever Young in Amber

The golden age of angelology was more accurately the amber age of the church scholar. Like Gregory, these men of words created ever more complex yet empty hierarchies of heaven and hell. At the core of this vast kingdom of paper angels lay a dogmatic assumption: that human beings were to be the replacements in Heaven for the fallen angels and that the Church was a reflection of the heavenly hierarchies on earth. Few of these canonical ideas and even fewer angels survived the public exposure of a corrupt clergy. By the 15th century the writings of Dionysius, that ultimate

Ezekiel's Vision, from the 17th century Bear Bible. Kabbalists claim that the prophet's vision was a mystical experience of the hierarchy of the Worlds of Action, Formation, Creation and Emanation. What is now known as the Kabbalah was once called the Work of the Chariot.

authority on the celestial hierarchies, were for the first time seriously challenged as being a fraud, while at the same time a deep rift appeared to cleave the Church as two opposing and equally infallible popes tried to lead the faithful flock, one from Rome and the other from Avignon in France. Any angels remaining in heaven after such a debacle of their "mirror-image" on earth were finally wiped out by the Black Death, which effectively also halved the human population of Europe. It was as if the plague struck at the very heart of these winged beings. Yet outwardly they were struck down at the very height of their powers in the golden age of the hierarchs. It was as if a cosmic pustule, a volcanic Vesuvius had erupted over a heavenly Pompei, encapsulating a whole age of angels under its black and deadly fallout. Angels never recovered from the blow of the plague. They were caught in an everlasting golden youth and have since then remained forever young. On the other hand the Dark, fallen angels and demons had acquired sturdy immune systems, doubtlessly due to their long association with corrupt humankind. Angels had no such resistance to the deadly virus.

The Aftermath

By the beginning of the 15th century when the worst ravages of the plague had passed, only art and popular piety with its strong pagan undercurrents really kept up the pretense that a host still existed in heaven. Theologians were already turning to the concept that Christ was enough and did not need vast legions of immaterial spirits behind him (who were for the most part Jewish anyway). The whole hierarchy of heaven had been so tainted with the corruption of the priesthood that when the apocalyptic plague descended few were surprised that ministering angels were nowhere to be found. But their absence and obvious impotence in the face of this terrible scourge was duly noted by the despondent survivors. The Church, in desperation, dropped any effort to defend their old winged allies. They quickly employed a diversionary tactic through the militant Inquisition and eagerly turned to attack the devil instead. And even if they couldn't actually tweak his tail they could destroy his fleshly handmaidens, the witches.

Where Did They Go?

But angels are supposed to be immortal, so even if the plague did claim them as victims they couldn't actually have died. So if they emptied the old mansions of Heaven where did they go? And where are they now?

Before answering this it will be helpful to examine the dossier of a modern encounter with a superior messenger from another world which might offer some clue as to their possible whereabouts.

CHAPTER THREE

Modern Encounters

Some Christian Writers have speculated that UFOs could well be a part of God's angelic host who preside over the physical affairs of universal creation...UFOs are astonishingly angel-like in some of their reported appearances."

Here is the voice of the popular evangelist Billy Graham in his book *Angels. God's Secret Agents* Although he may speak for many Americans it is not the only Christian view. Stuart Campbell, who seems to be of a more fundamentalist persuasion and who has the reputation of seeing fire and brimstone in the nakedness of a daisy, holds the opposite opinion. "The devil's angels...are calling themselves visitors from space today," he preaches, ominously adding: "The appearance of UFOs in our skies means the devil

is intensifying his satanic campaign against the good." We can all be grateful that he offers absolutely no evidence to support his claim. But neither does the more optimistic Billy Graham. Some writers even suggest that there are both angelic and satanic beings behind the helms of their flying chariots and that our skies will see the final apocalyptic battle between the forces of good and the hordes of evil by the end of this millennium. You can, of course, choose whichever scenario takes your fancy, but that germ, or seed

of an idea – that ETs are the new manifestations of angels or demons – is a very popular one. It fits very snugly with those who believe that earth has been visited by space travelers many times before throughout our history. It is equally acceptable to those who feel that angels assume the cultural or mythic form most acceptable for any particular era or milieu.

It becomes really fascinating, when comparing the angelic and the alien form, to find so many correspondences and similarities between the two phenomena.

The following list shows just a few of these.

1) Both angels and aliens are "Other Worldly" beings, whether they exist in inner or outer space.

2) They are superior entities who are either at a higher stage of development, being morally, spiritually or technologically superior, or are simply closer to the Deity.

3) The benevolent variety usually appear as the ultimate perfection of harmonious and youthful beauty. The vaguely androgynous nature of their appearance suggests a union of the male and female principles. However, it has to be admitted from the evidence of the ET reports that North American male witnesses tend to see more clearly defined and ravishing female aliens than their Russian, Euro-

pean and South American counterparts.

4) Both ETs and angels are clearly formidable linguists, speaking perfect English, German, French, Spanish, Russian, Dutch or Italian whenever necessary.

5) They all have a message to deliver. If there is any particular tendency to be observed, then angels do seem more inclined to the individual transfer of information, while the ET has a more global message. However, both usually have specifically chosen the witness in order to impart the word.

6) Both have remarkable means of aerial transportation, although there are very few reports of ETs with wings and these have to be filed away amongst the more suspect of accounts. However, both are known to use disks, wheels or saucers of light as their major mode of movement.

7) Both are beings of light. They seem to share a numinous, luminous essence which is most pronounced in their eyes which often glow with a brilliance that almost suggests rays; and in their faces which are said to shine.

8) They appear to radiate subtle auras of compassion, goodness, kindliness and a sense of peaceful harmony.

9) There is a remarkable similarity in their dress. Close fitting tunics or long flowing robes with a predominance of blue and white. Usually there is either a girdle of gold or bracelets, wristbands and rings of the same precious materials. It is actually a little curious that these beings always appear to the witnesses fully clothed. Surely only man, having sinned, found his nakedness evil. In this respect only the fallen angels would feel the need to wear clothes at all. Surely some ETs might find their nakedness beautiful in the sight of whichever Almighty they believed in.

10) Their height is usually given as human-sized, although there are a few cases which give the height as much as 8 feet.

11) Both aliens and angels show considerable concern at the state of man and the planet upon which we live. Invariably the general direction in which the peoples of earth are heading appears to cause alarm and concern. Oddly this is often attributed, by ET and angel alike, to the devil's work which does suggest that the "Enemy" has a long galactic arm. Otherwise a New Age flavor creeps in, which lays the blame of our behavior on poor attunement to the subtle vibrations of natural harmony. Whatever the detail might be, humans are in great need of the message which the beings have brought.

12) Although both ET and angel alike are impressively superior to any of us, they often talk as if we are equals, brothers or fellow travelers through space and time. However, they are seldom seen as free agents but rather as messengers bound by higher cosmic laws or, in the case of angels, by God.

13) The witness and the witnessed are intimately and inseparably bound together. The evidence is subjective and relies upon our acceptance or rejection of the sincerity and credibility of the beholder. Both the phenomena of angels and ETs rests upon trust, faith and belief.

This list, although in no way comprehensive, gives more than a hint that angels and ETs have a lot in common. This suggests we should be very wary of dismissing the possibility that present day sightings of UFO's or contacts with ETs might be similar phenomena. A comparison of a modern encounter with that of the earlier account by Ezekiel may here be useful.

It is difficult, however, to select one contemporary example which combines most of the typical characteristics of the whole genre. In comparison with the relatively modest number of encounters that can be traced in our ancient portfolio there are, literally, thousands of often convincing, disturbing and inexplicable reports in our times. One account, however, does stand out as being a classic case which fits both the contactee and the more recent abduction phenomenon. While the narrative exemplifies the whole mysterious and bizarre genre of UFOs and Alien meetings it is, at the same time, the record of a unique mystical experience. It managed to catch the shrewd eye of the veteran psychologist, C.G. Jung, who included it within his book on UFOs.

But before embarking upon this account it must be said that, like many who have told such stories before, the witness tells of the whole meeting in good faith and obviously is convinced, even if a skeptic might feel mistakenly, that the whole episode actually occurred. The particular epic chosen to exemplify the whole phenomenon of contactee and abduction drama must surely rank alongside with the angelic encounters of Enoch, Ezekiel or Elijah in powerful imagery. The very similarities suggest an uncanny central source, as if all of them have tapped into the same mythic circuit or have actually encountered the real thing.

If they have encountered the real and substantial angel or ET – or a combination of the two – then there is little left to say except that we should examine the message that they bring with great care. If, however, they have triggered some collective or individual process within the mind, then perhaps we can glimpse a pattern which all of us share and which makes the significance of the phenomenon of

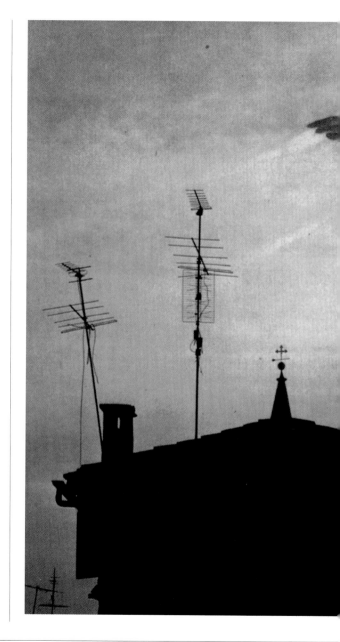

Angel by Sam Haskins.

angelic sightings far more revealing.

Taking this second option allows an examination of this truly remarkable story in terms of what we know about myth and dreams. One could imagine what a treasure trove this tale would be for any psychologist who was listening to his patient recounting it. It is a veritable powerhouse of mythic and archetypical elements. The annotations within the narrative point to the gems, those glistening archetypal jewels which unconsciously we all respond to.

These interpretations are in no way offered as an explanation of the narrators experience. If Angelucci's experience was real, objective and verifiable as a substantial and material phenomenon, it still doesn't invalidate this interpretation as a guide to how we all tend to think and feel within a mythic or archetypal framework.

The Case Study of a Modern Encounter

To start with, the name of the witness comes as an unexpected treasure – *Orfeo Angelucci*. At the outset we are immediately plunged into a mythical world. Center stage stands the modern Orpheus, the legendary Greek hero-poet who enters the "other world" in order to make himself whole through regaining his female part, Eurydice. Angelucci means *Little Angel* but also has overtones of *Angel of Light*. Either way it is difficult for this witness to go wrong. Having established his substantial, magical credentials, we discover on a more pedestrian level that Angelucci was a mechanic, employed by Lockheed Aircraft Corporation at Burbank, California at the time of his early contacts with what became known as the Space Brothers.

He had been working a night shift but had been feeling unwell, having a prickly sensation as if prior to an electrical storm.

Often psychics and mystics experience considerable discomfort before a visionary experience. It is not unusual; that this is expressed in terms of a restless electrical energy as if some static is running up and down the spine. In some cases this can even be the first stirrings of what Eastern Yogis have called the Kundalini or serpent power. Mystics attempt to awaken this through meditation but on occasion it arises spontaneously. If the recipient is unprepared or does not know of its import they can often experience its effect in very bizarre ways. The eastern mystic, Ramakrishna often experienced considerable discomfort before entering some of his ecstatic states.

As he drove home about 1 o'clock in the morning he saw a "red- glowing, oval-shaped object" flying in front of his car. "The object was now so close it seemed to be a master, commanding, almost breathing. There was not a sound from it.

This account is one of those which indicate that Jungs' firm and insistent belief that we use mandalic images to find our way around what seem to be complex or contradicting circumstances, does appear to have more than a grain of truth. The mandala is a circular cyclic and enclosed image which can manifest itself in a variety of images, one of which is of course the circular flying saucer or the flaming wheels described by Elijah or Ezekiel which were interpreted as the Ofarim, or the third order of angelic being. Even more interesting is the account by the modern yogi, Krishna Gopi, when he first awakened the kundalini current we have just mentioned. There were periods when he felt felt exhausted, drained

and depressed: "Whenever I closed my eyes I found myself looking into a weird circle of light, in which luminous currents swirled and eddied.

Orfeo felt impelled to follow the light as it led him off the main highway. It was as if he had become disconnected from the world and only associated with the ethereal object.

"Here we come to the classic moment of transition from one world to another. In Celtic myths the other world existed alongside our own. Yet it was a world of Other Time and to the denizens of that land our universe seemed a shadow world. But Orfeo was well prepared for this concept as he had written a book prior to his encounter entitled "The nature of Infinite Entities" in which he explored the nature of atomic evolution and involution. In myth and legend the hero cannot help but follow his destiny and often appears in a dazed or comatose state as he enters the quest.

Suddenly the red disk shot upwards at a colossal speed, releasing as it did so, two green balls of fire from which came the sound of a "most delightful masculine voice," which, in perfect English, reassured Orfeo that he was not to be afraid.

These cosmic brothers, like their angelic counterparts, do seem advanced enough to distinguish languages for they seldom seem to make any goofs over speaking Russian in California during the McCarthy era of communist witch hunts. For many observers this ability of angel and ET alike to converse in any tongue does stretch our credibility. The official language of angels is Hebrew yet few Americans find it odd that Gabriel or Michael can speak like a native when appearing in New York or Burbank, California.

188

The voice bade him to leave the car and told him that the lights were "instruments of transmission and reception,"

Immediately we are made aware of the tremendous extensions of the senses across space and time. This is the omnipresent, all seeing prerogative of the Gods alone.

and that he was "meeting friends from another world."

The "Other World" is an extraordinarily emotive archetypal image. It suggests a breakthrough from one set of laws of the universe into another. In the illustration" The Spiritual Pilgrim Discovering another World" we find a Rosicrucian Illumination where the pilgrim has broken through into another space/time continuum. We see the heavenly spheres reminiscent of Ezekiel's flying wheels or the rings of UFOs. Some of the strange and bizarre happenings claimed by other contactees or cases of abduction point to this other world as having an entirely different

sense of time. According to many different religious sources the gods don't live in our time. "For a thousand years in thy sight are but as yesterday when it is past, and as a watch in the night." (Psalm XC:4)

The voice, uncannily seemed to sense that Orfeo was thirsty and a crystal cup appeared on the fender of his car as if from nowhere. In it was the "most delicious nectar I had ever tasted."

The crystal goblet brings to mind the Holy Grail. The grail is Light; it is the Light connected to the Sun. There are many legends around this theme in which a magic goblet mysteriously fills with an ambrosia and yet no one can drink it unless they be pure. Even the Grail itself loses power if in the wrong hands. In folk lore fairies bring drinks to lost travelers appearing in lonely places. It is also the sign that Orpheus can enter the Underworld or the deeper levels of the unconscious.

A full luminous three-dimensional screen appeared in the space between the green disks.

This is a perfect example of the projection of a common cultural element. This was of course the period of novelty as far as a television screen was concerned. Television had only been in operation a few years so it is easy to see the context of the 1950's here. A later generation would surely have just "beamed" the space beings down in the style of Star Trek.

In it Orfeo saw the head and shoulders and the angel-like features of a man and woman "being near as possible the ultimate of perfection."

The extraordinary beings who seem so perfect and beautiful are simply off-the-shelf stereotypes which culturally we can all agree on. The attributes of compassion, love, care, harmony and higher spiritual lives which they exhibit are all qualities which have been agreed upon by popular consent. The images of the brothers correspond with 90% of all benign encounters in that they share our common cultural heritage. The fact that they would fit into the ranks of the angelic host, without raising the slightest suspicion, does indicate just how persuasive our stereotype is. It is small wonder that Jung suggests that Orfeo's cosmic friends, if not actual antique gods and heroes, are at least angels. Another cultural clue is that Angelucci only saw the head and shoulders of the two beings. This, of course, is perfectly in accord with what he had come to expect from watching television where announcers and personalities would be restricted to the size of the screen. It is unlikely that in the advanced technology of the space brothers such restrictions would apply.

They had huge shining eyes.

Angelucci was not the first to encounter beings from another planet. Helene Smith, the Swiss medium even created a Martian language assisted by her Guardian Angel, depicted above, as long ago as 1912. The imagery now would probably be more in the manner of the computer generated figure on the opposite page. Visionaries seldom depart from the contemporary images available even if the original phenomena might be totally outside their normal range of ideas.

This is an enduring image throughout the history of encounters. Its mythical content is of course an all knowing awareness, a bright penetrating look, the eye of Horus, the inner eye and higher consciousness. They seemed as if vaguely familiar.

"They conveyed kindness, understanding, experience, moderation, and a complete joy of the five senses. Life in full. All this and not a word spoken" They communicated telepathically.

This is a favorite theme of our own modern era for it seldom appears in myth and legend. However it does indicate a magical rather than technological achievement. It hints at a higher consciousness and a more advanced spiritual lifestyle.

They told Orfeo that Earth has been under surveyance for centuries.

This is the typical background of higher intelligences or cosmic guardians who are all seeing and omnipresent. Here we are introduced to the wise being, benevolently inclined to human beings and watchful over our destinies.

It seemed there was an especial interest in resurveying the planet. The vital statistics of each and every person on earth, they told him, is recorded on their crystal recording disks.

The eastern concept of the akashic records or the idea of memory fields is now introduced. That we are all important enough to be recorded in some higher cosmic file is a very reassuring theme, as is the concept that there is an all seeing eye which does the recording in the first place.

They felt a deep sense of brotherhood with earth because of some undisclosed kinship with their own home, the planet *Lucifer.* They asked Orfeo to look upon them as "older brothers." Cosmic law forbade them any spectacular revelations on Earth but they had to act now as the planet was threatened by greater dangers now than had been realised. They specifically mentioned the "creeping menace of communism that threatened the world."

At this point contemporary cultural and personal preoccupations are creeping into the narrative. This encounter happened just prior to the Communist witch hunts of Senator McCarthy. There was a paranoid atmosphere as the new threat of the vast destructive capacity of the Soviet nuclear arsenals became known. It is small wonder that, if Commu-

nism wasn't at the top of the space brothers priorities, it certainly was at the top of Angelucci's.

All this heady stuff had an electrifying effect upon the witness. He felt exhilarated "as though, momentarily, I had transcended mortality and was somehow related to these superior beings."

This is a typical timeless moment in any mystic or spiritual happening. The hero has now experienced a type of timelessness which gives him a glimpse of the nature of the Other Worlders who exist in a different time continuum. He has become one of them, or at least shares some of their mystery.

Angelucci's next meeting with the beings occurred precisely two months after that first overwhelming contact. On July 23rd 1952 Orfeo again felt unwell and tense. He took a walk in the evening and in another lonely setting saw before him a "huge misty soap bubble." This he entered, finding himself in a vaulted room about twenty feet in diameter,

in the center of which stood a reclining chair. As he sat down on it the chair adjusted to his body form.

This is an individual journey. We can see how different the significance would have been if the room was filled with chairs and yet he was the only occupant.

The walls were lit mysteriously and looked like "ethereal mother-of-pearl stuff."

Light is fundamental to most encounter experiences. Generally the background lighting in most of the meetings is soft and unified. It seldom comes from an identifiable source. Many of the "other world" situations in legends and myth are bathed in a soft twilight.

The UFO, as this is what it turned out to be, took off and Orfeo seemed to fall into a trance like state of semi-dreaming.

Here we observe one of the important transitional points which occur in all myths. The witness moves from reality to dream and back. The hero finds it difficult to distinguish one state from another

Through an opening in the walls he could see Earth a thousand miles away and he started crying. He heard a voice saying "Orfeo weep...we weep with you for earth and her children. For all its apparent beauty Earth is a purgatorial world..."

A favorite theme amongst most quasi-religious groups. It suggests the battleground for the forces of Good and the forces of Darkness. Even Georges Gurdjieff said that "Earth is a very bad place from the cosmic view – it is like the most remote part of northern Siberia. But the idea of purgatory is a late Christian invention and did not appear as a concept until the late Middle Ages."

...among the planets evolving intelligent life. Hate, selfishness and cruelty rise from many parts of it like mist." The voice went on to say that while every being on earth was divinely created some naturally were good while some gravitated towards evil.

One wonders how the concept of a dualist universe, which appears to be quite a latecomer to human thought, managed to permeate the rest of space. However, in terms of Earth myths, it is part of the hero's quest that he transcend all the polarities, that he unites the good and the evil, the earthly and the heavenly, the male and the female. This is the ultimate reward for his journey into the Other World.

Above: **A UFO** snapped by an amateur photographer in the early 1970's, in Virginia, U.S.A.. Concrete evidence of the power of folk legends of UFOs is to be found in backyards throughout America, from rockets to flying saucers and highway signs.

"We know where you stand Orfeo," they tell him reassuringly, for he has been chosen by them for a mission.

The Quest is seemingly imposed by a superior or higher entity: it is the quest to find the true Self. This is one of the most persistent themes to be found in UFO material. Most contactees express genuine surprise that they should be the ones singled out as being worthy of the mission. Few can believe that they have any of the required qualifications (save that of being very ordinary – Mr. or Mrs. Average. Many of the heroes of legend have similar misgivings and blame fate for the seemingly arbitrary nature of the choosing. However, on closer examination of the intricate webs of the cosmos, the hero discovers a deeper pattern which remains essentially unknowable, but one that he has to follow. We find such forces in action in the Hebrew accounts of the legends of the tribes of Israel. Here it is not just an individual who finds himself chosen but an entire people.
The question arises "Chosen for what?" In this respect Orpheo is more fortunate than many of his contemporaries for he actually has a gospel to impart to us. Most witnesses are told that they are amongst the chosen few and yet are left dangling when it comes to the fine print of the message. "Don't call us, we'll call you." is a too frequent tale in UFO accounts.

As part of their general explanation of how the forces of good and evil interact, the cosmic guardians mention Christ but only as an allegorical Son of God. In reality he was the "Lord of the Flame" and not of earth at all.

Most contactees have something to say about Christ. Invariably they offer new accounts of who he really was, often emphasizing the new age character of the space savior. The illustration of Christ as spaceman is
a familiar image of our times. Yet in this account Angelucci does add a touching and original note.

This "Infinite entity of the Sun" sacrificed himself for the children of woe and in doing so "has become part of the oversoul of mankind and the world spirit. In this he differs from all other cosmic teachers.

We have so few accounts of UFO sightings or contacts from the East that there seem to be no words of enlightenment concerning the cosmic nature of such spacemen as Gautama the Buddha, Mahavira, Lao Tzu, Chuang Tzu, Bodhidharma or Saraha. It does suggest a certain cultural bias exhibited by our cosmic watchers.

"Everyone on earth has a spiritual, unknown, self which transcends the material world and consciousness and dwells eternally outside of the Time dimension in spiritual perfection within the unity of the oversoul."

Orfeo is then baptized in the true light of the world eternal and undergoes a spiritual rite of passage. At that moment there is a lightning flash in which he sees into both past and future, understanding the mysteries of life. He thought he was going to die as he was wafted into "eternity, into a timeless sea of bliss."

This is the centerpiece of the drama. Here we have the typical rite of passage, the initiation to the mysteries and a landmark towards a final resolution of knowing the wholeness of Self. The description is remarkably similar, even though naively expressed, to many experiences of both Eastern and western mystics. Light is the most important element here. Literally, Orfeo saw the Light. We find a remarkable similarity of vision with the composer Jerry Neff,

Christ as Spaceman: Spaceman as Christ, *from Angeles ayer,
extraterretres boy.*

*who experienced the following during a trip on
LSD." In front of my eyes, as if in a dream, I could
only see a blazing pool of white or slightly golden
light...I did not so much see it as feel it, and that
feeling was one of absolute ecstasy, involving every
'good' sensation and every 'rightness' imaginable,
and in a moral sense as well. This bliss included benevolence, joy, and reconciliation of opposites – literally everything all at once...the absolute certainty
that what one is seeing is the real reality – a timeless
source of all that exists."While this is a far more
sophisticated expression than that of Orfeo the experience is uncannily alike.*

At the end of this remarkable episode, on returning to his home, Orfeo discovers a clear stigmata

*The hero always needs a symbol or sign which signi-
fies the nature of his search.*

...on the left side of his chest which was an inflamed circle with a dot in the center. He sees it as
the "symbol of the hydrogen atom" which represents the circle whose center is everywhere and
whose circumference nowhere.

*This is the hero's personal, manifest sign of a search
for the Unio Mystica, the totality of wholeness,
Jung's individuation or the alchemical transmuta-
tion. It is the symbol which Orfeo has chosen as Self.*

On August 2nd of the same year he, along with
eight other witnesses, claimed to have seen a UFO.
He went on alone to the lonely spot of the first encounter. Here he found a tall handsome man with
unusually huge, luminously expressive eyes.

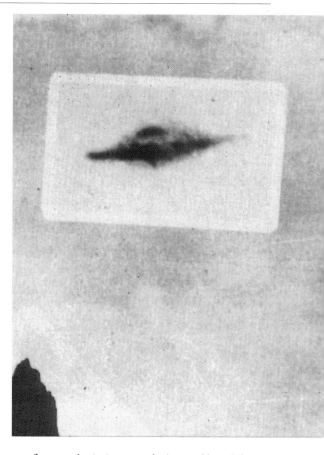

This is a persistent imagery, which can be found throughout history. Contemporary with the widespread religion of the Eye Goddess of Old Europe were those strange and enigmatic beings with luminous eyes which shone like the sun who appeared 12000 years ago in the Middle East and whose image gave rise to the stories of the angels.

This ethereal figure introduces himself as "Neptune."

This was the Roman god of the ocean deep. In Greece his name was Poseidon who arose from an even earlier deity Varuna. Varunas is the Sanskrit word for "The night firmament." All are emotive titles for the ruler of the ocean of the unconscious, the Other World or the vast firmament of the stars.

The edges of his majestic form seemed to ripple like wings or "water in the wind. *(Certainly an angelic characteristic)* He then tells Orfeo more of why earth was endangered and of its coming redemption.

Invariably in meetings in which some message is passed we find the same finger from the cosmic pulpit warning us about what we are doing wrong with ourselves and the planet. It is notable that these space or angelic emissaries don't sit down and laugh with the witnesses and cheerfully pass the bottle round congratulating the contactee on his good fortune to be a human being and making such a good job of it in the bargain. It is all so serious. Usually the message, the overall philosophy behind it, the pleas for humanity to give up its aggressiveness, to raise the low vibrations of our planetary consciousness to higher frequencies, is couched in such vague terms as to be virtually useless in practical ways of getting out of the mess they assure us we are in. It all sounds too much like a fundamentalist preacher wagging his finger and pointing towards Armageddon while getting his ecological facts all wrong. And so far the most damning evidence is that search as you might neither ETs nor Angels crack even one joke. If the accounts to date give some idea of the humor of our cosmic brothers or the laughter in heaven then we are in for a dull future.

In September of the following year Angelucci experienced a complete blankout for a week. In this time he was not consciously aware of his normal life on earth, although he still appeared to his friends and family as normal.

During this "absence" from Earth he somehow led a double life by appearing simultaneously on a planetoid which was a fragment of what had origi-

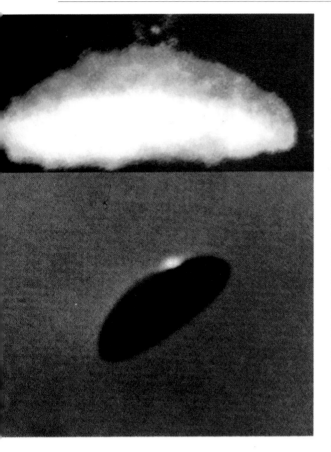

a glorious civilization, to Orfeo it was still seventh heaven. Without exception all the inhabitants were "statuesque and majestic." They moved through a world of colors, of flowers and delightful odors, delicious food, nectar and almost continual harmonious and celestial music.

Here the paradise garden is transported into space. However, from the descriptions given, it seems even this was a pale reflection of the golden Age on Lucifer itself.

Orfeo came to know that his true name was in fact Neptune while the being who posed as this was in fact called Orion.

The phenomenon of the UFO refuses to yield any really plausible explanation. Like angels, the occupants seldom leave any concrete evidence. But, at least, in our technological era they do leave a trace even though they seem pathologically camera shy. These three amateur snapshots have been judged genuine by experts. All three were confirmed by independent witnesses. The top, spectacular, glowing UFO was photographed from a Concorde jet in 1973 and the bottom one was seen in Peru. Below is a concrete sculpture by *Jene Highstein.*

nally been a planet Lucifer. All that remains of the planet is the ring of asteroids which orbit between Mars and Jupiter. It had once been ruled by a prince, "Son of the Morning," who, through personal ambition and pride, had seceded from the other "etheric Hosts" of the cosmos and had managed to contrive the destruction of his planet.

This is almost a straight, biblical account of Lucifer, the son of the Morning, Bearer of Light who fell from the heavens through pride. Angelucci suggests that here is a simple explanation for this story of Satan but we have mistaken the real source up until now.

However, even if the facilities of the planetoid were meager by comparison to what once had been

In other words he finds that he is both the superior being and the dark ocean of the unconscious himself. Now Orion holds even more dark secrets. The Persians named the constellation Orion as Nimrod, linking him with the rebel angel Shemhazai which would certainly fit the story of Lucifer's fall. Nimrod was also the evil creator of the Tower of Babel which instigated God's ruse to have 70 languages spoken instead of one, thus creating confusion amongst the Tower builders and preventing it from ever reaching heaven. The Greek Orion was a mighty hunter who also rebelled and offended his God. Strange company that Orpheus keeps.

He is increasingly in the company of Lyra, a beautiful female with long golden hair, large eyes and wearing a long Grecian robe.

Here is the age old theme which we find in the Celtic stories of Iseult who has the most outrageous hair as fair as Gold or the Sun. Grainne, another mythical heroine means Sun and as Queen of the fairies lives in a crystal palace, in which all the rays of the sun converge. In Orfeo's descriptions we find crystal buildings full of sunlight and prismatic colors. The Sun Goddesses are all initiators, having a deeper wisdom than that of the hero. Here the mythic archetype appears to Angelucci as he is skillfully guided by Lyra.

Telepathic communications reveal that she arouses erotic feelings in poor Orfeo and the whole company is rather primly shocked.

When she stimulates some pretty earthy instincts in Orfeo it shocks the otherwise calm and superior brothers who see this aggressive male principle as something to be ashamed of and which must be controlled and channeled into higher, almost Tantric realms. Arousal and generalized sexual themes often

appear in encounter reports. Most of the contactee reports of the 1950's tended to be rather prudish and adolescent in their attitudes to female ETs. Invariably, when the ET is human and female the woman conforms remarkably to the fashions of the times. As one enthusiastic contactee, Truman Bethurum wrote of his cute little telepathic ET.
"Her flesh was real and plenty firm,
Her shape was like an expensive urn.
She was just over four feet tall,
And certainly entrancing, all in all."
In the later abductee events the pattern has a more sinister ring. It starts in 1957 when a Brazilian farmer, one Antonio Villas-Boas, was taken on a space ship and forced to have sexual intercourse with an ET. The 1950's still had a certain romantic naivete for the ET turns out to be a very beautiful spacewoman. By the 1960's the Ets had taken a definite turn for the worse. The new breed of space being were often remarkably ugly and sinister. They continued to experiment with willing or unwilling victims, either through artificial insemination or other sexually centered activities.

But all ends well as he masters his baser instincts and is drawn into a more spiritual union with her." I turned and looked into Lyra's wonderful eyes shining with sympathy, compassion and purest love. My own heart swiftly responded. Then suddenly, miraculously we were as one being, enfolded in an embrace of the spirit untouched by sensuality or carnality."

Here, at last, we find the transforming culmination of the Quest. Like that of the Grail it is a search for the identity of the whole being. It is the Unio Mystica, which in Orfeo's case is both a union of the male and female principles but also a merging with the Light of all worlds as in his baptism.

One of the first contactees of beings from space was George Adamski. Here he poses with a rather idealized painting of one of them. While it is likely that his story was an elaborate hoax many accounts of contacts and abductions have an incontestable ring of truth.

The outward transformation in Angelucci is that he drops his former existence and becomes a prophet of the message even if his gospel is met with scorn and ridicule. One wonders whether Ezekiel, Enoch or Elijah had similar receptions to their accounts. Perhaps their times were more sympathetic to belief.

The Quest

Even a man like C.G.Jung offered a very patronizing interpretation of Orfeo's experience. He tells us that, "Orfeo's book is an essentially naive production which for that very reason reveals all the more clearly the unconscious background of the Ufo phenomenon and therefore comes like a gift to the psychologist." He goes on to say that, "The Individuation process, the central problem of modern psychology, is plainly depicted in it in an unconscious, symbolic form which bears out our previous reflections, although the author with his somewhat primitive mentality has taken it quite literally as a concrete happening."

Now, personally, I am surprised at Jung letting that last statement slip by as though it is a normal event of life. Orfeo believed it had happened to him and has "taken it quite literally as a concrete happening." This man, naive or not, has seen something so transforming and powerful that he will endure the ridicule and scorn of his friends and family in speaking out for what he sees as truth. How many of us have the courage of any of our normal convictions to do the same? This man doesn't even have any substantial evidence, save for his own subjective memory, and yet he sallies forth to fight the ever eager detractors, armed with nothing that they will believe in – that is except the emotional charge behind the story. It is that massive charge of energy which was able to shake even the most cynical amongst his critics. What is it within his story which, against all odds, has an authentic ring of truth?

Orfeo seems to have tapped a core of myth much as the ancient story tellers must have done. Perhaps they too re-enacted the events in their minds as if they were actually happening. Maybe in order to do so they took a little help from some drug, an ambrosia in a crystal goblet, before they started the tale. With the aid of a sacred mushroom the whole episode would become an elaborate piece of shamanic theatre – a display for the benefit of an audience who needed to know something about themselves. A play does simulate reality and in it we identify with the Other World.

Maybe the individual mind can put on such a display, for itself,devising a simulated reality in some dramatic episode in which the witness seems to encounter an other worldly being. The incident must be lifelike, so it is presented to the top layer of the conscious mind in such a way that it will be accepted as reality. The otherworldly figure has the necessary authority and power and mystery to resolve the needs of the visionary.

Stripped of all the ET or angelic trappings such encounters are clearly akin to legends of heroes, mighty quests, spirit guides and descents into the under or overworld. But investigators of the phenomena insist that such a story is not an exception. Tales far more bizarre and outlandish are appearing every day. The latest rash of reports of abductions is really quite alarming. Many peoples lives are drastically being altered by the encounters and many of the witnesses are far from being cranks, millennium riders or charlatans. They are as convinced of the validity and substantial nature of the encounter as someone who is sure that he or she has seen the sun rise in the morning.

As can be seen from this account the witness cannot be separated from what he or she has witnessed. The angel, the ET or the UFO are inseparable from the individual who claims to have seen them. And if the stories are true and we are meeting beings who are not of this earth, then it surely is one of the most important events in the history of humankind. If it turns out that it's not true then we

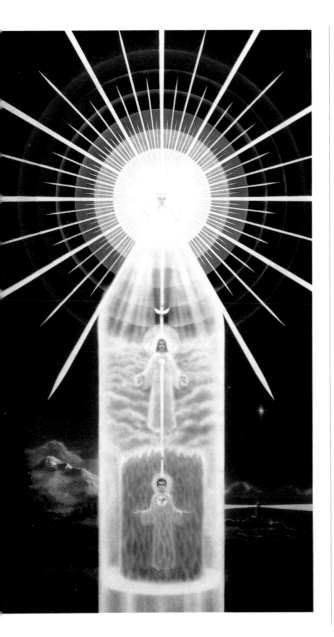

do have a situation which warrants our most careful scrutiny. If thousands upon thousands of people claim that they have seen angels or ETs, UFOs or aliens, and most seem genuine in their convictions that they have, then why on earth do they appear? What is the inner mechanism which triggers such concrete visions and what is the real message behind their appearances?

In order to explore at least one possible explanation it is necessary to turn to Jung's concept of the archetype.

The Image of the Real Self as envisioned by *Elizabeth Claire Prophet*. At the top is visualized the individual essence of God within each of us. Below that is the Mediator or Christ Consciousness which is the Inner teacher of the lower soul evolving through the body. On the left is the stained glass window at *Mare Island Naval Base, California*, showing the **Archangel Gabriel.** It is no accident that most modern representations of angels are to be found in military establishments. Some of the most notable angelic encounters of this century also come from sightings by the armed forces. The best known of these were the Angel of Mons in World War I and the stories from Air Chief Marshal Lord Dowding who tells of aircraft whose crews had been killed continuing to fight on in the Battle of Britain. Dowding was convinced that angels flew these planes. It was during World War II that sightings of alien, aerial craft were first reported. Pilots, at the time, on both Allied and Axis sides, believed their enemy had invented new and unknown craft.

CHAPTER FOUR
Archaic Memories

AFTER ALL THAT HAS BEEN UNCOVERED, still without any sign of concrete evidence, are we then to assume that angels are merely figments of a collective imagination? Are they, as many psychiatrists assert, projections of mysterious archaic memories which are somehow passed down from generation to generation in the form of archetypal images?

Carl Gustav Jung, in his introduction to *Man and his Symbols* tells of a patient, a theologian, who began to have visions. He had previously told Jung "that Ezekiel's visions were nothing more than morbid symptoms" and that when Moses and other prophets heard "voices" speaking to them, they were in fact suffering from hallucinations. You can imagine the panic that this religious scholar felt when something of a similar nature "spontaneously" happened to him.

We are so accustomed to the apparently rational nature of our world that it is scarcely imaginable that anything can happen which cannot be explained away by common sense. But the primitive man, confronted by a shock like that of the theologian, would not doubt his sanity; he would simply turn to his fetishes, his spirits, gods or angels.

Both Freud and Jung discovered exotic and bizarre elements occurring in their patients' dreams which seemed totally unconnected with the dreamer's personal experience. Freud called them archaic "remnants," or mental forms whose presence could not be explained by anything comparable in the everyday experience of that individual's life. They seemed to be aboriginal, innate and inherited shapes within the human mind. These he saw as biological leftovers from prehistoric and unconscious parts of the mind of archaic mankind.

Jung called these *archetypes* or primordial images. The archetype, in his view, was the tendency to build particular internal shapes and forms from more general over-images. He thought they were an instinctive trend, as the impulse for pigeons to "home" or termites to build huge towers. Such a thesis is clearly incompatible with the present conventional assumption that heredity depends upon information encoded within DNA molecules.

However, recent brain research does seem to confirm many of Jung's hunches and has uncovered some fascinating facts about the nature of phenomena which bear close resemblance to the archetypes. We have already been introduced to one model of how the brain functions which suggests that it is layered in three distinctive parts, each of which evolved at different stages of the human development. The oldest core of the brain is what has been popularly termed the "reptilian." The second layer which envelopes it is called the "neo-mammalian," while the third and very thin layer is a more recent acquisition. This thin shell which surrounds the other two brains is the "neo-cortex."

The core, or oldest, brain, in some way stores, or has access to, the archetype tendencies. These are ancient genetic memories, which can be stimulated by some outside situation or in the dream state. As they are evoked and struggle to the surface of consciousness they are inevitably colored and given form and detail by the other two more recent evolutionary layers. It would then seem that the final colorful and expressive form largely depends upon the cultural background and conditioning which is programmed within the neo-cortex. But sometimes the image evoked is so powerful and emotionally charged that the neo-cortex doesn't have the time, or inclination, to interfere.

Jung divided the symbols to which we respond so fiercely and irrationally into "natural" and "cultural." The natural symbols are derived directly from the unconscious contents of the psyche, or in our more recent terms, the reptilian brain. Cultural symbols are collective representations of some of the more persistent and common archetypes which have surfaced enough times to be recognized as "eternal truths" for those societies which have adopted them. These particular archetypes depend upon the various cultural and religious pressures which gave them outward expression.

Angels can be seen as a perfect example of such a cultural symbol which has been embraced in the West. Four thousand years of belief in such creatures has created just such an "eternal truth." It matters not whether they appear a bit tar-

nished in the cold light of our scientific morning; they still exert considerable unconscious power, for they retain much of their original numinosity or magic. Such archetypes continue to be capable of evoking deep emotional charges which are often expressed as irrational prejudices and overwhelming feelings against all reasonable evidence.

Although we are still vulnerable to the archetype, generally speaking, modern humans do appear to have otherwise lost the capacity to respond directly to the numinous world. This is a tragic loss which is probably due to the over-emphasis on rational learning and scientific thinking. So we tend to read *about* the numinous and mysterious rather than actually live it. And just because it is not central to our own

The benevolent guardian angel of the 1940's was, of course, *Superman*. While a cloak replaced the wings, this expression of the all powerful guardian archetype, who battled the evil dragons of satanic violence, greed and injustice, replaced the Archangel Michael in the popular imagination. On the one hand he was timid Mr. Everyman of the city streets and offices and yet in the next instant he was transformed into the supernatural, righteous angel of mercy. Of course he was also one of the very first popular ET's who's home planet was Krypton.

experience we are in considerable danger when some of the wilder aspects of the psychic underworld erupt to the surface and threaten our sense of sanity. This means that we are especially prone to fanatical ideas and to some of the more bizarre expressions of the more powerful symbols which haunt that underworld.

When an 84 year-old woman with rhinestone flecks on her eyelids, orange sherbet hair, wearing a purple chiffon gown arrives in an electric blue Cadillac with a flying saucer on the roof and announces that she is the Archangel Uriel, we are no longer in

Above: **Alchemical images** are perhaps the purest form of archetypes and show their multi-dimensional character most clearly. *Hypnos*, the Greek god of sleep, was the brother of Death and the son of Night. Dreams were once considered to be Divine messages and angels the messengers. †Below left: **Ruth Norman,** known to her 400 Unariun followers as the Archangel Uriel, poses before her electric blue Cadillac. Howsoever whacky this 84 year old widow might appear to many of us, those who have met her are impressed by what they call her "awesome ability to command and influence people and their behavior." And who is in the position to say that she is not an archangel or a reincarnation of a supreme being?

any position to judge whether she is speaking truth or is having a ball at our expense.† Because our belief is second hand we no longer can rely our own gut feelings to tell us whether things are true or false. The original Archangel Uriel might well have such kinky tastes, but in our confusion we cannot tell for sure. On the one hand we yearn for that archetype of higher consciousness, – a Wise man or woman coming from the skies or space to solve all our problems. On the other there is the rational, skeptical, "belief programmed" neo-cortex, censoring all such information which doesn't fit its conditioning. The conflict of these two processes within us all has become chronic.

The "Ancient Wise One" is the common archetype to which we are particularly prone. Children love the image of a guardian angel. However, as adults we are supposed to be able to distinguish between an encounter with an angel and the projections of our unconscious yearning for the comforting security of a father or mother figure to watch over us and guide our actions. From what can be seen of the general state of the world, it is all too obvious that most of us can't. So when someone like Brad Steiger recently writes a book like *The Star People* in which he goes as far as to propose that extra-terrestrial beings of "higher intelligence" may enter the bodies of common pets, there will be plenty of us who credulously accept that "in a sense these animals become guardian angels for a time." For where can we draw the line distinguishing

The photograph by *Joyce Tenneson*, below, shows the dreamlike visions we all share which are particular forms arising from an archetype over-image.

205

reality, fantasy or plain, unadulterated rubbish, if we are always in a triple-bind with our squabbling three brains?

Having lost contact with our emotional and unconscious centers many of us feel increasingly disquieted and alienated as scientific knowledge continues to proliferate. No longer do rivers contain "the spirit of the waters" otherwise we couldn't pollute them as we do. No voice speaks from the skies, otherwise we could not destroy the ozone layer, and no Pan or great Earth Goddess inhabits the soil to stay our hands from raping the lands. And no angel watches over every blade of grass, encouraging it to grow any more. This terrible loss of the numinous and the mysterious finds its desperate compensations through the archetypes which appear in our dreams, our nightmares and our irrational fears. Modern humans are a curious mixture of scientific convictions and ancient demons. We are so stuffed full of beliefs and outmoded habits of thought that we cannot deal with the emotional charge behind those dreams.

The angel archetype is the messenger of the higher self. It is the wise being, the advanced soul, the Shaman, the Enlightened master, Superman, or the saint. Our present fascination with highly evolved extra-terrestrial beings who have come to guide humanity, or the galactic messengers of peace and love who contact the chosen few (who will form the new Ark of earth when we blow ourselves up), appears to arise from this extraordinarily potent interior archetype.

Such symbols may represent an individual who is striving towards a full realization of his or her cosmic self. The whole episode in chapter 3, which we have already encountered, of Orfeo Angelucci, would seem to fit this theme.

So it is hardly surprising that the major characteristic of this archetypal image is one of flight. The wild and erratic flight of insects, the soaring flight of birds, the slow wheeling of an eagle, or the flight of the soul as it leaves the restrictions of the body, are images which give an immense sense of freedom and deep satisfaction to the dreamer. But in certain special circumstances, a crisis or an impossible situation, the consciousness of an individual divides. Then that self-same dream image can appear as real to the observer who literally has no way of telling whether the experience is internal or external. It is common for small children to find it difficult to distinguish between events which occur in their dreams and happenings when awake. Even the writer Carlos Castaneda was never quite sure whether the

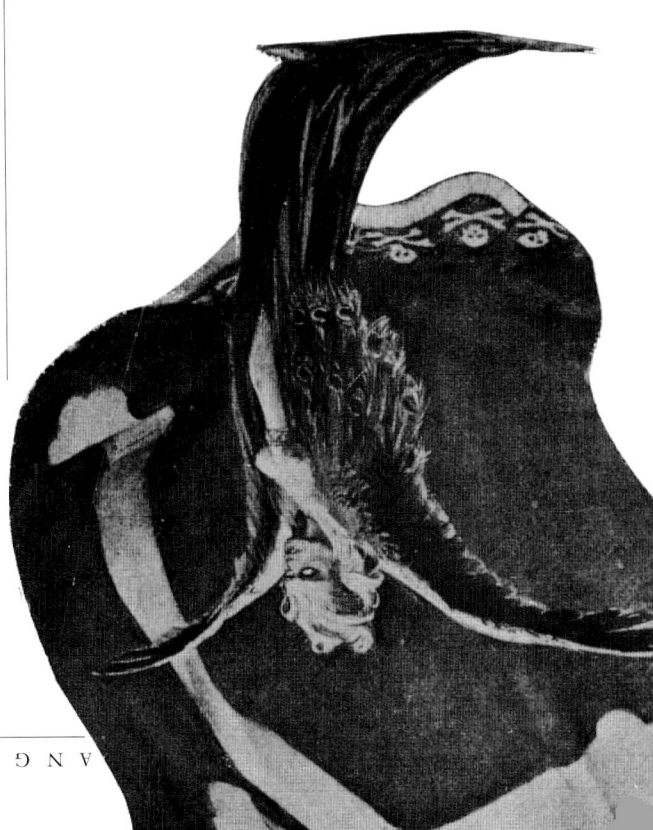

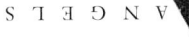

If anyone imagines that the old Superman image of the 1940's has lost its emotive charge then they should be directed to the Batman film of 1989 which was the all time box office hit. In this we have the age-old conflict of the good angel and the bad. Not so surprising is that Batman's Adversary is the Joker. This corresponds to perhaps the oldest archetype in the book which Jung identified as the Trickster. The Trickster has two faces; one is the Prince of Deception and Lies and the other is the Wise Man.

Although Jung felt the collective unconscious was planet-wide, he did suggest that different social conditionings would create different collective psyches as well. The diagram above, showing the overview of the collective unconscious, is by Marie-Louise von Franz. A = Individual ego consciousness; B = Personal unconscious; C = Group unconscious; D = National group unconscious; E = Unconscious which is common to all human beings containing the universal archetypes. Of course this could apply to smaller units like religious groups of those who believed in angels and those who don't.

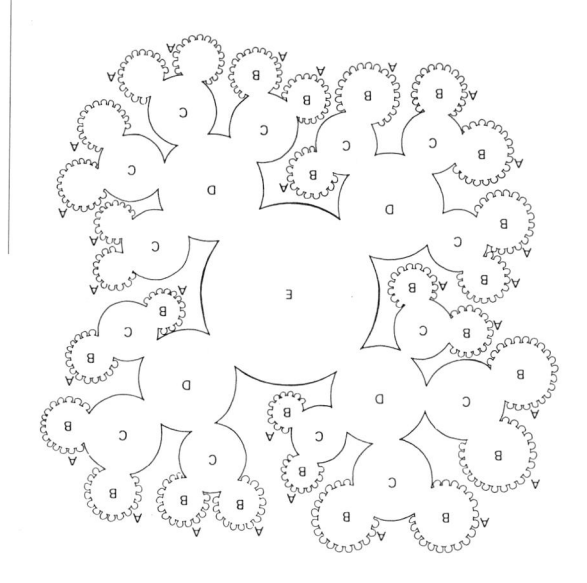

impossible antics of his sorcerer teachers, Don Genaro or Don Juan, were real flights, or an illusion induced by drugs or a dream state. Yet weird accounts of sages who are able to fly or walk on water are common in many cultures.

It would appear that one doesn't have to look far beyond the projected archetype to see a possible origin of the encounters with angels. In this century Jung has given us a plausible explanation for the phantoms which can materialize so convincingly. In more ancient days witnesses were not armed with such knowledge and may have accepted their own

projections of angels at face value. And in a case like that of Angelucci, today, the experience was so powerful that it does not ever seem to have crossed the witness's mind that one part of him might  have created the whole episode to in order to communicate to the other part.

An archetype appears to surface when something needs to be communicated. The angel only seems to appear when it has a message to impart.

These twin characteristics of communication and flight are significant. Flight is the hallmark on the sterling silver of the higher self, just as ang-els have "el" tacked firmly on the end of their tails. And the open communication of essential information throughout a whole organism is the hallmark of a healthy being. The appearance of an angel archetype can signify the first step on an individual's journey to become whole; to unify the divided consciousness. If sufficient numbers experience phenomena like angels or ETs then it would appear that the collective unconscious seeks to be healed in the same way.

Left: **Angels turning the Wheels of the Universe,** *14th century French Miniature.* The entire workings of the cosmos were once seen as being caused by a vast world of angels and spirits. The medieval mind loved a sense of the universe as having circular and fixed boundaries with simple divisions like the four compass points. The two mandalas, on the right, painted by one of Jung's patients exhibit the self-same archetypal spirit. Jung suggested that such mandalic symbols correspond most clearly to a psychological expression of the totality of the self and as such have a universal appeal. The modern computer generated image is a mathematical equation which has been transformed into a similar visual form.

CHAPTER FIVE
Elohim The Shining Ones

THERE IS A CERTAIN LAZY ARROGANCE in our modern assumptions of who we are and where we came from. We smile indulgently when we learn of the Anglican Archbishop of Armagh, Dr. James Ussher, who calculated the Creation of the World to have been at precisely 8 p.m. on the 22nd of October 4004 B.C.. We remain amused to learn that the Vice Chancellor of Cambridge University insisted that Adam was not actually created until 9 a.m. on the following day (Greenwich mean time of course).

Most 20th century citizens have Darwin's theory of evolution, with its vastly expanded time scale, firmly established in their minds when rea-

ding of such childish inventions. It is now acknowledged that any hypothesis which gives the age of the universe as less than ten billion years old is absurd. Virtually all the authorities from the various disciplines which examine pre-history, present a comforting assurance that Homo Sapiens Sapiens appeared simultaneously with the last of the Neanderthalers around 32,000 years ago. It was these new humans who created the awesome drawings and paintings to be found in the caves of Lascaux.

Orthodox theory then seems to lose track of these superbly gifted and visionary peoples until they turn up twenty thousand years later in Jerico, the Indus valley, Sumer, Crete and Egypt. But by then our ancestors had mysteriously, as if overnight, acquired the most miraculous skills in cutting building blocks, harvesting, storing grain, making long ocean trips in large seaworthy vessels and working metals.

Every year new discoveries in all parts of the world push this historical horizon further and further into the past. But, although there is concrete evidence that our old pre-historical view is wrong, outdated chronologies live on in our minds. The problem seems to be that the sheer weight and mass of archaeological opinion is about as movable as the Pyramids. Too much painstaking labor has gone into the whole theoretical framework for a few curious anomalies to make any dent in the superstructure. However, there are a number of unorthodox views as to how primitive, foraging, cavemen so abruptly acquired a superb civilization in the Middle and Near East as if from nowhere. Theories of how this could have come about range from the plausible to the outrageous. Van Daniken proposes that we are the experimental product of visitors from outer space. Charles Berlitz suggests that the legendary island of Atlantis once had a thriving and advanced culture even before the painters of Lascaux had found their caves, and that about 12,000 years ago it suffered devastating collapse. He maintains there were survivors who escaped to both the old and the new world with remnants of their once advanced technology. James Churchward spent his whole life searching for concrete evidence of a lost continent in the pacific which he called Mu, supposedly contemporaneous with Atlantis and almost as technologically advanced. He also believed that this great civilization was drowned by some terrible volcanic upheaval which caused the land mass to sink into the ocean. The survivors spread to the South Americas in the east and to China and India in the west, reaching as far as the coast of the Mediterranean. In a more sober account Christien O'Brien would have us believe that there was a small band of luminous individuals who appeared out of no- where, yet had such a profound

effect upon our ancestors that they remain in our memories, and in our myths and legends, as angels.

It is easy to dismiss those writers whose academic or

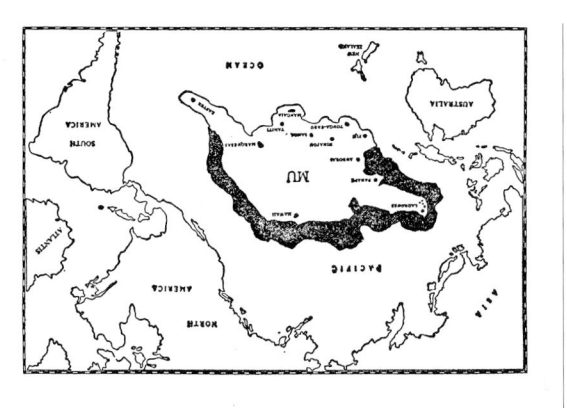

Far left: Completely recognizable prehistoric animals are seen in this scene from an incised stone of *Ica, Peru (3500 B.C.).* Even if such creatures were existing in the Peruvian highlands over 100 million years *after* they were supposed to have died out, it is even more remarkable that the hunters who seem to have domesticated these 50 ton pets have also invented the telescope. If a single image can collapse the orthodox historical palace of cards then it is surely this one. The clay statuette from the Julsrud Collection of Acambaro, Mexico appears to depict an allosaurus and the lively scenes of women with huge reptiles suggests that "dragons" still existed 5000 years ago in Mexico. Many so called legends may be far more factual than we have believed. Also from *Ica* the pictograms above can be compared with those immediately beneath from India. 10,000 miles separates these two sites and the pictograms are dated as being 7000 years old.

Below: A reconstructed map of the **Lost Continent of Mu,** with the position of Atlantis. This picture nearly fits the theory of continental drift and of the recently discovered Pacific plate although James Churchward forwarded his theory half a century before these discoveries.

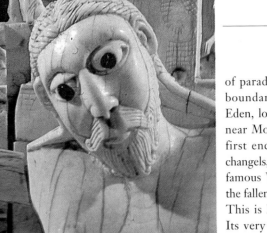

scientific backgrounds do not correspond to what an archaeological expert is supposed to be, but they do us the valuable service of questioning the holy cows of orthodoxy. O'Brien is of especial interest as he offers a closely argued case giving a plausible and very down-to-earth explanation of the origins of the angelic host. And it is an explanation we just cannot afford to ignore. It is a classic within the genre usually labeled "alternative history."

His action centers in the Lebanon and the Mesopotamian basin. Sumer has long been considered the crucible of civilization and about 5,500 years ago it had suddenly blazed forth in a number of closely connected centers within the valley of the Tigris and Euphrates. There was a prodigious explosion of art and artifacts which appeared with seemingly no transitional era between cavemen and the priest-kings who seemed to be the focus of all this activity. The archaeologist and writer, André Parrot, has suggested this sudden flowering could only be attributed to "the genius of the few."

Who these brilliant innovators could have been or where they came from formed the basis of O'Brien's speculation. He suggests that they were a group of advanced agriculturalists who physically appeared to be very different from the indigenous natives of the area. It was these great Lords of Cultivation who created a settlement in the region of present day Lebanon. It was this cultivated area, with its extensive irrigation schemes and rich orchards, which became the model upon which later scholars and priests based the various myths

of paradise. It was within the boundaries of this garden of Eden, located in the highlands near Mount Hermon, that we first encounter the seven archangels, their Lord and the infamous Watchers who became the fallen angels.

This is hardly a timid theme. Its very boldness becomes all the more attractive when we discover that there are at least two factual and relatively unadorned accounts describing this settlement and those who lived and worked there. It is a story of the building of a community which might well have been very like a modern Israeli Kibbutz. Between the two records we can build up a picture of its creation, its golden age and the steady decline when the so called angels dispersed and left the area.

What is fascinating about the whole epic is how the Sumerians, the Babylonians and the Hebrews, all of them incontinent "God Makers," managed to so embellish the original story that by the 4th century B. C. the leader of the settlement had

Right: **Anu**, *from the Temple of Abu at Tell Asmar, 2,700 B.C.* This figure and the one of Ninkharsag below, are part of a group of figures who, O'Brien suggests, could have been the original inspiration for the Hebrew Yahweh and His seven Archangels. In this case the female figure is the first representation of the Archangel Gabriel. The huge, staring eyes remind us of the descriptions of the Annanage,"and their eyes burned like lamps," or " his eyes were like fiery torches." We can see the continuing tradition in the 13th century carving of Christ from Madrid.

become God, His lieutenants had been transformed into the archangels and their working assistants were now flying around as angels.

The early Hebrews, in keeping with their wandering nature, were habitual exiles and thus a highly eclectic people. Their scholar-priests freely borrowed from whichever culture they happened to find themselves in, whether it was Egyptian, Sumerian, Babylonian, Assyrian or later Persian, Greek or Roman. Scholarship by its very nature, whether religious or secular, anthropological or archaeological, is notoriously inventive when describing the artifacts of ordinary life. The temptation to spice up an otherwise dull subject often has led to attributing great events to little happenings and creating supernatural phenomena where none actually existed. Thus a chair is transformed into the sacred throne of a priest-king, and a toothpick acquires the aura of a holy relic. In the following account we see how

such a process has probably been in action for over five millennia. Religious ideas were plastered over secular events creating legendary stories. Over the years these stories became "truths", which avidly fed upon themselves within whichever closed or "chosen" community they were found. In such greenhouse conditions even the most patently absurd ideas can become stronger and more incontroversial with each ritual and act of worship. In this way two very ordinary, secular events could have become "deified" and given a religious significance which they didn't originally warrant. One is the legend of the Garden of Eden and the other is that this Paradise was peopled by supernatural beings called Angels.

Origins of Heaven

According to eleven clay tablets from Sumer, backed by later Hebraic texts attributed to Enoch the scribe, a small band of mysterious but very much embodied beings arrived in what is now the Lebanon, about ten to twelve thousand years ago. From what we know they were physically unlike the local tribes, being considerably taller, having strangely shining faces with large and brilliant eyes. It is difficult to judge whether this was due to a cosmetic with some glowing property or whether they really were quite alien beings. Whatever the cause of this luminosity these peoples were known as the "Shining Ones." There are many descriptions of these peoples from early sources. Enoch describes them as being very tall and different from any that he had seen in the lowlands. "Their faces shone like the Sun, and their eyes burned like lamps." They were

 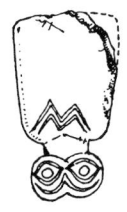 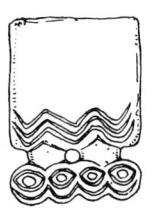 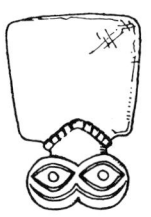  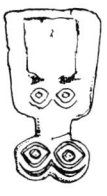

...peoples of southeastern Europe developed a unique civilization which owed nothing to the developments of the Near East and in fact pre-dated them. What is fascinating is that these peoples independently discovered how to work copper and gold and even evolved a rudimentary script. Their extensive worship of the Eye Goddess does suggest that another group of "Shining Ones" had sown the seeds of civilization two thousand miles from Eden at roughly the same time the first settlement appeared in the Lebanon. The two Egyptian eyes of Horus suggest a similar source of inspiration although these did not appear until five thousand years later.

 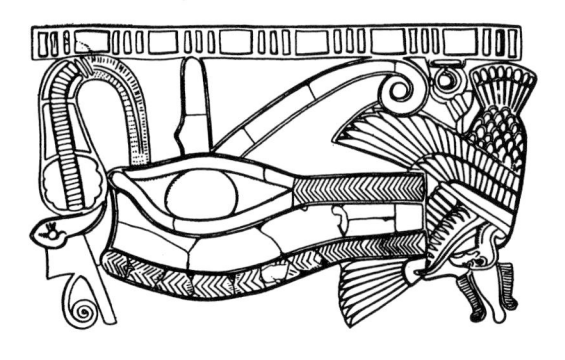

Above left: **The Kharsag Epic, 2700 B.C.** *from the original baked clay cylinder. Above:* **Eye Goddess** *statuettes from Old Europe.*

still around five millennia later when the Old Testament prophet, Daniel, sees one with a girdle of gold round his waist and the same shining characteristic: "His face shone like lightning, His eyes were like fiery torches."

We have already examined a description of an offspring born as a mixture of these peoples and the local inhabitants. This is the biblical Noah, whose supposed father, Lamech, was terrified of his weird baby who filled a darkened room with light. Lamech realizes that he is more likely to come from the loins of the "Sons of the Lord in Eden" than from his own. He complains to Methuselah that Noah "is not like you and me – his eyes are like the rays of the Sun and his face shines. It seems to me that he is not born of my stock, but that of the Angels" (En CVI:1-8).

It would seem that whoever these "angels" were, they were not restricted to the Middle East, for the Tibetan *Book of Dzyan* speaks of "luminous sons" who are the "producers of the form from no-form." One leader "shines forth as the Sun; he is the blazing divine dragon-serpent of wisdom." Thousands of miles away, in Sumeria, these same luminous

gar — sag
Kharsag

erim — an — ni
and assembly heavenly

im — tu — ne
entered they

an — ki — bi — da — ge
heaven   earth

dingir anu — a — nun — na — ge
lord Anu   sons great   (of)

es — a — zu
many wise ones

Kharsag Epic

The particular epic which concerns us is a very early version of this story and one which was recorded on eleven clay tablets which were copied sometime in the third millennium B.C. This so-called Kharsag epic actually described a period which dates back almost twelve millennia. The story is told in simple and secular terms with no religious or supernatural overtones at all.

A group of wise sages (it depends upon one's taste whether these are seen as aristocratic invaders, aliens, extra terrestrials, survivors from Atlantis or

peoples were called the One-eyed and Two-eyed serpents. "Listen ye Sons of Earth, to your instructors, the Sons of Fire" could as well be said in the Lebanon as in Tibet. Whichever part of earth they settled in, the newcomers set about teaching the local inhabitants the cornerstones of civilization such as writing, metal working, planting, cultivating and harvesting grain. Such knowledge would have been overwhelmingly impressive to the indigenous cave dwelling and foraging peoples. In the Sumerian tablet we are about to examine it says that before the coming of the shining dragon-serpents of fire, "Man had not yet learned how to make clothes, or permanent dwellings. People crawled into their dwellings on all fours; they ate grass with their mouths like sheep; they drank storm-water from the streams."

There are other Sumerian tablets which speak of "luminous beings" who drove through the sky in barks and disc-shaped ships of fire. In these epics they descended from the stars to teach and impregnate the daughters of Man in order to create a new kind of conscious being. Having completed their work they then flew back to the stars.

Mu, or just tall agricultural tribesmen) arrived near Mt. Hermon in the highlands near the present border of the Lebanon and settled in one of the high valleys. They called the whole area Eden and their major settlement Kharsag. They appeared very different

Left: **Stele of Naram-sin.** Christian O'Brien suggests that this could be a commemoration of the descent of the Annanage upon Mt. Hermon. His interpretation of the original Kharsag text reads, "At Kharsag, where Heaven and Earth met, the heavenly assembly, the Great Sons of Anu, descended – the many Wise Ones." The two brilliant disks do appear to be a mystery although the seemingly dismembered figure beneath the foot of the leading figure does suggest other interpretations. So many Sumerian artifacts are open to so many conjectures it is as well to remember most of what we know of these extraordinary peoples is just theory.

Above: **The scribe Dudu** (*Sumer 2,500 B.C.*) or as is believed by some, Enoch, the "writer of truth."

ferent from the indigenous tribes of the area who mostly inhabited the lowlands.

With the help of a separate group, who are later identified as the "Watchers" in a parallel version of the epic by Enoch (En VI:6): And they were in all two hundred, who descended in the days of Jared on the summit of Mount Hermon," these settlers ploughed the land, created enclosed fields, sowed grain of at least three different varieties, planted orchards and trees. They bred herds of cattle and sheep and housed them in pens and buildings which were well watered. In a relatively short space of time the settlement prospered and there was a surplus of food. But all this had required a tremendous physical effort. The Watchers, who seemed to bear the main burden of the manual labor, became restless and finally rebelled against their overlords. If these epics are anything to go by these lords then hit upon a solution which has affected us all. On later tablets, copied about 1635 B. C., called *Atrabasis*, we hear the lords agreeing to the workers' demands. "Their work was very heavy and caused them much distress...while Belet-ili is present let her create a 'lullu' – a man, and let the man do the work." And such a man was created from the "blood" of a Lord mixed with a mysterious "clay." We shall shortly return to this fascinating theme.

Building recommenced and a reservoir was constructed above the settlement to provide round-the-year water for a complex irrigation scheme. When all this was done the sages had residences built, especially one large principal house which was brightly lit by strange and unconventional means.

Now this, in very abbreviated terms, is the story of the golden age of Kharsag as told in the second of the eleven clay tablets and cylinders. This whole program was accomplished in seven clearly separated parts which could have contributed to the later Judaic and Christian version of the creation myth, also in seven parts.

When Enoch the scribe first visited the self-same settlement about nine thousand years ago, he had first been summoned by two very tall men whose faces shone like the sun, with burning and radiant eyes. Our attention is drawn to the next description: "Their clothes were remarkable – being purplish with the appearance of feathers; and on their shoulders were things which I can only describe as 'like golden wings'."

Enoch then attended a meeting in which a selection was to be made of those who were to receive an extension of their life span. This was supposedly granted by imbibing the life-extending fruits of the Tree of Life which grew within the settlement. Enoch attended this meeting seven millennia before the birth of Christianity and yet even by this time

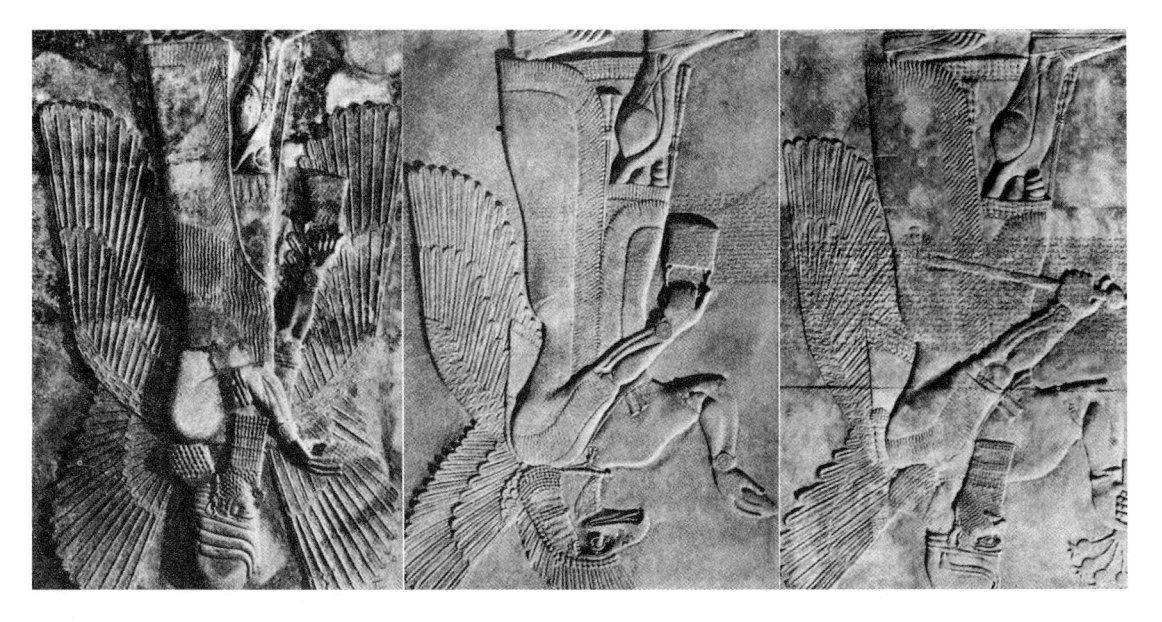

he was referring to the original Annanage or Shining Ones as Angels. It is difficult to tell when the transformation happened, as the accounts which have come down to us are copies made by later Hebrew scribes from other copies. There is no guarantee that the scribes have not translated El-ohim into angels in order to be comprehensible to their new readers.

Anyway, Enoch asks his angel companion who the four outstanding presences were who greeted the Lord of Spirits. (Enoch XL:1-10) "And he said, The first was Michael, the kindly and patient one; the second was Raphael who is responsible for treating illnesses and wounds among the people, here; the third was Gabriel, and the fourth was Phanuel (Uriel) who is responsible for dealing with those who are selected to receive an extension to their normal life-span."

From the general tone of Enoch's account it seems that even if there has been a change of name these angels remain very down-to-earth and even the reference to life extension is not necessarily supernatural. There has never been a shortage of life enhancing recipes throughout the ages including the daily advertisements in our own times.

So we now see how the Lords of cultivation, who were once identified with the original El-ohim or Shining Ones, became the angels. In the legends following Enoch's account, the Lord of Spirits, is deified and is transformed into the Hebrew God, Yahweh. The ordinary chair has become a throne in heaven.

Even without the addition of supernatural powers these peoples were obviously alien to the area. Whether they were alien to earth is one of those questions best left to more courageous investigators. For my money I would look towards either the Atlantic or the Pacific.

The settlement of Eden prospered for a while and then something went seriously wrong. First there was a sickness which seems to have been caused by eating contaminated food. This particular episode took on a more supernatural nature in a later and

Above left: **Assyrian Winged Genie,** *885-860 B.C.* Above: **The Assyrian Tree of Immortality,** *850 B.C.* This magical tree is to be found in legends as far apart as Polynesia, where a maiden is tricked into eating the fruit of a paradise tree by a serpent and so loses her immortality; in Iceland, where it is guarded by the goddess *Iduna* or in China where it becomes the Peach Tree of Immortality guarded by the serpent witch *Hsi Wang Kui*. In the Islamic version of the temptation of Adam and Eve the evil serpent tells them that "your Lord forbade you from this tree only lest you should become angels." In the Assyrian relief we see a mysterious winged chariot hovering above.

well known version of the Sumerian Paradise. In this we are told of a number of Lords who arose from the sea. (Adanus, Mu?). Their leader was Anu who was accompanied by Enki, Enlil and Nammu (Ninlil or Ninkarsag). They created a garden in the heavens and Ninlil fashioned a new creature who could be a servant to the Gods – man. At first it was a golden age of harmony and accord. The gardens flourished under the watchful eye of many goddesses of vegetation. Many new plants were created. But, so the story unfolds, Enki ate eight plants created by the Goddess Uttu before she had time to name them. This seemingly innocent act threw Uttu into a such a rage that she laid a terrible curse on Enki and he became ill. The other Gods were helpless as the gardens turned to desert and man had to go out into the wilderness.

In the earlier, secular, Kharsag epic the reason given was far more within our own experience. The food had been badly prepared. After, what appeared to have been a disastrous case of salmonella poisoning, the leader "established these wise precautions...In Eden, thy cooked food must be better cooked. In Eden thy cleaned food must be much cleaner... eating meat is the great enemy." This is hardly supernatural stuff, and these are the angels and archangels who had fallen ill.

Shortly after this, according to the *Atra-hasis*, another later Akkadian text of the same story, the Lady Ninlil appeared to conduct a genetic experiment with the local tribes. "She separated fourteen sections of the culture. She put seven sections on the right, and seven on the left, separating them by a partition. Fourteen experienced foster-mothers had been assembled. Seven were impregnated with the male cultures, and seven with the female cultures. The Birth-Lady, creatress of destiny, had them

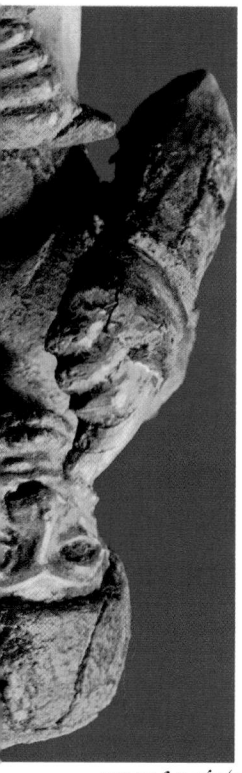

impregnated in pairs in her presence. So Ma-mi (Ninlil) laid the foundations of the human race."

Two of the fourteen were, as you might have guessed, Adam and Chawwah (Eve) and thus the first generation of the great patriarchal line of the Jews.

Now, according to the epic, this had been a controlled experiment which supposedly had been designed to combine some of the qualities of the Lords with those of the peoples of the lowland. And we are to find in the later story that the Annanage Lords were at considerable pains to keep the patriarchal line of what became the Jewish peoples an uncontaminated stock. Perhaps they just enjoyed Jewish humor. There are a number of current theories which have curious links with this story. The anthropologist, Stan Gooch, suggests that Jews are the direct descendants of a rare breed of half Cro-Magnon and half-Neanderthal stock which has been found to have lived in the area 20,000 years ago. Certainly there is no argument that the Hebrews have the greatest claim to be linked with the angels. As we have seen angels can be viewed as very much a Jewish invention. Is it possible that in their turn the Jews were very much an angelic creation?

The second calamity to disturb the peace of the paradise gardens happened when the socially lower artisan angels, who we now know of as the Watchers, or in Hebrew, as the *Eyrim*, dispensed with the artificial procedures altogether, finding the time-honored and sensual methods far more to their fancy.

This legend has already been introduced in the Treasury. They developed an insatiable lust for the daughters of men and begat many children by them.

The results were disastrous; the offspring were monstrous and aggressive. The Watchers were described as gigantic but their progeny were even larger. The whole lowland area was ravaged by these mutants, so much so that the Lords in Eden, albeit with much regret, decided to destroy them. This destruction coincided with the flood, or as one theory goes, the massive reservoir of water at the settlement was opened to devastate the valley below and drown the terrible brood.

The settlement itself seemed to have suffered from some natural disaster around 5000 B.C. and the various leaders resettled in the Mesopotamian Valley eventually founding the early Sumerian City-States. The "angels" eventually dispersed over the whole of the Near and Middle East, eventually moving into Europe and reaching as far as Britain. They left in their wake images of shining peoples, elven folk, Valkyries, and Giants. But, of course, their greatest legacy of all was the myth of angelic lore.

So far there is nothing to suggest for what reason, apart from being excellent farmers who, on occasions appeared with an oddly mysterious

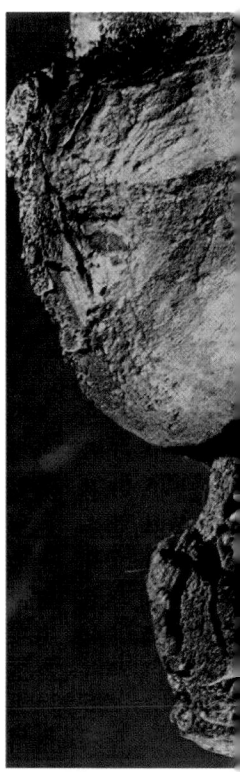

A Shining One, *from Sumer, 2600 B.C.:* The gold leaf on the face and hands heightens the effect and reminds us of the "face of burnished gold."

luminosity, these people attained the status of God and angel by the second millennium B.C. Certainly they did manage to teach the locals a thing or two and possibly they meddled a bit with their genes, but even so this would hardly generate the sort of worship and awe that later texts exhibit. The reason is both simple and yet difficult to swallow. It is recorded that they had two mysterious powers which were really awesome in those days: that of *flight* and that of *light.* These are the two major attributes they share with the angels.

Enoch is very specific here "They (the angels) lifted me up and placed me on what seemed to be a cloud, and this cloud moved, and going upwards I could see the sky around and, still higher, I seemed to be in Space." (Secrets of Enoch III:1)

Again in the Book of Enoch we find (XIV:8) :

"Behold, in the vision a cloud invited me and a mist summoned me, and the course of the stars and the lightnings sped by me, and the winds in the vision caused me to fly and lifted me upward and bore me to heaven." This is almost word for word the description given by Orfeo Angelucci in the 1950's when he was irresistibly drawn towards the UFO belonging to the space brothers of Lucifer. His first impression, before stepping inside it was of a "huge, misty soap bubble… The walls were lit mysteriously and looked like ethereal mother-of-pearl stuff." It is at this point in the narrative that our credulity can be stretched in one of two ways. Either these Shining Ones were really substantial beings who had supernatural powers, or they were in possession of a technology which put them ten thousand years in advance of their lowland competitors. Whichever way, where is the evidence to support either claim? This is of course the point at which any serious researcher finds it difficult to meet the eyes of the

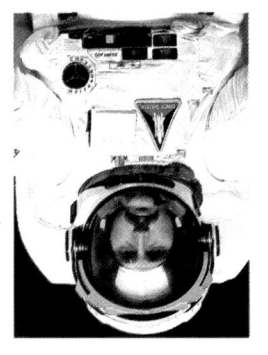

funding committees and when any reader starts to put the book down. Yet if half the citizens of the United States of America can accept the existence of a supernatural host of angels then surely our mind could be open to the possibility that there have been civilizations before us which had technologies equal or even superior to our own.

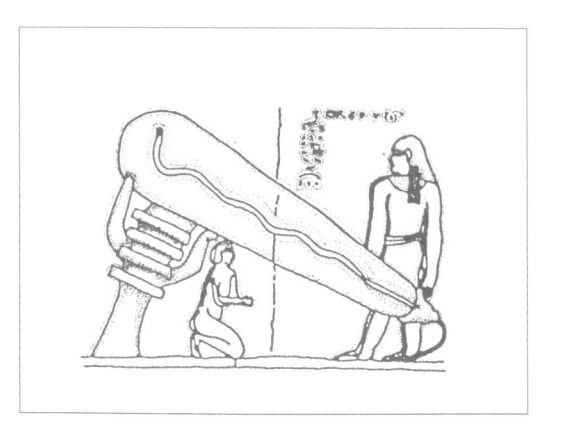

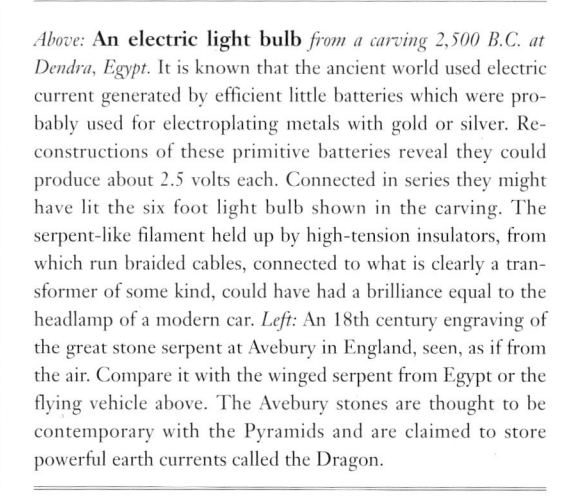

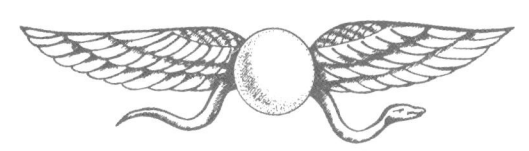

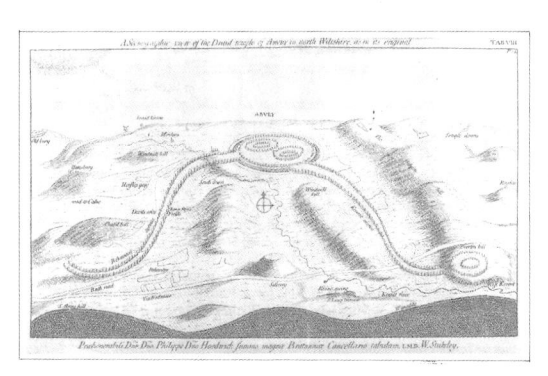

Above: **An electric light bulb** *from a carving 2,500 B.C. at Dendra, Egypt.* It is known that the ancient world used electric current generated by efficient little batteries which were probably used for electroplating metals with gold or silver. Reconstructions of these primitive batteries reveal they could produce about 2.5 volts each. Connected in series they might have lit the six foot light bulb shown in the carving. The serpent-like filament held up by high-tension insulators, from which run braided cables, connected to what is clearly a transformer of some kind, could have had a brilliance equal to the headlamp of a modern car. *Left:* An 18th century engraving of the great stone serpent at Avebury in England, seen, as if from the air. Compare it with the winged serpent from Egypt or the flying vehicle above. The Avebury stones are thought to be contemporary with the Pyramids and are claimed to store powerful earth currents called the Dragon.

As it happens, there are many intriguing examples throughout the world of ancient images of flying machines, from Egyptian toy gliders over four thousand years old to models of delta-winged jet aircraft found in Peru or mysterious rocket-like space vehicles found on the walls of temples deep in the jungles of South America.

But so far, it is true, an actual working example has not been unearthed or dragged up in a deep sea fishing net off the Azores.

So, not only are we understandably skeptical, but also, we still possess a mindset of civilization which is linear rather than cyclic. Yet Plato could be right when he insists, in his two books on Atlantis, that periodic catastrophes have left the few survivors "destitute of letters and education to begin all over again as children." In Plato's account, an Egyptian priest informs him of the many times that humankind has reached golden era's of knowledge and wisdom, only to lose everything in some calamity which erases all the evidence of those times. Yet those periods live on in myths of supernatural beings with legendary powers. With some justification the phenomenon of angels appears to fit this pattern.

Evidence of earlier epochs, when humans could have flown does exist. The Sumerians, Akkadians, Babylonians and Persians, all have records and pictures of flying machines and winged beings. Ahura Mazda, the Lord of Light, was supposed to fly in a disc and this was a very popular subject in bas reliefs. There are even the well known accounts in the Sanskrit texts of India which describe "an apparatus which moves by inner strength like a bird." That "...can move in the sky from place to place...The secret of building flying machines... that do not break, cannot be divided, do not catch fire... and cannot be destroyed. The secret of making flying machines stand still...invisible...overhearing con-versations in enemy flying machines... of taking pictures of the interiors of enemy flying machines...of making beings in enemy flying machines unconscious and destroying them." These brief extracts are from a text by Maharishi Bharadvaya, an Indian seer who lived thousands of years ago, who is almost offhand in giving details of aircraft. Similar details are to be found within the *Vedas* and the *Mahabharata* which supposedly dates back to 7016 B. C. This precise dating is valid if we are to reconstruct the time span required for the specific constellations described within the text to have appeared in the ancient skies. Add to these curiosities the little models of airplanes found within the Peruvian Highlands, or those winged toys of Egypt, and we begin to accumulate a modest, yet nonetheless solid body of evidence which clearly points to the possibility that silvery flying machines were probably climbing into the skies long before the two Wright brothers reinvented the device.

Friar Joseph, the Flying Monk

There is an alternative, yet no less startling explanation: these mysterious peoples could have learnt to fly without mechanical means. This is not so far fetched as at first may appear. Throughout history there have been a number of authenticated, although inexplicable cases of men and women who could sail into the air. One of the most famous of these cases was that of St. Joseph of Copertino whose miraculous flights in the 17th century were attested to by many influential and respected witnesses.

Except for this strange talent, Joseph was in no way remarkable. On the contrary, one Bishop even described him as *idiota*, which could be interpreted as innocent, although brother Joseph was also nicknamed "open mouth" as his lower jaw always hung open. Feeble-minded or not, Joseph could fly. It first occurred in the middle of mass: the monk could not restrain his ecstatic mood and drifted up from his seat to land on the high altar twenty feet away. Such zeal did not escape the Pope who ordered him to Rome. Joseph was so ecstatic in the Pontiff's presence that he floated off the ground for all to see. So high did he go that it was commented that he even showed due propriety by having on underwear for the occasion. In Assisi he was so overcome by the enthusiastic reception of the crowd that he sailed over the onlookers to land on the altar and embrace the statue of the Virgin. Once he flew into the topmost branches of a tree on overhearing a fellow monk remark on the beauties of the day. He demonstrated his bizarre power too many times for it to be dismissed as a mass hallucination. He could even help others to fly, as he demonstrated when he healed a demented aristocrat by seizing him by the hair and taking off. This time he flew for a record fifteen minutes. The Church is often a little embarrassed by such miraculous displays. But before they decided to canonize this rather awkward saint, the authorities examined the sworn testimonies of hundreds of witnesses including a Pope, two Kings, the Duke of Brunswick and his philosopher friend Leibnitz, who was certainly no credulous fool. Even when the doctor was cauterizing Joseph's leg just before he died, the surgeon was shocked to find that the friar was floating six inches above the chair.

It is certainly difficult to know quite what to make of this story. The sworn depositions of so many intelligent people suggest that Joseph could, indeed, fly. If a simpleton like this monk could do so, then surely it is not beyond others to use a human capacity which, for some reason or another, apparently lies idle. The Shining Ones of the Middle East could

Illumination

If it is difficult to unearth concrete evidence as far as flight is concerned, what of the second "advanced" technology? In the case of electric light there is at last real and substantial evidence of its use as far back as five thousand years ago. There are, for instance, actual examples of efficient electrical batteries which have been unearthed in Egypt and Baghdad. Many of these devices were actually used to electro-plate metals with gold and silver. There is, however, one example of a huge device depicted in a wall carving in Egypt, dating from 2500 B.C. which clearly resembles an electric light bulb.

Returning to the settlement for a moment we read in the earliest tablet:

"At the House of Joy and Life, the bright dwelling, Where the destiny of Man was established, The splendid place of Flaming Brightness.".

Another reference was to a "Brilliant, glowing House" which was obviously very different from the mud walled dwellings of the lowlands lit by either oil lamps or rush torches.

In Enoch's later account of the same house it is difficult to know whether his awed description is the genuine response of a simple country man who lived at the edge of pre-history and who had never seen brilliant light at night time, or a case of the "chair transformed to a throne." But Enoch was known as a writer of truth and most of his descriptions are remarkably free of religious or supernatural trappings. He enters a building with glistening white stone walls which was brilliantly lit. The floor

was white marble and illuminated fountains seemed to be playing ("fiery sentinels and heavenly rain") .

"In every respect, the inside was so magnificent, and spacious, that I cannot describe it to you. Its floor was brilliantly lit, and above that were bright lights like planets, and its ceiling, too, was brilliant.

"I looked and saw a high Chair, there, with the appearance of crystal, shining like the courses of the Sun; and I saw Cherubim. And from under the Chair came a blaze of light such that I could not bear to look at it.

"And on it was a stately Being – his clothes shone more brightly than the Sun, and were whiter than any snow."

This is a description, written over 9000 years ago, of a room which quite plausibly could have been lit by the electric power produced from the simple chemical batteries which have been unearthed in the region. So the dark pre-history of the cave dwellers might not have been quite so dark as our history books so solidly proclaim.

This tentative scenario of the origins of real, down to earth angels could explain how a group of beings, with far less miraculous powers than gods or angels, but having, nonetheless, an awesome technology compared with the primitive peoples in the area, could have been operating in the Bible lands over ten millennia ago. But where could they have picked up such a technology and where did these proto-angels come from in the first place? There are a number of plausible explanations without resorting, as many authors have done, to extra-terrestrial intervention.

Angels over the Oceans

There have been various theories as to the location

and fate of the legendary island of Atlantis or of the pacific continent of Mu. For the sake of brevity and following the meticulous Mayan calendar, the destruction and sinking of Atlantis was recorded as taking place in the year 8498 B. C. It is suspected that a small asteroid penetrated the Earth's atmosphere and crashed into what is now the Azores. Equally plausible was that overzealous Atlantaean scientists managed to blow themselves up, causing a similar catastrophe on the other side of the world. Whatever the reason, there is evidence to suggest that small parties of survivors from both Atlantis and Lemuria fanned out into their old colonies on the remaining continents. Some entered Southern Europe, North Africa, Egypt and the Middle East. It is surmised that some of these belonged to an elite scientific priesthood or aristocracy, who had advanced technologies and in some cases considerable wisdom. It was these who appeared with shining faces. Enoch did actually specifically state that these beings could, if they wanted, appear as normal, although exceptionally tall men, without this brilliant aura.

With such a background it is entirely feasible that such a group arrived in the Bible lands 12,000 years ago. It was they who transformed the myths and legends of the peoples who lived there. Of all the fabulous, supernatural, extra-terrestrial, psychic and psychological possibilities open to us, this explanation of how the whole phenomenon of angels suddenly appeared is one of the most persuasive and certainly one of the least suspect. It would also explain the powerful link between angels and the chosen peoples. For howsoever complex the later Christian heavenly hierarchy became, angels are at heart a Jewish creation. It must be remembered that the official language of angels was Hebrew long before they ever had to learn Greek or Latin.

CHAPTER SIX
Heavenly Hypotheses

S O Far, In The Search for what angels might really be, we have examined some of the most plausible explanations. But these in no way exhaust the hypothetical field.

In this chapter we will widen our vision and extend the horizons of speculation. It is regretted that space doesn't permit any "in depth" study of any of the various themes, but it does highlight the richness of the subject matter. We are beginning to appreciate that Angels can appear as all things to all men.

Creating What We Think

Modern day physicists and psychologists would agree that we tend to see what we expect to see. The moment a scientist attempts to observe atomic sub-particles, the very method he uses appears to influence the behavior of the particles. In fact his very presence, his mind frame and expectancies seem to basically alter their microscopic patterns. In quantum physics the observer becomes part of his observed world and can no longer be sure that so-called objective phenomena aren't just a thought cast in emptiness, or, at best, a shifting stream of thought-fields of possible worlds. The universe is no longer the solid substantive place as understood by the Victorians only a century ago. "You create what you think" has become one of the most fashionable idioms of our New Age.

We are familiar with the extremes of this concept. Psychiatric patients are known to sometimes live in interior worlds which they experience as being external and real. Their universe in no way corresponds to the one the rest of us collectively agree upon. But who is the final arbiter of what is real and what is dream? The visions of the schizophrenic are often closer to those of the mystic or the quantum physicist, than to those of the normal man in the street. Chuang Tzu once dreamt that he was a butterfly, but then asked his disciples whether it might be that the butterfly was actually dreaming he was Chuang Tzu.

Normalcy is a relative term which can only be supported by a mass composed of sheer numbers. What 99 out of every 100 people *agree* to witness is what we call both normalcy and reality. But normalcy is not necessarily reality. Truth has usually been found to be a lonely business and has seldom followed the majority.

So we cannot discount the possibility that witnesses of angels and other non-human beings could be the lonely one percent who see a reality which is denied to the rest of us.

Multiple Image

While most people could claim to be relatively sane, or at least normal in relation to those who are institutionalized, few can be said to be a whole and integrated entity. We are, what might be considered, a collection of fragments, a cluster of disparate parts. A schizophrenic is one extreme example of a personality which is divided in some way.

In an entirely different disorder of the brain, in which the bridge across its two hemispheres has in some way been damaged, the subject can be doing up the buttons of his coat with the right hand while the left hand is undoing them. Neither actions are being recognized by its the opposite compartment.

In some degree we all make unconsciously conflicting decisions most of the time. On one conscious level we are smiling at the wife or the boss, whilst on another "island" there is a volcano of resentment or anger which could explode any minute. A drunken state can suddenly bring back remembrances of similar occasions which have been totally forgotten when sober. Under deep hypnosis memories are uncovered of events which have otherwise been suppressed and therefore completely unavailable to the conscious part of the mind.

In a way everyone suffers from a weird kind of waking amnesia. Human beings are sleepwalkers who keep bumping into unrecognized chunks of their own drifting personalities. These fragments appear to retain memory stores which are lost or inaccessible to the rest of the conscious personality.

In attempting to show that such a mechanism could underlie encounters or visions of angels, it is instructive to briefly examine two of the most famous and well documented cases of fragmented or multiple personalities. These are those of Doris Fischer and Christine Beauchamp. These two, or more accurately nine, personalities enthralled psychiatrists and para-psychologists around the turn of this century and still are cited as classic cases.[†]

Stand Up the Real Me

By the time Doris Fischer was eighteen she had no less than *five* clearly separate personalities sharing her body. Doris herself was an intelligent, likable, conventional girl who blanked out every now and then. During these "blank outs", comas or sleep,

the other four characters emerged unbeknown to her.

The first was Margaret, who seemed in every way Doris's polar opposite. Margaret was noisy where Doris basically was quiet and amusing where Doris was serious. Margaret was a feisty, mischievous ten year old tomboy. She was aware of Doris and could "go in and out" apparently at will. Margaret was also aware of the third personality which she called "sick Doris". This one, called Mary Anne, appeared suddenly at the moment of the death of Doris's mother. She had no memory whatever and had to be taught how to speak by Margaret. Mary Anne remained a timid, shy and rather wooden personality who was often unwell, hysterical and generally nervous. Her major occupation was knitting. The lowest entity in the hierarchy was named Jane, who was little more than a tape recorder for the conversations of the others, which she could "replay" verbatim even if the original event had been years before. The most mature self of all was called Ariel, who appeared only when Doris was asleep. She was the wisest amongst the hierarchy and the only one who had an overview of all the other characters.

However, she claimed to be a separate spirit who had been summoned to help. Each personality profoundly changed Doris's whole physical form. Photographs taken when each of the characters was in command seem to show different persons who had a certain family likeness. Doris had no sense of smell or taste and was often unaware of her bladder through some form of anesthesia, so she often wet herself. Mary Anne appeared to have no sensitivity in her nerves especially below her waist. Margaret was the only one who was acutely aware of her body and could even see in the dark.

Christine 1, Christine 2, Sally and B-4

Equally famous at the time and as well documented was the case of Christine Beauchamp. She had fragmented into four main characters. Christine One was in poor health, nervous and suffered from uncontrolled movements of the body. When under light hypnosis Christine Two emerged was very relaxed, open and intelligent. The third of the company was Sally who, like Doris's Margaret was a mischievous and high spirited opposite to Christine One. She contemptuously referred to Christine as a "goody fool." As Christine had no idea of the existence of Sally she was often the butt of her "twin's" pranks, suddenly awakening to find Sally's cigarette still in her mouth and a glass of unlady-like wine in her hand. Physically Sally was as full of life and energy as Christine was depleted. Sally would take off for long walks, knowing well that poor Christine would suddenly find herself miles from home totally exhausted. The last personality that the Pittsburg psychoanalyst, Dr. Prince, discovered was labeled B-4: she seems much like Ariel in the case of Doris. B-4 was more mature, responsible and self possessed, but had a high opinion of herself.

Colin Wilson, to whom I am indebted for bringing these particular cases to my attention, neatly sums up, in his very perceptive *Mysteries*, a bewildering interaction between three characters locked in one body. "Sally and B-4 loathed one another. Christine accepted Sally's practical jokes with passive fatalism; B-4 hated them and often repaid in kind. On one occasion, Christine set out for New York to find a job. Sally got off the train at New Haven and took

a job as a waitress. Christine found the work exhausting; B-4 hated it as being below her dignity. One day B-4 walked out of the job, pawned Christine's watch and returned to Boston. Sally took over and decided to spite B-4 by refusing to return to her old lodging; instead she took a new one. Christine 'came to' in a strange bed, having no idea of where she was or how she got there."

Eventually we discover that both Doris and Christine were able to integrate, albeit a little uneasily, all their fragments into a single character. This was done at a cost. Doris's Mary Anne eventually regressed and knowing she was about to "die" wrote a letter to Margaret disposing of her things. Margaret herself became younger and younger until one day she appeared laughing and then left for good. In the case of Christine, Dr. Prince decided to suppress Sally who resisted the sentence. "I won't! I won't be dead," she screamed, "I have as much right to live as she has!" As it happened she did make an occasional appearance even when Christine was far more integrated, managing to play a few practical jokes on her more conventional counterpart.

Multiple Personality Disorder, (MPD), is now known to be far more widespread than was once believed. The recent case of a woman in Massachusetts called M. M.George (an amalgam of her three major personalities; Mary, Monica and George) is as extreme as that of Christine, eighty years before. She tells us, "My core personality went out at age six, and my host personality, Mary, took over. Only one person in my family knows. That's the case with most multiple personalities. You just don't see it if you are not looking for it. My first husband, poor dear, never knew what hit him. See, part of my personality went to sleep for a year and woke up married to Eddie – that's my ex-husband – and I could not tolerate him. Monica was the one who married him." Mary didn't know Monica even existed.

These two cases have been cited as extremes, but milder forms of multiple personality are not at all uncommon. Most of us exhibit less bizarre versions. Simultaneously driving a car, talking idly with a passenger and thinking about what you will do when you get home, effectively involves three minds which are operating independently of one another. It might be an unconscious robot which steers the wheel, a semi-conscious robot which politely exchanges smiling niceties and a raging jealous lover who is prepared to shoot his wife. If there is an emergency like a near collision with another car there is suddenly a total response of yet another vibrant consciousness which sweeps away all the others in a split second.

I have gone to some lengths to demonstrate that we are not the single entity most of us fondly imagine. Actually we are a crowd.

In order to know how this fact could generate an encounter with an angel or an ET, consider what Elias Canetti perceptively says of crowds. He distinguishes two sorts of crowd. One is an *open* crowd which is the universal phenomenon we all know. As soon as it begins to exist it wants to consist of more and more people. It is unbounded and continues to exist just so long as it continues to grow. The moment it reaches its goal or stops growing it disperses.

The *closed* crowd, by comparison, stops growth and opts for permanence. It defines clear boundaries which limit growth but also postpones dissolution. Both types exist so long as they have *"an unattained goal."* The implication is that this is true of our inner crowd as well, which only continue to exist while the goal of integration is unattainable. As soon as an individual gains some degree of individuation the crowds disperse. This happens as much with multiple personalities as with cases of abductions by ETs, or messages from angels.

This tendency to divide the self into separate parts which have separate memories and which are blocked from those of other "fragments" could form the basis of the encounter incident. Some powerful stimulus blocks the memory of an experience while at the same time leaving tantalizing and emotionally charged remnants within one or more of the other "fragments". We have already seen that the brain is composed of three evolutionary layers which have a degree of autonomy and independence, and that the archetypes seem to be triggered from or by the cerebellum. Any division of consciousness means that archetypal images which surface from the more primitive parts of the brain can actually manifest themselves to other less critical parts of our minds as if they were concrete reality. Under stress or unusual circumstances the likelihood of powerful exchanges, in the form of *waking dreams*, could occur between fragments. One fragment is the actor while the other becomes the audience.

As Jung suggests, the psychological and spiritual preoccupation of our times appears to be a striving towards unity, wholeness and individuation. This takes the form of a conscious or unconscious quest for a holy or *whole* answer to our increasing sense of feeling divided within ourselves and separated from the world about us. We all seem to be frantically trying to arrest the diaspora of our various parts which seem to be drifting off in every direction.

These drifting fragments are also trying to communicate with one another and will use any means to do so, including the images of ETs and angels. After experiencing a powerful encounter with an extra-terrestrial, one witness remarked with considerable insight: "I think the entire thing was a fantastic, beautifully executed theatre...a display solely for my benefit to convey something that right now is unbeknown to me".

Gregory Bateson, in describing a schizophrenic patient, has this to say: "It would appear that once precipitated into psychosis, the patient has a course to run. He is, as it were, embarked upon a voyage of discovery which is only completed by his return to the normal world, to which he comes back with insights different from those of the inhabitants who never embarked on such a voyage. Once begun, a schizophrenic episode would appear to have as definite a course as an initiation ceremony – a death and rebirth."

This must remind us forcibly of the experiences of the prophet, Ezekiel[†] and Orfeo Angelucci along with most of the abductee cases, like that of Whitley Striber who records his experiences in *Communion*. Both ETs and angels are the rare stuff of the "transformation myth."

This is the myth in which the plot hinges around the theme of *communication*. Angels are symbolic messengers of the Divine, just as ETs are the messengers of higher beings. In such myths of com-

munication these messengers of the gods bring about a higher transformation in the chosen individual. Could it be that we are observing the drama which surrounds an individual who is restoring all the fragmented parts of his or her being into one whole? The magic of the story can only work, however, if the hero or heroine is unaware that they are stepping inside their own myth.

The science fiction writer Philip Dick went beyond both angel and alien, for he went to the source. He experienced an encounter with God. The Almighty "fired a beam of pink light at my head." His own mind was then invaded "by a transcendentally rational mind, as if I had been insane all my life and had suddenly become sane." His ensuing confusion arose from the fact that "this rational mind was not human. It was more like an artificial intelligence. On Thursdays and Saturdays I would think it was God, on Tuesdays and Wednesdays I would think it was extra-terrestrial, sometimes I would think it was the Soviet Union Academy of Sciences trying out their psychotronic, microwave, telepathic transmitter." Dick didn't once consider the possibility that the whole phenomenon was born within himself, but insisted that it was an external happening. The conditions of the cure are that the hero doesn't know the real nature of his quest. Even a highly perceptive and imaginative writer like Dick could miss this option. It does suggest that even above average intelligence is no match for a division of the mind which makes one part so alien to another.

This would suggest a tentative explanation for the phenomena of cosmic guardians, archangels, spirit guides, ETs and demons. If the whole heavenly host and the diabolic citizens of the Infernal regions are of this order of reality then we know that the whole of heaven and hell fits neatly within the caverns of our skulls.

The Acid Test

In this New Age era the term "fragmentation" is almost a dirty word. And yet, if an individual is seen as a hierarchy of many possible beings, it implies that we are actually far vaster than we ever imagined. Many gurus, mystics and psychologists insist that the words "in your Father's house there are many mansions" should read "in *your* house"; yet for some unaccountable reason we all chose to live in the woodshed. Once the consciousness can be coaxed out of its cramped quarters the vision widens dramatically. Those who wrote of their experiences with LSD and other hallucinogens in the 1960's and early 70's were afforded glimpses which had, until then, been the exclusive territory of the sages and mages. Those on trips began to experience just how many halls these mansions contained. One of the best known experimenters, Dr. John Lilly, wrote in *The Center of the Cyclone*, of one occasion when he "became a focused center of consciousnesses and traveled into other spaces and met other beings, entities or consciousness's. "In a golden light which seemed to permeate in all directions," he met, what appeared to be, two guardian angels: "They say they are always with me, but that I am not usually in a state to perceive them. I am in a state to perceive them when I am close to the death of the body. In this state there is no time." One is reminded of Christ's description of Heaven: "There shall be time no longer", or the painter William Blake, on his death bed, "gloriously" singing of the sights of angels in heaven.

On a later trip the two guardian angels appear again and this time he is told: "You still have some evasions to explore before you can progress to the level at which you are existing at the moment. You can come and permanently be in this state. However, it is advisable that you achieve this through your own efforts while still in the body."

After extensive experimentation with LSD, hypnosis and meditation, Lilly became convinced that there were four levels above our normal consciousness and four levels below. This roughly corresponds to the Eastern concept according to which there is a level of superconsciousness above the normal range of awareness which then leads to a cosmic consciousness above that. The two balancing levels below are the unconscious and the collective unconscious. The phenomenon of angels appears within the realm of the superconscious and the devils within the unconscious.

Lilly's own proposition suggests a rich layered territory which could account for the "Guided Tours of Heaven and Hell" which have been experienced by saints and mystics.

In visiting the bottomless hell of one bad trip, Lilly describes what he maintains was the most punishing experience of his life. In it he seems to be a very small program in a huge and alien computer (Lilly was a computer expert so would find it a useful analogy). "The whole computer was the result of a senseless dance of certain kinds of atoms ...stimulated and pushed by organized but meaningless energies". In a total terror and panic he everywhere "found entities like myself who were slave programs in this huge cosmic conspiracy, this cosmic dance of energy and matter which had absolutely no meaning, no love, no human value."

From my own personal experience I have known a similar "bottomless pit" without the benefit of LSD.

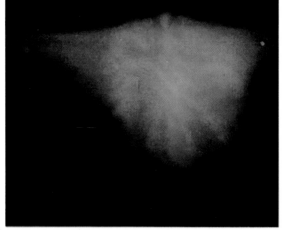

This happened on waking from a lucid dream in which I knew I was dreaming and had attempted to find out just who was directing the dream. There was the same totally alien space filled with what appeared to be black stars like so many thousands of acupuncture points or galaxies of molecules which were completely devoid of all such human qualities as love, life, laughter or light. Later I discovered that there is a long mystic tradition which describes this state as falling into "God's dark night". Supposedly there are times when God sleeps and in doing so vacates the void which is usually filled with Light. If a mystic is unfortunate enough to "flower" in meditation at the wrong point in the cycle he falls into this apparent hell. It is claimed that for some the experience is enough to put them off meditation forever. Equally, a glimpse of the upper layers has quite the opposite effect.

It will be recalled that we found a very similar layered hierarchy in the heavenly model in the Treasury. The contemporary channeled entity, Ramtha, has an interesting description of such layers. He says that, "when thought contemplated itself in your beginning, what it expanded itself into was the principle of thought called light. Light was created first, because whenever thought is contemplated and expanded, it always lowers into a vibratory frequency that emits light. Light is thus the first lowered form of contemplated expanded thought."

So all things are created by a thought which has no speed at all. By expanding it into something which does have velocity, that is light, and then slowing it down, it creates the manifest universe. The hierarchies of the angels found in the Treasury have identical principles. Lilly met the guardian angels on the second upper level, while on the highest level there was only a sense of being one with the Divinity. At last we have a clear location where beings who fit the description of angels appear to live.

Angelic locations

Many psychics and parapsychologists claim that Lilly's various layers of altered consciousness correspond to astral, ethereal and causal territories. According to the esoteric sciences we do not possess just one body but four, and each of these exists in a separate location. When someone experiences an out-of-body event, the *astral body*, for instance, moves in a world that is parallel to our own normal material universe.

Above: **Angel on Television** This image supposedly appeared during a Harmonic Convergence in Mt. Shasta, California. Postcards of the picture have an inscription, "Yes dear ones let it be known that the angels are truly here on Earth." This is certainly the first case of an angel who isn't camera shy. Opposite: **Angel appearing to the King in a dream**, *Lorenzo Monaco, 14th century, Firenze*. One possible explanation given for angelic phenomena is that some of us recall entering astral and ethereal territories and seeing wing-like auras surrounding other dream travelers.

There are many recorded and well documented instances of such phenomena. One of the classic cases is that of Robert Monroe who wrote of his experiences in *Out of the Body.* This otherwise very pragmatic American businessman discovered that he had the strange talent of being able to leave his physical body and travel in other realms or planes. He managed to explore three distinct localities with what he believes is his astral body. The first locale is our own physical world, but Monroe experienced that moving within this realm with an astral body feels very unnatural and the traveler is easily disorientated and exhausted. The second locality is a non-material, boundless immensity, which has very different laws of time and space, motion and matter to those found in locality one. In this world, as Monroe puts it, "as you think so you are". It is the natural abode of the astral body, the individual consciousness after death and the astral bodies of dreamers. Monroe's own theory is that there are "an infinity of worlds all operating at different frequencies". Just as wave vibrations can simultaneously occupy the same space, "with the minimum of interaction, so might the worlds of Locale II be interspersed in our physical matter world." A characteristic already observed in Dr. Lilly's account is that this corresponding level is a timeless zone. The past and the future co-exist with the here and now. However, the traveler can perceive what appears as solid matter as well as artifacts common to the physical world.

This locality is, "composed of deepest desires and most frantic fears", which are completely unshielded from others traveling in the same place. The zones nearest to the physical world are peopled by insane, emotionally driven beings who are still identified with their desires and fears. Passing through this region was like venturing into hell. There are precise descriptions in the ancient Tibetan Book of the Dead which closely correspond to Monroe's independent findings. His descriptions would also fit some of those Medieval visions of Heaven and Hell which we have already encountered. It will be recalled that at the borders of those heavens closest to our physical earth, demented and demonic creatures haunt the pathways and one of the specific duties of the angels of the order of Powers is to act as border patrols. The mystic Swedenburg would leave his body much in the same way as Monroe, and meet with angels and beings from the "Other World". In Celtic myths the "Other World" is parallel to our own and can be reached by crossing a stream, walking around a burial mound or meeting with the magical folk. But the hero is always warned that there is no sense of time in that nether region and he might re-

Above left: **The Silver Shield of the Mental Body,** *illustration by M. from "Dayspring of Youth."* The radiant field of energy currents which surround our mental, astral or ethereal bodies are remarkably suggestive of the wings of an angel. It is very possible that we experience seeing such images when moving in the astral or ethereal planes during sleep but do not remember in our waking hours. However the memory continues to haunt us at the edge of consciousness so that when we see a picture of an angel we feel some sense of recognition.

Above right: **Phane's Birth of the World Egg,** *117-138 A.D..* Phanes is known as "The Shining One," and in almost all respects shadows the image on the left, as if the artist has remembered more than most of us.

turn to the physical world hundreds of years older.

If we examine any descriptions or drawings of auras or of ethereal, astral or psychic bodies, then there is an uncanny resemblance to the wings of angels. Anyone who has experienced astral traveling or an out of the body experience will tell of the sheer exhilaration of flight. The forces around the astral body fan out behind the traveler like the electromagnetic fields around the planets and this could account for the angelic archetype. In similar modes to that of sleep we are able to leave the body. In this state we might see other astral travelers, but on returning to the substantive world forget the experience entirely, much as we forget most of our dreams. And somewhere we keep a memory, although the conscious mind seldom has access to it.

Monroe once "projected" himself into the study of a well known parapsychologist, Dr. Andrija Puharich. He had a long talk with him but when verifying the visit later Puharich had no recollection of the discussion at all. However, Monroe was able to describe the study in perfect detail and confirmed exactly what the psychologist was doing at the time. It does suggest that we might be able to communicate with other astral entities but that our physical memories retain no record of the transaction. Which also suggests that the phenomenon of multiple-entities might extend even into parallel worlds.

One ingenious explanation for the appearance of angels is that the astral bodies of those who sleep on the nightside of the planet can manifest to those awake on the dayside. There may be more to this seemingly wacky idea than first meets the eye. There are many cases of dreamers who pick up what is happening in other parts of the world. Earthquakes, plane disasters and wars are experienced in dreams. Millions of dreamers may forget actually experiencing a particularly awful flood on the other side of the globe or just put it down to a nightmare. But the frequency of those who pick up the newspaper or watch the television the next morning to see their nightmare in the flesh is too great to ignore. Unfortunately little respectable or serious research has been done in this area. But imagine a dreamer in Europe who tries to warn the occupants of a house of a coming earthquake. At first the physical occupants are oblivious of her existence and the dreamer feels impotent to avert disaster. Making a supreme effort she somehow manages to get through to them and they rush out of the building to see it collapse in rubble a few moments later. To the dreamer it is a satisfying conclusion to a nightmare, to the substantial Colombians it is hailed as a miracle and the dreamer as an unknown angel.

Having examined some of the more elaborate angelic speculations it is well to be reminded of William of Occam. He was the first Western thinker to expound the notion of *Notitia Intuitiva* or Intuitive Cognition. He believed that we are capable of perceiving things without the need of words or concepts. He insisted that, in the presence of any theory, parsimony was best. Occam's miserly "razor" prunes all unnecessary elaborations from any hypothesis and heads for the simplest and most obvious solution. With this in mind and armed with Samuel Butler's adage that "all reason is against it, and all healthy instinct is for it," we can turn to the Last Judgment.

CHAPTER SEVEN
The Last Judgment

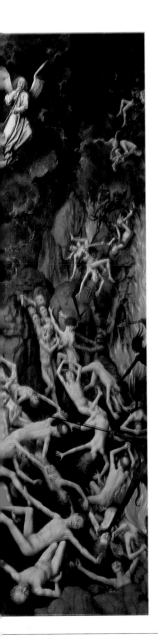

The Last Judgment *by*
Hans Memlinc, Brussels

HAVING EXAMINED SOME OF THE MORE EXOTIC SPECULATIONS as to who and what the angelic host might be and why they persist in our collective unconscious, it is clear that each hypothesis has had both its own peculiar merits and particular drawbacks. It remains largely a matter of individual taste which one seems to fit the facts. This is one of the problems fundamental to theorizing. If you are blind and have never seen the sun rise it doesn't matter how many hypotheses you can array, you still don't *know*. Belief is simply the adoption of someone else's idea. Once you have seen the sun you don't *believe* in it, you *know* it. But as far as angels are concerned, few have ever seen one, or if anyone has during some astral tour, he or she have managed to forget the whole episode. It is also surely evident by now that angels don't leave footprints so all that is left of their traces is a complex jumble of hypotheses. So this seems a perfect time to apply the sharp blade of Occam's "razor" to cut away all the excess ideas.

William of Occam is exactly the man for the job. He was the last great theologian of the Middle Ages who also helped to open up an entirely new vein of Christianity. As the brilliant pupil of Duns Scotus and a "theoretical" follower of St. Francis, he proposed the possibility of an immediate grasp and perception of singular objects, without any need for intermediary thoughts. This he called intuitive cognition. While, on the surface this doesn't seem to be an idea which could shake the foundations of the whole heavenly hierarchy, nevertheless it did. And his maxims are as relevant to our understanding of angels as they were seven centuries ago.

Occam argued that all concepts, like those to be found in our Treasury of Angelic Lore, were symbols devoid of reality, they were empty shells. This being the case the process of abstract reasoning is useless. The vast theoretical hierarchy of angels is actually constructed of concept, built upon concept or emptiness upon emptiness. In Occam's eyes the path to God could never be found through the intellect and of course what was known of angels at that time was almost entirely channeled through the minds of the scholars. The implications of Occam's principles were not lost on the brighter minds of the Establishment. For if one can perceive a thing without an intermediary thought, then it is not a very long road to travel before one can see God or Christ face to face without the mediation and interpretation of a priest or a Church.

Before being able to apply Occam's sword to the angelic theories of today, it is necessary to see how they affected those of the golden age of the host at the time of the great schism which split the Church of the 14th century. The true cause of this split was not that two politically hungry Popes faced off in France and Italy, but rather, that two completely irreconcilable paths suddenly appeared in one religion. The intellectual, Aristotelian reasoning of Thomas Aquinas clashed with the Mystical, Intuitive experience of St. Francis. A line up of the two sides might be helpful at this point.

Thomas Aquinas	St. Francis
Angelic Host	Christ as a Man
Scholasticism	Direct Experience
Male	Female
Intellect	Mysticism
Reason	Intuition
Knowledge	Love
Communication	Communion
Dionysius the Aeropagite	William of Occam
Albertus Magnus	Duns scotus
Aristotle	Plotinus
Via Antiqua	Via Moderna
The Dominicans	Franciscans
The Curia	Spirituals
Dante	Bonaventura
Human-like angel	Angel-like human

Above: **The Entrance to Heaven,** and Right: **The Last Judgment** *by Hieronymus Bosch, Venice, 1500*

Up until this point in history, the right wing of the intellect, the orthodox Church, had never been seriously challenged since the wild days of the Gnostics a thousand years before. But now a new type of Christian arose, exemplified by St. Francis of Assisi, the mystic who inadvertently and simply by his presence, toppled the whole angelic hierarchy.

Human-like Angels meet Angel-like Humans

About a century before the outbreak of the plague two minor monastic orders had been created within a few years of each other. They were at opposite ends of the Christian spectrum, like the two hemispheres of the human brain. The Dominicans were established in 1216 to combat heresy and defend the hierarchic authority. By 1231 this was transformed into the dreaded order of the Inquisition. In complete contrast were the Franciscans who, forming around Francis of Assisi, desired to reimbue the Church with the original Christian spirit. Their self-appointed task was to re-awaken popular piety and engage in scientific work. These two orders represented the polar extremes of intellectual and mystical worship. The Franciscans believed that the soul's eventual union with God could be attained, not by "imitating" angels, but quite literally by "becoming" angels. This was a monastic order which sought to know God or Christ directly, dispensing with the traditional clergy as intermediaries, which of course hardly pleased that clergy.

When the orthodox authority of the Church, with its legions of angels, had manifestly failed to halt the plague in any way, there was a turning towards the simple and direct mystic faith which Francis represen-

ted. As his order was dedicated to the road of poverty, it was a welcome change to what was seen as a grasping and greedy priesthood. The gentle and almost feminine receptivity of the Franciscans also appealed to a people worn out with the ravages of the period.

These Franciscan monks, with the exemplary life of Francis himself to guide them, were there to offer a new vision. They believed that only the "fire of Love" could renew the world and cure its wounds. Remember, that the highest order of angels in the old hierarchical system were the Seraphim, those "fiery serpents *burning with love*." It was no coincidence that it was a seraph who appeared to Francis to communicate the Stigmata of Christ. This was a transmission beyond the scriptures. "The seraphic ardor" of Francis had simply made him a seraph on earth. But the stigmata transmitted by the figure of Christ which appeared superimposed upon the angel was the mark which showed that Francis had become *more than an angel*. He had become a Christ.

So in looking back at those battle-lines and the last champions who opposed one another it was the human-like angel of the scholar who was simply loved to death by the angel-like mystic.

Tale of Two Cities

The great flying buttress of the Medieval Church was built upon the dogma of the twin cities of God. As already seen, one was held to be the Holy City, the New Jerusalem and the Heavenly abode of the angels. The other was the City of Earth. Within this lower City, in which we mortal sinners live, was the Mother Church. This was the only part which modeled itself upon the Holy City above and upon its equally holy inhabitants, the angels. So the hierarchy of the Church was supposed to be a mirror

Above: **The Earthly City of the Serpent**
Right: **The Holy City or the New Jerusalem**
Both images are from the *Apocalypse of Liebana,*
11th century, Paris, National Library
Here are the twin cities, one of Man and the other of the Angels. The Black Death decimated the City of Man but it left the City of the Angels completely deserted.

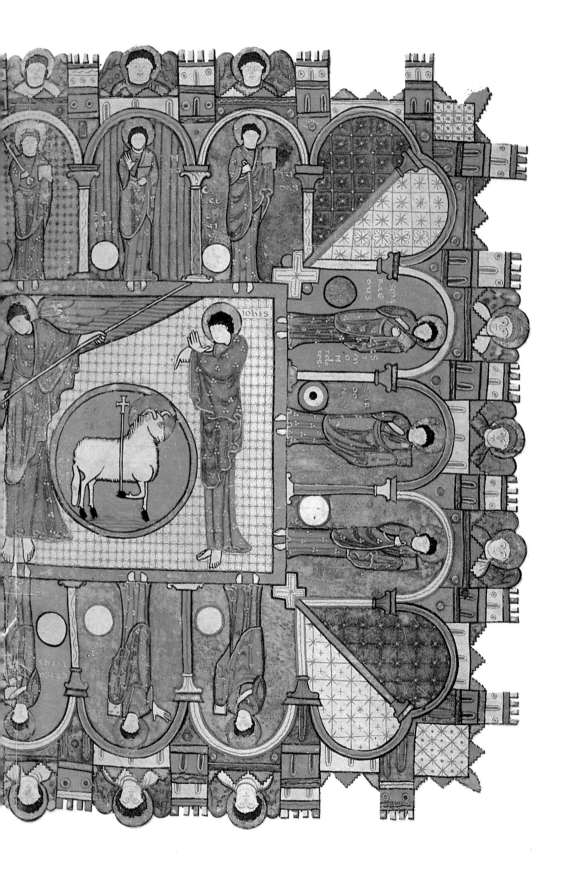

reflection of that superstructure of the heavens.

By the 14th century it was all too clear that something had gone terribly wrong with this model. All that the overtaxed and persecuted populace could see was the gross corruption of the clergy. Disenchantment with the ecclesiastical authorities boiled over when a deep schism appeared to split the Church of Peter, exposing its rotten and very earthly core. At this time the Holy vessel had two papal helmsmen: Clement VII elected in Avignon and Urban VI elected in Rome. After fifty years of stalemate, cardinals of both factions elected a third Pope. But just as the Church mirrored the Holy City with its complex angelic hierarchies, the reflection worked both ways, so the Heavenly abode must mirror the Church. Thus the entire celestial structure was seen to have also split and crumbled. The crash wiped out most of the angels who were supporting its pillars.

Simultaneous with the religious crisis, the horrified population of Europe of the 14th century had to face the terrible scourge of the plague. For most Christians the Black Death was the dreaded apocalypse come true, and was seen as the last trump and the end of the world. As half of Europe was dying, the Church vainly tried to rally its saints and its legions of angels to combat the menace.

Both saint and angel were supposed to be able to turn back such horrors, but neither did. Everyone could plainly see the emptiness and impotence of the Church's brave vanguard. Few angels escaped the effects of that plague in the memories of the masses.

Another significant Medieval dogma was that when a third of the rebel angels fell they were supposed to have left a vast gap in heaven. Humans were to have filled this gap by becoming "like unto the angels." We find many Christian ascetics stri-

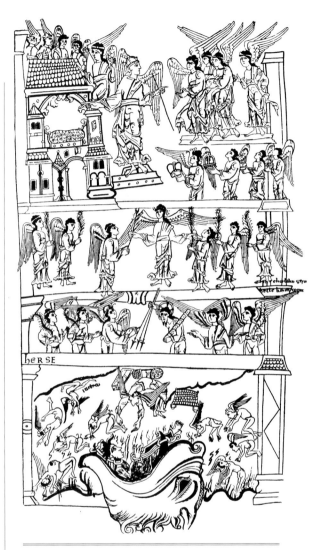

The Expulsion of Lucifer and the Rebel Angels from Heaven *Caedmon paraphrase.* When Lucifer fell he took with him one-third of the heavenly host. The empty places left in the Holy City were supposed to be filled by humans who became "like the Angels." By the middle of the 15th century this foundational concept of the Church was successfully challenged by the newly arising Humanism. In retrospect, it seems that quite the reverse actually happened. Angels came to Earth.

ving to rid themselves of the temptations of the flesh in order to meet that ideal. The corruption and desires of the flesh were seen to be the problem. Sex was obviously the real enemy, for of course angels were not supposed to have any. Taking pleasure in food was another hurdle to overcome, as it was generally acknowledged that angels didn't eat anything more substantial than God's Word. As we will shortly learn, a saint like Catherine of Siena most likely suffered from an acute eating disorder, probably anorexia, in her attempt to emulate this impossible angelic ideal.

Christ was only Human

In the aftermath of the plague a depression settled over Europe and with it a widespread distrust of all the Church's excessive religious ornamentation, its myriad spirits and impotent saints and holy martyrs. The new Humanist ideas which challenged the angelic hierarchies, the indulgences and the veneration of saints also perceived Christ in a new way. Since Christ was recognized as the real mediator between God the Father and humankind, or as one aspect of the Divine Trinity, why should anyone bother with an entire host of angels as well?

The very fact that Christ came to earth to share the sufferings of human beings makes him very human. Consequently it also makes him far removed from the angels who cannot share the experience of those self-same sufferings, without taking on the flesh themselves. And Christians knew all about angels who take on the corruption of the flesh – they're bad.

Yet another cherished concept was dealt a mortal blow as the early sciences began to gain respectability. In the harsh light of the new realities of astronomy, the whole concept of the seven heavens and the seven earths began to appear absurd. The old belief that it was the spirits and angels who kept the universe turning was replaced by a new belief in "natural forces" like gravity. As those proto-sciences expanded the horizons of their knowledge, so the whole angelic firmament of stars began to fade in the light of the new dawn. And as the old universe slowly crumbled, so too did the host of angels who had supported its existence for so long. The Heavenly City became deserted and was replaced on earth by the Book of Nature.

The mystical marriage of Christ and the Holy Jerusalem in Revelations, which once represented the pure female soul (and thus all saintly women were Christ's bride), gave way to a new marriage in heaven. This was the union of man and nature.

The immediate effect of the scientific approach was an acquisition of new knowledge, which further weakened an already wobbly house of angelic cards. Through the printing press that knowledge was disseminated in ways unthinkable in the 14th century. Knowledge up until that point, had been the prerogative of the Church and of the angels who were supposed to govern the workings of the cosmos. With the birth of scientific methodology that active angelic intelligence had either been superseded by humans or it had really come down to earth.

While, later on, the Reformation was to successfully challenge the Church's virtue (which anyone could see was a particularly weak spot) the Age of Reason challenged its intelligence. On most subjects its priests and scholars were shown to be ignorant and credulous. And these experts were the very champions of the angelic cause. Surely if the clergy were shown to be fools it was necessary to question the intelligence of the heavenly host itself. In the ensuing battle the angelic shocktroops were the first casualties.

Just like the Angels

So now man was no longer a replacement angel for the Holy City of God in Heaven, but a living example of the Redeemer within the City of Earth. The man-like angel became the angel-like man who could reach out, beyond the angels, to Christ Consciousness.

Francis's successor, Bonaventure, says of the Saint, "by the Seraphic ardor of his desires, he was born aloft unto God; and by his sweet compassion he was transformed into him who chose to be crucified because of the excess of his love." The transformation into more than an angel happens "not through martyrdom of the flesh but through the fire of his love consuming his soul."

Bonaventure goes on to tell us that Francis "was joined in a bond of inseparable love to the angels who burn with a marvelous fire." It was these Seraphim who would then "inflame the souls of the elect."

Whatever one's personal spiritual persuasions might be it, is difficult to remain unmoved by the story of Francis. But if he is the new angelic prototype then, at first glance, the species is likely to remain rare. At the same time, whatever remains of a living Christ within the boundaries of that religion must surely come from St. Francis. It is also no coincidence that his direct heirs are actually heiresses. For to be an angel on earth requires a receptive and female attitude. The virile angel of Thomas Aquinas, who remains, in essence, an intellectual, incorporeal, spirit has given way to the Seraphs of the "Fire of Love."

Strangely enough, a figure who appears to be one of Francis's spiritual daughters, Catherine of Siena, was a Dominican and therefore in the opposite camp. She would have been more familiar with

the intellectual teachings of Thomas Aquinas than those of Francis. Yet, while Aquinas, the "doctor of angels," was known to have a prodigious appetite, Catherine herself was anorexic and died at the age of thirty three having nourishment only from communion wafers. Like Francis, her overwhelming passion was to become what she called "an earthly angel".

Her approach was extreme, for in trying to imitate the angel she accepted a vision that the soul only becomes angelic by eating the right kind of food. And this is simply the Word of God. Her typical admonitions to her fellow sisters read: "Dearest daughter, contemplate the marvelous state of the soul who receives this bread of life, this food of angels, as she ought." In one of her visions God tells her that the Church has become a temple of the devil: "I appointed you to be earthly angels in this life, but you are devils who have taken up devils' work. "This is a very different message from that of before the Black Death. But by then even God had been forced to recognize that His servants on earth had found Satan's company more congenial.

With Francis the angel took on the flesh and experienced the divine in the same way as the mystic. The intellectual host of immaterial angels of Thomas Aquinas and the orthodox Church have descended to earth, but in taking on the flesh they have become receptive, like a female.

St. Francis receives the Stigmata, *by Giotto, Basilica S. Croce, Florence.* The six-winged, fiery Seraph of Love takes on the form of Christ. The Seraph was the highest expression of angelic consciousness and thus the perfect vehicle to communicate the stigmata. But the transformation of the angel into Christ meant a *communion* with Francis which went far beyond the angel, for in this supreme moment Francis became Christ Consciousness.

Even the stigmata of Francis, and those of Christ before him, show the signs of a vagina. The wound in the side of Christ has often been likened to a lactating breast. Perhaps nowhere is this image of the femininity of the seeker more poignantly expressed as in the rapturous vision of St. Teresa of Avila which we have already seen in Chapter Two. As the angel pierces her body with a long golden spear, it causes her a "pain so sharp that it made me utter several moans; and so excessive was the sweetness caused me by this intense pain that one can never wish to lose it, nor will one's soul be content with anything less than God."

The fanatic mystic, Bernard of Clairvaux, had already written of the Virgin: "A polished arrow too is that special love of Christ, which not only pierced Mary's soul but penetrated through and through, so that even the tiniest space of her virginal breast was permeated by love." A chaste virgin, according to Bernard, "Adores and worships one God, *just like the angels*; she loves Christ above all things, *just like the angels*; she is chaste, *just like the angels*, and that in the flesh of a fallen race, in a frail body that the angels do not have. But she seeks and savors the things that they enjoy, not the things that are on the earth...that as an exile on earth she enjoys the glory of celibate life, than that she lives like an angel in an animal body."

It was the pure Virgin of Siena who carried Bernard's image to a logical extreme by renouncing worldly foods in order to savor the food of angels. It is difficult to tell whether Catherine's visions were the hysterical outpourings of an anorexic or whether they were genuine religious experiences, but her obvious ecstatic states equal those of the angels. In talking of her soul she has this to say: "Her desire knows no pain nor her satisfaction any boredom...she often attains such union that she hardly

knows whether she is in the body or out of it." Just like the Angels.

Evolutionary Feathers

So, one might inquire, is this the end product of applying Occam's pruning knife to the elaborations from the earlier theoretical explanations of what angels really might be and why they persist in our times? Are we to surmise that in the Middle Ages angels had come down to earth and suffered from anorexia? Perhaps we might conclude that this is why someone like Catherine can fly and the fat Aquinas could never leave the ground?

The argument that angels have indeed come to ground is more far reaching than it might at first appear. It might imply that the phenomenon of the angel is a very particular, evolutionary, stage in the development of human spirituality. But it would be more precise to suggest that angels are an essential stage along western man's path to enlightenment.

In the East the major religious and spiritual path is through meditation. In the West the union with the Divine Source is usually sought through prayer. In meditation a witness needs no intermediator, although mystics can experience some very bizarre encounters with the deities of their particular background. The 19th century mystic, Ramakrishna, was totally absorbed with the Goddess Kali. She appeared to him as a completely substantial

Melancholia *by Albrecht Dürer.* With the rise of Humanism and the new proto-sciences, during the 15th century, much of the numinous and imaginative universe of the earlier centuries faded from the collective consciousness. Inevitably this cool intellectual and objective way of viewing the world brought with it a certain severing of the magical links with reality. Angels were amongst the first casualties.

being and he became obsessively stuck at that point simply because she was so beautiful and he loved her so much. Eventually it required a violent intervention by his Guru, to force him to destroy the image. Once accomplished, this destruction allowed Ramakrishna to move into a more comprehensive stage of consciousness. Likewise in our century the charismatic master Da Free John experienced both a real and substantial Virgin Mary, as well as a full and fleshy Goddess, before both faded and he moved to the final stage of his realization. Many mystics and spiritual seekers experience just such bizarre apparitions at certain times.

In a number of traditions there are particular experiences that help the seeker's progress along the so called spiritual paths and these have been carefully documented. For instance, there are certain meditations in which the seeker can explore the mysterious inner workings of the brain pathways. During this certain images and sounds seem to separate themselves from the observer and appear real and exterior. It is possible that on consciously entering the cerebellum or the brain core the observer actually triggers the archetypes hidden within its interior.

There is an equally powerful route to the Divine through devotion and prayer. In India this is exemplified by the *Bhakti*, or the Devotee. There have been many mystics who have worshipped the deity Krishna as if he was actually before them, in the flesh. Both men and women devotees accept that Krishna is the bridegroom and they are the brides. The process can be seen to be virtually identical to the one experienced by St. Francis. Whether in the form of Christ or Krishna, the ecstatic meeting with the Beloved is a meeting of the "fire of

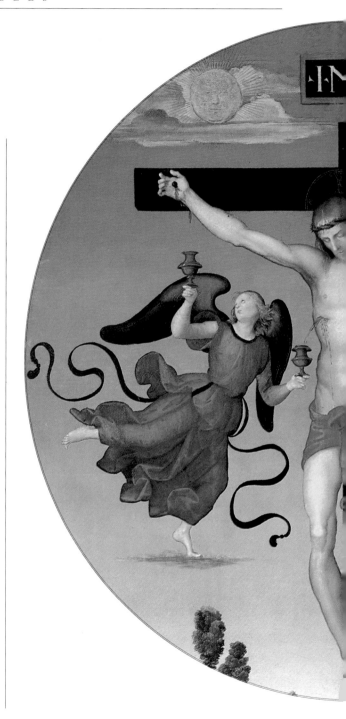

Love." The devotee in essence becomes one of the Seraphim, one of the innermost intelligences which surround the Divine Source as seen in the Heavenly Hierarchies. But now, instead of the process being an intellectual idea, the mystic lives the experience of that ecstatic vibration of Love. It recalls the experience of the composer Jerry Neff. "I could only see what seemed like a blazing pool of white or slightly golden light – what you might see if it were possible to look straight into the sun. But I did not see it so much as *feel* it, and that feeling was one of absolute ecstasy, involving every 'good' sensation and every 'rightness' imaginable, and in a moral sense as well. This bliss included benevolence, joy and reconciliation of opposites – literally *everything* at once." Just like the angels. But now the angel has come to earth and the human has arrived in Heaven.

Contacting the Higher Self

This New Age has brought to the surface many spiritual ideas which are odd combinations of the teachings of the East, of Western esotericism, of the occult and North American shamanism. One concept, which has its corresponding reality for those who practice it, is the belief in a Higher Self. This is the Inner Teacher of Claire Prophet or can even be seen as the "link" personality of those with MPD. It is the consciousness which has an overview of the

Angels of the Crucifixion *by Raphael, National Gallery, London.* The very fact that the Church was forced by the new Humanism to recognize that the Divine had come to Earth as a flesh and blood human being, who experienced the dualities of joy and suffering just as we do, meant that the angels, who could not (without falling), gradually faded from the picture.

individual. This Higher Self can be consciously contacted and sometimes it acts as a channeling entity. It has already been observed in the cases of multiple personalities that one of the "selves" is usually wiser and more mature than the others. Some even see this as the active angelic intelligence which is a hidden part living within one of the many mansions of our whole being. This higher self often tries to communicate with the normal everyday consciousness and sometimes does so in outlandish and bizarre ways such as creating an abduction episode or a contact with Other Worldly beings.

Now just suppose that this projection, which seems so real to the subject, can be seen by others who are in some way in a sympathetic space. Were the marks of the crucifixion on the body of Francis, those marks which supposedly were made by an angel, a mass hallucination on the part of his brother monks? This is the eye-witness report of the corpse of the saint: "His limbs were so soft and supple to the touch that they seemed to have regained the tenderness of childhood and to be adorned with clear signs of his innocence. The *nails appeared black against his shining skin, and the wound in his side was red like a rose in springtime.*" (Bonaventure). It was no wonder that the onlookers were amazed at the "miracle" and were confounded at how it was possible.

Equally miraculous is the Eastern concept that our normal consciousness is like the tip of an iceberg, or like Dr. Lilly's nine layers: we don't see the rest of a vast consciousness which is available to us. "Above us there is superconsciousness which is nine times as great as consciousness, while still higher there is cosmic consciousness which is ninefold that of superconsciousness. If that isn't enough the sages tell us: 'below', there is the unconscious, nine times as vast as our consciousness and below that there is the ninefold collective unconscious." At this point it might be wondered whatever happened to the Devil? Examining the model of the various layers of consciousness it is easy to infer an up and a down, an overworld of Heaven and an underworld of Hell. It does suggest that, just as angels can be seen as a stage in the development of awareness, so can devils. We are all perfectly capable of delighting or terrifying ourselves with visions from these ninefold layers, and we do.

The City by *Gustave Doré.* The Heavenly City or the New Jerusalem envisioned by John of Patmos remained empty of both angels and human-like angels. The reality of the paradise garden is most beautifully expressed in an old Zen saying. "This Very Place the Lotus Paradise, This Very Body the Buddha." For the Angels reside within us all and we are already standing in the Garden.

The Last Judgment

The Seraph which appeared to St. Francis could be seen as the last great visitation of the Angels. It was the turning point of a magnificent transformation and the last snip of Occam's razor. This glimpse was of the highest expression of angelic consciousness, burning with the fire of love. The image transformed into Christ who communicated the physical marks of the flesh to Francis. At that moment the spiritual man of the West made a great quantum leap. Man and angel merged in a consciousness higher than both. The essence of the higher angelic self, that higher vibration of Love became integrated with that of the lower vibration of the material world. All the multiple "personalities" became one whole. In the East such an integrity is known as enlightenment.

Eastern mystics have often commented, one might feel rather smugly, that the holy men and women of the West stop too long at a certain stage on the so-called spiritual path. That stage Meher Baba calls the "saintly" level. It corresponds to the opening of the third eye. It does appear that the experience is so ecstatic and literally miraculous that many mystics do get stuck there. Some maintain that this stage corresponds to the highest point of active angelic intelligence. It is said, that to pass beyond this point, is the whole reason that the soul must take on the flesh. It might be added that the same is true for the angel. Many religious traditions maintain that Enlightenment can only be realized for those who are in the body. That final release, the Liberation, needs something to be liberated from. If you have to transcend possessiveness it's no good having nothing to give up. A great hoarder or miser who can suddenly walk away from all his wealth without a backward glance is free.

In looking back over this whole survey it can be seen that our images of angels were just too perfect, perhaps just too good. They simply lacked contrast. Even when some rebelled they then merely became just too bad. Both good and bad were polarities. It requires the encapsulation of both principles within the boundaries of one body to really effect a true union of such poles. Humans live within the constant war of the dualities of the body and the spirit, good and evil, love and hate. While in the body no one can escape the responsibility which that entails. Only through enlightenment can a union emerge and a true flight of freedom happen. And those particular wings leave the angelic host far behind. In this respect St. Paul was right. Man is a higher form of life than the angel. But he didn't mention that such a human had to be *whole*.

Epilogue

In the course of this volume we have covered a great deal of territory in our quest to discover the real angels and why we all seem to care so much about them. Although it would have been tempting, at the outset, to accept that their nature is one of those inexplicable and unknowable mysteries of existence, we have chosen, instead, to examine both long established ideas as well as some often outlandish possibilities.

However, sooner or later, all such concepts reveal limitations, beyond which our normal minds cannot travel. Beyond this point we enter the realm of Grace or one's particular faith or belief. Ultimately we arrive at each person's own first hand mystical experience. For, even after all this exploration, angels still appear as inseparable from their witnesses as they did at the outset. When all is analysed and written, the hidden meaning of angels remains that they are an *inseparable part of each one of us*. We are One; the angel is one of our inner and most magical aspects; the angel is an integral part of *ourselves*. This is also William of Occam's gift to us. Our intuitive cognition, our direct knowing of that angelic aspect of our many selves is worth all someone else's paper angels of the intellect, howsoever beautiful and awe-inspiring they might at first appear. It is a far greater message than any separate and external archangel could ever bring.

If you really want to see an angel don't look for one outside: they reside within, and so long as human beings seek their own totality and wholeness, the angelic species cannot be endangered.

"But as for me, if thou wouldst know
What I was;
In a word
I am the Word who did dance all things
and was not shamed at all.
'Twas I who leapt and danced...Amen"
The Hymn of Jesus (The Leucian Acts)

Dedicated to One who danced all these things,
with Love and Light and Laughter.

The publishers wish to thank the following for their kind permission to use images found in this volume.

Scala, Italy: pages 14, 38, 50, 100, 129, 152, 156, 160, 236

– British Museum, London
– Museum of Art, Brussels
– Campo Santo, Pisa
– Sam Haskins
– Johfra
– Museum of Art, Madrid
– Historical Museum, Moscow
– Paris National Library
– National Gallery, London
– Uffizi Gallery, Firenze

ACKNOWLEDGMENTS

This book was compiled during the winter of 1989 and 1990 in a remote and exquisite part of Tuscany, between Florence and Siena. These Renaissance cities have more angels and demons gracing their walls than anywhere else on Earth. However this splendid isolation had its drawbacks and many of those I wish to thank for their help do not even know they gave it, for I only met them in the pages of their books. All the same my thanks to Colin Wilson, whose *Mysteries* (Grafton 1979) gave the necessary spark to the chapter on multiple personalities; to Christian and Barbara O'Brien for their thought provoking *The Chosen Few* (Turnstone Press 1985) which provided the theme for the chapter called The Shining Ones; to Gustav Davidson whose *Dictionary of Angels* (Free Press 1967) remains the most extensive compendium of Angelic Lore with a marvellous bibliography which cannot be bettered, and to Stuart Schneiderman for simply penning such a delightful *An Angel Passes* (N.Y. University Press 1988).

My very particular thanks to Deborah Bergman who, as consulting editor, was a transitional angel who I have only encountered in the extensive footnotes and deletions all over the first draft of the original manuscript. Any coherence the reader finds in the text can only be due to her labors. My heartfelt thanks to Philip Dunn of Labyrinth Publishing, for his ever optimistic attitude when visiting Hell, firmly believing Heaven to be just around the corner; to Simonetta Castelli for managing to fit text around so many feathers and membranes; to beloved Navyo who keeps me laughing and who was the original model for Lilith, and to the "Old Boy", who celebrated All and Everything and was the fieriest seraph of Love and the most devilish rogue I was ever fortunate enough to know.